CURRENT ISSUES IN INTERNATIONAL COMMUNICATION

LONGMAN SERIES IN
PUBLIC COMMUNICATION
SERIES EDITOR: RAY ELDON HIEBERT

CURRENT ISSUES IN INTERNATIONAL COMMUNICATION

L. John Martin
and
Ray Eldon Hiebert

Longman
New York & London

Current Issues in International Communication

Longman, 10 Bank Street, White Plains, N.Y. 10606

Associated companies:
Longman Group Ltd., London
Longman Cheshire Pty., Melbourne
Longman Paul Pty., Auckland
Copp Clark Pitman, Toronto

Cover photographs courtesy of AT&T Bell Laboratories.

Executive editor: Gordon T. R. Anderson
Production editor: Judith A. V. Harlan
Production coordinator: Ann P. Kearns
Text design: Renée Kilbride Edelman
Cover design: Renée Kilbride Edelman
Production supervisor: Kathleen M. Ryan

Library of Congress Cataloging-in-Publication Data

Current issues in international communication / edited by L. John
    Martin and Ray Eldon Hiebert.
            p.   cm.—(Communications)
    Includes bibliographical references.
    ISBN 0-8013-0121-1
    1. Communication, International.   2. Communication—International
cooperation.   3. Communication policy.   I. Martin, L. John (Leslie
John), 1921–   . II. Hiebert, Ray Eldon.   III. Series:
Longman Series in Public Communication
P96.I5C76   1990   89-36618
302.2—dc20   CIP

    3 4 5 6 7 8 9 10-ML-95949392

Contents

INTRODUCTION

Until the last half century, international journalism had always conjured up mysterious and romantic pictures of distant lands and strange customs. It has only been since World War II that international travel has become so common that there are few people left in the world who have not seen foreigners up close; distant people may still seem strange but are certainly no longer mysterious. The world has become a global village, as Marshall McLuhan termed it, in which everyone is everyone else's neighbor, and international journalism is becoming less and less the story of far away places with strange sounding names. This, more than anything else, accounts for the rapid changes we have been witnessing in international communication in recent years.

What are the media issues of an international nature that are being discussed by journalists, scholars, policymakers, and the general public? All people today, regardless of their public or private positions, are highly conscious of the role of the mass media in their lives. One reason is the sheer numbers of people who populate this earth—some five billion souls. As their numbers increase, they become more interdependent, but at the same time remaining in touch becomes more and more difficult. All the things that used to be possible through face-to-face interaction must be done through mass communication today. This goes for both keeping informed and being entertained. The piano or book or storyteller around which or whom a family used to congregate has been replaced by the television set or radio. Even the motion picture theater, where people could experience togetherness, will not be able to compete for long with the VCR, which isolates people into smaller groups.

Mass communication costs money, of course, and the question of how one should pay for it is an important one. The economics of mass communication has been changing in recent years. Printed media were not prohibitively expensive in the old days, and even radio could be supported with limited funds. But television requires a major investment, and, on a mass scale, the other media are quite expensive, too. Mass media ownership and control do provide military, political, economic, and social power by enabling the owner/controller to control large numbers of people or to rally them to joint action. Control and often ownership of mass media around the world has generally been in the hands of the government, the Church, a political party, a military entity, a wealthy individual, a private organization, the business community, or a union. While governments still control most television broadcasting and often radio broadcasting as well, especially in the Communist World and the Third World, commercial interests are making rapid inroads into their monopoly. At first, the business world is limited to buying a small amount of time to peddle its wares or other messages; but it will not be long before businesses will insist on having a say about the programs that are aired during the general time frame that they have been assigned for their commercials. Newspapers and magazines, too, are carrying more advertising by commercial interests than ever before even in government-owned and controlled media.

Meanwhile, ownership of the printed media by political parties, unions, religious organizations, and private individuals is decreasing, and, at the same time, newspaper chain and employee ownership is increasing in many countries.

Another change that is noticeable globally is the speed with which news reaches the outermost parts of the world. Technological advances, especially the use of satellites by news purveyors, has made news distribution almost instantaneous. Contrast this with the way news was transmitted until as recently as the 1940s and one can understand why McLuhan spoke of the global village. Except for the most urgent news, which was transmitted by cable in an abbreviated form referred to as "cablese" to save on the cost of transmission but at the risk of frequent misinterpretations, most international news was sent by mail, and quite often by sea mail. Most people in the world today read, hear, and see the same versions of the news, although the interpretations are different, of course. Because of the mounting cost of international news gathering, much news gathering is done cooperatively by national or regional wire services, or by the five major international wire services: the Associated Press, United Press International (both of the U.S.), Reuters (of Britain), Agence France Presse (of France), and TASS (of the Soviet Union). There also are national, regional, and international electronic media news services that are growing in importance with the increasing use and effectiveness of radio, television, and other telecommunications.

With technological advances has come the greater need for and appreciation of literacy. Governments worldwide have been encouraging it, and people have been accepting it for their children if not for themselves on a growing scale. But with literacy on the rise, expectations have been rising too. We will not deal with rising economic expectations, which are explosive, but with what people are expecting of their mass media fare. They are expecting more and better entertainment and they are also expecting more interesting and more accurate news about an ever growing number of things. Editors and producers are finding it more and more difficult to satisfy the voracious appetite of their audiences and readers. At international conferences of media people, one of the most frequent topics is where one can find more and better media content or how one can produce one's own on the available budgets. An analogy might serve to illustrate the problem, and it is an analogy from the health services. As we develop ever more sophisticated instruments, treatments, and drugs and find ways to cure or alleviate illnesses that used to kill us, we find we have to spend more money on health care because the treatments are now available. In the same way, our ability to gather, write, produce, and deliver news and entertainment of better and better quality and at increasing speeds has whetted the appetites of the public. But there is a parallel rise in costs that uses up an ever-growing share of our resources. Where will this all end?

After seeking to satisfy their own needs, people tend to look outward to see what their neighbors are getting, and this has led to another phenomenon in the mass communication field in recent years. People in the Third World, and to a lesser extent in the Communist world, have become concerned about what the Western world, which has enjoyed a higher standard of living than they have for some time, is being told about them. They found that the Western world had a low opinion of Africa, Asia, and Latin America, which comprise most of the Third World. While there are historical reasons for this, Third World and Communist world leaders feel that the mass media are perpetuating this feeling by emphasizing negative news over the more positive things that are happening in developing countries. So much noise was made about this unbalanced reporting about the Third World that the media and wire services have been making a conscious effort in recent years to provide a more balanced coverage of developing countries. This is evidenced in media content studies. What these studies show, however, is that, while there is an effort to report the good with the bad in Western media, the *amount* of coverage remains a function of the relationship between the country that is reporting and the country being reported on. Many countries are being completely ignored, although negative news about these countries would still be reported if the degree of negativeness were great enough. It is this controversy that led to the New World Information Order being introduced by UNESCO.

This book is divided into three parts. Part 1 deals with global communication processes, including the worldwide flow of communication, the development of national and international communication policies, and the ways in which different societies bring about control of the process.

Part 2 deals with current concerns, or those issues which have brought about discussion, research, and media coverage. This part is divided according to the three main media systems of the world, Western, Soviet-bloc, and Third World.

Part 3 deals with current problems in the field, including the impact that the transnational flow of communication has on cultures, the demands of the Third World for a New World Information Order, and the growing concern for the use of communication as a tool of social and national development.

In each section, the editors have included essays and reports that address the larger and more theoretical questions, and others which deal with more specific examples of those current questions as they are expressed in different countries. This process should help the student appreciate the more abstract concerns but also learn how those concerns are being translated into communication realities within various nations. These specific examples often portray countries whose communication problems have become newsworthy in the United States, and thus there are frequent examples from places such as the Soviet Union, China, South Korea, South Africa, and Israel, such high-visibility Third World countries as India, Nigeria, and Kenya, and regions such as Central America.

1 COMMUNICATION PROCESSES

Never before in history has so much been communicated so rapidly to so many people. We have entered the age of the global flow of information and entertainment as a result of the technological innovations that followed World War II. Chief among those innovations have been the full development of television, FM radio, the entire range of computers from large mainframes to mini and laptop models, and, most important for global communication, the use of space satellites orbiting above the earth's gravity zone to which electronic signals can be beamed so they can be reflected back to earth and received at any point on the globe in a matter of milliseconds.

The results may yet prove to be the most revolutionary experience that has ever happened to the human race. The end results could well be sweeping changes in politics, in cultures, in national systems, and in international relationships. But we are still at the beginning of this revolution. We do not yet know how it will turn out. All we can do at this point is to try to learn what is flowing back and forth between nations on this new electronic grid. That seems to be the best place to start in any examination of current international communication issues.

As global communication spreads, national and international communication policies are the inevitable results. Some Americans, especially those who have worked in the more traditional print media forms, have resisted national policies as inimical to freedom of the press as guaranteed by the first amendment to the Constitution. Nevertheless, most thoughtful observers think that national and international policies are essential to the future free flow of communication.

The dominant communication policy of most societies for most of human history has simply been the control of communication. Throughout history, communication and power have been intertwined. Those who have held power have used communication to maintain authority and have viewed unauthorized public communication as a threat. Some societies have taken the most extreme measures to control any communication viewed as critical. Such criticism was tantamount to blasphemy. It has not only been the Ayatollah Khomeini who has issued death warrants because of such blasphemy. European kings and early American religious zealots also sentenced communicators to death for getting out of control. Even today in the United Kingdom, blasphemy against the Church of England remains illegal.

Technological innovations have steadily eroded the ability of authorities to control the communication process. The development of movable type spread the printed word and made access to information far easier than it had ever been. More information for the people meant more power for the people, and less power for the central authorities. That process has continued as technological innovations have increased. In our time, the photocopy machine, the computer, the video-cassette recorder, the fax machine, and the personal computer have all made it more difficult to control communication and information. In the Soviet bloc, *glasnost* and *perestroika* may well be the results of communication technologies that have proved impossible to contain.

Our aim in organizing these readings has been to take the reader from the overview, the theoretical, and the abstract, to the specific, the concrete, and the real. Thus, we start with the broad picture, and move toward the specific illustration.

Unfortunately, things are changing so rapidly that research has not been able to keep up. Thus, we are presenting information here not as if it is the final word, but rather because it is only the best that is currently available. Hopefully, students of international communication will be as inspired by what is not here as they can be instructed by what has been done. And they will set forth to bring our understanding up to date.

1 INTERNATIONAL COMMUNICATION FLOW

Western Bloc nations have certainly dominated the flow of international communication for the past century. Theirs have been the news services which have carried most of the world's news and information. And increasingly theirs have been the entertainment production centers which have given the world's people much of their recorded music, motion pictures, and television amusements.

But that statement does not tell the whole story. It is, in fact, difficult to tell exactly how the West has come to dominate the communication channels. News about one's own region prevails in most of the world's news media, no matter what its origin. Furthermore, a variety of factors influence international news flow, not the least of which is the apparent "eliteness" in the minds of the information receivers of the country originating the message.

The new communication technologies have been perceived as a way of balancing the flow of news throughout the world. But in fact the new technologies require precisely the same kind of money and know-how that have led to the imbalance in the first place. And nowhere is this better illustrated than in the world of television drama. Many of the countries of the world simply do not have the creative and production capabilities to produce local entertainment that can compete with "Miami Vice," "Knight Rider," and "Diff'rent Strokes."

Even technologically competent countries *may not* be able to compete. Take Japan for example. Japan can produce the electronic equipment but it cannot create programming that would interest most of the world. Japan's talents are culture-bound and have been developed over the centuries for a closed and unicultural society. The United States, on the other hand, has been producing information and entertainment programming for an open, multicultural society. That kind of programming in America must appeal to blacks, whites, Asians, and Hispanics; to the rich, the middle-class, and the poor; to Protestants, Catholics, Jews, and Moslems; to people of European, African, Middle-eastern, and Asian ancestry. Little wonder that it might have more worldwide appeal than a Japanese television show.

Finally, there is the argument about the damage done by Western Bloc communication dominance. In some remote village in Peru, the inhabitants can now receive American TV. Is it ruining them? Should they remain ignorant of what television can bring them because it is American? A priest in Peru who is helping bring them American television asks, "Don't these people have a right to expand their horizons like everyone else?" This is one of the questions to be considered when we look at the dilemma of the imbalance in the flow of international communication.

THE "WORLD OF THE NEWS" STUDY

ANNABELLE SREBERNY-MOHAMMADI, KAARLE NORDENSTRENG, ROBERT L. STEVENSON, AND FRANK UGBOAJAH

This study of international news flow sets the stage. It is based on a UNESCO/ IAMCR sponsored project which surveyed the news coverage by press, radio, and television in twenty-nine countries. This study has brought forth negative reactions which should be noted. Robert L. Stevenson says this study does not show that Western media and news agencies ignore the Third World, provide predominantly negative coverage of the Third World, and/or portray the Third World through a filter of cultural bias. Nor does it indicate that Third World and Soviet bloc systems claim to represent an alternative model which operates much differently from Western counterparts. For Stevenson's complete response, see the *Journal of Communication*, Winter 1984, pages 134–138.

Perhaps no aspect of the New International Information Order debate has been more contentious and controversial than the question of international news. In the mid-1970s, argument about news flows and presentation, the imbalances of international communications structures, and the dominance of the Western news agencies agitated all concerned with the mass media: international organizations, national policy-makers, media researchers, and media practitioners. Bias in the flows of international news and distortion in its content, particularly regarding the image of the South, were the central themes. These were raised yet again at the General Conference of UNESCO in Nairobi in 1976, and a resolution was passed calling for study of this problem. This resulted in the joint study by UNESCO and the International Association for Mass Communication Research. (20)

This project was planned as an inventory of international news reporting. . . . It covers all "worlds of development," all the regions of the world, and includes data from both broadcasting channels and the press. There were 13 full participating teams and the U.S. team covered an additional 16 media systems, providing a very wide and significant data base of 29 media systems. The 13 participating teams were from Australia, Finland, the Federal Republic of Germany, India, Iran, Hungary, Lebanon, Malaysia, the Netherlands, Nigeria, Poland, the United States, and Yugoslavia. In addition, quantitative data were generated for Algeria, Argentina, Brazil, Egypt, Greece, Iceland, Indonesia, Ivory Coast, Kenya, Mexico, Thailand, Tunisia, Turkey, U.S.S.R., Zaire, and Zambia.

The idea for the project stemmed from a resolution passed at the 1976 General Conference of UNESCO in Nairobi; the responsibility for undertaking the research was transferred to the IAMCR in the summer of 1977, and by the summer of 1979 the above teams had volunteered as possessing the necessary resources.

All participants were to adhere to a core schedule for sampling, coding and analysis. While some undertook additional historical and other kinds of analysis, only the results of the core schedule are reported here; the other materials are available in the respective national reports. The press sample included three or four of the largest daily papers in each country. For the radio and television broadcasting sample, only the "main news bulletin of the day"

Annabelle Sreberny-Mohammadi, Kaarle Nordenstreng, Robert L. Stevenson, and Frank Ugboajah, "The World of the News." From the *Journal of Communication*, Winter 1984, pp. 121–134. Reprinted by permission of author.

was selected and taped for subsequent analysis. Beyond such general instructions, each national team was free to select those press and broadcasting channels that best represented their particular national system. Some reflected political diversity, as in the Finnish selections, while others focused on the diverse presentations of ethnic/linguistic communities, as in the Malay choices. Some focused only on national newspapers, while countries without a national press selected regional papers. The variations in selection mean that the figure used for some countries represents only a single channel (Greece, Turkey); it rises to a maximum of twelve channels studied (Malaysia).

We grouped the 29 media systems into seven geo-political regions for reporting large patterns, so many differences were equalized in collapsing these data. For example, the data on North American television are derived from a single national media system, that of the United States, while the data for Africa included seven media systems.

The time sample was based on one chronological week, in April 1979, and a composite week, which spanned April through June. Our week was in fact six days, since Sunday editions were excluded; these tend to break with the normal pattern of weekly presentation and many countries publish no Sunday or equivalent paper. Only the "general news" pages of the press were included. All specialized sections of a paper, such as finance, travel, women, etc., were omitted, as were any special reports and supplements that appeared during our time period. This was intended to maximize the comparability of results, cut coding time, and help make the press results more comparable with those from broadcasting, where no special programming of a news-oriented kind could be included.

To some extent, this focus on the "general news" pages biased the outcome of our findings, orienting the sample toward a comparatively limited set of hard news topics. Clearly, too, our study does not pretend to reflect the complete universe of news and news-related information available within any of the participating nations. It focuses only on the main formal mass media channels and their particular modes of news presentation and through the formal coding instrument provides information on the rough volume and overall structure of international news presentation.

The news item was the unit of analysis. Each item was coded on the following variables: *location*—where the news item originated; *source*—from whom the news item originated; *position and nationality of actor*—who made the news; *topic*—what the news was about; and *theme*—what is the news context. The length of an item was also coded, but since the correlations between the two sets of figures for frequency and length were high, we report only the total number of items here.

Not all items included were "foreign" or "external" news in terms of origin or strictly *international* in terms of dealing with events in more than a single country. The widely adopted story-type classification that allows for "foreign news at home" and "home news abroad" eliminates any neat dividing line between what is purely domestic news and what is international. There was also a high level of what we call "natiocentric coverage," or international news items being included in media output when their domestic relevance is clear. Thus, as soon as we began to examine the disparities between the total amounts of international news carried by the various systems and to try to determine what could be considered an acceptable or desirable balance between domestic coverage and international reporting, analytic difficulties arose. Sometimes a strong international focus would appear to draw attention away from necessary domestic investigation, while a weak international focus seemed to result in an isolationist and introverted outlook.

Table 1 shows the selected channels for each participating team, the total data base, and the average amount of international news carried by each channel daily. The results of the study can be presented here only in the most general and schematic manner. Results are presented in a single composite figure for each national media system. This leaves out the interesting question of differences between press and broadcast news. Perhaps what was most notable about the findings of the limited quantitative analysis was that, although the participating nations reflected different levels of development and a variety of political perspectives, the overall pattern of attention paid to certain kinds of events was remarkably similar.

In terms of the topics covered by international news, we found that politics dominated international news reporting everywhere (for results by region,

Table I

AMOUNT OF INTERNATIONAL NEWS ON AN AVERAGE DAY BY SELECTED
CHANNELS (PRESS, RADIO, AND TV)

	International News Stories			International News Stories	
	$\bar{x}$	% of all news*		$\bar{x}$	% of all news*
North America			Africa (Continued)		
U.S. (N = 1,487)			Television	14	77
New York Times	33	39	Zaire (N = 419)		
Washington Post	26	42	Elima	9	29
Los Angeles Times	21	25	Salongo	7	25
New York Daily News	14	19	Radio	18	61
Minneapolis Tribune	14	30	Zambia (N = 516)		
Charlotte Observer	11		Zambia Times	13	43
Television—CBS	4	19	Zambia Daily Mail	13	81
			Radio	10	47
Latin America			Television	7	80
Argentina (N = 1,017)					
Clarín	20	43	Middle East		
La Opinion	27	53			
Cronica	21	25	Egypt (N = 1,322)		
Radio—Rivadavia	11	n.a.	al-Ahram	30	25
Television—11	3	n.a.	al-Akhbar	38	17
Television—Tele Noche	4	n.a.	al-Gomhuria	30	12
Brazil (N = 630)			Radio	14	92
O Estado de São Paulo	29	33	Iran (N = 453)		
Jornal do Brasil	24	28	Kayhan	15	16
Mexico (N = 1,188)			Ettela'at	12	18
El Universal	40	33	Ayandegan	11	17
Excelsior	39	43	Lebanon (N = 2,049)		
			al-Nahar	48	35
Africa			as-Safir	57	41
Algeria (N = 935)			al-Amal	31	30
El Moudjahed	35	44	Radio Lebanon	22	62
Television	13	68	Tele-Liban	13	65
Ivory Coast (N = 390)					
Fraternité Matin	22	51	Asia		
Television	33	82			
Kenya (N = 501)			Australia (N = 1,032)		
Nairobi Standard	13	45	Australian	23	29
Daily Nation	14	36	Herald	30	28
Radio	15	64	Telegraph	16	46
Nigeria (N = 205)			Radio—ABC	7	52
Daily Times	9	5	Radio—2AD	2	18
New Nigerian	3	16	Television—ABC	6	30
Punch	2	13	Television—9/8	2	16
Radio	3	17	India (N = 1,649)		
Television	1	3	Hindu	24	24
Tunisia (N = 1,303)			Times of India	33	21
La Presse	36	76	Indian Express	22	24
L'Action	25	51	Hindustan Times	27	23
			Statesman	32	29

	International News Stories			International News Stories	
	$\bar{x}$	% of all news*		$\bar{x}$	% of all news*
Asia (Continued)			**Eastern Europe (Continued)**		
Radio	5	18	U.S.S.R. (N = 997)		
Television	6	34	*Pravda*	35	55
Indonesia (N = 811)			*Izvestiya*	25	55
Kompas	11	18	*Komsomolskaya Pravda*	15	46
Sinar Harapan	14	34	Television	8	32
Merdeka	27	44	Yugoslavia (N = 1,144)		
Radio	6	n.a.	*Delo*	50	60
Television	9	n.a.	*Dnevnik*	24	39
Malaysia (N = 2,070)			*Večer*	12	19
New Straits Times	39	39	Radio	11	36
Utusan Malaysia	18	16			
Sin Chew Jut Poh	37	26			
Tamil Nesan	18	23	**Western Europe**		
Radio (E)	7	54			
Radio (M)	13	35	Federal Republic of Germany		
Radio (C)	5	43	(N = 3,068)		
Radio (T)	5	38	*Bild-Zeitung*	31	41
Television (E)	10	54	*Die Welt*	59	52
Television (M)	10	39	*Frankfurter Allgemeine*	50	48
Television (C)	9	45	*Suddeutscher Zeitung*	65	60
Television (T)	7	30	*Frankfurter Rundschau*	37	41
Thailand (N = 500)			Television—ARD	14	17
Siam-Rath	9	17	Television—ZDF	15	24
Thai-Rath	18	20	Finland (N = 881)		
Dao-Sham	4	11	*Helsingin Sanomat*	26	39
Radio	2	19	*Aamulehti*	18	23
Television 3TV	14	58	*Kansan Uutiset*	14	22
Eastern Europe			*Savon Sanomat*	11	10
Hungary (N = 2,931)			Television	5	36
Népszabadság	55	32	Greece (N = 205)		
Népszava	43	25	*Ta Nea*	16	18
Magyar Nemzet	60	31	Iceland (N = 689)		
Magyar Hírlap	61	37	*Morgundbladid*	25	23
Esti Hírlap	25	30	*Thjódviljinn*	11	24
Radio	16	33	*Dagbladid*	11	16
Television	11	40	Radio	6	20
Poland (N = 713)			Television	4	18
Trybuna Ludu	42	73	Netherlands (N = 991)		
Zycie Warszawy	26	58	*Telegraaf*	16	26
Express Wieczorny	30	45	*NRC/Handelsblad*	38	42
Radio 1	9	41	*Tubantia*	23	17
Radio 111	6	55	Television—Nos	6	53
TV News	8	26	Turkey (N = 327)		
			Milliyet	27	33

General news–hole, omitting special sections and supplements.

Table 2   COVERAGE OF SELECTED TOPICS IN INTERNATIONAL NEWS BY REGION*

	North America	Latin America	Africa	Middle East	Asia	Eastern Europe	Western Europe
	%	%	%	%	%	%	%
International politics	18	20	32	42	16	26	18
Domestic politics	21	28	19	17	17	18	20
Military	16	9	11	14	12	10	10
Economic matters	9	11	8	6	13	12	10
Crime	12	10	8	4	9	4	9
Culture	2	2	2	2	2	8	2
Sports	2	3	2	3	1	4	3
Personalities	1	1	2	1	2	1	2
Natural disasters	4	4	2	1	3	2	3
Total	85	88	86	90	75	85	77

*The other topics were: international aid, social service, religion, science, entertainment, human interest, student matters, ecology, and other.

scc Table 2). Our two categories of international politics and domestic politics accounted for between 32 percent and 66 percent of all international news coverage in all participating media systems but three (Nigeria and Australia had less; Iran even more). Indeed, "hard" news, represented by these two political categories and by items on military and defense and economics, accounted for the majority of all stories. This was even more the case in the news media of the South, where few "soft" stories are either generated or reported. Similarly, we found that political figures dominate, embracing 25 percent to 60 percent of all actors in international news; few other categories of actors received significant mention. Political news with political actors constitutes the bulk of international news coverage everywhere.

The other overall finding was the prominence of regionalism. Every national system devoted most attention to events happening within and to actors belonging to its immediate geographical region. This focus characterized between 23 percent and 63 percent of all international news in every system. Thus, Nigeria was most concerned about African affairs and African actors, Argentina featured Latin American news most prominently, and so on. Table 3 shows this phenomenon by grouping the countries

into regions and ranking their focus of attention; the diagonal line of number-one-ranked regions is clear. Although there is little evidence of a "Third World perspective," a "continental orientation" is strong.

The only instances in which this regional focus did not hold true were in the Polish and Yugoslav systems, where as much attention was paid to news events in Western Europe as in the East. Indeed, the Eastern European region was the only one to be more fully represented in international news through its actors than through location of events within its territory (see Table 3). The separation of *actors* from *location* in the great mobility of international affairs again raises the question of how "balance" is to be achieved in international news production. Our data show that extra-regional concern for other developing areas is still weak, so that Galtung's assessment of a decade ago that "the peripheral nations do not read much about each other, especially not across bloc borders" still holds (2). Thus, again, balance can be achieved in the "reciprocity of indifference" whereby Latin America ranks last in the attention of the African media, and Africa ranks low in the Latin American. Western Europe and North America manifest a "reciprocity of concern," as each accords the other the most attention after themselves. Balance achieved by the equalization of the

Table 3   RANK ORDERING OF REGIONS IN INTERNATIONAL NEWS BY LOCATION OF EVENT

Regions	North America	Latin America	Africa	Middle East	Asia	Eastern Europe	Western Europe	Location	Actor
	Participating media systems								
North America	1	3	5	3	3	6	2	3	2
Latin America	6	1	8	6	8	8	8	7	8
Africa	5	6.5	1	4	5	7	5.5	5	6
Middle East	2.5	4	2	1	4	4.5	3	2	1
Asia	4	5	5	5	1	3	5.5	4	5
Eastern Europe	7	6.5	7	7	6	1	4	6	4
Western Europe	2.5	2	3	2	2	2	1	1	3
General	8	8	5	8	7	4.5	7	8	7

flow of news "bits" may still leave more basic issues unsettled.

In regard to news content, news everywhere appears to be defined as the "exceptional event," with coups and catastrophes being newsworthy wherever they occur. That the South is so often portrayed in such a manner is a function of the limited amount of attention paid to developing areas outside their own regions. The media of the South both exhibit less interest in covering and are less a source for "soft" news items such as human interest stories, culture, entertainment; further, the fewer the number of international news items, the more those items are concentrated in a few subject areas and reflect very immediate events. Only in the Eastern European media is any significant amount of attention paid to what might be termed "positive" news about culture and science.

The most contentious area of current debate on international communication has been the role of the Western news agencies as the dominant creators and gatekeepers of news flows. Our methodology proved rather crude for distinguishing the source of a news item. Examining the press only, we found a very high rate of non-attribution of news sources, as shown in Table 4. Given that constraint, however, there was a high reported use of local sources, mainly national news agencies, and of national correspondents. While this may mask the exact origination of a news item, it does reveal a significant amount of possible *secondary* gatekeeping in the

selection, interpretation, and processing of news that originally may have been culled from external sources. Yet it was indeed the "big four" Western agencies that figured as the second most important set of sources for international news, and our figures quite probably do not reflect all the news from these sources. It may be the case that the "big four" provide a limited news diet, but there was no evidence to suggest even a sampling of alternative news menus from the many other types of sources that now exist.

From the beginning of this project, we intended to balance the formal exercise in quantification with a more delicate, nuanced, interpretative analysis of the deeper content of international news presentation. This would provide the context for interpretation of the statistical data and a real taste of the news coverage available within each national system. Devising such an interpretative schema proved a bigger task than anticipated, and this great aim was reduced to an analysis of selected "dominant" stories. Decisions as to how "dominance" was constructed within each media system (by length of story, presence on front page, repetition throughout the period, etc.) were left to each national team. Three or four items were to be selected and a summary made of the perspective and news angle adopted and the journalistic devices and language styles used to report the item. Some differences emerged between the findings from the quantitative study and those of this qualitative analysis, which suggest that analysis

Table 4	ATTRIBUTED SOURCES OF INTERNATIONAL NEWS BY REGION (FOR PRESS ONLY)*						
	North America	Latin America	Africa	Middle East	Asia	Eastern Europe	Western Europe
	%	%	%	%	%	%	%
Home country agency	4	—	11	3	16	36	15
Reuters	6	—	5	12	14	2	14
UPI	9	10	1	7	5	2	4
AP	22	7	1	9	14	1	14
AFP	—	12	5	20	10	2	6
TASS	—	—	—	—	—	16	1
Other agency	—	17	—	12	2	2	3
Own staff	36	9	9	8	26	22	27
Other medium—home	1	—	—	—	—	1	1
Other medium—foreign	1	2	3	5	3	3	4
Other source	6	12	5	10	6	5	7
Unidentifiable	11	39	65	28	18	27	21

*Multiple coding was permitted, so totals may exceed 100 percent.

based on only one kind of evidence might be very misleading.

The categories used for quantification tended to reflect similarities in coverage, while the qualitative analysis revealed some differences in outlook. The qualitative analysis produced a different geographic focus from the quantitative findings. For example, Africa was repeatedly said to have furnished major news stories, relating to elections in what was then Rhodesia and to the routing of Idi Amin from Uganda. The statistical ranking of the region, however, was not high. Conversely, Western Europe and North America were not found to have produced many significant stories, yet both achieved a higher ranking for amount of news coverage than did Africa. These two regions seem to provide a second tier of attention after "own region" as "consistent newsmakers," even overtaking the global "hot spots." The implication of this divergence— whether a continual and low-key or a short-term and dramatic focus has the greater effect on audiences of media news—deserves attention.

Differences in focus, perspective, and value orientation became clearer in this qualitative analysis. Varying attitudes toward the Camp David agree-

ments were revealed, as was the contrasting jubilation or cynicism with which Salt II talks were greeted. Yet, at the same time, many national studies showed considerable reverberations of the concepts and descriptive terminology used by the big agencies themselves, as Weaver and Wilhoit have discussed in their study of agency output (see, e.g., 23). The widespread adoption of news agency language suggests that there is less real secondary gatekeeping than many would wish for. It is clear, however, that tone, moral judgments, and political orientations form the wider ideological frame of each media system and are as, if not more, important in the construction of social consciousness than the total amount of news coverage. The differences and contractions between the two—quantitative and qualitative—sets of data suggest that caution is needed in the evaluation of the project. Adequate understanding of international news presentation requires several levels of analysis; any one set of findings alone may be ambiguous and open to very different interpretations.

Given the vast amount of data generated by even the simplest of 29-country surveys, we limited ourselves to the central questions.[1] We made no special analysis of the position of a news item, so a front-page leader counted the same as a news brief on a middle page. We gave no ranking to the relative "influence" of the paper being analyzed nor to any of the radio and television channels, although this issue is legitimately raised in the national reports. According to our sample comparisons, the analyses based on the number of items and those based on total amount of space proved to be remarkably similar. Although differences do appear when the data are divided into small subcategories, at the level of analysis by country—which is the level we use in the final report—the similarities are striking. It seems to make very little difference whether the number of stories is counted or whether total space covered is measured: the results for each country are nearly identical.

Some tests were also made on a sample of U.S. papers of the effect of including only the general news sections from six-day samples (the method used in the study) as compared with analysis of international news items culled from the entire newspaper and including the Sunday editions. As the results in Table 5 show, care is needed with the interpretation of the data. Sports news in particular, but also other materials usually found in special sections of a paper, are underrepresented in our study. So too is material not written to meet a daily deadline, so that "soft" news is underrepresented, while the fast-breaking, event-oriented news of politics, foreign affairs, and war tends to be overrepresented. The total amount of international news available in the American press is also underrepresented, by about 45 percent, and this may hold true for other national systems. On the other hand, any kind of sampling procedure creates certain distortions and this study does not claim to have analyzed the total universe of international news available in any one country: that would be a quite formidable, albeit fascinating, task.

And yet, the validity of our quantitative findings is supported by and in turn reverberates the general findings of many other such studies conducted over the past decade. For example, a look at the geographic emphasis of international news from the data of 42 countries (culled from 10 separate empirical studies)[2] reveals a strong, consistent, and simple pattern. Regional news is emphasized in the media of all countries. Behind the dominance of own region, in second place, is news from North America and Western Europe, while the "invisible" parts of the world are Eastern Europe and the rest of the developing world outside own immediate area. Likewise with topic, where the degree of slippage between categories is greater, all the studies examined found that news emphasizes a narrow range of hard news topics and actors: politics, or politics-by-other-means such as war and economics, mainly through the activities of decision-making elites. But again, in this study as in most of the others, exactly those parts of the mass media and also alternative media were omitted where a more analytic, contextualized, and perhaps more positive approach toward international news might be found.

We would suggest that it is time to move away from this kind of study, since the accumulated data are vast and the central findings reasonably validated. We could do with more studies that focus on and help to explain how and why this almost universal process of news selection has evolved: studies of the news "gatekeepers," especially in Third World contexts, and their professional training, organizational contexts, news orientations; studies on the production and distribution processes and content of non-Western news agencies, particularly those aiming to promote a development orientation; studies that examine existing alternative perspectives on the news, from a feminist outlook on British Channel Four to a Third World perspective in an African paper, to see how "difference" is created.

We might concentrate more on the news product itself, to provide a "deeper" reading of the content of international news and thus improve on our attempt at qualitative analysis. Also, the inherent presumption that the mass media are central and crucial carriers of information and imagery about foreign countries itself needs to be tested again, balanced by investigations of exactly what various audiences do "receive" from such international news presentation and what alternative sources they use.

Finally, if the demands for a New International Information Order are to have any bite, then the rhetorical teeth need to be sharpened. Central notions like balance and distortion need to be clarified. Balanced news in an unbalanced world would be an empty victory.

Table 5   COMPARISON OF GENERAL NEWS SECTION, SIX-DAY ANALYSIS
AND TOTAL PAPER, SEVEN-DAY ANALYSIS IN U.S. MEDIA SAMPLE

	Full Sample (n = 2,675)	Limited Sample (n = 1,487)
	%	%
Geographic origin of news		
North America	35	26
Latin America	6	7
Africa	7	10
Middle East	11	16
Asia	13	14
Western Europe	17	16
Eastern Europe	7	6
General	5	5
	r = .94	
Main topic		
International politics	13	18
Domestic politics	15	21
Military, defense	11	16
Economics	14	9
International aid	1	2
Social services	2	2
Crime, justice, legal	9	12
Culture	7	2
Religion	2	2
Science	1	2
Sports	10	2
Entertainment	1	1
Personalities	4	1
Human interest	3	3
Student affairs	0	0
Ecology	2	2
Accidents, natural disasters	3	4
Other	2	2
	r = .84	

NOTES

1. This section draws heavily on an unpublished paper by Robert L. Stevenson (21).
2. The ten studies analyzed were by Dajani and Donohue (1), Gerbner and Marvanyi (3), Golding and Elliott (4), Harris (5), Hester (6), McQuail (11), Pinch (12), Rimmer (14), Schramm et al. (16), and Skurnik (17).

REFERENCES

1. Dajani, Nabil and John Donohue. "A Content Analysis of Six Arab Dailies." *Gazette* 19, 1973, pp. 155–170.
2. Galtung, Johan. "A Structural Theory of Imperialism." *Journal of Peace Research* 8(2), Spring 1971.
3. Gerbner, George and George Marvanyi. "The Many Worlds of the World's Press." *Journal of Communication* 27(1), Winter 1977, pp. 52–66.
4. Golding, Peter and Philip Elliott. *Making the News.* London: Longman, 1979.
5. Harris, Phil. "Final Report to UNESCO of a Study of the International News Media." Mimeo, University of Leicester, 1977.
6. Hester, Al. "Five Years of Foreign News on U.S. Television Evening Newscasts." *Gazette* 24, 1978, pp. 86–95.
7. Horton, Philip (Ed.) *The Third World and Press Freedom.* New York: Praeger, 1978.
8. "Humanising International News." Symposium in *Media Asia* 5(3), 1978.
9. International Press Institute. *The Flow of the News.* Zurich: IPI, 1953.
10. Kaiser, Jacques. *One Week's News.* Paris: UNESCO, 1953.
11. McQuail, Denis. *Analysis of Newspaper Content.* Research Series 4, Royal Commission on the Press. London: Her Majesty's Stationery Office, 1977.
12. Pinch, Edward T. "A Brief Study of News Patterns in Sixteen Third World Countries." Murrow Reports. Tufts University, Medford, Mass., 1978.
13. Richstad, J. and J. Anderson (Eds.) *Crisis in International News.* New York: Columbia University Press, 1981.
14. Rimmer, Tony. "Foreign News in UPI's 'A' Wire in the USA: A Descriptive Analysis of Content for February 13–18, 1977." Paper presented to the International Communication Association, Acapulco, 1980.
15. Schramm, Wilbur and Erwin Atwood. *Circulation of News in the Third World: A Study in Asia.* Hong Kong: Chinese University Press, 1981.
16. Schramm, Wilbur et al. "International News Wires and Third World News in Asia." Murrow Reports. Tufts University, Medford, Mass., 1978.
17. Skurnik, W. A. E. "Foreign News Coverage Compared: Six African Newspapers." Paper presented to the African Studies Association, Los Angeles, 1979.
18. Sreberny-Mohammadi, Annabelle. "More Bad News Than Good: International News Reporting." *Media Information Australia* 23, February 1982.
19. Sreberny-Mohammadi, Annabelle. "The World of the News: The News of the World." In *New Structures of International Communication? The Role of Research.* International Association for Mass Communication Research, 1982.
20. Sreberny-Mohammadi, Annabelle with Kaarle Nordenstreng, Robert L. Stevenson, and Frank Ugboajah. *Foreign News in the Media: International Reporting in Twenty-nine Countries.* Reports and Papers on Mass Communication No. 93. Paris: UNESCO, 1984.
21. Stevenson, Robert L. "Other Research and the World of the News." Unpublished paper, University of North Carolina at Chapel Hill, 1981.
22. "Third World News and Views." Symposium in *Journal of Communication* 29(2), Spring 1979.
23. Weaver, David H. and G. Cleveland Wilhoit. "Foreign News Coverage in Two U.S. Wire Services." *Journal of Communication* 31(2), Spring 1981, pp. 55–63.
24. "What's News?" Symposium in *Communications and Development Review* 2(2), 1978.
25. "A World Debate on Information—Flood-tide or Balanced Flow?" Symposium in *UNESCO Courier*, April 1977.

FACTORS INFLUENCING INTERNATIONAL NEWS FLOW

HERBERT G. KARIEL AND LYNN A. ROSENVALL

The factors influencing international news flow in one country are described in this case study of Canada. Herbert G. Kariel and Lynn A. Rosenvall found that the eliteness of a nation as a news source was the most important criterion for news selection in the Canadian press.

There is a wide disparity in the amount of news from various countries printed in the newspapers of other countries. This variation in the origin and destination of internal news flows has been looked at in a number of studies and can be confirmed readily by examining a set of daily newspapers. In order to understand these uneven patterns, researchers have proposed, at times rather nebulously, a number of political, economic, physical, and psychological factors. To date, however, no overview of this research has been presented, nor have the more persistently suggested factors been tested. The purpose of this study is to review what has been done and to test four of these factors in the flow of international news to Canadian daily newspapers.

Two global studies carried out in the 1950s, the International Press Institute's *The Flow of News*[1] and Unesco's, *How Nations See Each Other*[2] provided a descriptive look at the pattern of international news flows and appeared to have given an impetus to explaining observed variations. Within 10 years scholars formulated theoretical views to account for these patterns. Many of these early investigations were carried out by Scandinavian scholars. For example, Östgaard in 1965[3] isolated a number of determining factors, grouping them under the headings, "political" and "economic," and stressed that, "the news media tend to reinforce or at least to uphold the divisions of the world between high status nations and low status nations."[4]

In an attempt to systematize the factors influencing news flow. Galtung and Ruge,[5] following the work of Östgaard, presented numerous theories and hypotheses. They proposed, for example, that "the more the event concerns elite nations, the more probable that it will become a news item." They then tested some of these hypotheses against news flow data from four Norwegian newspapers. Other Scandinavian scholars, such as Sande[6] and Rosengren[7] attempted to test these factors and to refine the theoretical base of such studies.

More recently, researchers in other parts of the world, have also tested these factors against other news flow patterns.[8] As a result of these studies, numerous factors have been discussed and the following are some of the more persistently suggested ones: distance, cultural affinity, population, trade, gross national product, and eliteness.

FACTORS IN NEWS FLOW

Distance

The physical distance between the country of news origin and the country in which the items appear has been a tempting explanation of the volume of news flows. While MacLean and Pinna,[9] found that news interest declined with distance, Hicks and Gordon,[10] in their study of foreign news in Israeli and U.S.

Herbert G. Kariel and Lynn A. Rosenvall, "Factors Influencing International News Flow." *Journalism Quarterly*, Volume 61, Autumn 1984, pp. 509–516. Reprinted by permission.

The authors are professor and associate professor, respectively, in the Department of Geography at the University of Calgary, Alberta, Canada.

newspapers, found that other factors—ethnocentrism and elitism—were more important. In their study of news flows within Canada, Kariel and Rosenvall[11] found that no substantial relationship existed between news flow and physical distance; but when news flow from the U.S. to Canada were analyzed, some cross-border affinities were present.

Our conclusion, based on these and other studies, is that differences in findings are probably related to the distance itself: when relatively short distances are involved, there is some relationship to distance as news from these nearby sources could be considered local. When longer distances are involved, as in much international news flow, then distance is not an important variable.

Cultural Affinity

The importance of the influence of cultural affinity on international news flow has been observed by several researchers. Schramm,[12] for example, noted that the more a reader or editor identifies with a story, the greater the likelihood that it will be selected and the higher the possibility of it being sent along the news flow channels between countries.

In his identification of news flow factors Östgaard stated, "things or issues with which those handling and those receiving the news are most familiar, finds its way through the news channels more easily than news concerning unfamiliar persons, things or issues." Also, "the greater the possibilities of identification with the news, the greater will be the news flow, and conversely, that the less the possibilities of identification, the more the news flow will be hampered."[13] In a study of news printed in Canadian newspapers, Kariel and Rosenvall[14] found a significant relationship between cultural affinity and the amount of news from the country with which there is the affinity, that is, French-language newspapers favor news from French-culture countries and English-language newspapers favor news from the United Kingdom.

Population

Since most news is about people and their activities, more news items should be printed about nations with large populations. Rosengren and Rikardsson's study of Middle East news in Swedish newspapers found that "trade seems to be more important than population as a determinant of the news flow."[15] On the other hand, our study of news flows from the U.S. to Canadian newspapers showed that a positive relationship does exist between news volume and the population size of the state of news origin.[16]

Trade

The amount of trade between nations has been used as a factor to explain international news flow. Rosengren and Rikardsson,[17] for example, incorporated Swedish import trade figures in their study and concluded that it was an important predictor. Likewise, Anderson,[18] in a study of Copenhagen newspapers, found a correlation between amount of news and export-import figures.

Gross National Product

Gross national product per capita (GNP/C) has been suggested as a factor accounting for international news flows, primarily because it relates closely to the economic and political importance of nations as well as their level of technological development. As Hicks and Gordon stated, "the world flow of foreign news deals chiefly with a group of highly developed countries which are dominant in world politics."[19] Both Östgaard and Rosengren and Rikardsson[20] indicated that differential news flows relate to the relative wealth of nations.

Eliteness

The notion of "eliteness," the relative standing of nations in the eyes of others, has provided an interesting concept for the understanding of international news flows. This amorphous, but nonetheless apparently important concept, has not been defined precisely. Galtung and Ruge[21] mentioned the term. Sande operationally defined an elite nation as "one of the big powers."[22] Schramm identifies elite nations as a "group of highly developed countries which are also dominant in world politics."[23] Östgaard refers to "high status" and "low status" nations when ranking countries.[24] Rosengren and Rikardsson[25] investigated surrogate measures, such as population size and foreign trade. Although at times "elitism" rather than "eliteness" has been the term used, we use the term "eliteness" in order to emphasize a state of being.

This study pursues further the last four of these factors: population size, trade, GNP/C, and eliteness, but does not deal with physical distance or cultural affinity. Physical distance in international news flow does not seem to be significant except in border situations. Since cultural affinity has already been studied and shown to be important, and since it is a discrete variable, it was not included in this study which comprises continuous variables.

METHODOLOGY

This study extends our previous research on news in Canadian daily newspapers. A detailed discussion of the methodology and sampling procedure can be found in other articles.[26] Basically, a sample of 21 Canadian daily newspapers published in 18 centers, consisting of the federal capital, all provincial capitals, and population centers over 100,000 (which combined have about one-half of the Canadian population) was selected.[27] A random sample of 31 publishing days during a one-year period, representing 10% of all days on which Canadian newspapers publish, was used.

To determine the validity of the suggested variables, correlation analyses were carried out. The number of news items was the dependent variable. These were determined for each country by tabulating all the datelines of all 31 issues of these 21 newspapers. Since photographs are also news items but carry no datelines, they were assumed to originate in the country identified in the caption.

Although United States news items are part of the international news flow, they were not included in the present analysis, since in our sample they constituted nearly half (49.8%) of all international news items in all newspapers, overshadowing and usurping the international news flow to such an extent as to render any analysis difficult to interpret. Moreover, as McNaught[28] pointed out, U.S. news almost falls within the category of domestic news in Canadian newspapers.

Data for the independent variables were selected so as to correspond as closely as possible to the time period of the news item data. Population data were obtained from the *United Nation's Demographic Yearbook*. Data used for the amount of trade between Canada and the various countries was the total value of exports and imports given in the *Canada Yearbook*. Gross national product per capita data was used as given by the International Bank of Reconstruction and Development.

In order to obtain quantifiable judgments of each country's eliteness, all Canadian and American geographers who had indicated a topical proficiency in political geography in the *Directory*[29] of the Association of American Geographers were surveyed. These judges were asked to rate each country's eliteness on a five-point scale. Of the 80 questionnaires sent, 34 usable ones were returned. Mean values of the respondents' evaluations were computed, in a procedure similar to the one used by Driver.[30] These ranged from the most elite, 3.909 for the United Kingdom and 3.818 for the U.S.S.R. and Japan to 0.152 for Montserat and St. Vincent, the least elite.

Data Analyses

Simple correlation-regression analyses were carried out between each of the independent variables and the dependent variable to determine the relationship between them, as well as to identify which countries do not fit the general pattern; that is, those from which either more or fewer news items were printed than would have been expected on the basis of the independent variable used [Table 1]. A difference greater than ± 1.5 standard error untied from the regression equation was used to identify these deviant observations.[31] A multiple correlation analysis was then performed to determine the relative importance of each independent variable as well as the degree of relationship when all were used simultaneously. Logarithmic transformations were made where necessary to normalize the data.

FINDINGS

The correlation between population size and the number of news items was 0.599 ($r^2 \pm 0.359$), a statistically significant relationship at $\alpha = 0.05$. Inspection of the scatter diagram (Figure 1) shows that

Table I   CORRELATION MATRIX BETWEEN ALL VARIABLES

	Y	X_1	X_2	X_3	X_4
Y News items	1.000	0.599	0.586	0.469	0.845
X_1 Population		1.000	0.475	−0.085	−0.657
X_2 Trade			1.000	0.595	0.685
X_3 GNP/C				1.000	0.558
X_4 Eliteness					1.000

more items were printed from countries such as the United Kingdom, France, South Vietnam, and Iceland than would be warranted by their population size, and that from others, such as Mali, North Korea, Guinea, Honduras, and Albania, fewer news items were printed than would be expected considering their population. Several countries which were closely predicted, and may be of general interest, such as the U.S.S.R., West Germany, Egypt, India, Japan, China, and Brazil are also identified in the figures.

The correlation between the amount of trade and the number of news items was 0.586 ($r^2 = 0.343$), a statistically significant relationship. More news was printed from the United Kingdom, South Vietnam,

Kampuchea, Laos, and some other countries than would be expected considering the amount of trade, and countries such as Honduras, Mauritius, Fiji, Martinique, and Albania had fewer news items appearing about them (Figure 2).

The correlation between GNP/C and the number of news items was 0.469 ($r^2 = 0.220$). Although this is a statistically significant relationship, it accounts for less than a quarter of the variance. The United Kingdom, South Vietnam, India, and several other countries are those about which more news items were printed than would have been predicted on the basis of GNP/C, and fewer items were printed about some others, such as Qatar, Gabon, Honduras, and Fiji (Figure 3).

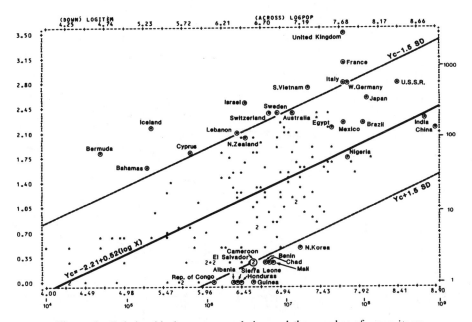

Figure 1 Relationship between population and the number of news items

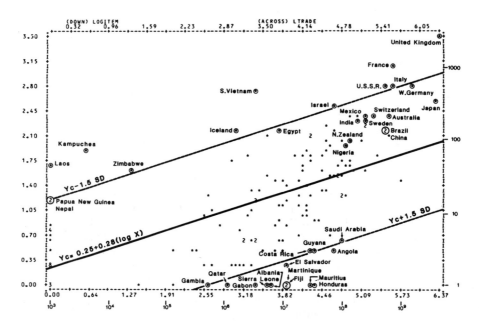

Figure 2 Relationship between amount of trade and the number of news items

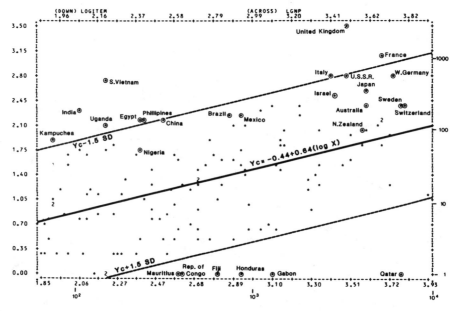

Figure 3 Relationship between Gross National Product per Capita (GNP/C) and the number of news items

22

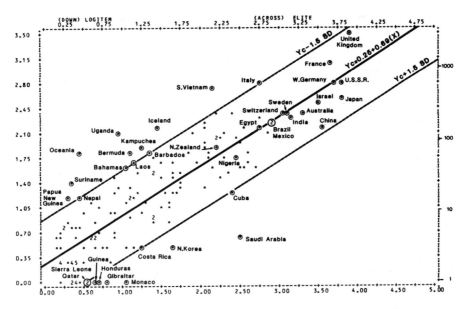

Figure 4 Relationship between eliteness and the number of news items

The correlation between eliteness and the number of news items was 0.845 ($r^2 = 0.713$). This relationship is both statistically significant and substantively important, since over 70% of the variance was accounted for. Countries about which more news was printed than their eliteness rating warranted included South Vietnam, Iceland, Kampuchea, Uganda and the islands of Oceania (Figure 4). Those about which fewer news items were printed included Saudi Arabia, North Korea, Monaco, and Honduras.

When these four variables were considered simultaneously in a multiple correlation-regression analysis it is found that eliteness contributed most to the size of the multiple correlation coefficient ($R = 0.850$, $R^2 = 0.723$), and that none of the other variables contributed statistically significant over the simple correlation ($r = 0.845$, $r^2 = 0.713$) which was found for eliteness alone. The additional variance accounted for by the inclusion of the other three variables is only 0.83 percent.

DISCUSSION

Two interesting conclusions can be reached as a result of these analyses. First, since the relationships are all statistically significant, the factors thought to

account for international news flows are valid. Since, however, the proportion of the explained variance is small in three instances, population 36%, trade 34%, and GNP/C 22%, their substantive importance appears to be minor, whereas that for eliteness is significant 71%.

Secondly, some countries are consistently under- or overpredicted, that is, more or less news, respectively, is printed about them than would be expected on the basis of these variables (Table 2). This is partly due to the particular events which took place in these countries during the time period of the study: for example the Boris Spatski–Bobby Fischer chess tournament in Iceland; the war in Vietnam, Laos, and Cambodia (Kampuchea); the special interest of Canadians in their favorite vacation spots, Bermuda and the Bahamas; several important events which took place during the year in Italy, including the eruption of Mt. Etna, a crackdown on the Mafia, an election, an unusual number of art thefts, an apartment explosion in Rome, Tito's visit, and an airplane hijacking by a former U.S. marine; the mystique of Nepal, and the flooding of several villages leaving numerous dead; and of course the cultural affinity of Canadians with the United Kingdom and France.

The fact that there is less news than expected

Table 2   COUNTRIES UNDER- AND OVERPREDICTED IN TWO OR MORE ANALYSES ON THE BASIS OF POPULATION SIZE, GROSS NATIONAL PRODUCT PER CAPITA, VALUE OF TRADE, AND ELITENESS

Country	Variable			
	Population	Trade	GNP/C	Eliteness
Underpredicted				
Bahamas	x			x
Bermuda	x			x
France	x	x	x	
Iceland	x	x		x
Israel	x	x		
Italy	x	x	x	x
Kampuchea		x	x	x
Laos		x		x
Nepal		x		x
Papua New Guinea		x		x
South Vietnam	x	x	x	x
Uganda			x	x
United Kingdom	x	x	x	
Overpredicted				
Albania	x	x		
El Salvador	x	x		
Fiji		x	x	
Gabon		x	x	
Guinea	x			x
Honduras	x	x	x	x
Mauritius		x	x	
North Korea	x			x
Qatar		x	x	x
Republic of Congo	x		x	
Sierra Leone	x	x		x

from some countries is more difficult to account for except in terms of self-imposed news suppression as in Albania, or that these countries are relegated to the extremely insignificant category in that many editors may never have heard of them, as with Honduras.[32]

The overwhelming importance of eliteness in the multiple correlation analysis reinforces the findings of the simple correlation analyses and raises a num-

ber of interesting questions. First, one can question the causal relationship between eliteness and news flow, that is, is the eliteness rating of a given country affected by the amount of news from that country, or, conversely, is the news flow determined by the country's eliteness? Further, what is it that makes nations elite and why is this factor so important? Do elite nations really have as many newsworthy events as are printed about them or do reporters, editors, and other gatekeepers perceive these countries accurately. How would the amount of international news in the newspapers of other countries correspond to the eliteness ratings by residents of those nations?

CONCLUSIONS

The importance of cultural affinity has already been assessed, but determining its importance relative to eliteness is more difficult. Our data suggest (and we suspect) that, on the average, eliteness is considerably more important; only for those nations where there are particularly close cultural ties, as with the United Kingdom and France for Canada, does this variable greatly influence the amount of news that is printed.

Special or unusual events, those which cannot be ignored in the world of economics, sports, politics, or the natural environment, tend to increase the number of news items from the country in which they take place. This is the result not only of the reporting of the events themselves, but in addition, since more reporters are on the scene, additional items are filed which might otherwise pass unnoticed.

The rapid change which can occur in the number of news items being printed about a country can be exemplified readily by the current situation in El Salvador, the earlier conflicts in Afghanistan and the Falkland Islands, and related to the time period of our study, Vietnam and Kampuchea.

Careful consideration of our data shows that most events reported from the countries underpredicted in the eliteness analysis were of interest to or directly involved an elite nation. That is, if more news is reported from a country than its eliteness rating would warrant, one or more of the world's elite nations has a stake in or is involved in the event.

NOTES

1. International Press Institute, *The Flow of News* (Zürich: International Press Institute, 1953).
2. UNESCO, *How Nations See Each Other* (Paris: UNESCO Publications, 1954).
3. Einar Östgaard, "Factors Influencing the Flow of News," *Journal of Peace Research*, 2:39–63 (1965).
4. *Ibid*, p. 55.
5. Johan Galtung and Mari Holmboe Ruge, "The Structure of Foreign News," *Journal of Peace Research*, 2:64–91 (1965). The quotation is on p. 68.
6. Øystein Sande, "The Perception of Foreign News," *Journal of Peace Research*, 8:221–237 (1971).
7. Karl Rosengren, "International News: Intra and Extra Media Data," *Acta Sociologica*, 8:96–109 (1970); and Karl Rosengren and Gunnel Rikardsson, "Middle East News in Sweden," *Gazette*, 20:99–116 (1974).
8. See for example, Gertrude Joch Robinson and Vernone M. Sparkes, "International News in the Canadian and American Press: A Comparative News Flow Study," *Gazette*, 20:203–218 (1977); Ronald G. Hicks and Avishag Gordon, "Foreign News Content in Israeli and U.S. Newspapers," *Journalism Quarterly*, 51:639–644 (1974); and Al Hester, "Theoretical Considerations in Predicting Volume and Direction of International Information Flow," *Gazette*, 19:239–247 (1973).
9. Malcolm S. MacLean Jr. and Luca Pinna. "Distance and News Interests: Scarperia, Italy," *Journalism Quarterly*, 35:36–48 (1958).
10. Hicks and Gordon, *op cit*.
11. Herbert G. Kariel and Lynn A. Rosenvall, "United States News Flows to Canadian Newspapers," *The American Review of Canadian Studies* 13:44–65 (1983).
12. Wilbur Schramm, "The Nature of News," *Journalism Quarterly*, 26:268 (Sept. 1949).
13. Östgaard, *op. cit.*, p. 46.
14. Kariel and Rosenvall, "Cultural Affinity Displayed in Canadian Daily Newspapers," *Journalism Quarterly*, 60:431–436 (1983).
15. Rosengren and Rikardsson, *op cit*, p. 104.
16. Kariel and Rosenvall, "United States News Flows to Canadian Newspapers," *op cit.*, p. 54.
17. Rosengren and Rikardsson, *op cit.*, p. 104.
18. Cited in Rosengren and Rikardsson, *op cit.*, fn 7, p. 103.
19. Hicks and Gordon, *op cit.*, p. 640.
20. Östgaard, *op cit.*, p. 43; and Rosengren and Rikardsson, *op cit.*, p. 106.
21. Galtung and Ruge, *op cit*.
22. Sande, *op cit.*, p. 238.
23. Wilbur Schramm, *Mass Media and National Development* (Palo Alto, California: Stanford University Press, 1964), pp. 58–90.

24. Östgaard, *op cit.*, p. 55.

25. Rosengren and Rikardsson, *op cit.*

26. H. G. Kariel and L. A. Rosenvall, "Circulation of Newspaper News Within Canada," *Canadian Geographer*, 22:85–111 (1978), and Herbert G. Kariel and Lynn A. Rosenvall, "Analyzing News Origin Profiles of Canadian Daily Newspapers," *Journalism Quarterly*, 38:254–59 (1981).

27. Since the Kitchener-Waterloo *Record* was unobtainable in the original or on microfilm, this newspaper and this center were left out of the analyses. The Montreal *Star* and the Ottawa *Journal* have ceased publication since the inception of the research.

28. Carleton McNaught, *Canada Gets the News* (Toronto: Ryerson Press, 1940).

29. Association of American Geographers, *AAG Directory*, 1982 (Washington, D.C.: Association of American Geographers, 1982).

30. B. L. Driver, "Quantification of Outdoor Recreationists' Preferences," *Research Camping and Environmental Education* University Park: Pennsylvania State University, HPER Series 11, 1975), pp. 165–87.

31. This procedure follows that suggested by, Edwin N. Thomas, *Maps of Residuals from Regression: Their Characteristics and Uses in Geographic Research*, Department of Geography Studies in Geography, No. 2 (Iowa City: State University of Iowa, 1960).

32. Peter Worthington, "Foreign Affairs: The Irrelevant Beat," in Walt McDayter, ed., *A Media Mosaic: Canadian Communications Through a Critical Eye* (Toronto: Holt, Rinehart and Winston of Canada, Ltd., 1971), pp. 54–83; material is on p. 57.

THE INTERNATIONAL FLOW OF TELEVISION PROGRAMS

TAPIO VARIS

This selection reviews specifically the international flow of television programs. Tapio Varis's research of sixty-nine countries found that changes in the pattern of program flow indicates a trend toward greater regional exchanges along with the continued dominance of a few exporting countries.

The global production and dissemination of information and knowledge can be approached by an analysis of the international flow of information through different media. A UNESCO study of the international flow of television programs and news in 1972–1973 (reported in [1]) found two clear trends: that there is a one-way traffic from the big exporting countries to the rest of the world, and that entertainment material dominates the flow. These aspects together represent what I have called a tendency toward concentration. This article summarizes a follow-up study undertaken in 1983 to examine the present situation in terms of both specific regions of the world and the broader global trends in the international flow of television programs.

Since the early 1970s, the number of television

Tapio Varis, "The International Flow of Television Programs." From the *Journal of Communication*, Winter 1984, pp. 143–152. © 1984, *The Journal of Communication*. Reprinted by permission.

The author is Director of the Tampere Peace Research Institute.

receivers and the size of the television audience have increased remarkably. In the beginning of the 1970s, there were approximately 273 million television receivers and an estimated audience of 883,900,000. During the decade these figures grew rapidly. For example, the worldwide television audience for the Olympic Games in Mexico in 1968 was estimated to be some 600,000,000 and for the Montreal Games of 1976 over one billion; the Moscow Games in 1980 were estimated to be watched by hundreds of millions more. This steady increase in audience size and coverage were key factors in the desire to chart current trends in the flow of television programming.

This project was conducted on a regional basis. Research centers within each region were chosen on the basis of their qualifications and experience. Each research center received a set of general instructions describing the method of sampling and categories of analysis and was responsible for collecting the data from its region in collaboration with other institutes. The representatives of these institutes also held joint consultations. The research centers and the regions for which they were responsible are: CIESPAL (Centro Internacional de Estudios Superiores de la Communicación para América Latina, Latin America), East-West Center (North America), Asia-Pacific Institute for Broadcasting Development (Asia), ASBU (Arab States Broadcasting Union, Arab States), CESTI (Centre d'Études des Sciences de Techniques de l'Information, Africa),[1] Centre for Mass Communication Research of Hungarian Radio (Eastern Europe), and the Tampere Peace Research Institute in cooperation with the Department of Journalism and Mass Communication, University of Tampere (Western Europe). The project was coordinated in Tampere.

Television programming was sampled for a two-week period, from January 31 to February 13, 1983, including weekends. Each center also determined the number of channels to be studied, depending upon available resources. Where possible and important, different types of broadcasting organizations—commercial, public, government, etc.— were sampled to give the range of available offerings. The categories of analysis for the types of programming were based on UNESCO's recommendations concerning the international standard-

ization of statistics on radio and television and on earlier UNESCO studies (see 1). The goal was to emphasize the international dimension of the flow within each program category and the programming as a whole, rather than to identify national characteristics of the television program structure. There were eight major categories:

1. *Informative programs.* These were programs whose content consisted of facts, events, theories, or forecasts or programs that provided explanatory background information. They included news bulletins and news commentaries (including sports news), other informative programs (such as those dealing with political, economic, scientific, cultural, and social matters), special events, and documentaries.

2. *Educational programs.* These were programs in which the pedagogical element was considered fundamental. They included educational programs related to a specific curriculum (schools, university, etc.), educational programs for rural development purposes, and other educational programs.

3. *Cultural programs.* These were programs that could be regarded as cultural performances or activities in themselves and those in which the spheres and phenomena of culture were reported in non-didactic ways.

4. *Religious programs.* These were programs based on different forms of religious service or similarly inspirational programs intended to edify the audience.

5. *Children's programs.*

6. *Entertainment programs.* These included films originally released theatrically, programs produced as plays, including serials, programs whose dominant content was "live" or recorded music, sports programs (but excluding sports news) and other entertainment programs.

7. *Unclassified programs.*

8. *Advertisements.* These were commercial or other advertisements for which payment was made.

Television programs were classified by type using their characteristics as described in written television program guides when available and by additional monitoring when possible. The resulting classification is meant to be suggestive of the nature of the program structure, rather than of an exact breakdown of categories, as different cultural and

Table I

PERCENTAGE OF IMPORTED TELEVISION PROGRAMS IN 1973, 1983, AND PRIME-TIME 1983 (MEASURED IN PROGRAMMING HOURS)

Country and Broadcasting Institution	Percentage of Programming Imported in			Country and Broadcasting Institution	Percentage of Programming Imported in		
	1973	1983	1983 (prime time)		1973	1983	1983 (prime time)
North America				*Western Europe (Continued)*			
Canada/CBC	34	32	24	Iceland	67	66	66
Canada/RC	46	38	31	Ireland	54	57	58
United States/comm.	1	2	2	Italy	13	18	19
United States/educ.	2			Netherlands	23	25	24
Latin American and Caribbean				Norway	39	30	28
				Portugal	35	39	—
Argentina/Canal 9	10	49	53	Spain	—	33	35
Brazil	—	30	23	Spain/EIT.B Regional	—	74	—
Chile	55	—	—	Sweden	33	35	28
Colombia	34	—	—	Turkey	—	36	49
Cuba	—	24	9	United Kingdom/ BBC	12	15	21
Dominican Republic	50	—	—				
Ecuador	—	66	70	United Kingdom/ ITV	13	14	20
Guatemala	84	—	—				
Mexico	39	34	44	United Kingdom/ Channel 4	—	26	15
Uruguay	62	—	—				
Venezuela	—	38	42	*Eastern Europe/ Soviet Union*			
Western Europe							
Austria	—	43	61	Bulgaria	45	27	21
Belgium/BRT	—	28	33	German Dem. Rep.	26	30	39
Belgium/RTBF	—	29	28	Czechoslovakia	—	24	25
Denmark	—	46	32	Hungary	24	26	35
Fed. Rep. of Germany/ARD	23	13	7	Poland	17	—	—
				Romania	27	—	—
Fed. Rep. of Germany/ZDF	30	23	23	Soviet Union	5	8	18
				Yugoslavia	27	29	22
Fed. Rep. of Germany/ Regional	—	24	—	*Asia and the Pacific*			
Finland	40	37	37	Australia	57	44	46
France	9	17	17	Brunei	—	60	28
Greece	—	39	—	People's Rep. of China	1	8	—

Table I	Percentage of Programming Imported in			Country and Broadcasting Institution	Percentage of Programming Imported in		
Country and Broadcasting Institution	1973	1983	1983 (prime time)		1973	1983	1983 (prime time)
Asia and the Pacific (Continued)				Vietnam	—	34	—
Hong Kong/Asia TV Chinese	31	24	16	*Near East and Arab Countries*			
Hong Kong/Asia TV English	40	64	72	Algeria	—	55	55
Hong Kong/Asia TV Ltd.	—	27	9	Egypt	41	35	41
				Israel	55	—	—
India/Calcutta	—	3	6	Kuwait	56	—	—
India/Delhi	—	11	10	Lebanon	40	—	—
Japan/NHK educ.	1	—	—	Saudi-Arabia/Riyadh TV	31	—	—
Japan/comm.	10	—	—	Saudi-Arabia/ Aramcu TV	100	—	—
Republic of Korea/ Tong-yang	31	—	—	Syria	—	33	35
Republic of Korea/ Munhwa TV	—	16	0	Tunisia	—	55	35
Malaysia	71	54	31	People's Rep. of Yemen	57	47	—
New Zealand/one	75	72	64	*Africa*			
New Zealand/two	75	75	66	Ghana	27	—	—
Pakistan	35	16	12	Kenya	—	37	60
Philippines	29	12	20	Nigeria	63	40	—
Philippines/Metro Manila	—	40	—	Republic of South Africa	—	29	31
Singapore/Channel 8	78	55	70	Uganda	19	38	38
Singapore/Channel 5	78	70	66	Zambia	64	—	—
Sri Lanka	—	24	22	Zimbabwe	—	61	—
Thailand	18	—	—				

social environments make it difficult to create fully comparable categorization of program types. In addition, the source of programming (domestic or imported and from what country) was coded, as was whether or not the program was shown in prime time (as defined by a given regional research institute).

Table 1 summarizes the percentages of imported versus domestically produced programs in each country studied. A comparison is made between 1973 figures, 1983 figures, and 1983 prime-time figures.

Overall, imported programs average approximately one-third or more of total programming time. In all parts of the world there are those countries that are heavily dependent on foreign imports in their programming as well as those that are only slightly dependent. The difference between figures for prime time and total time is not very great, with the exception of Latin America, where foreign programming tends to dominate more in prime time (but not in Brazil and Cuba).

Although one cannot generalize a worldwide trend, regions have exhibited notable changes between 1973 and 1983.

North America

The United States imports very few programs from abroad. Out of the quarter of a million program hours broadcast during the two-week period examined, less than two percent were imported from outside the United States. Most of these came from the United Kingdom and were shown on public television. The rest of the imported programs came from Mexico and other Latin American countries.

In Canada, six channels in the Montreal area were studied. The findings confirm that publicly owned networks (CBC) tend to show more Canadian programming than privately owned networks (RC). They also confirm that the private sector tends to displace Canadian programming during prime time. The United States accounts for the vast majority of imported programming except in the case of the educational network, Radio Québec, which imports most of its programming from Western Europe.

Latin America

Entertainment programming dominated the television schedules of all the countries analyzed, accounting for approximately half of the total transmission time (about a third in Cuba). Entertainment programming accounts for most of the imported materials, which also take up half of the total transmission time (slightly more during prime time). The United States (together with production by the multinational corporations) is the source of about three-quarters of the imported material. Programs from other Latin American countries make up twelve percent of the imported material, and Western Europe adds a few percent to the total.

Western Europe

Here, differences between various countries are notable. Overall, approximately thirty percent of the programs are imported. The bulk of them (44 percent) are from the United States, with U.S. programs accounting for more than ten percent of the total transmission time in Western Europe. The United Kingdom provides 16 percent of the imported programs in Western Europe, followed by the Federal Republic of Germany and France, which each provide 5 to 10 percent, as do other Western European countries combined. Eastern European and Soviet productions make up about 3 percent of the imported programs. They have a higher share in Finland and Yugoslavia than elsewhere, although France, Great Britain, and West Germany do import programs from the East.

Eastern Europe and the Soviet Union

Although the greatest number of imported programs is in the entertainment category, many of the cultural programs are also imported (21 percent). The Soviet Union imports only 14 percent of its entertainment programs. Eastern European television organizations together imported programs from 26 countries during the period examined. Forty-three percent of the aggregated total of imported material broadcast was produced in other Eastern European countries and 57 percent was purchased from countries outside Eastern Europe. The Soviet Union accounted for 21 percent of the imported programs in Eastern Europe.

Asia and the Pacific

The overall averages for imported programming are 36 percent of total transmission time and 36 percent of prime time. The greatest variation is by individual broadcast organization. The share of imported programs ranges from a high of 75 percent (Television New Zealand, Channel Two) to a low of 3 percent (Doordarshan India, Calcutta Station). On the average, Asian/Pacific audiences had access to about 10 hours of television programming every day, with a low of about 3 hours in Vietnam and a high of 20 hours in New Zealand.

There seems to be a direct relationship between the number of transmission hours and the percentage of imported programs. Entertainment and information programs together constitute about 75 percent of the total transmission time and 88 percent of prime time. A majority of children's programs are imported (53 percent of total transmission time), followed by entertainment programs (49 percent imported), whereas informational, educational, cultural, and religious programs are largely domestically produced. The United States and the United Kingdom are the main source of imported programs in Asia. Japanese children's programs, documentaries, and theatrical movies are also widely shown, as are films produced in India, Hong Kong, and Taiwan. The People's Republic of China produces most of its own programming; of its imported programs, the majority are educational programs and news material from the United Kingdom.

Arab Countries

Forty-two percent of television programs are imported, approximately one-third of them from other Arabic countries. Imported programs dominate the category of television plays and documentaries. The United States provides 32 percent of the non-Arabic imported programs in the Arabic region. U.S. programming is most prominent in Egypt, where it constitutes 54.5 percent of the imported programs. Of the rest of non-Arabic imported programming, France supplies almost 13 percent, the United Kingdom, Japan, and the Federal Republic of Germany each provide 5 to 7 percent, the Soviet Union provides less than 3 percent, and other socialist countries provide about 1 percent. Of the Arabic countries, the most important source of imports is the United Arab Emirates (10 percent of the imported programs), followed by Egypt (6 percent), Saudi Arabia (4 percent), and Kuwait (4 percent).

Africa

Television is not yet a major medium in many African countries, except in urban areas. Data from Kenya, Nigeria, and Uganda suggest that almost 40 percent of the programs are imported. In Zimbabwe, the figure is 61 percent. Of the foreign programs in Kenya, more than half originate in the United States, a quarter come from the Federal Republic of Germany, and the rest come from other Western countries.

The Republic of South Africa, which was introduced to television in 1976, was analyzed as a special case. Almost one-third of the programs are imported, coming from the United States (54 percent), the United Kingdom (30 percent), France (9 percent), Austria (5 percent), and Canada (3 percent). Entertainment programs make up some 70 percent of the imported material. Light entertainment originates mainly in the United States rather than Great Britain, because the British actors' union Equity forbids the sale of material involving its members to South African TV. No educational programs were broadcast during this period.

Table 2 summarizes the types of programming imported by region, with some further breakdowns. In the United States, imports from two nations, Mexico and England, account for almost half the television time devoted to imports. The Mexican programs are mainly TV plays, and the British imports are cultural programs.

In the Soviet Union, the imported programs shown on Central Television during the two weeks studied were produced in the socialist countries (Bulgaria, Czechoslovakia, German Democratic Republic, Hungary, Poland, Mongolia, Yugoslavia), Western countries (France, Federal Republic of Germany, Spain, United States), and developing countries (Sri Lanka). Imported material constituted 39 percent of all feature films and 33 percent of all sports broadcasts.

In Canada, movies and situation comedies account for the highest proportion of imports. Entertainment programs dominate in all Latin American countries, with approximately half of total transmission time devoted to entertainment (except in Cuba, where the figure is one-third). Most of the imported material falls in this category.

In Western Europe, too, entertainment programming is very dependent on foreign imports, but there are notable differences among Western European countries not shown in these cumulative figures. In Eastern Europe, entertainment programs tend to be imported; to some extent, so do children's programs and educational programs.

Table 2   DISTRIBUTION OF PROGRAMMING BY REGION AND CATEGORY*

Program Category	U.S.		Canada		Latin America		W. Europe	
	All (%)	Imp. (%)	All (%)	Imp. (%)	All (%)	Imp. (%)	All (%)	Imp. (%)
Informative	19	1	35	—	16	20	29	5
Educational	7	0	8	—	7	13	9	10
Cultural	6	9	8	24	2	14	6	12
Religious	3	—	2	28	1	18	1	11
Entertainment	40	2	36	72	44	71	35	53
Sports	4	2	3	—	5	18	8	36
Other (ads, children's, unclassified)	25	0	8	35	25	37	12	30
Total %	100		100		100		100	
Minutes	17,344,100		84,166		670,088		236,207	

*The figures are indicative to the regions as a whole as represented by the countries in the study. The Republic of South

In Asia and the Pacific region, imports appear mostly among children's programs, followed by entertainment programs. Informational, educational, cultural, and religious programs are largely domestically produced.

In the Arab countries, imported programs dominate the category of television plays and documentaries. In African countries, most of the theatrical films, TV plays, and educational programs are imported.

At a global level, the bulk of imported programs originate in the United States and—although to a much lesser extent—in Western Europe and Japan. The flow consists mainly of programs of a recreational nature, such as entertainment, movies, and sports. In some regions, such as Latin America, the United States is the source of as much as three-quarters of the imported materials.

In Europe, regional exchange has been well established for a long time. In both Western and Eastern Europe, more than forty percent of imported programming originates within other countries in the regions themselves. Considering the East and West as regions, the share of U.S. imports in Western Europe is on the average over 40 percent of imported programs, while Soviet-originated programs constitute some 20 percent of the imports seen in Eastern Europe.

The increase in regional exchange is particularly notable among the Arab countries, where approximately one-third of the imported programs come from other countries within the region, and among Latin American countries, where the figure for interregional imports is around ten percent. Of course, there remain great differences in the amount and origin of the flow between nations and regions.

The "North-South gap," a familiar term in discussing international economic, political, and military relations, holds for television program flow as well. But there are also certain imbalances in the East-West dimension. Of the programs imported by Eastern European countries, almost two-thirds come from nonsocialist countries; Western European countries get only about three percent of their total imports from the socialist countries. No programs from the socialist countries were shown in the United States during the period of this study. One interesting case is Cuba: during the period examined,

U.S.S.R.		F Europe		Asia		Arab Region		Africa	
All (%)	Imp. (%)	All (%)	Imp. (%)	All (%)	Imp. (%)	All (%)	Imp. (%)	All (%)	Imp. (%)
30	2	2υ	7	15	30	22	12	39	8
14	—	13	9	7	13	6	1	9	27
15	4	12	21	3	6	6	2	3	29
—	—	—	—	2	9	5	1	1	—
27	14	36	49	48	53	42	72	30	73
9	32	10	43	10	28	6	2	6	60
5	5	9	21	15	41	13	50	12	40
100		100		100		100		100	
22,080		60,097		152,978		48,689		30,524	

Africa is not in the figures. Yugoslavia, as a member of the European Broadcasting Union, is in Western Europe.

Cuba imported 20 percent of its foreign programs from the United States and 19 percent from the Soviet Union. During prime time, however, the main source of foreign programs was the German Democratic Republic (27 percent), followed by the United Kingdom (20 percent).

The situation surrounding the importation of traditional broadcast television as described here is undergoing rapid change, due to the new markets created for videocassettes and other nonbroadcast media. Little is known about the pattern of the international flow for these media, but it may prove to be characterized by even more concentration among a few sources than the traditional media. Videocassettes may also open new alternatives to minorities and foreigners. The importance of these new media is difficult to gauge so far, although they are certainly playing a role in the undermining of traditional broadcast systems in many countries, especially in Europe.

Under the present economic conditions, it is not easy to predict how rapidly the active civil deployment of the new communication technology will take place. Direct broadcast satellite channels, it is said, will soon be flooding Western Europe with television programming. According to one estimate, most households in Europe should be able to receive at least a dozen different satellite-delivered channels by the end of this decade; many densely populated areas with extra equipment could have double this number. So far, however, the introduction of satellites has not changed the basic patterns of the flow of television programs and news. Although they have contributed to the improvement of regional exchanges, in some cases they have enhanced a trend toward transnational concentration.

It has become a truism that present information flows are marked by serious inadequacy and imbalance and that most countries are passive recipients of information disseminated by a few other countries. The new communication technologies may offer some alternatives for the future. But they may also serve only to widen the gap between those who have access to information and the means of using it and influencing others, and those who do not have these capabilities. If access to information is dependent solely on wealth and income, no change in this current flow of information seems likely in the future.

NOTE

1. Data for Africa are still preliminary, with the exception of those for South Africa (provided by the author).

REFERENCE

1. Varis, Tapio. "Global Traffic in Television." *Journal of Communication* 24(1), Winter 1974, pp. 102–109.

MEDIA MARKETS AROUND THE WORLD

This selection deals with specific examples of the flow of international communication. From *Electronic Age* we reprint an item about media markets around the world which provides some specific facts about the media systems of ten countries.

Around the world, countries are grappling with the changing electronic media.

While some consider easing up on their regulations, other governments are looking into imposing stricter guidelines. Meanwhile, broadcasters are considering how to expand their program options.

Here are profiles of 10 countries, featuring a representative sample of what's been happening in the last year in the electronic media.

By comparison, the United States has 1,349 TV stations and 10,267 radio stations—4,908 AM radio stations and 5,359 FM stations.

Cable is in 51 percent of U.S. homes, while videocassette recorders are in 52 percent.

The country has 1,677 daily papers.

And "The Cosby Show" finished the 1987–88 prime-time season as the No. 1 show in the United States.

AUSTRALIA

TV stations: 67
Number privately owned: 54
Commercials allowed: on the private stations
TV networks: 3 commercial, 1 independent but government-funded
Radio stations: 239
Privately owned: 107
Cable TV penetration: None
Videocassette recorders: 2.4 million
Daily newspapers: 67, including three national and one in Chinese
Hottest domestic TV show: "60 Minutes"

Hottest American-made TV show: "The Cosby Show"
Quota on foreign shows: No, however stations must each run 104 hours of Australian-made drama each year, plus four "big-budget" specials.

A huge shakeup in the electronic media occurred last year after Rupert Murdoch's $1.8 billion takeover of the Herald & Weekly Times group forced him to sell his TEN television network under media ownership laws.

All three commercial networks subsequently

"Media Markets around the World." *Electronic Media,* April 25, 1988. Reprinted by permission.

changed hands: TEN moved from Mr. Murdoch to Frank Lowy, Nine Network from Kerry Packer to Alan Bond and Seven from H&WT/Fairfax group to Christopher Skase.

The non-commercial Australian Broadcasting Corp., which is federally funded but independently controlled, is currently considering allowing commercial sponsorship of some of its programs, such as sports and concert events.

Cable TV may be introduced after 1990, but by then closed-circuit satellite television is expected to have gained a foothold.

BRAZIL

TV stations: 196
Number privately owned: 186
Commercials allowed: yes
TV networks: 4
Radio stations: 2,222
Privately owned: 2,141
Cable TV penetration: none
Videocassette recorders: more than 3 million, many of which are smuggled into the country
Daily newspapers: 320
Hottest domestic TV show: "Mandala," a nightly telenovela that's a modern-day version of Sophocles' "Oedipus."
Hottest American-made TV show: "Hunter"

Quota on foreign shows: No

The country of Brazil has seen an increasingly looser television environment since a civilian government took office in 1985 following 21 years of dictatorship. TV censorship exists, but appears to be more concerned with political and religious questions than with sexual ones.

Meanwhile, audiences flock to watch the nightly soap operas, which start at 8:20 p.m.

One network also began running old black-and-white American TV shows such as "Lost in Space," "The Twilight Zone" and "The Untouchables."

CANADA

TV stations: 132
Number privately owned: 68
Commercials allowed: at 100 stations
TV networks: 6
Radio stations: 698 (422 AM, 276 FM)
Privately owned: 460 (315 AM, 145 FM)
Cable TV penetration: 78 percent
Videocassette recorders: 4.3 million
Daily newspapers: 110
Hottest domestic TV show: "Lance et Compte 2" ("He Shoots, He Scores.")
Hottest American-made TV show: "The Cos-by Show"
Quota on foreign shows: Varying limits on different networks

The number of Canadian homes with videocassette recorders continued to grow in the last year.

In 1987, 45 percent of the country's households had VCR, up from 35 percent the previous year and almost double the 1983 level.

At the same time, cable television penetration remained stagnant at 78 percent.

FRANCE

TV stations: 6
Number privately owned: 4, including 1 subscriber channel.
Commercials allowed: Yes
TV networks: None
Radio stations: 1,200
Privately owned: All but 2, France Inter and Radio France
Cable TV penetration: 100,000 households
Videocassette recorders: 5 million
Daily newspapers: 93
Hottest domestic TV show: "La Roue de la Fortune" ("Wheel of Fortune"), with same format as the U.S. show
Hottest American-made TV show: "Starsky & Hutch"
Quota on foreign shows: 60 percent of all TV material must be EEC-produced, except on TF1, which must run 70 percent. In addition, 50 percent must be of French origin, except on M6, which must air 52 percent.

In contrast to the preceding year or two, 1987 was a relatively calm year on the audio-visual scene in France.

Compared to 1985 and 1986, when television licenses and stations came and went, 1987's singular event was the privatization of one of the three government stations, TF1.

Last spring, it was officially turned over to construction magnate Francis Bouygues and some investors, despite the protests of many who were competing for the license.

La Cinq, one of the other private stations, run by Italian Silvio Berlusconi, is not realizing the lustrous results observers had hoped.

It started with big budgets for talent, for example, and while it hired people away from other stations, many have left because Channel 5 management didn't have the money to pay them.

The most important result is the broadening of the television advertising market in France, where space had previously been severely limted.

ITALY

TV stations: 1,397
Number privately owned: 1,394
Commercials allowed: yes
TV networks: 3 state-run RAI, 3 private and 9 part-time networks
Radio stations: 4,204, including 10 national and 5 state-run RAI stations
Privately owned: 4,199
Cable TV penetration: none
Videocassette recorders: 2 million, or 10 percent of all households
Daily newspapers: 72
Hottest domestic TV show: "Fantastico" variety show
Hot American-made TV show: "Dynasty"

Quota on foreign shows: No

In the continued absence of new and clear broadcasting legislation—current laws were designed to protect the state-run RAI monopoly—private TV and radio stations have popped up by the hundreds, often with low budgets and weak signals. However, the lack of clear legislation has also allowed the big players, especially in commercial TV, to make significant developments such as morning TV programs and airing news programs as options to the RAI networks' news.

While cable TV is still unavailable in Italy, the media industry here is enthused about the advent of satellite broadcasting early next year.

JAPAN

TV stations: 105
Number privately owned: 103
Commercials allowed: yes
TV networks: 5 private, 1 government owned, NHK
Radio stations: 73
Privately owned: 71
Cable TV penetration: 5 million, or 12.7 percent
Videocassette recorders: 21 million, or 53 percent
Daily newspapers: 94, including 5 national

Hottest domestic TV show: "Takeda Shingen," a samurai drama
Hottest American-made TV show: "Airwolf"
Quota on foreign shows: No

Cable growth will continue, and a number of new metropolitan services are expected to start in 1988.

The major event of 1987 was the start of NHK's Direct Broadcasting Service in July 1987. NHK expects 1 million homes to be equipped with DBS dishes by 1990.

MEXICO

TV stations: 402
Number privately owned: 134
Commercials allowed: yes
TV networks: 2, government-owned Imevision, privately owned Televisa
Radio stations: 842 (646 AM, 196 FM)
Privately owned: 815
Cable TV penetration: 400,000 households
Videocassette recorders: Not available
Daily newspapers: 415
Hottest domestic TV show: "Que Nos Pasa," a weekly comedy series
Hottest American-made TV show: "Knight Rider"
Quota on foreign shows: No

Televisa, the private consortium, consolidated its position as Mexican TV audiences' favorite over the last year, topping the ratings with a programming policy based on soap operas.

By January, the 10 most popular programs in Mexico were Televisa's, and five of those were soap operas.

Televisa also produced a blockbuster, serious drama series about the 21 post-revolutionary years before the Mexican oil industry's expropriation in 1938. The series was sold to dozens of TV companies throughout the world.

The past year saw a dramatic increase in the number of satellite TV dishes in Mexico, but many of these were pirates.

SWITZERLAND

TV stations: 3
Number privately owned: None
Commercials allowed: Yes
TV networks: 1 state-run network
Radio stations: 36
Privately owned: 30
Cable TV penetration: 100,000 households, although not an official estimate

Videocassette recorders: 1 million
Daily newspapers: 35
Hottest domestic TV show: "Temps Present," a news show resembling "60 Minutes"
Hot American-made TV show: "Dynasty"
Quota on foreign shows: No

An attempt to graft privately owned TV onto

the nation's three state-run channels appeared to founder in 1987 when cable channel Telecine announced it was going bankrupt.

The owners attempted to solve their problem by piping in the signal of France's Canal Plus, but this was rejected by the government "because it would destroy the Swiss character of the channel."

This prompted some wry comment from newspapers, since Telecine's programming is largely old movies, virtually none of which come from Switzerland.

The local radio scene is shaking out, with one or two of the fringe radio stations failing because of lack of money and others talking merger.

The proximity of Switzerland to a half-dozen neighboring countries with more powerful radio transmitters continues to be a problem.

The government from time to time has to ask the other countries, usually France and Italy, to tone down the power of their stations.

On the television front, the Swiss-Italian television channel has had to increase the power of its transmitters to drown out signals from more than 50 private stations located across the border in northern Italy.

UNITED KINGDOM

TV stations: 18
Number privately owned: 17
Commercials allowed: at 17 stations
TV networks: 2-BBC and ITV
Radio stations: 4 national, 78 local
Privately owned: 46 (all local)
Cable TV penetration: 254,500 homes
Videocassette recorders: about 11 million, roughly 50 percent
Daily newspapers: 12 national, 100 regional
Hottest domestic TV show: "East-Enders," twice weekly soap
Hottest American-made TV show: "The A-Team"
Quota on foreign shows: 14 percent, excluding other EEC countries

Prime Minister Margaret Thatcher's government has recently announced several measures on broadcasting which have shaken the commercial TV industry.

The biggest, revealed in February, was that the franchises for the 15 ITV stations would be auctioned off to the highest bidder when they come up for renewal in 1992. Previously, the franchises have been allocated on merit so the companies with the biggest names and most impressive programing plans got the business.

The government has also declared that it is looking into the possibility of allowing a fifth all-day TV channel.

In an effort to get more competition in program making, the government has got both the ITV and stations and BBC to agree that a minimum 25 percent of their programing should be made by independent production companies.

The ITV stations have come under fierce criticism from advertisers after losing 5 percent of their audiences last year.

In January, the government published plans for three new national commercial radio stations and for several hundred local and community stations.

WEST GERMANY

TV stations: 8

Number privately owned: 5

Commercials allowed: Government-owned ARD and ZDF restrict commercial time, while 3 SAT bans commercials; the five private stations do allow commercials.

TV networks: none

Radio stations: 94

Privately owned: 81

Cable TV penetration: 12 percent

Videocassette recorders: 40 percent

Daily newspapers: 375

Hottest domestic TV show: "Black Forest Hospital," a soap opera

Hottest American-made TV show: "Dallas"

Quota on foreign shows: No

The debut of new radio stations was the most significant development here in 1987.

The ZAW, Association of German Advertisers, in Bonn expects that in a couple of years the number of radio stations may more than double to 200.

Media watchers, on the other hand, are cautious and expect that not all new stations will survive.

The private TV stations SAT 1 and RTL Plus can now be received by 12 percent of German households; however, 22 percent more households could be linked to cable TV, but the German Post Office failed in its attempt to sign them up.

THE GLOBAL PICTURE

JONATHAN MILLER

Jonathan Miller describes some of the specific examples of how "the global picture" is affecting different societies. The new technologies, in particular, are changing television and mass media around the world, as Jonathan Miller shows.

America's balance-of-payments deficit may be huge, but at least in one field the United States has demonstrated a genius for export. This involves not a set of products but a cluster of new technologies, dubbed Television II, that are remaking the medium worldwide.

These new media, along with the growing realization that they need not, indeed cannot, be tightly controlled by monopoly broadcasting organizations, are transforming the global information system. In the new arrangement, the traditional gatekeeper's power is eroding, and the viewer's power is becoming supreme.

None of this is new in America, where it has been clear since the late '70s that the hegemony of traditional broadcasters is ending. What *is* new is the

Jonathan Miller, "The Global Picture." *Channels, 1986 Field Guide*, pp. 16–17. Reprinted by permission.

The author is a free-lance journalist.

evidence that the new American television revolution is becoming a global phenomenon [see Table 1]:

- In Estonia, the Soviet territory across the Baltic from Finland, enterprising residents hook up elaborate antennas to receive American television shows transmitted from Helsinki. In Moscow, there's a thriving market in *samizdat* videocassettes.

- In Hong Kong, the Communist-run Chinese Friendship Stores do a roaring business in videocassettes, and sell video recorders that can play them back in any of the world's three color television formats.

- In Jamaica, more than 15,000 backyard earth stations have been installed to pluck American cable programs from the sky. The Jamaican Broadcasting Corporation fears it will be unable to recover from the inevitable loss of viewers.

The new age of television thrives where viewers enjoy political and economic freedom. Nowhere on the planet is television so free as in America, where a relaxed Federal Communications Commission allows almost anything. Yet even in countries that lack America's democratic traditions, video is escaping control.

Throughout the world, the technology that appears most resistant to control is the videocassette recorder. Increasingly portable and inexpensive, the VCR on its own is a formidable technology. Just as Xerox machines permitted printed information to be distributed widely and inexpensively in private networks, video recorders allow viewers to share programs that have never received the imprimatur of governments.

Two kinds of campaigns are being waged by governments still under the illusion that they can control television. In authoritarian and totalitarian countries, the efforts are undisguised.

In the Soviet Union, the press wages a coordi-

Table I   MONDO VIDEO

(More than 90 percent of the homes in developed countries can receive broadcast television, and growing numbers have cable or videocassette recorders. Following are estimates of media penetration in 11 major countries.)

	Broadcast TV	Cable TV	VCRs
United States	99%	46%	30%
Canada	98%	61%	13%
Japan	99%	#	35%
United Kingdom	98%	5%	38%
France	93%	2%	7%
West Germany	97%	4%	21%
Belgium/Luxembourg	97%	83%	11%
Sweden	97%	5%	20%*
Switzerland	96%	48%	7%**
Ireland	90%	29%	7%**
Italy	90%	0%	7%**

Average in Scandinavia.
**Average in selected European countries.*
#Currently, only Japanese hotels have cable TV.*
Chart compiled by Jane Lusaka. Sources: For Europe, 1985, CIT Research; for Canada, 1984, Canadian Bureau of Statistics; for U.S., 1985, Motion Picture Association of America; for Japan, 1985, Japan Broadcasting Corporation (NHK) and Sony Corporation.

nated campaign to persuade viewers of the evils of Western television. The government backs its propaganda with more forceful measures. Estonia has stopped the sale of materials that can be used to make television antennas, and has forced viewers to hook up to a cable network that carries only officially sanctioned programs.

In Western Europe, efforts to control television are more subtle. The French have used import duties and quotas in efforts to stem the flow of VCRs from Japan. (The project has been a failure—French viewers smuggle the machines from Belgium.) In Italy, the government tried for years to maintain the fiction that only the state broadcasting organization was entitled to operate a national television network. The anarchist Italians ignored the injunction. Hundreds of local television stations have started grouping together into networks in open defiance of the bureaucrats in Rome.

Efforts by Western European governments to introduce new television distribution systems on a planned basis have been futile. For almost five years, every major government in Western Europe has been attempting to introduce cable television. In Britain, government policy permits cable construction by private entrepreneurs; in France and Germany, responsibility for cable has for the most part been seen as a governmental function. Neither form has shown signs of working. Despite some widely publicized experiments, the continent is being cabled only very slowly—in Britain because the government has promulgated regulations that make cable an unattractive investment; in France and Germany because the authorities haven't financed it adequately.

Europe is often seen as the place where direct broadcasting from satellites is likely to make a big splash. Here, too, there are reasons to be skeptical. The high-power satellites that the Europeans want to use have been plagued with technical and economic problems, and are years behind schedule.

The French and Germans plan to launch their first TV satellite in 1986, but they still have to work out who will get to put programs on them. Also, because the satellites will be able to transmit only a handful of channels, viewers may not be prepared to pay for the dishes necessary to receive those channels, especially when a similar investment will buy

access, through a VCR, to thousands of available cassettes.

In Britain, the direct broadcasting plan has collapsed altogether. (The government insisted that the system be placed in the control of the existing broadcasting organizations, which proved incapable of agreeing on what to do with it.)

Several other satellite plans in Europe appear equally problematic. Ireland wants to launch one, but its partner in the project, America's Hughes Aircraft Company, acknowledges that the financial and organizational obstacles are formidable. Luxembourg's effort to launch a direct-broadcast satellite has collapsed; Italy's plan looks for the moment like a nonstarter.

The Europeans may now be learning that using high-power satellites dedicated to direct broadcasting is a less effective approach than the American scheme, which relies on the use of far more economical general-purpose satellites. Swedish, Luxembourgois, and British groups are now trying to raise money to launch these American-style satellites, which will offer Europeans a larger selection of channels than the official direct-broadcasting satellites.

The new distribution patterns for television programs are commercially attractive but, given the prevailing anarchy in the marketplace, hard to exploit. Increasing numbers of studios and other copyright holders are losing control of their products. There are widespread fears that the uncontrollable nature of many of the new video techniques will lead to an erosion of program standards. In Britain, especially, this topic has engaged the attention of broadcasters and editorial writers. The argument goes that an environment of abundant video will foment the bad and drive out the good. BBC executives, sounding much like their American counterparts a few years ago, claim that support of "public service" broadcasting will wither away when viewers are distracted by the choices presented in the new age of television.

But for the most part, the new video environment appears to be an improvement over what preceded it. Television, which began its life as a power-centralizing medium, is in its maturity dispersing that power, democratizing society by putting the control of images into the hands of viewers. As such, TV around the world is becoming analogous to print. As viewers equip themselves with VCRs, satellite dishes, video cameras, and the other accessories of the new television, a new generation of viewers are coming to look upon television not as a mystery, but as something over which they have mastery.

GLOBAL TELEVISION FLOW TO LATIN AMERICAN COUNTRIES

Maria C. Wert and Robert L. Stevenson

Maria C. Wert and Robert L. Stevenson describe the "global television flow" as it affects Latin American countries, specifically in three Central American countries, Panama, Costa Rica, and El Salvador. They show that American TV still dominates in these countries.

Nothing in the decade-long international debate over the dominance of the West—especially the United States—in global communication has raised more controversy than the issue of television programming. And nothing apparently has changed less than the ubiquity of Anglo-American news and entertainment on TV screens in most countries of the world. An extensive study in 1983[1] concluded that, on the average, at least one-third of programming in the 50-plus countries studied was imported and that the United States was the dominant source.

Yet these general conclusions obscured several important changes that had occurred since a comparable study a decade earlier.[2] One was a decline in the proportion of imported programming in most Third World countries; a second was the rise of regional production centers in the Middle East and Latin American, a phenomenon also noted in Hong Kong.[3]

A special issue of *Communication Research*, also published in 1984, documented the trends in Latin America but emphasized different aspects of this change. In it, Antola and Rogers[4] concluded that viewer interests were moving U.S. imports to the periphery of the television screen and replacing them with domestic or regionally produced programs, especially the unique Latin American soap opera. They identified Mexico and Brazil as the main regional exporters and Mexico, where most non-Spanish programs are dubbed, as the key gatekeepers through which programs from outside the region must pass.

So beneath a rapidly growing TV world, still dominated by Anglo–American imports, important new currents can be detected. Countries such as Mexico and Brazil are important producers in their own right (according to Varis, they produce, respectively, 66% and 68% of their programs domestically) and as sources of programming for their neighbors.

How does this trend affect smaller countries, which cannot realistically compete with either the

Maria D. Wert and Robert L. Stevenson, "Global Television Flow to Latin American Countries." *Journalism Quarterly*, Volume 65, Number 1, Spring 1988, pp. 182–185. Reprinted by permission.

Maria C. Wert was, at the time this article was written, a graduate student in the School of Journalism of the University of North Carolina at Chapel Hill, where Robert L. Stevenson is professor.

Anglo–American giants or the new mini-giants closer to home? Does it reduce their use of Anglo–American imported programs? Or substitute Mexico and Brazil for the United States and Britain? Has it encouraged them to expand their own production or merely to import from a wider variety of suppliers?

To answer these questions, we turned to three relatively small Latin American countries that must live in the shadows of the United States and their larger Latin American neighbors, Panama, Costa Rica and El Salvador.

BACKGROUND

Compared to other regions of the Third World, Latin America, of course, has a well developed mass media system.[5] El Salvador, the poorest and most densely populated of the three countries, was the first to put a TV station on the air in 1956. Panama and Costa Rica followed four years later. By 1984, El Salvador had four stations (three privately owned, one government and a fourth commercial station due on the air in 1985), while Panama had five and Costa Rica six. In both countries, one station was government run.

Although less developed economically than Costa Rica (1980 per capita GNP of US $1,116 compared to US $2,238), Panama had a greater concentration of TV receivers. According to BBC estimates, Panama had 18 TV sets per 100 people in 1985 (up from 13 per 100 in 1975), while the comparable figure in Costa Rica was 12 sets per 100 (up from 7 per 100 in 1975). El Salvador was the least developed economically (per capita GNP of US $470 in 1980) and in media (8 TV sets per 100 population in 1985, up from 3 per 100 in 1975).

All three countries developed their TV systems in the shadow of the United States and, partly because of technical assistance from and investment by U.S. commercial interests, followed the North American model of private ownership with minimal government oversight. From the beginning, programming was heavily oriented toward entertainment and relied on imports from the United States. Even today, three to five stations, dividing small and relatively poor markets, cannot realistically be expected to produce much of their programming.

But are they still dependent on imports from the United States? Or are other, larger Latin American producers an alternative? And are they dependent on one or two regional gatekeepers that decide which U.S. programs will be dubbed and made available for further distribution?

METHOD

Our study focused on commercial TV offerings—schedules for the government stations were not available—for the last two weeks of November, 1984. TV listings in newspapers or TV magazines were the starting point. Then, as always happens in such projects, the study became as much a detective search as quantitative analysis. By contacting people from the three countries, their embassies and even the TV stations themselves, we were able to identify and classify programs listed in the printed schedules. Without this effort, we could not have known that "El Precio del Deber" ("The Price of Duty") in Costa Rica was the NBC series "Hill Street Blues" or that "Vecinos y Amigos" ("Neighbors and Friends") in El Salvador was the CBS series "Knots Landing." Programs were classified by type according to the scheme used by Varis with minor modifications and the addition of "telenovelas" as a separate category because of their unique importance in Latin American television.

RESULTS

Clearly the trends toward local production and regional exchange documented in the larger Latin American countries have not reached these three small countries (Table 1). They still import 80 to 90% of their programming, most of it—two-thirds to three-quarters of all imports—from the United States. Only Mexico is visible as a significant supplier. And that, we may suspect, represents mostly the ubiquitous telenovela.

For the standard entertainment part of the schedule, which represents about half the total programming, the three countries rely totally on imports (Table 2). Their own modest production resources are directed toward news and education (limited in

| Table I | ORIGINS OF IMPORTED TV PROGRAMMING IN PANAMA, EL SALVADOR AND COSTA RICA |

	Panama	El Salvador	Costa Rica
Percent Imported	80%	88%	78%
United States	64.9%	75.0%	73.9%
Mexico	14.6	15.0	12.3
Venezuela	5.7	2.5	2.6
Puerto Rico	4.1	1.6	4.0
Brazil	2.1	0.0	0.0
Argentina	1.3	0.3	2.7
Chile	0.4	0.0	0.3
Japan	1.9	4.0	0.9
Britain	1.0	0.4	0.3
Spain	0.5	0.0	2.2
France	0.4	0.0	0.0
Italy	0.4	0.9	0.0
Australia	0.0	0.3	0.0
Germany	0.0	0.0	0.8
Others	2.7	0.0	0.0
n = (hours)	527.8	395.5	614.3

Table 2   TOTAL PROGRAMMING AND PERCENT IMPORTED BY TYPE OF PROGRAM

	Panama		El Salvador		Costa Rica	
	Total	Imports	Total	Imports	Total	Imports
Information	7.4%	0.0%	1.7%	0.0%	9.2%	0.0%
Education	1.3	94.1%	2.4	56.2%	3.1	55.4%
Sports	3.6	76.0%	6.4	68.0%	10.2	68.0%
Series	20.9	100.0%	20.8	100.0%	25.7	100.0%
Telenovelas	15.9	92.0%	12.1	100.0%	11.0	100.0%
Movies	18.9	100.0%	23.4	100.0%	12.5	100.0%
Variety	5.1	85.0%	2.0	22.6%	3.7	58.6%
Drama	0.0		0.4	0.0%	0.0	
Children	15.4	93.0%	20.4	98.0%	12.9	92.1%
Religion	2.7	64.7%	2.5	88.2%	3.9	52.4%
Music	3.1	43.8%	5.8	61.1%	4.1	85.3%
Other	5.7	0.0%	2.1	0.0%	3.7	18.0%
n = (hours)	658		449.5		792.3	

program hours), music and variety shows (a legitimate forum for local pop culture) and, to a lesser extent, sports. Even religious shows are mostly imports; curiously enough in a heavily Catholic part of the world, they are mostly fundamentalist Protestant programs from the United States.

Matching categories of programs flowing to these three countries from the United States, other Latin American countries and the rest of the world, we find the diet of programs from the United States heavily oriented toward entertainment—the action series, movies—and children's programs (Table 3). The latter includes both the popular "Sesame Street" and cartoons.

As was suspected, a majority of imports from other Latin American countries are telenovelas, supplemented by limited offerings in other categories of entertainment and some children's programming. Children's programs, in fact, are the most catholic of imports, representing significant proportions of programming from countries outside the western hemisphere as well. Otherwise, the non-American world provides some sports (in Panama), some educational programs (Costa Rica) and some movies (El Salvador).

These data suggest that the great trends in Third World broadcasting—an explosion of receivers and expanded services, the rise of regional producers, perhaps a lessening interest in U.S. entertainment programming—have had little influence on the TV diet of these three small countries.

Imports still dominate the schedule in every category except news and some music and variety programs, which are sensible uses of scarce local production resources. But little use is made of the flood of programming available from countries around the world. For every hour of programming imported from the United States—mostly movies and adventures series—these smaller countries show about 30 minutes of Latin American programs—mostly telenovelas from Mexico. Programming from Europe and Asia is all but invisible on the TV screens of Panama, El Salvador and Costa Rica.

It could not be determined precisely how much of the non-Spanish programming passed through the dubbing studios in Mexico, but most of the experts and insiders contacted in the course of the project agreed that the international distributors remain the key gatekeepers; the only foreign programs available to the small, language-specific countries in Latin America are those selected and dubbed by regional distributors.

The trends noted in the intensive study of Latin

Table 3	TYPE OF IMPORTED PROGRAMMING BY ORIGIN								
	Panama			*El Salvador*			*Costa Rica*		
Imports from:	*USA*	*LatAm*	*Other*	*USA*	*LatAm*	*Other*	*USA*	*LatAm*	*Other*
Information	0.0%	0.0%	0.0%	0.0%	0.0%	0.0%	0.0%	0.0%	0.0%
Education	2.1	0.0	2.8	2.0	0.0	0.0	1.9	0.0	26.4
Sports	1.2	0.0	39.1	6.6	0.0	0.0	11.4	0.0	15.1
Series	36.0	9.4	0.0	29.8	6.5	0.0	43.6	2.9	5.1
Telenovelas	0.0	63.6	0.0	0.0	70.3	0.0	0.0	64.8	0.0
Movies	33.6	2.4	16.1	33.0	5.2	13.6	17.4	12.7	11.3
Variety	1.4	12.5	14.0	0.3	0.0	0.0	1.8	6.7	0.0
Drama	0.0	0.0	0.0	0.0	0.0	0.0	0.0	0.0	0.0
Children	18.7	12.1	28.0	22.4	9.3	77.3	15.7	9.9	35.8
Religion	4.3	0.0	0.0	3.4	0.0	0.0	3.3	0.0	0.0
Music	2.6	0.0	0.0	2.5	8.7	9.1	4.9	0.0	3.8
Other	0.0	0.0	0.0	0.0	0.0	0.0	0.0	3.0	2.5
n = (hours)	342.8	149.8	35.8	296.5	77.0	22.0	454.5	134.2	26.5

American programming and extensive study of TV around the world have not reached the three small countries of Central America. For them, imports, especially from the United States, still dominate the television screen.

NOTES

1. Tapio Varis, "The International Flow of Television Programs," *Journal of Communication*, Spring, 1984, pp. 143–152.

2. Kaarle Nordenstreng and Tapio Varis, *Television Traffic: a One-Way Street?* (Paris: Unesco, 1974).
3. Robert L. Bishop, "Regional Media Export Centers: the Case of Hong Kong," *Gazette*, 35:61–70 (1985).
4. Livia Antola and Everett M. Rogers, "Television Flows in Latin America," *Communication Research*, 11:183–202 (April, 1984).
5. Data are from various sources cited in Maria C. Wert, *The Flow of Television in Panama, Costa Rica and El Salvador*, unpublished master's thesis, School of Journalism, University of North Carolina at Chapel Hill, 1984. Economic statistics are from the World Bank, TV estimates from the BBC.

TV OPENS UP REMOTE VILLAGERS' WORLD

BRADLEY GRAHAM

Bradley Graham describes how the flow of U.S. television programs is changing a remote Latin American village. Even in the backwoods of the world, satellite technology can bring in television from the modern, sophisticated, cosmopolitan world.

OCOBAMBA, Peru—Each day as the sun goes down, the Quechua Indians in this remote Andean village file into the sparsely furnished living room of the Rev. John Jeremias Pashby for an electronic glimpse of the outside world.

Huddled on wooden benches, they stare at a small television wired to a parabolic antenna that Pashby, a Catholic priest from Boston, has installed among the town's squat adobe houses.

A local Army captain calls Pashby a "magician" and "messiah" for introducing television to this all-but-forgotten corner of Peru. Word of the priest's feat has spread through nearby mountain valleys, prompting appeals from other peasants to be tuned in, too.

Television is finally arriving in the backwaters of Latin America, reaching distant villages like Ocobamba often before running water, telephones, regular mail service and—thanks to battery-powered sets—even before electricity. In many of the poorest homes, a TV set now ranks as the treasured next addition after a kerosene stove.

"Before phones, people in this part of the world want television," said Carlos Romero, director of Peru's National Institute for Research and Training in Telecommunications.

Bradley Graham, "TV Opens Up Remote Villagers' World." *The Washington Post*, Thursday, March 10, 1988, World News Section. Reprinted by permission.

The author is a *Washington Post* Foreign Service correspondent.

For thousand of peasants, television is providing the first images of places beyond the primitiveness and isolation of their own rugged existence. Experts see both positive and negative influences in this exposure to the airwaves.

Advocates of TV's proliferation stress the medium's educational potential. But others worry that current programming—particularly its heavy reliance on U.S.-made series dubbed into Spanish—is suffocating folk cultures and stunting the growth of national identities.

Moreover, some specialists contend that TV is contributing to a swelling migration of villagers to urban shantytowns. Lured by pictures of city life, peasants have been abandoning their impoverished communities in growing numbers.

Pashby's project is one of the most dramatic examples of TV's penetration. He built his first giant antenna with the help of local youths, who hammered and shaped sheets of corrugated tin from a discarded schoolhouse roof. Aiming the homemade metal dish skyward, the priest spent weeks trying to locate one of the many TV satellites that circle the Equator. At last he picked up a signal: a Mickey Mouse cartoon in Spanish from Argentina.

Since then, Pashby has learned to beam in programs from Lima to London. As his living room fills every evening, the soft-spoken, amiable 54-year-old cleric known here as "Padre Jeremias" is besieged with requests for such favorites as "Miami Vice," "Knight Rider" and "Diff'rent Strokes."

"These people have literally been walled in by the mountains for generations," said Pashby, who was sent to South America 25 years ago by the Society of St. James in Boston. "Little of the outside world gets here. No newspapers, no magazines. Now with TV, people want to watch all they can get."

A Canadian entrepreneur did something similar in Iquitos, a jungle city in northeastern Peru. He installed a parabolic antenna a few years ago and linked viewers there with cable connections. More often, though, to receive TV broadcasts Peru's isolated communities end up collecting funds on their own for the purchase of a microwave tower.

The multiplication of TV sets has been phenomenal. Gladys Otero, director of programming at Peru's state-run Channel 7, estimates that the number of sets nationwide has doubled since 1984, to roughly 4 million. Assuming an average of four viewers per set, Otero figures that 16 million of the country's 22 million people can now tune in.

Unfortunately, what they see on most channels tends to have little to do with Peruvian reality. "Latin America is the region of the world with the highest level of imported TV programs," said Rafael Roncagliolo, director of the Lima-based Center of Studies about Transnational Culture. "About 60 percent of the programs are imported, and about 80 percent of those come from the United States."

Some networks in Brazil, Mexico, Colombia and Venezuela produce sophisticated and popular *telenovelas*, or soap operas, that compete with U.S.-made series. But most Latin American stations lack the money to make high-quality programs.

"Although laws exist mandating a certain percentage of national programming—60 percent in Peru, 50 percent in Venezuela and Colombia, 30 percent in Ecuador and Bolivia—they are not realized," a recent study by Roncagliolo's organization concluded.

Preoccupied with problems of terrorism, inflation and poverty, Latin American governments have little time to think about improving television. But thanks to increasingly cheap and compact forms of TV-related technology, people like Pashby have begun to take matters into their own hands.

The American priest is convinced that TV can become an important teaching tool. Using a video camera and enlisting local teen-agers as actors, he has put together a series of short video spots on dishwashing, bathing, lavatory habits, breast feeding and the proper treatment of children with diarrhea (a principal cause of infant mortality). With a small transmitting antenna on top of his house, Pashby hopes to broadcast the blurbs—in Quechua, the language of the Peruvian Andes—during commercial breaks in the programs he intercepts.

Ocobamba's population is only about 400, but Pashby's parish spans the upper part of Apurimac Province and includes thousands of Peru's poorest and most isolated citizens. Pashby dreams of eventually rigging TV sets, video cameras and mini-transmitters into a regional two-way communication system.

Impressed with the results so far a government

development agency has funded parabolic antennas for two other tiny villages—Uripa and Huaccana— at a cost of about $1,200 each. Pashby, meanwhile, has put up a second dish here to give viewers a choice of stations.

The people of Ocobamba are sold on TV. "My kids are more alert now as a result of television," said Jorge Palacios, a child care instructor who lives beside the giant saucers and recently bought a TV. "Television is helping to educate us. It has advanced us more than anything."

Yet not everyone is enthusiastic. "Sooner or later, television was bound to arrive, but why rush it?" asked Pierre de Paepe, a Belgian doctor in nearby Andahuaylas. "The aim should be to try to fortify local culture, but most TV programming has little to do with Indian culture."

Some Indian customs do survive here, but as Pashby and others note, Ocobamba is hardly a pre-serve of Inca civilization. One out of three people born here die in infancy, and most of the rest do not live past age 40.

Pashby acknowledges that the consequences of bringing TV here are not entirely predictable, but he argues that its advantages are already evident. He says television has awakened villagers to the size and diversity of the rest of the world, made them more curious about how things are done elsewhere and caused them to be more attentive to caring for their own health, houses and work.

"I know," said the priest, "that some people ask why bring television here, as if TV is impure and will ruin some kind of natural state. But the notion that a Shangri-La exists in this place and needs protecting just isn't true. Besides, don't these people have a right to expand their horizons like everyone else?"

2 INTERNATIONAL COMMUNICATION POLICIES

Communication has come to be so extraordinarily powerful that everyone is concerned with public policies that deal in some manner with mass media. Individual nations have created policies for coping with both internal media as well as the communications that cross their borders. The United Nations, UNESCO, and international commissions have suggested or initiated policies concerning global communication issues.

The United States has come slowly and somewhat reluctantly to communication policy-making. Many Americans still cling to the Jeffersonian ideal that there should be no laws placing limits on communication. In the field of electronic communications, we realized at the dawn of the radio era that limited frequencies and the use of public airwaves required the administration of national radio policies. Those laws were later expanded to television specifically, and to telecommunications in general. The United States now also accepts the fact that some international policies are required to sort out global communications.

On what basis should those policies be made? Economic? Technological? Cultural? Political? While some would argue one way or another, few countries are willing to abide by international policies inimical to their own values. Americans by and large reject ideas embodied in UNESCO's "new world information order" precisely because those policies are seen as harmful to American ideals.

Interestingly, while American news and entertainment media have played large roles in the world, American policies have not prevailed. Few of the world's societies have embraced the Jeffersonian notion. The Soviet Bloc obviously has not, but neither have many nonaligned Third World nations. Even in the case of advertising, United States's great gift to free enterprise, America's laissez faire attitude has not prevailed. Some countries prohibit advertising altogether, and most countries place more careful control on it than America does. Increasingly, policies of global advertising control are being advocated, and these may well come to influence American advertising policy as well.

TOWARD A THEORY OF THE STATE AND TELECOMMUNICATIONS POLICY

Vincent Mosco

Vincent Mosco reviews the range of policies that have been or that can be brought to bear upon national and international communication. He concludes that only by a greater appreciation of the *political* dimension can the discussion of policy issues expand "beyond dichotomous thinking—to regulate or not to regulate."

Policy research in telecommunications, especially research on deregulation, is more descriptive than analytical, identifying the major participants in the policy arena—equipment manufacturers, service providers, regulators, users—and describing the major issues over which they contend—industry structure, pricing, the extent of regulation. This research is useful in keeping us abreast of developments in technology, services, and changes in the players and their relationships. However, the lack of analytic focus leads to simplistic conclusions. Will the arena be technology-, market-, or regulation-driven? How can we adjust to inevitable deregulation and privatization?

According to one observer, by

posing the issue as a struggle between free enterprise and stifling government control, [this approach] has obscured the central issue of how we organize and maintain that set of rules and constraints which we call the market. The conservative's idyllic "free market," unencumbered by government meddling, is a logical impossibility. The important question . . . is whether these "rules of the game" ease and encourage economic change, or forestall it (35, pp. 48–49).

In this view, deregulation does not lessen government action and may actually increase it because deregulation is "only a shift in the nature of govern-

Vincent Mosco, "Toward a Theory of the State and Telecommunications Policy." From the *Journal of Communication*, Winter 1988, pp. 107–124. © 1988, *The Journal of Communication*. Reprinted by permission.

The author is a professor of sociology at Queen's University, Kingston, Ontario.

ment action, from commanding specific outcomes to creating and maintaining new markets.'' As many of those familiar with the process of telephone deregulation in Judge Greene's court would agree, creating new markets can mean more government intervention and more bureaucracy.

Where telecommunications policy research is analytical rather than descriptive, it has tended to rely excessively on technological and economic—typically neoclassical economic—reasons for what propels policy making. According to this view, natural monopoly regulation may have been the appropriate policy for an industry characterized by a narrow range of technologies and widespread economies of scale and scope; but the rise of a technologically driven service economy, a complex array of buyers and sellers, and the development of markets that are, if not fully competitive, then at least ''contestable,'' invite deregulation and privatization (7, 40).

Analysis that departs from strict technological or economic explanation has done so either through attempts to apply neoclassical economic models to the political domain, in so-called public choice theory, or through detailed investigation of micropolitics, with studies of how administrative staffs ''capture'' regulatory and public policy bodies (30, 33, 45).

This article is a modest step toward developing a distinctly *political* perspective on telecommunications policy and regulation. How does contemporary political theory, particularly the theory of the state, contribute to our understanding of this field? Specifically, I draw on political and social theory in two ways. First, I identify and chart the relationships among modes of intervention to settle social claims and forms of governance. This provides a broad perspective within which to situate current developments, assess their significance, and consider the prospects for the future structure of telecommunications policy and regulation. Second, I outline three models for understanding the state in democratic capitalist societies and show how these offer different ways of explaining the *functional* and *political* importance of recent developments in telecommunications policy, particularly the turn to deregulation and privatization. Rather than offering definitive conclusions on the best way of seeing the

relationship between the state and telecommunications policy, I suggest concepts that broaden our means of explaining this relationship and draw out the logic of different models that provide alternative approaches to explanation. Since my aim is to be suggestive, I limit my critical assessment to a modest critique from within each perspective.[1]

My first goal is to broaden the range of available concepts for explaining the relationship of the state to telecommunications beyond the simplistic dualism of regulation/deregulation. Drawing on recent work in sociological and political theory, I begin by identifying mechanisms that developed capitalist societies use to process social claims or demands and suggest how these mechanisms are organized into forms of governance.

Drawing on the work of Luhmann (27), we can identify four modes of processing social claims in developed capitalist societies: *representation* or political power, the *market* or monetary and exchange power, *social control* or power derived from socialization, values, norms, etc., and *expertise* or power based on the possession of information, what Bell (4) has called the codification of theoretical knowledge. These forms are present in less advanced and noncapitalist societies, but those societies also contain other forms and tend to structure the relationship among forms differently. The specific configuration identified here applies to the developed capitalist world, and each of these modes possesses strengths and weaknesses that serve or fail to serve specific needs of developed capitalist societies at particular historical junctures.

Representation incorporates a wide range of social claims but subjects the system to regular bouts of ''demand overload.'' The result is a decline in the ability to govern or to manage the range of demands.

The *market* provides a more calculable means for structuring social claims but tends to particularism in the definition of claims, i.e., subject to monetary calculation, to the concentration of power to structure the market for processing claims, and to rigidities in the exercise of claims, what Hirschman (22) calls a bias in favor of ''exit'' over ''voice.''

Expertise has the value of drawing on socially sanctioned views of what constitutes correct information, knowledge, and truth. The twentieth century has defined scientific and technical knowledge as privileged truth sources that carry the weight of inevitability. Rather than enter the long-standing debate on the power of experts and intellectuals in a technocratic age, suffice it to say that expert-based decision making is particularly valuable in a system whose leaders are eager to reduce the claims on its resources (17). Success in reducing claims depends crucially on the ability of experts to show convincingly that expertise achieves satisfactory results and that only a select few, highly trained individuals can claim expert status. These tasks are all the more essential because the technocratic class lacks a natural power base. Technological failures such as Three Mile Island and the space shuttle program have made it more difficult to accept expertise as a legitimate mode of settling social claims. According to Winner (46), technological solutions are bound to fail because technocrats, almost by definition, do not consider the diversity of information sources.

Finally, *social control* over cultural values or norms is a powerful mechanism for settling claims because it is rooted in the daily lived experience of people, in the structure and rhythms of day-to-day life. Nevertheless, the successful inculcation of values requires a complex institutional apparatus for socializing people sufficiently to agree on what values are appropriate and how they are to be realized.

There are different ways to configure these four modes of settling claims. I situate them here in this particular way because representation and expertise, on the one hand, and market and social control, on the other, are fundamentally different modes. In principle, representation incorporates the widest range of claims; expertise, only those that meet strict truth tests. The market is an indirect and opaque means of settling claims; social control is direct and explicit.

These four modes combine to provide four fundamental forms of governance in developed capitalist societies: regulation, private competition, expert boards, and corporatism. Within each of these forms, variation exists depending on which of the modes is emphasized. For example, in advanced capitalist societies, nationalized enterprises embody regulation with a bias to representation. Regulatory bodies whose purpose is limited to setting market rules for private companies constitute regulation with a bias to the market. Although I will offer brief

descriptions of each form of governance in a Weberian ideal type construction, a range of forms can be identified along the axes shown in Figure 1. A fundamental premise of the discussion is that developed capitalism has no form for settling social claims that precludes state intervention. One can acknowledge degrees of state intervention within each mode, from low in a facilitative role to high in a directing capacity. But the state is involved in each form, including the market.

Regulation offers representation within a private market structure. For example, the Federal Communications Commission is responsible for representing the public interest by taking into account the views of those whose lack of market power would give them little voice in a pure market structure. Nevertheless, the FCC's core responsibility is to maintain a private market in communications.

Private competition is a form of governance that relies on the market to clear social claims and privileges the ability of experts to make fundamental decisions about the best use of the market mechanism. According to this view, technical, management, and investment experts are those most appropriate to decide what to produce and how markets should be structured for distribution. Contrary to popular myths about the market, fostered in part by systems theories that reify component parts, the market is not a self-creating and self-sustaining mechanism. The key questions are who creates and sustains markets and to whose benefit.

Although regulation and competition are familiar modes of governance in the United States, some perceive them to have shortcomings. Prominent among these shortcomings is that they fail to control a political system that permits too many claims. The system suffers from the "excesses of democracy" or "excessive expectations . . . generated by democratic aspects of the system" (6, 10).

Following Offe (32), one can identify two ways of dealing with this perception that the political system suffers from demand overload. First, reduce the number of social claims. The market does this but with a bias to short-run gains and an unstable arena that makes overall management difficult, particularly for long-term planning. An alternative is to provide authority to *expert boards* or groups of people whose right to governance is based on social-

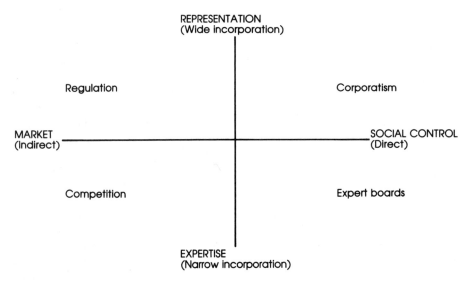

Figure 1   Forms of governance for processing social claims in developed capitalist societies

ly defined expertise. Such bodies proliferate in an advisory capacity throughout the government; some have suggested the need to make them more powerful. George Kennan, former U.S. ambassador and a policy adviser since the late 1940s, has called for legislation that would create an expert board

> advisory both to president and to Congress, but standing outside them, and made up of persons remote from participation in partisan political activity but qualified by training, experience and temperament to look deeply into present trends and possible remedies and to tell both the legislative and executive branches of the government of the things they *must* do, whether they like it or not, to head off some of the worst eventualities that seem now to be, almost unhindered, in the making (24, p. 6).

Such an expert body would reduce the legitimacy of social claims that conflict with a grounding in its definition of expert-based authority, thereby providing a tighter source of social control.

The other way to deal with demand overload is to increase the steering capacity of the state. In principle, regulation provides some managerial control by concentrating power to define the public interest in a small group of individuals. Recent proposals depart

from the regulatory model by calling for strengthening executive control and introducing explicit corporatist principles into American governance. The 300-member Committee on the Constitutional System, led by Senator Nancy Kassenbaum, Republican of Kansas, C. Douglas Dillon, Secretary of the Treasury under President Kennedy, and Lloyd Cutler, former counsel to President Carter, has identified "chronic deadlock" as the fundamental problem of the U.S. constitutional system. To overcome the resulting "governmental gridlock," the committee calls for constitutional amendments that would strengthen executive power and introduce strict party discipline (9).

A more explicit form of representation increases the control powers of the state through *corporatism*. This form of governance gives authority to individuals who represent specific components of the economic division of labor, particularly different sectors of business. Depending on the power of labor and consumer interests, these groups may play a role, typically secondary, in the corporatist system. Rather than reducing social claims, this form of governance brings social claims to the fore and gives them voice through economic representation. It also better manages and controls social claims because it vests authority directly in a body that reflects what the state defines as legitimate and forces all claimants to channel demands through this body. Moreover, corporatist powers are rarely as clearly defined as traditional constitutional ones. This provides what Offe calls the benefits of "organized formlessness" or the informal contact and extralegal activities that enable decision-makers to deal rapidly with changing conditions without attracting the publicity that comes with formal governmental action.

One early U.S. effort at a corporatist solution was the National Civic Federation, which from 1900 to 1918 created and implemented a social reform agenda put together by leaders in industry and finance with the support of the American Federation of Labor and the United Mine Workers. In so doing, the Civic Federation was able to gain recognition for collective bargaining, the minimum wage, and other reforms, thereby undermining the growing power of independent trade unions and explicitly socialist political organizations (see 44).

A more recent example of a corporatist governing body is the Municipal Assistance Corporation (MAC), which brought together government, business, and labor to produce the financing package and governance reforms to steer New York City out of bankruptcy. In fact, MAC's architect, investment banker Felix Rohatyn, proposes to extend this model with a national corporatist strategy. Rohatyn premises his call on the failure of market-based deregulation. In an article with the auspicious opening, "the United States today is headed for a financial and economic crisis," Rohatyn decries "a climate of deregulation pushed to dangerous extremes":

For the sake of competition, we have broken up AT&T, and the result has been both bad service and higher prices. We have deregulated the airlines and the resulting price wars did, indeed, lower fares. However, one airline after another is on its way to bankruptcy or to being acquired by another. The result will be a few huge airlines, with questionable financial structures, poor service with possibly higher prices, and worrisome safety factors. Deregulation of the financial markets has resulted in an explosion of private debt, unprecedented market speculation, and the sordid abuses in the financial industry that have been coming to light in recent months. Deregulation, as with most things in life, has to be done in

moderation; it has been carried too far. The free market is not always right; it surely is not always fair. It should not be turned into a religion (37, p. 3).

To address these and other concerns, to bring the United States back from where Rohatyn sees it, "on the brink," he calls for a commission that would include members of both political parties, people in business, and labor and academic experts who would at best propose solutions and at least "provide a coherent frame for debate of the economic alternatives."

The United States lacks the militant trade union activity and socialist politics that have made corporatism a more prominent feature of the European political landscape (38). This helps the U.S. state to avoid the danger of corporatism which, according to Jessop, is to risk introducing problems of fundamental class conflict into the heart of the state apparatus (23). Nevertheless, there are those, Rohatyn and Reich included, who call for forms of corporatism or "collective entrepreneurialism" to overcome what they see as unmanageable anarchy. In Reich's terms, "opportunistic individualism . . . induces collective gridlock" (35). Reich's remedy is corporatism, based on a new spirit of "collective trust" among business, government, and labor.

This overview of the relationship among modes of settling social claims and forms of governance broadens our conceptual powers for moving toward a theory of the state and telecommunications policy. The next step is to consider how major perspectives in political theory make use of these concepts to explain the role of the state in telecommunications policy.

Alford and Friedland (1) and others identify pluralist, managerial, and class perspectives as the major ways of seeing the role of the state in developed capitalist societies. One can further distinguish between the major focus, or, to use Bell's language, axial principle, of state activity in each perspective (functional domain) and the primary social tension or conflict that arises out of state activity (political domain). Each perspective, while acknowledging several focuses of state activity and numerous sources of conflict, concentrates on the one principle function and source of conflict which, it claims, offers the most explanatory value.

The *pluralist* **perspective starts from the view that power is situational, that it operates in specific circumstances over specific issues.** The pluralist sees the state as one among numerous organizations, including business, unions, voluntary associations, and churches, around which sets of interest coalitions focus their attention to meet their needs. The state is held together by a legal structure and an organizational culture that reflect widely held values. The state acts on these values to structure impartially the preferences of competing interests (11, 12, 14).

Pluralist analyses of deregulation begin with a shift in political values from a concern with detailed regulation in the public interest to a commitment to promote private competitive markets (13). This shift reflects a groundswell from below, in the form of public support for private marketplace solutions over government intervention, and from above, as intellectuals and policy-makers coalesce in their agreement on the need to minimize regulation. There is a general shift from representative- to market- and expert-based solutions (see Table 1), leading the state to assess the pressures of competing interests in a different fashion. The claims of those who would have the state intervene directly to support public interest norms of fairness and equity lose out to those who would have the state expand competition through private markets.

In essence, the state oversees a marketplace of competing interests, with no single one capable of controlling decision making. Rather, the range of competing participants marshal resources to back the claim that the state should meet their demands. An interest succeeds to the extent that it can convince the state that its political clout is substantial *and* that it conforms to the dominant value preference of the day better than do competitors. Pluralists offer the functionalist view that deregulation and privatization grow out of a shift in values that prompts a restructuring of the interest arena in favor of those seeking greater reliance on private markets for settling claims.

When pressed to identify the source of changing values, pluralists tend to emphasize developments in technology which, in this case, have broadened the range of telecommunications services (29). Furthermore, they point to the difficulty of managing the wide range of claims that were accepted out of legal and political necessity under the public interest standard. An "overloaded government" cannot manage change successfully (15). The government overload problem is deepened by the tendency of regulators to use the rules to their own benefit—what Wilson calls "staff capture" of the agency (45). The shift to a market principle streamlines the process of settling claims, eliminates many as illegitimate, and undermines the organizational power of regulatory bureaucrats (31). Finally, pluralists point to changes in policy analysis that, over time, created a critical mass of experts who supported the shift in government's role from directly regulating to overseeing markets (13).

From a policy point of view, pluralist theory sees two problems with the turn to deregulation that are likely to lead to a pendulum swing in the other direction. First, though deregulation resulted *from* a shift in attitudes and values about government intervention, it resulted *in* the replacement of a societal value, however murky the "public interest" may have been, with a largely instrumental solution that begs the question of values. Consequently, Reich, for example, suggests that the fundamental problem of American governance cannot be solved by turn-

Table I	PERSPECTIVES ON THE STATE AND TELECOMMUNICATIONS POLICY	
	Domain of Explanation	
Perspective	*Functional*	*Political*
Pluralist	Realize values	Clash of interests
Managerial	Manage complexity	Clash of elites
Class	Accumulate capital	Hegemony/struggle

ing to the competitive marketplace because the market works against building the spirit of trust among businesses and between business, labor, and government that he feels is essential for achieving collective solutions to the complex problems posed by the contemporary world economy. According to Reich, regulation fails not because regulatory bodies are populated by a class of anticapitalist civil servants and social engineers—the explanation that Kristol and other neoconservatives use to press for deregulation—but because businesses lack trust or a commitment to the spirit of the law. As a result, rather than comply, businesses deepen "the miasma of regulation": "Each maneuver generates a countermaneuver from within the regulatory bureaucracy and Congress. . . . The result, over time, is a profusion of legislative and regulatory detail that confounds American business" (35, p. 219).

Reliance on the marketplace may free up resources that had been contained by monopolistic and regulatory constraints, but it is likely to exacerbate the failure of U.S. business to join with government and other interests in developing collective responses to the pressures of a world economy. Consequently, Reich and others call for a fundamental reorientation of socialization practices to emphasize the mutual trust and collective action essential to corporatist- and expert-based forms of governance.

The turn to deregulation also represents a problem for "neopluralists" like Dahl and Lindblom (11, 12, 21, 26), who fear that pluralism no longer explains politics in the United States because the balance of interest forces has become distorted by the growth of corporate power. In contrast to his 1956 *Preface to Democratic Theory*, Dahl now argues that "corporate capitalism" tends "to produce inequalities in social and economic resources so great as to bring about severe violations of political equality and hence of the democratic process" (12, p. 60). For Dahl and others, the turn to the marketplace will aggravate this problem. Instead, they call for greater representation, for explicit state measures to ensure fuller equality and participation from groups who would otherwise be submerged beneath the marketplace power of business.

Where the pluralist views power as situational, tied to specific events and circumstances, the *managerial* theorist sees it as structural, embedded in the rules governing the operation of organizations and institutions. Managerial theory sees power in elite conflicts over the policy agenda that frames a series of discrete decisions, such as the general shift in the framework of regulation from public interest to private marketplace. The pluralist asks who won and lost in this decision; the managerial theorist asks who controls the policy agenda.

For managerial theorists, the fundamental driving force in developed capitalist, as well as socialist, societies is the need to manage the growing complexity brought about by technological change and the division of labor. Managerial perspectives draw their inspiration from several streams of thought. Prominent among these is the work of Weber (42) and Schumpeter (39), whose focus on bureaucratic rationalization and control over the means of administration marked a managerial departure from the pluralist view of Durkheim and the class analysis of Marx.

For Weber and Schumpeter, bureaucratic elites take a central place in the twentieth-century arena of power as a result of their critical role in technological and political management. Consequently, pluralism is strictly circumscribed by managerial necessity. The substance of democracy is limited to conflicts among elites, though the rituals and symbols of democracy proliferate, chiefly as forms of social control. An ill-informed citizenry is unable to distinguish between substance and symbol. Following the work of Skocpol (41) and other "state-centered" theorists, the international arena is increasingly characterized by competition and cooperation among centralized states reflecting internal elite conflicts over national versus global solutions to problems.

Managerial theorists explain deregulation as a response to the growing complexity of the telecommunications industry and the failures of representative regulation to manage the industry successfully. There are several sources of this complexity. The growth of technology provides a quantitative increase in available services. More important, it creates qualitative changes in industry structure. These changes amount to the blurring of distinctions among technologies and services that have heretofore provided the basis for regulation. For example, the distinction between communication and data processing had its roots in both technology—the difference between a telephone and a computer—and in industry structure—A.T.&T. was regulated, IBM was not. Microelectronics diminishes the ability to make functional distinctions among technologies—telephones contain microprocessors, computers communicate. Industry structure blurs as computer firms enter telecommunications and vice versa. The growing stakes in computer communications lead many large information users into the market so that banks, insurance firms, retailers, and others become information providers. In essence, several discrete and manageable technologies and industry sectors merge into an increasingly integrated and decreasingly manageable electronic services arena. Managerialists point to the experience of the FCC in the United States; the Canadian Radio-television and Telecommunications Commission, and state authorities in Europe to show that it is difficult, if not impossible, to apply old regulatory categories to this new arena or to develop new ones that might improve regulatory categories to this new arena or to develop new ones that might improve regulation and management.

In the absence of fundamental structural change—that is, a new policy agenda—more powerful interests in the industry resist challenges from competitors by using the regulatory apparatus to maintain their power. This managerial version of the familiar "capture" thesis has A.T.&T. and major television broadcasters, for example, building alliances with regulators and their congressional overseers to shape what change takes place in the arena to their advantage, even if that means maintaining a fragmented system whose rules bear little relationship to reality. Deregulation, according to this view, results from the development of a coalition powerful enough to undermine these old-line established powers. In telecommunications, the new coalition includes, chiefly, the executive and judicial branches of government and large corporate users. In function, deregulation is a form of state intervention that advances managerial efficiency by overcoming the fragmentation caused by dominant interests' capture of state agencies. Politically, it results from the formation of a new power bloc that seizes the policy agenda from a bloc linked to an established regulatory agenda. The new group wins out because it is

able to apply its economic, political, and informational resources more effectively—though, as the restructuring of A.T.&T. would indicate, not without significant compromises with this and other established powers. Much of the cost of the conflict is shifted to those groups in society least able to offer successful opposition (2).

The major policy concern from within the managerial view is that the market is not the best long-term vehicle for effective management of the sector. Deregulation and privatization may provide the jolt that was needed for an industry characterized by both rapid technological change and stagnating regulation. But the result may be excessively fragmented markets that fail to provide necessary coordination, guidance, or planning for the new arena or, more likely, lead to a reconcentration of power in the hands of industry leaders followed by a return to the cycle of regulatory stagnation.

We are already observing concerns raised on both of these counts. Weinhaus and Oettinger worry about how well a fragmented telecommunications sector can meet complex U.S. defense needs (43). A Brookings Institution report argues that the United States needs a managerial solution in the form of a National Technology Office. This government agency would underwrite basic research in information technology and support creation of what are increasingly called "precompetitive" joint commercial ventures to strengthen the U.S. computer industry in global markets (16). Others worry about the rapid reassertion of A.T.&T. power in the postdivestiture period, following the pattern of reconcentration established in the airline industry (18, 25).

As a result of these concerns, managerial theory leads us to anticipate growing discussion of nonregulatory alternatives to private markets, including forms of corporatism, particularly where oppositional forces are strong enough to require cooptation, and expert panels or boards, where opposition is not strong.

***Class theory* sees power as systemic and consequently calls on the analyst to comprehend more than its manifestation in situation and structure.** In general, situational and structural power are the realization of systemic power relations. To understand telecommunications policy we need to expand the focus beyond the divestiture case or the agenda of decision making that has come to be called deregulation. Class theory sees control over decisions and agendas as expressions of dynamic processes and power relations in the entire social system, in this case developed capitalist societies.

Two major strands of class theory encompass the functional and political dimensions of this perspective. Each grows out of and responds critically to earlier theories of state monopoly capitalism (23).

The first or *state derivationist* view derives the state from the fundamentals of capitalism, particularly from the need to overcome contradictions inherent in the system. According to this perspective, the state tries to function as the ''ideal collective capitalist,'' serving the interests of capital in general, not just the monopoly sector. These interests include first and foremost advancing capital accumulation by providing and maintaining a productive infrastructure, creating and enforcing a legal order that makes markets and commodity exchange possible, regulating conflicts between capital and labor, and promoting the total national capital in world markets (23).

As the state works to meet these goals, it faces problems that derive from a fundamental contradiction. The state is called on to perform a wide range of managerial activities but is denied the opportunity to enter the private productive core to generate the revenue necessary to perform these activities. Consequently, state action on behalf of capital depends on the state's capacity to secure revenues from the privately generated surplus. The state is faced with the challenge of promoting accumulation as it seeks to withdraw revenues from the accumulation process. The globalization of capital adds to pressures on the state because it is additionally responsible for achieving the degree of international coordination necessary for markets to work *without* advancing the creation of a global state (3). Although day-to-day relationships between the state and capital are characterized by bargaining and compromise, capital retains the ultimate discipline: the institutionalized right to withhold capital.

Responding to the view that state derivationist theory is too functional, too focused on legitimate, integrative state activities, a second or *state power* variant of class analysis addresses political conflict in capitalist society. Drawing on the work of Gramsci, state power theorists see the capitalist state as a vehicle for maintaining class power without directly appearing to do so. Although force and coercion remain means of control, developed capitalist states increasingly work hegemonically, that is, by mobilizing and reproducing the active consent of nondominant classes through moral, political, and ideological means.

In this view, the state faces systemic conflicts deriving from class antagonisms that originate in the labor process. The state is responsible for controlling antagonisms before they become systemic conflicts. Two complementary means of hegemonic control are particularly important. Combining Poulantzas and Jessop, we can call these the *isolation-unification effects*. The isolation effect is the process whereby the state identifies the agents of production not as members of antagonistic classes—capital and labor—but as individual legal subjects. As a result, economic agents tend to experience capitalism not as a system of class relations but as relations of competition among mutually isolated individuals and/or fragmented groups of workers and managers. Complementary to this, in the unifying effect, the state presents itself as the strictly political public unity of the people as nation, the abstract sum of formally free and equal legal subjects. As a corollary to these processes, the state will, from time to time, shift the locus of actual power from one part of the state apparatus to another, depending on the balance of pressures on different parts of the state. In essence, the state presents itself as the agent for solving the problems of individual juridical citizens until such time as pressures threaten to aggregate into a major organizational or class-based threat. At that point, the state can introduce direct coercion or re-form itself by eliminating that part of the state apparatus which serves as the arena of fundamental conflict (23, 34).

These responses meet with mixed results. They sometimes fail because the more limited and structured sets of interests that state actors form in their particular sector of the state clash with the long-term needs of capital. As Benda (5) has shown, state managers do not necessarily operate out of a sense of long-term systemic interests; rather, they advance bureaucratic rationalization, which does not always correspond to systemic interests. Responses also fail because they clash with people's lived experience and with the organizing efforts of nondominant class members. They also can get in the way of another major state project: maintaining some degree of class unity, chiefly through the creation of dominant power blocs at the top of the class hierarchy. To the extent that they fail, there is movement away from what Poulantzas calls the "normal" to the "exceptional" form of the state, one that eliminates democratic institutions and the autonomous organization of nondominant classes. Corporatism is situated between the normal and exceptional states. It is looked on favorably because it allows policy to be formulated outside the normal voting, party, or regional apparatus. It also allows for more of the necessary ad hoc decision making that permits supportive groups to be incorporated in the nondominant classes and more radical elements to be completely excluded.

From a class perspective, deregulation is a response to the recognition that telecommunications and its related informatics and communications sectors have come to occupy a central place in the capital accumulation process. Under the shaping influence of capital, with considerable state (particularly military) assistance, technology has deepened and extended the ability to make the products of computer communications, such as data and information, marketable commodities. The data/information commodity is a value in its own right and also enhances the value of more traditional commodities.

In general terms, information and the technology that produces and circulates it overcome the space and time constraints that have inhibited capital from expanding in territory and function while retaining centralized control. The application of communication and information technology is vital to building an international division of labor that permits capital to take advantage of the most profitable and most stable markets for financing, raw materials, and labor (8).

Deregulation and privatization accelerate the information commodification process by rupturing traditional relationships among business, the state, and labor. These relationships provided a workable regulatory solution in an era of continuous economic growth, developing national markets, and a strong

labor movement. The dense network of relationships among the old A.T.&T., the Congress and the FCC, the Communications Workers of America, and individual phone users is a prime example of the earlier, so-called Fordist, solution. In return for providing secure employment and near-universal phone service, A.T.&T. was guaranteed a near monopoly and a steady and secure return to shareholders. This relationship is called into question by increasing reliance on telecommunications for economic growth, the centrality of global markets, and weakened trade unionism. Deregulation and its corollaries, divestiture, privatization, etc., are instruments to forge the global expansion of telecommunications and information, both as industries and as sources of transnational capital expansion generally. Part of this process of expansion is removal of such principles as employment security and low-cost local service. A.T.&T. has eliminated thousands of (mostly union) jobs since divestiture. New telecommunications companies, like their counterparts in the deregulated airline industry, pay lower wages and are less likely to be unionized. Even proponents of deregulation admit that phone bills have increased for individual households and are likely to increase further as deregulation advances (29).

This emphasis on capital accumulation risks an overly economistic view, however. Deregulation is additionally a political instrument, one that "unleashes" new instruments of social control. As Robins and Webster put it:

> There is a sphere in which capital seeks to influence, not ideas or profits, but the very rhythms, patterns, pace, texture and discipline of everyday life. Within our wider focus upon power relations in society, this represents—to use Foucault's term—the terrain upon which operate the "systems of micro-power." For us, the "communications revolution" is socially significant insofar as it represents a recomposition of the microstructures—and of the experience—of everyday life (36).

The capacity of telecommunications and information technologies to measure and monitor transactions expands the potential for workplace and consumer surveillance, thereby providing a substantial increase in opportunities for social management and control. Analyses that concentrate solely on the economic potential, the financial winners and losers, miss what is most significant about the technology. It hold the potential to be, at the same time and in all aspects of social life, an instrument for capital accumulation *and* social control.

The stakes in social management and control add significance to the struggle over eliminating regulation. Indeed, it was when nondominant groups were beginning to achieve success in applying pressure on the regulatory apparatus to implement public interest values more forcefully that the movement to deregulate undermined this success. It was not until 1969 that a court made the FCC end what the court termed ''a profound hostility to the participation of Public Intervenors and their efforts'' and grant standing to public interest groups in Commission proceedings (20, pp. 499–501). This resulted in a decade of strong public pressure on the FCC, particularly in mass electronic media. According to a class analysis, deregulation is a response to this pressure, to mounting social claims on the communications system. It is a means of eliminating social claims that the courts decided not be cut off by FCC administrative action. Deregulation is one way that state reforms itself to eliminate an arena of potential class conflict.

However, the result of deregulation is to increase pressure on the market to realize those values that regulation sought to achieve, or to put increased pressure on the social welfare apparatus of the state (Lifeline services, Link-up America, etc.) to offset the anticipated failure of the market to meet nonmarket goals. As Keane puts it:

> The implication is that the overall survival of the ''unregulated'' sphere of capitalist exchange depends upon the continuous application of forms of ''collective regulation''. . . .
> In a word, welfare state policies are required to do the impossible; they are forced to reorganize and restrict the mechanisms of capitalist accumulation in order to allow those mechanisms to spontaneously take care of themselves (quoted in 32, pp. 15–16).

Politically speaking, these solutions are not likely to satisfy nondominant groups, particularly the beneficiaries of earlier regulatory arrangements. We already see evidence of coalition building in opposition to deregulation. However, the strength of deregulation, particularly the divestiture of major impetus to regulation, makes a return to the old form unlikely. The balance of forces in opposition, particularly the ability of trade unions and the public interest lobby to recover from a decade of decline, will influence the mix of regulatory, corporatist, or expert-based alternatives that are introduced. Offe and other class analysts would deny the possibility of a satisfactory long-term solution. Reich is correct, they would contend, in arguing that some form of collective solidarity or trust is necessary to provide a buffer against the uneven distributional consequences of globalization. But the private market is an economic and technical instrument for settling claims. It is rooted in individualistic self-interest. It cannot be expected to succeed at this *and* support collective actions for which meaningful and norm-oriented behavior is essential.

In essence, what we have is ''market overload,'' the class theory counterpart to government overload in managerial theory. Or, as Gramsci put it: ''The crisis consists precisely in the fact that the old is dying and the new cannot be born; in the interregnum a great variety of morbid symptoms appear'' (quoted in 32, p. 276).

Class theories of the state have flourished in the past two decades, giving rise to considerable debate both within the class perspective and with pluralist and managerial theories. A major concern within class analysis is the significance of nonclass factors in creating the conditions for effective opposition. Although class is a dimension of the politics of deregulation, particularly in the debate on universal service and employment, much of the organized opposition in the United States and other developed capitalist societies comes from groups whose cohesion is indirectly tied to social class. Gender, age, religion, the environment, and nationality are among the bases of solidarity in opposition. Although class analysts have taken steps to incorporate nonclass factors in understanding opposition and the formation of social movements, most of these are simply catalogues of nonclass forces. To my knowledge, Haight and Weinstein (19) have offered the only analytic argument that seeks to understand, in the tradition of Piven and Cloward's work on social welfare movements, the relationship of movement activity to the policy process in communications.

In 1400 a.d., 1,300 years after the death of Ptolemy and 70 years before the birth of Copernicus, astronomers persisted in stretching the model of an Earth-centered universe to fit what their observations told them was not so. In 1987, neoclassical economists persist in stretching the model of an open, competitive marketplace to fit a world of oligopoly and monopoly. We can eliminate telephone price regulation, even though markets are not competitive, because they are "contestable."[2] We can support government-subsidized corporate cartels in the computer industry because these are now "precompetitive arrangements." The descendants of Ptolemy believed that by adding a few more cycles to their diagrams, they could avoid a paradigm shift. The descendants of Adam Smith believe they can do it with euphemisms.

This article has been a modest effort, by no means Copernican, to suggest ways of accentuating the *political* in the political economy of telecommunications. Specifically, by drawing on contemporary work in political and social theory, I have pointed to concepts and conceptual schemes for viewing the political dimension of telecommunications policy and regulation. Concretely, I have offered ways of expanding the discussion of policy issues beyond dichotomous thinking—to regulate or not to regulate—and ways of seeing the politics of policy that do justice to the central role of telecommunications in contemporary social life.

NOTES

1. Moreover, in order to give substantial attention to conceptual issues, there is here little of the analysis of specific developments in telecommunications policy and regulation that I offered in a paper for the congressional Office of Technology Assessment (28).
2. This is of more than conceptual interest. According to the *Wall Street Journal*, A.T.&T., not the consumer, is "the bigger winner" in those states that have lifted profit regulation. In Maryland, "which AT&T con-

siders a model of how price—rather than profit regulation—should work," the company earned a 125 percent return on investment for the year ending March 31, 1987. In Pennsylvania it is earning a 20 percent return, and in South Carolina A.T.&T. has gone from an operating loss to a rate of return on investment of 43.6 percent (18).

REFERENCES

1. Alford, Robert, R. and Roger Friedland. *Powers of Theory*. Cambridge: Cambridge University Press, 1985.
2. Aufderheide, Patricia. "Universal Service: Telephone Policy in the Public Interest." *Journal of Communication* 37(1), Winter 1987, pp. 81–96.
3. Barker, Colin. "A Note on the Theory of the State." *Capital and Class* 4, 1978, pp. 120–124.
4. Bell, Daniel. *The Cultural Contradictions of Capitalism*. New York: Basic Books, 1976.
5. Benda, Charles G. "State Organization and Policy Formation: The 1970 Reorganization of the Post Office Department." *Politics and Society* 9, 1979, pp. 123–151.
6. Brittan, Samuel. *The Economic Consequences of Democracy*. London: Temple Smith, 1977.
7. Bruce, R. R., J. P. Cunard, and M. D. Director. *From Telecommunications to Electronic Services*. Toronto: Butterworths, 1986.
8. Castells, Manuel. "High Technology, Economic Restructuring, and the Urban-Regional Process in the United States." In Manuel Castells (Ed.), *High Technology, Space, and Society*. Beverly Hills, Cal.: Sage, 1985, pp. 11–40.
9. Committee on the Constitutional System. *A Bicentennial Analysis of the American Political Structure*. Washington, D.C.: CCS, 1987.
10. Crozier, Michel, Samuel Huntington, and Joji Watanuki. *The Crisis of Democracy*. New York: New York University Press, 1975.
11. Dahl, Robert A. *A Preface to Democratic Theory*. Chicago: University of Chicago Press, 1956.
12. Dahl, Robert A. *Dilemmas of Pluralist Democracy*. New Haven, Conn.: Yale University Press, 1982.
13. Derthick, Martha and Paul J. Quirk. *The Politics of Deregulation*. Washington, D.C.: Brookings Institution, 1985.
14. Deutsch, Karl. *The Nerves of Government*. London: Free Press, 1963.

15. Easton, David. *A Framework for Political Analysis.* Englewood Cliffs, N.J.: Prentice Hall, 1965.
16. Flamm, Kenneth. *Targeting the Computer: Government Support and International Competition.* Washington, D.C.: Brookings Institution, 1987.
17. Gouldner, Alvin. *The Future of Intellectuals and the Rise of the New Class.* London: Macmillan, 1979.
18. Guyon, Janet. "AT&T Profits on Price-Cap Alternative." *Wall Street Journal*, September 2, 1987, p. 6.
19. Haight, Timothy R. and Laurie R. Weinstein. "Changing Ideology on Television by Changing Telecommunications Policy: Notes on a Contradictory Situation." In Emile G. McAnany, Jorge Schnitman, and Noreene Janus (Eds.). *Communication and Social Structure.* New York: Praeger, 1981, pp. 110–144.
20. Head, Sidney W. with Christopher H. Sterling. *Broadcasting in America* (4th ed.). Boston: Houghton-Mifflin, 1982.
21. Held, David. *Models of Democracy.* Stanford, Cal.: Stanford University Press, 1987.
22. Hirschman, Albert O. *Exit, Voice and Loyalty.* Cambridge, Mass.: Harvard University Press, 1970.
23. Jessop, Bob. *The Capitalist State.* Oxford: Martin Robertson, 1982.
24. Kennan, George. "In the American Mirror." *New York Review of Books*, November 6, 1986, pp. 3–6.
25. Kilman, Scott. "An Unexpected Result of Airline Decontrol Is Return to Monopolies." *Wall Street Journal*, July 20, 1987, pp. 1, 3.
26. Lindblom, Charles E. *Politics and Markets.* New York: Basic Books, 1977.
27. Luhmann, Niklas. *The Differentiation of Society.* New York: Columbia University Press, 1982.
28. Mosco, Vincent. "The Communications System from a Regulatory Perspective." Paper prepared for the U.S. Congress, Office of Technology Assessment, 1987.
29. Noam, Eli M. "The Public Telecommunications Network: A Concept in Transition." *Journal of Communication 37*(1), Winter 1987, pp. 30–48.
30. Noll, Roger (Ed.). *Regulatory Policy and the Social Sciences.* Berkeley: University of California Press, 1987.
31. Nozick, Robert. *Anarchy, State, and Utopia.* New York: Basic Books, 1974.
32. Offe, Claus. *Contradictions of the Welfare State.* Cambridge, Mass.: MIT Press, 1984.
33. Posner, Richard A. "Theories of Economic Regulation." *Bell Journal of Economics and Management Science 5*(2), 1974, pp. 335–358.
34. Poulantzas, Nicos. *State, Power, and Socialism.* London: New Left Books, 1978.
35. Reich, Robert. *Tales of a New America.* New York: Times Books, 1987.
36. Robins, Kevin and Frank Webster, "Cybernetic Capitalism: Information, Technology, Everyday Life." In Vincent Mosco and Janet Wasko (Eds.), *The Political Economy of Information.* Madison: University of Wisconsin Press, 1988, pp. 44–75.
37. Rohatyn, Felix. "On the Brink." *New York Review of Books*, July 11, 1987, pp. 3–6.
38. Schmitter, Phillipe. "Modes of Interest Intermediation and Models of Societal Change in Western Europe." *Comparative Political Studies* 10, 1977, pp. 7–38.
39. Schumpeter, Joseph. *Capitalism, Socialism, and Democracy.* London: Allen & Unwin, 1943.
40. Shepherd, William G. "Concepts of Competition and Efficient Policy in the Telecommunications Sector." In Eli M. Noam (Ed.), *Telecommunications Regulation: Today and Tomorrow.* New York: Harcourt Brace Jovanovich, 1983, pp. 79–120.
41. Skocpol, Theda. *States and Social Revolutions.* Cambridge: Cambridge University Press, 1979.
42. Weber, Max. *Economy and Society.* Berkeley: University of California Press, 1978.
43. Weinhaus, Carol and Anthony G. Oettinger. "Behind the Telephone Debates—2 Concepts: Understanding Debates Over Competition and Divestiture." Program on Information Policy Research, Harvard University, Cambridge, Mass., 1987.
44. Weinstein, James. *The Corporate Ideal and the Liberal State, 1900–1918.* Boston: Beacon Press, 1968.
45. Wilson, James Q. (Ed.). *The Politics of Regulation.* New York: Basic Books, 1980.
46. Winner, Langdon. *Autonomous Technology.* Cambridge, Mass.: MIT Press, 1977.

COMMUNICATIONS POLICY MAKING IN WESTERN EUROPE

ROLAND S. HOMET, JR.

This article looks at the specific case of communication policy in Western Europe. The study by Roland S. Homet, Jr., concludes that commercialism has not been the dominant feature of Western European communication policy, but rather fragmentation, political control, and paternalism.

New communications techniques—many of them directly competitive with the traditional services of broadcasting, telephony, the mails, and the press—have begun to make their presence felt in both Europe and the United States. The challenge is not just to the continued vitality of established services on which people now depend for their information, entertainment, and social and business discourse. It is also to the institutional structures by which these services are provided and to the regulatory or supervisory arrangements under which they operate.

In the 1976–1978 period, four full-scale reports were produced by independent committees of inquiry appointed by Western European governments. In West Germany, the Commission for the Development of the Telecommunications System (the KtK), under the chairmanship of Eberhard Witte, looked at the new electronic communications technologies and services and addressed the problem of integrating these developments into established patterns of industrial and government organization (2). In Britain, there were three reports, each published in 1977. The Committee on the Future of Broadcasting, chaired by Lord Annan (the Annan Committee), examined possible arrangements for a fourth broadcasting channel, for newer technologies such as broadband cable and teletext, and for various institutional and procedural innovations (see 1, 3). The Post Office Review Committee, chaired by Charles Carter (the Carter Committee), dealt with both postal and telecommunications services and with the organizational structure for them (4). And the Royal Commission on the Press, chaired by (the now Lord) McGregor (the Royal Commission) inquired into the economic health of a highly concentrated industry and into the advisability, among other things, of government subsidies and of a strengthened Press Council (5). Parochial considerations seem to have played a good part in creation of these inquiry committees, but their reports are nonetheless valuable for the insights they provide into the process of policy formulation.

There is no single or uniform Western European approach to communications policy making. Significant differences exist between countries and among various classes of communications services. The press is unregulated, posts and telecommunications tightly controlled. Yet some governments favor press subsidies, while others at least formally shy away.[1] Some governments foster technical and service innovation by their PTTs (post and telecommunications organizations), others struggle and hold back. There is wide divergence in the amount of freedom allowed to broadcasting entities and in the degree of pluralistic participation in broadcast programming. When it comes to admitting new services like broadband cable or teletext or packet switching, with the potential for undermining the economic viability of established service, inertial resistance is fairly uniform, but emphases differ considerably.

Roland S. Homet, Jr., "Communications Policy Making in Western Europe." *Journal of Communication*, Volume 29, Number 2, Spring 1979, pp. 31–38. Reprinted by permission.

The author was with the U.S. Information Agency in Washington, D.C., when this article was written.

But if there is no uniformity, there are common tendencies in Western European policy making, which can be made to stand in relief when they are contrasted to the ways that communications policy is decided in North America. The independent regulatory commission, enshrined in the communications landscape of America and Canada, finds no counterpart in any Western European country. Commercial broadcasting, the premier service in the United States, is given at best a secondary place in the broadcasting systems of Western Europe. The stress in American policy debates on the invigorating virtues of marketplace competition is given some lip service in Europe as regards the press, control over which is falling into ever fewer hands, but virtually no recognition in other sectors of communications policy.

The print media are generally free from government control in Western societies, while electronic communications services are subject to varying degrees of government supervision. The point-to-point services, like telephony and the mails, are governed as common carriers, having a duty to carry without discrimination any messages presented to them. The mass electronic media, on the other hand, are expected to choose messages for transmission (news, entertainment, information) exercising their own editorial judgments subject to certain standards imposed on them by governments. Switched services operate to link people (or computers) together individually, one-to-one, whereas distributed services like publishing or broadcasting emanate to an audience from a central point, one-to-many.

These categories have been generally accepted by both Western Europeans and North Americans for structural and policy purposes. Differing institutional and regulatory consequences have flowed from the placement of a service in one category or another. Today those categories are breaking down as a result of new and versatile communications and computing technologies whose service capacities overflow the conventional boundaries. But for comparative purposes it is still useful to start with the traditional set of shared assumptions.

Point-to-point services in Western Europe are organized into post and telecommunications administrations, under the form of nationalized monopoly industries or government departments. The British Post Office, an independent state corporation, responsible for the mail and telephone systems, looks rather like the U.S. Postal Service but does not at all resemble the Bell System. Management prerogatives on the telephone side of the business are curtailed by the appointment of senior officers at the pleasure of a government minister, by the habit of treating staff as part of the civil service, and by the absence of any clear line of demarcation between governmental and business responsibility. The division of authority between regulation and management in North America, where independent regulatory agencies oversee the telephone industry, is much more pronounced than is that between management and political supervision in Western Europe, where there are no such agencies.

In Britain there are privately owned commercial programming companies, sharing television time on a third (ITV) channel alongside the two public networks BBC–1 and BBC–2. The BBC itself is an independent state corporation. So are the West German broadcasting stations, which have the added independence of being subject to state and not federal control. Two of the three French television networks derive the majority of their income from the advertising market and not from governmental appropriations. Sveriges Radio in Sweden is owned by a group of private organizations including the "popular movements" of evangelical, temperance, consumer, and labor groups. The Netherlands has adopted an "access" form of broadcasting that allots radio and TV transmission time to affiliation groups in proportion to the size of their membership. Italy has even been forced under court order to liberalize the state monopoly, RAI, to begin its own experiments with access programming, and to open up local broadcasting on an essentially unrestricted basis.

Yet with all this there is still no disposition to adopt the American model of broadcasting as a dominantly commercial enterprise exercising itself to maintain the maximum possible separation from government. In Western Europe, governments appoint the governors and/or managers of broadcasting systems who again serve at the pleasure of politicians. Financing of the public networks is mainly through a license fee levied on radio and television receivers.

Perhaps the major distinction from U.S. practice is the steadfast resistance of all Western European countries to commercial domination of their broadcasting systems. Brand advertising is permitted on at least some channels in virtually all these countries, but each has adopted measures designed to restrain competitive programming aimed at the lowest common denominator of mass audience tastes. Western Europeans want to avoid the dispiriting uniformity of programs that can result when all channels are reaching for the same audience. They also want to preserve a public resource for public uses; that is, they are unwilling to cede control over a principal means of communication to forces driven by the profit motive. This fear of commercial distortion is every bit as strong and pervasive as is, in the United States, the fear of government intervention.

The tradition of a free and independent print press, supported by advertising as well as circulation, on the other hand, is observed with fair similarity on both sides of the North Atlantic. Subsidies to newspapers are rather more cheerfully dispensed and accepted in Western Europe, with little evidence of concern as yet about impairment of editorial integrity. In Britain and in Sweden, the Press Councils operate as organs of industry self-regulation with much wider acceptance than their counterpart body enjoys in the United States. West Germany has adopted a statutory right of reply, for persons aggrieved by a false or misleading newspaper story.

But these differences between European and American practice, significant as they may be, are less important than the similarities. There are no government agencies with authority to supervise the output of the press, no requirement of "fairness" or balance in newspaper coverage. There are ritual expressions of concern about the growing concentration of ownership among newspapers, but just as in the United States very little is done about it.

The high costs of labor and of newsprint are forcing a search for cost savings, which, with recent technological advances, may be found through such expediting techniques as electronic editing, computer adjustment, and photocomposition. If labor unions can be persuaded to overcome their resistance to these innovations without exorbitant compensation for the loss in jobs, newspapers will establish themselves in the electronic publishing business, and it is not too far from there to go into electronic distribution as well.

Here is where European innovation is ahead of the United States. The British Post Office and the British broadcasting authorities have produced two different species of "teletext," or alphanumeric displays on television screens. In one system, the text travels as a tiny part of the broadcast signal from a central text-storing computer. In the other, the text is carried over telephone wires. The wired teletext system has a much higher information capacity, and is interactive—which means that a viewer can order the exact information needed. The service is well suited to the presentation of classified advertisements and of financial information such as stock market results. Under protocols adopted by the British Post Office and likely to be copied elsewhere in Europe, newspapers could offer these traditional press services over the wired teletext system and charge subscribers who order them. Electronic composition of the print newspaper would make this much easier.

Teletext is one of a family of new communications developments pressing on established institutions and confusing the conventional categories of print vs. electronic, mass media vs. point-to-point. Broadband cable, though it can scarcely be regarded as new, still confounds conventional categories because of its ability to deliver broadcast signals along with telephone or telegraph messages or facsimile or its own wired teletext. Satellites may be used for either point-to-point or mass communications or both at the same time. "Teletext" itself quite literally means a written output from an electronic transmission.

Of the new technologies, only video discs and cassettes have escaped government control. Cable in Western Europe is licensed or operated as part of the postal monopoly. Satellites are distant microwave stations and therefore fall under the same control. The flourishing private cable television industries of Canada and the United States are unknown in Western Europe, and there is nothing to compare with private satellite operation of the sort practiced—with U.S. government encouragement—by an A.T.&T., an RCA, or an IBM. In Europe, the curtailment of private opportunity to offer these services has resulted in a lessened state of development.

When it comes to wired teletext, however, Western Europe may find room for private entrepreneurs. There are jurisdictional stalemates between broadcasting and telephone monopolies, and struggles for control over text editing between the broadcasting and newspaper industries. Furthermore, there is precedent for private operation: computer service bureaus offer an analogous service for business users, and they have been authorized as private commercial entities.

This possibility of competitive entry into telecommunications is atypical. No competition is presently permitted for such things as telephone terminal equipment, specialized business services, or satellite communications—all of which have been opened to competitive entry in the United States. Engineering predilection for a single, standardized telecommunications system has prevailed in Western Europe over economic or legal arguments in favor of encouraging technical and service innovation, just as the engineering profession dominates decision-making within the PTTs.

Sweden has two separately programmed television networks, France three, Britain three, and West Germany two. In a number of these cases, however, the senior controlling authorities are the same people; when that is not the case, harmonization measures are taken to enforce diversity of programming even at the cost of lessened viewing audiences for one or another channel. Competition in this context is an instrument of control rather than openness.[2]

There are significant departures from this theme. In the Netherlands, while the networks themselves are under uniform state control, programming on those networks is open to any group that can demonstrate (1) it has something to say and (2) it has a specified minimum number of members who share its social outlook—in practice, who subscribe to its program magazine. (In recent years, the first criterion has been relaxed to the point where programming for the mass rather than for distinctive audiences has begun to take over the system.) In Britain, the Annan Committee has proposed a somewhat comparable "open system" for the fourth television channel, to allow independent producers among others to have an outlet for their viewpoints. And in Italy, a series of mid-1970s decisions by its Supreme Constitutional Court have mandated open entry for both imported and local broadcasts, with the result that there are now about 1000 local radio stations, which can draw as much as half the prime-time audience away from RAI.

To date there has been no disposition to promote cable as a competitive alternative to the over-the-air broadcasting. In the smaller Western European countries like the Netherlands and Belgium, cable subscription is relatively widespread. It serves as a means of bringing in broadcasts from the larger neighboring countries—France, Britain, West Germany—which themselves have little cable penetration to speak of and only a few intermittent local experiments to show what services cable could provide. A recent French regulation defines cable so as to exclude program origination, and the Annan Committee made no secret of its distaste for pay programming on cable. In West Germany and Britain, as well as in France, cable is treated as a local service of limited utility whose expansion would entail unwelcome costs both for the national economy and for the national broadcasting system which is supposed to impart the nation's cultural heritage in ways the government can assure.

The formal controls over broadcasting content are similar to those in the United States. Programming is required to be balanced, objective, and impartial—very like the second part of the "fairness doctrine." In Sweden the balance need not occur within the same program, and the younger commentators in both Sweden and West Germany are allowed subjective expressions of views which are not universally welcomed. Yet editorializing by broadcast management is generally not permitted. Subversive doctrines—dictatorship, racism, terrorism—are exempted from the balance requirement and journalists are expected to refrain from coverage or to condemn these doctrines.

As for "equal time," in Western Europe this tends to take three forms. Sessions of Parliament, the legislative debates among the parties, are covered for the record; as yet there is very little live transmission, although BBC radio did begin regular afternoon broadcasting of the Question Period in the spring of 1978. Ministers who ask for broadcasting time to make a political statement are subject to televised rebuttal by spokespersons for opposition parties. Beyond that there is the institution of the party political broadcast both during elections and more regularly throughout the year; time is usually allotted in accordance with electoral strength. The opportunity to make these appearances is evidently valued by politicians, despite probable audience apathy.

In Britain these derive from the extraordinarily sweeping "reserve powers" in the BBC's license, permitting the government to dictate what shall and shall not be shown and even to take over the whole apparatus of broadcasting without recourse to Parliament. The powers have never been exercised as such, but they are thought to induce anticipatory compliance with substantive government policies on such matters as Northern Ireland. In Sweden, comparable taboos have been imposed by the insistence of the "popular movements" represented on the board of Sveriges Radio. In France, and in Italy before the recent court decisions, political polarization causes the coverage of news and current affairs to reflect with some fidelity the views of the government in power. In West Germany, independence of expression is curtailed by the *proporz* system of political party appointments to key positions in the broadcasting stations.

These are all monopoly or oligopoly situations and the content controls both formal and informal are correspondingly stiff. In the Netherlands, where programming arrangements are pluralistic, the content controls are much more relaxed. There is no balance or "fairness" requirement since a balance among contending viewpoints is built into the system. Offense against the security of the State, public order, or morality can lead to suspension of broadcasting rights, but this has been leniently applied and under currently pending proposals could only follow a judicial judgment. The Dutch system is also hospitable to the work of free-lance producers, whose access to other broadcasting institutions has been steadily declining.

Electronic alternatives already with us (like computer conferencing) and others that will shortly be introduced (like interconnected magnetic-card typewriters) can deliver business and eventually personal messages faster, more frequently, and more cheaply than conventional mail delivery. The technical and economic aspects of the likely shift-over are being examined internally by the post and telegraph ad-

ministrations of Western Europe, but there is very little published discussion of either economic or social consequences. The KtK in West Germany conceded there is a problem but offered no analysis of its implications. In Britain the Carter Committee, which was asked among other things to assess "the social significance of the Postal Service," saw no problem and urged the Post Office to hold firm against the kind of pessimism it found in the United States regarding future postal prospects. Although the postal service and telecommunications both fall under the same roof in Europe, it is not clear that the losses on one side of the house will be made up by the gains on the other, and it does seem likely that there will be serious transitional strains, which call for advanced planning.

What "electronic mail" could do to the mails, "electronic publishing" might eventually do to some parts of the press. Newspaper proprietors have moved to protect themselves by, among other things, seeking a prescriptive right of participation in ownership and management of the wired teletext medium. The Royal Commission on the Press turned that down. But there seems no question that the press can participate as electronic information suppliers and even as competitive operators of computer-retrieval or teletext systems. The real issue is what measures may be called for to protect the interests of readers. On that question there is as yet no public discussion at all.

It is a confusing time for analysts and planners. The old categories are breaking down. There is no independent regulatory forum to serve as a catalyst for new perceptions about established industry and governmental structures. Policy is arrived at largely behind institutional doors and without the involvement of the public or the participation of knowledgeable outsiders. Communications policy competence is fragmented among a variety of ministries—broadcasting in one place, the postal service and telecommunications in another, the press in a third—with no coordinating mechanism to draw them together. The arrival of a new technology or service typically precipitates a struggle over which ministry shall control it, rather than a questioning of whether existing lines of responsibility are appropriate.

European legislatures could make up the deficiency but they do not. Party loyalties have been so tightened that majority members are loath to criticize their ministerial colleagues or even to go very far to encourage constructive change. Most Parliamentary committees have a very general jurisdiction that precludes careful examination of communications policy, and continuing oversight of the sort practiced by committees of the U.S. Congress is not done; still less are there "foresight" responsibilities of the kind adopted by the U.S. House of Representatives for its committees in 1974.

Insistence on retaining political control and an underlying paternalism are dominant features of Western European communications policy making. Quality is a very important consideration, in terms both of engineering design and of cultural merit, and these matters cannot be decided by popular preference.

Americans would probably criticize European policy making on several grounds, among them that it does not foster service innovation or economic efficiency, that it unnecessarily restricts consumers' freedom of choice, and that it does not allow democratic involvement in the decision process. Europeans, on the other hand, would criticize the American scene for a wasteful insistence on both market competition and procedural regularity, claiming that each glorifies a process instead of the end result. Neither system is readily translatable from one side of the ocean to the other, but there are features of each that on patient examination may have more cross-relevance and utility for the future than they have been accorded up till now.

NOTES

1. See the article by Milton Hollstein on "Government and the Press: The Question of Subsidies," *Journal of Communication*, Autumn 1978.
2. For details see the symposium on Western European broadcasting in the *Journal of Communication*, Summer 1978.

REFERENCES

1. Annan, Lord. "United Kingdom: Broadcasting and Politics." *Journal of Communication* 28(3), Summer 1978, pp. 59–67.
2. Commission for the Development of the Communications System, Report. Federal Ministry of Posts and Telecommunications. Bonn, 1976.
3. Committee on the Future of Broadcasting. Cmnd 6735. London: H.M.S.O., 1977.
4. Post Office Review Committee, Report. Cmnd 6850. London: H.M.S.O., 1977.
5. Royal Commission on the Press, Report. Cmnd 6810. London: H.M.S.O., 1977.

GLOBAL INFORMATION:
THE NEW BATTLEGROUND

ELIE ABEL

The typical thoughtful view of American mass communicators toward national and international policies is represented in Elie Abel's essay. As a former newspaper reporter, editor, television correspondent, and academic dean, Abel agrees that communication policies are going to bring about heated debate. His conclusion is that the policies which had been developed by agencies such as UNESCO are not apt to serve the interests of those seeking to insure a free flow of global communication. His solution is to urge greater presence of American communicators and scholars in the international policymaking debate.

The first thing to be said about the need for decisions in both the private and public sectors is that policy has not kept pace with the blistering speed of technological development over the last ten to fifteen years. The new ways in which humankind is learning to communicate, to transfer basic economic and business data from point to point instantaneously, to collect, edit, and distribute news, along with technical and scientific information and entertainment, are changing so rapidly that a policy lag was, I suppose, inevitable. It seems to me apparent, nevertheless, that the United States has been slower than, say, Japan or Canada or several European countries, to come to terms with the brute fact of a world in transition; I find this remarkable in view of the fact that the technological revolution we are living through owes so much to American invention and drive.

The computer and the communications satellite, in tandem, are the principal agents, though not the only agents, of this surging tide of change. American scientists and American corporations are showing the rest of the world the way to a more abundant future. At the same time, Americans are frequently reduced to the use of borrowed words ("télematique" or "informatique" from the French) to describe what they are about. The lag I have been talking about is, in short, not scientific or industrial. It has more to do with our culture and our governmental processes.

The House Committee on Government Operations in 1981 published a report titled "International Information Flow: Forging a New Framework," which attempts in weighty detail to examine the positions and policies of the United States with respect to international communication issues. That report finds that many countries, not alone third world countries, are raising new barriers to the international flow of information across national boundaries. These barriers include restrictions on the introduction of technology, limitations upon the ability of telecommunication and dataprocessing firms to enter foreign markets, the imposition of tariffs and, most galling to the community of journalists, restrictions upon the content of information that is being communicated. These barriers, so the Congressional report contends, are damaging to U.S. business and to the national interest, but our government till now has not come up with a coordinated policy for dealing with them. Our private sector, for its part, has grappled with these problems on a case-by-case and ad hoc basis. We are still a

Elie Abel, "Global Information: The New Battleground." *Political Communication and Persuasion*, Volume 1, Number 4, 1982, pp. 347–357. Reprinted by permission of Taylor & Francis, Publishers.

The author is a professor in the Department of Communications at Stanford University.

long way, in short, from the consistent and comprehensive policy that is called for by the House Committee. . . .

Dissatisfaction with the existing order of international communication is not limited to the nonaligned countries, which have kicked up such a storm over certain of these issues in UNESCO and other agencies of the UN system. Canada, for example, is an ally as well as a good neighbor. Yet a great many Canadians, jealous of their separate identity, will tell you that they dislike being dominated—that is the word often used—by the vast power of the United States to inform, influence, and persuade spilling over that long, undefended border. It was Canada, after all, which imposed quotas on the amount of imported (chiefly from the United States) programming that could be shown on Canadian television. Canada, moreover, by tax legislation specifically directed against foreign-owned periodicals, forced our friends at Time Inc. to abandon their Canadian edition. And it is our European friends and allies who want to curb the flow of information or personal data across national frontiers in the guise of safeguarding their citizens' right of privacy.

The rhetoric becomes less polite when certain officials of the so-called third world enter the debate. Not so many years ago these officials used to define underdevelopment in terms of poverty, disease, illiteracy, and too rapid population growth. Increasingly over the last decade they have added the criterion of foreign domination. They complain of cultural imperialism—in the form of news, motion pictures, television programs, books, and magazines exported by the advanced industrial countries, with the United States cast in the role of arch-imperialist.

The case rests on a number of undisputed facts—and a bundle of myths, embellished by far-fetched ideological theorizing. It is true that roughly two-thirds of humankind lacks access to modern communication systems; that these peoples of the developing countries lack a great many other things associated with the good life is, of course, a truism. Advanced industrial societies tend to possess advanced communication systems; less developed economies make do, on the whole, with less elaborate systems. The imbalance in news flow that results from these disparities is closely linked to the

wide, and still-widening, economic gap between countries of the North and the South.

It is true that four Western news agencies—the Associated Press and United Press International, based in New York; Reuters, based in London; and Agence France Presse in Paris—account for something between 80 percent and 90 percent of world traffic. News flows, in short, predominantly from North to South, from the developed to the developing societies. *Time, Newsweek,* and *Reader's Digest* (published abroad in 13 languages the last time I checked) are distributed round the world. The United States remains the world's largest *distributor* of motion pictures, even though it is no longer the biggest producer. (India turns out more titles than Hollywood.) The global traffic in television programs is, of course, tilted heavily in Hollywood's favor as council members must know from their travels about the world. The last time anyone undertook to gauge this flow, the United States was exporting roughly twice as many programs as all other exporting countries taken together.

It is clear, moreover, that in the field of computer and satellite technology, the United States leads the world by a very wide margin, although the Japanese are making considerable headway in this competition. IBM alone is said to account for 70 percent of total world business in computers.

These facts are not seriously disputed by Americans or others in the West who are familiar with present-day traffic patterns. The disputation in and out of UNESCO arises over the proposed remedies, notably the demand pushed by the nonaligned group in the United Nations for something called a New World Information Order. Although you will find the concept endorsed in resolutions adopted by the General Assembly, it has never been defined by any international body, not even by UNESCO. It was not until the Twenty-first General Conference of UNESCO in Belgrade in October 1980, that a Venezuelan resolution was adopted calling for the initiation of studies to elaborate, by 1983, the principles that might characterize such a new order. It is sometimes difficult to distinguish reality from fantasy in the debate that has raged over this issue.

It is, however, possible to trace back the origins of the nonaligned movement's concern with communication to the Algiers summit conference in

1973. It began modestly enough with an agreement to exchange information between and among developing countries and to strengthen the national media. The more ambitious goal of a new information order began to be discussed in the following year or two, in parallel with the demand for a New World Economic Order. This demand for a radical restructuring of world trade in terms more favorable to the raw-material producers of the southern hemisphere was, I suspect, heavily influenced by the success of OPEC in forcing up the price of petroleum so dramatically after the Arab oil embargo. In any event, the parallel notions of a new information order and of a new economic order both seem to me attempts to apply on a global scale the principle of what John Rawls has called *distributive justice*.

I must leave to others the intricacies of a new economic order. So far as the information order is concerned, the plain fact is that nobody knows what it would mean. A Finnish Marxist communication scholar of my acquaintance, who is enchanted with the idea, has said that it points to "a global structure not far from Lenin's theory of imperialism" and "a call for war against the 'old order.'" If his analysis is correct, then surely we can expect the Soviet Union to embrace the concept, right? Well, not entirely. The most scathing denunciation of the idea that I have heard came from a ranking member of the Central Committee of the Communist Party of the USSR, who said it reminded him of another New Order which a certain European dictator had attempted to impose some forty years ago with disastrous results for all mankind. A Latin American proponent of the new order concept, when I pressed him for a definition, replied: "I grant you, it is not a perfectly definable concept."

The new world order obviously means different things to different people. It is more slogan than plan of action. Among Latin American radicals, clustered in certain universities and research institutes, it suggests a blueprint for dispossessing the rich and powerful owners of advertiser-supported newspapers, radio and television stations in that part of the world. The radicals accuse these publishers and broadcast executives of enhancing their profits and their power by working hand-in-glove with large multinational corporations, based chiefly in the United States. What the radicals want to see is a

process called "democratization" of the media, one that can perhaps be interpreted as leading to nationalization or some form of community ownership.

Africa is quite another matter. Here the demands are less ideological and, as I see them, rooted in real material needs. Of the three continents commonly thought of as comprising the third world, Africa certainly is the poorest in terms of media. It has the lowest newspaper circulation (14 copies a day per thousand inhabitants); the lowest number of radio receivers; the least access to telephone, television, computer and satellite service. It also is characterized by weak private sectors; this means that most African media, existing or projected, are financed and directed by the government. What Africans look for when they talk about a new order is, among other things,

1. Material assistance from the developed countries in building their communication capabilities, that is, infrastructure.
2. Help in training their media professionals, i.e., journalists, technicians, film makers, television producers, and the like.
3. More systematic—and more sympathetic—coverage of their affairs by the big Western media. I recall the complaint of a Nigerian official that the visit of his President to Washington had been all but totally ignored by our media, while visits of certain other foreign leaders were front-page news.

Asian attitudes toward the new order are harder to define. The Chinese till now have shown no great interest in these matters. The Japanese, with their own enormously powerful media and their highly sophisticated electronics industry, need no help from any quarter. For that matter, Taiwan, Hong Kong, Singapore, and South Korea are anything but hardship cases. India has a fairly sturdy free press. Many of its editors and publishers, if not in every case its government officials, oppose meddling by UNESCO, or by their own government, with the flow of information into or out of the country.

Proponents of the new order, no matter what country they come from, share a number of questionable assumptions, some rooted in myth, others in a lack of relevant research data. One such assumption, for example, is that the major international news agencies are so immensely profitable that they should (as some enthusiasts have suggested) pay a special tax for the benefit of developing countries. Yet the stubborn fact is that not one of the four major agencies shows a profit on the operation of its news service. Another myth has it that the peoples of the developing countries are passive receivers, literally awash in a tidal wave of unwanted, irrelevant, alien information. The fact, amply documented, is that only a handful of third world governments, chiefly in Latin America, allow their newspapers and broadcasting stations to subscribe directly to foreign agencies. One study as shown that in roughly three-quarters of the countries studied, the subscriber is the government itself, or a government agency which filters out any information that the regime considers to be irrelevant, unduly critical, lacking in balance, or socially harmful. Much of the information barred from circulation to the general public is reserved for official use only. It is then distributed among trusted, upper-level politicians and bureaucrats who, presumably, have a need to know what is happening in the outside world. (This process of official filtration has long been the rule, incidentally, in countries of the so-called second world, that is, Soviet-bloc countries, where the service of the Associated Press, for example, or Reuters, is available to a state agency such as Tass, rather than to individual newspapers such as *Izvestia*.)

The word "domination," it should be added, hardly applies to a business transaction where the purchaser has, and exercises, the right to buy—or not to buy—services or TV programs for internal distribution. If a program executive in a developing country chooses to show an imported series, such as *Kojak, Hawaii Five-O*, or in another period reruns of *I Love Lucy* and *Bonanza*, it is not because an American salesman held a gun to his head. The reasons, one may safely conclude, are that these programs are cheap, far less costly than filling an hour of television time with a home-made production; also that programs of this type have mass audience appeal, even if highbrows here at home and abroad sniff at them.

There is, I believe, only one sure road to a degree of media independence; that is for the developing countries to produce more of their own news, TV programming, and motion pictures. Americans, who have talked so much and done so little about reducing *their* dependence upon, say, foreign sources of petroleum, ought (I believe) to understand and support the aspirations of many third world leaders to reduce *their* dependence upon foreign sources of information, entertainment, and instruction. Building self-reliant media will, however, take a great deal of time and money, more of both than most poor countries in a hurry can afford. That is one dilemma.

Another dilemma (for those in the West who remain sympathetic to the plight of the poorest among nations) is the authoritarian nature of so many third world regimes. Like the Church and European monarchies of an earlier era, which regarded the printing press as a natural instrument of subversion, many leaders of newly independent countries seek to control the flow of information and ideas that reaches their populations. They dismiss the principle of free flow of information, commonly regarded in the liberal Western countries as an essential human right. It seems to them a principle that favors the strong over the weak, the information-rich over the information-poor, another way of ensuring neocolonialist dominance over the minds of their peoples. At home many third world regimes. Like the Church and European monarchies mobilizing the masses in support of national development schemes. They demand protection against what they see as irresponsible reporting, whether by international agencies or their own media people, through the imposition of codes of conduct and a range of other controls on the flow of information. The effect, if carried much farther, will be to constrict or block existing international channels by state action, with the blessing of majority votes in the United Nations system.

What is at stake in this debate? you may ask. To begin with, a world that is less open than the world we know today, a world on guard—neighbor against neighbor—seeking a false security in xenophobia. Second, a less informed world in which the developing countries may feel that they enjoy UNESCO's blessing when they censor their own media, harass foreign correspondents, prohibit or censor foreign publications, jam foreign broadcasts, and push legislation to inhibit or control the operations of multinational or, as they are sometimes called, transnational corporations, including news services, advertising agencies, dataprocessing outfits, publishers, and TV program suppliers.

We have been hearing a great cry of pain on the part of our major exporters of news—AP, UPI, *The New York Times* and *Washington Post–Los Angeles Times* services, *Time, Newsweek*—and the TV program packagers in Hollywood, whose products reach out to the most remote corners of the world. All of these corporations have an obvious stake in the traditional American doctrine that news, ideas, and images should be allowed to flow freely. There is a larger financial stake that we don't hear so much about: the stake of our major computer companies, data processors, and other high-technology companies whose operations circle the globe and whose economic power (in the case of IBM, for example) dwarfs that of many a sovereign country.

Some third world governments are tempted by the universal linkages that satellites can provide at a tiny fraction of the costs in labor and capital that an earthbound system would entail. But they worry that the advanced technology, once installed, will make their societies even more dependent upon Western suppliers in the future, dependent upon imported software as well as hardware.

It is, as I warned you at the outset, a perplexing set of issues we confront. The new technologies which make possible transborder data flows, remote sensing, and the prospect of direct-broadcasting satellites, have annihilated distance and made frontier controls obsolete. Americans may believe that they have made the adjustment to life in that kind of world. It is Americans, after all, who build and sell the computers and the satellites that make possible this somewhat spooky traffic. Our satellites routinely overfly the territories of other nations to map *their* natural resources and military dispositions.

But peoples on the receiving end, the observed, not the observers, cannot be expected to take the same relaxed view of the future. Their nationalism is new, their pride easily bruised. They are not ready to live in a world without borders. Here is the central paradox: That our new communication technologies refuse to be cramped within national boundaries, their reach being truly global, while the nation-states in most of the world still jealously guard their sover-

eignty. All of which suggests that the issues I have outlined briefly are likely to be with us for a good many years to come.

Let me in conclusion say a few words about the role of UNESCO in dealing with these matters. You will have read in *The New York Times* that a meeting was convened in Paris, ostensibly designed to agree upon measures for the protection of journalists on dangerous assignments. It was supposed to approve a plan for an international commission that would issue identity cards to journalists working outside their own countries, particularly in war zones. The commission, according to the French political scientist who drew up the plan, would also adjudicate complaints about the professional conduct of the journalists it was seeking to protect, a scheme that presumably opens the door to withdrawing credentials from those whose work is found to be in violation of "generally accepted" professional ethics.

I cite this scheme because it offers a revealing case study of the far-from-subtle ways in which the UNESCO Secretariat pursues its own agenda, substantially ignoring Western sensibilities and, in this case, also the recommendations of its own international study commission, headed by Sean MacBride of Ireland, which after two years' work explicitly rejected the idea of any special privileges for journalists. The MacBride report, noting that a Protocol to the Geneva Convention for the Protection of Journalists on Dangerous Missions is already on the statute books, went on to say: "To propose additional measures would invite the dangers entailed in a licensing system, since it would require some body to stipulate who should be entitled to claim such protection."

To make matters worse, the organizations invited to take part in the Paris meeting pointedly excluded all American or West European professional groups except one, the International Federation of Journalists, based in Brussels. The Federation might well have found itself in a minority of one if word had not leaked out of Paris alerting some of us to the stacking of the deck. The original invitation list, all too predictably, had been weighted in favor of Soviet-bloc and third world organizations: the Prague-based International Organization of Journalists, for example, and regional organizations that claim to speak for Africa, the Middle East, Asia, and Latin America.

As on some past occasions, the Director-General of UNESCO, when confronted with last-minute protests from the West, disclaimed personal knowledge of the matter and promptly directed his staff to invite the World Press Freedom Committee and several other groups of the libertarian stripe. We were asked, in short, to treat as an oversight what more closely resembled a deliberate and systematic exclusion of Mr. M'Bow's UNESCO staff of bodies and viewpoints hostile to the idea of licensing journalists.

I do not wish to be misunderstood. Having worked overseas myself for a good many years, I need no reminder from UNESCO or anyone else that journalism is a dangerous calling in some parts of the world. One need only recall the murder of an ABC correspondent in Nicaragua, the recurring death threats and fusillades directed at correspondents in El Salvador, or the disapperance in Cambodia so many years ago of Welles Hangen, whom some of you will remember as an Edward R. Murrow Fellow at the Council of Foreign Relations. But I see no shed of effective protection in UNESCO's identity-card scheme; only a fresh excuse for oppressive rules to tighten their control over newsmen and women by moving to revoke their credentials, supposedly on ethical grounds. When government, any government, becomes the judge of journalistic ethics we are, I firmly believe, on the slippery slope to an international system of mind control.

The game played in Paris tended to confirm my conviction that UNESCO has long since forfeited any claim to evenhanded neutrality in dealing with communication issues. I have learned from personal experience that the Secretariat *does* have a policy commitment that is fundamentally hostile to the obligation embodied in the Universal Declaration of Human Rights and UNESCO's own constitution: to promote the free flow of ideas. I contend that ranking members of the Secretariat not only propagate the positions and demands of particular countries in the nonaligned movement but actively inspire and orchestrate these demands. It is, of course, technically true that the General Conference of member governments sets policy at three-year intervals. But it is the Secretariat that largely determines the conference agenda.

Surely, it is time, as Gerald Long of Reuters has argued, to take UNESCO matters more seriously than we or the British have done in recent years. I do not advocate withdrawal from the organization. If we are to influence the outcome of the debate, we must stay and listen and do a better job of fighting for *our* beliefs. Not at the very last moment, when the lines have been drawn and positions have hardened, but in the day-to-day conduct of UNESCO business.

That means keeping a strong permanent delegation in Paris and encouraging larger numbers of qualified Americans to compete for policy-level jobs in the Secretariat; their number has been pitifully small in recent years. We have a right and a need to demand stronger representation. Above all, we must (as I see it) draw a line in the dust, serving notice that we will refuse to discuss, let alone negotiate, any regulation of news content, now or ever.

PRIVATE SECTOR PARTICIPATION IN PUBLIC SERVICE BROADCASTING: THE CASE OF KENYA

CARLA W. HEATH

A Third World country, Kenya, provides the setting for a country-specific study of communication policy and its impact on one national communication system, with particular reference to public service broadcasting. Carla W. Heath concludes that commercial advertising and religious broadcasts are allowed in Kenya in order to raise revenues, but at the same time the public broadcasting policies have been developed to ensure that the ability of the state is not threatened by alternative voices.

Public service broadcasters in market economies have always been faced with private sector demands to participate in their broadcasting operations. In the early decades of broadcasting, public service systems were generally reluctant to open their doors to such participation in either production or sponsorship. However, facing increasingly high production costs, competition from popular commercial systems, and the recent move toward privatizing public services, public service broadcasters in Western Europe, North America, and Japan have found it necessary to find ways to utilize commercially generated revenues without compromising public service standards (21, 28, 31). In light of these developments in post-industrial economies, it is interesting to examine the relationship between public service broadcasting systems and the private sector in non-industrialized market systems such as can be found in Africa.

Government ownership and direct control of broadcasting are the rule in Africa, where leaders have considered it unwise to allow radio and television to fall into the hands of those who might use them to challenge state policies or introduce alien perceptions. Even in countries where private ownership of newspapers is permitted, private ownership of radio and television services is not. Leaders argue that a government monopoly on broadcasting must be retained in order to ensure political stability, promote national unity and development, and minimize foreign cultural influence.

Despite the presumed dangers to the state that are inherent in permitting alternative voices access to the public through broadcasting, most African systems do allow some form of private sector participation. The nature and extent of that participation vary with each country's ideology, strategies for development, and distribution of power. Many systems, even those in socialist nations, carry commercials; nearly all offer opportunities for religious leaders to speak to the people.

This article is concerned with the situation in Kenya. It sketches the ideology that informs policies governing private sector participation and examines the nature of private sector broadcasts and the arrangements that have been developed to incorporate them into the state-run system. Finally, it considers some of the implications of these arrangements for cultural autonomy and social development.

Kenya's ideological orientation and model of economic development demand that the private sector be permitted to participate in broadcasting. But such participation gives alternative voices a national hearing and thus threatens to undermine the authori-

Carla W. Heath, "Private Sector Participation in Public Service Broadcasting: The Case of Kenya." From the *Journal of Communication*, Volume 38, Number 3, Summer 1988, pp. 96–107. © 1988, *The Journal of Communication*. Reprinted by permission.

The author is an assistant professor in the Department of Communication at Randolph-Macon Woman's College.

ty of the state. This contradiction poses serious challenges to broadcasting professionals, who must devise strategies that permit private sector participation but do not permit that participation to threaten the state. These inherently conservative strategies, designed to protect broadcasters and to ensure the survival of established broadcasting institutions and practices, legitimize and strengthen the country's other established institutions and entrenched interests.

Kenya is a democratic country firmly committed to participation in a global market economy. Elections for president and National Assembly have been held on a regular basis since independence in 1963. Campaigns are lively, and members of Parliament who have failed to look after their constituents' interests have not been returned to office. Within fluctuating boundaries, "constructive" dissent and criticism are tolerated. The major forums for criticism and public debate are the General Assembly, whose sessions are open to the public and reported by the press and national broadcasting service; the press, which is commercial and competitive;[1] and the churches, whose leaders are frequently quoted in the press and whose sermons are broadcast live on the radio.

Kenya's political-economic ideology and strategies for economic growth and development where most clearly articulated in a 1965 government white paper (18) and have subsequently been reaffirmed in national development plans, addresses, and national day speeches (e.g., 16, p. 38; 23). As outlined in the white paper, Kenya's objectives are: "political equality; social justice; human dignity including freedom of conscience; freedom from want, disease and exploitation; equal opportunity, and high and growing *per capita* incomes equitably distributed" (18, pp. 1–2). Attainment of those objectives, the paper contends, depends upon rapid economic growth that can best be achieved through Kenya's version of African socialism.[2] This approach to development draws from traditional values those that seem best and most appropriate to the task of nation building: humanism, political democracy, and mutual responsibility. This approach, according to its proponents, is flexible and adaptable to changing internal and external conditions. It is a policy based on political an economic non-alignment.

In accordance with this philosophy, many forms of ownership are permitted. Government policies encourage participation by the private sector, which includes small-holding farmers, producer and marketing cooperatives, Kenyan entrepreneurs, and foreign investors. Volunteer agencies, self-help organizations, and churches have been urged to complement government efforts to provide food, housing, health care, water, and education. The government's major roles have been to orchestrate development through planning, regulation, and fiscal policies and to maintain a stable and peaceful environment that is attractive to investors (see 16). The government has also been largely responsible for building the physical infrastructure needed to attract investors and has invested in some enterprises that initially were not attractive to private capital. In the 1984–1988 plan period, the government set about to divest itself of many of these enterprises and to adopt additional policies to encourage the private sector, especially in export-oriented enterprises.

What is most important about Kenya's development strategy in the present context are the government's expectations that the private sector will share with the state both the cost of economic expansion *and* the burden of providing social services. These expectations are supported by policies designed to encourage personal and institutional contributions to social services and welfare projects as well as individual, small-group, and corporate enterprises. For example, individuals are urged by government representatives to contribute to churches and *harambee* (self-help) fund raisers. Religious organizations are urged to build health clinics and community centers as well as churches. The strategy implicitly acknowledges that private enterprise and individual accumulation result in inequalities in wealth and distribution of resources that must be ameliorated by private charity. "African socialism" in Kenya entails redistribution of wealth through the private sector rather than exclusively through the state.

In a society where the private sector is expected to make significant contributions to economic and social development, it is reasonable to expect private sector participation in broadcasts. Such participation takes two principal forms: commercial participation, primarily in the form of advertising and program production; and voluntary agency participation, notably religious broadcasts.

Kenyans have been of two minds regarding commercial participation in broadcasting. On the one hand, there is a long tradition of privately owned, commercially supported broadcasting. Kenyaradio, the service catering to Europeans and Asians from 1928 to 1959, was a commercial operation (7, chap. 3; 25, pp. 39–45). On the other hand, some Kenyans have habitually argued that commercial considerations have no place in a public service system and that programs to uplift and educate the people should take precedence over commercial fluff (e.g., 12; 13, Vol. 66, May 19, 1956, cols. 701–708; 14, Vol. 29, April 25, 1973, col. 839 and Vol. 53, Oct. 22, 1980, cols. 1912–2010.) Such sentiments clearly reflect the influence of the BBC model of broadcasting.

A modest broadcasting service for African Kenyans begun during World War II was supported entirely by government appropriations. In contrast to Kenyaradio, the programs of the African Broadcasting Service (ABS) were primarily educative and informative, intended to support social and economic change and to win approval for government policies. However, when the colonial government expanded broadcasting services at the end of the 1950s and consolidated the ABS and Kenyaradio, it was expected that advertising revenues would be sought to keep government subventions to a minimum (11).

Kenya broadcasting moved more completely in the direction of a commercial service in 1962, when the colonial government established the Kenya Broadcasting Corporation (KBC) in order to introduce television. Television Network Ltd., a consortium of eight communication companies (only one of which was not foreign-owned), contracted to build and operate a television service in Kenya at no expense to the government. The debate surrounding the establishment of a television service (11; 13, Vol. 80, May 28, 1959, cols. 1396–1442) and the 1961 agreement between the government and the Television Network (Ordinance No. 24f, 1961) clearly indicate that the government and contractors alike expected the corporation to make a profit within three years.

Although the KBC did manage to increase revenues from radio ads, it was not able to raise the funds needed to maintain the new television service.

By the time self-government was achieved in June 1963, the KBC was deeply in debt. Between July 1963 and July 1964 the government voted £329,000 (approximately U.S. $921,000) in loans and supplementary appropriations to keep the corporation afloat (14, Vol. 3, pt. 1, June 24, 1964, cols. 530–531). That degree of financial dependence, plus concern on the part of many Kenyan leaders that the young country could not risk the threat to its national sovereignty posed by foreign ownership of such powerful media, led to the nationalization of the KBC in June 1964 (Kenya Broadcasting Corporation [Nationalization] Law, No. 12, 1964). The Voice of Kenya (VOK), as the broadcasting service was renamed, was returned to the Ministry of Information, Broadcasting and Tourism and resumed its role as the voice of the government. Private ownership was precluded by the new law, but private sector participation was assured (17, p. 5).

During the 1960s, the VOK operated on the understanding that it was to become self-supporting and, with the assistance of a team of advisers from the United States Agency for International Development, set about to streamline business practices, increase advertising revenues, and produce and import more popular television shows (27). These developments led to public and parliamentary concern about overcommercialization and cultural imperialism. A 1971 cabinet decision limited imported programs to a maximum of 30 percent and urged greater attention to local production.

Additional funds were appropriated for television in the following years (15), but they fell far short of what the VOK needed to free itself from dependence on imported entertainment programs or commercial support. Still, the VOK has had no clear mandate to become financially self-sufficient by increasing commercial billings (2). Government policy on the matter is clearly contradictory. On the one hand, the state is ideologically committed to encouraging private—foreign and domestic—enterprise, which includes businesses that wish to advertise on the VOK. On the other hand, it is reluctant, for political as well as cultural reasons, to allow the VOK to become a self-supporting operation. Kenyan policymakers seem to appreciate that a self-sufficient broadcasting institution would be at once stronger and more and more independent of government and more vulnerable to foreign commercial and cultural interest than an institution that must make an annual request to the government for all its funds.

Rather than formulating a clear policy with regard to commercial participation, the government has placed the burden of intuiting the correct path on the VOK. Consequently, the VOK staff have evolved strategies to mollify cultural nationalists while simultaneously filling air time and permitting commercial participation.

The most apparent form of commercial participation is advertising. Commercial spots are sold for all three radio services and for television; arrangements to sponsor television and radio programs are also made. The National Service (radio), which broadcasts 16½ hours a day in Swahili and can be received throughout the country, is the most popular service with advertisers, bringing in 54 percent of the VOK's advertising revenues in 1983. The General Service (radio), which broadcasts nationwide in English, earned 9.5 percent, the Vernacular Services (radio) 15 percent, and television 22.5 percent (32). Commercial revenues are sufficient to meet the recurrent expenses of the three radio services, but revenues for television ads cover less than 25 percent of annual recurrent television expenditures (15).

Advertising in Kenya is almost entirely controlled by foreign capital. Of the 11 Nairobi-based advertising agencies, 4 are subsidiaries of multinational firms and 6 are local corporations with a large share of foreign capital; only one is fully Kenyan-owned (8, p. 441). The advertisers, likewise, are predominantly multinational corporations that manufacture, assemble, or process consumer goods in Kenya.

Commercials are subject to a fairly stringent set of regulations (8, 19). A code adopted by the Kenya Broadcasting Service in 1959, which limits the content, length, and timing of commercials, is still in use. All ads must be reviewed by the VOK Censorship Committee to make sure they are "suitable," in "good taste," and contain no exaggerations or misleading claims. Drugs advertised on the VOK must have prior approval from the Chief Government Pharmacist, and commercials must be followed with a warning, "if pain persists, see your doctor." Tobacco ads may not show or mention advantages of smoking. All ads must be produced in Kenya by either the VOK or an independent production house.

Kenyan talent must be used in these ads, and the sound and look must be Kenyan.

Imported programs are, in theory, subject to similar formal monitoring procedures. VOK staff select imports from what is being marketed that year (24), guided by past experience with popular and official reactions and by personal taste. Pilots are previewed by the Censorship Committee, which includes VOK executives and representatives from the Ministries of Home Affairs, Education, and Culture and Social Services and the Children's Department. The committee is primarily concerned with preventing the airing of violent and immoral programs. Once decisions are made, lists of programs available for sponsorship are presented to potential advertisers. Sponsors can arrange for exclusive identification with a series by agreeing to pay rental and shipping costs as well as the commercial air time. Although allegations in the press that sponsors influence program selection are officially denied, it has been well established in general that advertisers seek an appropriate environment in which to situate their commercial messages (3, 6). Advertisers in Kenya are known to be reluctant to sponsor VOK productions, ostensibly because they do not wish to be associated with the staff's technically sloppy work.

Although money for television ads is quite limited (less than $.5 million in 1984), some companies do want to reach the television audience. A clear cabinet directive to sell commercial time only to advertisers who agree to support local productions would provide much-needed incentives to producers to "pull up their socks." Alternatively, the VOK could agree to purchase programs produced by independent Kenyan-owned production houses. To date, the VOK has exhibited considerable reluctance to move in that direction, rejecting independent offerings on religious and moral grounds.

Sponsored radio programs are more important than commercial television programs in terms of revenue raised and audience reached. Programs are in Swahili and English. Some are educative; others are entertaining. Sponsored programs are produced in local, privately owned recording studios in conjunction with advertisers and, in the case of programs featuring popular music, record companies. Sponsors foot the bill for productions and pay the VOK for commercial air time. Many advertisers prefer this arrangement to buying spots on VOK-produced programs because it allows them to control the technical quality as well as the content of the shows with which they are identified. The radio programs, like advertisements, are subject to VOK oversight. However, as Wallis and Malm have commented, "This arrangement does not give the VOK overall control of the music policy of the station; outside gatekeepers with clearly defined commercial interests are allowed to decide part of the phonogram output" (33, p. 245). Indeed, commercial interests are allowed to decide other output as well.

As they were in U.S. radio in the 1920s, sponsors' products and program content tend to be closely linked. For example, Trigga Industries, manufacturers of agricultural chemicals, sponsors "Hatua Kwa Hatua" (Step by Step), which answers farmers' questions about the proper use of pesticides and fertilizers. Explanations are integrated with commercial jingles familiar to regular radio listeners. "Kahawa" (Coffee), sponsored by the Coffee Board of Kenya, provides agricultural and marketing information to coffee growers. Pepsi sponsors "Sounds Like Hits," on which only records produced by Kenya-owned AIT are played; Polygram and Sanyo are responsible for a similar Swahili program, "Kuwa Juu Kuwa Tops."

In addition to supplying records for independently produced Top 10 shows, major recording companies[3] regularly supply the VOK with new releases. It is alleged that small, local production groups slip disc jockeys cassettes of their latest recordings along with a little cash to make sure that the tapes receive favorable airplay. VOK officials tend to look the other way, perhaps because copyright fees are not paid for noncatalogued recordings. This may be regarded as a way to support local entrepreneurs and thus somewhat offset the influence of the multinational companies and celebrity artists; or perhaps it is simply a matter of taking advantage of one's position as a broadcaster to augment a civil service salary.

Although sponsored radio programs are aired on the two national channels and thus are heard by pastoralists and factory workers alike, they are all directed to the modern sector of the economy: the farmers who produce for export and can afford fertilizers and pesticides, urban youths who have their own radios and have cash for soft drinks and cassettes. In this regard, the incorporation of commercials and commercially produced programs into the VOK's schedule is consistent with and lends support to development strategies intended to promote "growth and modernization" (16, p. 38).

Participation in broadcasting by voluntary social service agencies and the churches has been generally unchallenged. Although some Kenyans question the place of religious messages on radio and television, their reservations are seldom expressed publicly. When the question of religious broadcasts has been raised in the General Assembly, it has been to request additional time, especially for Islamic programs; these requests have generally been met.

In 1984 the VOK allotted, without charge, 24 hours a week on the radio to the Christian churches and another 8½ hours, primarily on the Somali and Coast-Swahili services, to Muslims. In addition, religious organizations provided nightly epilogues on television, and time was made available on radio and television for special programs during Christian, Muslim, and Hindu religious holidays. These programs were typically produced by the religious communities concerned. VOK radio also scheduled time each week for programs produced by voluntary organizations, such as the African Medical Relief Emergency Fund and the Family Planning Association of Kenya.

In order to avoid charges of state interference in religious matters, the VOK has delegated responsibility to the religious institutions themselves for deciding which denominations shall have access to the airwaves. Christian churches can participate only through the National Council of Churches in Kenya (NCCK) and the Muslims only through the Chief Kadhi. Churches that are too small or whose beliefs and practices are too controversial to qualify for membership in the NCCK, or Islamic sects that do not meet with the approval of the Chief Kadhi, do not have access to the broadcast media. In 1984 there were more than 800 registered religious societies in Kenya. Only 35 were members of the NCCK[4] and only 15 of these regularly contributed radio programs.

VOK recording facilities are available free of charge to religious institutions whose programs are to be aired. However, the churches seem to prefer to use their own facilities because they are generally better equipped and maintained and more convenient for churches not located in Nairobi and Mombasa. Thus, by virtue of its policy of avoiding charges of state interference in religious matters, the VOK makes sure that only large, fairly prosperous, established religious institutions—those most likely to support the state—will be heard.

The cooperation between the VOK and the NCCK is an excellent example of the kind of public/private cooperation the government is so anxious to promote. For many years the NCCK and the Catholic Mission have maintained a joint Broadcasting Committee charged with formulating Christian broadcasting policy, evaluating existing programs, and proposing new ones (22). The committee is responsible for scheduling participating churches for daily services, nightly epilogues, and Sunday services and for determining which churches are to produce programs for which vernacular services. These decisions are affected by the relative popularity and influence of particular churches with different ethnic groups. Through the Broadcasting Committee, missions and churches that have their own studios and professional staff provide the VOK with special weekly programs such as "Singing I Go" and "Maisha ya Jamaa" (Family Living), which combine music with religious and prosocial messages intended to strengthen the modern family and to inculcate Christian values.

Perhaps most important, the NCCK Broadcasting Committee functions as a gatekeeper, making VOK censorship unnecessary. Although VOK staff reserve the right to review all tapes, ostensibly to assure high technical quality, this is a *pro forma* procedure, and there is no preview of the live Sunday services that are broadcast from Nairobi churches, a tradition dating from 1928. The committee has clear guidelines for religious broadcasts. Church spokesmen must avoid appearing denominational. They must speak on behalf of all churches in Kenya and must not ridicule or criticize other churches or religions. They may preach against social ills but must be careful not to blame the government for them or to give messages that might "confuse the people or cause them to despise the government or other people" (22).

The churches are important forums for public debate. Sermons and clerical statements constitute a substantial element both in the print media and on the VOK. Leading churches have ready access to the broadcast media, and uncensored sermons are broadcast live to the entire nation. On numerous occasions, church leaders have severely criticized government policies and have called upon the nation's leaders to mend their ways. For example, Anglican bishop the Right Reverend Henry Okullu has spoken against corruption in public office, economic inequality, and detention without trial (5, 30). Prior to the 1983 general election, the Catholic bishops issued a pastoral letter "calling for the election of leaders who valued honesty and commitment to national interests and who had a sense of justice" (30). In 1987 clergymen were strongly critical of President Moi's scheme for party selection of candidates for the 1988 General Election, which required voters to queue behind the candidate of their choice (4).

Some politicians have accused the clergy of abusing the constitutionally guaranteed freedom of worship and demanded that clergy stay out of politics. To these charges the clergy counter that as Kenyans they have the duty to point out what is wrong in Kenyan society. The church, they say, "must fulfill its role of watchdog over the state and remain in principle critical of every state and ready to warn it against transgression of its legitimate limits" (5). Kenyans are reminded that freedom of worship is a right, not a privilege to be granted or taken away by politicians.

Although most powerful church leaders in Kenya are critical of what they perceived to be abuses of power and do make oblique references to government policies they think are wrong, they are seeking to reform the system, not overthrow it. They deliver sermons on charity—material and spiritual—to the rich and powerful. They preach cooperation with the state in ameliorating the conditions of the poor and provide leadership for such projects. The government clearly recognizes the power and influence of the church in Kenya and is keen to enlist the cooperation of all religious organizations and leaders in its nation building and development projects. Generous access to the public through the broadcast media is, in effect, for that cooperation. Should a churchman become too outspoken or obvious in his criticism of present leaders or policies, he is likely to find his access to the broadcast media blocked.

Private sector participation in Kenya's public service broadcasting system is an essential com-

ponent of Kenya's strategy for economic and social development. If Kenya is to be a player in the international marketplace, policy-makers believe, its citizens must acquire a taste for consumer goods and international cultural products. If multinational enterprises are to be encouraged to invest in Kenya, they must be allowed to hawk their goods and services. On the other hand, if a model of development that places a greater value on growth as measured in per capita income than on equality and social welfare is to be sustained without social dislocation, private organizations must be encouraged to provide those social services that the state is unable or unwilling to provide. Above all, Kenyans must be taught by teachers, preachers, and the media to respect authority and to prefer stability to potentially disruptive change.

The VOK clearly serves the interests of those in positions of authority and influence by giving voice and legitimacy to cultural attitudes and assumptions that favor the status quo. There is nothing exceptional about this situation; the mainstream media everywhere serve the interests of the powerful (1). Nevertheless, the situation in Kenya is fraught with contradictions.

Most apparent to those familiar with the New World Information and Communication Order debate is the fact that the VOK's policies with regard to commercial participation are not in line with the MacBride Commission recommendations to which Kenya has given its support. Several of those recommendations are applicable: "Developing countries should establish national cultural policies, which should foster cultural identity and creativity, and involve the media in these tasks" (2, p. 259). Care should be given to reduce the influence of advertising on editorial policy and broadcast programming, and preference should be given to noncommercial forms of mass communication. Communication should be democratized, decentralized, and diversified in order to provide "opportunities for real direct involvement of the people in the communication process" (23, p. 267). These views are echoed by Kenya's former Director of Broadcasting, James Kangwana: "African broadcasting organizations have the historic duty to encourage and nurture the creativity of their own societies," and they must balance their professional biases and advertisers'

preferences for polished Western material "against the needs and wishes of rural audiences who form the majority" (9, p. 262).

The government's failure to adequately fund the VOK has forced broadcasters to depend upon outside financial support. This dependence is exacerbated by the fact that VOK equipment is so inadequate and in such bad repair that the VOK staff is all too grateful for material produced in better-equipped privately owned facilities. As we have seen, these materials are naturally designed to meet the needs of the producers, which in many cases match the interests of Kenyan elites. By catering to the tastes and interests of privileged classes and reinforcing a pattern of development from which they benefit, the VOK is abrogating its responsibility to "encourage and nurture the creativity" of its own society and its responsibility to provide a communications vehicle that will facilitate and encourage popular participation in genuine social development.

Because the VOK is an arm of the government, if change is to come it will have to come from the top, with a reworking of definitions of development and strategies to achieve it and a serious financial and moral commitment to broadcasting that strengthens cultural identity and facilitates social progress. It is not necessary to exclude the private sector; indeed, that would be a move in the wrong direction. But arrangements for private sector participation can be reworked so that participation is in accordance with new perspectives.

NOTES

1. The majority of the shares of the Nation Group, which publishes the *Daily Nation, Taifa Leo*, and the *Sunday Nation*, are held by His Highness the Aga Khan. The *Standard*, which publishes a daily and a Sunday paper, is owned by Lonhro, a big multinational corporation with considerable interests in Africa. Since April 1983 the ruling party KANU has published the *Kenya Times, Kenya Leo*, and the *Sunday Times*. The *Weekly Review*, an extremely influential news magazine, is published by the totally Kenya-owned Stellascope.
2. Alternative forms of African socialism have been articulated in (10, 26, 29).

3. In addition to AIT, the recording business in Kenya is dominated by Polygram and CBS (33, pp. 350–356).
4. The NCCK Constitution of 1983 stipulates that to qualify for full membership churches must have 10,000 adherents, have been registered in Kenya for 5 years, and be sponsored by a NCCK member from the same district.

REFERENCES

1. Altschull, J. Herbert. *Agents of Power*. New York: Longman, 1984.
2. Anabwani, Simeon. Commercial Manager, Voice of Kenya. Personal interview, Nairobi, 1984.
3. Barnouw, Erik. *The Sponsor*. New York: Oxford University Press, 1978.
4. "The Catholic Voice." *Weekly Review*, September 4, 1987.
5. "Debate over Religion and Politics." *Weekly Review*, August 31, 1984.
6. Gitlin, Todd. *Inside Prime Time*. New York: Pantheon, 1985.
7. Heath, Carla Wilson. "Broadcasting in Kenya: Policy and Politics, 1928–1984." Unpublished Ph.D. dissertation, University of Illinois, Urbana, 1986.
8. Jouet, Josiane. "Advertising and Transnational Corporations in Kenya." *Development and Change* 15, 1984, pp. 435–456.
9. Kangwana, James. "Making Programme Policy." In G. Wedell (Ed.), *Making Broadcasting Useful*. Manchester, England: University of Manchester Press, 1986.
10. Kaunda, Kenneth. *Letters to My Children*. London: Longman, 1973.
11. Kenya, Colony. *Report of the Television Commission*. Nairobi: Government Printer, 1958.
12. Kenya, Colony. *Sessional Paper No. 4 of 1957/58*. Nairobi: Government Printer, 1958.
13. Kenya Legislative Council. *Debates*. Nairobi: Government Printer, various years.
14. Kenya National Assembly. *Official Report*. Nairobi: Government Printer, various years.
15. Kenya, Republic of. *Appropriation Accounts*. Nairobi: Government Printer, various years.
16. Kenya, Republic of. *Development Plan for the Period 1984 to 1988*. Nairobi: Government Printer, 1983.
17. Kenya, Republic of. *Government Observations on the Report of the Lutta Commission of Investigation into the Financial Position and Administration of the Kenya Broadcasting Corporation*. Nairobi: Government Printer, 1964.
18. Kenya, Republic of. "African Socialism and Its Application to Planning in Kenya." *Sessional Paper No. 10 of 1965*. Nairobi: Government Printer, 1965.
19. Komu, Patrick. Commercial Manager, Voice of Kenya. Personal Interview, Nairobi, 1983.
20. MacBride, Sean et al. *Many Voices, One World*. Paris: UNESCO, 1980.
21. MacCabe, Colin and Olivia Stewart (Eds.). *The BBC and Public Service Broadcasting*. Manchester, England: University of Manchester Press, 1986.
22. Maingi, Charles. National Council of Churches in Kenya, Communications Department. Personal interview, Nairobi, 1984.
23. Moi, President Daniel arap. Speech to the National Assembly presenting the Fifth Development Plan, reported in the *Daily Nation*, December 10, 1983.
24. Muthui, Eliud. Head of Television Operations and in charge of imported programs, Voice of Kenya. Personal interview, Nairobi, 1983.
25. Mwaura, Peter. *Communication Policies in Kenya*. Paris: UNESCO, 1980.
26. Nyerere, Julius. *Ujamaa: Essays on Socialism*. London: Oxford University Press, 1963.
27. "Project Agreement AID in Kenya #134-1-614 (1966)." Kenya National Archives I&B/44.
28. Rowland, Willard. "The Challenge to Public Service Broadcasting." *Report on a Joint Conference of the Aspen Institute Berlin and the Aspen Institute Program on Communications and Society*. Aspen, Colo.: Aspen Institute for Humanistic Studies, 1986.
29. Senghor, Leopold. *On Socialism*. Translated and with an introduction by Mercer Cook. London: Pall Mall, 1964.
30. "A Sensitive Issue." *Weekly Review*, June 22, 1984.
31. Shimizu, Shinichi. "Public Service Broadcasting in Japan: How NHK Faces the Future." NHK, Tokyo, 1987.
32. Voice of Kenya Commercial Department. "Commercial Billings Jan.–June 1983." VOK, Nairobi, 1983.
33. Wallis, Roger and Krister Malm. *Big Sounds from Small Peoples*. London: Constable, 1984.

THE GLOBAL SPREAD OF ADVERTISING REGULATION

J. J. BODDEWYN

We now look at the rise of global policymaking in one specific area of mass communication—advertising. J. J. Boddewyn reviews the changes that are occurring worldwide and concludes—from an American perspective—that advertisers must be vigilant as the social climate changes and as pilot nations develop their own policies about mass communication advertising.

U.S. regulatory developments quickly spread abroad, but foreign concerns gain audience and support here, too, since the United States does not exercise overall leadership in the regulation of advertising.[1]

Americans like to think of themselves as always being first and foremost in everything. But we have historically lagged behind the Europeans in the areas of consumer policy and advertising regulation. The countries to watch are Sweden and Norway where most innovative legislations begin. Generally it is picked up by the United Kingdom and Germany, and makes it way to the United States with a time lag of six to eight years. The world is a laboratory.[2]

One can quibble with this listing of pilot nations, but the point remains valid: There are nations to watch because they are often imitated by others. Exhibit 1 illustrates a number of issues and leading countries.

Also, an increasing number of developing nations are reacting against Western advertising languages, themes, and illustrations; they are stirring themselves to develop consumer protection rules. For that matter, the United Nations Economic and Social Council has commissioned a 1981 report that will include proposals for consumer protection standards and regulations in the less developed nations. Consequently, advertising regulation is becoming a global phenomenon well worth the keen attention of domestic as well as international advertisers. No country is a regulatory island.

This global multiplication of advertising regulations arises because of certain key factors, listed in Exhibit 2.[3] It also invites a number of business initiatives, illustrated in Exhibit 2 and discussed in subsequent sections.

Beyond the fine legal points best left to the experts, advertisers must pay attention to the following regulatory developments and the problems they raise as they spread from nation to nation.

Prove It Beforehand

Advertisers used to be able to take their chances: "Raise the flag and see who salutes" was Madison Avenue's motto. If a complaint or suit ensued, one only had to gather evidence to prove, if possible, that the claim was truthful or not misleading. This little game is increasingly difficult to play. The new rule is: "Get your facts straight *before* you run the ad."

■ In the Pfizer ("Unburn") case, the Federal Trade Commission (FTC) ruled that in the area of health and safety, the advertiser should have *sub-*

J.J. Boddewyn, "The Global Spread of Advertising Regulation." *MSU Business Topic*, Vol. 24, No. 2, Spring 1981, pp. 5–13. Reprinted by permission.

The author is professor of international business at Baruch College, City University of New York.

Exhibit I   ISSUES AND PLACES TO WATCH

Advertising to children	Canada, Scandinavia, United States
Class action by consumer associations	European Economic Community (EEC) Commission, United States
Comparison advertising	EEC Commission (encouragement), France (relaxation), Philippines (ban), United States (encouragement)
Consumer protection in general	EEC Commission, Scandinavia, United Nations organizations, United States
Corrective ads	United States, EEC Commission
Feminine hygiene commercials (mandatory prior screening)	Canada (British)
Food, drug, and cosmetics commercials (mandatory prior screening)	Canada, Mexico
Infant formula promotion	World Health Organization/UNICEF
Reversal of the burden of proof on the advertiser	EEC Commission, Scandinavia, United States
Sexism in advertising	Canada, Netherlands, Scandinavia, United Kingdom, United States
Use of foreign languages in advertisements	France, Mexico, Quebec Province
Use of foreign materials, themes, and illustrations	Korea, Moslem countries, Peru, Phillipines
Wording used in food and drug ads	Belgium, EEC Commission, United States

stantiation in hand before a claim is made. (The FTC used the term a *reasonable basis.*) In any case, to avoid legal hassles and consumer complaints, private and public networks worldwide increasingly require the facts quoted in commercials be substantiated when the ad is submitted to them. This requirement is spreading to print media.

▪ Twenty-four of forty major advertising countries have at least one government requirement for prior clearance. These apply to such health-related products as prescription drugs, over-the-counter medicines, medicated toiletries, and cosmetics. A smaller but growing number of countries, for example Canada and Mexico, require prior clearance of all food and drink ads, particularly if therapeutic claims are made. Clearance is mandatory for *all* commercials in Australia and the United Kingdom. In Canada, adherence to the Broadcast Code for Advertising Directed to

Children requires prior clearance and is now part of a station's licensing requirement.

▪ The law and court decisions are shifting the onus of proof to the advertiser, as exemplified by the proposed European Economic Community (EEC) directive on misleading and unfair advertising: "Where an advertiser makes a factual claim, the burden of proof that his claim is correct shall in civil and administrative proceeding lie with him." Even if that directive is not adopted, EEC member nations are likely to change their rules accordingly. Such a reversal of the burden of proof is a fact in at least fourteen countries, including Denmark, France, Hong Kong, Norway, Spain, Sweden, and Venezuela. It is, in effect, practiced under self-regulatory systems, that is, participating advertisers, agencies, and media agree to justify their advertisements when challenged by consumers, competitors, and media.

Exhibit 2   REGULATION AND RESPONSE

Key Regulatory Factors	*Major Regulatory Developments*	*Suggested Business Responses*
Consumer protection (for example, against untruthful, unfair, misleading ads)	Prior substantiation of advertising claims is becoming the norm.	More self-regulation by industry
Protection for competitors (for example, against the misuse of comparison and cooperative advertising)	Growing product restrictions affect the advertising of them.	Collaboration with consumer organizations
	More informative ads are in order.	Greater self-discipline by advertisers
Environmental protection (for example, against outdoor advertising)	Advertising language is being restricted.	Expanded lobbying and public advocacy
Civil rights protection (for example, against sexist ads)	Vulnerable groups such as children are becoming the target of advertising regulations.	Revised marketing and promotion policies
Religion (for example, against the advertising of contraceptives)	More groups and people can now sue advertisers.	
Standards of taste and decency (for example, against sexy ads)	Penalties are getting stiffer.	
Nationalism (for example, against the use of foreign languages, themes, and illustrations)		

This trend is nearly irresistible because it makes sense to require advertisers to be sure about their facts before they use them. It is also perceived by self-regulatory bodies as a way of warding off unnecessary criticism of advertising.

Ban the Product or Ban the Ad?

Advertising regulation increasingly reflects restrictions imposed on the product or service itself. If the latter is considered immoral, unsafe, or unhealthy, its promotion is likely to be restricted. Thus, most countries ban or severely limit the advertising of cigarettes, alcoholic beverages, lotteries, and pharmaceuticals because their use, misuse, or overuse is considered undesirable.

This issue is not easily resolved. On the one hand, governments point to their duty to protect consumers. On the other hand, there are constitutional and legal provisions for freedom of speech (for example, in Norway, Sweden, and the United States) that shield advertising against undue restrictions. Besides, if cigarette smoking is dangerous to

one's health, why not prohibit its manufacture and sale instead of its advertising? Considering the growing stringency of regulations and voluntary guidelines regarding validation of advertising claims, it is unlikely that cigarette or liquor ads would lay claim to health-enhancing properties. Moreover, bad habits do not necessarily originate with paid advertisements, as the popularity of unadvertised marijuana and cocaine readily attests.

Clearly, this situation calls for a balance of commercial, consumer, and societal interests. Unfortunately, general censorship and mandatory prior clearance may not be far away, because governments are showing a tendency to ban or restrict any good that can be abused.

Decrease the Mood; Increase the Information

Critics of advertising grudgingly accept its informative role. They would, however, prefer to have such information gathered and disseminated by impartial bodies and publications of the *Consumer Reports* type. The critics' ideal advertisement is what the French call a *réclame*, something like a supermarket ad announcing that a brand of butter is on sale. They object to emotional appeals that go beyond fact and reason, such as "things go better with Coke."

Creative advertising people are adamant about making people imagine themselves in new roles and situations. We are back to the old debate about whether to sell the sizzle or the steak. Advertisers, like politicians, know that buyers need more than information to get past the awareness and interest stages and into evaluation, trial, and adoption. After all, U.S. presidents have asked the electorate to "dream again," to want "the Great Society," if not "to be born again."

But this argument goes just so far. *Whatever their emotional content, ads will have to be more informative.* Even if advertisers are not obliged to tell all the facts, they will clearly have to tell more.

- Regulatory bodies in the United States and Europe, as well as many consumer associations around the world, have been supporting comparative advertising precisely because it is *more informative* and because it identifies brand and contrasts them in terms of specific attributes.

   Increasingly, it is the net impression or total effect on the audience that counts. Hence, advertisers are well advised to use disclaimers ("Not available at this price in stores!") and warnings ("Cigarette smoking is dangerous to your health") as well as to mention negative product features when a claim of overall superiority could be incorrectly assumed by the public.

- In Sweden, comparative ads must be "significantly complete," and all major differences between the products, including shortcomings, must be mentioned. The EEC Commission draft directive on misleading and unfair advertising proposes to ban and prosecute ads that "omit material information, and by reason of that omission give a false impression or arouse reasonable expectations which the advertised goods or services cannot satisfy." In Spain, the Maizena cornstarch package can no longer show a baby's picture lest it be believed by mothers that *by itself* this product would "help raise healthy and strong children" (the brand's former slogan).

Watch Your Language

A major battle is shaping up regarding the wording of advertisements. Health and fair trade authorities make more stringent demands about the wording on packages, labels, and informative enclosures. That is all to the good, but what about the ad extolling the same product? Regulators would like approved food, energy, and health claims to become the basis of advertising copy.

- An FTC staff report recently recommended that claims made in advertising regarding the use of over-the-counter drugs should not significantly differ from those that the Food and Drug Administration permits on drug labels, and that only FDA-approved terms be used in most cases. (The FTC dropped this proposal in February 1981.)

   Advertisers, however, resist this harmonizing of labeling and advertising. After all, how much can you say and show in a 30-second commercial or even in a full-page print ad without cluttering the message and losing the reader's or viewer's attention? Ads are not consumer reports, securities announcements, or medical bulletins. They should inform, of course, but persuasion is the stuff of advertising, too. Where will it end? Should you tell potential buyers of a quadrophonic set that they could go deaf if they play it too loud, too long, or too close? Still, such *warnings, noncommercial messages, and compulsory wordings are increasingly being mandated.*

- The Swedish government is now requiring that safety messages be included in ads to children. ("Always wear a helmet when skateboarding.") In the Netherlands, candy ads must display a toothbrush. The FTC staff has proposed that public service messages about good nutritional habits be financed by commercial advertisers.

- Many countries regulate the use of such words as *gratis* and *free.* The U.S. government as well as the EEC Commission may soon restrict expressions that have become fairly meaningless— such as *health, home-made, natural,* and *organic* when applied to food. (Belgium has already taken such action.) The FTC limits references to *energy, low-calorie,* and *fat/fatty acid/cholesterol* in ads and would like to further regulate nutritional claims.

- The regulators are now trying to tell advertisers, who pride themselves on their expressive skills, how to tell their story. No more *cough remedies* but *cough suppressants* according to an FTC staff proposal. *Calories* is out in Europe and *joules* is in. Say *Succès du jour* rather than *hit* on French radio and television.

Vulnerable Groups

Some people do not like advertising and would prefer to do without it. There are, however, too many vested interests and good legal and economic arguments in favor of it for this to occur. So they concentrate on specific advertising targets against which a decent if emotional case can be made.

Essentially, the argument that it is unfair to advertise to such vulnerable groups as the young, the old, the poor, the sick, the recently bereaved, and the ignorant. In particular, children are considered incapable of distinguishing between program and commercial materials, and overly susceptible to certain messages ("Get that toy and be popular!") and techniques (for example, the use of TV personalities and comics characters.)

- The FTC staff proposed banning TV ads directed at children under the age of 8, and of sugared food products to those under 12. This proposal is dormant, but a similar ban is in effect in Quebec. The EEC Commission and various countries also are looking into this issue.

- The use of premiums is severely restricted in Sweden and West Germany, where they are considered overly attractive—too strong an inducement. Some jurists consider them a form of misleading information because of the complexity of combined offers. (How much is that box of detergent really worth if it includes a dinner plate?)

- The partial ban on promoting infant formulas in developing countries falls under the same heading of vulnerability and unfairness on the grounds that relatively uneducated parents may misuse such products to the detriment of their children's health.[4]

Additional Suitors

More people and organizations can now legally sue advertisers or at least take some legal action. The traditional notion that only injured parties can sue is rapidly being eroded on the ground that everyone has an interest in having false, unfair, and misleading advertising stopped *before* harm is done. Besides, a number of countries (for example, Belgium) already allow *bona fide* consumer associations to sue on behalf of their members and the constituencies they represent. This tendency is embodied in the EEC draft directive, which would mandate its ten member countries to allow customers and competitors, as well as their legitimate associations, to start legal action against unfair or misleading advertising if they merely run a risk of injury.

Governments welcome this development to the extent that it reduces the need for more bureaucrats to police business behavior. It is better to let the courts referee the regulatory system as the prompting of concerned competitors and consumers. Needless to say, this will burden the judiciary system and expose business to more legal action—unless advertising review boards are allowed to handle most of the complaints.

Stiffer Penalties

The violation of commercial regulations no longer leads only to cease-and-desist injunctions, moderate fines, or payment of mild compensation to injured parties.

- In 1977, the Danish Consumer Ombudsman handled 2,112 cases. Most were settled by negotiation, but thirty were brought before the Copenhagen Maritime and Commercial Court. In each case, the verdict favored the ombudsman.

- In settling the suit brought by the FTC, the STP Corporation, under the terms of a consent order, agreed to spend $200,000 to place notices in three newspapers and eleven magazines with an estimated readership of 78 million people. The notices told, in part, that tests conducted for STP cannot be relied upon to support its claim that it reduces oil consumption. The FTC reported in September 1979 that more people are aware of a problem with STP's advertising and will not buy the product.[5]

▪ In Canada, untrue, deceptive, and misleading advertising can lead to five-year sentences and up to $25,000 fines. The size of fines is increasing.

▪ The EEC Commission draft directive on misleading and unfair advertising would permit courts to issue cease-and-desist injunctions "even without proof of intention or negligence or of actual prejudice." Courts also would be allowed to require publication of a corrective statement and of the court decision, as well as to impose penalties taking into account the extent of the harm. (This is already the case in France and the United States.)

Obviously, mistakes will be more costly in the future. Advertisers are well advised to double-check with their legal counsel.

CONTAINING THE GLOBAL SPREAD

There is no stopping the multiplication of advertising regulations. Some nations still lack adequate regulations, and societal concerns will continue to evolve and require new responses. Still, the advertising industry can do much to minimize problems.

Develop and Support Self-Regulation

Anglo-Saxon countries (including South Africa) are taking voluntary self-regulation very seriously. Advertising associations are developing codes and guidelines, setting up monitoring and complaint processing systems, making the public and government cognizant of their efforts, and turning over to the authorities evidence against recalcitrant wrongdoers. They hope thereby to reduce the need for further regulations as well as the number of complaints. Continental Europe is getting better organized to do the same under the goad of various EEC draft directives and national bills. Similar developments have taken place in Argentina, Brazil, Japan, Korea, Mexico, the Philippines, and Singapore, among others.

Self-regulation abroad is getting a boost from the well-publicized U.S. reactions to the costs of restrictive laws and rules. Still, self-regulation has its limits. Scandinavian countries seem satisfied with their consumer ombudsman system, leaving to the ombudsman most of the advising and arbitrating connected with the supervision of advertising behavior. Besides, most developing nations are in no position to establish self-regulatory systems; they lack collaborative tradition, interest, and resources. After all, it has taken industrialized countries decades to design and use such machinery. Of course, developing countries will be increasingly able to learn from that experience.

Some governments and the EEC Commission support self-regulation because it simplifies their own task and is a useful complement to the judiciary system. Thus, the Philippine Board of Advertising and Brazil's CONAR have been deputized to set up and administer advertising standards. Other governments (Canada, Japan, and the United Kingdom, for example) are moving in the same direction.

This quasi-governmental role is flattering to advertisers but also disturbing. It raises the specter of corporatism with its train of collusive restrictions on advertising. Also, business should think twice about accepting quasi-judicial power that would destroy the spirit of *voluntary* compliance underlying self-regulation. Besides, industry guidelines and codes could no longer be changed without government permission.[6]

Collaborate with Consumer Organizations

This approach can take several forms. A recent French government report urged that codes be negotiated between trade and consumer associations. The EEC Commission will do likewise in its 1980–1985 Consumer Protection and Information Program. Jointly developed codes are probably premature; the two groups are still very much at loggerheads. Exceptions occur only when governments can control the situation, as in the case of state-owned broadcasting networks.

An intermediate solution is the appointment of consumer and public-interest representatives to advertising review boards. This approach, however, raises questions about the nature of *self*-regulation if outsiders participate in the screening. Hence, this solution is limited to specialized committees dealing with advertising to children, pharmaceuticals, and feminine hygiene products (for example, in Canada). Still, it is likely to spread as experience is gained and mutual trust develops.

More readily achievable is consultation. In Germany, the Central Advertising Board (ZAW) is working in concerted action with the corresponding consumer association (AGV) through the Coordinating Committee on Consumer Advertising. In Belgium, the government-sponsored Consumers Council includes representatives from all economic sectors. They advise the administration and parliament on legislative and regulatory proposals and policies bearing on consumer affairs.

Develop Self-Discipline

Some U.S. firms have their own code of ethics (for example, Procter & Gamble, General Foods, and Revlon). Other countries have done more. In the Netherlands, industry has encouraged the appointment in all agencies, advertising firms, and media of an ethical officer responsible for overseeing the application of the Dutch Advertising Code as well as of general principles of ethical behavior. Similar developments have occurred in Norway, South Africa, and Sweden. German advertising people discuss questions of advertising law first and creative problems second when planning advertising. The legal counsel in U.S. firms serves a related function, but more companies will have to make such a procedure formal in order to cope with growing regulations.

Speak Up

The best defense is a good offense. This widely known precept should be heeded by advertisers with a clear conscience. Some proposed regulations go too far; they should be nipped in the bud through

individual and collective lobbying. Ruthless denunciation of violators will also help business's image.

The U.S. advertising industry has been in a fighting mood in recent years because of bold and possibly overreaching attempts by the FTC to apply its rulemaking powers to advertising to children and the wording of health- and food-related ads. In 1980, these efforts paid off; the FTC's powers to issue regulations about trade rules on the basis of unfairness were restricted by Congress (until 1982). The 1975 Supreme Court decision affirming that advertising is protected under the First Amendment, as well as the now popular reaction against overregulation, has given the industry strong legs on which to stand and fight.

Abroad, the International Chamber of Commerce, the European Advertising Agencies Association, and various national advertising bodies (particularly in the United Kingdom and West Germany) have strongly reacted against the EEC draft directive. It has been toned down if not permanently stalled. Similar reactions against overregulation or undesirable restrictions have occurred in Australia, Brazil, Canada, and Mexico.

Lobbying does not have to be offensive. It is most effective when based on research. This was evidenced by the facts marshalled by the breakfast cereals industry to counter the proposed FTC ban and restrictions on junk foods and on advertising to children. In any case, the more strident U.S. methods are not accepted abroad, where more conciliatory and discreet approaches are preferred.

It is time for business to point out that the most common abuses are not always committed by major advertisers but by individuals, governments, and nonprofit organizations.

- There are more lies in personal ads than by all business combined—from "apartment with river view [from the bathroom]," to "car in perfect condition [to die on you]," to "attractive woman wants to meet man."

- Some government ads are downright misleading, too—from savings bond announcements that do not warn buyers about their woefully inadequate interest rates to armed forces recruitment posters that promise you will "see the world" but do not include a warning (from the Surgeon General?) that you could be shot at and die. Fittingly enough, Public Advocates Inc.—a consumer group—filed a complaint with the FTC regarding the Treasury Department's allegedly misleading promotion of U.S. savings bonds as a good investment. This practice could have cost the public $2.4 billion in 1979 alone and may well have been "the most costly series of deceptive acts engaged in by any corporation or government agency in recent American history."[7] The Treasury Department has since toned down its claims. In summer 1979, the FTC chairman offered to make his staff available for advertising consultation to twelve government agencies.

- Regulation and self-regulation usually restrict advertisement wording to claims that can be substantiated. This sharply contrasts with the advice given by some journalists to their readers in such matters as diets and other health habits.

Freedom of speech is, of course, involved in editorial matters, but business has an improved record to stand on, and can request that its opponents and regulators also be better informed, more truthful, and not misleading or unfair in their statements, criticisms, and demands.

Revise Policies

A recent discussion of marketing strategy stressed the need for more ethical and anticipatory responses, as well as for a greater value and conservation orientation on the part of business people.[8] These suggestions have implications for advertisers.

Above all, business will have to be more technologically innovative in developing products and in translating significant product advantages into fact-based advertising. The growing restrictions on misleading advertising may spell the decline of product differentiation and market segmentation based on cosmetic differences. We may still dream, but after the fact.

Similarly, recent ethnic, religious, and nationalistic developments in Iran, France, Malaysia, Peru, and the Philippines suggest reconsidering the wisdom of standardizing advertisements around the world. There is a reaction abroad against Western cultural influences that advertising embodies in a highly visible and vulnerable manner. Just as protective coloration has long helped various animals to survive, so must advertising tone down its foreign or multinational appeals and use more indigenous touches. We will still be raising the flag to see who salutes, but the flag had better have the right colors.

CONCLUSION

Advertising regulations will continue to spread, even though much variety will remain. The Scandinavian countries have their Consumer Ombudsman approach; the Anglo-Saxon nations have their strong reliance on self-regulation; and the developing world has its emphasis on protecting cultural identity. Still, threading through this variety are common regulatory developments that will require both domestic and multinational firms to learn to communicate effectively and legally. In this process, eternal and global vigilance will help.[9]

NOTES

1. Recent surveys conducted by the International Advertising Association as well as other sources provide both facts and insights about such regulatory trends. See J. J. Boddewyn and Katherin Marton, *Comparison Advertising: A Worldwide Study* (New York: Hastings House, 1978). Other IAA international surveys (mimeo) include: J. J. Boddewyn, "Premiums, gifts and Competitions" (1978); "The Use of Foreign Languages and Materials in Advertising" (1978); "Government Pre-Clearance of Advertisements" (1979); "Outdoor/Billboard Advertising Regulation" (1979); "Advertising to Children" (1979); "Decency/Sexism in Advertising" (1979); "Energy and Advertising" (1980); "New Regulatory Developments: Reversal of the Burden of Proof, Corrective Advertising, and Suing Advertisers" (1980); and "Direct Mail/Direct Response Advertising" (1981). Also, see J. P. Neelankavil and A. B. Stridsberg, *Advertising Self-Regulation: A Global Perspective* (New York: Hastings House, 1980); and

J. J. Boddewyn, "Advertising Regulation, Self-Regulation and Self-Discipline around the World," *International Journal of Marketing* 1 (1981). The taxation of advertising is not discussed here but represents another growing form of government intervention around the world.

2. Graham T. T. Molitor, "U.S. Far from Top in Most Ad Regulations," *Advertising Age*, 12 November 1979, p. 110. Molitor is president of Public Policy Forecasting.

3. For further analysis of these factors and pressures, see J. J. Boddewyn, "Advertising Regulation in the 1980s: The Underlying Global Forces," working paper, Baruch College, January 1981.

4. At the October 1979 World Health Organization/UNICEF meeting in Geneva to debate the selling and promotion of infant formulas in developing countries, major manufacturers agreed to curb advertisements and sales promotion that would discourage breast-feeding. This issue will be further negotiated in 1981.

5. Until 1975, the only way the Federal Trade Commission could enforce its rules on trade regulations was through a cease-and-desist injunction. Fines came only after an order had been violated. The FTC Improvement/Magnuson-Moss Act now gives the FTC the right to ask the courts for penalties as soon as a company breaks a rule, and to automatically apply similar penalties to firms guilty of comparable violations.

6. Compulsory membership in self-regulatory bodies is illegal in the United States for antitrust reasons. Other countries are more lenient in this respect.

7. "Treasury Secretary Target of Complaint over Savings Bonds," *Wall Street Journal*, 26 September 1979, p. 1.

8. Gene R. Laczniak and Jon G. Udell, "Dimensions of Future Marketing." *MSU Business Topics* 27 (Autumn 1979): 33–44.

9. The author gratefully acknowledges the helpful comments of Sylvan Barnet (International Advertising Association), Helmut Becker (University of Portland), Maurizio Fusi (Torino, Italy), Eric D. Haeuter (CPC International), Robert E. Oliver (Canadian Advertising Advisory Board), Elaine S. Reiss (Ogilvy & Mather), Helmut Soldner (University of Augsburg), and Roger Underhill and Richard Hunt-Taylor (Advertising Association, United Kingdom).

3 COMMUNICATION CONTROL IN DIFFERENT SOCIETIES

Western Europe, prior to the nineteenth century, went through different phases of communication control that seem, on the surface at least, to correspond to Soviet Bloc and Third World control in successive eras. At first, these European countries exercised absolute dictatorship over communication, much as has the Soviet Bloc. Later these European countries adopted more subtle means of control, some quite similar to techniques that have been used more recently in many Third World countries. Only in the late eighteenth and nineteenth centuries did many European countries adopt policies that would largely free communicators from government control.

Studies of more recent times indicate that control exists in a great variety of ways now, but that basically the world still divides into three categories: those countries with strict control (mostly Soviet Bloc), those with moderate control (mostly Third World), and those with little control (mostly Western Bloc).

No matter what the system or the ideology, there are real life factors that must be considered. Some countries which might ideologically adhere to policies of control nevertheless in reality offer considerable freedom (as the case of Botswana shows). Other countries which might believe in little control actually have their communication sometimes controlled externally by another government (as the case of South African manipulation of American news demonstrates).

Some countries might openly espouse few controls over privately owned media, but perceived threats to those countries by internal and external forces might bring about public pressures which can place severe limits on the media (as the case of Israel shows). In some countries, the freedom accorded one group of communicators may not be given to another group (as the case of the Palestinians demonstrates). And in yet other countries the media institutions might be totally free of legal controls but occupy a monopoly position, and without competing voices and messages in those societies, the media may simply serve as mouthpieces for the ruling few (as the case of Costa Rica shows).

The cases presented in this section are merely illustrative. Many countries fall into these categories. In fact, even in the United States control has a variety of faces, and all of the conditions described in these cases have prevailed in some way in some places at some time or other.

LIMITS ON THE "FREED" PRESS OF 18TH- AND 19TH-CENTURY EUROPE

CHARLES A. RUUD

This essay points out how European governments in the eighteenth and nineteenth centuries coped with the new freedom of the press. Charles A. Ruud shows that while preliminary censorship was abolished in most of Europe by the 1850s, governments were able to devise other means to influence what appeared in print.

In response to the printing press, the Church in 15th-century Europe imposed preliminary censorship, or the precirculation screening of all printed works. In the years that followed, "freedom of the press" came into common use to mean the abolition of preliminary censorship; but the granting of that reform by state after state—England led the way in 1695—repeatedly came because preliminary censorship proved unworkable. Given all the philosophical arguments for a free press, however, lawmakers could proclaim the dismissal of censors a liberal reform. In turn, they imposed yet other press controls. The limits on publishing by the governments of England, France, Germany and Russia, for exam-

Charles A. Ruud, "Limits on the 'Freed' Press of 18th- and 19th-century Europe." *Journalism Quarterly*, Volume 56, Number 3, Autumn 1979, pp. 521–530. Reprinted by permission.

The author is associate professor of history at the University of Western Ontario.

ple, in the two centuries before our own underscore two realities that persist to the present: the relativity of press "freedom" and the basic intolerance of state officials to criticism by the press.

Finding preliminary censorship unsatisfactory and faced with the growing influence of the periodical and newspaper press on public opinion, European governments in the 18th and 19th centuries applied other pressures on a press they could no longer effectually censor. Each state under discussion consequently granted "freedom of the press" (a term commonly understood to that time to mean the freedom granted by the abolition of preliminary, or pre-publication, censorship); but, contrary to the expectation of leading political philosophers, these same states in turn used their judicial systems and yet other devices to shape what appeared in print.

The first to abolish the system of preliminary censorship, which all states imposed following the establishment of printing presses, was England in 1695. Just over 50 years before, in 1644, Milton had given the rationale for freedom of the press—or "liberty," as he put it—basic to Western free press doctrine today: truth can emerge, he said in *Areopagitica*, only by struggling with falsehood. "What wisdom can there be to choose, what continence to forbeare without the knowledge of evil?"[1] (Milton was justifying his having by-passed state censorship in publishing his pamphlet favoring divorce without obtaining the license required under the Parliamentary order of 1643.)

Still, when Parliament finally abandoned licensing in 1695, the legislators did not act simply to clear the way for truth. Rather, they rejected an unpopular and unworkable system. Strongly persuasive was the 1695 memorandum of Locke opposing the licensing act because it preserved the publishing monopoly of the Stationers' Company and gave the government power to search homes and seize books adjudged seditious. The common law, Locke further argued, provided adequate protection against abuses of the press: "I know not why a man should not have liberty to print whatever he would speak; and to be answerable for the one just as he is for the other, if he transgresses the law in either."[2]

Although he said little about the necessity of press freedom, Locke assumed an informed citizenry. in framing his theories of dissent and consent on the part of citizens toward their government.[3] In a

like vein, his *Letter on Toleration* in 1685 had advocated freedom for differing religious viewpoints because none monopolized the truth. Locke set limits on public discussion, however: the civil magistrate must not permit freedom of discussion to those who, like Catholics, sectaries, or atheists, would use freedom to attack the "laws of the commonwealth and the liberty and property of the citizen."[4] Recalling the excesses of religious enthusiasm during the Civil War, Locke wanted a political framework that would accommodate disagreement without permitting the opponents of the Protestant monarchy to destroy it. Kept within the law, dissent would prevent despotism—another tenet of modern Western free press doctrine.

Midway through the 18th century, Hume similarly argued that a free press was essential to the British political system, in which republican and monarchial principles balance one another. Referring to the capacity of public opinion to thwart any wrong ambitions of the royal court, Hume saw nothing "so effectual to this purpose as the liberty of the press by which all the learning, wit, and genius of the nation may be employed on the side of freedom and everyone be animated to its defence."[5]

In Koenigsberg in the last quarter of the century, when England alone had as yet abolished preliminary censorship, Kant saw fit to argue that free discussion in public, even on basic political and religious issues, would pose no threat to the established order but would advance enlightenment and promote human freedom. In "What is Enlightenment?" (1784), Kant explained that although one must at all times obey the law and perform one's duty to the state, the citizen is free to voice as a scholar his considered and informed views even when they conflict with his public duty. Kant expected tensions in defining precisely that point at which criticism of the existing order became unreasonable and illegal, but such tensions within a just and rational order would advance knowledge and benefit both the citizen and the ruler.[6]

In Russia, where the printing press had not long been in private hands and preliminary censorship was itself just getting established (both began in 1783), Radishchev advanced the Miltonian argument in 1790, emphasizing, like Hume and Kant, that a free press would check despotism. "The rulers of nations will not dare to depart from the way of truth," wrote Radishchev, "lest their policy, their wickedness, and their fraud be exposed."[7] Such words in his *Journey from St. Petersburg to Moscow* so angered the Empress Catherine II that she exiled Radishchev to Siberia. He had merely wanted to start a constructive debate among educated Russians on questions of reform, including that of the censorship, Radishchev told police interrogators. The Empress saw the matter differently: Radishchev was infected with the "French madness," she said.

With the onset of the 19th century, English radicals upheld the Miltonian tradition through arguments directly related to representative government as advanced in the Reform Bill of 1832. Again, the censure of public institutions and of public men was positively necessary to avoid tyranny. To his own question—"Under a government of laws, what is the motto of a good citizen?"—Jeremy Bentham had answered: "*To obey punctually; to censure freely.*"[8] In turn, James Mill wrote that laws must protect the reputation of individuals, especially in private matters, but that the public must know even the "slightest suspicion" of a man in his official capacity.[9]

John Stuart Mill accepted his father's argument for free discussion but emphasized that the resultant emergence of truth would be a slow process. Truth would become known only "in the course of ages" because fallible man can readily misconstrue false ideas as true ones. Even truth itself could become dogma and stifle thinking about new truths. These problems of fallibility and conformity being paramount, Mill in *On Liberty* said little about the danger of government controls on the press but stressed the danger of men collectively standardizing thought.[10]

The philosophers, mainly English, who opposed censorship stirred discussions across Europe. Optimism about the increasing enlightenment of the general citizenry underlay arguments that a freespeaking press would benefit states by providing information on all sides of questions. Press freedom would not only lead men to truth but also would restrain despotism.

In legal terminology, "liberty of the press" in the 18th and 19th centuries meant that printed works could reach the public without advance screening by censors. Eighteenth century English jurists—notably Blackstone, Mansfield, and Kenyon—repeatedly stressed that liberty for the press meant no restraints prior to publication. Blackstone closely echoed Locke: "Every free man has an undoubted right to lay what sentiments he pleases before the public: to forbid this is to destroy freedom of the Press; but if he publishes what is improper, mischievous, or illegal, he must take the consequences of his own temerity."[11]

One long-standing law which governed published works was the one prohibiting seditious libel, the very limit on public utterances set by the Star Chamber: because, in order to maintain peace, order, and stability, the government must preserve its good name, an utterance—whether true or false—becomes seditious libel if it is adjudged able to undermine the political order. The crime of seditious libel remains in the British criminal code today; but, notably, the other nations here discussed were readier than England to charge the press with this kind of crime.[12] Germany, France, and Russia all defined seditious libel very broadly in the 19th century. Their searchers after sedition were to identify published passages that could not only undermine the political system but also discredit morality and religion or provoke "tensions" among social classes. The prosecutions of these imprecise crimes tended to peak—and, especially so, once preliminary censorship had ended—during periods of political unrest. In every nation, laws against seditious libel predated press censorship and remained a judicial weapon against the press once censorship ended.

As already shown, a free press had emerged in Britain in 1695 when Parliament allowed licensing to lapse. Subsequent legislation and judicial acts over the next century and one-half were further to enlarge publishing rights in England. Although initially Parliament had continued to guard jealously its own debates and proceedings and in 1738 specifically prohibited their publication, Parliament began in 1771 to give the press access to its deliberations and permission to report them. Going further, Parliament in 1840 applied the doctrine of "privilege" to such reporting (a writer who described Parliamentary proceedings fairly was not subject to persecution) and later extended it to reportage about other public assemblies. Meanwhile, in 1792, Fox's Libel Act gave to the jury in cases of seditious and defamatory libel the right to decide not merely the fact of publication but also whether or not printed material was libelous.

On the continent, the elimination of preliminary censorship came much more belatedly than in England. The Bourbon's system of preliminary censorship first ended in France in 1789, as confirmed in the Declaration of the Rights of Man and Citizen. The First Republic's still born constitution of 1793 also contained an article establishing freedom of the press, but the Republic acted instead to reinstate censorship and especially directed it against monarchists. In turn, Napoleon I imposed his own censorship. Not until the Charter of June 4, 1814, did the French have a document forbidding preliminary censorship of lasting effectiveness (with some few exceptions). However, although unwilling to overturn the Charter, French governments in the first half of the 19th century, whatever their ideology, relied on administrative measures, a lengthening list of libels, and quasi-judicial tribunals to restrict the press. Even the Second Empire, although no longer restrained by the Charter, avoided preliminary censorship. Instead, the government of Napoleon III, upon discovering that only 16 of 200 papers in 43 prefectures supported the government, issued the press law of February 17, 1852, following the *coup d'etat* of the previous December. In it, Minister of Justice Rouher established a "warning system" to give the government administrative, or non-judicial, means to suppress those hostile publications which did not violate the precise terms of the criminal law.[13]

First of all, publishers had to secure government permission to publish and could be turned down. Then, if the minister of the interior or one of his prefects discerned a dangerous trend in a publication (an undefined, subjectively-determined tendency), he could issue a warning. A third warning to a publication would cause temporary closure for up to two months or even its permanent closure. In the course of 16 years, the government issued against newspapers in Paris 109 warnings, 8 temporary closures and 5 permanent closures. By 1862, according to government figures, the circulation of pro-government papers far exceeded that of the oppositional press. Such seeming success was to make the warning system attractive to other continental governments, as well. Not until 1881 did the French secure a freedom comparable to that of the English

when the Third Republic ended all administrative press restrictions and made writers and publishers subject solely to the general laws and the courts.

As for the German states, the revolutions of 1848 had destroyed their systems of preliminary censorship. Prussia proceeded to include the principle of press freedom in its Constitution of 1850 and the other German states followed; but after 1850, the German states turned to a mix of administrative restrictions and judicial controls over the press. Under the Prussian press law of May 12, 1851, persons who published or sold printed matter had to secure a government license.[14] The law of March 6, 1854, gave new powers over publishing to the government by restricting juries in press cases, and the Federal statute of July 6, 1854, imposed new controls on the press in all German states.[15]

In 1863, faced with a constitutional crisis over the military budget, Bismarck dealt with the opposition press by having the king of Prussia prorogue the Diet and use the emergency powers accorded the king when the Diet was not in session to decree a press law containing a warning system like Napoleon III's. His officials could issue warnings for vague offenses to a publication and, after three warnings, could temporarily or permanently close it. Again, as in France, the object was to avoid the courts, where the canons of evidence required rigid proofs of wrong-doing. When it reconvened, the Diet rejected this press law and ended Bismarck's experiment with the warning system after only several months.[16] Bismarck clearly distrusted the press, especially newspapers, and he saw free expression as a step toward constitutionalism and popular representation.[17]

A decade later, the press law of the German Empire of May 7, 1874, confirmed freedom of the press, but gave the public prosecutor and the police considerable leeway in delaying the publication of the newspapers and in confiscating them. Then, in its anti-socialist legislation of October 1878, the Reichstag empowered the police to seize publications thought to be socialist or communist and bent on overthrowing the established order. The law permitted appeals to an Imperial Commission—four members appointed from the Bundesrat and five from the bench, one of whom the emperor named chairman.[18] But the Commission set its own rules and judged press appeals against police seizures almost exclusively from documents furnished by the police themselves.

The Commission was to assess a publication's "total tendency" (*Gesamttendenz*) over several issues and in light of the persons who were publisher, editor and printer. Of the 608 police actions against periodicals, the Commission heard 105 appeals and upheld 35. Of 1,241 actions against non-periodical publications, only 123 were appealed and 25 upheld.[19] Decisions were final and not subject to judicial review, the liberals in the Reichstag maintaining that the necessarily loose prohibitions in the law— those against agitation, creating animosity between social classes, and casting disrepute on the state— could be judged only by a group not bound by the formal proofs required in court.[20] The government actually wished the 1878 law to apply to the press as a whole, but failed in that plan because the National Liberals opposed it.[21] Bismarck's attempt to toughen the anti-socialist legislation failed in 1890, and the Reichstag did not renew the law.

Of the four states under discussion, Imperial Russia was the last to abolish preliminary censorship, doing so, finally, in 1905. In October of that year, Nicholas II granted the freedom of the press long sought by writers and publishers. Three earlier major attempts to liberalize press controls had all involved retention of censorship and all had been undercut by arbitrary police interference in times of emergency (such moments were frequent in Imperial Russia). The first two, through decrees in 1804 and 1828, had promised fair, clearly-stated, and uniformly-applied press rules.[22] The third was a statute of 1865, which was hailed as a "reform" and which did, in fact, free many works from preliminary censorship—all books over 10 printed signatures (160 pages), translated books having more than 20 signatures, and periodicals and newspapers in St. Petersburg and Moscow. Alexander II, who four years before had liberated the serfs, said that he was granting the press "all possible relief and convenience," but did not pronounce, at least in public, the word "freedom." Under the terms of the 1865 statute, once the new system of courts under the judicial reform of 1864 had come into being, Russian judges decided whether individuals and publications had committed criminal offenses through

the printed word. But government dissatisfaction with the outcome of prosecutions contributed to Russia's relying on the warning system invented under Napoleon III, a system which lasted from 1865 to 1905.[23]

For displaying a "dangerous orientation" (*vrednoe napravlenie*), a Russian periodical or paper that received three "warnings" from official overseers (most usually from within the Ministry of the Interior) could be suspended for up to six months or closed permanently with Senate approval. The impending threat of a third warning could hang over the head of an editor for years, although a time limit was finally set. During the 40 years Russia used the system, the Imperial government issued 280 warnings and suspended for varying periods 64 journals and papers, a number of them two or more times.[24] Relatively few such publications were closed permanently, but the constant threat of closure caused editors themselves to avoid sensitive statements. In this same period, the Imperial government used other penalties not subject to court review to keep papers and journals in line—for example, suspension of street sales and of advertisements and the outright prohibition of any commentary on sensitive topics.

In summary, the abolition of preliminary censorship took place in England in 1695, in France in 1789 and again in 1814, in Prussia in 1850, and in Russia in 1905 (forty years after a substantial cutback of censorship in 1865). In each country, the government abandoned preliminary censorship when that system proved too cumbersome, ineffectual, or odious as a control over what appeared in print. The authority to decide the legality of printed content *after* publication became the responsibility of each state's court system; but in three of the four states here discussed (England is the exception) the government found the court system too slow or too lenient and therefore empowered administration or police officials to ban works and close presses— measures which were "administrative" rather than judicial.

When, on the other hand, a government felt no need for immediate suppression of a printed work, the very slowness of the courts made prosecutions useful. Prosecution offered a means to retrain the press by engaging publishers, editors and writers in expensive, time-consuming and unpredictable judicial procedures. England's attorney general in the 18th century could file an *ex officio* information against journalists, for example, and thereby avoid a Grand Jury investigation and the danger that the jury would dismiss a case. He could also delay a press trial, permitting the indictment to hang over the head of a writer as a form of intimidation.[25] Not until 1819 did one of the Six Acts put a year's limitation on bringing a case to trial. In France, the police perfect of Paris, Giquet, admitted that prosecution itself was a form of harassment of unfriendly papers in the 1830s under the July Monarchy. He approved, for example, that the Republican *Tribune*, facing its 111th law suit, chose in 1835 to cease publication.

In Germany, the relatively liberal press law of 1874 was followed by an increase in federal prosecutions in 1874 and 1875, usually under the criminal law forbidding insult to the emperor, the chancellor, the state and its institutions. According to the most recent study of the 1874 law, imperial officials were convinced that they could control the opposition press, when necessary, by stepping up the number of prosecutions; and some 3,287 press trials took place between 1874 and 1890.[26]

Although the Russian Imperial government, through its press reform in 1865, attempted to rely on the courts to restrain the opposition press (an uncomfortable anomaly in an autocratic state), Russian officials had within a few years all but abandoned that course. The warning system and other administrative measures virtually supplanted taking members of the press to court, except in personal libel suits. Only in 1905, when the government finally declared freedom of the press, did the Russian court system begin hundreds of prosecutions against periodicals and papers, often under a provision of the criminal code which prohibited incitement to civil disobedience, as in encouraging students to leave their studies to participate in street demonstrations.[27]

Another readily available weapon against hostile or dangerous writers and publishers was financial in nature. All four governments used taxes, fines, or caution money (or all three) to make publishing expensive and discourage the radical press. Only 17 years after allowing censorship to lapse, Parliament

in Great Britain placed duties on all newspapers through the Stamp Act of 1712, with the result that subscription costs rose and circulations fell. Duties increased in Britain throughout the 18th century and were eventually levied not only on copies of papers and journals but on advertisements and paper, as well. Violations of the Stamp Tax led to prosecutions which could result in fines and even destruction of stocks and equipment. Duties reached their peak around 1815, when the government feared social upheaval. Then, once more secure, Parliament set aside the taxes one by one, repealing the last of the "taxes on knowledge," that on paper, in 1861.[28]

French governments similarly used stamp duties to limit publications, especially radical ones. In 1826, a dozen years after the Charter had ended preliminary censorship, Charles X's prime minister, the Comte de Villele, raised stamp duties and postal rates. These expenses for papers and journals fluctuated in the years that followed, reaching their height under Napoleon III, when the stamp duty fell on the number of copies produced rather than the number sold. Furthermore, publications could only be sold on the streets of the department in which they were stamped—an effective means of restraining distribution.[29] Duties of this kind remained in effect in one form or another until the Third Republic abolished them in 1870.

In Prussia, Joseph von Radowitz, the conservative advisor to King Frederick William IV, distinguished between literary works which required little control and newspapers and pamphlets—products as dangerous as narcotics or gunpowder—which required a great deal.[30] Not surprisingly, the Prussian press law of 1851 established a newspaper tax that rose with circulation.[31] That same law extracted deposits from publishers in the form of a surety bond, or caution money, from which fines, if incurred, would be deducted—a measure also used by France and Russia. In France in 1852, for example, deposits doubled to 50,000 francs for newspapers in Paris and Lyons and 25,-30,000 (depending on the importance of the location) for those published elsewhere. In like fashion, the Russian government required all publications released from preliminary censorship by the statute of 1865 to deposit caution money: 5,000 rubles for newspapers and 2,500 rubles for journals. All these government-imposed costs increased the capital-funding requirements for periodicals and caused publishers to observe the press laws with greater care.

As they withdrew preliminary censorship, then, governments used other restraints—litigation, taxes, warning systems, fines,—to control what appeared in print; for government leaders and security officials commonly retained their view of critical journalists as instruments not of truth but of disruption, whether as captives of some political party or as self-proclaimed spokesmen for the "public." As a logical corollary governments themselves set about to capture press loyalties and to garner favorable press commentary which would serve to neutralize the writings of those critically opposed.

Toward that end, states had to abandon the traditional view that a state's cultivating relations with journalists was demeaning—a point Metternich made in 1808 when, as Austrian ambassador to France, he reported to Vienna with alarm the Emperor Napoleon's skill in manipulating the press of Europe.[32] Still other European officials in the first half of the 19th century, identifying writers and publishers as wielders of power in their own right, favored conciliating rather than antagonizing the press. The second-in-command of the Russian secret police, von Vock, warned his chief in 1826 that press repression would cause writers to infect the general public with their anger.[33] So, too, Joseph Fouché, as Louis XVIII's minister of police, held that governments faced a new problem: "the previously unknown pressure of public opinion"—a phenomenon greatly influenced by the press. No longer could religion, the moral structure, or repression keep order, he wrote the Duke of Wellington, and a government was best advised to seek to "influence" rightly its people through the press.[34] Of the same mind was Louis Philippe's minister, Guizot: the press was the best means by which the government could defend itself and advance its policies. In turn, said Guizot, politicians must react sparingly against press criticism lest they provoke greater irritation against the government.[35]

In England, in 1831, Lord Henry Brougham had contended that the proper role of the press was not to represent public opinion but to observe and to report the conduct of public men.[36] By 1854, an influential Tory member of Parliament, John Wilson Croker, was complaining to Brougham that political life had become "precarious" because no man can "venture to brave the press." The Reform Bill, he thought, had made public opinion tyrannical and newspapers ministers of the tyranny. Newspapers insisted that they "represent public opinion, and, of course, the people, in a more direct and authoritative manner than even the House of Commons."[37]

All in all, the power of the press and of public opinion had proved real enough. Governments continued to set limits on what they would tolerate in print, but they tolerated more and made greater efforts to win friends among the press and to influence publicity on affairs of state. Winning press loyalty and garnering favorable publicity could be by open or covert means. The just-mentioned Tory, Croker, for example, advocated that a single cabinet minister "supervise" the British government's relations with the press, a service he had himself informally performed. That minister's objective would be to convey to the press officially-sanctioned articles and, with the "most profound secrecy," to keep from the public the source of those articles by including in each a few calculated errors.[38]

The British government, especially under Robert Walpole in the 18th century, passed secret service funds from the Treasury to friendly papers and writers, although this practice had largely ended by the 1830s.[39] An alternative form of subsidizing was the purchase of subscriptions which served also to circulate more widely a friendly publication. In addition, the government placed advertisements in cooperative papers and gave them special postal privileges.[40] Granting access to political news, or "intelligence," similarly played a role in winning over writers eager to best their competition. As prime minister of Great Britain, Earl Russell saw clearly the political utility of such information. He wrote in the 1870s that the government "can exercise and does exercise a great influence over part of the press by communicating from authority intelligence which has been received and the decisions which have been arrived at by persons holding high office."[41]

So, too, when French governments in the 19th century could no longer fall back on preliminary censorship, they regularly channeled funds to friendly publications. For example, during the July Monarchy, Guizot subsidized *Epoque*, a daily which failed to live up to its extravagant ambitions and soon failed; and the government of the Second Empire subsidized progovernment papers and journals. Even before the *coup d'etat* of December 1851, Louis Napoleon cultivated the journalist Cassagnac and sent him 5,000 francs to pay a fine imposed by the National Assembly.[42]

In Germany, Bismarck proved especially inclined to bribe journalists and subsidize editors, both at home and abroad. He drew from monies solely under his control, for which he had to account only to the monarch, from the so-called Guelph Fund (*Welfenfond*), the annual income from the sequestered property of the Hanoverian royal family. This arrangement gave rise to a term of fairly wide usage—''reptile fund.'' It originated from the chancellor's derogatory labeling of the Guelph family and its supporters as ''reptiles,'' but Bismarck's opponents and others soon applied the term to fund recipients, that is, to journalists accepting bribes from the government.[43] In 1872, Guelph money purchased the London-based *Englische Correspondenz*, almost the only source of English news for German newspapers. The paper's editor and publisher went so far as to plant stories in English papers favoring Bismarck's policies so that he could quote them to show his German subscribers that English public opinion supported Bismarck.[44]

Russian emperors also gave favors and funds (and signet rings) to sympathetic writers and editors, although documentation of such largesse in Russia—as elsewhere—is sketchy. Unquestionably, Alexander I gave the mystical journal *Messenger of Zion* and its editor funds and a favored censorship position because its religious views approximated his own in 1816.[45] Nicholas I gave similar favors to the first extravagantly successful commercial journalist in Russia, Faddei Bulgarin of the *Northern Bee*, because Bulgarin used his columns to heap praises on the Emperor.[46] The Emperor despised Bulgarin but valued his influence with his readers. Such subsidies and government purchases of subscriptions took place in Russia throughout the 19th and early 20th centuries, just as a pro-government editorial line often brought editors gentle treatment from the censorship and even the privilege of receiving publications from abroad untouched by Imperial censors.

Even as governments of the states under discussion traded funds and favors behind the scenes for press support, many officials favored overt use of state press bureaus. By issuing stories and arranging for their publication in private publications, the press bureau influenced papers and journals to put the government and it policies in the best possible light.

In England, the state most inclined to laissez faire treatment of the press in the 18th and 19th centuries, a state press bureau got no further than the proposal state. One failed recommendation came forward in the early 1830s for a press bureau under the Treasury and the Foreign Office, along with a daily official paper to give a fair and accurate summary of affairs of state.[47] Among such state enterprises in France, the July Monarchy established the *Bureau de L'esprit publique*, which openly issued articles but covertly subsidized and covertly used the press agency, Havas (found by Charles Havas in 1835), to counteract bad publicity and to distribute progovernment stories to more than 300 papers in France.[48]

Prussia's minister of the interior in 1850 founded the Prussian Central Office for Press Affairs (*Zentralstelle für Pressangelegenheiten*). This office reported to the prime minister on the state of the unofficial press, supported loyalist journalists with information and subsidies from a fund for ''higher police purposes'' and, generally, conducted an active program to shape favorable public opinion.[49] It also published two newspapers, one for official announcements and the other, the *Preussische Correspondenz*, to campaign against oppositional groups and newspapers.[50] Creation of the powerful press bureau in the foreign office came under Bismarck, who also secretly controlled the one German news wire service. Not even the Diet knew of the formal contract signed by the Prussian State Ministry and the Central Telegraph Company (the Wolff Bureau) in 1869 giving the company a monopoly on news transmission and the government prior control over political dispatches wired to subscribers, the right to demand dismissal of agents, and the right to have its own observer on the Board of Directors.[51]

In Russia, all attempts to establish a state press

bureau—whether for foreign or domestic news—failed, although the ministries of the government published a number of official papers to influence opinion in favor of the government. One open attempt to influence the press by means of a press bureau was the 1859 Committee on Press Affairs appointed by and directly responsible to the Emperor.[52] The four highly-placed bureaucrats who were members tried to call in writers and editors for "useful" conversations, as well as to arrange for pro-government stories in unofficial papers and journals. For the most part the Russian press refused to cooperate with the committee. The committee even failed in its attempt to launch a newspaper to speak with one voice for the government. In the 19th century, not even the autocratic Russian government could bend public opinion at will to its own purposes. One decade later, the government did found the *Government Messenger* to speak with a single voice, but it acquired no popular support.

By the middle of the 19th century, the principle of granting freedom of the press by abolishing preliminary censorship had become law—through formal recognition in constitutions and legal codes—throughout most of Europe. Even in Imperial Russia, the autocrat had, by 1865, freed the major publications from preliminary censorship. In keeping with the arguments of liberal political philosophers and jurists, the press became subject not to administrative review under special laws prior to publication but to court review under the general laws after publication. The philosophers, however, had not foreseen that what they called freedom of the press would prompt states to continue old means and devise new ones, both open and covert, to influence what appeared in print. In other words, whereas "freedom of the press" had appeared to be guaranteed by the ending of preliminary censorship, once laws had abolished that censorship, new restraints caused the cry for "freedom of the press" to continue. The phrase then came to mean an end to all government meddling in what citizens chose to publish and, later on, an end to the government's withholding information, the primary meaning it has today.

The contrast between the principle that governments endorsed and the rationale on which they

acted clearly emerges in the history of the relationships between governments and the press in Europe during the 18th and 19th centuries. With good reason, every government is sensitive to the ideas and criticism expressed by the press. Every government seeks to withhold information that journalists wish to publish or broadcast. The pattern common to the four states discussed here testifies that governments imposed whatever limits they could justify within the law and, for better or worse, beyond.

NOTES

1. *Areopagitica*, commentator Sir Richard C. Jebb (1918; reprint ed., New York: AMS Press, 1971), p. 20.
2. Maurice Cranston, *John Locke, A Biography* (London: Longmans, Green, 1957), p. 387.
3. M. Seliger, *The Liberal Politics of John Locke* (New York: Praeger, 1969), pp. 297–300.
4. *Epistola de Tolerantia. A Letter on Toleration*, trans. J. W. Gough, ed. Latin text Raymond Klibansky (Oxford: Clarendon Press, 1968), pp. 131–35.
5. *Essays, Literary, Moral, and Political*, reprint of the 2 vols., 8vo ed. (London: Ward, Lock & Tyler, 1870), p. 13.
6. "What Is Enlightenment?" in *The Philosophy of Kant*, ed. Carl J. Friedrich (New York: The Modern Library, 1949), p. 139.
7. *A Journey from St. Petersburg to Moscow*, trans. Leo Wiener, ed. Roderick Page Thayer (Cambridge, Mass.: Harvard University Press, 1958), p. 171.
8. Philip Wheelright, ed., *Jeremy Bentham. An Introduction to the Principles of Morals and Legislation. James Mill, Essays on Government, Jurisprudence, Liberty of the Press, and Law of Nations. John Stuart Mill. On Liberty. Utilitarianism* (Garden City, N.Y.: Doubleday, Doran & Co., Inc., 1935), p. xiii.
9. *Ibid.*, p. 275.
10. *On Liberty*, ed. Currin V. Shields (Indianapolis: Bobbs-Merrill, 1956). p. 25.
11. Fredrich Seaton Siebert. *The Rights and Privileges of the Press* (New York: D. Appleton-Century Co., 1934), pp. 8–9.
12. Laurence Hanson, *Government and the Press, 1695–1763* (London: Oxford University Press, H. Milford. 1936), pp. 17–18.
13. Irene Collins, *The Government and Newspaper Press*

in France, 1814–1881 (London: Oxford University Press, 1959), pp. 118–35.

14. Ernst Rudolf Huber, *Deutsche Verfassungsgeschichte Seit 1789*, Vol. 3 (Stuttgart: W. Kohlhammer Verlag, 1963), p. 172. I wish to express my thanks to Prof. Erich Hahn for his assistance in translating from this and other German sources.

15. *Ibid.*, pp. 172, 137.

16. Ernst Rudolf Huber, ed., *Dokumente zur Deutschen Verfassungsgeschichte*, Vol. 2 (Stuttgart: W. Kohlhammer Verlag, 1964), pp. 65–67. For a discussion of the decree of June 1, 1863, and its cancellation see Huber, *Deutsche Verfassungsgeschichte Seit 1789, op. cit.*, pp, 318–20.

17. Robert H. Keyserlingk, "Bismarck and Freedom of the Press in Germany, 1866–1890," *Canadian Journal of History*, 11:34 (April 1976).

18. "Law against the Publicly Dangerous Endeavors of Social Democracy," in Vernon D. Lidtke, *The Outlawed Party: Social Democracy in Germany*, 1878–1890 (Princeton: Princeton University Press, 1966), pp. 341–43.

19. Karl-Alexander Hellfaier, "Die Sozialdermokratie under Ausnahmegesetz, 1878–1890," in Leo Stern, ed., *Der Kampf der deutschen Sozialdemokratie in der Zeit des Sozialistengesetzes, 1878–1890: Die Tatigkeit der Reichs-Commission* (Berlin: Rutten & Loening, 1956), pp. 9–10.

20. *Ibid.*, pp. XVII–XVIII.

21. Hans-Wolfgang Wetzel, *Presseinnenpolitik im Bismarckreich (1874–1890): Das Problem der Repression oppositioneller Zeitungen* (Bern: Herbert Lang, 1975), p. 291.

22. The Statute of 1804 is described in M. Lemke, "Propushchennyi iubilei. 100 letie pervogo russkogo ustava o tsenzure. 1804–1904," *Russkaia Mysl'*, 9:34–62 (1904). The 1828 statute is in the complete code of laws of the Russian Empire: *Polnoe Sobraine Zakanov Rossiiskoi Imperii*, ser. 2, 3, no. 1979 (April 22, 1828). pp. 459–78.

23. The statute of 1865 is described in C. A. Ruud, "The Russian Empire's New Censorship Law of 1865." *Canadian Slavic Studies*, 3:235–45 (Summer 1969).

24. V. Rozenberg, "V mire sluchainosti," in V. Rozenberg and V. Iakushkin, *Russkaia pechat' i tsenzura v proshlom i nastoiashchem* (Moscow: M. and S. Sabashnikov, 1905), pp. 137–38, 140.

25. Arthur Aspinall, *Politics and the Press, 1780–1805* (London: Home and Van Thal, 1949), p. 40.

26. Wetzel, *op. cit.*, p. 299.

27. *Polnoe Sobranie Zakonov Rossiiskoi Imperii*, ser. 3, 25, sec. 1, no. 26926 (November 24, 1905), p. 839.

28. Collett Dobson Collett, *History of the Taxes on Knowledge: Their Origin and Repeal* (London: Watts & Co., 1933), p. 184.

29. Collins, *op. cit.*, p. 134.

30. James G. Legge. *Rhyme and Revolution in Germany: A Study in German History, Life, Literature and Character, 1813–1850* (1918: reprint ed. New York: AMS Press, 1970), p. 173.

31. Keyserlingk, *op. cit.*, p. 26.

32. Prince Richard Metternich, ed., *Memoirs of Prince Metternich*, 1773–1815, trans. Mrs. Alexander Napier, Vol. 2 (New York: C. Scribner's Sons, 1880), p. 225.

33. Peterburgskoe obshchestvo pri vosshestvii na prestol imperatora Nikolaia po doneseniiaem M. M. Foka— A. K. Benkendorfu," *Russkaia Starina*, 32:583 (November 1881).

34. Donald E. Emerson, *Metternich and the Political Police: Security and Subversion in the Hapsburg Monarchy, 1815–1830* (The Hague: M. Nijhoff, 1968), p. 137.

35. Francois Guizot, *Memoirs to Illustrate the History of My Time*, trans. J. W. Cole, Vol. 3 (1860; reprint ed., New York: AMS Press, 1974), pp. 201–04.

36. Aspinall, *op. cit.*, p. 3.

37. *The Croker Papers, 1808–1857*, ed. Bernard Pool, New and abr. ed. (New York: Barnes & Nobel, 1967), pp. 257–58.

38. *Ibid.*, p. 124.

39. Aspinall, *op. cit.*, pp. 67–69.

40. Hanson, *op. cit.*, p. 109.

41. Quoted in Aspinall, *op. cit.*, p. 383.

42. Collins, *op. cit.*, p. 114.

43. Stewart A. Stehlin describes Bismarck's use of the Guelph Fund in *Bismarck and the Guelph Problem, 1866–1890: A Study in Particularist Opposition to National Unity* (The Hague: M. Nijhoff, 1973). In particular, see chapter eight.

44. Fritz Stern, *Gold and Iron: Bismarck, Bleichröder, and the Building of the German Empire* (New York: Alfred A. Knopf. 1977), p. 272.

45. N. F. Dubrovin, "Nashi mistiki-sektanty." *Russkaia Starina* 84:127 (December 1894).

46. On Bulgarin, see M. Lemke. *Ocherki po istorii russkoi tsenzury i zhurnalistiki XIX stoletiia* (1904; reprint ed., The Hague: Mouton, 1970), pp. 369–427.

47. Aspinall, *op. cit.*, pp. 234, 151.

48. Natalie Isser. *The Second Empire and the Press: A Study of Government-Inspired Brochures on French Foreign Policy in Their Propaganda Milieu* (The Hague: M. Nijhoff, 1974), pp. 6, 14.

49. Huber, *Deutsche Verfassungsgeschichte Seit 1789, op. cit.*, p. 171.

50. *Ibid.* The *Correspondenz* in 1852 made the mistake of criticizing Bismarck, then the Prussian delegate to the Diet of the German Confederation at Frankfurt. The head of the Press office, Dr. R. Quehl, soon found himself in diplomatic exile in Copenhagen. His successors as head were Immanuel Hegel, son of the philosopher, and then Dr. Ludwig Metzel, who later headed the powerful press bureau in the foreign office.

51. Stern, *op. cit.*, pp. 265-66.

52. M. Lemke, "Ocherki po istorii tsenzury: Komitet po delam knigopechataniia." *Russkoe Bogatstvo*, nos. 3-4 (1903), pp. 186-212, 158-86.

PRESS FREEDOM, MEDIA, AND DEVELOPMENT, 1950–1979: A STUDY OF 134 NATIONS

David H. Weaver, Judith M. Buddenbaum, and Jo Ellen Fair

Looking at a more recent time frame, 1950–1979, David H. Weaver, Judith M. Buddenbaum and Jo Ellen Fair have studied 134 nations for their press freedom and media development. They conclude that, while more developed countries have viable independent media and greater press freedom because of economic productivity, in less developed countries the media still "tend to be used to facilitate the functioning of the economy and to perpetuate the power of the rulers."

The importance of a free press, usually defined to mean a press free from government control, and the relationship of such a press to the form and stability of government and to economic growth and the quality of life have been the subject of debate for centuries. That debate seems to have heated up in recent years. Looking at nearly a quarter century of various countries' experience in trying to implement development in accordance with the Lerner (13) paradigm, scholars have begun to raise many questions both about the development paradigm and its assumptions, particularly the importance and value of a free press system. This new look at the free press system does not imply a lack of faith in democracy as an ideal, but rather an attempt to deal realistically with conditions as they exist in the developing nations (9).

Many Third World spokespersons have come to

David H. Weaver, Judith M. Buddenbaum, and Jo Ellen Fair, "Press Freedom, Media, and Development, 1950-1979." From *Journal of Communication*, Volume 35, Number 2, Spring 1985, pp. 104–117. © 1985, *The Journal of Communication*. Reprinted by permission.

David H. Weaver is professor of journalism and director of the Bureau of Media Research in the School of Journalism at Indiana University. Judith M. Buddenbaum is assistant professor of journalism at Colorado State University. Jo Ellen Fair is a doctoral student in mass communication at Indiana University.

believe that a free press is a luxury that they cannot afford and can do without for the time being. Their explanation is that, given the conditions of scarce resources, a colonial legacy, a poorly educated population, tribal and ethnic rivalries, and a subservient position in the world economic and information systems, a free press can too easily lead to an inability of government to junction and to internal chaos (1). Thus, some form of press controls is seen as both necessary and desirable for national development and political stability in some less developed countries.

For the most part, this debate has been conducted at the ideological level. The sparse empirical evidence with which to address the contending views that press freedom either is necessary for development, the establishment of democracy, and the stability of the political and social system, or that it is, for the time being at least, counterproductive, comes largely from correlational studies made at a single point in time and from more general media effects studies (4, 5, 12, 16). While most of the scholars involved have been wary of speaking in terms of causal relationships, their work clearly suggests that such relationships may exist, and a handful of studies have been conducted to explore this possibility, with somewhat mixed results.

In 1967, McCrone and Cnudde (15) proposed the following model of democratic political development: urbanization→education→communications→democratic political development. They then tested and partially confirmed this model using the Simon-Blalock technique of comparing actual and predicted correlations based on data from a single year and supported it fully by computing path coefficients from the original correlation coefficients. Meanwhile, Schramm and Ruggels (20) were using cross-lagged correlations on data collected in 1950–1951 and 1960–1961 from 23 less developed nations to test causal relationships. They found that urbanization, literacy, gross national product, and mass media development seemed to be related in different ways in differing developing regions of the world.

Seven years later, Weaver (29; see also 28) used path analysis over time to test relationships between amount of government control of the press and six other characteristics of a society. Using data collect-

ed for 137 countries during four different time periods between 1950 and 1966, he found evidence to suggest that mass communication development plays an important role in the growth of participant forms of government in many areas of the world and evidence to support Siebert's observation that "the more direct the accountability of the governors to the masses, the greater the freedom of the press" (24).

In addition to support for links between media development, accountability of governors, and government control of the press, the evidence also suggests that increases in resources or economic productivity, as measured by gross national product and energy consumption per capita, often lessen the stress on or disruptions to the political system of a country. This, along with greater accountability of governors, led to less government control of the press—but only in North America, Western Europe, and Asia (29). These findings raise doubts about the universality of suggestions by Siebert, Field, Stevens, Schramm, and others (6, 18, 21, 24, 25, 29) that an increase in stress leads to an increase in government control of the press. The Weaver study also found little support for the first part of Lerner and McCrone's developmental model which specifies that greater urbanism leads to increased education, which in turn leads to increased mass media growth (14).

In addition, increased resources generally lead directly to increased levels of education and media development, and increased media development contributes to an increase in resources, probably because the media are industries that contribute to the economy while consuming energy. Growth in urbanism and media had a substantial positive impact on levels of education in all countries of the world analyzed together between 1950 and 1966 (29).

These findings suggest that there is some merit in models relating media development and a free press system to national development and to the form and stability of government, but that the relationships are much more complex than the original linear models of development had anticipated. Furthermore, the relationships most likely change over time.

The criticisms of other scholars suggest that resources, urbanism, education, and media development are related to each other in complex ways and that these measures of development do not necessarily go hand-in-hand with democratic government and a stable society in the way predicted by the original development paradigm (8, 17, 23). In fact, this is what Weaver's earlier study found for the time period from 1950 to 1966—little support for a linear pattern of development but important links between media development and accountability of governors and between increases in accountability of governors and decreases in government control of the press. But these patterns were complex, and they varied somewhat by the period of time analyzed and the region of the world under study (29).

These patterns may change noticeably or become clearer as data covering a longer time span become available. Such patterns, analyzed over time for groups of countries, can give us a baseline against which to compare patterns and processes within individual countries. They can also provide a more general understanding of what societal conditions are conducive to greater freedom of expression— and what conditions work against it—than can studies of individual countries.

Although the experiment is the traditional and preferable approach to analyzing causal relationships among variables, sociological studies such as this one are rarely amendable to experimental analysis because of ethical and practical problems. The next best strategy is to collect data over time, using a longitudinal study design and cross-lagged correlation or path analysis to analyze the relationships among variables. The object of such an analysis is not just to find what correlates with what, but to get estimates of causal linkages among variables so that one can better understand how changes in one variable affect the values of the other variables in the system under consideration.

Of course, there are real problems in working with aggregate cross-national data. Such measures can be taken only as rough estimates of the conditions prevailing in any given country at any given time. However, if the purpose of using such data is to identify *patterns* of relationships among variables rather than to determine the precise functional relationships (in mathematical terms), then such data can be useful, since Heise (10) has shown that even low-reliability measures are not likely to obscure general patterns of relationships.

In this study, path analysis over time is used to analyze the relationships among the key concepts. Path coefficients estimate the degree of *change* in a dependent variable, given a one-unit change in independent variables, whereas correlation coefficients indicate the degree of covariation between variables.[1]

When dealing with more than two variables over time, as Heise (10) points out, a series of multiple regression analyses must be carried out to obtain the estimates of the path coefficients. Each variable in the system is treated as a dependent variable, and its time 2 (later) value is regressed on the time 1 (earlier) values of the other variables, including the time 1 value of the dependent variable itself. This procedure is continued until the time 2 values of each variable in the system have been treated as dependent variables predicted by all time 1 variables. The standardized partial regression (beta) coefficients resulting from these analyses are estimates for the path coefficients.

To estimate the path coefficients between the seven variables in Weaver's model, we carried out a series of multiple regressions, taking the time 2 value each variable as dependent across the 1950–1979 time period. Separate regressions were attempted for six different regions of the world, in keeping with Weaver's 1974 study, but were not possible because of the missing data and low numbers of cases across the 29-year time period. However, it was possible to carry out separate regression analyses for the more developed and less developed countries of the world.[2]

On the basis of this literature review, composite measures for each concept were constructed whenever possible and then tested for reliability and validity. The actual data for each measure were drawn from the best available sources for each year. In 1979, again, every effort was made to use composite measures whenever possible, but some of the necessary data were not available. No attempt was made to find new measures, because this would have destroyed the comparability of the measures across time. Instead, only one or two measures for each concept were used when necessary, because the high correlations among the various measures of each concept included in the original study suggested that this strategy would not seriously affect the overall findings.

Government Control of the Press

This takes into account only those restrictions initiated by the government of a country, and it does not measure the actual free flow or diversity of opinions and ideas within the mass media of a country (although an inverse correlation is assumed between the degree of government control and such diversity). The amount of government control of the press in 1950 is measured by Schramm and Carter's Guttman scale (19). The items in this scale include government ownership of newspapers, economic pressures by government on mass media, political censorship, restrictions on free criticism of government policies, and government ownership of broadcasting facilities. Scores on this scale range from 0 (very little control) to 5 (very great control).

The 1979 measure for government control of the press is constructed from Gastil's (7) table listing the print and broadcasting media of each nation as "free," "partly free," or "not free." In making these assignments, Gastil takes into account government ownership of the media, government censorship, restrictions on criticism, and other forms of government pressure on the media. For this study, a rating of "free" was coded as 1, "partly free" as 2, and "not free" as 3. The scores for the print and broadcast media were then added together to produce a scale ranging from 2 (very little control) to 6 (very great control).

Accountability of Governors

This concept was defined in the original study as executive and legislative dependence on public support and voting behavior. The indicators used to measure accountability of governors in 1950 are drawn from Banks's *Cross-Polity Time-Series Data* (2) and include (a) type of selection of the effective executive (direct election, indirect election, or nonelective); (b) effectiveness of the legislature (effective, partially effective, ineffective, no legislature); (c) competitiveness of the legislative nominating

process (competitive, partially competitive, largely noncompetitive, no legislature); and (d) an aggregate competition index score based not only on the effectiveness of the legislature and the competitiveness of the nominating process but also on the existence of competing factions within a legislature and the existence of recognized competing political parties. These indicators were selected via a principal-factor solution (with iterations) using varimax rotation.

For the 1979 portion of the study, a measure of accountably of governors was constructed by adding together measures of political rights and civil liberties compiled by Gastil (7). The political rights measure rates states on a seven-point scale in which those judged "most free" have a fully competitive electoral process and those elected clearly rule. Those states judged "least free" are ruled by "political despots" who "appear by their action to feel little constraint from either public opinion or popular tradition" (7, p. 16). The civil liberties measure is also a seven-point scale that takes into account the degree (a) to which courts protect individual differences of religion and of political opinion, (b) to which private rights and desires in education and residence are respected, and (c) of freedom of the press from pressure to serve primarily as a channel for government propaganda. In adapting Gastil's measures to this study, these measures were added together and inverted to produce a new measure ranging from 2 (very little accountability) to 14 (very accountable).

Stress on Government

This concept is defined here as any period of great demands on, or significantly lessened support for, the existing government, as indicated by any relatively rapid changes or disruptions to the established pattern of social interactions between the governors and the governed.

Stress in 1950 is measured by data on the number of revolutions, taken from Banks's *Cross-Polity Time-Series Data* (2), the number of protest demonstrations, riots, armed attacks, deaths from domestic violence, and government sanctions in response to perceived threats, taken from Taylor and Hudson's *World Handbook of Political and Social Indicators* (26).

The measure of stress on government in 1979 is drawn from Gastil's table reporting levels of political terror in each nation. This table provides five levels of terror based on "the extent to which the people live under a recognizable and reasonably humane rule of law" (7, pp. 37–40). This judgment takes into account the number of occurrences of and number of people subject to political murders, torture, exiles, passport restrictions, denial of vocation, ubiquitous presence of police controls, and threats against individuals and their relatives.

Mass Media Development

Mass media development is defined as the level of availability of mass communication products per person in any given country. This definition does not include consideration of the type or quality of information conveyed by the media but does indicate the general availability of such information.

Two indicators from Banks (2) were used to measure the level of media development in 1950—number of radio sets per capita and newspaper circulation per capita. These same two measures were used for 1979, but the data were drawn from the 1981 U.N. *Statistical Yearbook* (27).

Level of Education

Level of education is defined as the relative effort a society is exerting toward educating its population at a given time. Therefore, school enrollment ratios are used as indicators.

For the 1950 portion of the study, the indicators from Banks (2) include primary and secondary school enrollment per capita and total school enrollment per capita. For 1979, figures on primary and secondary school enrollment per capita were taken directly from the U.N. *Statistical Yearbook*. A measure to total enrollment per capita was also constructed by adding the primary and secondary school enrollment per capita figures to data on per capita enrollment in higher (third level) education (27).

Urbanism

Shaw's suggestion that one way of operationally defining urbanism is to employ "such available data as volume of mail or number of phone calls, with due attention paid to 'the necessity for contextual operational definitions' " (22, p. 22) is followed on the assumption that those scholars who define and measure urbanism and urbanization in terms of the concentration of population are really trying to tap the amount of participation in multiple information networks, and that this participation is what chiefly distinguishes the interests, knowledge, and attitudes of relatively urban from relatively rural inhabitants. Therefore, urbanism is measured in the 1950 portion of this study by an index composed of three indicators from Banks (2): volume of mail per capita, number of telephones per capita, and number of highway vehicles per capita.

For the 1979 portion of the study, an index was composed of the number of passenger cars per capita taken from the 1981 *Europa Year Book* (3) and number of telephones per capita taken from the 1981 *Europa Year Book* and *Yearbook of Common Carrier Telecommunication Statistics* (11).

Availability of Resources

Availability of resources is defined as the relative supply of material goods per person in a country, including such diverse "goods" as food, shelter, clothing, transportation, and energy. This variable is measured for 1950 with an index composed of four indicators from Banks (2): gross national product per capita, gross domestic product per capita, energy consumption per capita, and revenue per capita. For 1979, data on the single measure of gross national product per capita, taken from figures compiled by the World Bank (30), are used to measure availability of resources.

The revised model in Figure 1 illustrates the strongest relationships among all concepts for all countries taken together during the 1950–1979 time period. First, the relationships among resources, media development, accountability of governors, and government control of the press are mostly reciprocal during the 29-year time period under study, supporting the arguments of those such as Golding (8, p. 46) who view modernization and development as "a total nexus of relationships" and not an immutable process of distinct developments. These reciprocal relationships conform top Weaver's original theoretical model in sign but not in direction (29). There are positive path coefficients

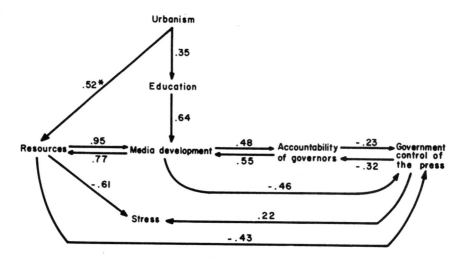

Figure 1   Predictors of government control of the press,ᵃ 1950–1979 (for all countries,
n = 134)

*ᵃStandardized regression coefficients (Betas) for the strongest paths between variables during the
1950–1979 time period. Paths with Betas and/or correlations of less than .20 are not shown.*

between resources, media development, and accountability of governors, and negative path coefficients between accountability of governors and government control of the press, as predicted by the theoretical model. But these characteristics of societies reinforce one another, rather than leading to each other in a step-by-step process. This casts doubt on Weaver's earlier model, which specifies that increased media development leads to increased accountability of governors, which in turn leads to less government control of the press. The findings from this present study do suggest, however, that resources, media development, accountability of governors, and minimal government control of the press are all linked to each other and mutually reinforce each other when all countries are considered together.

Although the original theoretical model specifies that increased resources are linked to increased mass media development through increased urbanism and higher levels of education of the populace, findings from this study suggest that resources and media development are directly related to each other and reinforce each other. Urbanism does contribute positively to educational levels, and higher educational levels do lead to increased media development from

1950 to 1979, as predicted in the original model, but the strongest predictor of mass media growth is the economic productivity of a country and media growth contributes to that productivity. In addition, increased urbanism (as measured in this study) contributes to increased economic productivity, rather than the other way around, as predicted by the original model.

Figure 1 also shows that increased economic productivity lessens stress on a society, as Weaver had predicted, but less stress does not lead to a decrease in government control of the press. Instead, increased government control of the press leads to increased stress, rather than vice versa, during 1950–1979, at least for all countries combined.

Finally, there are two direct paths not predicted in the original model. The first is from media development to government control of the press, reinforcing Weaver's earlier conclusion that mass communication development may play an important role in reduced government control of the press in many areas of the world. The second is from resources to government control of the press, underscoring the importance of economic productivity to lessening government control of the press. Another way of interpreting these findings is to point out that the

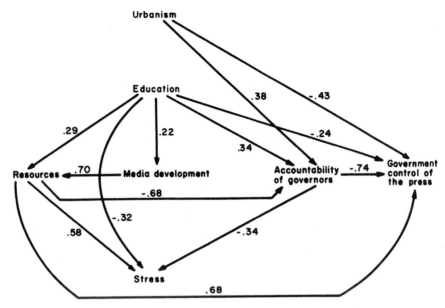

Figure 2   Predictors of government control of the press,[a] 1950–1979 (for Third World countries,
n = 105)

*[a]Standardized regression coefficients (Betas) for the strongest paths between variables during the
1950–1979 time period. Paths with Betas and/or correlations of less than .15 are not shown.*

stronger the media are economically, the less likely the government is to control these media.

Figure 2 illustrates the path coefficients for 1950–1979 for only those 105 countries classified as less developed in this study. This classification was based on various measures such as gross national product per capita, media (radios, televisions, and newspapers) per capita, school enrollments, and levels of urbanization. From these measures, an index score for each country was calculated, ranging from 10 (highest level of development) to 1 (lowest level). The dividing point between less developed and more developed countries was 8, but nations with scores of 6.0 to 7.9 were reexamined and categorized on the basis of both index scores and geographic, economic, political, and social considerations. Generally, the nations of Africa, Asia, the Middle East, and Central and South America form the less developed group, as one would expect. Israel is classified as a more developed nation because of its relatively high index score (7.17) and its economic, political, and social ties to the United States. South Africa is classified as a less developed

country because of its relatively low index score (5.6).[3]

The path coefficients in Figure 2 indicate no reciprocal relationships among the less developed countries, in contrast to all countries combined (see Figure 1). In addition, there are more direct predictors of the amount of government control of the press among Third World countries than among all countries combined. Greater accountability of the government is linked to less government control of the media in Third World as well as in all countries, but the level of media development does not predict the amount of government control in Third World countries as it does for all countries combined. Higher levels of resources directly predict less government control of the press, as is true for all countries, but in the less developed countries increased resources in 1950 are strongly associated with increased (rather than decreased) government control of the press in 1979. This suggests that, in the more prosperous of the Third World countries, the governments have been unwilling to reduce controls on the media, perhaps because these media tend to be used to facilitate the functioning of the economy and to perpetuate the power of the rulers.

Another striking difference between Figures 1 and 2 is the lack of a positive path from resources to media development in Figure 2, suggesting that increased economic productivity generally has not led to increased levels of media development in Third World countries as it has in more developed nations.[4] Nor have increased resources led to less stress in the less developed countries, possibly because the distribution of resources is so uneven in many of these countries. In all countries combined, however, increased economic productivity is a strong predictor of increased media development, less stress, and less government control of the press (see Figure 1). Thus, it is clear that between 1950 and 1979 in the less developed countries of the world, higher levels of economic productivity did not generally decrease stress, increase media development, and decrease government control of the press, as was true in the more developed countries. Figure 2 also indicates that those Third World countries that were most prosperous in 1950 tended to have the least accountable governments in 1979. Clearly, economic prosperity isn't everything, especially in the Third World.

What *does* predict increased media development, increased accountability of government, less stress, and less government control of the press in Third World countries is education, measured in terms of school enrollment per capita. Even though it is not a terribly strong predictor, increased educational effort in 1950 is consistently associated with what most Western observers would agree are desirable characteristics of a society (see Figure 2), perhaps because the model for many educational systems in Third World countries was a colonial one. Increased urbanism is also associated with more accountability of government and less government control of the media.

Thus, in the less developed countries of the world, at least from 1950 to 1979, it seems that more emphasis on education, rather than increased economic productivity, contributes most consistently to stability, media growth, democracy, and press freedom from government control, whereas in the more developed countries, economic productivity is a more important predictor of these characteristics.

These findings suggest that for most Third World countries, the amount of government control of the press in the post—World War II period is an indicator, rather than a predictor, of the kind of political, educational, and communication systems present in these countries. Unlike the case in the more developed countries of the First and Second Worlds, increased economic productivity in the Third World has not been associated with increased media development, increased public accountability of government, and decreased government control of the press. In the Third World, education is more likely than money to bring about many of the characteristics of society valued by most Westerners.

In short, this analysis of data from 134 countries of the world during 1950–1979 suggests that there are different predictors of the amount of government control of the press in Third World countries than in the more developed First and Second World countries. Moreover, there appear to be real problems with simple, linear models of development which predict that increased urbanism leads to increased literacy, which in turn leads to increased development of the communication media, to greater political participation, and then to less government control of the media. Whereas there is some support for these models among the 32 more developed countries in our study and among all countries considered together, such models do not apply to the 105 less developed countries, where there is no link between urbanism and education or between media development and accountability of governors. It should be remembered that many of these are highly intercorrelated, making it difficult to untangle causal relationships. In addition, 29 years may be too short a time period in which to understand fully the relationships among such concepts as urbanism, education, media development, accountability of governors, and government control of the press, especially in view of the fact that the modern histories of some of the developing countries are not as long as this study's time period.

Nonetheless, our findings allow us to speculate that sudden increases in economic productivity in Third World countries may have exactly the opposite effects that are intended by many interested in promoting development via a Lerner-type dominant paradigm model, unless these increases in finances are counterbalanced by increases in educational efforts. At the same time, our data provide no support to those who advocate controlling the press in an effort to stabilize society and promote development. No increase in educational, media, or economic development during this time period was found for countries in which government control of the press was increased.

NOTES

1. Such coefficients are calculated by using standard multiple regression, with the path coefficients estimated by the standardized regression coefficients (betas), providing that one makes the assumptions of linearity, homoscedasticity, noncolinearity, and constancy and equivalence of causal relations. When using path analysis over time, it is also necessary to assume that there are no instantaneous effects in the system, that the lag periods for all relationships are about the same, that the time required to measure the variables at one point in time is less than the causal lag period, and that the time between measurements is about the same as the causal lag period. Although this seems to be a formidable set of assumptions, Heise (10) has shown that they need not be unduly restrictive if one is interested in general *patterns* of relationships rather than in precise prediction.

2. Although there were 137 countries in Weaver's original study from 1950 to 1966 (28, 29), there are only 134 nations in this study because Papua and New Guinea, and North and South Vietnam, are each treated as one country in the 1979 data, and separate data from 1979 are not available for Zanzibar, which is now part of Tanzania. A list of these countries is available from the first author, or see Weaver (29).

3. The list of more developed (First and Second World) nations includes the following 32 countries: Australia, Austria, Belgium, Bulgaria, Canada, Czechoslovakia, Denmark, Finland, France, East Germany (GDR), West Germany (FRG), Greece, Hungary, Iceland, Ireland, Israel, Italy, Japan, Luxembourg, the Netherlands, New Zealand, Norway, Poland, Portugal, Romania, the Soviet Union, Spain, Sweden, Switzerland, the United Kingdom, the United States, and Yugoslavia. All other countries were classified as less developed (Third World). Complete data were not available for Cambodia, Papua and New Guinea, Somalia, Taiwan, North and South Vietnam, and Zanzibar.

4. Separate path analysis over time was carried out for the more developed countries, so these comparisons are based not only on Figures 1 and 2 but also on the separate correlations and betas for the more developed countries.

REFERENCES

1. Aggarwala, Narinder. "Press Freedom: A Third World View." *Development Communication Report* 19 July 1977, pp. 1–3.
2. Banks, Arthur S. *Cross-Polity Time-Series Data.* Cambridge, Mass.: M.I.T. Press, 1971.
3. *The Europa Year Book.* London: Europa Publications, 1981.
4. Farace, Vincent. "A Study of Mass Communication and National Development." *Journalism Quarterly* 43, Summer 1966, pp. 305–313.
5. Farace, Vincent and Lewis Donohew. "Mass Communication in National Social Systems: A Study of 43 Variables." *Journalism Quarterly* 42, Spring 1965, pp. 253–261.
6. Field, Marshall. *Freedom is More than a Word.* Chicago: University of Chicago Press, 1945.
7. Gastil, Raymond D. *Freedom in the World: Political Rights and Civil Liberties.* New York: Freedom House, 1980.
8. Golding, Peter. "Media Role in National Development: Critique of a Theoretical Orthodoxy." *Journal of Communication* 24(3), Summer 1974, pp. 39–53.
9. Gunter, Jonathan E. "An Introduction to the Great Debate." *Journal of Communication* 28(4), Autumn 1978, pp. 142–156.
10. Heise, David R. "Casual Inference from Panel Data." In Edgar F. Borgatta and George W. Bohrnstedt (Eds.) *Sociological Methodology 1970.* San Francisco: Jossey-Bass, 1970.
11. International Telecommunications Union. *Yearbook of Common Carrier Telecommunication Statistics.* Geneva: ITU, 1980.
12. Katz, Elihu. "Can Authentic Cultures Survive New Media?" *Journal of Communication* 27(2), Spring 1977, pp. 113–121.
13. Lerner, Daniel. *The Passing of Traditional Society.* Glencoe, Ill.: Free Press, 1958.
14. Lerner, Daniel. "Toward a Communication Theory of Modernization." In Lucian W. Pye (Ed.) *Communications and Political Development.* Princeton, N.J.: Princeton University Press, 1963.

15. McCrone, Donald J. and Charles F. Cnudde. "Toward a Communications Theory of Democratic Political Development: A Causal Model." *American Political Science Review* 61(1), March 1967, pp. 72–79.

16. Nixon, Raymond B. "Factors Related to Press Freedom in National Press Systems." *Journalism Quarterly* 37, Winter 1960, pp. 13–28.

17. Rogers, Everett M. "Communication and Development: The Passing of the Dominant Paradigm." *Communication Research* 3(2), April 1976, pp. 213–240.

18. Schramm, Wilbur. "Communication Development and the Development Process." In Lucian W. Pye (Ed.) *Communications and Political Development*. Princeton, N.J.: Princeton University Press, 1963.

19. Schramm, Wilbur and Richard F. Carter. "Scales for Describing National Communication Systems." Unpublished manuscript, Institute for Communication Research, Stanford University, 1960.

20. Schramm, Wilbur and W. Lee Ruggels. "How Mass Media Systems Grow." In Daniel Lerner and Wilbur Schramm (Eds.) *Communication and Change in the Developing Countries*. Honolulu: East-West Center Press, 1967.

21. Shaw, Donald L. and Stephen W. Brauer. "Press Freedom and War Constraints: Case Testing Siebert's Proposition II." *Journalism Quarterly* 46, Summer 1969, pp. 243–254.

22. Shaw, Eugene F. "Urbanism as a Communication Variable." Paper presented to the Association for Education in Journalism, Berkeley, Cal., August 1969.

23. Shore, Larry. "Mass Media for Development: A Reexamination of Access, Exposure, and Impact." In Emile G. McAnany (Ed.) *Communications in the Rural Third World*. New York: Praeger, 1980.

24. Siebert, Frederick S. *Freedom of the Press in England: 1476–1776*. Urbana: University of Illinois Press, 1952.

25. Stevens, John D. "Press and Community Toleration: Wisconsin in World War I." *Journalism Quarterly* 46, Summer 1969, pp. 255–259.

26. Taylor, Charles Lewis and Michael C. Hudson. *World Handbook of Political and Social Indicators*. New Haven, Conn.: Yale University Press, 1972.

27. United Nations. *Statistical Yearbook*. New York: United Nations, 1981.

28. Weaver, David H. "The Press and Government Control: International Patterns of Development from 1950 to 1966." Unpublished Ph.D. dissertation, University of North Carolina at Chapel Hill, 1974.

29. Weaver, David H. "The Press and Government Restriction: A Cross-National Study Over Time." *Gazette* 23(3), 1977, pp. 152–170.

30. *World Bank Atlas: Gross National Product, Population and Growth Rates*. Washington, D.C.: International Bank for Reconstruction and Development/World Bank, 1982.

GOVERNMENTS AND PRESS CONTROL: GLOBAL VIEWS

JOHN C. MERRILL

John C. Merrill uses a reasonably simple model to determine the degree of press control in various countries. Using his model, Soviet bloc and Third World countries rank highest for strict control, while countries aligned with the West rank lowest on the control scale.

John C. Merrill, "Governments and Press Control: Global Views." *International Communication Bulletin*, 23:1–2, Spring 1988, p. 12. Reprinted by permission.

The author is professor of journalism at Louisiana State University and professor emeritus of journalism at the University of Missouri.

This study has focused on *government opinion* concerning freedom and control of the press in various countries. The following basic question prompted the study: *What is the inclination of governments to see a restricted or disciplined press—by whatever means—in their respective nations?*

Interviews were completed with information/press officers at U.N. missions in New York and embassy press attaches in Washington, D.C. The interview forms concentrated on six main factors believed important in determining "control" in a press system:

1. in-country licensing;
2. international licensing;
3. identification cards or accreditation;

4. university education;
5. in-country codes of ethics;
6. international codes of ethics.

The various government representatives were asked their opinions on these factors (i.e., whether they favored the application of each of these six factors to journalists). Responses to each question were given scores reflecting the strength of attitude on that factor (**very much in favor = 4; in favor = 3; neutral = 2; against = 1; very much against = 0**). For example, if a nation's spokesperson was very much in favor of in-country licensing of journalists, that country would score 4 on the factor. This score would be combined with scores on the other five factors to result in the Control Inclination

Table I	RANK ORDER OF COUNTRIES BY CII SCORE

	Strict Control
24	German Democratic Republic, Iraq, Peru, Cuba, People's Republic of China, Syria, Tunisia.
23	Bulgaria, Jordan, Paraguay.
22	Ethiopia, U.S.S.R., Lebanon.
21	Angola, Czechoslovakia, Egypt, Yugoslavia, Panama.
20	Central African Republic, Kuwait, Bolivia, Zimbabwe, Malaysia.

	Moderate Control
19	Ivory Coast, Hungary, Guyana, Pakistan, Ecuador, Argentina.
18	Nigeria, Poland, Portugal, Bangladesh, South Korea, Indonesia.
17	Austria.
16	Denmark, Turkey, Chile, Costa Rica, Guatemala.
15	The Sudan, Finland, Spain.

	Little Control
14	South Africa, Philippines.
13	New Zealand.
12	Norway, India.
11	Sweden, Australia, Japan.
10	Netherlands, United Kingdom, West Germany, Mexico.
9	Greece, Canada.*
8	United States of America.

NOTE: *These scores reflect views of government representatives of the countries listed. Actual control of the press in any of these countries may be more or less than shown here.*
Questionnaire, not interview.

Index (CII), ranging from a possible high of 24 to a possible low of 0. Thus, a higher CII score would indicate a greater inclination on the part of the government to see the press controlled.

Table 1 shows CII scores of countries included in this study. Based on these figures, the region of the world most inclined to control the press is the Middle East, with the highest average total score of any region (21.7). Latin America had the second-highest CII score (19), followed by Africa and Eastern Europe (18.5 each). The group of countries representing Western Europe and North America had the lowest CII score (12.5). Rather surprisingly, Asian countries, as a group, had a second lowest score (16.2).

More than twice as many countries favored in-country licensing as did not; half were in favor of international licensing. Most agreed on the necessity of an accreditation or identification system, and on the benefit of higher education for journalists (but very few saw it as compulsory). Very few countries were opposed to in-country codes of ethics; and twice as many favored an international code of ethics as those opposed to it.

REGIONAL PRESSURE AND THE EROSION OF MEDIA FREEDOM IN AN AFRICAN DEMOCRACY: THE CASE OF BOTSWANA

JAMES J. ZAFFIRO

Some specific regions show how the process of media control works out in reality. First, two cases in southern Africa, Botswana and South Africa. James J. Zaffiro shows that in Botswana, regional pressure from South Africa has come to affect the unusually free exercise of media, suggesting a clear link between media freedom and government perceptions of legitimacy and security.

Any journalist must weigh the consequences of his reporting if it is prejudicial to the nation. The National Security Act is not meant to abridge civil rights. Rather, it should be looked at in the "peculiar" times in which we live in Southern Africa.

O. T. Maptise, Assistant Attorney-General of Botswana, June 1986.

Government is by nature allergic to criticism. It would be ludicrous not to expect it to interfere with editorial policies. There is an inherent conflict between the media and government.

Andrew Sesinyi, Director of News, Radio Botswana, September 1987.

James J. Zaffiro, ''Regional Pressure and the Erosion of Media Freedom.'' From the *Journal of Communication*, Volume 38, Number 3, Summer 1988, pp. 108–120. © 1988, *The Journal of Communication*. Reprinted by permission.

The author is assistant professor in the department of political science at Central College, Pella, Iowa.

Most recent research on African media and democratic politics has focused on Nigeria, a multiparty, federal state with an unprecedented degree of media pluralism, at least during periods of civilian rule (37). Botswana, by contrast, is not nearly as diverse. Yet the Western-style, democratic character of its media institutions appears similarly striking and politically significant, particularly when examined in the context of the country's exceptionally open political life. What connections, if any, exist between political democracy and media freedom in Botswana today? What accounts for this media freedom? Perhaps most significant, what are the prospects for survival of both political and media democracy in the face of mounting domestic and regional stresses?

Regional pressures are beginning to have a noticeably negative effect on democracy and system legitimacy in Botswana. For the first time cracks are appearing in representative processes and institutions, and a young, vocal private press, a relatively unencumbered state-managed radio service, and sometimes critical stands in the government's own daily paper are being jeopardized. This article will discuss recent shifts in government attitudes and policies toward the Botswana media that have been fueled by the intensifying spiral of violence in its neighbor to the south and east, South Africa. These shifts have propelled the first major challenge to the inherited legitimacy of the Botswana Democratic Party (BDP), which came into power by election when the nation gained independence from Britain in 1966.

Since achieving independence, Botswana has distinguished itself for consistently free and fair elections, enduring political institutions, and the operational efficiency of its civil service. A state-capitalist, pro-West orientation has made it a darling of foreign donors. Because it is relatively homogeneous ethnically, the "problem of tribalism" has never been a major threat to human rights, representative democracy, or economic development in the country.[1] Its largely successful strategy for coping with a serious five-year drought also sets it apart from many similarly affected African states (15, 23).

At times, however, these qualities have blinded observers to Botswana's near-total economic dependence on and military vulnerability to South Africa. The applicability of the Botswana model to other states is beginning to be questioned (26). With 70,000 absentee workers employed largely in South African mines and looming prospects of non-renewed contracts for workers from Mozambique in the wake of Western economic sanctions, the potential for regime-shaking ripple effects throughout the Southern African region increases daily.[2] Foreign revenues from citizens of Botswana (known as Batswana) who are employed abroad have become critical to the economic health of the nation (7, p. 172). One of the most striking examples of recent South African economic pressures directed against Botswana has been the continuing effort to link a $300 million Sua Pan soda ash project in the northeast with "security cooperation" (1, p.158).

Military vulnerability has also been driven home several times since 1985 through South African Defense Force (SADF) commando raids and border harassment, resulting in a notable rise in tensions and distrust among both the government and the general public (see 8, 9).[3] The South African propensity to preemptive action of this sort has been described as "buttressed by a concept of 'special responsibility' toward Southern Africa similar to the Monroe Doctrine and justified by analogy to U.S. actions in Grenada" (43).

The intensifying struggle in South Africa is hastening Botswana's entrance into a period of accelerated political change. Traditional political harmony and an overall atmosphere of tolerance and respect for dissent, in media as well as in politics, are in danger. Some feel that the legitimacy of the regime is also under siege; this has led to greater awareness of the potentially harmful effects of an uncontrolled opposition that is being given voice for the first time through an influential, unregulated mass media sector (2, 20, 28, 50).

Botswana has a number of opposition parties, the most influential of which is the Botswana National Front (BNF); the Botswana Independence Party (BIP), the Botswana Peoples' Party (BPP), and the Botswana Liberal Party (BLP) are less prominent. Despite this multiparty character, over twenty years in power the ruling BDP—one of very few ruling parties in Africa that has had to remain concerned with the pressures of impending competitive elections—has never been seriously challenged electorally through five free contests. Party leaders have enjoyed unquestioned access to and dignified, extensive coverage by state-funded and administered radio and press, publicizing programs and gaining exposure for candidates. Only since 1982 has the rise of a private press offered opposition parties the possibility of similar coverage.

Media institutions reflect complex connections between dominating and dominated groups of society on all levels of relations with the state (10). Throughout Southern Africa, crisis and change are coming to be reflected in increasingly tense relations between media and government. As the private press becomes more critical, government unease grows, feeding the demands of some for greater control.

Why have the mass media in Botswana been more open and free to print or broadcast items critical of official policy than is the case in other African political systems? Recent trends aside, glimpses of likely futures are possible only with knowledge of details of past connections between political communication, mass media, and legitimacy (51, 53).

In the words of Al Osman, editor of the weekly private newspaper the *Gazette*,[4] "the press was never used to fight for independence, and in fact press and broadcasting were created by colonial authorities to manage and suppress nationalist pressures within the Territory; independence was given on a silver platter" (22). This history is very different from events in West Africa, where the press was the main vehicle through which leading nationalist figures and parties emerged, or in Southern and East Africa, where settler media long predated independence struggles and later fought for information legitimacy with new nationalist "counter-media" (see 47).

To a greater extent than was true of the vast majority of states in Africa at independence, national leaders in Botswana inherited legitimacy, both for the system and for channels of political communication, via existing ties between politicians of the new regime and traditional sources of authority in the

territory (51). With credibility and authority fairly well established countrywide, it was not as necessary or important to set up nationwide mass media systems or attempt to strictly control existing media channels. Press and radio were not seen as the most crucial means of political communication, nor were they perceived by leaders as necessary for the transmittal to citizens of national unity, regime legitimacy, and party-government policies, goals, and values (53).

Today's private press, born through commercial rather than political pressures, has an opportunity to play a vigorous role in the emergence of genuine opposition parties. Botswana media are beginning to serve as important nontraditional mechanisms of political acculturation, providing new conceptual and linguistic points of reference for the public's evaluation of policies. The central question has become the extent to which this growth will be tolerated by the ruling BDP party.

The alliance between the BDP, chiefs, and district and local authorities made it politically unnecessary for some time for the government to attend to the development of an extensive countrywide system of broadcasting and press distribution. Moreover, opposition parties and politicians stood to gain from this development because they lacked these connections with traditional authority and channels of political communication (with the exception of Chief Bathoen's BNF ties after 1969 in his region [25]). By contrast, most new African regimes lacked comparable ties with traditional sources of authority, legitimacy, and political communication. They therefore placed a high priority on gaining control of pre-independence systems or immediately setting up modern statewide radio networks to construct and maintain these vital prerequisites for legitimation, entrenchment, policy dissemination, mass mobilization, and national unification (14, 19, 33, 45, 49).

Leadership style is also a factor in how Botswana deviated from the imperative of legitimacy construction elsewhere in Africa.[5] Although press and radio were organized and administered as a formal department of government and in the 1970s actually became a part of the Ministry of Presidential Affairs, Botswana's first president, Sir Seretse Khama, did not dominate government media during his 14-year rule to nearly the same extent as other African leaders. Part of this was in no small measure due to his strong customary standing and legitimacy; he did not need mass media exposure. A Western liberal in many respects, Khama held ideas about the role of mass media in Africa that were less attuned to developmental journalism notions than those of his contemporaries elsewhere in former British Africa. Indeed, in some respects his views had more in common with United States perspectives on the role of media in politics.

On the other hand, President Masire, in office since Khama's death in 1980, has made more extensive, conscious use of government press and radio to build and maintain recognition and support at the mass level, both for himself and the BDP regime. Unlike Khama, Masire must work to solidify the personal legitimacy of his rule, given that he lacks the same degree of customary standing and given the presence of potential challengers from within his cabinet, party, and the political arena at large.

The views of the president and the most media-conscious of his ministers are rapidly coming to resemble those of contemporaries who have wholeheartedly embraced the values and goals of developmental journalism. This new view attempts to fit the goals of developmental journalism to particular national and regional circumstances while working to overcome legacies of settler-serving media systems inherited from the colonial era and unwanted intrusions from multinational media institutions into national cultural, economic, and political development. In the states in the "frontline" (in terms of the struggle against apartheid and for South African independence), particularly Tanzania, Zambia, and Zimbabwe, the media are to varying degrees expected to promote values that foster national unity and reflect favorably on the current political-economic system and particularly those who have power within it (13).

Botswana's present Agriculture Minister, Daniel Kwelogobe, had attempted during his years in the mid-1970s as Minister for Information Services to incorporate a developmental journalism perspective into Botswana government media policy and administration. Recent years have seen a growing number of more pointed pronouncements by high government officials concerning a "mission" or "roles" for radio and the press. Minister of Presidential Affairs Ponatshego Kedikilwe has begun to more explicitly lay down interpretations of a development journalism perspective for Botswana journalists, including

playing the role of a public watchdog to nurture the process of democracy, acting as sentinel and mirror of corruption, public morality, public conscience and consciousness; exercising self-restraint on sensational, inflammatory reporting likely to mar individuals, groups or Government for no justifiable cause; exhuming truth; showing sensitivity to the plight of Government [by] refraining from making mountains out of frivolous issues; and walking the tightrope of playing its legitimate role without taking advantage of rifts and frictions, strains and stresses that are inevitable in fledgling nations:

Media commands the strength to help Government overcome its problems through constructive reporting. If media tends to promote developments that build the nation and play down those that tend to push the nation down the drain, they will in my view be moving in the right direction. If they find pleasure in promoting developments that tend to tear the society apart and leave it bleeding to death, the media will be doing a great disservice to humanity and nation-building.[6]

As an illustration that press freedom does exist in Botswana, the minister quoted several sections of the Constitution relating to freedom of expression.[7] He told the press that they have nothing to fear because the government respects the rule of law.

The government's changing media ideology bodes ill for partisan opposition. African varieties of developmental journalism have taken a dim view of the idea of investigative reporting, coverage of competing views, allowing criticism of government policy, and affording access to opposition spokespersons. The BNF charged in late June 1986 that

Radio Botswana had begun to censor opposition party news, in the wake of the station's failure to broadcast a taped interview with a former BDP councillor (see 29).[8] The government has been careful to assert its continuing commitment to political opposition parties, acknowledging the fact that peoples' ideas, in the words of Vice-President Peter Mmusi, are not always homogeneous (see 16). The existence of private media also seems ultimately to be anathema for regimes genuinely committed to this path of media development.

As long as they remain to some degree separated from the government, mass media in Botswana will continue to help define and reflect political authority. As the audiences grow larger and more sophisticated, this role will grow in importance. Before the 1984 parliamentary elections, mass media played only a limited role in structuring mass participation and reinforcing popular attitudes about politics, parties, policy, and the system itself. This role has changed rapidly. The government has become more conscious of the media's presence, not just as a public address system but as a potentially threatening political adversary. All evidence suggests that the media will play a crucial role in the 1989 electoral campaign; pressures for media access by political opposition have already begun to markedly increase. In the words of former *Botswana Guardian* editor Kgosinkwe Moesi:

> In the past they were too weak to expect media access. Now they want it and government is nervous; it has no real policy to deal with these demands. Now that the parties are stronger, especially the BNF, they can no longer be ignored by the media . . . so we try to cover them. They are already talking of setting up their own papers, and government is keeping a close eye on them. During the '84 elections, BDP claims against the opposition were always printed [by the official paper, the *Daily News*] without asking them to respond first, yet the opposition had to allow a spokesman to answer charges leveled at government, before they could be printed in the *Daily News*. There is a general fear of criticism among policymakers now (17).[9]

Following Moesi's stormy 1979 departure from the *Guardian*, the paper went through two editors within one month before settling on a former Department of Information employee.

The BDP has made no concerted effort to forge a central place for broadcasting and the press in national development and political life. Although the media have played an important role in legitimizing authority in Botswana, especially over the past few years, attempts to likewise legitimate the idea of an institutionalized, loyal opposition have not been as successful. Rapidly changing political and economic conditions, as well as intensifying social inequalities, do not bode well for future success in this area (25, 26).

Since independence, opposition parties have regularly complained about insufficient access to and coverage in mass media. Besides the BNF, smaller parties have added their occasional voices. The Secretary-General of the BPP, John Mosojanc, accused both private and government press of "perpetuating false images of the BPP" and complained of overemphasis on coverage of Gaborone and the BDP/BNF (see 5, 6). The onset of a viable private press in the early 1980s appeared to be at least a partial solution to their problems. That press's equally rapid demise (for financial reasons, among others) spells trouble for the opposition parties as the next national election approaches, given their extreme lack of financial or technical resources for nationwide campaigning and organizing that has hampered them in past elections.

Compared with the rest of Africa, however, opposition access and coverage have been at least minimally possible throughout the entire post-independence period. Opposition coverage, like that afforded the government and the ruling party, has emphasized interviews or parliamentary remarks by top party leaders (especially Dr. Kenneth Koma of the BNF). The chief complaint of opposition politicians has been the lack of access for their candidates, along with insufficient coverage of their criticisms of BDP policies. Only those able to win election to Parliament or skilled in the ways of the media themselves have been able to gain regular access.

The next national election promises to be the

most media-intensive contest to date. The BNF plans to make heavy use of radio in major urban centers (see 3).[10] At its July 1985 party conference the governing BDP called upon its Central Committee to devise a strategy to counter the inroads being made into the BDP by the opposition in urban areas (see 21). The chief stumbling block for most parties, aside from lack of funds to purchase air time, has been their ignorance of how to maximize opportunities for press or radio coverage of their rallies, speeches, or views. In the words of former *Guardian* editor Moesi:

> The opposition is still very . . . raw, unsophisticated; they still don't know how to manipulate, to use the mass media; even a simple thing like a press conference, when to call one. On matters of campaign strategy they still follow the BDP; when they do something, the opposition slowly follows. The BDP is a very efficient organization with people who know how to campaign and get publicity. By the next election some people, like Paul Rantao at the BNF, will be somewhat more effective in their use of media (17).

At least for the present, private papers continue to be able to transmit political information and opinion independent of regime or traditional society-structured lines. Traditional lines of communication remain vitally important, given the extreme mobility of people from city to village to lands at different times of the year. However, radio and the press have begun to succeed in introducing new lines of formal political communication, particularly among semi-permanent urban residents under the age of 25. Media coverage is coming to reflect some of the frustration and alienation directed at the ruling elite and its party by these younger citizens, many of whom lack the inclination of their parents and grandparents to equate the realm of the politically possible and desirable with the party and leadership of their ethnic heritage, the BDP. Given growing unemployment and proliferating external threats to prosperity, security, and stability, different political generations tuned in to increasingly differentiated

channels of political information may be expected to characterize the electoral landscape of the country from now into the near future.

The future of the mass media in Botswana is inherently connected with the evolving nature of the state and social system, which in turn are fundamentally affected by the shadow of Botswana's powerful neighbor to the south. The political history of media-government relations over the entire life of the country vividly bears this out (51, 53). This dynamic relationship is even more relevant today, given conditions that could provide opposition parties unprecedented electoral gains at the expense of the ruling party.

Central to understanding the future character and direction of media-government relations is the question of the extent to which media credibility and regime legitimacy rest on the same foundation. Given environmental pressures and constraints, will there continue to be enough common ground to encourage government to allow for the continued existence of media that may criticize it? Until quite recently the private press believed that it was not their business to protect government from the negative effects of policy shortcomings or implementation failures. If the press were not allowed to report uncomfortable truths, how could policy-makers and voters get necessary feedback?

Former *Guardian* editor Moesi:

> As a free paper, we believe it was our duty to investigate certain issues which we thought the government was not being completely open about . . . legitimate news. Government attacks on [BNF Member of Parliament Kenneth] Koma . . . that he was a South African agent, had to be looked into. We found no truth to government charges. They called us a BNF paper . . . but we believed that the government party should be put under the microscope too, in fact more, because as rulers they should have a greater responsibility (17).

Such explicit articulations of the media's perspective were seen as generally unnecessary for preserving a relatively unfettered position during the days of expanding export earnings and largely peaceful foreign relations. Now, in the face of regional crisis, the "state of war" argument for limiting press freedom is beginning to be heard.

Unlike the vast majority of African states, the government of Botswana has never faced a crisis of these proportions. It never had to deal with the painful dilemma of using its own media to exhort citizens to support it while at the same time actively seeking to eliminate or prevent media not under its control from questioning official exhortations. As long as an overwhelming national policy consensus existed, the media had little to report that was damaging. Indeed, during parts of the post-independence period private newspapers did not exist simply because there was no widely perceived need to provide counterpoint to Radio Botswana or *Daily News* reporting of news and current affairs.

What is the likely future of private media in Botswana? Editors are increasingly pessimistic:

> The press in Botswana has not yet built bridges with vested interests which can protect it from government. We are very vulnerable: the president could shut us down tomorrow. I have very little reason to believe that over time and crises our democracy can withstand the pressures and so eventually, we may come to more closely resemble other African media systems, where government takes control to a great degree. South Africa still affects us greatly. As this pressure grows, there will be more talk of limiting the press. Government's record in handling crisis is unfortunate . . . they tend to overreact and forget about democracy (17).

Sociopolitical and economic forces in Botswana and throughout the Southern African region will continue to rapidly restructure media-government relationships over the months ahead, with or without formal attempts by those in power to participate in or control the process (35, 48). As potential threats to legitimacy mount, political leaders will be sorely tempted to monopolize and strictly control mass media. Increasingly specific government policies for media use and control may soon reflect similar efforts to narrow and control the political arena. One can only hope that the outcome will not too closely resemble media-government dynamics of other African regimes threatened by crises.

For scholars of mass communication in developing countries, this analysis of patterns of media-government relations in Botswana suggests that a regional as well as country-specific perspective can help in evaluating a government's use of mass media. Artificial, dated, or externally imposed categories and classifications or broad, ethnocentric "theories of the press" (34) may prove dangerously misleading when used as the basis for analysis of complex, dynamic, culture-specific trends in media-government relations. Conversely, although cross-national comparisons that examine dozens of cases do provide a baseline against which to examine patterns and processes within individual countries (40, p. 107), they are of limited utility for those seeking to understand the role of mass media in processes of political change and regime legitimation efforts in particular national or regional contexts. The case of Botswana does tend to support the general argument that the amount of government media control is one significant indicator of the type of political system present in a state (40, p. 115).

The work of Weaver, Buddenbaum, and Fair suggests that increased press controls in the face of South Africa pressures are unlikely to help stabilize Botswana's social and political environment. To the contrary, greater controls may actually encourage further instability and system stress. (40, p. 112). The Botswana case also tends to provide support for the proposition that the stronger the media are economically, the less likely the government is to control them (40, p. 113). As the financial position of the press deteriorated in late 1985 and through 1986, government efforts to provide media with guidelines increased.

In Botswana, as elsewhere, present dynamics in media-government relations reflect past experiences. For the press and radio in Botswana, this necessitates looking to the pre-independence period for a fuller understanding of present realities. The nationalist period, when mass circulation newspapers emerged and radio was developing, is particularly crucial (51, 52, 53).

Even in democratic systems it is government that maintains the upper hand in the media-government relationship, shaping it according to its own needs and perceptions. The Botswana case illustrates the extent to which government media philosophy and policy may vary from what has been the norm in African states, under a regime that attained and has held power and legitimacy through nonrevolutionary, noncoercive means. For the researcher, it suggests the value of seeking out direct, mutually reinforcing connections between regime perceptions of legitimacy and local definitions and levels of media freedom (49). Politically significant variations in state media policies may exist between regimes with high self-perceptions of legitimacy and those that feel more threatened, both domestically and internationally. To paraphrase Siebert, the more threatened the government, the less free the press and mass media in general.

In African states, particularly those with one party political systems, media access and media controls tend to converge. Because broadcasting and the press are vital to the exercise of power, the tendency is for access to give way sooner or later to control. Botswana may prove to be no exception.

NOTES

1. President Masire attributes the durability of Botswana democracy to strong, commonly held traditions: "unlike many countries in Africa, we haven't divided into tribal entities and broken into war. Our history instilled discipline in us" (11; see also 4).

2. An estimated one-quarter to one-third of Botswana's male labor force works in South Africa; recruiting for mining jobs averages approximately 19,000 per year (*Europa Yearbook*, 1985, p. 1248). This comes at a time when the government is unable to absorb its own mushrooming labor force, particularly those who have not completed primary school. Just over 100,000 Botswana citizens are estimated to be employed in the country's own formal wage sector (see 24).

3. Botswana media coverage of the June 14, 1985, SADF raid filled the press for months, with tensions remaining high (see 31, 32, 36, 38, 39, 41, 42, 44).

4. Of the three private newspapers presently in existence, the *Gazette* may be considered the least controversial. It began as the *Business Gazette*. From November 1984 to February 1985 it made an attempt to go daily, but cost considerations forced it to return to a weekly format in March.

5. Post-independence Zimbabwe under the new ZANU (PF) government of Prime Minister Robert Mugabe provides an important example of a regime faced with the daunting task of building credibility and legitimacy for itself through, among other things, radio, television, and the press, which had lost credibility among audiences under the years of control and abuse of Ian Smith and the Rhodesian Front (see 12, 46, 49).

6. For the full text of the minister's speech see (18). The government's own newspaper played down the threatening elements of Kedikilwe's remarks in its coverage (see 27).

7. The Constitution of Botswana states in Chapter II, part 3 (b): "freedom of conscience, of expression and of assembly and association; part 12 (1): no person shall be hindered in the enjoyment of his freedom of expression . . . freedom to communicate ideas and information without interference (whether the communication be to the public generally or to any person or class of persons); 12 (1)(b) extends this to operators of broadcasting or television."

8. The Department of Information and Broadcasting had reportedly censored a BNF press release concerning the recent defection of a former BDP District Council member, Keorapetse (Bright) Segwagwa, to the BNF. In response to these allegations, Director of Information and Broadcasting Margaret Nasha stated that "it is not Department policy to report defections; we cannot allow ourselves to be used by partisan organization."

9. These impressions of the situation were shared by the other editors of private newspapers in Botswana. One, interviewed in October 1985, predicted problems: "I think you will see the media threatened, in the context of a threatened democracy. You will also see a more threatened elite and intensification of rivalries among them . . . the emergence of a Botswana Breoderbond which will be very vicious when threatened internally. Troubles of this nature will be reflected in the press; we will have to tread very cautiously" (30).

10. Beginning with the 1984 parliamentary elections, BDP ministers and members of Parliament made extensive use of mass media for campaign-related coverage. Many took Radio Botswana crews and *Daily News* reporters with them to their districts and made a point of using media coverage of drought relief programs to gain heightened visibility and take credit for policy successes.

REFERENCES

1. Ajulu, Rok and Diana Cammack. "Lesotho, Botswana and Swaziland: Captive States." In David Martin and Phyllis Johnson (Eds.), *Destructive Engagement: Southern Africa at War*. Harare: Zimbabwe Publishing House, 1986, pp. 138–169.
2. "Bloody Riot." *Botswana Guardian*, April 3, 1987, p. 1.
3. "BNF Urged to Work Hard to Assume Power." *Botswana Daily News*, July 17, 1985, p. 1.
4. "Botswana Cobbles Together Success." *Christian Science Monitor*, October 23, 1986, p. 1.
5. "BPP Answers Critics." *Botswana Guardian*, June 28, 1985, p. 1.
6. "BPP Shedding Off Its Regional Image." *Gazette* (Gaborone), August 28, 1985, p. 1.
7. Colclough, Christopher and Steven McCarthy. *The Political Economy of Botswana: A Study of Growth and Distribution*. Oxford and New York: Oxford University Press, 1980.
8. Cownie, David S. "The Wolf at the Door?" *ACAS Newsletter* No. 18, Spring 1986, pp. 21–28.
9. Cownie, David S. "Bantustan Illegitimacy and Pressure on the Frontline States." *ACAS Newsletter* No. 22, Winter 1987, pp. 37–43.
10. Dassin, Joan R. "The Brazilian Press and the Politics of Abertura." *Journal of Inter-American Studies and World Affairs* 26(3), 1984, pp. 385–413.
11. Foster, Richard. Interview in Gaborone with Quett Masire. Reported in "Botswana Rises Above Woes," *Milwaukee Journal*, June 17, 1986, p. 6.
12. Frederickse, Julie. *None But Ourselves: Masses v. Media in the Making of Zimbabwe*. Johannesburg: Raven Press, 1982.
13. Hachten, William A. *The World News Prism: Changing Media, Clashing Ideologies*. Ames: Iowa State University Press, 1981.
14. Head, Sydney W. (Ed.). *Broadcasting in Africa: A Continental Survey of Radio and Television*. Philadelphia: Temple University Press, 1974.
15. Holm, John D. and Richard G. Morgan. "Coping with Drought in Botswana: An African Success." *Journal of Modern African Studies* 23(3), 1985, pp. 463–482.
16. Modikwe, Kwapeng. "Presence of Opposition Essential—Mmusi." *Botswana Daily News*, August 27, 1985, p. 1.
17. Moesi, Kgosinkwe. Personal interview, Gaborone, October 23, 1985.
18. Molefhe, Rampholo. "Kedikilwe Lays It Down for Press." *Botswana Guardian*, February 11, 1986, p. 1.
19. Mytton, Graham. *Mass Communication in Africa*. London: Edward Arnold, 1983.
20. "Newsman Is Held." *Botswana Guardian*, April 3, 1987, p. 1.
21. "Old Guard, New Faces." *Gazette* (Gaborone), July 24, 1985, p. 3.
22. Osman, Aludin. Editor of the *Gazette* (Gaborone). Personal interview, Gabarone, October 26, 1985.
23. Parson, Jack. *Botswana: Liberal Democracy and the Labor Reserve in Southern Africa*. Boulder, Colo.: Westview Press, 1984.
24. Parson, Jack. "Class, State and Dependent Development." *Mmegi wa Dikang* (Gaborone), June 22, 1985, p. 8.
25. Picard, Louis A. (Ed.). *The Evolution of Modern Botswana*. London: Rex Collings, 1985.
26. Picard, Louis A. *The Politics of Development in Botswana: A Model for Success?* Boulder, Colo.: Lynne Rienner, 1987.
27. Ramongkga, Edison. "Media Has Great Potential as Tool for Development." *Botswana Daily News*, February 11, 1986, p. 1.
28. "RB Gagged." *Botswana Guardian*, September 25, 1987, p. 1.

29. "RB News Censored?" *Botswana Guardian*, June 27, 1986, p. 1.
30. Rensburg, Patrick van. Reporter for *Mmegi wa Dikang*. Personal interview, Gabarone, October 1985.
31. "SA–Botswana Communique." *Mmegi wa Dikang* (Serowe), March 1, 1986.
32. "SA Looks for Excuse to Invade." *Botswana Daily News* (Gaborone), January 10, 1986, p. 1.
33. Sesinyi, Andrew. News Director, Radio Botswana. "A Paper on Mass Media and Culture." Unpublished paper delivered to the Botswana Society, Gaborone, September 28, 1987.
34. Siebert, F., T. Peterson, and W. Schramm. *Four Theories of the Press*. Urbana: University of Illinois Press, 1956.
35. "Socio-Political Trends Will Change." *Botswana Daily News*, November 25, 1985, p. 1.
36. "Threats Fly Over SA's ANC Plot Accusations." *Star* (Johannesburg), April 10, 1987, p. 3.
37. Uche, Luke Uke. *Mass Media, People and Politics in Nigeria*, 1987.
38. "Ultimatum: Take Action or We Come In, SA Warns." *Daily Gazette* (Gaborone), January 8, 1986, p. 1.
39. "Warnings of Imminent Attacks." *Star* (Johannesburg), April 9, 1987, p. 1.
40. Weaver, David H., Judith M. Buddenbaum, and Jo Ellen Fair. "Press Freedom, Media, and Coming Development, 1950–1979: A Study of 134 Nations." *Journal of Communication* 35(2), Spring 1985, pp. 104–117.
41. "We Don't Want Conflict With SA—Masire." *Daily Gazette* (Gaborone), February 3, 1986, p. 1.
42. "We Don't Want War—Dr. Chiepe." *Botswana Daily News*, January 9, 1986, p. 1.
43. Weisfelder, Richard. "Peace from the Barrel of a Gun: Non-aggression Pacts and State Terror in Southern Africa." In Michael Stohl and George Lopez (Eds.), *Foreign Policy and State Terror*. Westport, Conn.: Greenwood Press, 1986.
44. "We're a Victim of SA Bouts of Blind Rage." *Botswana Daily News*, January 27, 1986.
45. Wilcox, Dennis L. *Mass Media in Black Africa: Philosophy and Control*. New York: Praeger, 1975.
46. Windrich, Elaine. *Mass Media in the Struggle for Zimbabwe*. Gweru, Zimbabwe: Mambo Press, 1981.
47. Zaffiro, James J. "Broadcasting and Political Change in Zimbabwe, 1931–1984." Unpublished Ph.D. thesis, University of Wisconsin, Department of Political Science, 1984.
48. Zaffiro, James J. Remarks to a seminar for Botswana journalists sponsored by the National Institute of Research, University of Botswana, 1985.
49. Zaffiro, James J. "Political Legitimacy and Broadcasting, The Case of Zimbabwe." *Gazette* (Amsterdam) 37(3), 1986, pp. 127–138.
50. Zaffiro, James J. "The Press and Evolution of Political Opposition in an African Democracy: The Case of Botswana." Paper presented to the Conference on Culture and Communication, Philadelphia, October 1986.
51. Zaffiro, James J. "A History of Radio in Bechuanaland, 1927–1954." National Institute of Research, Gaborone, 1987.
52. Zaffiro, James J. "Twin Births: African Nationalism and Government Information Policy in the Bechuanaland Protectorate, 1927–1954." Unpublished manuscript, Central College, Pella, Iowa, July 1987.
53. Zaffiro, James J. "Under the Shadow of South Africa: Failure of Commerical Radio in the Bechuanaland Protectorate, 1936–1966." Unpublished manuscript, Central College, Pella, Iowa, July 1987.

THE IMPACT OF CENSORSHIP OF U.S. TELEVISION NEWS COVERAGE OF SOUTH AFRICA

C. ANTHONY GIFFARD AND LISA COHEN

In South Africa, the government's perception of threat from violent unrest has led to increasingly stringent restrictions on coverage by both domestic and foreign media, in spite of the relative freedom enjoyed in that country. C. Anthony Giffard and Lisa Cohen describe the ensuing censorship. In later sections of this book, we provide evidence of the impact that censorship has had on media in other countries, including the United States.

Since the start of the most recent spasm of racial violence in South Africa in 1984, the government has clamped increasingly stringent censorship on news media, both domestic and foreign. In the case of domestic media, the aim has been to prevent the spread of violence and preserve a semblance of normality. In the case of foreign media, the curbs are intended to force news of the conflict off the front pages of the world's newspapers and from its television screens.

This study seeks to determine the impact of varying degrees of censorship on the amount and kind of reporting from South Africa through a chronology of events and a content analysis of U.S. network TV coverage of South Africa from January 1982 through May 1987.

The South African government has long had an uneasy relationship with the media, especially the foreign press.[1] On the one hand it wants to be accepted as an upholder of Western democratic values, including a free press. That is one thing that distinguishes South Africa from Marxist one-party states to the north, and helps justify white rule. The government seems to believe also that if people abroad were to get objective coverage of South Africa's problems, they would better understand the country's policies.

As a result, South Africa has accepted a large contingent of foreign correspondents. As of January 1987, there were about 170 accredited foreign media representatives there—far more than in the rest of Africa. U.S. news organizations with bureaus in South Africa included the Associated Press, United Press International, Time, Newsweek, ABC News, CBS News, NBC News, the Christian Science Monitor, the Los Angeles Times, The New York Times, the Washington Post and the Washington Times. Other newspapers are permitted to send correspondents to South Africa from their bases elsewhere in Africa. In addition, scores of South African journalists serve as stringers for overseas media. The country makes communications facilities available to them, including a satellite uplink for TV video. Yet, faced with the current crisis, the government has clamped down on the media, evidently preferring a reputation for press censorship to nightly scenes of violence on the world's television screens.

BACKGROUND

For purposes of analysis, we identified six periods between January 1982 and May 1987, each characterized by different levels of unrest in South Africa and different degrees of censorship.

C. Anthony Giffard and Lisa Cohen, "The Impact of Censorship of U.S. TV Coverage of South Africa." School of Communications, University of Washington. Reprinted by permission.

C. Anthony Giffard is a professor and Lisa Cohen was, when this article was written, a student in the School of Communications, University of Washington.

Period 1 (January 1982–December 1983): This is a control period. There were only occasional incidents of racial strife and the media—especially the foreign correspondents—were not subject to any unusual restraints.

Period 2 (January 1984–October 1985): This was a period of growing racial unrest, but the media were free to report on events. The current spate of unrest began in January 1984 when black students boycotted schools to protest apartheid. The protests escalated in August when white voters went to the polls in a referendum for a new constitution that extended national voting rights to Asians and Coloreds, but excluded the 24 million blacks. Serious rioting broke out in September when residents of black townships near Johannesburg called a strike to protest rent increases. More rioting took place after a strike over pay for black mineworkers. Thousands of workers staged a general strike in November to protest the use of troops to seal off the troubled black townships. The rioting spread to Cape Town in February 1985 after rumors that the government was going to move 100,000 black squatters from the Crossroads shantytown. In July 1985, after about 500 people had died in the violence, the government declared a state of emergency in 36 black cities and towns.

The emergency decree provided for press censorship. One section stipulated that police could prevent the publication of any information on or comment about the emergency. The regulations were not strictly applied at first, although the media were forbidden to identify the hundreds of people detained by the security forces, or to enter areas declared off limits.[2] Foreign correspondents continued to move freely about the rest of South Africa, filing reports without restriction. In September, however, the government expelled *Newsweek* bureau chief Ray Wilkinson because it objected to a *Newsweek* cover story on South Africa. The Minister of Home Affairs, Stoffel Botha, said the image of South Africa created by the media abroad was distorted. "As a result, an emotional campaign was started against South Africa resulting, amongst others, in sanctions" against the country.[3]

The Deputy Minister for Information, Louis Nel, warned that the government was considering measures against foreign correspondents. Nel told a National Party congress in September that "there are

people in South Africa who send out untruths, half-truths, selective reports and create a false and twisted impression." It was time, he said, for the government to reconsider "whether its hospitality should be extended to people who share in organized lying."[4]

Period 3 (November 1985–March 7, 1986): The crackdown came on November 2, 1985 when the government banned the televising, photographing, recording or drawing of unrest in any area affected by the emergency decree. The ban applied to any disturbances, riots, strikes, boycotts, attacks on property and assaults on individuals, as well as to action taken by the security forces. Print journalists were still allowed to report on the unrest, and TV and radio journalists could still give eyewitness reports of what they had seen. But they could not take pictures, nor distribute pictures taken by someone else in the areas under emergency rule. Media were free to operate in the rest of the country, however. Penalties for contravention of the law included confiscation of equipment, substantial fines, or up to 10 years in jail.[5]

Foreign Minister R. F. Botha said the action was taken to end the "vicious and venomous coverage by foreign TV crews." And he accused the foreign press of ignoring government reform initiatives and presenting a one-sided, distorted picture of South Africa, offering TV viewers abroad a "tunnel vision of South Africa aflame."

Foreign media executives believed the restrictions were having a significant impact on coverage, with television being particularly hard hit. George Watson, ABC News vice-president, told the *Washington Post* four months after the curbs took effect that the "sad fact" was that the South Africans had "mostly succeeded in what they wanted to do." Watson said the ABC, deprived of live coverage of the rioting, had done "stand-ups" with a correspondent standing before the camera and telling the story. They had also used graphics instead of film, "but the truth is it doesn't make good television." CBS Evening News anchor Dan Rather said they were "having a hell of a time trying to make it accessible and interesting, but we are determined to continue to report the reality, not the unreality that the government would like us to report."[6]

South African officials clearly felt that the curbs on reporting had been successful. The South African ambassador to the United States, J. H. Beukes, said that there had been less trouble in areas where the cameras were banned. "There has indeed been a reduction, no question about that . . . but what is more important is that there is no way of telling how much more violence could have occurred if this had not been done."[7]

Period 4 (March 8–June 11, 1986): The decline in violent protests prompted the government to lift the state of emergency on 7 March 1986, seven months after it was imposed. This also lifted the media restrictions. At the same time, however, the government ordered three CBS newsmen to leave the country because CBS had broadcast a film of a funeral for black riot victims in Alexandra Township, violating a ban on cameras at the ceremony. Home Affairs Minister Stoffel Botha accused CBS of showing "flagrant contempt" for the order, and of regularly seeking film that would damage the public image of the South African government.[8] The government reversed the expulsion order after CBS executives conceded "more care could have been exercised in covering the funeral."[9]

The end of the state of emergency and its accompanying press restrictions meant that TV cameramen were again free to film scenes of unrest. And there was plenty to film in May and June as rival black factions battled for control of the Crossroads squatter camp near Cape Town. A free-lance cameraman working for Britain's Independent Television News Network, George De'Ath, was fatally injured by a machete-wielding mob in Crossroads on June 10, and several journalists were briefly detained by security forces.[10] CBS cameraman Wim de Vos, one of the three threatened with expulsion earlier, was again ordered to leave the country. This time his appeal was refused.

Period 5 (June 12–December 11, 1986): The violence continued, and on June 12 the government declared a new state of emergency, now covering the entire country, and including a nationwide ban on TV coverage of the unrest. The emergency was declared to avert what President P. W. Botha said was a threat of huge and violent protests planned to coincide with the 10th anniversary of the Soweto uprising of 16 June 1976 that had sparked off a year of violence and nearly 600 deaths. Once again the security forces were given sweeping powers to make

arrests without charge, conduct searches without warrant, and ban meetings. The decree also gave the authorities far greater powers of censorship that had been the case in the earlier, partial state of emergency. It forbade TV, radio or photographic coverage of violent protest or of police action to curb it anywhere in the country. The decree also made it an offense to publish a wide range of "subversive" statements, including calls for strikes or economic sanctions. It stipulated also that all news about the emergency would be channeled through the government's Bureau for Information.

Two days later, foreign journalists were ordered not to transmit abroad statements that could be considered subversive. Nel said he had given instructions to the Bureau for Information to "monitor very carefully media reports in this regard."[11] Also on the eve of the Soweto anniversary, the Commissioner of Police, Gen. Johann Coetzee, barred all journalists from the black townships and forbade all reporting of the movements or actions of the security forces.[12] The only exception was if they were disclosed by the Bureau for Information.

TV reporters bore the brunt of the new restrictions. For three weeks they had been able to show dramatic scenes of violence from the Crossroads squatter camp. Now they could not, although the rules stopped short of directly censoring broadcasters. They could file reports but were responsible for the content if they did. It was left to the news organizations to interpret the vaguely-worded restrictions on quoting "subversive" statements. They were obliged to weigh the importance of reporting a particular piece of information that might violate the guidelines against the risk that their correspondents might be expelled. News organizations hired lawyers in their South African bureaus to review tapes before they were transmitted abroad.

One stratagem used briefly by the networks to report dissident views was to beam live interviews back to the United States or Europe by satellite. That way, if the person being interviewed said something illegal, the TV organization could claim it had no control over it.[13] But the government quickly banned live transmissions over the satellite uplink. This meant that if broadcasters taped an interview locally, then transmitted it, they could be held accountable for what was said.

Meanwhile, questions asked by reporters at the Bureau for Information's daily briefing apparently irked the government. And on June 19 the bureau announced that it would "no longer allow the news conference to be turned into a circus." Media would in future have to telex their questions at least four hours in advance to get an official response.[14] The same day, President Botha, in his first public appearance since declaring the emergency, complained about hypocrisy in the West regarding South Africa. "A carefully calculated propaganda campaign is unfolding against us internationally and even internally, especially with the assistance of some of the media," he said.

Britain's Independent Television News challenged the restrictions on June 23 when it broadcast an interview with Winnie Mandela, wife of the imprisoned black nationalist leader Nelson Mandela. In addition to calling for sanctions, Mandela said that the media restrictions were intended "to prevent any reports about what is happening to our country . . . the idea is to conceal from the rest of the world the deepening crisis within the country."[15] No immediate action was taken against ITN, but its correspondent, Peter Sharp, was expelled some months later. *Newsweek* correspondent Richard Manning was ordered to leave the country on June 23 after the magazine carried a critical cover story, and a correspondent of Israeli Army Radio, Dan Sagir, was expelled the next day. The government threatened further action against journalists on June 25. Louis Nel summoned foreign correspondents to a meeting in Pretoria and warned that the government "will not hesitate to take whatever steps we deem necessary to ensure compliance with the state of emergency regulations."[16]

The Bureau for Information—the sole source of official news about the unrest—announced on June 25 that it was suspending its daily briefings because the state of emergency had reduced unrest to the point that there was little to report. It would continue to issue daily written reports, and special briefings would be held on major events. The government continued its crackdown on foreign reporters on June 30, expelling Heinrich Buettgen, correspondent for West Germany's ARD television channel.[17]

The networks encountered further difficulties when tapes they sent from Johannesburg to London

vanished en route. ABC, NBC and Britain's ITV all complained in mid-August that tapes had been tampered with or had disappeared after being handed over to South African Airways for shipment.[18] Foreign correspondents also reported they had been called in by the Bureau for Information to discuss "problems" with their work monitored overseas. A bureau spokesman said South African missions abroad might see reports that were obviously biased, omitted facts or were not fair. "Instead of jumping down on a correspondent, or refusing a renewal of permit—and in order to promote better communication—the bureau was talking to journalists."[19]

Nevertheless, some restrictions on reporting were eased. At the end of July the ban on naming detainees crumbled when the Johannesburg daily *The Star* published a list of more than 3,400 people held under the emergency regulations. The *Star* said the names had in effect been disclosed once the authorities notified the families of the prisoners. The government took no action, encouraging other media to follow suit. On August 20 a court overturned restrictions on reporters entering black townships and the ban on unauthorized reporting of security force actions, on the grounds that the curbs had not been properly promulgated. Journalists still were barred from quoting subversive statements. Television crews remained more tightly constrained than print journalists, however. The order prohibiting unauthorized filming of unrest and security force activity remained in effect, as did the ban on live TV news transmissions.

Although the unrest continued—albeit at a lower level of intensity—TV coverage in the months that followed shifted from what was happening in South Africa to the growing calls for sanctions abroad, and to diplomatic efforts to defuse the crisis. The U.S. Congress adopted tough new limits on trade with South Africa, and denied landing rights in the United States to South African Airways. A veto of the bill by President Reagan, who preferred a policy of "constructive engagement," was overridden by Congress. Similar sanctions were adopted by the Commonwealth nations and by the European Common Market. Louis Nel blamed foreign media coverage for the setback: "To a remarkable degree, foreign television has succeeded in pushing governments to take steps against South Africa."[20] Nel complained that "the peaceful side, reflecting perhaps 95 percent of our national life, is simply not aired."

Period 6 (December 12, 1986–May 14, 1987): Threats of massive antiapartheid protests over the Christmas period by the United Democratic Front, a coalition of political, labor and church groups, and a renewal of violence in the townships, led to the most severe censorship of the emergency. The regulations, promulgated on December 11, extended the ban on reporting of violent unrest, but also of nonviolent campaigns organized by the United Democratic Front. The front's "Christmas Against the Emergency" campaign was to have included black consumer boycotts of white-owned stores. The new rules made it illegal to publish statements that encouraged the public to participate in a boycott; discredit the system of compulsory military service; oppose any member of the government in his role of maintaining public order; stay away from work, or attend a restricted gathering. Unless permitted by the authorities, media were not allowed to publish reports on any security force action; the time, date, place or purpose of any restricted gathering, or give an account of any speech made at such a gathering; or anything relating to the circumstances, treatment or release of detainees. It was also ruled illegal to describe rent boycotts in the black townships.

For the first time the government imposed prepublication censorship. It set up a panel to examine all news copy and film about the unrest before it could be published or broadcast. All unrest stories had to be submitted to the body, known as the Interdepartmental Press Liaison Center, which operated 24 hours a day and was coordinated by the Bureau for Information.[21] Anyone who distributed material without first submitting it for approval was liable to a fine of up to $9,000, or up to 10 years in prison. The government continued to crack down on foreign journalists. In January it expelled Alan Cowell, bureau chief for the *New York Times*. In April, after a court ruling that seemed to invalidate the media curbs, police nevertheless seized ten journalists working for foreign news organizations and confiscated their film of street battles between police and striking railway workers. Among those arrested were two NBC News cameramen. NBC said its bureau in Johannesburg received a phone call from the Bureau of Information offering "friendly advice from on high" that NBC should not use pictures of police operations. In May, the government expelled two TV journalists working for the Australian Broadcasting Corporation. They were kicked out for trying to send out "reports containing gross untruths about South Africa." A week later, BBC TV correspondent Michael Buerk and ITN's Peter Sharp were expelled. Buerk and Sharp had been reprimanded by government officials in April after the BBC and ITN had broadcast film of clashes between police and students in Cape Town.

On May 14, however, the government ended prepublication censorship and disbanded the Press Liaison Center, saying that a sharp decline in political violence had prompted the move. And the police Public Relations Directorate in Pretoria assumed the role of the Bureau for Information in releasing the daily unrest bulletins. The ban on filming unrest or security force action remained in effect, and was continued when the state of emergency was renewed in June, 1987.

Clearly, to the South African government the restoration of law and order is far more important than abstract notions of press freedom. Its objective in censoring the media has been to reduce the level of violence internally, and externally to mute the negative publicity the country is receiving. Joseph Leyleveld, foreign news editor of the *New York Times*, told National Public Radio in March that "I am afraid that the South African authorities have largely succeeded in what they set out to do." At the height of the crisis in June 1986, the *New York Times* published 45 articles with South African datelines. Of these, 16 appeared on the front page. In January 1987, the first month of the most severe restrictions, it published 24 such articles, only one on page 1.[22] Independent Television News correspondent Peter Sharp said that in March 1986 he sent an average of 19 different reports to Britain by satellite each week. In March 1987 the average was about four a week. "We're not getting those very, very dramatic pictures of confrontation in the townships which any TV editor would find it very hard to resist," said Sharp.[23]

The incidence of violence also has declined. South African authorities report that since the emergency was declared, incidents have dwindled to just a handful a day. Government figures show that the number of deaths in racial conflicts dropped from 665 in the first half of 1986 to 251 in the second half. Further evidence of a return to normality in the townships is that in February 1987 thousands of black students returned to their classrooms after two years of turmoil and boycotts.[24] Business activity has picked up and foreign tourism has recovered since nightly scenes of rioting, burning and looting disappeared from the world's TV screens.

All of this suggests two questions. One is whether curbs on TV coverage of conflict situations can in fact force a story off the nightly news. As expelled *Newsweek* correspondent Richard Manning puts it, TV faces a stern test: "whether it has reached a level of sophistication that will allow it to report consistently from South Africa without the 'bang-bang'." The second question is whether the curbs have changed the type of news reported from South Africa.

METHOD

To find an answer we have undertaken a content analysis of U.S. network coverage of events in South Africa, using the Television News Index and Abstracts prepared by Vanderbilt University. These are not ideal because they don't tell much about the pictorial content of the newscasts. But they do indicate who said what, when and on which channel. The study focuses on the events of 1985 and 1986, but to establish a baseline we coded all newscasts from January 1982 through May 1987. This yielded a population of 1,262 news reports, with an average of two main themes each.

Each newscast dealing with South Africa was coded as to date, the network, whether it was a studio report or included a reporter in the field, whether it had new video or file footage, the length of the report, and its location. The unit of analysis was the theme. The content categories were derived from a purposive sample of the abstracts for the entire period. About 80 distinct themes were identified. These were collapsed into 16 larger topic areas. In each case we noted whether a theme was supported by a "sound bite"—that is an interview with a person on camera, and, if so, who that person

was. We also noted whether a person was quoted by the reporter without appearing on camera.

FINDINGS

The 1,262 reports were broadcast in roughly equal numbers by the three networks: CBS and NBC each had about 35 percent, and ABC carried 30 percent of the total. We divided the reports into two broad categories: those dealing with events inside South Africa, and those occurring outside. Most of the themes (67 percent) dealt with events inside South Africa. Of the remainder, most occurred in the United States, with occasional reports on events relating to South Africa from Europe and Africa.

By far the most common topics for internal coverage were violent protest against apartheid (26 percent), and security force actions to suppress antigovernment activity, including the state of emergency, police actions, press censorship and bannings and detentions (27 percent). These two topics alone account for more than half of the internal coverage. Add peaceful demonstrations against apartheid—marches, strikes and boycotts—and one finds 70 percent of the themes dealing either with protests of the government's effort to suppress them. Other frequent themes dealt with visits to South Africa by foreigners trying to negotiate and end to the apartheid system, and the effects of sanctions on the economy.

By contrast, only three percent of the themes dealt with what the government would regard as positive news, that is steps to move away from apartheid, such as the repeal of laws prohibiting sex or marriage between whites and other race groups, and the abolition of the pass laws that prevented blacks from moving from place to place. These were significant steps—the first real moves away from apartheid since the National Party came to power nearly 40 years ago. Yet they were seldom mentioned, and when they were it usually was followed by an interview with an opponent of the government who declared that the changes were merely cosmetic.

Coverage of events outside South Africa was dominated by reports on demands for sanctions to bring about change (35 percent); of protests abroad against events in South Africa—for example, demonstrations and arrests of assorted celebrities at the South African Embassy in Washington (20 percent). In these reports, arguments in favor of sanctions were quoted almost twice as often as those against. Another 27 percent of the external coverage dealt with condemnations of apartheid by the United States or other governments.

We tested several hypotheses against the data.

HYPOTHESIS 1:

Censorship would result in a drop in the number of reports about South Africa on U.S. network television.

This hypothesis is not borne out by the data. During the whole of 1982 and 1983 (Period 1), the three U.S. networks between them carried 51 reports about South Africa, or events abroad relating to South Africa, a combined average of one story every two weeks. When the violence flared in 1984, and TV was still free to film it (Period 2), the combined total jumped to an average of five stories a week (Table 1), partly because the networks sent full-time crews to South Africa. Then came the partial restrictions during the first state of emergency (Period 3). Instead of declining, the number of reports increased to an average of nearly eight a week. The number rose again to more than eight a week during the ''free'' period between the emergencies (Period 4). The biggest jump, however, coincided with the imposition of strict controls during the second, nationwide state emergency (Period 5). The average for the three networks combined

climbed to 15 stories as week—or five reports a week for each network TV evening news show. During the height of the crisis in June 1986, all three networks had reports every evening. Clearly the state of emergency itself made news, as did efforts to censor the media. There was as marked drop after the introduction of prepublication censorship in Period 6. Even so, the average number of reports—six a week—was still higher than during the 1982–83 control period when there were no restrictions.

A much stronger predictor of the level of coverage than censorship is the amount of violence that was occurring. One measure of newsworthy violence is the number of unrest-related deaths—whether caused by blacks incinerating other blacks with gasoline-soaked tires around their necks, or by security forces shooting protesters. The number of reports per month peaked at the same times as the number of violent deaths in August 1985 and June 1986. As the level of violent deaths declined, so generally did the number of reports (Figure 1).

HYPOTHESIS 2:

Censorship would result in less reporting specifically about unrest in South Africa.

The purpose of the restrictions was to limit television coverage of violence. The first curbs in November 1985 (Period 3) banned filming of disturbances, riots and strikes in areas under the partial state of emergency, as well as action taken by the security forces to control them. The second emergency, in June 1986 (Period 5), extended these curbs to the entire country and also banned the reporting of sub-

Table 1   AVERAGE NUMBER OF REPORTS RELATING TO SOUTH AFRICA PER WEEK

Period	ABC	CBS	NBC	Total
1	0.2	0.1	0.1	0.5
2	1.4	1.6	1.8	4.7
3	2.2	2.5	2.8	7.7
4	2.0	3.1	2.6	7.8
5	4.4	5.5	5.1	14.9
6	1.7	2.3	2.4	6.9

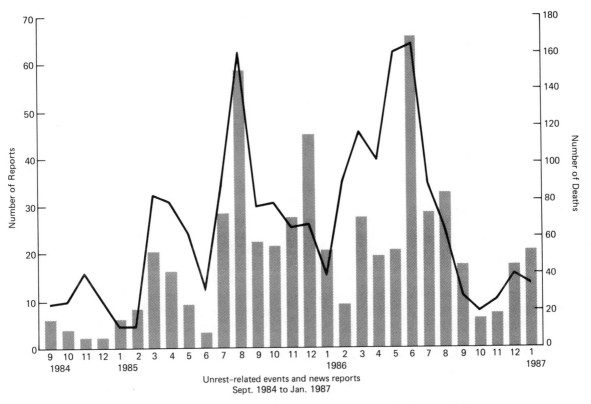

Figure 1   Unrest-related events and news reports Sept. 1984 to Jan. 1987

versive statements. The most severe restrictions, from December 1986 (Period 6), not only broadened the range of topics that were off-limits, but applied prepublication censorship to reports on the unrest. We expected that the progressively more stringent curbs would result in fewer reports about events that could not be filmed. This was generally not the case. During Period I, when things were relatively quiet, there was just one report every eight weeks on average relating to internal unrest—defined here as demonstrations, riots, strikes, school and economic boycotts, political protests, security legislation, police action and media censorship (Table 2). In Period 2, when the school boycotts and strikes began and TV could still film them, this jumped twenty-fold to an average of two reports a week on the three networks combined. This increase coincided with the arrival in South Africa of more TV correspondents, drawn by the events there. When the partial state of emergency was declared (Period 3), the

number tripled again to six reports a week on the three networks. Many of these concerned the state of emergency itself, and unrest in areas outside the emergency zones, like the Crossroads riots near Cape Town. In Period 4, the lull between the two emergencies, coverage of the unrest continued at a relatively high level, with an average of five reports a week. The imposition of a nationwide state of emergency (Period 5), with even stricter controls on the media, did not curtail the unrest coverage: it rose again to an average of nearly six reports a week. This was in spite of a decline in the number of unrest-related incidents and deaths reported by the South Africa authorities. Only the imposition of prepublication censorship in Period 6 saw a decline in the coverage, which dropped to an average of less then four reports a week. But this period is marked also by a continued decline in the level of violence as the emergency measures took effect.

Reporting on unrest as a proportion of all reports

Table 2   AVERAGE NUMBER OF REPORTS PER WEEK ABOUT INTERNAL UNREST

Period	Number of Reports
1	0.1
2	2.3
3	6.0
4	5.0
5	5.7
6	4.3

about internal events in South Africa also varied. In the first, quiet period, about 32 percent of all reports dealt with internal unrest (Table 3). This rose to 73 percent when the disturbances began in Period 2, and peaked at 85 percent during the partial state of emergency (Period 3). Between the emergencies, when the press restrictions were lifted (Period 4), the proportion of unrest reports was 84 percent. This dropped back to 70 percent during the nationwide state of emergency (Period 5) and rose again to 74 percent during the period of prepublication censorship. clearly, to the networks the South African story was racial violence, and media curbs did little to change that perception.

HYPOTHESIS 3:

Censorship would result in proportionately fewer reports about events in South Africa and more about events relating to South Africa that took place abroad.

In the first two periods, before the partial emergency, reports about internal events in South Africa accounted for about two-thirds of all reports about the Republic. One would have expected that during the first state of emergency (Period 3) the press restrictions would have forced a decline in the proportion of reports from South Africa. Instead there was a large increase, with nearly 93 percent of the reports dealing with events in the Republic (Table 4). This can be attributed to three main factors. First, South Africa became part of the international news agenda and more correspondents were sent to the scene. Second, the restrictions applied only to certain parts of South Africa, leaving the TV crews free to report on violence in areas not covered by the emergency regulations. And third, attention in the United States was diverted from American anti-apartheid demonstrations by the explosion of the shuttle Challenger in January 1986 that dominated news coverage for weeks.

During Period 4, between the two states of emer-

Table 3   REPORTS ABOUT UNREST AS A PROPORTION OF ALL REPORTS ON INTERNAL EVENTS IN SOUTH AFRICA

Period	Unrest	Other Topics
1	45	55
2	73	27
3	85	15
4	83	17
5	67	33
6	79	21

Table 4   REPORTS ABOUT INTERNAL EVENTS IN SOUTH
AFRICA AND RELATED EVENTS ABROAD

Period	Internal (%)	External (%)
1	68	32
2	67	33
3	93	7
4	75	25
5	54	46
6	78	22

gency, the proportion of reports about events within South Africa continued at a high level—75 percent of the total. But coverage of related events outside South Africa, primarily in United States, increased considerably to reflect the growing protests against apartheid and calls for divestment and sanctions. In Period 5, the second and more rigorous nationwide state of emergency, while the absolute number of reports about internal South African events increased dramatically, the proportion they formed of the total coverage dropped to its lowest level in the five-year period under review—54 percent. This reflects the extensive coverage of U.S. Congressional action on economic sanctions, culminating in the overriding of President Reagan's veto of the legislation. The proportion of reports about internal South African events increased to 83 percent in Period 6, despite prepublication censorship, largely because once Congress had adopted sanctions public interest in the United States switched to other issues—most notably the Iran-Contra scandal.

HYPOTHESIS 4:

There would be a change in the format of the reports.

We expected that restrictions would result in fewer reports about unrest in South Africa from correspondents in the field and an increase in the proportion of news about the unrest read by network anchors in the United States. The restrictions did have a marked impact on the format of the reports. During the relatively quiet Period 1, about 40 per-

cent of the reports about unrest in South Africa featured live coverage by correspondents on the scene: the rest were read by anchormen in New York (Table 5). Once violence began in Period 2, and correspondents flocked to the country, the proportion of "reporter-wrap" presentations from South Africa rose to 63 percent. It dropped to 57 percent during the partial state of emergency (Period 3), and to 55 percent between the two emergencies (Period 4). Despite the nationwide emergency (Period 5), the proportion rose again to 62 percent and remained at the level during the period of prepublication censorship.

While the absolute number of reports continued at a high level, therefore, the networks compensated for their inability to get live coverage from correspondents by having news anchors present "copy stories." Often these were a summary of the day's death toll and violence as released by the South African Bureau for Information or by the police.

HYPOTHESIS 5:

Media restrictions on quoting "subversive" statements would result in fewer interviews with South African anti-apartheid leaders.

Of all the people shown expressing their views on camera during the five years studied, more than half (57 percent) were South Africans. About 60 percent of these people were clearly identifiable as opponents of apartheid. The person shown or quoted most frequently was Bishop Tutu, followed by Winnie Mandela and the Rev. Alan Boesak, then other

Table 5 "REPORTER-WRAP" REPORTS ABOUT INTERNAL UNREST FROM CORRESPONDENTS IN SOUTH AFRICA AND "COPY STORIES" READ BY NEWS ANCHORS

Period	Reporter Wraps (%)	Studio Reports (%)
1	39	61
2	77	23
3	67	33
4	63	37
5	69	31
6	58	42

antiapartheid black leaders. The government spokesman shown on camera or quoted most frequently was President P. W. Botha—although he appeared only half as often as Tutu. The impact of the curbs on the proportion of South African and American sources is not consistent. In the first two periods the proportion of South Africans quoted was about 60 percent of the total. During the first state of emergency this proportion increased markedly to nearly 80 percent. That proportion held constant during Period 4, between the states of emergency. Once the second state of emergency (Period 5) was declared, however, with its ban on quoting "subversive" statements, the proportion of South African sources dropped sharply to 50 percent—the lowest level of the five-year survey. This decline, however, can also be attributed to the increasing attention the networks paid to South Africa's critics abroad, particularly in the United states. The curbs did not appear to silence South African blacks. In fact Tutu was shown proportionately more often during the second state of emergency than during the periods that preceded it. But fewer reports featured interviews with Winnie Mandela and other antiapartheid leaders after the ban on reporting subversive statements. One reason for Tutu's continued prominence is that he often was televised while delivering church sermons or while traveling abroad where he could be quoted with relative impunity.

CONCLUSIONS

The study shows that in the short term at least the amount of coverage of South Africa did not decline after curbs were placed on the media, but rather

intensified. The networks clearly were determined to get stories out in spite of the restrictions. As previous studies have shown, the presence of correspondents in an area ensures that it will be covered. Once the networks had committed reporters to the Republic, those correspondents had to justify their presence there by sending a regular flow of reports. And the networks had to justify the expense by using them.

The question as to whether the nature of the reports changed is more ambiguous. The data show that the focus remained on violent protests against apartheid, despite the censorship. Yet there is a perception that the restrictions have blinkered the cameras. Richard M. Cohen, senior producer of foreign news for CBS Evening News, believes that the American consciousness about South Africa "was formed and maintained by the constant television images of brutal repression in many forms: the image of the padded, faceless policeman, club raised; the image of the black youth with fear covering every inch of his face as he throws a rock. These were constant and common images, and now they are missing . . . Those images are no longer on American television because we cannot broadcast them, for fear of being expelled from South Africa."[25]

It is possible that the nature of the coverage has indeed changed, and that analyzing abstracts of TV newscasts rather than the video itself masks the differences. But it is also likely that the reason for the change in the amount and kind coverage is that the level of violence has declined. Coverage peaked in August 1985, the start of the emergency, when 116 reports were broadcast by the three networks together. The declaration of the second state of emergency spurred 108 reports in June 1986. By September this had dropped to 60. In December it was down to 24. There has been a corresponding decline in violence as reported by the Bureau of Information. The Bureau reported in June 1987 that unrest-related incidents had dropped by 80 percent since the start of the emergency.

The curbs did seem to have some positive effects on television as well. TV is notorious for being "event-oriented" rather than concerned with explaining issues. With the imposition of the curbs, correspondents were forced to look for other angles rather than simply the number of deaths that day: to give background on the stories and explain "why" rather than just "what happened."

One cannot demonstrate, as South African authorities maintain, that curbs on foreign media are responsible for the decline in violence, although a stronger case could possibly be made for censorship of South Africa's domestic media. It cannot be disputed that both the level of violence and the level of TV coverage declined. This could be because, as South African authorities claim, there are no longer highly-visible TV crews in the townships whose presence turns peaceful demonstrations into riots. It is more likely, however, that the actions taken by the security forces, including the detention of thousands of political activists, have led to a decrease in the amount of violence and hence in the level of coverage. Many antiapartheid news sources used by the media are in detention, or in hiding. Finally there is the boredom factor. The media are easily distracted by new sensations. Perhaps the best thing the South African government had going for it in forcing the story off the nightly news was not curbs on the media, but the Iran-Contra scandal.

One lesson seems to be that if a country wishes to black out news about its internal affairs it needs to do what Iran or Afghanistan have done—that is to exclude foreign correspondents completely. Allowing correspondents in, then trying to control what they report, clearly is doomed to failure.

NOTES

1. See W. A. Hachten and C. Anthony Giffard, *The Press and Apartheid: Repression and Propaganda in South Africa* (Madison: University of Wisconsin Press, 1984).
2. South African Society of Journalists, *The Journalist*, August 1985.
3. *New York Times*, 11 September 1985.
4. United Press International, 11 September 1985.
5. *Christian Science Monitor*, 4 November 1985.
6. *Washington Post*, 10 March 1986.
7. *Washington Post*, 10 March 1986.
8. Associated Press, 9 March 1986.
9. *Seattle P–I* 12 March 1986.
10. Associated Press, 11 June 1986.
11. United Press International, 16 June 1986.
12. *New York Times*, 16 June 1986.
13. *New York Times*, 18 June 1986.
14. United Press International, 20 June 1986.
15. Associated Press, 23 June 1986.
16. *New York Times*, 25 June 1986.
17. *New York Times*, 30 June 1986.
18. Associated Press and *New York Times*, 20 August 1986.
19. South African Society of Journalists, *The Journalist*, August 1986.
20. Associated Press, 15 August 1986.
21. *The Argus* (Capetown), 11 December 1986 and *The Pretoria News*, 12 December 1986.
22. *New York Times*, 1 March 1987.
23. National Public Radio, "All Things Considered," 6 March 1987.
24. South–North News Service, 26 February 1987.
25. Richard M. Cohen, "To Reporters: Quit South Africa," *New York Times*, 31 August 1987.

ISRAEL AND THE PRESS

JIM HOAGLAND

Israel has had similar problems. Because of the threat to its security posed by rebelling Palestinians within its borders on the West Bank, Israel, the most liberal democracy in the Middle East, has nonetheless sought strict control of certain kinds of communication. Jim Hoagland discusses the problem from an American perspective.

Is South Africa now the world trend setter in press censorship, a Giorgio Armani for governments that want to shut off foreign and local coverage of embarrassing scenes of unrest?

That seems to be the surprising suggestion by some of Israel's American friends who have aired the idea that Israel should practice censorship "a la South Africa" by cracking down more brutally and banning the press from covering the Palestinian revolt.

The idea of a South African-style crackdown in Israel was floated last month in a private meeting of American Jewish leaders in New York. Its paternity remains in dispute, with Henry A. Kissinger stoutly and persuasively denying that he urged such action, despite one participant's memo to the contrary.

But the thrust of this proposal has now been echoed publicly by Mayor Ed Koch of New York, who asked this week in a column for *The Jerusalem Post* why Israel should be alone in allowing coverage of riots to be flashed on the world's television screens. In Paris, Israeli Ambassador Ovadia Soffer also argued that "By sticking to the rules of democracy, Israel suffered severe damage to its image."

Israel should ignore the intellectually flawed advice that presents the South African censorship experience as a success story in which the tactic of banning coverage brings more benefits than costs.

The reverse is true for countries like South Africa and Israel, which actively seek the support and understanding of the West by describing themselves as embattled democracies struggling to preserve societies based on American and European models and values.

South Africa's image in the outside world has not improved an iota since its press restrictions were enacted. Sanction talk is growing again in the West as more organizations are banned. Black dissent and journalistic enterprise continue inside South Africa at a level unimaginable 15 years ago.

Those who would push Israel down the South African path appear to be worried about the pressures and influence of western opinion supposedly inflamed by television images of the Army's brutal handling of the Palestinians.

But banning the press from the West Bank and Gaza will do little to restrict outside pressure on Israel. Such censorship would in fact backfire. It would instead restrict Israel's own ability to influence public opinion in the West, still a vital asset for the Jewish state.

Erecting legal and physical walls to keep the press from covering political uprisings does not improve a country's image, no matter how painful the scenes that would be suppressed. The main impact of censorship in such cases is to limit a country's chance to change a negative image.

Critics of the press should stop to consider that the totalitarian countries that have the severest forms of censorship, such as the Soviet Union or Syria, are

Jim Hoagland, "Israel and the Press." *The Washington Post*, March 19, 1988, p. A2. Reprinted by permission.

The author is a correspondent for the *Washington Post*.

precisely those countries about which the American public feels most negatively and which it is most prepared to confront if necessary.

My professional bias as a working journalist is clear in this matter. My professional experience is perhaps no less relevant.

Writing and editing news involving Israel is one of the most exciting and demanding challenges offered in American journalism. Virtually every sentence you produce is subject to intense scrutiny for fairness, accuracy and comprehension.

The complaints that follow about slights and failures, real and imagined, are often time-consuming, aggravating and the cause of tempers boiling over in newsrooms. As a senior editor having to deal directly with such complaints, I was at first thankful that other countries did not have the articulate, focused constituency among our readers that Israel has.

But I came to realize that newspapers benefit from this kind of scrutiny. Coverage of Israel in the American press is likely to be more factual and carefully worded than coverage from any other foreign country. I have no doubt that coverage of all countries, including the United States, would improve under such informed testing.

When they involve closed societies, where the walls of censorship block off verification, such complaints are likely to carry little weight with editors where there is no possibility of cross-checking reports and allegations.

Censorship a la South Africa might save Israel a few immediate headaches. But it would cancel most of the impact that active and articulate supporters of Israel have on public opinion and on western media. Israel deserves better advice from its friends and officials.

CENSORSHIP IN ISRAEL

Yaacov Bar-Natan

Yaacov Bar-Natan looks at the problem of control from an Israeli point of view. He concludes that it is public opinion in Israel which is the main threat to press freedom.

During the many months of turmoil in the West Bank and the Gaza Strip, there has been a marked difference between what Israeli Television (ITV) has shown its viewers and what the foreign TV networks operating in Israel have been transmitting to the rest of the world. The international networks have shown Israeli troops beating captured Palestinians. ITV has not. Television crews, Israeli and foreign, are frequently excluded from the scene of a disturbance, and, in at least two cases, cameramen were roughed up by troops, though the Israel Defense Forces (IDF) spokesman apologized in both cases.

In the same period a radical Israeli Arabic and Hebrew weekly was informed that it is to be closed down, and one of its Arab editors was arrested. On Israel's cultural scene, plays of a left-wing political flavor were threatened with expulsion from the country's 40th anniversary celebrations, although the threat was not carried out. Does all this add up to

Yaacov Bar-Natan, "Censorship in Israel." *St. Louis Journalism Review.* July 1988. Reprinted by permission from New Outlook.

The author is a freelance journalist living in Jerusalem.

a tightening of censorship in Israel on the background of the riots in the occupied territories? To answer this question, it is worthwhile reviewing the various forms of censorship, de jure and de facto, existing in Israel.

The 1945 Defense Regulations empower the military censor to stop the publication, not only of sensitive military secrets, but also of anything he deems prejudicial to public order. In 1949, shortly after the War of Independence, there was a move to abolish the regulations and replace them with an act of the Knesset that would restrict censorship to security matters. The government even drafted a bill for the purpose, but at the last moment it was withdrawn. Instead, the censor made an agreement with the Editors Committee, a body representing the main Hebrew daily newspapers and Israel Radio (at that time there was no television). The censor promised not to practice political censorship against news organizations represented on the committee nor to use his power to prosecute them for censorship violations. In return, the bill to restrict his statutory powers was dropped. This left the censor free to use his powers at will against newspapers not represented on the committee, with the compliance of those that were. In those days it was the Communist Press (Hebrew and Arabic), the sensationalist left-wing weekly *HaOlam Hazeh*, and the organ of the right-wing opposition Herut party, led by Menachem Begin, that were regarded as radical. Today it is the East Jerusalem Palestinian press.

Among the Israeli papers, *HaOlam Hazeh*, the weekly *Koteret Rashit*, and the new tabloid daily *Hadashot* are not members of the Editors Committee and are not protected by the censor's promise. The same applies to the foreign press corps operating in Israel. In practice, however, the censor usually refrains from political censorship of Israeli or foreign media.

For the Arabic-language papers in East Jerusalem the situation is different. They are subject to persistent interference by the censor, despite the fact that East Jerusalem was annexed by Israel in 1967 and the press there, whether Israeli or Palestinian, is supposed to enjoy the benefits of Israeli democracy. Sometimes these papers are forbidden to publish reports that have already appeared in the Hebrew press, even when they are translated verbatim, if the

censor thinks that they will inflame their Palestinian readers.

Even with the "establishment" press, the censor has not always kept his promise to refrain from political censorship. During the 1982 Lebanon War, for example, the censor altered a report in *Ha'aretz* to create the impression that the Syrian army had attacked Israeli forces on the Beirut-Damascus highway, when in fact it was the Israelis who had launched the offensive. Since the Syrians obviously knew this, the reason for the alteration could not have been national security. It transpired that Defense Minister Ariel Sharon was trying to keep the information from Acting Prime Minister David Levy (Prime Minister Menachem Begin was in Washington at the time) because he (Sharon) had told Levy that Syria started the battle, and he did not want the already suspicious Levy to learn the truth from the morning paper.

As if military censorship were not enough, no newspaper can appear in Israel without a license from the local district commissioner, who is a regional director of the Ministry of the Interior. Under the 1933 Press Ordinance Law (also inherited from the British Mandate), the commissioner can revoke or refuse to grant such a license without even explaining why. Israel's High Court of Justice has condemned the law as "a draconian provision passed by a colonial regime . . . incompatible with the basic values of a democratic state," but it is still in force. It was under the Press Ordinance Law that Jerusalem District Commissioner Eli Suissa recently informed the Israeli Hebrew and Arabic weekly *Derekh Ha-Nitsots* (The Way of the Spark) that he was about to revoke its license, on the grounds that the journal had links with Nayef Hawatmeh's Democratic Front for the Liberation of Palestine, one of the organizations in the PLO. The journal's editor, Assaf Adiv (an Israeli Jew), denied this. He said the journal reflects the views of the Israeli Communist Party, of which he is a leading member. Shortly thereafter, one of the journal's Arab editors was arrested. Suissa wrote that he had been informed of the paper's alleged links with the DFLP by the security services. He gave no details about the charges.

The Emergency Regulations also empower the authorities to prevent the publication of books.

Again, this power is seldom used against Hebrew writers. One notable exception was the journalist Matti Golan, who was forbidden to publish *Conversations with Henry Kissinger*, a remarkable book giving almost the entire protocol of Kissinger's Middle East shuttle negotiations. In the end, the book was published after Golan agreed to cut certain passages the Israeli authorities regarded as particularly sensitive.

In addition to all of the above, the Editors Committee sometimes indulges in a kind of voluntary censorship, at the request of the government or the armed forces. In return for briefings from cabinet ministers and generals, which give the editors a certain advantage over the non-establishment press, they agree to tone down or not to publish information the officials regard as damaging to the national interest. The most notorious case was in the autumn of 1973, just before the outbreak of the Yom Kippur War, when the chief-of-staff, Lieut. Gen. David Elazar, asked the editors not to make too much of the concentration of Egyptian and Syrian troops, as this might cause panic. The editors agreed, and did not give the reports the kind of coverage their military correspondents believed was warranted. In retrospect, the editors felt that they shared responsibility for the disaster of October 6, for if they had rejected the general's request and sounded the alarm, the public might have demanded a general mobilization, and the armed forces might not have been caught off guard.

The chairman of the Press Council, Dr. Yehoshua Rotenstreich, points out that the Editors Committee never agrees to suppress or restrict information unless the decision is unanimous. If one paper disagrees, they all publish. It is also true that some other Western democracies have press censorship in one form or another. Britain has its D-Notice procedure in which an army brigadier informs the papers that this or that item is sensitive; it is then automatically dropped. The British Official Secrets Act is also something of a catch-all. During the Falklands War there was simply no primetime TV coverage, and the picture presented to the British people was strongly influenced by the government's censors. The French authorities also have the power to close newspapers, although it has not been used since the Algerian war. However, the defects of the British and French systems offer no justification to Israelis for the defects of their system, and no excuse to Israeli editors who have long since given up the fight for a better system.

It was soldiers from the crack Golani Brigade who roughed up Israeli TV cameraman Moshe Ben-Dor, damaging his camera, as he was trying to film a demonstration in Gaza. CBS bureau chief Bob Simon told *New Outlook* that the army frequently tries to prevent the filming of disturbances, either by declaring the scene of the riot a closed military area, or by harassing the crew or otherwise hindering their work. "To a large extent they are successful," Simon says, "and this is why a great deal of what is going on is not being shown even by the foreign networks. What we do get on the screen is only the tip of the iceberg."

On the other hand, there has been very little formal censorship of TV footage since the outbreak of the riots. "The military censor has been commendably absent," Simon says. By contrast, during the Vanunu, Poland, and Irangate affairs, relations between the foreign media and the military censor broke down completely, and many foreign correspondents simply stopped submitting their copy to the censor. This was because they (and the Israeli media) were being forbidden to publish important material, which Israeli officials would then leak to a selected foreign paper, usually *The New York Times*. By no stretch of the imagination, the reporters argued, could such censorship be considered necessary for the country's security. After a while, relations between the censor and the foreign media returned to normal, but as one veteran reporter pointed out, it is in times of crisis that the system is tested.

The crisis in the territories has presented ITV with a challenge it has failed to meet. ITV has not brought to Israeli screens the harrowing pictures of the beatings the rest of the world has seen. ITV is a monopoly, obliged by law to keep the public informed, and Israelis are totally dependent on it for serious Hebrew-language coverage.

The failure is not due to interference by the military censor nor the ITV management. ITV editors insist that they have not cut any important footage the crews have brought in. The editors even point to one or two scoops that ITV has had during the disturbances, for instance, pictures of a General Security Service agent shooting in the general direction of stone-throwers (he did not hit any, and was subsequently dismissed from the service). Yet ITV staffers admit that they have failed to catch the scenes of violence that constitute the main news story. They have seldom been on the spot at the right time.

There are two reasons for this: one is organizational, the other loosely connected with censorship. ITV is an inefficient, bureaucratic organization that is incapable of covering a major event such as the riots in the territories in the manner that the foreign networks can and do. On one occasion, a crew did not leave the office until 1:00 P.M. because the management was unable to provide a security guard to escort them. Reporters and cameramen are grossly underpaid and demoralized, particularly in the wake of a long and unsuccessful strike. Even the life insurance provided by the Broadcasting Authority in the case of death or injury is pitifully low. During the Yom Kippur and Lebanon wars these same crews risked their lives to bring pictures to Israeli viewers. Now they just don't care. Foreign crews, or Israelis working for foreign networks, are highly paid, heavily insured, equipped with the latest communications equipment, and employed on the basis of free competition. They are out in the field at 7:00 A.M. because they have the incentive to be there, and are at the scene of events because they have the facilities.

To make matters worse, ITV cameramen say they have been warned time and again by their superiors that the riots are a very sensitive issue. "If you are told seven times over to be careful and responsible," one cameraman explained, "you get the message. So why should you bust a gut or risk your neck?"

If ITV director-general Uri Porat were genuinely interested in showing the Israeli public what is going on, he could easily obtain footage from the foreign networks, as ITV has exchange agreements with a number of them. But Porat is a political appointee of the Likud, and regards the foreign coverage of the riots as distorted and unbalanced. He even criticized one of his own reporters, Victor Nahmias, for an interview with a Palestinian that Nahmias included in one of his on-the-spot reports.

In spite of the wide statutory powers of censorship the authorities possess, the main threat to press freedom in Israel lies in the attitudes of the Israeli public. A recent opinion survey showed that barely 30 percent of Israelis have democratic attitudes toward the media. The rest do not really want to read or hear views opposed to their own. Most of the available evidence suggests that if ITV had broadcast the same pictures as the foreign networks, a majority of the viewers would have resented this. Most viewers believe that even the partial and rather pale coverage provided by ITV is heavily biased against the Jewish settlers in the West Bank and Gaza Strip and against the armed forces.

There is no doubt that the right-wing political leadership has exploited the anti-media sentiments of its voters for all they are worth. Prime Minister Yitzhak Shamir never loses an opportunity to pillory the media. It is hard to say how much of the hostility is generated by the politicians, or to what extent they are merely capitalizing on the resentments of their following to increase their popularity. Whatever the case, the riots in the territories have shown that Israel's continued control of more than a million hostile Arabs poses as big a threat to the freedom of the news media as to other aspects of Israeli democracy. Few believe that the territories will return to the degree of normality that existed before the wave of disturbances, and it is likely that the news coverage of what is happening there will continue to bring criticism upon Israel Television, Israel Radio, and Israeli papers, whether they succeed in their function or fail.

THE PALESTINIAN PRESS: LIFE ON A LEASH

ELLEN CANTAROW

Ellen Cantarow views media control in Israel from the vantage point of a journalist who has been looking carefully at the "other" side. She writes that the Israeli press is not nearly as controlled as the Palestinian media in the Palestinian territories.

Some people are trained to find news, but news and history came to Jawdat Mana'a's door. Born in 1952 in Dehaishe, a West Bank refugee camp, he began to write about it in 1980, after the camp was punished with a weeks-long curfew for the burning of an Israeli army jeep. He started sending stories to Palestinian newspapers, and people started sending him news of strife in other camps. He developed a sizable archive—"I have information about the camps, and photos, that go back to when I was born"—and he made contacts not just with Palestinian reporters, but with Israeli, European, and American journalists as well. Opening the Bethlehem Press Service in 1982 seemed only logical.

Last March 13, armed Israeli soldiers, police, and secret service officers entered Mana'a's offices, ordered them temporarily closed, and arrested him. Two of the soldiers carried M16s. "They took all my negatives, hundreds of photographs and papers, even the music cassettes I like to listen to when I work," he says. Like many Palestinian reporters with nationalist sentiments, Mana'a had been arrested before. This time he was jailed twenty days without being charged, and then he was accused of possessing material that could incite his people to rebel—photographs of demonstrations and people wounded in clashes with the army, a Fax machine; a cassette with Palestinian nationalist songs; and most damaging of all in the eyes of the authorities, one of the thousands of leaflets, issued by the leaders of the intifadah, as the Palestinians call their eleven-month-old uprising. Well-liked by his foreign colleagues, Mana'a assumes it was articles published

abroad about his arrest that spurred the military authorities to release him without making him pay the bail—4,000 shekels, or $6,400—the court had imposed. His driver's license was lifted, however, and he returned to find his phone lines cut.

Mana'a is one of the forty-seven Palestinian journalists jailed between the start of the intifadah last December and August 20, according to the Arab Journalists' Association in the Occupied Territories. During that period, eight newspapers suffered temporary bans on distribution in the territories, the licenses of two magazines were permanently revoked, and three press services besides the one in Bethlehem were closed. At least one more journalist was arrested after that list was compiled, a copy editor for Al Fajr, whose editor, Hanna Siniora, is considered a spokesman for the most moderate wing of the Palestine Liberation Organization. Al Fajr has been particularly hard-hit, with eight journalists jailed and three deported.

Israel justifies these harsh measures on security grounds. The legal rationale comes from the Defense Security Regulations of 1945, which, along with some 1,300 military orders, impose restrictions on many aspects of life in the territories, including free expression. They were used sparingly until the mid-seventies and an upsurge of nationalism in the territories. Over the past eleven months they have been wielded unremittingly against the Palestinian press. Under the regulations, newspapers and magazines in the territories must submit to the military censor two copies of everything to be printed—from the weather to political analysis. The censor may

Ellen Cantarow, "The Palestinian Press: Life on a Leash." Reprinted from the *Columbia Journalism Review*, November/December 1988 ©. Reprinted by permission.

The author is a free-lance journalist who has been writing about the occupied territories since 1979.

remove anything deemed to be of "political significance."

That phrase is broad enough, in the words of a 1986 report by Law in the Service of Man (a West Bank affiliate of the International Commission of Jurists), to include "any suggestion that West Bank inhabitants are suffering under occupation . . . and [any] representation of national aspiration."

So the Palestinian press can't even report on its own problems. Asked whether *Al Fajr*'s remaining staff had been able to write about their jailed and deported colleagues, an editor shrugged. "Write? It's a big word. We can write that they have been arrested. We can say, 'This man was arrested on such and such a day,' but no one will know the details." Another editor, who like most who were interviewed would not allow his name to be printed, says many reporters are reluctant to do legwork. "They say, 'Why should we go out? The story will only be censored.' "

Still, some Palestinian reporters have found a partial detour around the censor. They feed their tips to foreign wire services, then reprint the resulting stories; once articles are published outside Israel's borders, the censors seem to be less harsh. News of interest to residents of the West Bank and Gaza may also reach the Palestinian press by way of Palestinian reporters working for West Jerusalem-based foreign media. All ten front-page stories published September 10 by the East Jerusalem daily *Al Quds*, for example, were taken from foreign wire services. "I titled one story AMERICAN DELEGATION CALLS ON U.S. TO STOP MILITARY AID TO ISRAEL," says Samaan Khoury, a West Bank journalist who works for Agence France-Presse. "The day after AFP ran it, I saw it with the same headline in five East Jerusalem papers."

In theory, Israel could censor its own press. From time to time the prime minister and the defense ministry may decide that certain issues are national security matters (Israel's 1982 invasion of Lebanon, for example). Israeli reporters must then submit stories about those issues to the military censor, who usually makes few, and minor, changes. "Censorship is really not a problem for us," says Dani Rubinstein, a veteran correspondent of the Israeli daily *Davar*.

In fact, the Israeli press publishes vivid accounts of events that would be instantly censored in the territories, and are even fairly rare in the U.S. press: detailed descriptions of villages under siege for long periods, deprived of water, electricity, and food; eye-witness accounts of beatings and shootings of unarmed civilians; soldiers' accounts of their feelings about meting out such punishment (see "Telling the West Bank Story," *Columbia Journalism Review*, July/August).

But such stories rarely get into the Palestinian press. In early September, Mana'a covered an *intifadah* birthday party in a hospital. A patient had just turned seventeen, a boy from Mana'a's birthplace, Dehaisha, who had been critically wounded in the stomach by a soldier's bullet the month before. Unable to eat, fed by intravenous tubes, he was clearly dying. Flowers bedecked the room; there was a picture of the illegal Palestinian flag over the bed. Someone blew out the candles on a three-tiered cake, and a doctor fed the patient two forkfuls of it. Young men from the camp, along with his parents and relatives, surrounded him. As at an *infitadah* funeral, they weren't mourning the young man's impending death, but celebrating his martyrdom to the Palestinian cause. Mana'a reported the event for the foreign and domestic clients of his wire service, taking care to give only the barest facts and not to use the charged word *infitadah*. But it came back censored in full. "I *always* write," Mana'a says, when asked if he gets discouraged. "Whether or not it gets censored, I must try."

UNHIDDEN AGENDA

ANDREW REDING

Andrew Reding describes the problems of control in the Central American country of Costa Rica, long known as the most democratic country in Central America. As in many democracies, the media there are controlled by the wealthy owners and operators, while the masses and the bureaucracy of government have less media authority.

In its streets, Costa Rica does not seem to be a land at war with itself. The only Central American country with a long-standing democratic tradition and, not coincidentally, the only one without an army, Costa Rica has been an oasis of relative peace and prosperity in a region better known for repression and misery.

Yet a war is being waged there—a war of words, ideas, and images, not guns and grenades. The war is between the right-wing establishment that controls the electronic and print media, and a growing collection of former presidents and government ministers, artists, writers, and other citizens who fear that the media are trying to redesign the country's social traditions. In particular, the media are attacking Costa Rica's lack of an army, its tradition of neutrality, and its tolerance of domestic leftists.

The message from the media is that Costa Rica must change its ways and raise an army or be overrun by its neighbor to the north, Nicaragua. Four of the five privately owned major TV stations broadcast a barrage of sensationalized news reports warning of the *sandinocomunista* threat. (The fifth station is all sports.) While the stations never interview the Nicaraguan ambassador, they give considerable time to the Reagan administration's viewpoint. In Channel 7's recent half-hour interview with American ambassador Arthur Lewis Tambs, for instance, Tambs was allowed to make unsubstantiated—and unchallenged—claims that the Nicaraguans are harboring Basque, Lebanese, Palestinian, and Colom-

bian terrorists, and that they have proclaimed "a revolution without borders"—an intention the Sandinistas have repeatedly foreworn.

Since April 1980, executives of the major TV stations and newspapers have held joint meetings on editorial strategy concerning issues of importance to the Reagan administration, often with U.S. embassy officials attending, according to Juan José Echeverría Brealey, former minister of public security, and other well placed sources. Since then the media have played up Nicaraguan totalitarianism and aggression and begun a witch hunt of supposed Sandinista sympathizers in the government, hounding from office the public security minister Angel Solano Calderón for his zealous enforcement of the country's neutrality.

In addition, many informed Costa Ricans believe journalists receive monetary encouragement from the United States. Former Nicaraguan contra leader Edgar Chamorro testified in the World Court last fall that CIA money was used to bribe journalists and broadcasters in both Costa Rica and Honduras. But there's a more fundamental reason that television stations and newspapers take a uniform approach to geopolitical news, according to the two-time former Costa Rican president José Figueres Ferrer: "Because they're owned by a minority—the Costa Rican oligarchy—and now they find they are backed by U.S. dollars."

"The upper classes of Latin American countries normally control by means of the army," says Pablo

Andrew Reding, "Unhidden Agenda." *Channels*, April 1986, pp. 62–63. Reprinted by permission.

The author is a fellow of the World Policy Institute, New York.

Richard, a prominent Chilean theologian living in exile in Costa Rica. "Since there's no army here, they do so through the media of communications." Ownership of the five private stations is extensively linked with that of the major newspapers in large family stock holdings, according to Carlos Morales, director of the journalism school at the University of Costa Rica.

Though these owners and their media are considerably to the right of the general population, alternative media haven't been able to develop. "We have tried many times," says Daniel Oduber, a former president who is among the country's most popular political figures. "The problem is, the owners of the media are the same group as the owners of the businesses that advertise, and without advertisements, no media can survive." There is a state television channel, but it's devoted to education and few Costa Ricans watch it.

What they do watch, on the commercial channels, is Venezuelan and Mexican soap operas, soccer matches, and dubbed U.S. shows such as *Comisario Lobo, Los Héroes de Hogan, He-Man y los Amos del Universo*, and *La Cruzada de Jimmy Swaggart*. Despite a law limiting imported programs to 75 percent of broadcast schedules, about 90 percent are, in fact, imports. In addition, U.S. programs dominate the cable systems in parts of the capital, San José, and are available on an ad hoc TV station operated as a hobby by a suburbanite named Erick Roy.

Roy, a manufacturer of satellite dishes, runs a small UHF transmitter that retransmits the Chicago superstation WGN and, in the evening, the pay cable network Showtime, both of which he picks out of the sky with a backyard satellite receiver. WGN's baseball broadcasts have given the Chicago Cubs a substantial following in San José. The U.S.-educated broadcaster's project is nonprofit but not without motive, as he admits. "Either we get Americanized, or we get communized from the north," says Roy.

Getting Americanized, however, does not appeal to a number of Costa Rican intellectuals, including Professor Morales, who believes that violent U.S. shows such as *Los Magníficos* (*The A-Team*) and *Kojak* are affecting Costa Rica's pacifist ways. "This degrades our society," he says, "so that little by little we are losing our values."

Talk of national values might be easier to disregard in some countries, but Costa Rica's are indeed long established and unusual in Central America. Costa Rica began universal free public education in 1879 and social security in 1942, abolished the death penalty in 1882, and has elected its president and legislature since 1889. It has the region's highest standard of living, and a life expectancy comparable to the United States.

The country has also tried to foster political tolerance and dialogue—deep-rooted Costa Rican traits—through laws like the one that requires broadcasters to accept political ads during campaign periods. It was through recourse to that rule, in fact, that the freedom-of-information issue was raised briefly on television late last year. CODELI, a coalition of prominent writers, artists, and former government ministers, broke into prime time with a series of attractively produced ads warning that "the freedoms of information and opinion have become impoverished in Costa Rica . . . threatening a climate of intolerance that could be manipulated to lead us into authoritarianism and the loss of our freedoms."

The media immediately denounced the ads as a campaign to discredit "the watchdogs of public morals," as one editorialist described the media, and shortly thereafter TV newscasts picked up on a newspaper story that painted former president Figueres as a traitor and implied that CODELI and Costa Rican neutrality play into a Nicaraguan-Cuban plot. The news reports were based on a highly incriminating letter, supposedly sent by the Nicaraguan ambassador to Figueres—a letter that police later determined was forged.

While CODELI's ads on behalf of free speech were soon withdrawn from the air, the broadcasters have had no objection to carrying "Let's Activate Costa Rica" ads from the Costa Rican Coalition for Development Alternatives (CINDE), a recipient of grants from the U.S. Agency for International Development. CINDE's ads show workers and management climbing a hill together, then standing on the summit as the Costa Rican flag rises behind them. The objective: associating the country's anti-union but pro-U.S. business establishment with patriotism, and promoting the passage of laws favoring exports—which is consistent with U.S. advice to Costa Rica and other countries deep in debt. "In the context that the U.S. government is aiding us massively,'' says Lafitte Fernandez of CINDE, ''the idea is that I'll help you, but you must change.''

Up-to-date video persuasion was also employed in TV advertising during this winter's presidential campaign. Right-wing candidate Rafael Angel Calderón Fournier, a godson of former Nicaraguan dictator Anastasio Somoza Garcia, was shown talking one-on-one with Ronald Reagan, Margaret Thatcher, and Pope John Paul II. Calderón's opponent, Oscar Arias Sánchez, the candidate of the incumbent centrist party, brought in liberal American consultants Bendixen & Law, who used polling to identify what was worrying the large bloc of undecided voters and refocus the campaign appropriately. By promising jobs, housing, and peace, Arias was able to overcome Calderón's wide lead in early polls to win the presidency in February.

The fact that Arias—certainly not the oligarchy's favorite for the presidency—was allowed to advertise on television indicates that the Costa Rican media carry a wider range of views than those of less democratic Third World countries. Its government also doesn't seriously threaten freedom of the press. But CODELI wasn't defending freedom of the *press*. The group's complaint, given a brief and rare airing this winter, was that the media themselves, controlled by a small minority, act as censors, threatening the citizens' freedom of *information* that is essential to democracy. Throughout the Third World this concern had lead to calls for a ''new information order'' and the removal of media from foreign and private control. ''The owners of the media,'' warns former president Oduber, ''should be aware that they are provoking an attack against the media.''

2 CURRENT CONCERNS IN THREE MAIN SYSTEMS

Whether or not it makes sense to divide up the world into three main camps, it is the division that many communication researchers have used to generalize about world mass media systems. Politically, the Western bloc, the Communist bloc, and the Third World have tended, with notable exceptions, to be in agreement on many issues, especially on issues pertaining to international communication. Historically, these are the alignments that have prevailed since World War II. That is why we have chosen this breakdown. We recognize that in many instances there are more differences than similarities within the systems. But they have enough in common to make this a meaningful approach.

The Western bloc is made up mostly of developed countries. Their wealth is relatively great, ranging from gross domestic products of more than four billion in Luxembourg to more than four trillion in the United States. Technologically it contains the most advanced countries in the world with the most extensive and sophisticated lines of communication. Because of the area's wealth, it tends to produce and disseminate more news and entertainment, and, because of the great volume of its production, it can do so more cheaply since many more consumers of its news and entertainment share in the cost of the overhead. It can also pay its producers more than poorer regions can, and it therefore manages to attract the best talent.

It is not surprising, therefore, that poorer regions and nations complain about "media imperialism," "cultural hegemony," "electronic colonialism," and other terms indicating, as Jeremy Tunstall put it, that "the media are American," or, at any rate, Western. Four of the five international wire services are Western. They not only gather and disseminate world news, often selling it to national and regional news agencies, but they practically dictate what is news and how it should be presented. The fifth wire service—the Soviet Union's TASS—is used far less often than is the Associated Press and United Press International of the United States, Reuters of Britain, and Agence France Presse of France, even by those media that subscribe to it.

Because modern technology is heavily concentrated in the Western bloc, most of the knowhow is concentrated there, too. Television programming, videocassette production, data bases, computer networks, and satellites are available elsewhere, but nowhere as cheaply, in as large quantities, and in the quality that the world has developed a taste for. If the Western bloc has been changing in the years since World War II, the changes have been due to the exponential development of technology. There also has been a growing concentration of mass media ownership in the hands of a few press lords and syndicates. Media content, however, has not changed markedly in recent years.

The Communist bloc probably has seen greater changes than either of the two other areas, especially in the late 1980s. While these changes did not occur overnight, everyone will agree with the election of Mikhail Gorbachev to leadership had a lot to do with the reforms and the openness that we have witnessed in the Soviet Union in particular, and in the whole Communist bloc in general. Gorbachev believes that *glasnost*—or "giving people a voice"—is necessary for *perestroika*—generally interpreted as "economic reform." The second half of the 1980s, therefore, has witnessed a steady decline in state secrecy and open discussions about many—though not all—issues that have long been festering in Communist bloc countries. Heads of government departments have been holding regular press conferences and answering tough questions. The writings of dissidents are being serialized in the Soviet press, and television is showing facets of both Soviet and foreign life that had never been seen before. Soviet editors have been showing signs of being preoccupied with reader interest rather than with reader enlightenment, which used to be their major concern. China, however, has, in recent years, been slower in its press reforms than has the European branch of the Communist world. In fact, it seems to have slowed down somewhat.

Third World mass communication has been making rapid technological advances, although the bloc is still behind in the organization of broadcast programs, especially television, which requires higher levels of skill and more capital than most Third World countries can muster.

The preoccupation of communication scholars interested in the Third World has been with the question of the area's dependence on "imperial centers" such as the United States. Many recent studies have dealt with the effect on Third World media of Western dominance. Questions have centered on whether Western media coverage has been balanced and accurate, and, indeed, whether Third World countries have been ignored by Western journalists. Scholars in Third World countries have largely focused on government–press relations in their countries.

4 WESTERN BLOC SYSTEMS

The issues affecting the communication process vary from country to country and region to region. We have chosen to divide the world's press and mass media into three main systems—the Western Bloc, the Soviet Bloc, and the nonaligned countries of the Third World. Since the issues are different in each of these regions, we have taken a slightly contrastive approach in each of the following chapters.

In the Western Bloc, the communication issues have not revolved much around government control, technological competencies, or interference from outside sources; rather, the main issue has been bias. Do freedom and advanced technology guarantee objectivity? The answer is of course not. To what extent, then, is bias preventing the Western Bloc public from getting the truth? What is bias doing to perceptions of reality? Is it possible to learn the truth from mass media? Or is there ever even a truth?

Western Bloc broadcasters, on any given day, seem to agree to a large extent on what is the important news of the day. But when they focus on news from Third World Countries apparently, the tend to focus on news about natural disasters. Americans are getting more international news than ever before, thanks largely to the new cable and satellite technologies. But is it news of consequence, and consequential to whom?

Some countries and some issues get more coverage and more favorable coverage in Western Bloc media than others. If you are Arab, you are very likely to regard Western coverage as biased in favor of Israel. If you are South African white, you are likely to regard Western coverage as biased in favor of nonwhites, so internal policies are changed to manipulate the coverage of Western journalists. If you are Chinese, you have witnessed an interesting change in American coverage of China as the relationship between America and China has developed. Which portrayal of China was real?

Western Bloc media are perceived as biased not only in their coverage of Soviet Bloc and Third World issues. When we turn the spotlight around and look at the way other Western nations view the United States, as we see in the case of Canada and Mexico, their biases about Americans are quite obvious to American observers.

Increasingly, we understand that all communication is biased. We are trapped in our own skins, our own cultures and social groupings. These condition every aspect of our sending and receiving messages. Journalists and mass communicators do not transcend this simple fact of life. They are just as guilty as all the rest of humanity.

WORLD NEWS COVERAGE OF U.S. AND INTERNATIONAL BROADCASTERS

KIM ANDREW ELLIOTT

We start with an analysis of the news which seven major western nations broadcast to the rest of the world. Although Kim Andrew Elliott surveyed these broadcasts to find out what Americans were hearing from other nations, his work also provides an index of the kinds of news that western governments feel they want to communicate across national boundaries.

At any moment of any day, hundreds of transmitters are sending radio programs across international boundaries. This is the activity of international broadcasting, conducted by some 100 countries, in more than 100 languages, with programs directed to all parts of the world.[1] North America is the target for international broadcasts in English from about 35 nations.[2] One recent study suggests that there are more than one million persons in the United States listening, at least occasionally, to foreign shortwave broadcasts.[3]

While many types of programming exist in international broadcasts, this brief study focuses on the world news coverage of international radio stations commonly audible in North America. Does the U.S. shortwave listener obtain significant additional world news coverage by tuning to foreign broadcasts as well as to domestic broadcast news sources? It was expected that world news of the various international broadcasters would be redundant but would provide breadth.

METHOD

Evening newscasts were monitored during the five-day period from February 11 through 15, 1980. U.S. domestic sources of news for comparison were taken from National Public Radio's "All Things Considered" and ABC Television's "World News Tonight." The foreign stations monitored were the BBC World Service, Radio Canada International, Deutsche Welle (West Germany), Swiss Radio International, and Radio Nederland. These stations were selected because they deliver consistently clear signals to North America and because they include world news in their broadcasts, as opposed to news limited to the station's own country or region. Radio Moscow was excluded because, following the communist journalistic tradition, it was expected to be more persuasive than informational. Monitoring was at 6 p.m. (NPR), 7 p.m. (ABC and BBC), 8 p.m. (Canada), 8:30 p.m. (West Germany), 8:45 p.m. (Switzerland), and 9:30 p.m. (Netherlands).

The unit of analysis is the *news item*. Not included is a comparison of time spent on each item or the content of the items. Of interest here is the *breadth* of news coverage provided by international radio.

FINDINGS

During the five days, the five international stations reported 55 world news items not covered by the two U.S. broadcast sources.

The *BBC World Service* is a 24-hour English-language service of information and entertainment directed to all parts of the world. It can be heard

Kim Andrew Elliot, "World News Coverage of U.S. and International Broadcasters." *Journalism Quarterly*, Volume 58, Autumn 1981, pp. 444–449. Reprinted by permission.

The author was assistant professor of communication studies at the University of Massachusetts, Amherst, when this article was written and is now director of research for the Voice of America.

Table 1   NEWS STORIES PRESENTED ON MONDAY, FEBRUARY 11

	NPR	ABC	BBC	RCI	DW	SRI	RN
1. Iran on hostages; U.S. response	X	X	X	X			X
2. Tito's condition	X		X	X		X	X
3. Mugabe assassination attempt	X		X	X		X	
4. Sentencing of former SS officers		X					X
5. Three Mile Island accident		X		X			X
6. Int'l Olympic Committee on Taiwan		X		X			
7. Discussion of Olympic site change		X		X		X	X
8. U.S. and Soviet clash at human rights conference			X			X	
9. Polish Congress and Economy			X			X	
10. Debate on West Bank			X			X	X
11. Thai Cabinet shakeup			X				
12. Afghanistan seeks Pakistan accord				X			
13. Greece and NATO					X		
14. EEC ministers on spending					X		
15. Iran internal fighting						X	
16. El Salvador developments						X	
17. Guatemala violence						X	
18. Northern Ireland bombings			*			X	
19. French conviction in toxic baby powder case						X	
20. Namibia fighting							X
21. Occupation of embassy in Peru							X

Covered in separate BBC program, "News About Britain"
NPR—National Public Radio (U.S.)
ABC—ABC-TV "World News Tonight"
BBC—British Broadcasting Corporation
RCI—Radio Canada International

DW—Deutsche Welle (German Federal Republic)
SRI—Swiss Radio International
RN—Radio Nederland

Table 2   NEWS STORIES PRESENTED ON TUESDAY, FEBRUARY 12

	NPR	ABC	BBC	RCI	DW	SRI	RN
1. Iran hostage developments	X	X	X	X			X
2. U.S. Gold Medal to Kenneth Taylor	X			X			
3. Olympic hockey begins	X	X					
4. Tito's health	X	X	X				
5. Lebanon fighting	X		X				
6. West Bank developments	X		X			X	
7. Khomeini speaks against Soviets		X					
8. U.S. troops to Persian Gulf		X		X	X		

Table 2 NEWS STORIES PRESENTED ON TUESDAY, FEBRUARY 12 (*Continued*)

	NPR	ABC	BBC	RCI	DW	SRI	RN
9. Carter press conference		x					
10. Afghanistan developments		x					
11. Gromyko in India		x	x	x		x	x
12. Olympic Site not to be changed		x	x	x		x	x
13. Three Mile Island developments		x					
14. Carter on nuclear waste		x					
15. Israel on Palestinian arms deal		x					
16. North-South Commission report		x			x	x	x
17. Iran internal fighting			x				x
18. Rhodesia campaign developments			x			x	
19. El Salvador developments			x			x	x
20. Taiwan Olympic team			x				
21. Human Rights Commission on Argentina						x	
22. Soviet diplomat dies							x

Table 3 NEWS STORIES PRESENTED ON WEDNESDAY, FEBRUARY 13

	NPR	ABC	BBC	RCI	DW	SRI	RN
1. Iran hostage developments	x	x	x	x		x	x
2. Carter/Kennedy on hostages	x	x	x				
3. Soviets suggest Afghanistan withdrawal	x						x
4. New group to aid Afghan refugees	x						
5. Opening of Winter Olympics		x	x	x		x	x
6. Taiwan athletes leave Lake Placid		x		x		x	
7. Soviets on IOC site decision		x		x			x
8. Tito's health		x	x	x		x	x
9. U.S. to rejoin I.L.O.		x		x	x		
10. Japan auto production		x					
11. Three Mile Island		x					
12. El Salvador developments		x	x	x		x	x
13. Gromyko talks in India			x			x	
14. Iran internal fighting			x				
15. Lebanon/Syria developments			x				
16. West Bank developments			x			x	
17. Rhodesia situation			x			x	x
18. Kenya base offer to U.S.			x				
19. Pakistan on Afghanistan relations					x		

Table 3	NEWS STORIES PRESENTED ON WEDNESDAY, FEBRUARY 13 (*Continued*)						
		NPR	ABC	BBC	RCI	DW	SRI	RN
20. U.S. asks U.N. Human Rights Commission to condemn Soviets on Afghanistan							x	
21. Egypt requests U.S. arms							x	
22. E.E.C. committee calls for fuel tax								x

Table 4	NEWS STORIES PRESENTED ON THURSDAY, FEBRUARY 14						
		NPR	ABC	BBC	RCI	DW	SRI	RN
1. Iran hostage developments		x	x	x	x		x	
2. Spain expels Aeroflot official		x			x		x	x
3. El Salvador developments		x		x			x	x
4. Gromyko leaves India			x	x				x
5. Rhodesia developments			x	x			x	x
6. Lebanon fighting			x		x			
7. Olympic events			x					
8. Violence in Turkey				x				x
9. Tito's health				x	x	x	x	x
10. Iran asks aid after flooding				x	x			x
11. I.O.C. on Moscow Olympic site					x			
12. U.S. decision on Summer Olympics					x			
13. West Bank developments					x			
14. Soviet ships barred from Australia						x		
15. UN Human Rights Commission on Soviets							x	
16. India on U.S. Navy in Indian Ocean							x	
17. Belgium/G.F.R. leaders meet on Afghanistan situation						x	x	

Table 5	NEWS STORIES PRESENTED ON FRIDAY, FEBRUARY 15						
		NPR	ABC	BBC	RCI	DW	SRI	RN
1. Iran hostage situation		x	x	x	x	x	x	x
2. Winter Olympics events		x	x		*	'		x
3. U.S./Europe on Soviet		x	x	x	x	x	x	x
4. U.S. secret aid to Afghan rebels		x						
5. Tito's health		x	x	x	x	x	x	x

Table 5 NEWS STORIES PRESENTED ON FRIDAY, FEBRUARY 15 (*Continued*)

	NPR	ABC	BBC	RCI	DW	SRI	RN
6. U.S. inflation	x	x				x	
7. Polish Prime Minister loses job		x	x	x	x	x	x
8. Rhodesia developments		x	x	x		x	x
9. More Soviet spies in Spain			x			x	x
10. Plot in Greece to blow up U.S. embassy			x				x
11. Turkish violence			x				x
12. Fire in Thai refugee camp			x	x			
13. Red Cross flood aid to Iran			x				
14. Iran protests on Canada				x			
15. British inflation	x		**	x			
16. El Salvador developments						x	x
17. Lebanon fighting						x	
18. U.S. on possible Persian Gulf actions							
19. Schmidt on attempt to divide U.S./Europe					x	x	
20. Swedes and Swiss criticized by Soviet Union on arms exports						x	
21. British abortion bill			**				x
22. Catholic theologian Kuhn wants new hearing							x

*Covered in special RCI program on Winter Olympics
**Covered in the BBC's "News About Britain"

most of the day and night in North America, with reception quality enhanced by relay transmitters located in the Caribbean, South Atlantic, Canada and the United States itself. Eight-minute world news summaries are presented 17 times per day, with numerous other informational features throughout the day. During the five-day period, the BBC provided 25 news items not covered by the two U.S. sources. Examples are coverage of the Polish Communist Party Congress (Feb. 11), regional fighting in Iran (February 12), disruptions in El Salvador (Feb. 12) and a plot in Greece to blow up the U.S. embassy (Feb. 15).

Because shortwave listeners interested in world news are likely to tune to the BBC because of 1) its reputation for news, 2) convenience of schedule and quality of lead-in programming, and 3) clarity of signal, the remaining four stations will be compared to U.S. coverage and to the BBC coverage. Do they

present additional world news worth returning from the BBC to meet their less convenient schedules?

Radio Canada International has a daily half-hour English broadcast to the Americas. During the five days, RCI provided six items not covered by the U.S. networks, seven items not included in the BBC newscasts and six items mentioned in neither the BBC nor U.S. broadcasts. This coverage included a report of Afghanistan seeking to normalize relations with Pakistan and two items concerning the Olympic Games.

Deutsche Welle, the West German international station, has a daily 20-minute English broadcast for North America. The station emphasizes news about Germany. However, some items not concerning Germany are included, usually at the end of the newscasts, suggesting their function as a time "pad." Deutsche Welle sent six items not covered by the U.S. sources, seven not on the BBC and six not included by either the U.S. or British sources. Two of these stories had some German connection. Another exclusively covered item reported on negotiations with Greece to bring that country back into the NATO integrated military structure.

Swiss Radio International has a daily half hour in English. During the period of analysis, this station covered 26 items not mentioned by the U.S. sources, 21 not included in the BBC newscasts and 15 not on either the BBC or U.S. networks. The unique items included three on Latin American affairs and two on matters concerning the U.N. Human Rights Commission.

Radio Nederland has a 55-minute daily English broadcast to North America beginning with a world news summary. The Dutch station provided 18 items not contained in the two U.S. newscasts, 16 not on the BBC and 8 not included in the combined NPR/ABC/BBC newscasts. News updating may explain some of this. Radio Nederland was the last station to be monitored each evening. A unique item was a report of a Common Market committee's call for a fuel tax in Europe.

DISCUSSION

It appears that international broadcast listening would indeed widen the scope of the U.S. listener's awareness of international events. An average of 11 world news items per day, in addition to domestic news, were offered exclusively by the various international stations. This may be important in many parts of the United States with limited access to such elite newspapers as the *New York Times*. However, there may be little incentive to tune beyond the BBC, whose most formidable news competitor, Swiss Radio International, averaged only three items per day not heard by those who had already listened to NPR, ABC, and BBC newscasts.

For all the importance attached to international broadcasts, international radio listening is basically a *leisure* activity, and the international radio listener's appetite for world news, background reports, analyses, and commentaries should be considered finite. The frequent, easily-heard newscasts of the BBC and the Voice of America probably greatly diminish the utility of the international news coverage of other stations for listeners in many parts of he

world to non-English as well as English broadcasts,[4] especially if their objective is comprehensiveness of coverage.

A possible alternative for the "welterweight" international broadcast station is to emphasize news of their respective countries or regions. This is already being done by such stations as Radio Finland, Israel Radio, and Radio Australia. Third world nations have opportunities here to counter imbalance in news flow between industrialized and developing countries by bringing news of Africa, Asia, and Latin America to the many shortwave listeners in North America, Europe, and Japan. Another alternative is more human-interest and entertainment features, designed to attract and retain listener attention by catering to the "armchair traveler" motive for tuning in shortwave broadcasts.

How would such lighter programming benefit the government sponsoring the international broadcast? First, the alternative programming might attract and retain listener attention for brief segments of information or commentary, thus in the long term accomplishing a useful information mission. Second, the programming may increase the listener's interest in and attraction toward the broadcasting country, with positive effects on trade and tourism, as well as more long-term affective outcomes.

NOTES

1. See summary of world's international broadcasting activity in J.M. Frost, ed., *World Radio TV Handbook* (New York: Billboard Publications, 1980).
2. *Popular Electronics*, four times each year, carries a schedule of English-language shortwave broadcasts audible in North America. For a discussion of the news contained in these broadcasts, see Glenn Hauser, "A World of News," *Popular Electronics*, January 1980, p. 84.
3. Radio Canada International, "Short-Wave Listening in the United States," Unpublished results of Gallup Poll, April 1975.
4. Audience research conducted by the U.S. International Communication Agency, and its predecessor, indicates that in most areas of the world, BBC is first and VOA is second in numbers of listeners, with the other stations trailing. See for example USICA's report, *International Radio Listening in Urban India*, R-18-78, August 1978.

WHOSE LIVES COUNT? TV COVERAGE OF NATURAL DISASTERS

WILLIAM C. ADAMS

William C. Adams tests geographical bias in American television's international news coverage by looking at the way TV treats natural disasters. His study helps show how U.S. media prioritize the rest of the world.

How do the U.S. news media prioritize the rest of the world? Recent research on television news has helped describe the way countries and regions are treated (e.g., 1, 2, 7, 9, 19). Larson (9), for example, calculated detailed country-by-country coverage by ABC, CBS, and NBC each year from 1972 through 1981. But describing patterns in international coverage is far easier than explaining the factors that produced that coverage; describing is also easier than critiquing the content. The academic literature and the New World Information Order debate are filled with arguments over the causes and merits of U.S. television's apportionment of attention to various countries and various issues (e.g., 7, 19). It is popular, for example, to call for more in-depth coverage of the Third World, but at which countries' expense should such coverage come? Ultimately, the television news agenda, in terms of relative attention, is a zero-sum game. If Ghana and Peru are to receive more coverage, then France or the Soviet Union and some other objects of news attention must receive proportionately less.

Much of the analytical quagmire derives from the difficulty in defining news on a uniform standard. (Is an economic crisis in France more "important and consequential" to the world than one in Ghana? Are all coups equally significant?) What can be said about content data apart from assertions of personal preferences and apart from comparisons with other content data?

Rosengren (14; see also 15) has argued that, where possible, research should begin with "extra-media data" in order to "establish a universe of events, and this universe of events, rather than the universe of news reported during a given time period, provides the starting point for the investigation." Rosengren then advocates using extra-media data in regression analyses to determine what proportion of the variation in media coverage can be explained by various factors. Although this approach is not without problems—extra-media data and ideal measures of explanatory factors are often difficult to secure—Rosengren makes an important contribution to addressing some of the comparative and explanatory issues that pervade studies of media content.

Earthquakes, hurricanes, and floods all strike and kill ordinary people. An appropriate measure of the severity of the disaster is the total number of people who lost their lives. The initial hypothesis to be tested is that the amount of attention U.S. television news devotes to a natural disaster reflects the magnitude of that disaster. Is it true, as Sreberny-Mohammadi (18) wrote, that "coups and catastrophes [are] newsworthy wherever they occur"? Or does the locale of the catastrophe make all the difference in the world? A commonly used formulation raises these questions in a dramatic way: "A hundred Pakistanis going off a mountain in a bus makes less of a story than three Englishmen drowning in the Thames" (13); "One dead fireman in Brooklyn is worth five English bobbies, who are worth 50

William C. Adams, "Whose Lives Count? TV Coverage of Natural Disasters." From the *Journal of Communication*, Volume 36, Number 2, Spring 1986, pp. 113–122. © 1986, *The Journal of Communication*. Reprinted by permission.

The author is professor of public administration at George Washington University.

Arabs, who are worth 500 Africans'' (5); ''One thousand wogs, fifty frogs, and one Briton'' (17). To what degree are these cynical ratios accurate?

If the magnitudes of these tragedies, as measured in number of dead, do not correlate with their prominence on U.S. television, then it will be useful to go to Rosengren's second step, estimating the explanatory power that can be attributed to other factors in the treatment of these events.

From January 1972 through June 1985, according to *World Almanac 1986* (11, pp. 688–689), 35 major natural disasters occurred that each took the lives of at least 300 people. These 35 disasters included 17 major earthquakes, the most devastating of which killed 800,000 people in Tangshan, China, in July of 1976. In this same 13.5-year period, there were 11 major tidal waves and floods, the most severe in Morvi, India, where an estimated 10,000 people died. Seven major cyclones, typhoons, hurricanes, and monsoons were also recorded; the most damaging was the cyclone that struck Bangladesh in May of 1985 and killed 10,000 people.

U.S. television's attention to these events was measured with the use of the Vanderbilt *TV News Index and Abstracts*. A period of one month after each natural disaster was examined to discover exactly how much time each network devoted to news about each locale. All coverage of all 35 major natural disasters was calculated for ''ABC World News Tonight,'' ''CBS Evening News,'' and ''NBC Nightly News''—the flagship network newscasts with audiences far surpassing those of all other network news efforts. Intercoder reliability among the four coders, measured as percent agreement, was 98 percent.

In measuring the severity of the natural disasters, it was tempting to use the total number of lives lost (as recorded in the *World Almanac*). However, these official figures are usually announced many days or weeks after the early tentative reports to which broadcast journalists must respond. So the best measures of the perceived magnitude of the tragedies are the preliminary reports from the region. Initial estimates of lives lost in each disaster were drawn from the wire services and other reports in the *New York Times* and *Washington Post* as well as early network stories; after each episode, the highest estimate quoted within the first three days was selected.

Had the starting point of the analysis been television news, a few of these events would have been missed entirely because they were totally ignored on nightly newscasts; others were given so little news time they might well have been overlooked in any search. By beginning instead with extra-media data on disaster deaths, a more thorough examination was possible. Substituting the preliminary death estimates for the subsequent official figures then corrects for the information available at the time. As expected, the amount of newscast time devoted to each disaster correlates more with the early estimates than with the official figures, although both associations turned out to be weak.

Coverage priorities on all three networks were highly similar. Correlations for the volume of coverage each network gave the 35 disasters all exceeded .80: ABC and CBS, .94; ABC and NBC, .84; CBS and NBC, .83. In very few instances did one network focus on a story that the others ignored. This strong comparability made it reasonable to merge all three networks into a ''mean TV'' variable. The composite TV variable had a correlation of .97 with ABC, .96 with CBS, and .94 with NBC and is used for the rest of the analyses.

Overall, attention paid by TV shows no relationship to disaster severity. The r^2 correlation for estimated natural disaster deaths and the corresponding volume of television news coverage is .03. One might expect that tragedies causing 10,000 or 25,000 deaths would attract and deserve more attention than those causing 300 or 1,000. Yet the estimated loss of life statistically explains only three percent of the variation in the amount of coverage disasters were given on nightly network newscasts.

Six major earthquakes rocked the globe in 1976—Guatemala in February, Italy in May, Indonesia in June and July, China in July, the Philippines in August, and Turkey in November. Table 1 shows the sizable differences in the magnitudes of each tragedy, ranging from about 800,000 deaths in China and 23,000 in Guatemala to less than 1,000 in Italy. The table also shows curious discrepancies in coverage.

Earthquake coverage in 1976 reflects the disparities in television coverage of natural disasters found throughout this period. Contrast, for example, coverage for the earthquakes in Turkey and in the

Table 1   COVERAGE OF EARTHQUAKES IN SIX COUNTRIES, 1976

	Early Est. Deaths	Mean Network TV News Time	TV Minutes per Est. 1,000 Deaths	Later "Official" Deaths
Italy	1,000	7.6 min.	7.60	946
Guatemala	5,200	12.5 min.	2.40	22,778
Turkey	3,000	7.2 min.	2.38	4,000
Philippines	3,130	2.9 min.	.93	8,000
China	100,000	8.5 min.	.09	800,000
Indonesia	9,000	0.3 min.	.04	943

Philippines. Originally, the disaster in the Philippines was thought to be as severe as the one in Turkey, but it received less than half as much coverage. Guatemala experienced one of the worst earthquakes in this century in the Western hemisphere. Yet, proportionate to the number of victims, it received one-third of the coverage given the Italian earthquake.

Asian countries received the shortest shrift, with the Phillipines, China, and Indonesia given the least attention. The disaster in the Philippines caused eight times as many deaths as the one in Italy, but it received less than half as much coverage. And the earthquake in Indonesia was initially announced by the networks to have killed 9,000 people—nine times as many as the one in Italy—but Indonesia's losses received about 20 seconds of airtime (on a single night), compared with those of Italy, which received coverage for more than a week (typically including four nights of major—1.5- to 2.5-minutes—stories).

The greatest outlier of all was the Tangshan quake of 1976, which caused the greatest loss of life of any natural disaster in the twentieth century. For example, the number of dead—800,000—was 160 times greater than the 5,000 people killed in the Italian earthquake of 1980. Even using the very early estimate of 100,000 dead, the Tangshan quake was worse than all other recent earthquakes (1972–1985) combined.

The enormous scope of the disaster contrasts sharply with its failure to register on the world's consciousness. China's near-total embargo on news during this period led to average U.S. network evening newscast airtime of less than 9 minutes devoted to the earthquake and subsequent flooding. The disparity between casualties and coverage is so enormous that the Chinese data skew the statistics and are excluded from the balance of the data analysis.

One other natural disaster—1979's Hurricane David—is also excluded from subsequent data analysis, but for a different reason. Available resources did not make it feasible to disentangle coverage about the hurricane's approach and landfall in the United States from coverage about its rampage in the Caribbean, where most of its real victims resided.

If all Chinese and Hurricane David cases are excluded, there are still 30 major natural disasters to examine in more detail. Excluding these outliers, the r^2 correlation between estimated disaster deaths and TV coverage increases only from .03 to .08.

Massive loss of life is so difficult to fathom that there may be some sort of automatic psychological logarithm at work. An earthquake with 20,000 deaths may not be comprehended as ten times worse or as meriting ten times more coverage than one with 2,000 deaths. If that is so, then the logarithm of estimated disaster deaths may correlate better with TV coverage than does the raw number believed dead. And, in fact, the log of estimated disaster deaths does produce a modest increase, raising the r^2 from .08 to .18, but this still explains less than one-eighth of the variation in nightly network news attention.

Table 2 shows the broad pattern in coverage. Western Europe (Italy) is indisputably on top. Eastern Europe (Romania) is a distant second and Latin

Table 2   NATURAL DISASTER COVERAGE BY REGION

	TV Minutes per Est. 1,000 Deaths	Coefficient of Relative Variation[a]	Number of Major Natural Disasters	TV Minutes per Official 1,000 Deaths
Western Europe	9.20	.28	2	6.72
Eastern Europe	3.60	—	1	2.53
Latin America	1.02	1.24	7	.92
Middle East	.87	.74	7	.83
Asia	.76	.96	13	.63

[a]Standard deviation/mean.

America (Brazil, Colombia, Guatemala, Honduras, Nicaragua, Peru) a distant third. The least relative news time is given to the Middle East (Turkey, Algeria, Yemen, Iran) and to Asia (Bangladesh, India, Pakistan, Indonesia, the Philippines). Were we to set up an equation of relative coverage using our data, the death of 1 Italian would equal those of 3 Romanians, 9 Latin Americans, 11 Middle Easterners, and 12 Asians.

Regional differences are not entirely definitive, however; the standard deviations suggest some lack of uniformity within regions. Especially in the case of Latin America, the coefficient of relative variation (CRV = standard deviation/mean) indicates that the mean masks considerable variation in television's treatment of disasters in that area.

U.S. evening newscasts allocate more newscast attention to human death in some parts of the world than in others. Factors other than the actual magnitude or even rough order of magnitude of the tragedy must influence broadcast journalists' decisions on how to apportion coverage. What other factors help predict these patterns?

Epstein (6) has stressed the importance of factors such as logistics and the organizational imperative of dramatic stories that will appeal to a broad U.S. audience. Lichter and Rothman (10) have emphasized the role of journalists' personal world views. Paletz and Entman (12) and others have weighted heavily the power of the government and capitalist elites to sway media coverage. Walter Cronkite and other journalists of the "that's the way it is" school have maintained that the news simply reflects events. Graber (8), Roscho (16), and others have

suggested that television news echoes society's general cultural norms and dominant values.

For the multiple regression equations, these factors were operationalized in a variety of ways. The severity of "actual events" was operationalized with three different variables: the number of estimated disaster deaths, the logarithm of estimated deaths, and the later "official" number of deaths. Measures of the objective significance of the "event's country context" were the population of the country in which the natural disaster occurred, the gross national product of the country, and the gross national product per capita (24). Sympathies of the U.S. government and power elites were calibrated with four indicators: The extent to which countries vote with the United States in the United Nations' General Assembly (3); the amount of foreign aid and credit granted by the Untied States (23); the amount of U.S. exports (23); and exports per capita (23).

Social and cultural affinities of leading journalists and U.S. citizens at large were gauged in three different ways: the number of U.S. tourists to each country (21); the number of Americans who identify their ancestors (or parents or themselves) as coming from each country (22); and the proportion of leading journalists with ethnicity in common with each country (10).

The networks' penchant for drama was partially measured by creating dummy variables for each type of disaster (e.g., earthquakes vs. floods, vs. cyclones) and by coding each country's share of international news time during the two years preceding the disaster. The latter variable was an effort to capture any effects from "continuing saga" coverage (whereby a country already in the news would have an established priority). The logistical, and perhaps psychological, impact of geographical proximity was estimated by the variable of miles from New York City to the capital of each country. One final important organizational factor—the competition of other events for the finite "newshole"—was not amenable to a convenient measurement and will be discussed below.

Following Rosengren, the next task is to see how much of the total variation these independent variables explain. Accordingly, all 16 variables were entered in a multiple regression equation to try to predict the amount of newscast time devoted to each major natural disaster. Three of these 16 variables stood out, together explaining 61 percent of all variation in coverage. The other variables could all together explain only an additional nine percent of the variation. (Thirty percent of the variation in coverage remained unexplained.)

These three most potent factors were (a) number of U.S. tourists (i.e., cultural proximity and social interest), (b) logarithm of estimated disaster deaths (i.e., severity of the news event, modified by a logarithmic scale), and (c) distance from New York City (i.e., geographical proximity). As long as these three variables were in an equation, no other variables came close to absorbing more than three percent of the variation. These three independent variables were entered as the sole predictors in a multiple regression equation used to calculate the unique variation explained by each one.

Their independent contributions to the total explained variation can be partitioned using the coefficient of partial determination, which "measures the proportion of variation in the dependent variable that is explained by each independent variable while controlling for, or holding constant, the other independent variable(s)" (4, p. 280). The coefficient of partial determination for U.S. tourists is .331; for the logarithm of estimated deaths, .201; and for distance from New York City, .047. Since these variables are highly orthogonal to one another, most of the explained variation is unique rather than overlapping explained variation (.032).

Rosenblum (13) sees tourism as emblematic of ethnic and cultural affinity. In discussing why an earthquake in Italy gets more coverage than one in Guatemala, he notes:

> [It occurs] partially because Italy is easier to cover than Guatemala, and more reporters are immediately available. But it is mainly because Italians are seen as individuals, with physical and cultural characteristics familiar to Americans. Many editors and readers have been to Italy, and they recognize place names in the stories. Guatemalans are seen, on the other hand, only as faceless residents of the underdeveloped world.

Note that tourism had a correlation (r) of .84 with U.S. exports; .91 with the ethnic ancestry of elite journalists; and .66 with the ancestry of the U.S. public. This further suggests that the tourism variable is a reasonable and convenient surrogate for the sociocultural affinity of the United States for other countries.

In the equation, the tourism figure is calculated in a way that at least technically controls for "distance from New York." Geographical proximity explained one-twentieth of the variation in coverage, independent of the magnitude of the disaster and the social proximity (tourism). And, not to overlook "reality," logarithms of the preliminary numbers of deaths uniquely explained another 20 percent of the variation.

What about the remaining variation that is left statistically unexplained? One strong candidate to account for the balance is one for which no suitable measure was found to incorporate into the multiple regression equations—the newshole of competing stories. It is axiomatic that a story's rank on the news agenda depends on what else is happening in the world at the same time. Could competing stories account for much of the unexplained variation in disaster coverage?

One way to investigate this matter is to select those instances that are most poorly predicted by the three-variable multiple regression equation. Inspection of the residuals revealed three cases at or beyond two standard deviations. Those cases were the Nicaraguan earthquake in 1972 and the Italian earthquake in 1980—both of which received substantially more coverage than the regression equation predicted—and the Italian earthquake of 1976, which received less coverage than predicted by tourism, distance, and lives lost.

The Nicaraguan earthquake's unusually high degree of airtime in December 1972 may be attributed to three factors: (a) Roberto Clemente, a popular baseball player for the Pittsburgh Pirates, was killed in a plane crash as he was taking part in a relief effort to aid his native land; (b) the earthquake occurred December 23, and much of the story emerged during the period between Christmas and New Year's Day, traditionally considered a slow news week; and (c) other top stories were almost all ongoing stories about the continuing anti-war efforts in the United States.

The Italian earthquake occurred on November 23, 1980, after the presidential race was over. It clustered nicely with a "disaster array" that included news about a big Las Vegas hotel fire, a Reno hotel fire, and California brush fires, with the brief counterpoint of a small tremor in western Nevada. These stories would appear to bolster rather than minimize events in Italy. Without dramatic developments in the Iranian hostage crisis, Italy was well situated to compete for air time.

In contrast, another Italian earthquake was given much less coverage than tourism, distance, and deaths predicted was its due after May 6, 1976. At that time, the competition was substantial: the unusual challenge of Ronald Reagan to the renomination of President Gerald Ford as well as various last-ditch efforts to stop Jimmy Carter from locking up the Democratic nomination, amid assorted primaries and caucuses held during this period.

Retrospective searches do run the risk of mistakenly confirming the researcher's presumptions. Nonetheless, these three cases lend plausible support for the notion that newshole competition can account for much of the otherwise unexplained variation in the way these 30 natural disasters were treated.

One widely voiced complaint has been that far too much of the coverage of the Third World consists of natural disaster stories (although Stevenson and Cole [19, p. 59] "could find no evidence that more attention was paid to this category of news in the Third World than in any other part of the globe"). The present research has concluded, however, that earthquakes, typhoons, and floods in the Third World, given their severity, have received proportionately little attention.

Stevenson and Gaddy (20), who argued that coverage of the Third World was somewhat heavy with negative and conflictual stories because there was more actual conflict in the Third World, speculated that a count of "the coups and earthquakes around the world" would yield "results comparable to the data we have presented here: violence and conflict get reported pretty much the same way wherever they occur." This research suggests that this is not the case, however. Where earthquakes occur makes a great deal of difference. The severity of natural disasters alone explains little (less than one-tenth) of the variation in their coverage on nightly U.S. newscasts. A little more (about one-fifth) of the variation in news attention can be explained using logarithms of estimated disaster deaths. Overall, the globe is prioritized so that the death of one Western European equaled three Eastern Europeans equaled 9 Latin Americans equaled 11 Middle Easterners equaled 12 Asians.

REFERENCES

1. Adams, William C. (Ed.) *Television Coverage of the Middle East.* Norwood, N.J.: Ablex, 1981.
2. Adams, William C. (Ed.) *Television Coverage of International Affairs.* Norwood, N.J.: Ablex, 1982.
3. Anti-Defamation League, B'nai B'rith. "Keeping Score at the U.N." New York, 1980–1982.
4. Berenson, Mark, David Levine, and Matthew Goldstein. *Intermediate Statistical Methods* and *Applications.* Englewood Cliffs, N.J.: Prentice-Hall, 1983.
5. Boyer, Peter. "Famine in Ethiopia." *Washington Journalism Review* 7, January 1985, pp. 18–21.
6. Epstein, Edward Jay. *News from Nowhere.* New York: Vintage, 1974.
7. Gerbner, George and Marsha Siefert (Eds.) *World Communication.* New York: Longman, 1984.
8. Graber, Doris. *Mass Media and American Politics.* Washington: Congressional Quarterly Press, 1980.
9. Larson, James. *Television's Window on the World.* Norwood, N.J.: Ablex, 1984.
10. Lichter, S. Robert, Stanley Rothman, and Linda S. Lichter. *The Media Elite.* Washington, D.C.: Adler & Adler, 1986.

11. Newspaper Enterprise Association. *The World Almanac*: 1986. New York: NEA, 1985.

12. Paletz, David and Robert Entman. *Media Power Politics*. New York: Free Press, 1981.

13. Rosenblum, Mort. *Coups & Earthquakes*. New York: Harper & Row, 1981.

14. Rosengren, Karl Erik. "Four Types of Tables." *Journal of Communication* 27(1), Winter 1977, pp. 67–75.

15. Rosengren, Karl Erik. "International News: Methods, Data and Theory." *Journal of Peace Research* 11, 1974, pp. 145–156.

16. Roscho, Bernard. *Newsmaking*. Chicago: University of Chicago Press, 1975.

17. Schlesinger, Philip. *Putting "Reality" Together*. London: Constable, 1978.

18. Sreberny-Mohammadi, Annabelle. "Results of International Cooperation." *Journal of Communication* 34(1), Winter 1984, pp. 121–134.

19. Stevenson, Robert and Richard Cole. "Patterns of Foreign News." In Robert Stevenson and Richard Cole (Eds.) *Foreign News and the New World Information Order*. Ames: Iowa State University Press, 1984, pp. 37–62.

20. Stevenson, Robert and Gary Gaddy. " 'Bad News' and the Third World." In Robert Stevenson and Richard Cole (Eds.) *Foreign News and the New World Information Order*. Ames: Iowa State University Press, 1984, pp. 88–97.

21. United Nations. *1982 Statistical Yearbook*. New York: United Nations, 1985.

22. U.S. Bureau of the Census. *Ancestry of the Population*, 1980. Washington, D.C.: U.S. Bureau of the Census, 1983.

23. U.S. Bureau of the Census. *Statistical Abstracts of the United States: 1986*. Washington, D.C.: Bureau of the Census, 1985.

24. World Bank. *1983 World Bank Atlas*. Washington, D.C.: World Bank, 1983.

THE DEVELOPING STORY OF CABLE'S INTERNATIONAL NEWS COVERAGE

DON FLOURNOY

Don Flournoy describes the growing international reach of American television as a result of Cable Network News, now covering the world for American cable viewers more thoroughly than wireless television has ever done before.

Most of you probably missed it—*CNN World Report* on Monday Oct. 26, 1987, midnight to 2 a.m. EST.

I know that I would have, except that I was flat on my back in the hospital recovering from a lumbar laminectomy (disk surgery) and wide awake from a pain killer intended to help me sleep.

What I caught quite by accident was the inauguration of one of Ted Turner's new international newscasts, without a doubt the most striking assortment of news items I have ever seen strung together. What made it unique was that it consisted of a two-hour package of "unedited and uncensored" local news from around the world reported by native news anchors.

I counted at least 30 countries contributing mate-

Don Flournoy, "The Developing Story of Cable's International News Coverage." Reprinted with permission from February 22, 1988 issue of *Broadcasting* magazine.

The author is an associate professor at the School of Telecommunications, Ohio University, Athens.

rial, all of it collected, packaged and redistributed out of Atlanta. I was getting it in Columbus, Ohio, about the same time it was being distributed across six continents.

There were news items from Zimbabwe, Thailand, Venezuela, Poland, Guam, Grenada, Switzerland, Portugal and Cyprus—places you only hear about if there is some disaster, an attempted coup, an earthquake or a terrorist bomb.

Some of it was indeed that kind of news. Nepal sent news of its latest flood; a water contamination problem was offered from Puerto Rico. Both of these were covered, in English, by local reporters.

There were also items more closely resembling the kind of news you often see when you are in a Third World country—"development communication" news—such as the opening of the new airport in Brunei; a fish breeding operation in Czechoslovakia; celebration of commonwealth status for Guam, and a procession of royal barges on a river in Thailand.

To accomplish this feat, CNN has gone a big step beyond regional satellite news exchange. This is not just a matter of local stations collecting and contributing the news they deem worthy of wider distribution to a national network. Nor is it a parallel and competitive service to the regional services of neighboring states, such as Intersputnik, Eurovision and Asiavison, which operate within geographic and political borders. It is the first truly planetary newscast to which any country in any part of the globe is free to contribute and free to use as it will.

I am one who likes to see the other side of the news. When I go abroad I like to find out where that country's news comes from, whether its people get the same news I do at home, and observe whether the news editors take the same or a different view of that news. I like to see what types of news they give priority to and note how they handle it.

The *CNN World Report* doesn't appear to be a true test of that. That is, it isn't really the evening news as you would see it on TV sets abroad. It's in English, and it is abbreviated news in the Western tradition. In the U.S. we are used to seeing "all the news that is fit to broadcast" whittled down to bitesized pieces of two minutes or less. In the developing world, especially, news items are more leisurely presented. Time pressures are less intense. But the story is more fully developed.

On the following Monday morning I wasn't up to view the second newscast, nor was I there for the third or the fourth. I did arrange to have each event taped and I did make a commitment to myself to view them all. As that goes, it wasn't until the fifth week that I found the two hours to sit down with the Nov. 23 tape.

What was it like? There were 38 news items from 28 countries. CNN contributed the most. Their five items covered the Iran-Contra report, U. S. budget deficit, Denver plane crash, tornadoes in Texas and the return of the aircraft carrier, Saratoga. The USSR contributed three items: icy temperatures in the USSR, a new technique in heart surgery and a rally in Latvia against U.S. interference in Soviet internal affairs. All the other countries sent single items.

I estimate that half of the contributions were human interest stories. A skateboard contest in Czechoslovakia, the dropping of rural rail services in Finland, tattooing of tribal chiefs in American Samoa, wheelchair sports for the disabled in Zimbabwe, the split between Swiss Catholics and Rome, and the deterioration of Australia's celebrated opera house in Sydney were the types of stories offered.

Hard news, which represented a quarter or fewer of the total items contributed, consisted of reports on kidnappings, assassinations and other violent acts in Spain, Argentina, San Salvador and Colombia; South African military operations in Southern Angola and the fire in Kings Cross tube station in London.

Most of the remaining items (using a classification system that is admittedly a little fuzzy) were political. That is, they told the story of an upcoming economic referendum in Poland, pre-election maneuverings in Haiti, the visit of the Spanish President to Uruguay, reduction of the Brazilian President's term of office from six to four years, House Speaker Jim Wright's peace efforts in Nicaragua, confiscation of illegal firearms in Hong Kong and the Latvian piece from the USSR.

Actually, very few of the items were blatantly promotional. I would have expected more. In the opening newscast, Colombia had given a self-congratulatory piece and Aruba had contributed what appeared to be old tourism footage. In the fourth newscast, St. Lucia's story on its new duty-free shopping center, United Nations TV's story on the UN Children's Fund and Costa Rica's interview with its President Arias came across to me as borderline promotional.

When I got home from the hospital, I called Stuart Loory, the producer, to congratulate him. He told me CNN now has signed agreements with 87 countries and is working on others. Money is not changing hands, since each country is responsible for its own uplink and downlink costs, and Comsat, Intelsat and the Armed Forces Satellite Network are all contributing connect time. Copyright is not at issue. He is uncertain how many countries are using the material. He knows that some countries are using the whole two hours, some may be using no more than a few minutes, if at all.

Why is it that I haven't read anything about *World Report*? Here it is February and nobody is talking about what I thought was the biggest breakthrough in international news flow, ever. I know that I am not typical of the American viewing public and certainly can't predict how the rest of the world will react to anything, but are my interests that unrepresentative? Maybe everybody up at that time of the morning is watching Letterman and we haven't yet got the mail from abroad. At this point, it appears the introduction of our first planet-wide news program is a nonnews story.

ARAB VS. ISRAELI NEWS COVERAGE IN THE *NEW YORK TIMES*, 1976 AND 1984

Deborah A. Barranco and Leonard Shyles

Bias in American coverage of the Middle East is suggested in this study of *New York Times* treatment of Israeli and Arab news. They determine this by comparing the amount of coverage given to Israel and Israelis with the amount of coverage given to Arabs and Arab countries in headlines.

No region in the world is as volatile, as strategically important . . . as the Middle East. From the Arab oil embargo [and] the murder of U.S. marines in Beirut, [to] the Iranian hostage crisis . . . recent events have underscored the growing American dependence on and involvement in, this complex and confounding region.[1]

Since Ze'ev Chafet's observations, American-targeted terrorist activities, including the murder of an American Jew upon the ill-fated Achille Lauro, the hijacking of TWA Flight 847, and the bombing of a West Berlin night club frequented by American military personnel, have brought Mideast turbulence and frustrations closer to home.

As a leading superpower, the United States has the potential and the responsibility to help promote peace in the region. But before one can begin to understand the causes of Mideast hostilities, a balanced view of the Middle East is essential.

As James Abourezk has noted, ''The unfortunate

Deborah A. Barranco and Leonard Shyles, ''Arab vs. Israeli News Coverage in the *New York Times*, 1976–1984.'' *Journalism Quarterly*, Volume 65, Number 1, Spring 1988, pp. 178–181. Reprinted by permission.

Deborah A. Barranco was, at the time the article was written, a master's student and Leonard Shyles a faculty member in the Department of Communication Arts and Theatre at the University of Maryland.

fact is that the vision most Americans hold of the Mideast situation has been badly blurred since 1948 by [an] imbalanced presentation in the American media.''[2] According to Ze'ev Chafets:

> The Middle East is an area that produces a great deal of news—but very little real information. . . . A national debate on the wisdom of American involvement and the parameters of American policy in the Middle East depends upon the flow of reliable, comprehensive and balanced information from the area. It is the job of the American press to provide that information . . . anything less will distort America's view of the region.[3]

Daniel Pipes contends that deliberate bias is rare compared to the prime source of misinformation about the Mideast, which is an American journalistic tendency to focus the majority of news reports on but two Mideast topics: Israel and American Mideast involvement.[4] All associated events and persons ordinarily capture prominent coverage, not only in the American news agenda, but world-wide, as the same stories are disseminated internationally. Subsequently, unrelated Mideast news escapes with minimal or no mention. Some experts believe the amount of news coverage devoted to Israel, in comparison to other Mideast nations may be over-emphasized; some believe such over-emphasis prevents clear understanding of important issues. For example, from 1972 to 1980, the three major U.S. television networks devoted an average of 98.4 minutes per year to Israel, 54.7 to Egypt, 42.4 to the Palestinian Liberation Organization (PLO), and to all of Syria, Lebanon, Saudi Arabia, Jordan and Iraq combined—a mere total of 72.5 minutes annually, compared to an average of 152.7 minutes of TV news devoted to the U.S. in the Mideast.[5]

Similarly, Richard Hofstetter's *Bias in the News*, finds an effect which he labels ''aggrandizement of values,'' and he distinguishes this from outright ''lying'' or ''distortion'' by the press.[6] He concludes that ''ideological commitment probably accounts for most television newscasts that have created charges of bias in recent years.''[7] The disproportionate amount of coverage accorded to Israel may be symptomatic of a special interest taken in Israel by the American press, and may be due to an ''aggrandizement'' of values.

But whose values?—those of the American press, or more generally the public? Because Israel is culturally, politically and ideologically closer to the U.S. than other Mideast nations, and because she is our major ally in a key region, it is predictable that Americans would find news concerning Israel and the U.S. to be of greater interest. What danger, therefore occurs when a narrow focus on but two players in an arena of more than 20 threatens to impair the world view and comprehension of vital developments in the Mideast? The problem may run deeper yet: for the way the American press covers the Mideast may influence public opinion formation,[8] and therefore Washington's policies.[9]

For these reasons, this study evaluates the accuracy of the claims of contemporary critics of Mideast journalism practice. Specifically, it is the purpose of this research to determine if ''aggrandizement'' bias exists in *New York Times* Mideast press coverage; that is: are Israeli and American issues, events and leaders more salient than are those issues, events and leaders of the following ten prominent Arab nations: Egypt, Syria, Libya, Iraq, Saudi Arabia, Lebanon, Palestine/PLO, Sudan, Jordan and Kuwait. For this study, analysis was limited to articles appearing in the *New York Times* for two time spans (May 3, 1976 to November 3, 1976 and January 21, 1984–July 21, 1984). The *New York Times* was selected because it is considered to be the ''newspaper of record'' and because it may be viewed as one of the major vehicles of the American prestige press.

METHOD

To determine whether the subtle news bias (labeled ''aggrandizement'' by Hofstetter) exists in current *New York Times* coverage of Mideast issues, we conducted a content analysis of a random sample of articles about Mideastern issues, events and leaders for the six-month periods beginning May 1976 and January 1984. These two time spans were selected for analysis in order to acquire data during periods of time distant enough from one another so that the events of one phase are relatively unrelated to events of the other. However, during the 1976 phase civil war broke out again in Lebanon, this time with the intervention of Assad's Syrian troops, despite strong

Iraqi and Egyptian opposition. Similarly, the 1984 phase saw a welter of military/political events: the withdrawal of American Marines from Beirut, talks between King Hussein and PLO chairman Arafat, the Lebanese abrogation of the 1983 withdrawal agreement with Israel, continued Israeli and Syrian occupation of Lebanon, the U.S. sale of Stinger missiles to Saudi Arabia for defense against Iran, and Israeli elections. The periods selected for analysis were chosen to obtain coverage not directly influenced by the flood of news resulting from the Iranian hostage crisis, (which, arguably, might not accurately reflect the standard pattern of Mideast subjects chosen for coverage).

Data Collection

A sample of 30 publication dates was randomly selected from each six-month period for analysis. From these 60 *New York Times* issues, 30 each from 1976 and 1984, 136 and 173 articles respectively, or a total 309 articles, were analyzed. All articles included for analysis had the Mideast as their primary focus, as determined by the headlines.

Category Development

Articles were evaluated according to two separate measures of news focus. To answer the research question, whether the "aggrandizement" bias exists in *New York Times* press coverage of Mideast countries (in other words, to see whether the issues, events and leaders of Israel and America are significantly more prominent in Mideast news than those issues, events and leaders of Arab-world nations on a country-by-country basis), we used a "Headline Proper Mention"[10] measure which examined the frequency of each Mideast country's appearance in the headlines. An average was computed across all Arab nations by dividing the Arab world total by the Number of Arab nations coded (10). The headline was selected as the unit of analysis because of its acknowledged function as a reliable summation of article content. Two coders reviewed the headlines (both main and sub) for all articles, recording all proper nouns and proper adjectives ("proper mentions") appearing in each headline, as well as the frequency of each proper mention's appearance. The

1976 sample yielded 30 different proper nouns (e.g., "Cairo," "Mubarak," "Egypt," etc.), and proper adjectives (e.g., "Egyptian", "Lebanese", "Saudi", etc.). The 1984 sample yielded 38 such items. These initial proper mentions were then sorted by country; either Israel, America or one of 10 Arab countries (i.e. "Assad", "Syria" and "Syrian" are all placed in the "Syria" category). The reliability of coders' judgments was assessed according to coders' agreement on the proper mentions assigned independently to each category. Coders' judgments yielded an 80% agreement rate (N = 30) for the 1976 sample and an 84% agreement (N = 38) for the 1984 sample.

A second analysis known as "Primary and Secondary Focus Nation" was also conducted to see whether Israel and America were featured in articles significantly more often than Arab countries. For this analysis, each article's headline and first two paragraphs were read and coders designated each article by primary and secondary focus by nations. For this phase, coders agreed in 85% of all coding decisions. This rate was deemed acceptable. In all cases, disagreements were resolved by discussion among the coders and principal investigator.

The proportion of articles devoted to Israel was compared with that devoted to each Arab nation, as were those items devoted to America. It was expected that if the *New York Times* features America and Israel over other nations in the region, then the proportions of headline proper mentions and primary and secondary focus nation mentions devoted to Israel and the U.S. should be significantly greater than those devoted to the "Average Arab Nation."

RESULTS

As Table 1 indicates, the frequencies of proper mentions attributed to Israel and the U.S. were significantly greater than those attributed to Arab nations in 1976 ($X^2 = 119.05$, d.f. = 8, p < .005); and 1984 ($X^2 = 131.35$, d.f. = 8, p < .005). Israel and the United States each received about one-fifth of the total proper mentions, or a combined total of 38.5% in 1976 (N = 85) and nearly identical proportions in 1984 (N = 115).

An "Average Arab Nation" sum was then com-

Table 1   HEADLINE PROPER MENTIONS DEVOTED TO TEN ARAB NATIONS, ISRAEL, AND THE U.S. IN 1976 AND 1984, IN PERCENT

	Headline Proper Mentions	
Country	*1976*	*1984*
Lebanon	26.2	23.4
Syria	10.4	5.5
Palestine	9.5	4.4
Egypt	7.7	4.4
Libya	2.7	5.8
Saudi Arabia	2.7	4.0
Jordan, Kuwait, Iraq, & Sudan[a]	2.3	11.3
Israel	20.4	21.1
United States	18.1	20.1
N	221	274

1976: $X^2 = 119.05$, d.f. = 8, p < .005.
1984: $X^2 = 131.35$, d.f. = 8, p < .005.
N = total number headline proper mentions.
[a]The frequencies of Jordan, Kuwait, Iraq, and Sudan were combined to retain expected cell frequencies of 5 or more in order to perform a valid test of chi-square.

puted by dividing the total number of Arab proper mentions by the number of Arab nations coded (ten), so that an Arab vs. non-Arab comparison could be made. As shown in Table 2, Israeli and American proper mention percentages in both 1976 and 1984 were significantly greater than those of the "Average Arab Nation" ($X^2 = 14.1$, d.f. = 2, p < .005 in 1976; and $X^2 = 25.5$, d.f. = 2, p < .005 in 1984).

Because Lebanon's proper mention count was noticeably greater than that for all other Arab nations (accounting for more than one-third of the total Arab proper mentions), the researchers found it worth comparing Israeli and American proper men-

Table 2   COMPARISON OF AVERAGE ARAB COUNTRY HEADLINE PROPER MENTIONS WITH PROPER MENTIONS OF ISRAEL AND THE U.S. IN 1976 AND 1984, IN PERCENT

	Headline Proper Mentions	
Country	*1976*	*1984*
Arab[a]	15.8	12.4
Israel	44.6	45.0
United States	39.6	42.6
N	101	129

1976: $X^2 = 14.1$, d.f. = 2, p < .005.
1984: $X^2 = 25.5$, d.f. = 2, p < .005.
N = total number headline proper mentions.
[a]Represents the average number of headline proper mentions devoted to an Arab country, computed by dividing the total number of Arab proper mentions by 10.

Table 3 AVERAGE ARAB COUNTRY'S PRIMARY AND SECONDARY ARTICLE FOCUS VS. ISRAEL AND THE UNITED STATES IN 1976 AND 1984, IN PERCENT

Country	Primary and Secondary Focus	
	1976	*1984*
Arab[a]	16.5	11.2
Israel	47.0	40.5
United States	36.5	48.3
N	100	100

1976: $X^2 = 12.46$, d.f. = 2, $p < .005$.
1984: $X^2 = 26.31$, d.f. = 2, $p < .005$.
N = total frequency of primary and secondary focus.
[a]Represents the average frequency of primary and secondary article focus for an Arab country = total Arab frequency divided by 10.

tion totals against the sum of *nine* Arab nations, excluding Lebanon. This sum amounted to just more than twice the magnitude of either the Israeli or American totals. Further, Lebanon captured the largest percentage of proper mentions across both time periods, thus dominating Mideast headlines in 1976 and 1984, followed by Israel which received an average of 20% and the U.S. 19%. The second and third leading Arab nations in 1976 were Syria (10.5%) and Palestine/PLO (9.5%), and, in 1984, Iraq (6.6%) and Libya (5.8%) (see Table 1).

Overall, the Headline Proper Mention analysis demonstrates that almost 40% of all Mideast proper mentions across both periods are devoted to just two countries—Israel and the United States. It appears from this that the issues, events and leaders of Israel and the U.S. are the subject of Mideast headlines significantly more often than nine of 10 Arab nations examined. In addition, U.S. and Israeli references were present significantly more often than those for the "Average Arab Nation." In fact, Israeli proper mentions appeared at least twice as often as did the proper mentions for any single Arab country, with the exception of Lebanon, whose civil war developments flooded the news agenda.

Table 3 displays results combining the frequency of primary and secondary country focus, which correspond closely to those of the Headline Proper Mention measure. Israel and America significantly exceeded the "Average Arab Nation's" frequency of primary and secondary article focus in this mea-

sure for both sample years ($X^2 = 12.46$, d.f. = 2, p < .005 in 1976; and $X^2 = 26.31$, d.f. = 2, p < .005 in 1984). The 1976 percentage of 10 Arab nations' primary and secondary focus was 65.6% with Lebanon accounting for more than one-third vs. the Israeli sum of 18.4% and the U.S. sum of 16%, while the 1984 Arab world total came to 55.6% vs. the Israeli and American sums of 20.3% and 24.1% respectively. Israel's presence in the headlines was consistent in both periods, capturing primary and secondary billing in at least one-fifth of all stories.

CONCLUSIONS

Israel, its issues, events, and leaders, receive more coverage in *New York Times* news reports than its Arab neighbors. Such coverage of the Mideast has the potential to mar the American, as well as the international, comprehension of issues and events in that region. To the extent that coverage favors one segment of a geopolitical region over another, one may argue that there is less possibility for clear understanding, and therefore a lack of appreciation for the causes, effects and cures of regional turbulence. Such a bias not only holds Israel up to unrealistic expectations, but further aggravates Mideastern wounds by infecting the international news agenda with disfigured perceptions of the Mideast.

NOTES

1. Ze'ev Chafets, *Double Vision* (New York: Morrow, 1984), inside cover.
2. See preface by James Abourezk in Edmund Ghareeb, ed. *Split Vision* (Washington: Arab-American Affairs Council, 1983), p. ix.
3. Chafets, *Double Vision*, p. 297.
4. Daniel Pipes, ''The Media and the Middle East,'' *Commentary*, 1984, vol. 77, p. 29.
5. William C. Adams, *TV Coverage of the Middle East* (Norwood, New Jersey: Ablex, 1981), p. 9.
6. Richard C. Hofstetter, *Bias in the News* (Columbus, Ohio: Ohio State University Press, 1976), p. 9.
7. *Ibid.*
8. See, e.g., Shelly Slade, ''The Image of the Arab in America: Analysis of a Poll on American Attitudes,'' *The Middle East Journal*, 1981, p. 143. 35:143–162 (1981).
9. See preface by Abourezk in Ghareeb, *Split Vision*, p. xiii.
10. ''Proper Mentions'' refers to ''proper'' nouns (e.g., Jerusalem, Assad, Lebanon) and ''proper'' adjectives (e.g., Israeli, Lebanese, American) appearing in article headlines; common nouns, pronouns, and adjectives were disregarded.

WHY HAS THE U.S. MEDIA SPOTLIGHT TURNED AWAY FROM SOUTH AFRICA?

TREVOR BROWN

The coverage of South Africa poses special problems. The violence that attracted the American press to South Africa before it passed the "Comprehensive Anti-Apartheid Act of 1986" continues. But coverage of the violence has declined.

Americans' questions to a native South African have changed. From the 1960s through the early 1980s they used to ask, ''When do you think the revolution will occur?'' Now they ask, ''What's really happening there?'' Guided by the information and images of the press, Americans have shifted from prediction to confusion, from ''apocalypse now'' through ''the fire next time'' to ''engage or disinvest?'' Even that question may have been tabled. South Africa was on the nation's agenda in 1985–86. It is not now, not unless the Rev. Jesse Jackson can lure it back by insisting that the Democratic Party define South Africa as a terrorist state. The apartheid story, it seems, has almost disappeared.

The sad irony is that the press is better prepared in 1988 to help the public tackle the South African issue than it was when South Africa exploded into American consciousness in March 1960 with the shooting at Sharpeville. Edward Hoagland's later judgment on the American press may have applied for the period 1960–1976. A stay-at-home intellectual community, he wrote, ''has resulted in a stay-at-home journalism, a press that travels only belatedly and as a thundering herd, so that as a nation we

Trevor Brown, ''Why Has the U.S. Media Spotlight Turned Away from South Africa.'' *American Society of Newspaper Editors Bulletin*, July–August 1988, pp. 34–35. Reprinted by permission.

The author is dean of the School of Journalism at Indiana University.

are perpetually astonished after the fact at whatever goes on in the world."

Sharpeville did not so much astonish attentive citizens as confirm their expectations. "For years it had been predicted," *Newsweek* wrote on April 4, 1960, "last week it happened." The magazine did not define "it," but the apocalyptic tone left little doubt as to what "it" was. Two weeks later *Newsweek* wrote, "South Africa may be headed for massive racial war, flaring up sporadically in the middle '60s, setting the whole continent alight in the '70s."

During those weeks journalists from all over the world thundered to South Africa, trying after the fact to understand how initiative for protest had passed from the hands of the African National Congress led by Albert Luthuli, "a typical embodiment of moderate African nationalism," as the *New York Times* described him in 1959.

"With the responsible leaders regarded as moderates banned or banished," the *Times* wrote in March 1960, "the extremist elements are left to whip up anti-white sentiment through organizations such as the Pan African Congress, headed by Robert Mangaliso Sobukwe."

The labels "moderate," "responsible," and "extremist" were not only serviceable shorthand for reporters suddenly projected into another foreign crisis. They were the currency of white South African liberals on whom American reporters relied for analysis of Sharpeville and later, at least for the first few weeks, of the Soweto uprising in 1976.

Novelist Alan Paton, in fact, almost single-handedly interpreted South Africa to the United States for 16 years. Only on June 24, 1976, did Paton acknowledge in the *Times* that he was "not writing for all the people in South Africa. I am writing for its white people. White people cannot write for black people any more."

Sharing that awareness, American reporters significantly matured in their analysis of South Africa. In 1976 they had once again thundered late to the scene, no more informed about Steven Biko's black consciousness movement in the late 1960s and early 1970s than they had been about Sobukwe's PAC in 1960.

In August 1976 Anthony Lewis expressed the puzzle for American reporters this way: "In the past, the common pattern has been a single incident,

met by unyielding repression. But the trouble that began with the riots in Soweto last June 16 has not stopped. . . . For protest to continue so long is extraordinary under the conditions of black life in South Africa."

American reporters worked after 1976 to describe and understand those conditions, no longer relying on white South African liberals who had intelligent and moral understanding of apartheid but virtually no experience of the lives South African blacks lived. Such reporting was to win Pulitzer Prizes for Joseph Lelyveld's 1985 book, "Move Your Shadow," and for Michael Parks of the *Los Angeles Times* for his "comprehensive and balanced coverage of South Africa'" in 1986.

So why has the apartheid story seemingly disappeared? In a study published in 1987 sociologist Eleanor Singer and statistician Jacob Ludwig hypothesized that the South African government's ban in November 1985 on photographic and sound recordings of protest activities would reduce American media coverage of protest-related stories, the overall volume of coverage, and the prominence of the South Africa story.

They found that coverage had already begun to decline before the ban, which turned out not to have had the effects they predicted during the period studied. As the South African government tightened press restrictions in 1986 and 1987, however, American journalists persuaded Singer and Ludwig that these later restrictions had reduced coverage.

Here is another hypothesis. Media coverage after 1976 informed attentive American citizens of the complexity of the South African story and contributed with very newsworthy domestic activism to establishing apartheid as an issue on the national agenda. South Africa became a problem requiring more vigorous bipartisan response than the Reagan administration's benign diplomacy of constructive engagement.

Through its representatives in Congress and against the wishes of its president, the concerned American public made its statement on South Africa with the passage of the Comprehensive Anti-Apartheid Act of 1986. Its conscience was essentially salved. South Africa had been dealt with and other items crowded the agenda.

At the same time the South African government

made life awkward for the thundering herd and, by brutal oppression as in the past, painful for newsworthy protest. South Africa is not the photo opportunity in 1988 that it was in 1960, 1976 and 1984.

So what is really happening there? One fears that *Newsweek* in 1960 may have had it right: "In South Africa, a land so lovely even those who hate it can hardly bear to leave it, masses of black men chanting 'kill, kill, kill,' clashed with white men shouting "Back you black b------s!" *Newsweek*'s melodrama of hate may not be that lurid in contemporary South Africa. Nevertheless the violence that attracted the American press to the scene continues now largely out of the international spotlight. South Africa threatens still to fulfill this nation's dismal predictions, but our attention is elsewhere.

THE NEWS AND U.S.-CHINA POLICY: SYMBOLS IN NEWSPAPERS AND DOCUMENTS

TSAN-KUO CHANG

It is easy to trace the relationship between the United States, China and Taiwan by checking how the "two Chinas" are referred to in the *Washington Post* and the *New York Times*. Regardless of how the public feels about a foreign country, the press reflects the closeness of the two governments—or is it the other way around? Do governments and the press reflect public opinion? This study suggests that even in a recognized democracy such as the United States, the climate of opinion in regard to relations with other countries is set by the government.

For average citizens, foreign affairs are often beyond direct experience and involvement. Their involvement and perception of the world outside depend largely on how the issues and consequences are symbolized by policy makers and transmitted through the mass media. There is little doubt that symbols are created for public consumption by foreign policy makers to reflect foreign policy issues.

In the political world, symbols often appear in either referential or condensational format. These two symbolic formats differ in the scope of meanings and emotions associated with the political message: "Referential symbols are economical, concrete, and not prone to attract emotional baggage. They refer to things in specific and precise terms. Condensational symbols, on the other hand, appear in contexts with abstractions that are often ambiguous in meaning or have a history of powerful emotional concerns for the audience."[1]

The use of different symbols could have policy implications for decision makers. When public concern or involvement in an issue is undesirable, policy makers tend to use referential symbols. If, on the other hand, public involvement is called for, the issue may be defined in condensational terms.[2] For the general public, symbols could have different meanings and cognitive as well as emotional effects, depending on how they are used in specific contexts.[3]

Tsan-Kuo Chang, "The News and U.S.–China Policy: Symbols in Newspapers and Documents." *Journalism Quarterly*, Volume 65, Number 2, Summer 1988, pp. 320–327. Reprinted by permission.

The author is an assistant professor in the Department of Communication at Cleveland State University.

In the case of the word Communist, Cobb and Elder suggested that for most Americans this symbol is related to "oppression, totalitarianism, or other negative terms."[4] Such symbols, like cultural symbols, make us focus on some things rather than on others.[5]

This study examines how political symbols were used in the U.S.-China policy-making process during the past three decades. Specifically, the following research questions were addressed: What was the symbolic representation of China in news coverage of U.S.-China policy? How did it shift over time? To what extent were these shifts determined by shifts in the U.S.-China policy?

While studies on Sino-American relations over the years have been voluminous and diverse, a less systematic examination has been conducted of the relationship between the news and U.S.-China policy.[6] Some evidence has suggested that before 1950 the press played a major part in the making of U.S.-China policy.[7] Yet, China after 1950 was something totally different from what it used to be to most Americans, officials and civilians alike.

The defeat of the U.S.-supported Nationalist regime and the takeover of China by the Soviet-backed Chinese Communists in 1949 stirred a wide and bitter debate in the United States over responsibility for the failure of U.S.-China policy. The rise and fall of Sen. Joseph R. McCarthy and his relations with the press in the 1950s was one notable, and notorious, example of how China could be entangled in American domestic policies and become both a national issue and a political symbol in the mass media for many years to come.[8] For a brief period, American mass media even became part of the instruments of the U.S. government used to block contacts between the world's most powerful country and the most populous nation.[9]

Political symbolism in the making of U.S.-China policy is important and deserves close examination. First, in the absence of diplomatic relations and direct official interactions between the two countries from 1950 through 1971, China refused to go away and managed to be on the U.S. political agenda, both internationally and nationally. As *Newsweek* put it, "for more than two decades, China has been out of sight but rarely out of mind."[10] Second, "the real China is alien," as Cumings saw it, "but 'China,' as an issue and a symbol in American politics since 1945, is familiar and central."[11]

METHOD

China policy news was defined as news and opinions regarding U.S. relations with both the People's Republic of China and the Republic of China on Taiwan (hereafter Taiwan). The study period covered 35 years, from 1950, the first full year after the People's Republic was founded in Peking in October 1949, through 1984, the end of President Ronald Reagan's first term. Two sets of data were used: newspaper items and government documents.

Front page news and editorials were selected from the *New York Times* and the *Washington Post*.[12] The two papers were chosen because of their prominence and influence.[13] In the case of the *Times*, some researchers argue that it "ends up influencing the content" of other mass media[14] and that it "may not be a bad indicator of the general thrust of news" that reaches the U.S. citizenry.[15] For government policy, presidential documents on U.S.-China relations during the study period were used based on non-duplicate items listed in the *Public Papers of the Presidents of the United States* and the *Weekly Compilation of Presidential Documents*.

The paragraph in the newspaper items and government documents was the coding unit. The whole item was too broad for the study and the paragraphs could, of course, be used as "cues or indicators"[16] of the overall content for the items. All paragraphs coded in the same year—the unit of analysis—were aggregated and transformed into percentages based on the frequency distribution of paragraphs in a given category. Each category then became a new variable with the percentage as its value.[17]

Three types of symbols were examined: ideological, geographic and legal. Ideological symbols attached ideology to the words, including Communist China, Red China, Chinese Communists, Chinese Communist regime, Nationalist China, Chinese Nationalists, Chinese Nationalist regime, and Free China. These terms might be considered as condensational symbols as they invite emotional associations and private interpretations. Geographical symbols tended to be neutral, showing no political connotations. They were Peking/Peiping, mainland China, and Taiwan/Formosa/Taipei. Legal symbols implied acceptance of legitimacy and existence as a political entity, involving the official titles of China and Taiwan: People's Republic of China (PRC) and Republic of China (ROC). Unlike the ideological symbols, the last two types of symbols tend to be more specific, leaving little room for individual sentiments and projections.

RESULTS

Table 1 shows the symbols associated with China in the two papers. News and editorials were combined to show the overall picture. In the first decade of Sino-American relations, the ideological symbols of China looked quite salient in the two newspapers. China was often identified as Communist China, Red China, the Chinese Communists or the Chinese Communist regime. Its official title, the People's Republic of China, was seldom mentioned.

While the geographical and general symbols—mainland China and Peking or simply China—were relatively visible throughout the 1950s, the two newspapers mostly used ideologically loaded labels to refer to the world's most populous country. The use of ideological symbols seemed more apparent in the two papers during those years when China's external behavior became increasingly violent and aggressive, such as in the 1954–55 and 1958 Taiwan Strait crises.

The representation of China in the news appeared to be parallel to the use of symbols by the government during this period (Table 2). As can be seen, the United States rarely mentioned China by its official title. The most often used symbols used by the government were "Communist China" and "China," with the ideological symbol being the dominant one. When the tension between the two countries escalated in the Taiwan Strait in 1954–55 and in 1958, the United States frequently referred to China as Communist, a symbol clearly echoed in the news.

Unlike the first decade, the second decade of Sino-American relations saw a steady decline in the news of the use of ideological symbols and a growing use of geographical and general symbols with reference to China. When the Senate held the China hearings in 1966, the use of ideological symbols in the two papers dropped for the first time in nearly two decades below the level of the use of general symbols. During the same period, while the use of ideological symbols by the government remained relatively stable, there was an apparent increase in non-ideological symbols (Table 2).

The drastic decrease in the papers' use of ideological symbols came in 1971 when President Nixon announced that he would visit China, thus beginning the process of Sino-American normalization. During the following years and until 1984, the symbol "Communist China" vanished from the government's representation of that country. Replacing "Communist China" was the increasing use of the precise title of China, which undoubtedly spoke for the American acceptance of the Peking regime as a fact in the world and a legitimate political entity in Chinese politics.

The disappearance of the label "Communist China" and the emergence of the legal and specific symbol, "People's Republic of China," in the government's dealings with China was closely reflected in the news coverage. The increased appearance of the legal symbol in the news seemed to follow the pattern of government policy during the last decade of Sino-American relations. The drop of the loaded labels might be a result of the new-found friendship between the two countries. As the *Washington Post* put it, "suddenly it seems a bit *ungracious* to say 'Communist China'."[18] (emphasis added)

The use of symbols with respect to Taiwan in the two newspapers was not as clearcut as the pattern shown in the use of symbols concerning China. Table 3 reports the results. While the symbols "Nationalist China" and "Taiwan" evidently dominated the news coverage, no clear representation of Taiwan could be identified in the first two decades of American-Taiwan relations. For the most part, both the ideological and geographical symbols appeared interchangeably in the two papers. The legal symbol "Republic of China" and the general symbol "China" remained largely inconspicuous.

On the part of government policy, there appeared to be some degree of ambivalence toward Taiwan from 1950 through the early 1970s (Table 4). The U.S. government often used "Nationalist China," "the Republic of China," and "Taiwan" interchangeably. It seldom used the symbol "China" to refer to the Nationalist government on that island, which was driven out of Chinese mainland by the Communists in 1949.

Table 1   SYMBOLS OF CHINA, 1950–1984, IN TWO NEWSPAPERS:
FROM COMMUNIST CHINA TO CHINA

Year	Communist[1] China	PRC[2]	Mainland[3] China	China	Peiping (Peking)	N*
50	54.8%	1.7%	4.6%	33.6%	5.3%	1069
51	64.8	2.0	1.9	21.9	9.7	739
52	64.9	—	7.8	22.1	5.2	77
53	69.4	0.3	11.8	15.3	3.2	340
54	75.8	1.0	4.4	12.3	6.5	682
55	70.4	1.0	7.1	12.3	9.1	1729
56	70.7	1.5	1.1	17.5	9.1	263
57	53.4	0.6	6.1	35.3	4.6	479
58	76.4	0.9	7.5	9.6	5.7	1164
59	58.4	0.5	4.2	26.6	10.3	214
60	67.4	—	9.7	18.9	4.0	175
61	59.0	0.7	5.2	20.7	14.4	271
62	59.5	1.2	14.5	13.9	11.0	173
63	45.0	—	24.0	31.0	—	100
64	49.3	1.9	19.0	29.9	—	211
65	46.5	0.5	17.8	35.1	—	243
66	31.6	—	19.4	39.0	—	830
67	26.5	—	13.9	59.6	—	166
68	20.2	—	33.7	46.1	—	89
69	27.4	0.8	28.6	43.1	—	248
70	26.0	4.1	34.6	35.3	—	269
71	9.5	9.5	35.5	45.5	0.2	1370
72	3.3	5.2	26.3	65.2	—	692
73	1.5	6.0	28.7	63.9	—	335
74	0.9	5.2	19.1	74.8	—	115
75	0.9	6.0	30.1	63.0	—	216
76	1.5	3.5	28.6	66.3	—	199
77	2.6	5.7	27.2	64.5	—	265
78	2.5	9.4	28.4	59.6	—	394
79	0.4	5.3	23.9	70.5	—	570
80	—	7.1	17.6	75.2	—	210
81	2.9	5.1	27.0	65.0	—	274
82	1.9	2.5	38.9	56.6	—	316
83	0.7	2.2	17.0	80.0	—	270
84	1.4	1.4	12.0	85.1	—	349
Total	38.7%	2.9%	16.4%	38.3%	3.6%	15048

[1]This symbol includes Communist China, Red China, Chinese Communists, Chinese Reds, and Chinese Communist regime.
[2]PRC: People's Republic of China
[3]This symbol includes Mainland China, Chinese mainland, and Peking
*Entries are number of paragraphs. Paragraphs with no symbols were excluded.

Table 2   SYMBOLS OF CHINA USED BY GOVERNMENT, 1950–1984*

Year	Communist[1] China	PRC[2]	Mainland[3] China	China	Peiping (Peking)	N
50	26	1	1	10	—	38
51	9	—	—	6	—	15
52	2	—	—	3	—	5
53	7	—	—	3	1	11
54	10	—	—	4	—	14
55	25	—	1	2	—	28
56	4	—	—	1	—	5
57	5	—	—	6	—	11
58	49	1	—	2	—	52
59	7	—	—	7	—	14
60	9	—	1	2	2	14
61	26	—	—	9	—	35
62	15	—	—	8	—	23
63	12	1	1	9	—	23
64	35	—	1	6	1	43
65	13	—	—	2	1	16
66	17	1	8	12	—	38
67	6	—	4	8	—	18
68	—	—	—	1	—	1
69	33	—	3	2	—	38
70	23	—	2	7	—	32
71	12	64	54	24	—	154
72	—	95	24	41	—	160
73	—	38	9	16·	—	63
74	—	8	—	2	—	10
75	—	27	—	6	—	33
76	—	30	2	10	—	42
77	—	15	2	19	—	36
78	—	48	3	30	—	81
79	—	39	—	57	—	96
80	—	53	—	70	—	123
81	—	10	—	3	—	13
82	—	13	—	14	—	27
83	—	12	—	3	—	15
84	2	25	—	138	—	165
Total	347	481	116	543	5	1492
	23.3%	32.2%	7.8%	36.4%	0.3%	100.0%

*Entries are number of paragraphs. Paragraphs with no symbols were excluded.
[1]This symbol includes Communist China, Red China, Chinese Communists, Chinese Reds, and Chinese Communist regime.
[2]PRC: People's Republic of China.
[3]This symbol includes Mainland China, Chinese mainland, and Peking.

Table 3   SYMBOLS OF TAIWAN, 1950–1984 IN TWO NEWSPAPERS:
FROM NATIONALIST CHINA TO TAIWAN

Year	Nationalist[1] China	ROC[2]	Taiwan[3]	China	N*
50	30.0%	0.2%	58.9%	11.0%	644
51	41.5	3.2	49.0	5.7	282
52	44.6	4.6	41.5	9.2	65
53	60.4	0.7	36.9	2.0	149
54	35.5	1.5	60.4	2.6	273
55	36.7	3.6	56.3	3.4	1203
56	27.1	0.8	68.6	3.4	118
57	24.6	3.1	70.8	1.5	65
58	48.8	3.1	44.8	3.2	864
59	17.4	2.2	78.3	2.2	46
60	40.3	3.4	55.5	0.8	119
61	50.9	4.3	36.8	8.0	163
62	61.3	2.2	35.5	1.1	93
63	46.7	6.7	26.7	20.3	15
64	36.7	4.1	36.7	22.4	49
65	53.8	3.8	26.9	15.4	26
66	31.9	6.0	32.8	29.3	116
67	33.3	—	11.1	55.6	9
68	26.7	—	66.7	6.7	15
69	37.5	2.5	52.5	7.5	40
70	41.2	7.4	41.9	9.5	148
71	33.8	8.0	51.1	7.1	523
72	23.3	3.0	73.3	0.4	236
73	22.1	1.1	70.5	6.3	95
74	21.4	21.4	57.8	—	14
75	6.3	3.1	90.6	—	64
76	10.0	4.5	85.5	—	110
77	19.6	0.6	79.1	0.6	163
78	10.6	5.0	83.8	0.7	303
79	7.5	2.1	89.7	0.7	292
80	2.3	1.6	93.8	2.3	129
81	8.4	1.3	88.3	1.9	154
82	8.1	0.3	90.6	1.0	297
83	6.8	—	90.5	2.7	74
84	2.6	1.3	94.7	1.3	76
Total	31.2%	3.1%	61.0%	4.7%	7032

[1]*This symbol includes Nationalist China, Free China, Chinese Nationalists and Chinese Nationalist regime.*
[2]*ROC: Republic of China.*
[3]*This symbol includes Taiwan, Taipei, and Formosa.*
*Entries are number of paragraphs. Missing values were excluded.

Table 4	SYMBOLS OF TAIWAN USED BY GOVERNMENT, 1950–1984*				
Year	Nationalist[1] China	ROC[2]	Taiwan[3]	China	N
50	4	—	17	6	27
51	3	—	2	—	5
52	—	1	1	2	4
53	2	—	2	1	5
54	2	2	1	—	5
55	11	12	13	—	36
56	—	—	5	—	5
57	2	2	4	1	9
58	11	11	30	1	53
59	—	3	4	1	8
60	—	11	11	3	25
61	—	9	1	3	13
62	2	5	4	—	11
63	2	—	2	—	4
64	2	1	—	—	3
65	2	3	—	—	5
66	—	1	3	—	4
67	3	16	5	2	26
68	—	—	2	—	2
69	—	4	5	—	9
70	—	3	—	—	3
71	—	6	7	1	14
72	—	5	4	—	9
73	—	1	3	—	4
74	—	1	—	—	1
75	—	4	—	—	4
76	—	—	5	—	5
77	—	8	11	—	19
78	—	1	27	—	28
79	—	—	28	—	28
80	—	—	29	—	29
81	—	—	1	—	1
82	—	—	14	—	14
83	—	—	4	—	4
84	—	—	7	—	7
Total	46	110	252	21	429
	10.7%	25.6%	58.7%	4.9%	100.0%

*Entries are number of paragraphs. Paragraphs with no symbols were excluded.
[1]This symbol includes Nationalist China, Free China, Chinese Nationalists, and Chinese Nationalist regime.
[2]ROC: Republic of China.
[3]This symbol includes Taiwan, Taipei, and Formosa.

Not until 1971 did the use of symbols concerning Taiwan in the two newspapers clearly shift from "Nationalist China" to "Taiwan." Within a short period of time, the symbol "Taiwan" became ubiquitous in the news coverage of U.S.-China policy. In government policy by 1968, the United States had dropped the symbol "Nationalist China" and the use of the precise title, the Republic of China, declined significantly.

Following the Nixon trip to China, the recurring use of the symbol "Taiwan" in the two newspapers' coverage of U.S.-Nationalist China relations seemed to follow the path of government policy. This was particularly true after the United States severed its diplomatic relations with the Nationalist government on Taiwan in 1979 and recognized the Communist government on the Chinese mainland as the sole representative of China.

After the 1972 Shanghai communique, the United States gave up the idea of two Chinas and switched to the concept of one China of which Taiwan was a part. The use of symbols concerning Taiwan in the two newspapers stuck to the official line. The two papers not only discarded the idea of two Chinas, but also considered the talk as "reckless" or "careless."[19]

DISCUSSION

During the 35-year period from 1950 through 1984, news coverage of U.S.-China policy seemed to reflect the ups and downs of Sino-American relations over time. Representations of both China and Taiwan in the two papers shifted from the use of ideological and emotional symbols in the first two decades to that of legal and precise symbols in the last decade. Such shift appeared to follow closely the change of U.S. policy toward China and Taiwan. For example, after 1971, the symbol "Communist China" became virtually non-existent in U.S.-China policy, as shown in the presidential documents (see Table 2); so did the two papers' use of the symbol.

Underlying such a clear shift of symbols from "Communist China" to "PRC" or "China" was, of course, the U.S. desire to improve relations with the world's most populous nation and the American willingness to treat China as an equal counterpart.

On the other hand, the change of symbols might be designed by policy makers to prepare public opinion for the changing U.S.-China policy. Between 1950 and 1970 public opinion polls had shown that the public sentiment was consistently against "Communist China."[20]

Given the fact that from 1972 through 1978 the United States still maintained diplomatic relations with the Republic of China on Taiwan, the use of an official title for another Chinese authority by the U.S. government not only defied any diplomatic protocol, but also was suggestive and provocative. It signified the decreasing importance and status of the Nationalist government as a realistic alternative to the Communist government as ruler of China and as representative of the Chinese people.

If the use of symbols is any indication of the official status of Taiwan as a legitimate country, an observer would have no difficulties seeing the fact that over the past 35 years the status of Taiwan has gradually but steadily shifted from that of one China, the Nationalist China, to a province of China with its capital in Peking. For government-to-government relations, news coverage of U.S.-China policy in the last decade unquestionably affirmed the American official stand since the 1972 Shanghai communique that there was only one China of which Taiwan was a part.

Considering the fact that in the foreign policy area the mass media tend to rely heavily on official sources for news and opinions regarding foreign relations,[21] symbols for China and Taiwan in the news during the past 35 years have reflected U.S.-China policy. Such use of symbols might, as Nimmo has suggested,[22] be created and planted by foreign policy makers.

NOTES

1. W. Lance Bennett, *Public Opinion in American Politics* (New York: Harcourt Brace Jovanovich, Inc., 1980), p. 256.
2. *Ibid.*
3. Roger W. Cobb and Charles D. Elder, *Participation in American Politics: The Dynamics of Agenda-Building* (Baltimore: The Johns Hopkins University Press, 1972), p. 131; and W. Lance Bennett, *News:*

The Politics of Illusion (New York: Longman, 1983), p. 43.

4. Cobb and Elder, *Ibid.*, p. 131.

5. Michael Schudson, *Advertising, the Uneasy Persuasion* (New York: Basic Books, Inc., 1986), p. xxii.

6. See, for example, T. Harrell Allen, "U.S.-Chinese Dialogue, 1969–71," *Journal of Communication*, Winter 1976, pp. 81-86; Tsan-Kuo Chang, "How Three Elite Papers Covered Reagan China Policy," *Journalism Quarterly*, 61:429–432 (Summer 1984); and Carolyn Lin and Michael B. Salwen, "Three Press Systems View Sino-U.S. Normalization," *Journalism Quarterly*, 63:360–362 (Summer 1986).

7. Gertrude C. Byers, "American Journalism and China, 1945–1950," (Ph.D. dissertation, St. Louis University, 1980).

8. See, for example, Edwin R. Bailey, *Joe McCarthy and the Press* (New York: Pantheon Books, 1981).

9. Tsan-Kuo Chang, "The Press and U.S.-China Relations: A Long Journey," paper presented at the annual conference of the American Journalism Historians Association, University of Nevada, Las Vegas, October 2–6, 1985.

10. "An Open Door, a People Dimly Seen," *Newsweek*, Feb. 21, 1972, p. 40.

11. Bruce Cumings, "Chinatown: Foreign Policy and Elite Realignment," in *The Hidden Election*, ed. Thomas Ferguson and Joel Rogers (New York: Pantheon Books, 1981), p. 210.

12. Indexes of the two papers were used to search for items. The proportion of agreement between the index and the newspaper was unity for the *Post* (1.00) and near perfect for the *Times* (0.98).

13. See, for example, Bernard C. Cohen, "Foreign Policy Makers and the Press," in James N. Rosenau, ed., *International Politics and Foreign Policy*, (New York: The Free Press, 1961), p. 221; W. Phillips Davison, "Mass Communication and Diplomacy," in James N. Rosenau, Kenneth W. Thompson, and

Gavin Boyd eds., *World Politics* (New York: The Free Press, 1976), pp. 389–390; Carol H. Weiss, "What America's Leaders Read?" *Public Opinion Quarterly*, 38:5 (Spring 1974); Doris A. Graber, *Mass Media and American Politics* (Washington, D.C.: Congressional Quarterly Inc., 1980), p. 245; and Charlotte Saikowski, "Reagan Reading List: 'Coolidge' to 'Hondo,' " *Christian Science Monitor*, Dec. 29, 1983, p. 4.

14. Todd Gitlin, *The Whole World is Watching* (Berkeley: University of California Press, 1980), p. 299.

15. Benjamin I. Page and Robert Y. Shapiro, "Presidents as Opinion Leaders: Some New Evidence," *Policy Studies Journal*, 12:651 (June 1984).

16. Richard W. Budd, Robert K. Thorp and Lewis Donohew, *Content Analysis of Communications* (New York: The Macmillan Co., 1967), p. 34.

17. Using the Holsti formula, the average intercoder agreements were .89 for symbols of China and .95 for symbols of Taiwan. Ole R. Holsti, *Content Analysis for the Social Sciences and Humanities* (Reading, Mass.: Addison-Wesley, 1969), pp. 137–140.

18. *Washington Post*, April 15, 1971, p. A18.

19. *Washington Post*, July 8, 1981, p. A22; and *New York Times*, Jan 13, 1982, p. 22.

20. Robert Weissberg, *Public Opinion and Popular Government* (Englewood Cliffs, New Jersey: Prentice-Hall, Inc., 1976), p. 158.

21. Tsan-Kuo Chang, "The Press and U.S. Foreign Policy: Some Theoretical and Methodological Considerations," paper presented at the 67th annual convention of the Association for Education in Journalism and Mass Communication, Gainesville, Florida, August 1984.

22. Dan Nimmo, "Political Communication: From Area of Inquiry to Emergence of a Field," in Jerry Lynn, ed., *Communications Research Symposium: A Proceedings*, vol. 2, (Knoxville, Tennessee: The University of Tennessee, 1979), p. 13.

CANADA AND MEXICO: WHAT THEY SAY ABOUT US ON TV

RODERICK TOWNLEY

They both view the U.S. ambivalently: while they admire it, they are wary of their big and wealthy neighbor. They feel they are misunderstood in the U.S. and taken for granted—or, worse still, largely ignored.

"God bless America!" What resonance in those words, and in those celebrated places, Big Sur, the Grand Canyon, Washington, New York, Chihuahua . . .

Chihuahua??

That's right, and Manitoba, too. Mexico and Canada are as much a part of America as we are, though we tend to forget that, and our network newscasts mostly ignore events to the north and south of us.

News organizations in Canada and Mexico, though, are certainly very much interested in *us*, because they know how much their countries are affected by events in the United States. Their economic vulnerability is particularly worrisome, and the dollar is watched closely, reported on frequently. "If you have a recession," says Yolanda Sanchez, Washington bureau chief for the Mexican newscast *24 Horas* (*24 Hours*), "it affects Mexico tremendously. Our exports come to the United States." Canadian Broadcasting Company (CBC) correspondent Bruce Garvey made a similar point on the air last April, when he spoke of "Canada's dependence on the U.S. economy. If their interest rates rise, then so do ours. If they sink into a recession, then so do we."

Unlike the U.S., Canada and Mexico each have one dominant TV news program. In Mexico, it's Televisa's *24 Hours*; in Canada, it's the CBC's *The National*, followed by a MacNeil/Lehrer-ish news-feature supplement called *The Journal*.

Author Jane Jacobs, a U.S.-born urban theorist who moved to Canada 20 years ago, considers the CBC more even-handed and less partisan than American news organizations, particularly when the subject is U.S. military actions abroad. "The CBC isn't taking the American point of view. It isn't taking the other point of view, either, whether it be the Nicaraguan, the Salvadoran or whatever."

And Canada's news programs can be quite aggressive at times: for instance, investigating reports that Prime Minister Brian Mulroney's official residences were lavishly renovated with political contributions. Mexican news stories, on the other hand, seem perfunctorily reported and studiously uncontroversial. It would be a cold day in Cuernavaca before the finances of President Miguel de la Madrid were questioned on television.

The huge, privately owned virtual TV monopoly Televisa, writes Alan Riding in his book *Distant Neighbors: A Portrait of the Mexicans*, "readily accepts official guidelines on how specific news items are to be handled and rarely criticizes the government directly. Yet its treatment and selection of news are consistently slanted to the right . . . on foreign affairs, the slant is even sharper, with Televisa effectively endorsing Washington's anti-Communist view of the world."

Other observers think it's not so much a question of "left" or "right" but of being pro-establishment, whatever the establishment happens to be. After all, Televisa has strong links to both the United States

Roderick Townley, "Canada and Mexico: What They Say about Us." Reprinted by permission from *TV Guide* ® Magazine. Copyright © 1988 by Triangle Publications, Inc. Radnor, Pennsylvania.

Roderick Townley is a free-lance writer.

and to the Mexican government. (Indeed, Televisa's president, Miguel Aleman, is the son of a former president of Mexico.) It would be only prudent to avoid offending the government of either country. The result is often muted, even timid, coverage of news events.

Mario Lechuga, the *24 Hours* correspondent in Los Angeles, says he covers everything from immigration to movie stars but concentrates on "lighter news, like festivals and sports." He did a story on the death of Lorne Greene "because Mexico buys all those series, *Bonanza, Highway Patrol, The Fall Guy.*" Mexicans, he says, love American sports and American entertainers.

From looking at several weeks of Mexican broadcasts last spring, one might conclude that the U.S. was composed primarily of baseball players, Donna Rice and Secretary of State George Shultz (usually seen huddled with a fellow named Shevardnadze). Mickey Mantle has chest pains. Prospects for an arms agreement improve. It is, to say the least, a fragmented view of American life.

Jorge Castañeda, a political analyst living in Mexico City, sees Dan Rather's newscast on cable TV at 8 P.M.; then at 10:30 he can see the Mexican news. Often, it contains some of the exact same footage but with a Spanish voice-over. It particularly annoys him that the Mexican newscast takes "the feature stuff that Dan Rather likes to do. You know, the heartland, the farmer in Iowa, the world's largest hamburger. . . . They like that a lot on Televisa." Such U.S.-generated life-style features, he thinks, are absurdly irrelevant to the lives of the Mexican people.

Clearly it's cheaper for Televisa to buy video from CBS or NBC (which also supplies footage to Canadian TV) than it is to send film crews around the States shooting stories. This wholesale use of American footage may account for the surprisingly full coverage of the U.S. Presidential campaign. "You don't get that amount of coverage for [political campaigns in] Spain," notes Sergio Sarmiento, journalist and editor-in-chief of Spanish-language publications of *Encyclopedia Britannica* in Mexico. "And we have closer cultural links to Spain."

Mexican TV has used a good deal of footage of campaign dropout Bruce Babbitt, says Sarmiento,

because Babbitt is from Arizona, which has close links with Mexico. Other campaigners seen frequently on Mexican TV are Robert Dole, George Bush, Richard Gephardt and Michael Dukakis.

Coverage, of course, is not the same as understanding. Just as the U.S. is full of clichés about Mexico, declares the renowned Mexican poet Octavio Paz, so Mexico has its clichés about the United States. Many Mexicans, for instance, assume from images they see on television that life in the States is more luxurious than it really is. They also think it's more violent than it is. "We are living in a period of clichés," says Paz. "I'm afraid television has been decisive in the extension and dissemination of these clichés."

Such "mutual ignorance," he continues, "is a pity, because more and more we're going to suffer the same problems." Among the problems we currently share with Mexico are drug trafficking, the Mexican debt and illegal immigration. But it's hard to find any forthright or detailed reporting on such issues on *24 Hours*.

The handling of the drug-enforcement problem is perhaps typified by the lead story on *24 Hours* last April 13. The army seized 850 kilos of cocaine in Jalisco, announced anchorman Jacobo Zabludovsky. Two Colombian smugglers were arrested. A load of marijuana was also discovered on a plane in San Luis Potosi. A positive, upbeat report, in other words, on how efficiently the government is taking care of things.

"You'll never see a program on people in the army who are accused by the U.S. of drug smuggling," says Juan Ruiz-Healy, a news commentator who worked as a reporter for Televisa for 16 years, than anchored and produced a Mexican version of *60 Minutes* for five years more.

When the U.S. publicly criticizes Mexico on the drug issue, he says, the ruling party (the Institutional Revolutionary Party, or PRI) generally issues a strong denial, which is duly carried on the newscasts. "What the PRI says will always have an uncritical forum on TV," he says.

The matter of illegal immigration is also treated superficially on Mexican newscasts, says Ruiz-Healy, who now works for Ch. 41, a Spanish-language station in San Antonio. He recently completed a tough documentary on Mexican workers crossing illegally into the U.S., but he has little hope it will be seen on Mexican TV. In newspapers, he says, there is more independence. But on TV, "you live with censorship or you don't survive."

Canadians share with Mexicans the feeling that they're misunderstood and taken for granted by their colossal neighbor, but drugs, debt and immigration are not the grating conflicts they are for Mexico. The biggest U.S.-Canada issue these days is free trade.

The new trade agreement, which would do away with most tariffs between the two countries, is not something most Americans know about. "It's invisible in the States," says John Owen, chief news editor of CBC's newscast, *The National*, "but it's a raging issue here. . . . I've got a printout behind me of items we've done [about it on the newscast], and it's extraordinarily thick."

Another subject about which it seems impossible to get the attention of Americans is acid rain, the forest-destroying fallout from factories, many of them located in the United States. That's why *The National* paid a lot of attention to the perjury trial of Michael Deaver, the former White House deputy chief of staff. He was accused of lying under oath about using his White House connections to bring a number of issues, including acid rain, to the attention of the Administration.

Not all the Canadian news items about America concern weighty subjects, however. CBC correspondent Terry Milewski finds "there's a lot of interest in the weird and wacky world of the United States." There was enormous reaction, he says, to a story he did on the PTL and fallen evangelists Jim and Tammy Bakker. The Ivan Boesky insider-trader story was covered, too, and the arrest of Wall Street brokers for trading in cocaine. John Hinckley's bid to be allowed home for Easter, Amy Carter's acquit-

tal of charges of trespassing and disorderly conduct, Oliver North's testimony, Gary Hart's trip to Bimini, surrogate mother Mary Beth Whitehead's visits to her daughter—all these seem as foreign to Canadians, says Milewski, "as a Japanese tea ritual. We don't suffer the same afflictions in Canada, where everything is nice and bland and medium."

And what image of America emerges from all this? "We look at the United States," says Milewski, "as our best friend and as a battered, slightly crazy giant that we have to be nice to."

From the evidence of its newscasts, Canada's view of the U.S. is as ambivalent as Mexico's, a combination of admiration and wariness, with an underdog's sense of competitiveness thrown in.

That's why it was such big news in Canada when CBC's national correspondent Peter Mansbridge was wooed by CBS. He was offered a prince's ransom to come to New York and co-host the new *CBS This Morning* program with Kathleen Sullivan. He decided to turn CBS down and stay in Canada. "It was a huge story here," says Mansbridge's boss at the CBC, John Owen. "A lot of instant hero-worship. . . . People were writing in and saying, 'Thank God someone said no to the Yanks!'"

Such nationalistic sentiments, understandable though they are, can only perpetuate the fragmentary and sometimes distorted images of the United States presented by Canadian and Mexican newscasts. Juan Ruiz-Healy, a journalist with a reformer's zeal to improve TV news, hopes that one day the three largest countries sharing the North American continent will be able to get beyond defensiveness and stereotypes.

"We need to show the reality of the United States," he says. "And our own reality. Let people speak out for and against. Let them be seen. We don't know each other. We've got to open things up!"

FOREIGN NEWS GATEKEEPERS AND CRITERIA OF NEWSWORTHINESS

SOPHIA PETERSON

Sophia Peterson shows how cultural differences among the editors, reporters and stringers of *The Times* of London affect their judgment of what is newsworthy.

In a democratic society newspapers, especially elite papers, play a central role in providing information for decision-makers and the attentive public.[1] The selection of news is, therefore, crucially important. If newsmen share a pattern of preferences as to what is newsworthy, and that pattern does not represent reality, they will present a distorted image of the world which may contribute inappropriate decisions and policies.

This is an inquiry into news selection by newsmen responsible for the foreign news printed in *The Times* (London), commonly regarded as one of the world's great newspapers.[2] It concentrates on two questions: (1) What events in countries other than Great Britain are likely to be preferred by *The Times* newsmen as being newsworthy, and (2) Is there a consensus about the comparative newsworthiness of events or is there some divergence arising from the diverse cultural backgrounds and/or organizational positions of the newsmen?

To answer these questions a mail questionnaire was administered to the 98 persons in London and abroad who gather and process foreign news for *The Times*. This staff is made up of three major subgroups: the home office editorial staff, the staff correspondents, and the stringers.[3] The questionnaire tested a group of hypotheses derived largely from the work of Galtung and Ruge, and Smith.[4] Briefly stated, their research suggests that news is structured because newsmen more readily perceive events with certain properties as newsworthy. Galtung and Ruge also believe these preferences may vary with the cultural background of the newsmen. Other research points to the importance of organizational position in affecting news choices.

RELEVANT THEORY AND RESEARCH

News Selection

The news selection process is sub-divided into news gathering and news processing. News gatherers are the correspondents and stringers who select from the multitude of events those which they will transform into news copy. News processors are the home office editors and sub-editors (copy editors in the U.S.) who select from the news copy those stories which will eventually appear in the newspaper.[5] Although their different organizational functions may cause news gatherers and processors to have somewhat divergent views, nevertheless they influence each other greatly. Because of this relationship, Cohen argues that the "flow of news" should more accurately be termed the "circle of news."[6]

Gatekeeping

For many years, Kurt Lewin's concept of the "gatekeeper" provided the organizing principle for studies on news selection. Lewin conceived that news flowed along a channel containing several gates controlled by gatekeepers each of whom would

Sophia Peterson, "Foreign News Gatekeepers and Criteria of Newsworthiness." *Journalism Quarterly*, Volume 56, Number 1, Spring 1979, pp. 116–125. Reprinted by permission.

The author was at the University of West Virginia when this article was written.

make a decision as to whether the news item should continue on through the channel. Lewin's framework focused research upon the individual gatekeeper, although Lewin indicated that one should also investigate the forces acting upon the gatekeeper.[7] The limitations of this basically linear and individual-oriented model are cogently expressed by Bailey and Lichty:

> Earlier gatekeeping models were deficient primarily because of a narrowness of perspective. To take the individual as the gatekeeper is to deny the great body of knowledge about the social and organizational context of individual behavior.[8]

Organization Theory

Awareness of the drawbacks of an over-simplified model led researchers to utilize an organizational model to explain news selection.[9] In her study of American press treatment of the Indochina War, Welch emphasized the organizational constraints in news selection:

> Any organization has characteristics that shape and reinforce the attitudes of those who are part of it and thereby influence the content of decisions made. Despite, or because of, the hierarchical structure of organizations that gives particular individuals key roles in decision-making, these decisions are made within an organizational context. The totality of an objective situation is never perceived by any individual. Since reality is so complex, only a limited part of it can be observed and assimilated. Organizations in their divisions of labor and responsibility inherently specify a set of limits on a member's definition of reality.[10]

In sum, perceptions of reality depend upon a person's role in an organization.

The influence of organizational position upon perspective is explained further by the concept of "uncertainty absorption."

> The further an individual is from the entity about which he is receiving information, the greater are the cumulative biases which enter into [his] . . . perception of reality. Each person in the chain of information that connects him to the event will make judgments about what he has actually seen or been told, and draw certain conclusions. These selections from the total mass of information that serves to make judgments simpler and more consistent constitute "uncertainty absorption."[11]

The individuals in the news process farthest from the actual events are those in the home office—the editorial staff which selects from raw news copy the small fraction which will actually appear in *The Times*. It may be expected, therefore, that uncertainty absorption is greatest in the home office. The "cumulative biases" which would be used to interpret events are the criteria for newsworthy events to which newsmen are socialized by a variety of means (interaction with other newsmen, reading newspapers, reinforcement when their judgments are upheld by superiors, *etc.*). The reliance upon traditional news criteria by the home office would presumably be challenged least frequently by actual confrontation with events. This is in contrast to the staff correspondents and stringers who, at least part of the time, directly observe the events they report and thus need rely somewhat less on traditional news criteria.[12]

The different orientations of the home office as compared with the correspondents and stringers may also contribute to a difference of perspective. The former are audience-oriented; the latter are source-oriented: "The processors regard gatherers as over-involved in their particular subjects; the gatherers see the processors as playing *down* to the audience."[13]

Cultural Background

One final factor must be explored in discussing possible divergent news choices among the three main sub-groups—cultural difference.[14] Galtung and Ruge speculate about the role that the particular cultural orientations of newsmen with a European-North American background might have in news selection, although they do not analyze this factor in depth.[15] Because of the lack of research along this avenue of inquiry, however, one can only conjecture as to the possible effects of cultural differences between newsmen of the industrialized, complex, modern cultures of Europe and North America (almost all the home office staff and correspondents) and those of the cultures of the rest of the world (a large proportion of the stringers).

At one obvious level, news selection may be influenced by homophily—interaction with those like ourselves.[16] That is, the cultural similarity of newsmen from the European-North American region may predispose them to select news about their own region as more newsworthy. Or, since Europe and North America contain most of the elite nations in the world, newsmen from this region, more than those from other regions, may be likely to select news events involving elite nations both in and out of their region.

At another level, divergence in news selection may arise between newsmen from Europe and North America and those from other regions because of the comparatively more individualist cultural orientation of the former; in other words, divergence arises from the nature of the culture itself. As discussed by the cultural anthropologist Hsu, this individualist orientation is most characteristic of European (or European-derived) societies:

> Individualism is that conception of each human being as unique and as possessing God-given rights which cannot be taken away from him by men, society, or tradition. To express this uniqueness he must have freedom and, to safeguard his right, his due is equality. Individualism so defined was only initiated and exemplified by Occidental peoples of our Type B [societies of a majority of the Western peoples—Europeans and the peoples of European origin throughout the world] and was unknown among all other peoples before the impact of the West.[17]

Other anthropologists have also differentiated the more modern western culture from others in terms of individualism (recognizing, of course, that there are variations within all cultures).[18] This value orientation may affect news selection by establishing a preference among newsmen from Europe and North America for news events in which individual human beings (rather than social forces) are clearly the focus of the story.

An individual-oriented culture entails greater competition and momentum for change in contrast to traditional societies where obedience to authority and interdependence are stressed.[19] Competition and a change-orientation leads to greater conflict.[20] Thus newsmen who are members of a more conflict-oriented culture may regard conflictual events as more newsworthy since conflict figures more prominently in their world view.

At the same time, cultural divergence in news selection may be mitigated by the fact that *The Times* stringers of all regions are socialized professionally to western news criteria and they are all aware that they are writing for a British audience.[21] It is probable, however, that the home office and correspondents are more effectively socialized to western news criteria. Even if correspondents are stationed abroad, almost all are British born and educated, almost all learned their profession in Britain serving on *The Times* and/or other British news media, and remain in daily contact with the home office.

Properties of Events[22]

Galtung and Ruge developed a framework of analysis consisting of a list of "news-factors"—the properties of events which increase the likelihood that an event will be perceived as newsworthy. They hypothesize that the following news factors, all other things being equal, will increase the probability of an event being perceived and recorded.[23]

Frequency. A news event will be perceived as more newsworthy if it takes place within the same time frame (frequency) as the news medium operates (in the case of a daily newspaper, 24 hours).

Threshold. An event must make a "big enough splash" before it will be perceived. There are two dimensions of this phenomenon: *absolute intensity* (the more violent the murder, the more newsworthy), and *intensity increase* which relates to the degree of change regarding the event.

Unambiguity. An event whose interpretation is clear and direct will probably be perceived as more newsworthy than one which is not. Closely related to unambiguity is simplification—the less complicated the event, the easier it is to draw conclusions.

Meaningfulness. Meaningfulness involves two dimensions: cultural proximity and relevance. An event will be perceived as meaningful because it occurs in a nation culturally familiar or in close association to your own (to *The Times* home office, this is West Europe, the United States, and former members of the British Empire). Or, an event may be meaningful even if it occurs in a culturally distant nation because of special relevance to your own (for example, it produces an important product).

Domestic News. This hypothesis is supplementary to the cultural proximity hypothesis.[24] It maintains that domestic news about a foreign country is perceived as more newsworthy than international news involving the same actor. The majority of foreign news is in reality domestic news about foreign countries, not international news (that is, news involving interactions between international actors, or news with clear ramifications for other international actors). Such a preference may occur because domestic events seem more proximate (psychologically closer) to a correspondent or to a stringer who has probably lived in the country most of his life. This may be, therefore, a test of proximity as a news factor.

Consonance. Consonance involves two dimensions: predictability and demand. What is expected to happen is both what one predicts is likely to occur and what one wants to occur.

Unexpectedness. This news factor is not merely the opposite of consonance. It is the unexpected "within the meaningful and the consonant" that increases the likelihood of perception of the event. Given a set of events both meaningful (culturally familiar and relevant) and consonant (predicted and desired), that event will be perceived as newsworthy which is unexpected or rare.

Elitism. The preference for reporting events involving elite nations and/or elite persons may reflect the recognition that at least in the immediate future, the actions of such actors have more impact than those of non-elites. In addition, the elites possess a natural salience which raises them above the threshold necessary before an actor and the act will be perceived. The special attention paid to elite nations and persons may thus be another example of the operations of the threshold news factor.[25]

Personalization. A personal orientation in news selection emphasizes events as the individual acts of human beings instead of the results of social forces. Events clearly associated with individual human beings may be regarded as more newsworthy because of the ease of identifying with human beings and the techniques of newsgathering which depend heavily on personal interviews. Further, personalization relates to frequency and elitism. People can act within the news medium time span—social forces move more gradually. And, obviously, elitism is an attribute of persons, not of social forces.

Negativity. Negative, or conflictual, events fulfill several requirements: frequency, unambiguity, consonance, and unexpectedness. Although Galtung and Ruge found a preference for negative events in their study, Smith did not. Because of his negative findings, Smith speculated that negativity contributed to newsworthiness, particularly when the consequences of the events were negative "*as perceived by the recorder.*"[26] This, in effect, combines meaningfulness (especially its relevance dimension) with negativity.

The Replication Hypothesis

Finally, the replication hypothesis posits: "*the process of selection* [of those events which satisfy the news factors] . . . *will take place at all steps in the* [news] *chain from event to reader.*"[27] The data will permit comparison of the news gatherers (correspondents and stringers) with the news processors (the home office staff) to determine whether replication occurs between the two stages. Many students of journalism affirm the existence of a "news consensus" among newsmen—agreement as to what constitutes news.[28]

On the other hand, while a news consensus may exist defining general agreement as to newsworthiness, within that area of agreement there is reason to expect some divergence of perspectives among newsmen because of their functional and/or cultural diversity. Thus, this study tests the hypotheses against the three different organizational units with the following expectations:

1. that the home office staff will tend to confirm the hypotheses most strongly because of their organizational position and common British background;
2. that the stringers who do confirm the hypotheses most strongly will be those from Europe and North America since their criteria of newsworthiness will probably be similar to those of the predominantly British home office and correspondents.

THE RESEARCH DESIGN

Most research attempting to determine newsmen's preference for certain types of events has suffered from the same problem—lack of an objective standard of the real world. Comparison of one newspaper's output with another's or with a non-newspaper (such as a set of documents) does not answer the question as to what has been systematically excluded from all sources.

To avoid this problem, the strategy of this study was to create its own universe of events constructed to test the hypotheses. This was done by means of a 16-item questionnaire made up of 15 sets of two events, and one set of three events, in which the respondents (the 98 *Times* newsmen) were asked to rank the events in each set according to which they thought had a better claim to be published in *The Times*. It was not necessary that they think the events should be published—only relative, not absolute, judgments were requested. The mail questionnaire, which included questions about personal and professional background, was administered during the spring of 1975 to 98 newsmen, everyone who gathered or processed foreign news for *The Times*. The response rate was 74.5%.[29]

FINDINGS: NEWS CRITERIA HYPOTHESES

Table 1 presents the results of the questionnaire including the actual news items which the newsmen ranked according to newsworthiness. Each set of news items is ordered so that the item which the hypothesis held should be given preference for publication is listed first.

With one exception, the responses were in the predicted direction. The exception was the consonance hypothesis, in which only 15% of the entire group ranked the "correct" news item first. The set of news items devised to test this hypothesis was designed to test predictability (assuming that it is to be expected that a Socialist nation will recognize a Marxist government) and demand (assuming that it is in the British tradition to extend recognition to whatever government establishes effective control over a country). It is possible that the questionnaire instructions to "regard the events as bona fide events reported by reliable sources" undercut the consonance hypothesis.

Although the three sub-groups ranked news items, by and large, similarly, it is interesting to note those cases where the greatest differences appeared. For example, in testing the meaningfulness hypothesis, although all three sub-groups agreed that the item involving New Zealand (rather than Thailand) was more newsworthy, 63% of stringers did so in contrast to 83% of the home office. Although respondents were asked to rank events in terms of what they thought should be printed in *The Times* (and, therefore, presumably kept in mind the British audience), it appears that what was meaningful for the home office was not quite so meaningful to the stringers.

Another hypothesis on which there was as large a difference of opinion was the domestic news hypothesis. All three subgroups agreed that the item involving the purely domestic American news item should be published in preference to the news item with international relevance, but 78% of the home office and 75% of the staff correspondents ranked the domestic event first in contrast to 58% of the stringers. The considerable support of both the home office staff and the correspondents for the American domestic event may reflect the clear priority given by *The Times* to the United States (the only nation in which it stations three correspondents). Stringers from more diverse backgrounds may not share so strongly the sense of newsworthiness of purely domestic American events.

Finally, in testing the personalization hypothesis,

Table I   STORY CHOICES OF *THE TIMES* NEWSMEN, IN PERCENT

Hypothesis and News Items	Home Office N = 18	Staff Corre- spondents N = 12	Stringers N = 43	All N = 73
Hypothesis 1: Frequency News Factor				
A new program was inaugurated today to deal with rising crime rate due to economic recession in Nation B.	78%	67%	72%	73%
Nation A's crime rate is rising in the midst of a continuing economic recession.	17	25	26	23
* * *				
Today representatives from Nation C and Nation D signed an agreement providing for construction of a new bridge which will link their two countries	78	83	79	80
Work is proceeding on schedule in building a bridge which will link Nation A and Nation B. Four pilings are being constructed to support the structure.	17	17	16	16
Hypothesis 2: Threshold News Factor (Absolute Intensity)				
The Foreign Minister of Nation A has been shot to death by an assassin.	94	92	95	95
The Foreign Minister of Nation B has died as a result of injuries in an automobile accident.	0	0	0	0
Hypothesis 2: Threshold News Factor (Intensity Increase)				
During the last week the epidemic in Nation A has claimed three times more victims than in the previous week.	72	75	70	71
Death due to starvation and disease continues as drought in Nation B persists in the central provinces.	22	8	23	21
Hypothesis 3: Unambiguity News Factor				
A large fish kill was reported as a result of radioactive leakage from Nation A's submarine anchored off shore of Nation B.	94	100	91	93
Nation C and Nation D disagree about the dangers of contamination resulting from leakage from nuclear plants seeping into the ocean.	6	0	7	5

Table I   *(Continued)*

Hypothesis and News Items	Home Office N = 18	Staff Corre- spondents N = 12	Stringers N = 43	All N = 73
Hypothesis 4: Meaningfulness News Factor (Cultural Proximity)				
New Zealand has signed a trade agreement with Nation B	83	75	63	70
Thailand has signed a trade agreement with Nation A	6	0	28	18
Hypothesis 4: Meaningfulness News Factor (Relevance)				
Coffee-growing nations of South America announced a rise in the export price of coffee next year.	94	92	88	90
Thailand has announced a rise in the export prices of teak next year—other teak-producing nations will follow suit.	0	8	7	5
Hypothesis 5: Domestic News Dominance				
Today the U.S. Congress passed a new Omnibus Education Bill.	78	75	58	66
The United States has signed a new cultural-education exchange agreement with Nation A today.	17	25	37	30
* * *				
The government of Nation A has been overturned in a bloodless coup d'etat.	83	67	84	81
Nation B and Nation C have broken off relations with one another.	0	8	12	8
Hypothesis 6: Consonance News Factor				
A (Socialist) nation has promptly established diplomatic relations with the new Marxist government of a South American nation.	17	17	14	15
A (Socialist) nation is resisting pressure to recognize the new Marxist government of a South American nation.	72	83	81	79
Hypothesis 7: Unexpectedness News Factor				
The USA and the USSR are expected to announce at their summit meeting an agreement as to additional controls regarding underground nuclear tests.	72	75	72	73

Table I (*Continued*)

Hypothesis and News Items	Home Office N = 18	Staff Corre- spondents N = 12	Stringers N = 43	All N = 73
The UN Disarmament Commission, amongst whose members are the USA and the USSR, is expected to announce agreement as to additional controls regarding underground nuclear tests.	22	25	23	23
Hypothesis 8: Elitism News Factor (Persons)				
The King of Nation B was married today to a member of the nobility.	90	100	88	91
Mr. and Mrs. John Doe were the hundredth couple to be married in the capital city of Nation A today.	0	0	9	5
Hypothesis 8: Elitism News Factor (Nations)				
The Chinese People's Republic signed a treaty with Nation C today.	78	75	84	81
India signed a treaty with Nation A today.	0	0	12	7
Indonesia signed a treaty with Nation B today.	0	0	0	0
Hypothesis 9: Personalization News Factor				
President John Doe of (developing) Nation A sees his political future jeopardized unless he pursues industrial development as vigorously as possible whatever the environmental cost.	61	58	47	52
The struggle to maintain worldwide environmental quality is complicated by the different stages of industrial growth between the developing and the developed countries. The former see their immediate problem as raising the standard of living of their people through rapid industrialization despite the environmental cost, while the latter have achieved high standards of living and already face the dramatic deterioration of their environments resulting from previous years of uncontrolled development.	39	25	44	40
Hypothesis 10: Negativity News Factor (General)				
Nation C and Nation D have abrogated their mutual defense agreement.	67	83	70	71

Hypothesis and News Items	Home Office N = 18	Staff Corre-spondents N = 12	Stringers N = 43	All N = 73
Table I				
(Continued)				
Nation A and Nation B have signed their mutual defense agreement.	17	0	21	16
Hypothesis 10: Negativity News Factor (Specific)				
Turkey has withdrawn from NATO and will no longer participate in European defense.	89	92	93	92
Argentina has withdrawn from the Organization of American States and will no longer be bound by its decisions.	0	0	2	1

Note: This table reports the percentages of respondents who picked the given story first in the particular pair or triplet. Percentages do not add to 100 for each pair or triplet because for each question there were some "no answer" responses.

although all three groups preferred the news item focusing on an individual, the stringers divided almost evenly (47%–44%) on whether the personalized news item should be preferred. Since many stringers live in developing countries, they many be more aware of the social forces operating in their countries. They may also, as previously discussed, not share the individualist orientation of westerners.

In summary, the results suggest strongly that news criteria shape a picture of the world's events characterized by erratic, dramatic, and uncomplicated surprises, by negative or conflictual events involving elite nations and persons. Furthermore, a certain parochialism surrounds news selection with a preference for the domestic over the international event, and for the event narrowly relevant to the particular culture of the newspaper.

FINDINGS: THE REPLICATION HYPOTHESIS

The replication hypothesis states: ". . . *the process of selection* [of those events which satisfy the news factors] . . . *will take place at all steps in the* [news] *chain from event to reader.*"[30]

The Times respondents occupy two different points in the news chain—news gathering and news processing. It is clear from the findings that by and large the three sub-groups agreed in the general direction of their rankings of the newsworthiness of events. In all tests of the hypotheses they shared the same modal position in ranking the same event first. The replication hypothesis is supported.

FINDINGS: SUB-GROUP DIVERGENCE

While news consensus was anticipated, it was also suggested that the three subgroups might disagree to some extent because of organizational and/or cultural differences. Research expectations were:

1. that the home office will tend to confirm the hypotheses most strongly;
2. that the stringers who do confirm the hypotheses most strongly would be those from Europe and North America since their criteria of newsworthiness will probably be similar to those of the predominantly British home office and correspondents.

One way to determine if there are differences

among the three sub-groups in their judgments of the newsworthiness of events is to correlate the pattern of responses for each respondent over all rankings of the events against a "perfect" response pattern confirming all the hypotheses. Thus one could answer the question: Which of the sub-groups ranked the events most closely to the predictions of the hypotheses? Seventy respondents were ranked according to the similarity of their response patterns with the "perfect" hypotheses-confirming pattern. The highest rank correlation was .75; the lowest was .20. The median was .54.[31] Those above and below the median were divided according to the three sub-groups to which they belonged. A majority of the correlations for home office editors and staff correspondents were above the median. A majority of the correlations for stringers were below the median. Cultural differences seem to explain disagreement on rankings more than does organizational position.

The importance of cultural factors in influencing news preference is further substantiated by looking more closely at those stringers who were above the median in support of the hypotheses. Eleven (44%) of the total group of 25 stringers born and educated in Europe or North America were above the median. Only four (25%) of the 16 stringers born and educated in the rest of the world were above the median. This also confirms the importance of the cultural factors in shaping news choices.

CONCLUSION

In contrast to past research, which by and large has inferred news criteria from newspaper *output*, this is a study of *input*—it provides evidence directly from newsmen as to the nine news criteria guiding their news choices. It also provides evidence of news consensus and of divergence within that general consensus. Newsmen socialized to the news norms of Europe and North America, but born and educated in other parts of the world, diverge somewhat from those news norms. Different cultural regions doubtless maintain varied perceptual maps of the world, and the press aids in sustaining those divergent perceptions.

Future research may well utilize Galtung and Ruge's framework for analyzing news selection in other settings. For example, a modified questionnaire could be utilized to determine whether newsmen of other non-western newspapers such as *Al Ahram* of Egypt or the *Times of India* rely upon similar news criteria. Or, it might be applied to the study of other types of news media, for example, radio and television. The latter are particularly important because for many citizens in developing countries radio is a very significant source of news, while television is heavily relied upon in the developed countries.

Finally, since one of the findings of this study is that cultural differences affect news selection, this question might be pursued in greater depth since it is a relatively unexplored area. A more systematic scientific understanding of the effect of cultural differences would be a contribution not only to our understanding of news selection, but also to the current debate on western news coverage of the Third World. That debate often revolves around the issue of press freedom. An awareness of cultural bias might introduce an important missing element in that debate.

NOTES

1. In a study of what top leaders of American political and economic institutions read, Carol H. Weiss found *The New York Times* to be the most widely read. Further, in the area of foreign policy the media were the leading information sources and provided highly regarded input for the leaders' debate and decisions. "What America's Leaders Read," *Public Opinion Quarterly*, 38:1–22 (Spring 1974). For further discussion of the role of newspapers see Johan Galtung and Mari Holmboe Ruge, "The Structure of Foreign News," *Journal of Peace Research*, 2:64 (Spring 1965).

2. John C. Merrill, *The Elite Press: Great Newspapers of the World* (New York: Pitman Publishing Company, 1968), pp. 170–177.

3. Stringers are not usually full-time reporters for *The Times*. They provide stories from time to time on a retainer and/or linage basis but are also simultaneously employed by other media organizations and are usually foreign nationals. Edwin Samuel, "The Administration of the Times," *Public Administration in Israel and Abroad 1973*, 14:226 (1974).

4. Galtung and Ruge, *op. cit.*, Raymond F. Smith, "On the Structure of Foreign News: A Comparison of the *New York Times* and the Indian *White Papers*," *Journal of Peace Research*, 6:23–36 (Spring 1969).

5. See Bass' illustration of this two-stage flow of news. Abraham Z. Bass, "Refining the 'Gatekeeper' Concept: A UN Radio Case Study," *Journalism Quarterly*, 46:72 (Spring 1969).

6. Bernard C. Cohen, *The Press and Foreign Policy* (Princeton: Princeton University Press, 1963), p. 91.

7. Kurt Lewin, "Frontiers in Group Dynamics: II Channels of Group Life: Social Planning and Action Research." *Human Relations*, 1:145–146 (Summer 1947).

8. George A. Bailey and Lawrence W. Lichty. "Rough Justice on a Saigon Street: A Gatekeeper Study of NBC's Tet Execution Film," *Journalism Quarterly*, 49:221–9: 238 (1972).

9. Leon V. Sigal, *Reporters and Officials: The Organization and Politics of Newsmaking* (Lexington: D.C. Heath and Company, 1973); Jeremy Tunstall, *Journalists at Work* (Beverly Hills: Sage Publications, 1971).

10. Susan Welch, "The American Press and Indochina, 1950–1956," in Richard L. Merritt, ed., *Communication in International Politics* (Urbana: University of Illinois Press, 1972), pp. 227–228.

11. *Ibid.*

12. Leo Bogart reports that "First-hand observational reporting represents a source . . . for a fourth of the stories [filed by the typical foreign correspondent]." "The Overseas Newsman: A 1967 Profile Study," *Journalism Quarterly*, 45:305 (Summer 1968).

13. Tunstall, *op. cit.*, p. 279. John T. McNelly's research on intermediary communicators in foreign news gathering and processing provides a bridge between the concept of "uncertainty absorption" and audience- versus source-orientation. "Intermediary Communicators in the International Flow of News," *Journalism Quarterly*, 36:26 (Winter 1959). Tunstall confirms that "Processing lends itself to a greater degree of routine than does gathering. Rules are more applicable in processing." Tunstall, *op. cit.*, p. 41.

14. Almost 40% of the stringers were born and educated in regions outside Europe and North America where almost all the home office and correspondents were born and educated.

15. Galtung and Ruge, *op. cit.*, pp. 68–70. Culture is defined as "the integrated system of learned patterns of behavior, ideas, and products characteristic of a society." Paul G. Hieberts *Cultural Anthropology* (Philadelphia: J. B. Lippincott, 1976), p. 25. The discussion of culture in this study focuses on the ideas, in particular the values, of modern western cultures in contrast to the more traditional cultures of Asia, Africa, and Latin America. See Mary Ellen Goodman, *The Individual and Culture* (Homewood: Dorsey Press, 1967), pp. 228–229.

16. James C. McCroskey, Carl E. Larson, and Mark I. Knapp, *An Introduction to Interpersonal Communication* (Englewood Cliffs: Prentice-Hall, 1971), p. 237.

17. Francis L. K. Hsu, "Kinship and Ways of Life: An Exploration," in Francis L. K. Hsu, ed., *Psychological Anthropology* (Homewood: Dorsey Press, 1961), p. 418. In the same volume see also Hsu, "American Core Value and National Character," p. 217: "A qualified individualism with a qualified equality has prevailed in England and the rest of Europe."

18. Hiebert, *op. cit.*, p. 360; Goodman, *op. cit.*, pp. 226–228.

19. Hsu, "American Core Value," p. 224; Francis I. K. Hsu, *Clan, Caste, and Club* (Princeton: D. Van Nostrand, 1963), p. 221.

20. Hsu, *Clan, Caste, and Club*, pp. 215, 236, 244–245; Hsu, "American Core Value," pp. 224–225.

21. Einar Ostgaard, "Factors Influencing the Flow of News," *Journal of Peace Research*, 2:42 (Spring 1965). See also James W. Markham, "Foreign News in the United States and South American Press," *Public Opinion Quarterly*, 25:262 (Summmer 1961).

22. The properties of events are clearly not the only factors which influence news selection. See Sophia Peterson, "News Selection and Source Validity," in Don Munton, ed., *Measuring International Behavior: Validity Problems in Event Data* (Halifax: Dalhousie University Centre for Foreign Policy Studies, forthcoming).

23. For a full explanation of these news factors see Galtung and Ruge, *op. cit.*, pp. 65–71. Several media studies corroborate the role such news factors in news selection: Walter Gieber, "Across the Desk: A Study of 16 Telegraph Editors," *Journalism Quarterly*, 33:432 (Fall 1956); Gene Gilmore and Robert Root, *Modern Newspaper Editing* (Berkeley: The Glendessary Press, 1971), pp. 110–111; Delmer D. Dunn, *Public Officials and the Press* (Reading: Addison-Wesley Publishing, 1969), pp. 25–27; Cohen, *op. cit.*, p. 94; Markham, *op. cit.*, pp. 249–262.

24. This hypothesis was not derived from Galtung and Ruge, but from a review of research and analysis of newspaper output. There are many reasons why do-

mestic events may be perceived as more newsworthy. Correspondents and stringers rely heavily for news upon the newspapers in the countries they cover, which typically concentrate on domestic news.

25. Elite nations include the superpowers (USA and USSR), potential superpowers (CPR and Japan), or the upper range of the middle powers (France, Great Britain, West Germany, Italy, and India). Categorization derives from Trygve Mathisen, *The Functions of Small States in the Strategies of the Great Powers* (Oslo-Bergen-Tromsco: Universitetsforlaget, 1971), pp. 17–20. Elite persons are defined as the top leaders of a country (head of state, prime minister, president, *etc.*).

26. Smith, *op. cit.*, p. 33.

27. Galtung and Ruge, *op. cit.*, p. 71.

28. Sigal, *op. cit.*, p. 3; Gilmore and Root, *op. cit.*, p. 117; Cohen, *op. cit.*, p. 90; Emery L. Sasser and John T. Russell, ''The Fallacy of News Judgment,'' *Journalism Quarterly*, 49:280 (Summer 1972).

29. Of the 30 members of the London home office, 18 responded; of the 14 staff correspondents, 12 responded from 8 of the 10 countries in which they were stationed (West Germany, Italy, South Africa, Chinese People's Republic, Japan, Israel, Lebanon, Belgium, France, and the United States); of the 54 stringers, 43 responded from 36 of the 43 countries in which they are employed.

30. Galtung and Ruge, *op. cit.*, p. 71.

31. The correlations were based on 35 questionnaire items—the 16 items reported here plus 19 more items which tested the complementarity hypothesis: ''If the event is low on one dimension or factor *it may compensate for that by being high on another*, and still make the news.'' Galtung and Ruge, *op. cit.*, p. 72. Space did not permit presentation here of the results of testing the complementarity hypothesis. In computing correlations, three respondents were excluded because they answered fewer than $\frac{1}{3}$ of the 35 different questions (two stringers and one home office member). ''No answer'' responses were excluded so that the correlations are based on actual rankings only. The Spearman rank correlations were performed on the IBM/360 using the SAS program.

5 SOVIET BLOC SYSTEMS

Communism was conceived of as a *supra*national political party, uniting the ''workers of the world'' in a dictatorship of the proletariat over the capitalist bourgeoisie. Among the earliest international radio broadcasts were those of the Bolsheviks, calling on the workers of the world to unite—''you have nothing to lose but your yokes!''

It wasn't, however, until World War II, starting in 1939, that the Soviet Union, through military action and negotiation, was able to start exporting communism to neighboring countries. At the end of the war, the Soviet Union was in effective control of Lithuania, Latvia, Estonia, Poland, East Germany, Czechoslovakia, Romania, Bulgaria and Hungary. Yugoslavia, while Communist, rejected Stalin's attempt to dictate its policies, but accepted aid from both the Communist bloc and the West. Soon after the People's Republic of China was proclaimed as a Communist state, it signed (in 1950) a treaty of ''friendship, alliance and mutual assistance'' with the Soviet Union. Other countries that have also joined the Communist bloc are Mongolia, North Korea, Vietnam, Laos and Cuba. Albania has run an independent course, siding with the more conservative government of Mao

Tse-tung's China, when the Soviet Union began de-Stalinization in 1960, but breaking with China, too, in 1978, after Mao's death. In 1955, the Soviet Union created the Warsaw Pact, to counter the North Atlantic Treaty Organization alliance of Western nations.

Since the election of Mikhail Gorbachev to various leadership posts (most recently to that of President) in the Soviet Union, there has been a marked easing of tensions between the Western and the Communist bloc, and a trend toward greater openness and involvement of the public in the governments of Communist Europe. Asian Communist governments have been slower in following suit, as we show in the articles that follow.

SOVIET MEDIA IN THE AGE OF GLASNOST

ROBERT L. STEVENSON, HOYT CHILDERS, PETER WEST, AND SUSAN MARSCHALK

Changes in the appearance and content of Soviet mass media have been developing over the past 35 years. But ever since Mikhail Gorbachev took over the leadership of the Soviet Communist party and government in the spring of 1985, Soviet media have been far more open in revealing the "bad news' as well as the good. Journalists on both television and in the principal party newspaper, *Pravda*, have been given greater latitude in who or what may be criticized. The authors, however, find that the staple of Soviet news content has changed little. It remains "the full texts of speeches, greetings and toasts that fall under the category of protocol news," as well as progress in the building of socialism.

A specter is haunting Eastern Europe. It is the specter of glasnost. Glasnost, which comes from the same root as the Russian word for "voice," is usually translated as "openness" and refers to a wide-ranging series of reforms introduced into the Soviet Union by party General Secretary Mikhail S. Gorbachev (Aksyonov, 1987; Baranov and Seleznez, 1987). The reforms appear to be intended mostly to breathe life into a creaky economic system but are reflected publicly in new cracks in a closed political system and, most dramatically, in changes in the mass media the political system controls. If *Pravda* reveals the truth of the Soviet reality, it appears that its truth may be undergoing something close to revolutionary change (Cullen, 1986; Quinn-Judge, 1986; Moody, 1986; Lee, 1987; Mickiewicz, 1987; Remnick, 1987).

In this paper, we will look at the content of the main organ of the Communist Party of the Soviet Union, *Pravda*, and the main news program on

Robert L. Stevenson, Hoyt Childers, Peter West, and Susan Marschalk, "Soviet Media in the Age of Glasnost." International Communication Division, Association for Education in Journalism and Mass Communication, meeting in San Antonio, Texas, August, 1987. Reprinted by permission.

Robert L. Stevenson is professor of journalism at the University of North Carolina, where Hoyt Childers, Peter West, and Susan Marschalk are graduate students.

Soviet TV, *Vremya* or "Time," as they promote and reflect glasnost in early 1987. Our analysis will be both quantitative and qualitative and will focus on two areas. The first is a new style of coverage of mostly domestic affairs that would not have appeared in earlier regimes. The key elements of glasnost-era news are information and criticism, both traditionally scarce in Soviet media. The second is foreign coverage and particularly reporting about the United States, the longstanding bete noire of the Soviet Union and its current rival for world opinion. As prelude to our analysis, we begin with a discussion of the role of mass media in the Soviet Union and the changes in the Soviet system that have made glasnost a familiar word around the world.

SOVIET THEORY OF THE PRESS

Ever since Siebert and his colleagues introduced their four theories of the press (Siebert et al., 1956), we have talked about a communist press theory (or Soviet Communist theory, as they called it), but there is no single source for such a theory. Marx himself wrote frequently about the press but most while a young man in Germany defending his radical journal from government attack (Padover, 1974). Although he usually defended free expression, it was for himself and not his critics. His actions in later life—certainly his monopoly of information in the years of the Communist Internationale—argue against any belief in Western pluralism.

It was Lenin, more than Marx, who defined mass media as an instrument of the party, a role that we still associate with a "communist theory" of mass media. In his famous outline for revolution, *Where to Begin*, Lenin (1973) argued that the press was a superstructure on which a political party organization could be built. And he assigned tasks that are still the basis of a communist press:

The role of a newspaper, however, is not limited soley to the dissemination of ideas, to political education, and to the enlistment of political allies. A newspaper is not only a collective propagandist and a collective agitator, it is also a collective organiser. In this last

respect it may be likened to the scaffolding round a building under construction, which marks the contours of the structure and facilitates communication between the builders, enabling them to distribute the work and to view the common results achieved by their organised labour.

With some minor accommodations to leadership style and outside forces, Soviet mass media continue to the mold established by Lenin. They are an instrument of the party, a part of the control apparatus, and always a monopoly of the political leadership. Hopkins (1970, ch.2) notes how the personalities of the first three Soviet leaders influenced mass media. He argues that neither Stalin nor Khrushchev added significantly to Lenin's press theory. Under Stalin, the media became a servile "company press," while in the Khrushchev years, they were allowed some independence consistent with the intellectual and political thaw that marked his regime.

The imprint of the Soviet leader's personality continued after Khrushchev. The media under Brezhnev fell into the same kind of lethargic stupor that infected the Soviet economy. But unlike earlier times, the Soviet people could not be isolated from the outside world. Brezhnev's policy of detente matched an active engagement with the word of foreign affairs with a tightening of social control at home and persecution of dissidents unlike anything since the Stalin purges. Despite that, however, more and more Soviets had first- or at least secondhand contact with the West (and with the icons of the Western information age and pop culture) and seemed less willing to accept a media reality that ignored real events in favor of a predictable litany of socialist achievements and exhortations (Hollander, 1972). Smith (1976) and Kaiser (1976), both reporters in Moscow in the early 1970s, describe the difficulty of verifying even the most simple datum of fact: a thick pall of smoke from a forest fire covered Moscow for weeks but went unexplained; a family learned only unofficially and after months of inquiry that a daughter had died in a plane crash officials never acknowledged; changes in the party hierarchy had to be inferred from pictures of officials atop Lenin's tomb—and sometimes even the photos were altered before publication. Despite occasional efforts to brighten the media, notably a campaign to compete with foreign radio (Lisann, 1975), the Brezhnev reign was noted more for the popularity of underground samizdat publications and probably greater reliance on outside information sources than for innovation in the domestic Soviet media. After the dull Brezhnev years and the short regencies of Andropov and Chernenko, it is not surprising that the energy and personality of Gorbachev appeared with the refreshing vigor of a Russian spring after a cold, gray winter.

GLASNOST

Kremlin watchers are still debating the source and purpose of glasnost, and no one pretends to know how it will permanently influence Soviet society (Walker, 1986; Roxburgh, 1987; Nagorski, 1987; Doder, 1986). However, fragments of an outline explaining glasnost might look something like this: Gorbachev inherited a stagnant economy that was steadily falling behind the West in innovation and productivity; several of Brezhnev's foreign policy initiatives—establishment of client states in the Third Word and introduction of a new generation of missiles in Eastern Europe, for example—had led to costly financial obligations with little political pay-off; the solution was a massive overhauling of the top-heavy bureaucracy that ran every aspect of the country and encouragement of the kind of individual initiative that apparently was working in China. The goal, it should be remembered, was a more efficient dictatorship, not Western liberalism. The glasnost model was certainly the disciplined efficiency of East Germany, not the open pluralism of West Germany.

For Gorbachev, glasnost meant enlisting the nation's huge mass media apparatus to outflank the entrenched party and government aparatchiki who had profited from the existing system and to mobilize the mass of ordinary citizens who had never known individual responsibility and who, quite sensibly, saw dangers in getting too enthusiastic about a reform that could be withdrawn as quickly as it was introduced. Curiously enough, his greatest allies were the intellectuals and growing middle class, increasingly well educated, well acquainted with the

shortcomings of Soviet life and the strongest critics of the old regime.

For journalists, glasnost meant an opportunity to delve into areas that had been off-limits. The turning point may have been the explosion at the Chernobyl nuclear reactor in April 1986. It began in the traditional fashion of Soviet reporting. The incident was not even acknowledged until authorities were pressured by Western European governments and media. Then came a few details, grudgingly admitted while Gorbachev himself withdrew from public view. After 10 days, however, he reappeared and began to comment on the disaster with the candor and criticism that had characterized his public style from the beginning. Soviet journalists then took their cues from him and began to report details and criticism with a vigor that must have surprised—and perhaps terrified—their readers and viewers. Some limits were quickly established—*Pravda* was criticized for its candor in reporting the privileges of high party officials—but the notion that journalists were the shock troops of Gorbachev's reforms caught on, and most seemed anxious to test their new independence.

What is new about glasnost journalism? A panel assembled by *Public Opinion* magazine (Pell, 1987) argued that Soviet media now present more information and more criticism, but "more" is relative. Since Lenin's time, Soviet media have functioned as a kind of inspector general corps for the regime, encouraging whistle-blowing on low-level bureaucrats and managers and calling attention to malfeasance, misfeasance and simple failure. All within narrow limits, of course. Now the limits have been stretched significantly, but they still exist. According to the *Public Opinion* panel, taboo areas still include almost half of Soviet history, the party itself and its leaders and, of course, communist ideology, including peripheral aspects of it such as atheism.

Still, the waves of fresh air sweeping through Soviet mass media are important enough that they remain newsworthy outside of the Soviet Union. Almost weekly, our own media report breakthroughs in Soviet journalism: critical investigations of the aftermath of Chernobyl, glowing reports on the advantages of McDonald's-style fast food, even stories on the excesses of the KGB (Breath of Fresh Air, 1987; Barnathan and Strasser, 1987; Cuddly

Russia?, 1987; Different Degrees of Candor, 1986; Igiebor, 1987; Mickiewicz, 1987; Moody, 1987; Pipes, 1987; Quinn-Judge, 1987; Remnick, 1987; Smith, 1987; Trewhitt, 1987; Walker, 1986). Not everyone is impressed, however. Vassily Aksyonov (1987), who was expelled from the Soviet Union in 1980 after a novel was published in the West, checked out a sampling of new Soviet journalism:

What's new? Can I distinguish today's Soviet papers from those of yesteryear, which made me so instantly nauseous? Yes, there are things that are new: the mention of some previously taboo problems, a certain critical intonation borrowed from dissident groups of the sixties, some steaming rebukes to the "bureaucracy." But . . . should I state it openly?—the papers still make me nauseous. The foundations of Soviet journalism remain unshakable: not "all the news that's fit to print" but "*our* interpretation of some news that fits *our* print." How could it be otherwise if the press is still "the sharpest weapon of the party"?

Some Western journalists also remain skeptical (Daniloff, 1986; Walker, 1986; Nagorski, 1987; Roxburgh, 1987), but whatever the long-range influence of glasnost on Soviet journalism—a fresh wind or cosmetic coverup—such a departure from the traditions of tightly controlled, predictable journalism deserves a closer look.

PURPOSE

Until recently, our ability to examine Soviet mass media systematically was limited to the tiny handful of researchers who combined an interest in communications with knowledge of Russian. Even then, of course, the vast body of journalism in the non-Russian languages of the Soviet Union was beyond scrutiny, and regular access to domestic Soviet broadcasting was impossible outside the country. The translations, such as the *Current Digest of the Soviet Press* and Foreign Broadcast Information Service reports, were incomplete and selective, and special English-language media, such as *Soviet Life,*

Moscow News, or Radio Moscow, were specially edited for foreign audiences. It was very difficult for most of us to see the world as the Soviet public saw it.

Now the situation is different. With the publication of the English-language translation of *Pravda*, the daily newspaper of the Central Committee of the Communist Party, we have full access to the single most important organ of the Soviet Union. With its 16-million-plus daily circulation, *Pravda* is the largest-circulation daily in the world and, as the voice of the only political party in the Soviet Union, one of the most important. Its influence extends to papers of the smaller units of the party—*Moskovskaya Pravda, Komsomolskaya Pravda,* for example—for which it serves as a model.

With the U.S.-produced English version of *Pravda*, we have—with not unreasonable delay—every word, every picture, every headline of the Russian edition in a format that mirrors the original, even down to the typeface of the distinctive "Pravda" nameplate. In our library, we often find the Russian and English versions mixed in their adjoining bins, evidence, we suspect, that browsers sometimes overlook the difference between the Cyrillic and Roman alphabets.

The Soviet equivalent of the evening network news—the 30-minute *Vremya*—is also now available in English and Russian thanks to the unique circumstance that the Soviet Union's northern geography requires a series of polar satellites rather than geostationary satellites over the equator to distribute programs to ground transmitters throughout the world's largest country. With a relatively simple tracking system, it is possible to monitor Soviet national programming live from most of North America. A new service from World View, Inc., in Oakdale, Iowa, now markets a package of Soviet news, including the full English and Russian texts of *Vremya* with excerpts of the program itself on a weekly videotape compendium.

With this new and unique access to the full text of the most important paper and most important television news program of the Soviet Union, we decided to examine for ourselves the evidence of radical change in Soviet journalism. Rather than testing any specific hypotheses about the impact of glasnost on *Pravda* and *Vremya*, we chose to undertake a relatively straightforward, traditional, descriptive analysis of the two, circa early 1987, with special attention to coverage that seemed to be inspired by glasnost and coverage of the United States, which might also be the test of a new, open style of politics.

METHODOLOGY

Descriptive content analysis is always a risky business because the decisions about what variables to measure and what categories to use are guided more by pragmatics and convention than theory. Nevertheless, the body of recent cross-national comparative studies (Sreberny-Mohammadi, et al., 1985; Stevenson and Shaw, 1984; Mowlana, 1986; Larson, 1984) points to a standard inventory of variables—topic, geographic location, etc.—that any descriptive study should include. We took these studies as a starting point and modified their procedures to suit our specific interests.

Variables

Some variables, such as those noted above, were obligatory, but several others were added to help us focus our analysis on the elements of Soviet media content that seemed most pertinent to the purposes of the study. Several of the variables were related to the Unesco New World Information Order debate, which tried to articulate new functions for the mass media and new definitions of news. The variables were:

1. *Type of news.* One of the major concerns in most content analyses has been the mix of foreign and domestic news, with the argument that Western media (or media in general) fail to pay adequate attention to the rest of the world. The figure for international news coverage depends heavily on its definition because a great deal of news concerns relations between the home country and another. Rather than decide arbitrarily whether a story about the Soviet Union and another country was foreign if it took place abroad but domestic if it took place in the Soviet Union, we opted for a three-category variable: purely domestic, international (involving the Soviet Union and a foreign country, regardless of geographic location) and foreign (with no reference to the Soviet Union).

2. *Geographic location.* This followed the Unesco/IAMCR study definition of geographic regions, but we pulled the Soviet Union itself out of Eastern Europe as a separate category.

3. *Main topic.* This, too, was taken from the Unesco-IAMCR study with one change. Because so much news in the Soviet media deals with economics, we broke that category into two, one essentially macro-economics—international items, performance of the Soviet economy, goals and accomplishments, etc.—the other basically micro-economics, including stories of individuals, housing projects and labor relations.

4. *Time frame.* Stories were coded as happening today/yesterday, recently (but with no specific time mentioned) or without a reference to time. This was of interest partly because of the argument in the New World Information Order debate that news should be less concerned with specific events and more with the processes of social change and partly because of the traditional Leninist definition of news as the unfolding of history rather than discreet events. While most of the NWIO debate has been between the Third World and the West, the Soviet media are closer to the model of "development journalism" than are the Western media.

5. *Type of story.* This category, too, is a product of NWIO debate and Soviet theory. On one hand, Western journalism has been criticized for its orientation toward "coups and earthquakes" and other kinds of disruptive events. In contrast, what is often put forward as more appropriate are protocol and development news. Protocol news is the official comings-and-goings of public officials, exchanges of greetings, etc.; development news is that which is supposed to promote development and to reflect it as well.

6. *Source.* We coded the source—TASS, other media, Western agencies, etc.—to see where the Soviet Communist Party's flagship newspaper and TV newscast turn for their information.

7. *Coverage.* We classified each item in *Pravda* according to whether it was a news story, document or statement, column or commentary, picture or cartoon, or part of a roundup of items. For the television material, the categories were on-location

correspondent report, story read by news anchor, and commentary, usually read by an outside journalist or public official.

8. *Glasnost*. Finally, we tagged each item according to a loose definition of glasnost. Glasnost is something like Justice Stewart's famous comment on pornography: it is hard to define it, but you know it when you see it. In this case, we operationalized glasnost as stories that were characterized by unusual openness and/or criticism, especially those in the tradition of American investigative reporting. Excluded were the traditional how-we-solved-the-problem stories and simple factual reporting of events even though this style of journalism is apparently new. Stories were tagged as glasnost only if they contained significant facts that traditionally had been excluded from the Soviet media, particularly those that reflected badly on the regime, such as comparisons with other countries, negative trends or failures to meet goals. Almost all stories classified as glasnost-related were domestic.

Sample

The *Pravda* sample consisted of 18 days drawn systematically from the first nine weeks of 1987. The constructed week included Monday and Thursday from the first week, Tuesday and Friday from the second and Wednesday and Saturday from the third; the sequence was repeated to provide two more weeks. For TV news, we were limited to what must be considered an availability sample of four weeks. It was used because the regular World View service did not begin until February, 1987. We used the first two weeks of that service and added to it two weeks from January, which had been distributed as a market test. A more rigorous sample could be drawn now, but we have no reason to believe that our sample is significantly non-representative. Tests of the Unesco/IAMCR data (Stevenson and Shaw, 1984, ch. 2) and other earlier similar investigations showed that general patterns of news content are not seriously affected by the sample design.

All separate editorial items were coded (*Pravda*, of course, has no advertising). If a cartoon or picture was typographically and editorially related to a story, it was considered part of the story. If not, it was coded as a separate item. Each item of a roundup—a common editorial device—was coded separately. Similar criteria were used for coding TV data, for which we used the printed English transcript rather than the videotapes themselves.

Coding

Several coders worked together to develop coding procedures and to refine the operational definitions of the variables. After we had established adequate coder reliability coders worked independently.

RESULTS

We have chosen to present the results of this probe into Soviet journalism in the era of glasnost two ways. In this section, we discuss the quantitative findings, supplemented occasionally with examples and other evidence. A selection of specific stories, which together give the reader a sense of the *Pravda* and *Vremya* style that the numbers cannot, is included as an appendix.

We have put most of the results of this analysis of the Soviet Union's premier print and TV news media into Tables 1 and 2 that summarize the results of the quantitative analysis. A few comments will help put them into perspective.

There are differences between the two media that cannot be explained as flukes. Television is more internationally minded than *Pravda* and more oriented toward glasnost-inspired reporting. This can be seen in its greater attention to foreign and international news, greater concern with today's and yesterday's news and even greater attention to disruptive events. Simple, straightforward pieces that are the staple of Western reporting—fighting in Beirut, an earthquake in Latin America, protests in Paris—appear with some regularity. They must be eye-opening to viewers accustomed to a diet of foreign news traditionally limited to labor and social unrest in the West and steady progress toward socialism elsewhere. This trend is in line with Richard Pipes's (1987) comment that Soviet television has been more enthusiastic about glasnost than *Pravda*, which is still under the influence of the older, more traditional party bureaucrats.

Still, to anyone accustomed to Western report-

Table 1   CHARACTERISTICS OF *PRAVDA* AND *VREMYA*

	Pravda (n=530)	Vremya (n=417)
Type of news		
Domestic	49%	35%
International	24	29
Foreign	27	37
Location		
Soviet Union	53%	38%
East Europe	7	5
West Europe	11	19
Nor. America	8	13
Lat. America	5	6
Africa	3	3
Asia/Pacific	8	10
Middle East	3	3
Multi-region/none	3	4
Main topic		
International politics	28%	32%
Domestic politics	11	24
Military/defense	3	5
Macro-economics	9	12
Micro-economics	16	7
International aid	0	0
Social services	3	1
Crime/law/justice	2	2
Culture/arts	6	7
Religion	0	0
Science/technology	9	4
Sports	3	0
Entertainment	1	0
Personalities	1	1
Human interest	4	1
Education	2	0
Ecology/environment	1	1
Natural dis/accidents	2	3
Other	1	0

	Pravda (n=530)	Vremya (n=417)
Time frame of event		
Today/yesterday	29%	36%
Recently	42	28
None	29	37
Type of news		
Protocol	3%	19%
Development	26	18
Disruptive events	8	13
Non-disruptive events	25	30
Routine, recurring event	6	8
Background to event	16	3
Non-event background	16	9
Source		
Staff	31%	72%
TASS	34	22
Western media	2	0
Other Soviet media	3	1
Public officials	3	1
Private citizens	5	1
Unidentified	21	3
Type of item		
News story	47%	
Letter	4	
Document/statement	3	
Roundup	31	
Picture/cartoon	6	
Column/commentary	9	
Correspondent report		26%
Anchor report		72
Commentary		2
Glasnost		
Yes	9%	17%
No	91	83

ing, both *Pravda* and *Vremya* come across as slow, plodding and frequently professionally inept. The language—admittedly in a foreign translation—is dull and burdened with ideological excess. After reading only a few issues or transcripts, these two flagship Soviet media become predictable. The stories that get reported in Western media as examples of glasnost—the kind words about American fast food, the criticism of perks for high-ranking party officials—are newsworthy here because they are exceptional events. The non-exceptional events remain the staple of Soviet news. These include the full texts of speeches, greetings and toasts that fall under the category of protocol news, the stories of

Table 2   CHARACTERISTICS OF NEWS IN *VREMYA* AND *PRAVDA* BY TYPE OF NEWS

	Vremya			Pravda		
	Dom *(n = 144)*	Intl *(119)*	For *(154)*	Dom *(259)*	Intl *(128)*	For *(143)*
Location						
Soviet Union	100%	15%	0%	100%	20%	0%
East Europe	0	6	8	0	16	9
West Europe	0	25	32	0	32	21
Nor America	0	11	25	0	16	16
Lat America	0	3	12	0	6	12
Africa	0	2	7	0	2	8
Asia/Pacific	0	24	9	0	1	17
Middle East	0	2	6	0	1	10
Multi-region/none	0	13	1	0	6	7
Main Topic						
Intl politics	8%	85%	12%	4%	66%	38%
Domestic politics	10	3	53	9	7	20
Military/defense	3	3	9	1	2	9
Macro-economics	30	3	2	11	6	6
Micro-economics	17	1	3	27	4	9
Intl aid	0	0	0	0	2	0
Social services	1	0	1	5	0	1
Crime/law/justice	1	0	5	0	0	5
Culture/arts	15	3	3	11	2	1
Religion	0	0	1	0	1	0
Science/technology	10	0	1	16	3	3
Sports	0	0	1	2	6	0
Entertainment	0	0	0	1	0	0
Personalities	2	1	1	2	2	0
Human interest	0	1	1	6	0	3
Education	0	0	0	2	0	4
Ecology/environment	1	1	0	1	0	1
Natural dis/accidents	1	0	7	2	1	2
Other	1	0	0	1	0	0
Time						
Today/yesterday	41%	46%	23%	24%	41%	27%
Recent	29	24	29	40	40	47
None	30	29	49	36	19	26
Type of story						
Protocol	13%	47%	3%	2%	7%	1%
Development	47	3	2	44	9	10
Disruptive event	3	1	31	4	2	20
Non-disruptive event	14	35	42	14	41	32
Routine event	8	7	9	5	9	18
Background to event	3	1	5	13	20	18
Non-event background	12	7	8	19	12	15

Table 2   (*Continued*)

	Vremya			*Pravda*		
	Dom (n = 144)	*Intl* (119)	*For* (154)	*Dom* (259)	*Intl* (128)	*For* (143)
Source						
Staff	97%	64%	57%	25%	37%	35%
TASS	2	24	38	33	43	29
Western media	0	1	0	0	0	8
Other Soviet media	1	0	1	4	2	2
Public official	0	4	0	4	4	1
Private citizen	0	3	0	9	2	1
Unidentified	0	4	0	26	13	24
Coverage						
Correspondent report	46%	22%	11%			
Anchor report	54	75	86			
Commentary	0	3	3			
News story				47%	59%	36%
Letter				6	2	0
Document/statement				2	2	6
Roundup				27	23	44
Picture/cartoon				7	5	6
Column/commentary				11	8	8
Other				0	1	0
Glasnost						
Yes	38%	7%	6%	15%	6%	3%
No	62	93	94	85	94	97

progress in building socialism that are the heart of development news and the orchestrated view of the world that seems to consist mostly of support for Gorbachev and condemnation of the United States around the world.

It is curious that Western Europe gets more attention than Eastern Europe in both media, an exception to the general global pattern of regional focus in foreign news and a change from the Soviet media analyzed in the 1979 Unesco/IAMCR study (Sreberny-Mohammadi, 1985; Stevenson and Shaw, 1984). And the United States is something of an obsession, particularly to *Vremya*, which devoted 13% of its total coverage to stories from North America; if the total included those datelined in other countries but about the United States, the total would be considerably higher.

A non-rigorous look at *Pravda's* coverage of the

United States (Lichter, et al., 1987), concluded that the appearance of some bad news about the Soviet Union in the glasnost-era Soviet media is not matched by any good news about the United States. In fact, much of the coverage of the United States— and the West in general—seems to be an obviously orchestrated effort to match Western criticism of the Soviet Union. Cases in point are the persecuted intellectual dissident stories that are blatant efforts to find Western equivalents of Andrei Sakharov and the Soviet response to charges of listening devices in the new American embassy in Moscow.

The comparisons in Table 2 show that indeed glasnost is concentrated in domestic coverage. Other differences between domestic and international or foreign coverage are also more or less what one expects: "bad news" of disruptive events does get considerable attention in foreign reporting; the heavy emphasis on economics is largely a domestic phenomenon; TASS is a significant source for foreign and international stories but not for domestic items.

These simple crosstabs only hint at the kind of analysis that can be carried out with even a simple content analysis. A better flavor of the two premier Soviet media can be gained from a reading of the short excerpts we have provided as an appendix to the paper. From these, one detects a style of reporting and writing quite at odds with the standards of a Western newspaper. *Pravda* and *Vremya* today probably have more in common with Lenin's style of journalism than with, say, *The New York Times*. The style is subjective and preachy but probably appropriate to media that are openly agents of the government and instruments of its control of the population.

CONCLUSIONS

We offer three tentative conclusions about Soviet news media in the age of glasnost. One, based on the quantitative analysis, is about glasnost itself. The second is based on a comparison of the results of this study with the earlier Unesco study. And the third is a serendipitous observation about the emphasis on equivalence between the Soviet Union and the United States.

1. *Glasnost.* Those who expect Soviet mass media to have assumed a glasnost role similar to that of the critical, watchdog Western media will be disappointed. *Pravda* and *Vremya* in early 1987 remain more like they were in 1967 than like today's Western media. But there are changes, important changes, that are evident even without the benefit of a comparable assessment 20 years earlier. There is open and critical reporting—up to a point, of course—but these two premier Soviet organs do seem to be on the cutting edge of great changes taking place in the Soviet Union.

2. *Change.* There is change in the kinds of news the two premier Soviet media cover and the way they cover it. Events not immediately linked to the Soviet Union or to the Marxist theory of history do get reported. More attention is paid to today's and yesterday's events rather than to the unfolding of

history. The Soviet Union's focus of attention has shifted from its neighbors in Eastern Europe to its competitors in Western Europe and especially to the United States.

3. *Equivalence.* To the extent that *Pravda* and *Vremya* reflect the world view of Soviet leaders—and no one suggests they do anything but that—there is almost an obsession with equivalence between the two superpowers. For every Sakharov, there must be a Hyder; for every bug in the new American embassy in Moscow, there must be two in the Soviet embassy in Washington; for every Western offer to destroy a nuclear missile, there must be a Soviet offer to destroy two.

To talk of glasnost in Soviet journalism as revolution seems clearly to be an overstatement. It is reform, significant but controlled reform. Martin Walker (1987), the *Guardian's* experienced Moscow correspondent, may have found the best metaphor to describe changes in the Soviet media:

> It is important to keep this [new openness] in perspective. Freedom of the press was not breaking out across the Soviet Union; simply, the straps of the straitjacket were being loosened slightly, to allow the press to report the corruption and bureaucracy, and air and criticism that the Kremlin found useful. This amounted to a subtler form of media management.

REFERENCES

Aksyonov, Vassily. 1987. Through the Glasnost, Darkly. *Harper's Magazine* (April), pp. 65–67.

Baranov, Alexander, and Gennady Seleznev. 1987. That New Word "Glasnost." *World Press Review* (April), pp. 16–17.

Barnathan, Joyce, and Steven Strasser. 1987. Gorbachev's Gamble: Opening a Closed Society. *Newsweek* (January 5), pp. 12–23.

Breath of Fresh Air, A. 1987. *The Economist* (January 31), p. 42.

Cuddly Russia? 1987. *The Economist* (February 14), pp. 13–14.

Cullen, Robert B. 1986. Live From the Launch Pad; the Kremlin Calls for Peppier Press Coverage. *Newsweek* (March 24), pp. 18–19.

Daniloff, Nicholas. 1986. New Words, Same Story. *U.S. News and World Report* (June 9).

Different Degrees of Candor; Soviets Cover Home More Openly, but the West Is Another Story, 1986. *Time* (December 15), pp. 68–69.

Doder, Dusko. 1986. *Shadows and Whispers; Power Politics Inside the Kremlin from Brezhnev to Gorbachev.* New York: Random House.

Hollander, Gayle Durham. 1972. *Soviet Political Indoctrination; Developments in Mass Media and Propaganda Since Stalin.* New York: Praeger Publishers.

Hopkins, Mark. 1970. *Mass Media in the Soviet Union.* New York: Pegasus.

Igiebor, Nosa. 1987. The Soviets' New Look; But Will the Old Guard Stand Still for so Much Reform? *World Press Review* (April), pp. 9–10. [From *Newswatch*, Lagos, Nigeria, March 2].

Kaiser, Robert G. 1976. *Russia; the People and the Power.* New York: Pocket Books.

Larson, James F. 1984. *Television's Window on the World: International Affairs Coverage on the U.S. Networks.* Norwood, NJ: Ablex.

Lee, Gary. 1987. Soviets Extend 'Glasnost' to Airwaves. *Washington Post* (May 4), p. A18.

Lenin, V. I. 1973. *What Is to Be Done?* Beijing: Foreign Languages Press.

Lichter, S. Robert, Linda S. Lichter, Daniel R. Amundson and Jessica M. Fowler. 1987. The Truth About Pravda: How the Soviets See the U.S. *Public Opinion* (March-April), pp. 12–13, 60.

Lisann, Maury. 1975. *Broadcasting to the Soviet Union; International Politics and Radio.* New York: Praeger Publishers.

Mickiewicz, Ellen. 1987. Soviet Viewers Are Seeing More, Including News of the United States. *New York Times* (February 27), Sect. II, p. 29.

Mickiewicz, Ellen. 1984. Policy Issues in the Soviet Media System. In Erik P. Hoffman [Ed.], *The Soviet Union in the 1980s. Proceedings of the Academy of Political Science*, 35(3):113–123.

Moody, John. 1986. New Messages for the Masses; Gorbachev Loosens the Restrictions on His Country's Press, *Time* (June 30), p. 16.

Mowlana, Hamid. 1986. *Global Information and World Communication.* New York: Longman.

Nagorski, Andrew. 1987. *Reluctant Farewell; an American Reporter's Candid Look Inside the Soviet Union* [paper ed.]. New York: Henry Holt.

Padover, Saul K. [Ed.]. 1974. *Karl Marx on Freedom of the Press and Censorship* [Karl Marx Library Vol. IV]. New York: McGraw-Hill.

Pell, Gene [Mod.]. 1987. Gambling on Glasnost: a Chronical of Current Events. *Public Opinion* (March-April), pp. 4–8.

Pipes, Richard. 1987. The 'Glasnost' Test: Gorbachev's Push Comes to Shove. *The New Republic* (February 2), pp. 16–17.

Quinn-Judge, Paul. 1986. Aim of Soviet 'Openness' Policy. *Christian Science Monitor* (October 22), p. 1.

Remnick, David. 1987. Taste of Freedom a Challenge for Editor. *Washington Post* (May 4), p. A25.

Roxburgh, Angus. 1987. *Pravda; Inside the Soviet News Machine.* New York: George Braziller.

Siebert, Fred S., Theodore Peterson and Wilbur Schramm. 1956. *Four Theories of the Press.* Urbana: University of Illinois Press.

Smith, Hedrick. 1976. *The Russians.* New York: Ballantine.

Smith, William E. 1987. Sounds of Freedom; Moscow Releases Some Dissidents, but Cracks Down on Refuseniks. *Time* (February 23), pp. 52–53.

Sreberny-Mohammadi, et al. 1985. *Foreign News In the Media: International Reporting in Twenty-Nine Countries.* Paris: Unesco.

Stevenson, Robert L., and Donald Lewis Shaw [Eds.]. 1984. *Foreign News and the New World Information Order.* Ames, IA: Iowa State University Press.

Trewhitt, Henry. 1987. Gorbachev on the High Wire. *U.S. News and World Report* (February 9), pp. 36–39.

Walker, Martin. 1986. *The Waking Giant.* London: Michael Joseph.

Walker, Martin, 1986. The Party Men Who Looked West and Saw the Warning. *The Guardian* (Manchester) (July 22) p. 19.

Walker, Martin. 1987. Gorbachev Plans Reforms From Below Too. *The Guardian* (Manchester) (January 18).

DEVELOPMENTS IN SOVIET JOURNALISM

PHILIP GAUNT

> Despite developments, the Soviet press still functions as a public relations arm of the government, but the author feels that there are signs of changes as the result of pressures from the Soviet public.

Over the past few years, there has been a steadily growing research interest in journalists, newsroom procedures and news values both in the United States and Western Europe.[1] However, with a few notable exceptions, this interest has failed to extend to the countries of Eastern Europe, partly for linguistic reasons, but, above all, because of the difficulty of access to journalists and media organizations in these countries. And yet, the Eastern bloc, with a combined population of 400 million, more than 30% of the world's industrial production, enormous military power and considerable ideological influence all over the globe, cannot be ignored.[2] It is important to know how the media operate in this region, particularly in the Soviet Union, which plays a leading role throughout the Communist world.

While the news values and objectives of Soviet journalists are quite distinct from those of their American counterparts, there are nonetheless certain similarities between professional journalistic practices in the United States and the Soviet Union. Taken together, they can provide a much better framework for understanding the roles and functions of the Soviet journalist. In particular, a parallel may be drawn between party-controlled journalism in the Soviet Union and routine newsgathering procedures in the United States, for it is here, rather than on an ideological level, that similarities are the strongest. Soviet journalism, it may be argued, functions very much like a large institutional or corporate public relations department in the West and this perspective may offer some useful avenues for further research. Finally, there is evidence that Soviet journalism is beginning to show signs of slow but significant change, brought about, perhaps, by a more mature audience and a greater demand for timely information which characterizes states with modern systems of mass communication.

Previous studies have already argued that similarities exist between Soviet and American journalists. In particular, Dean Mills has suggested that Soviet journalism is moving toward a more objective form of reporting "with which few American reporters would disagree."[3] Mills also insists elsewhere[4] that the prevailing view of "kept" Soviet journalists is a naive one fostered by such Cold War writings as Wilbur Schramm's chapter on Communist press systems in *Four Theories of the Press.*[5]

Lilita Dzirkals and colleagues have also warned against adopting Western rules of interpretation which might lead one to assume differences that do not exist and point out that "journalist are *people* and therefore unpredictable."[6] Thomas F. Remington, writing about professionalism in Soviet journalism, sees some noticeable differences. In his view, the Soviet journalist has a very different set of occupational values than the American journalist, identifying more with the priorities of the party than with the interests of the people.[7]

METHOD

The study of news values in the Soviet Union poses some challenging problems, in particular those caused by language and access.

For this study, a systematic review was made of translations published by the United States Joint

Philip Gaunt, "Developments in Soviet Journalism." *Journalism Quarterly*, Volume 64, Autumn 1987, pp. 536–542. Reprinted by permission.

The author was a doctoral student at Indiana University when this article was written.

Publications Research Service and the Foreign Broadcast Information Service between 1978 and 1985. These translations cover a wide selection of Soviet publications, including the journalists' professional monthly *Zhurnalist*. Other sources examined included research reports from Radio Liberty, the *Democratic Journalist*, the organ of the International Organization of Journalists, other publications of the IOJ and reports and studies published by IAMCR and UNESCO.

Most of these sources provide only an "official" view of the journalist role, but by comparing what is expected of the journalist on the one hand, and, on the other, the extent to which these expectations are, or are not, being fulfilled, it is possible to extrapolate a fairly accurate idea of how journalists actually go about their work.

In attempting to paint a portrait of the Soviet journalist one must first make a distinction between official phraseology about the journalist's idealized role and the constraints under which he labors. The official image of the Soviet journalist is that of "ideological warrior" working to further the aims of the party. Lenin's classic definition of the journalist describes him as "propagandist, agitator and organizer."[8]

The task of the "propagandist" is to present a complete picture of society and class struggle. The "agitator" seeks to explain a single idea to the masses. The role of the "organizer" is to motivate the masses. These definitions have changed a little over the years, but Soviet officialdom continues to think of the journalist as a "warrior of the party."

Mills outlines further roles for the Soviet journalist: literary craftsmen, publicist (meaning a writer on public affairs), investigative reporter, citizens' friend and member of the collective.[9] Some of these roles will be examined later and compared with U.S. equivalents. For the moment, however, perhaps the best overall definition of the ideal Soviet journalist comes from the article, "A master of his trade," by Alexsandr Levikov.[10] This article praises the work of Anatoliy Agranovskiy, a "remarkable master of commentary" who in the 1960s wrote such apparently genuinely popular pieces as "Sergeants of Industry," "Meeting with an Old Fashioned Mercantilist," "Waste of Education" or "Science Takes Nothing on Faith."

Levikov's description of Agranovskiy at work reveals the master as a kind of Soviet Sinclair.

> Struck by the discouraging absurdity, the great significance which here and there covered up the most ordinary bungling, he again and again burst into offices, cities and construction sites and wanted to dig everything up, to think it through and to argue it through.

Agranovskiy was a master of words, according to Levikov, but that is not the only reason why he captured the reader's heart. No, it was because people *believed* him. He was convincing. "The core of commentary," wrote Agranovskiy himself, "is the author's ideological conviction."

Such is the official image of the Soviet journalist, an ideological worker dedicated to furthering the aims of the party, fired by conviction and feeling for his fellowmen, eager to uncover sloth, inefficiency and bungling, and able, through his mastery of words and other journalistic skills, to convey stirring and mobilizing ideas to the masses.

What is the reality? From official criticism—and there is plenty of it—it is possible to deduce that journalists are not living up to this ideal. One editorial in *Sovetskaya Rossiya* sums up this criticism in a few, hard-hitting lines:

> The most important shortcoming—and this should be said with the utmost frankness—is that our press, radio and television often avoid analysis of the complex socio-political, economic and moral problems that are engendered by life itself. Instead of an in-depth examination of them and a search for ways of resolving them, readers, listeners and viewers are frequently offered articles and programs containing irksome lectures and stereotyped appeals to "strive," "intensify and improve."[11]

THE GORBACHEV ERA

There has been much speculation that the arrival of Mikhail Gorbachev would have an effect on the Soviet media. As a former Department of Propaganda official, he is known to have a strong and informed interest in the media and has spoken out in favor of a more open and responsive press.

It is true that his impromptu speeches and "walk-abouts" have been given wide and immediate coverage, but the Soviet media, with their strict planning and control seem to be too ponderous to reflect rapid change. In his report to the 27th Congress of the Communist Party of the Soviet Union on February 25, 1986, Gorbachev recognized that "editorial collectives have boldly tackled complex questions that in many respects are new." But he went on to say that the media were not fully realizing their potential:

> There is still a good deal of dullness, sluggishness has not been overcome, and deafness with respect to the news has not been cured. People are dissatisfied with insufficient promptness in covering events and with the superficial portrayal of the struggle for the advanced things that are entering our practice.[12]

Why does the Soviet journalist fail to live up to expectations? There appear to be three reasons. The first is that the journalist is hampered in his work by a number of constraints inherent in the Soviet media. The second is that training does not appear to prepare him properly for his professional duties. The third is that the profession is losing prestige and is no longer attracting the right kind of recruit.

The Soviet journalist has to labor under a number of constraints. First of all, the editorial process removes virtually any initiative from all but the best-known and politically safest writers. Content, emphasis and approach are established by the chief editor and transmitted to lower level journalists through assistant editors. The chief editor either takes his directives straight from the Propaganda Department or is so much in tune with the priorities of the Central Committee as to know himself exactly what is required and to act as the representative of the Propaganda Department within the editorial office.[13] Consequently the editorial process has a very direct influence on how the journalist works.

There are, however, a number of indirect factors influencing and constraining the Soviet journalist. Analyzing a variety of sources, in particular the finding of a survey conducted under the auspices of the Moscow University School of Journalism by Svitich and Shiraeva[14] and published in 1979, Thomas Remington paints a dismal picture of the journalistic profession:

> Journalists routinely complain that they are overworked and have to spread themselves too thin over too many subjects. Most newspapers set line quotas for their writers, on a per-issue or per-month basis or both. Many writers must work up 100 to 200 lines per issue or 2,500 or 3,500 lines per month.[15]

This is not always typical of the central press but it is particularly true in local newspapers, sometimes known as "juice-squeezers." Income is modest for beginners and since they have to meet their quotas before qualifying for a bonus, journalists will tend to stick to "safe" subjects and concentrate on quantity—hence the frequent accusations of uninspired writing.

Censorship is often thought of as a factor. There is of course a highly organized system of censorship. Everything that is published in a newspaper has to be approved before it can appear and there is a very precise list of subjects that may not be dealt with at any one time. But with the constraints mentioned above, there is hardly any need for censorship. Self-censorship is sufficient to keep the journalist out of trouble. In any case, censorship is more a question of what the journalist is required to do rather than what he may not do. It would appear that Soviet journalists are more concerned with overwork and what they perceive to be inadequate coverage than with censorship.[16]

JOURNALISM TRAINING

Many Soviet journalists are also dissatisfied with the training they receive. Most of them feel that they have too much theory and not enough practice and are unprepared for their jobs when they leave journalism school.[17] On the other hand, journalism educators complain about the "low intellectual level" of students. "Increased practical training is not the only answer," affirms Zdorovega, claiming that the training given to journalists is better than that dispensed to engineers, agronomists or economists.[18] The main problem, Zdorovega continues, is that first year students just do not have the necessary language skills. Another academic, P. Tkachev, who is dean of the Department of Journalism at the Byelorussian State University, believes that it is important to determine more precisely the specialty of the future journalist and train him specifically for, say, the secretariat of a newspaper, a branch department or the letters-to-the-editor department.[19]

There seems to be little doubt that the profession is losing prestige and that educators are concerned. "At a time when the role of journalist is increasing more and more," writes Zdorovega, "it seems to me the prestige of our profession is decreasing to some extent."[20] Tkachev notes that, although there are 23 universities providing journalistic programs, there is still a shortage of journalists to fill positions in raion (local) and city newspapers.[21] This is partly due to the fact that new journalism graduates just do not want to work in local papers where pay is low and working conditions are notoriously bad.

Gennadiy Seleznev, chief editor of *Komsomolskaya Pravda*, the country largest youth newspaper, worries about where future journalists are going to come from. "The feeling is created that the prestige of journalistic work is declining in the youth environment."[22] And Seleznev concludes, "One thing is certain: more effective forms of introducing creative young people into journalism are needed today."

It was suggested earlier that there are parallels between Soviet and American journalism. If there are, they are not very obvious. On the face of it, they seem to be very far apart. As J. Clement Jones has written:

> It is important to recognize the fundamental differences which exist between the mass media of socialist countries and Western hemisphere countries. Put in the simplest and most direct terms, it is a direct function of the former to act as a socializing force and an implicit requirement of the latter that they be independent and be economically viable.[23]

JOURNALISTIC VALUES

Mills argues that "Soviet reporters value a concept of objectivity that seems close to the American understanding of that term."[24] If they do, they do not

show it. The idea of impartiality, which is fundamental to an American understanding of objectivity, even with the "ritualistic" qualifications advanced by Gaye Tuchman,[25] appears to be entirely foreign to Soviet thinking in this matter. The Marxist definition of objectivity as "the expression and defense of the interests of those forces which are the vehicles of progress and embody the requirements of social development,"[26] may be a little outmoded today, but modern commentators such as Avraamov flatly reject the idea of impartialty in journalism:

> The journalist addresses himself to society not for the sake of impartially presenting the results of his observations. He is always in favor of or against something and tries to influence the thoughts and feelings of the reader, the viewer or the listener in such a way as to turn him into a like-minded person.[27]

The notion of "investigative reporting" is one area in which Soviet and American journalists may have a little more in common. Of course, the Soviet journalist will rarely undertake investigative reporting on his own government but even if the American journalist has such a prerogative, in practice it is extremely rare for him to "investigate" the Federal Government. In the United States, investigative reporting tends to concern itself more with business, industry or, at the most, local government, which is very similar to what goes on in the Soviet Union.

The differences examined so far are based in reality on ideological considerations. Where the two systems really come together is not on a theoretical or ideological level but on the level of everyday news gathering and processing. American journalists like to point out that, in an open democracy, they are free to report on whatever they want, and that is true. But, in actual fact, as Leon Sigal's 20-year content analysis of the *New York Times* and the *Washington Post* has shown,[28] a very large proportion of news—as much as 60%—comes through routine news channels, which are subject to control.

Furthermore, government officials, both American and foreign, account for more than 75% of all news sources. The economics of news gathering has become such that more and more reliance is being placed on routine sources to fill news holes, and this is particularly true of local news operations. As a rule, local reporters just do not have the time or the resources to initiate more than a very few original stories.

Compare this to what Remington describes in the Soviet Union. "Overworked, writing on every conceivable topic, under pressure to turn out a sufficient quantity of copy, the raion (local) journalist turns to official sources for ideas and information."[29] In other words, leaving aside a small proportion of original reporting, most of which tends to be devoted to local events of relatively minor importance, the mechanisms of news gathering in the United States and the Soviet Union appear to rely on the same routines and the same types of sources. The similarity is striking.

Even more striking is the way in which the Soviet system resembles a major institutional or corporate public relations department. There is the same channeling-down of information from the top, the same interpretation of information in accordance with current "policy," the same hierarchical structures, the same preoccupation with the quirks and whims of the leadership, the same partiality, even the same criticisms from above to the effect that writing should be more colorful and imaginative.

This parallel appeared to be particularly true during the aftermath of the Chernobyl nuclear accident when the Soviet media acted exactly like the public relations department of, say, the U.S. Atomic Energy Commission, or NASA or Union Carbide, all of which have been known to be more than a little guarded—perhaps understandably—about certain "incidents" that might have affected their public image.

Perhaps this resemblance offers a new perspective from which to view the Soviet system of journalism; a new model with which to explain how Soviet journalists interact with both the prevailing power structure and their audience. As has been suggested, comparative studies of Soviet and American journalists have tended to stress *ideological* differences. A public relations model might throw fresh light on the everyday professional activities of the Soviet journalist which appear to be dominated more by organizational constraints, hierarchical controls and bureaucratic priorities than by ideological considerations.

The Soviet media system is showing signs of change. The rigid planning that has always been a traditional feature of "news" production in the Soviet Union is perhaps starting to soften under the impact of the electronic media. Perhaps journalistic styles are changing too. Writing in *Zhurnalist*,[30] Dmitri Lyubosvetov, a senior instructor at the Moscow State University School of Journalism, states: "In journalism, there is a longstanding practice of structuring information according to the principle of the so-called inverted pyramid." Lyubosvetov goes on to say that this is not necessarily good since opening sentences tend to be too heavily loaded. There is a need to capture attention with an unusual beginning.

Does this mean that Soviet journalists are becoming more concerned with audience needs? Lyubosvetov also writes about "Mayak," a successful radio station:

> The appearance of Mayak was dictated not only by the public demand for greater information about events in our country and abroad. It was no less important to provide for the fastest possible dissemination of news, to create, as the scholars say, a continually active information field.

The *idea* of "the fastest possible dissemination of news" is not a completely novel one in Soviet journalism. The need for faster news has been recognized since the late 1960s. Mayak, for example, was launched in August of 1964, but until recently little actual progress has been achieved. Lyubosvetov, writing in 1982, reveals that journalists on radio Mayak are reluctant to use "time indicators" such as "yesterday" or "last night" in their newscasts, since these would date the news. There is a strong aversion to presenting "cold" news.

This is significant since it suggests that newscasters are aware of their audience's desire for up-to-the-minute information. Another point of significance is that this audience appears to be "maturing" and developing more sophisticated needs and tastes. It is interesting to conclude that the changes taking place in Soviet journalism are caused less by ideological factors than by an apparent thirst for fresh news on the part of the audience, as well as by structural factors within the media themselves.

Judging by past performance, these changes will be slow. Gorbachev's calls for more timeliness do not seem to have had much effect. The Chernobyl incident has illustrated that the Soviet media are too bureaucratic and hierarchical to respond to rapid change even at the insistence of the country's leadership. At a time of crisis, which would have been an excellent opportunity to demonstrate innovations, the media immediately reverted to their monolithic public relations paradigm. Change, when it occurs, is likely to come from within.

CONCLUSION

Despite irreconcilable differences in certain areas, journalistic practices in the United States and the Soviet Union resemble each other in their reliance on routine and official news sources. Furthermore, the Western-style public relations department may provide a better model to describe the work of the journalist in the Soviet Union. Most studies on Soviet journalists have tended to stress the irreducible *ideological* difference which separate them from their American counterparts. The application of a "deideologized" perspective, such as that provided by a public relations model, might offer a more scientific method of studying Soviet journalists.

Finally, changes taking place within the Soviet media are less the result of ideological exigencies than "bottom-up" pressure from the audience and structural changes within the media themselves. These changes are small as yet but highly significant, and will make the study of Soviet journalism even more fascinating in the years to come.

NOTES

1. Early studies include Warren Breed, "Social Control in the Newsroom: A Functional Analysis," *Social Forces*, 33:325–335 (1955) and Gaye Tuchman, "news, the Newsman's Reality," unpublished Ph.D. dissertation, Brandeis University, 1969. Among more recent studies are Jeremy Tunstall, *Journalists at Work: Special Correspondents, their News Organizations, News Sources and Competitor-Colleagues* (London: Constable, 1971); John W. C. Johnstone, Edward J. Slawski and William D. Bowman, *The News People: A Sociological Portrait of American Journalists and their Work* (Urbana: University of Illinois Press, 1976); Herbert J. Gans, *Deciding What's News: A Study of CBS Evening News, Newsweek and Time* (New York: Vintage Books, 1980); Philip Schlesinger, *Putting Reality Together: BBC News* (London: Constable, 1978); David H. Weaver and G. Cleveland Wilhoit, *The American Journalist: a Portrait of U.S. News People and Their Work* (Bloomington: Indiana University Press, 1986).

2. Stephen White, John Gardner and George Schöpflin, *Communist Political Systems: An Introduction* (New York: St. Martin's Press, 1982).

3. Dean Mills, "The New Soviet Journalism: More Facts?" *Newspaper Research Journal*, 4:28–33 (Fall (1982).

4. Dean Mills, "The Soviet Journalist: A Cultural Analysis," unpublished Ph.D dissertation, University of Illinois, 1981, p. 3.

5. Fred Siebert, Theodore Peterson and Wilbur Schramm, *Four Theories of the Press*, (Urbana: University of Illinois Press, 1974), Chapter 4.

6. Lilita Dzirkals, Thane Gustafson and A. Ross Johnson, *The Media and Intra-Elite Communication in the USSR*, Rand Report No. R-2869 (Santa Monica, Calif., September 1982), Chapter 2.

7. Thomas F. Remington, "Politics and Professionalism in Soviet Journalism," *Slavic Review*, 44:489 (Fall 1985).

8. M. Saifulin, ed., *Lenin About the Press* (Prague: International Organization of Journalists, 1972), pp. 48–52.

9. Mills, *op. cit.*, p. 100.

10. Alexsandr Levikov, "A Matter of his Trade," *EKO*, Novosibirsk, October 1985.

11. "The Party's Combat Arsenal," *Sovetskaya Rossiya*, July 12, 1983.

12. "The Political Report of the CPSU Central Committee to the 27th Congress of the Communist Party of the Soviet Union," *Pravda*, February 26, 1986.

13. Dzirkals *et al., op. cit.*, pp. 43–45.

14. L. G. Svitich and A. A. Shiraeva, *Zhurnalist i ego rabota* (Moscow: Moscow University Press, 1979).

15. Remington, *op. cit.*, p. 493.

16. Svitich and Shiraeva, *op. cit.*, p. 127.

17. Remington, *op. cit.*, p. 491.

18. Vladimir Zdorovega, "Only by Common Efforts," *Zhurnalist*, September 1982, pp. 14–15.

19. P. Tkachev and I. Novikov, "Training of Journalists for Local Newspapers Examined," *Pravda*, June 2, 1984.

20. Zdorovega, *op. cit.*

21. Tkachev and Novikov, *op. cit.*

22. "Where Will the Journalists Come From?" *Zhurnalist*, April 1985, pp. 37–38.
23. J. Clement Jones, "Media Councils in the Western Hemisphere," in Lars Bruun, ed., *Professional Codes in Journalism* (Prague: International Organization of Journalists, 1979).
24. Mills, *op. cit.*, p. 31.
25. Gaye Tuchman, "Objectivity as Strategic Ritual: An Examination of Newsmen's Notions of Objectivity," *American Journal of Sociology*, 77:660–677 (1972).
26. *Soviet Encyclopedia*, 3rd Edition, Moscow 1972, vol. 18, p. 772.
27. D. Avraamov, *Kommunist*, No. 15, October 1980, p. 15.
28. Leon Sigal, *Reporters and Officials: The Organization and Politics of Newsmaking* (Lexington, Mass.: D. C. Heath and Co., 1973).
29. Remington, *op. cit.*, p. 494.
30. Dmitri Lyubosvetov, "You are Listening to Mayak," *Zhurnalist*, July 1982, pp. 15–17.

SATELLITE INCIDENT SHOWS LIMITS OF SOVIET OPENNESS

James Oberg

There is a limit, however, to what the Soviet government is willing to reveal, and one of the areas that remains taboo involves national security. On that subject, the USSR is no more open than are most other countries, including the United States.

As the Western news media continue to swoon over Soviet *glasnost* and its revelations about some Soviet secrets, Moscow has just provided a jarring reminder of where the limits of openness remain. Another Soviet space nuclear accident is in the making, and Moscow has reverted to pre-Chernobyl-style denials, cover-ups and lies.

For most of April, Western space watchers were keeping their eyes on the Soviet satellite Kosmos-1900, launched last December. As it skimmed the atmosphere on its naval reconnaissance mission, frequent altitude boosts were needed to restore height lost to air drag. But by midmonth, the watchers noted with interest and growing alarm, the weekly boostings had ceased and the satellite's altitude was steadily dropping.

Aboard the Soviet satellite is a nuclear reactor to power its radar system. Over the past 20 years, dozens of this type of satellite were launched into low, unstable orbits on military missions. Although most safely boosted their radioactive cargoes into high, graveyard orbits, in 1978 and 1983 two tumbled back into the atmosphere, causing global concern. In 1969 and 1973, two others fell back to Earth during launch phase, without public awareness or Soviet admission.

Western analysts called them RORSATs, for Radar Ocean Reconnaissance Satellites. The Soviets labeled them "Kosmos" research satellites for peaceful scientific investigation of the universe. Moscow was lying.

By May 10, the Kosmos-1900 had gone a month

James Oberg, "Satellite Incident Shows Limits of Soviet Openness." *The Christian Science Monitor*, June 1988. Reprinted by permission of the author.

James Oberg wrote *Uncovering Soviet Disasters: Exploring the Limits of Glasnost*. New York: Random House, 1988.

without altitude boosts and slipped well below the normal operating range. Clearly something was wrong, and it was falling back to Earth out of control. Geoffrey Perry, a respected British space watcher and leader of the "Kettering Group" of amateur satellite trackers, told his news contacts that the satellite's uncontrolled orbital decay hinted at some sort of failure, and at the prospect of another Soviet space nuclear accident.

The announcement in London prompted Moscow to respond with a brief acknowledgement. They had known about the failure for a month, but announced it only two days after Perry revealed it.

The official Tass statement admitted "radio contact with the satellite was lost in April 1988," and that is would fly in orbit "till August-September 1988" when "it will cease to exist." Moscow admitted there was a reactor on board but claimed the satellite "has systems ensuring radiation safety on completion of the flight."

However, knowledgeable observers realized this statement consisted almost entirely of evasions, distortions, omissions and lies.

- Moscow did not even admit the obvious: The satellite was going to fall back into the atmosphere and spread radioactive contamination over the Earth. They implied it would just vanish.

- The timing of the fall, late summer, depends entirely on another feature mentioned by TASS: the "oriented flight" of the satellite.

- The phrase about "cease to exist" is nonsense. Satellites that fall back into Earth's atmosphere are subjected to immense destructive forces, both from deceleration stress and from the heat of atmospheric compression. But numerous large and small fragments survive to reach the surface.

The result is that the highly radioactive reactor core will fall back to Earth protected by the main satellite body, three tons of metal shielding. As in Canada in 1978, dangerously "hot" pieces of scrap metal are going to hit the Earth's surface.

This might occur over the ocean and endanger only the whales. Or it might occur over land between latitudes 65 North and South. The risk is not

that someone might be hit on the head. The finite danger is that passersby in an inhabited area might pick up the scrap. In 1978, pieces recovered in Canada were sufficiently radioactive to kill anyone who kept them nearby for several days.

Yet the TASS statement assured the world that the satellite would cease to exist and that radiation safety was ensured. By Moscow's word, no search, recovery or decontamination efforts will be needed.

The Soviets themselves clearly recognize the danger they deny. Even the fuel-expensive technique of boosting their used-up satellites into a permanent orbital graveyard is testimony to their private concern, since other used-up satellites (without reactors) are dumped back into the atmosphere over the remote southern Pacific Ocean. If the "safety systems" on the RORSATs are so perfect, why don't Soviet space controllers dump the old satellites onto Siberia and save fuel and complexity? They don't because they know it would be dangerous.

On May 13, at a Washington, D.C. press conference that turned out to be incredibly ill-timed, top Soviet space scientist Roald Sagdeyev joined with the Federation of American Scientists to call for a ban on nuclear reactors in space. Their target clearly was the United States' SP-100 program under development for the Strategic Defense Initiative, but some reporters asked Sagdeyev about the Soviet RORSAT program. He denied any specific knowledge about it except what he'd read in the Western press. And although the Sagdeyev/FAS motivation for banning all nuclear reactors in space was supposed to be safety, nobody at the press conference was willing to admit that Soviet assurances of perfect safety with Kosmos-1900 were phony.

Moscow refuses to discuss the satellite's true military mission, or to provide photographs of the vehicle and its reactor. It refuses to help other nations prepare search and decontamination procedures (while probably dusting off its own secret contingency plans). Without pressure in the form of pointed inquiries from skeptical Western newsmen, Moscow's stonewalling continues.

It may take radioactive reality, in the form of official disinformation over a genuine Soviet space disaster, to shock many Westerners out of their euphoria over *glasnost*.

SOME FACTS ABOUT PRAVDA

VIKTOR AFANASIEV

The importance of *Pravda*, the mouthpiece of the Communist party in the Soviet Union, should not be underestimated. Hundreds of thousands of readers pour out their hearts to its editors each year.

On the seventieth anniversary of the founding of *Pravda*, *The Democratic Journalist*, organ of the Prague (Czechoslovakia) based International Organization of Journalists, had this to say about the Soviet Communist party's flagship newspaper:

PRAVDA can truly be called the biggest newspaper in the world. It appears seven times a week in a daily edition of 10.6 million copies. In the past five years its edition has increased by more than 3.5 million copies.

PRAVDA has a readership in 153 countries of all continents.

In view of the enormous expanse of the USSR, PRAVDA is printed in 48 places around the Soviet Union—from Kiev to Vladivostok and Yuzhnosakhalinsk. Copies of finished pages are transmitted from Moscow to 42 cities photo-telegraphically via communication satellites.

The PRAVDA staff consists of 350 journalists of whom 44 work as correspondents abroad and another 67 as correspondents in various parts of the Soviet Union.

Readers' letters to the paper average about 1,400 a day; last year PRAVDA received a total of 514,000 readers' letters.

70 YEARS OF PRAVDA

V. I. Lenin characterized the essence of the communist press as a collective propagandist, agitator and organizer, comparing it to the scaffolding put up around a building under construction, indicating the outlines of the structure, facilitating contact among the individual masons, helping them to divide the work and to watch the overall results attained through organized labour. At the same time, in this allegorical picture of a "future building" we see in various stages of our history, in the spirit of Lenin's teachings, the real justification and the building of the party itself, the preparations for the victorious social revolution, and the construction of a new society.

Embodying Leninist ideas, the first working class daily in Russia—*Pravda* (Truth) came into existence 70 years ago. Written into its masthead today are the words: This paper was founded on May 5, 1912 by V. I. Lenin. The first number of the paper was issued on the day marking the birth of Karl Marx, and this was not by accident. The data personifies the linkage of the new paper, its fidelity to Marxism with the cause of the proletariat. The editorial of that number stated: "The working class must know the truth. The workers' paper *Truth* must correspond to its name . . .".

Lenin's "*Pravda*" heralded the October Revolution, which opened the road to socialism for many countries and peoples. It carried the appeal:

"To the Citizens of Russia", the news that the great revolution had triumphed, and the famous De-

Viktor Afanasiev, "Some Facts about Pravda." *The Democratic Journalist*, July–August, 1982, pp. 35–38. Reprinted by permission.

The author is a Communist Party functionary and editor in chief of *Pravda*. He is also chairman of the Union of Journalists of the Soviet Union.

cree on Peace, which was the first-ever in social-ism's life-giving practice of striving for peace implicit in it. In a historically brief period, the new system raised the Land of the Soviets to the summits of social progress, bringing the people to a developed socialist society and the building of communism. Throughout this period, "Pravda", the organ of the CPSU Central Committee, grew together with the party, acquiring new qualities and becoming the flagship of the Soviet press and the most widely read newspaper of our times.

Socialist development raised the people's political consciousness, activity, education and cultural requirements to a high level. When the Soviet public is described as the most widely-read in the world, the justification for this rests directly on, among other things, the popularity of the Soviet press. It consists of 8,000 newspapers in 55 languages of the peoples of the USSR. Their total daily printing exceeds 176 million copies. For every family in the Soviet Union there are upwards of four periodicals. . . .

It is alleged that in a socialist society there is no real freedom of criticism. However, even a cursory reading of "Pravda" and other Soviet newspapers, that daily print serious and sharply critical matters on various problems of our life and regularly feature whole pages devoted to public control, will show the worth of this allegation. Moreover, the criticism carried in our press is not hot air. It helps to remove shortcomings in the work of the most diverse organs—party, people's Soviets, and economic management.

However, while criticizing defects in all spheres of social life, the Soviet press sees its main task in convincingly demonstrating the new system's historic gains, in speaking out about its makers and heroes, its achievements and prospects. We are convinced that precisely this approach, which conforms to the optimistic truth of life, is the only sure one for the communist press. . . .

In a socialist society the people's direct participation in the work of the press is eloquent testimony of its democratic nature. With good reason this attracts considerable attention in the world. A book of letters from the people printed in our newspaper was re-cently brought out in Paris under the heading "Ivan Ivanovich Writes in Pravda". The foreword says: "When you start reading this book your first reaction is perplexity: 'What is this strange world? What sort of organization, rules, social mechanisms, and psychology are these?'" Gradually, step by step, without your noticing it, you see that this is life".

Let us give some illuminating statistics to back up these words. In the Soviet Union there are over seven million worker and rural correspondents: these are regular contributors.

"Pravda's" mailbag consists of nearly half a million letters annually from workers, collective farmers, and intellectuals, while the total mailbag of all Soviet newspapers consists of between 60 and 70 million letters. Letters are a barometer of public opinion, a rich fountain nourishing the press and giving journalists a better knowledge of reality. Moreover, they are a channel by which the people directly influence the solution of social problems. Decisions not only of a local but, to a large extent, of national significance are often adopted on the basis of letter containing criticism or recommendations.

The enhancement of the role of the press as a vehicle for the fulfilment of managerial tasks is one of the laws of its development under socialism, a law springing from the democratic character of socialist society's mass media. Here we can distinguish three essential elements. First, the press, television, and radio quickly spread social information, bringing it to the entire people and giving it a Marxist-Leninist orientation making it easy to understand and turning it into a means of mobilization. The people thus receive information in order to come forward as the subject of administration. Second, the press ensures not only a direct but also a reverse link—from the people to leading organs, which is of particularly great significance for promoting the sociopolitical activity of citizens. Lastly, with the support of public opinion the press comes forward as the organizer of efficient management, disseminating positive experience, analyzing pros and cons, and identifying potentialities for a more effective utilization of information in the diverse elements and institutions of society. . . .

CANDID LETTERS TO THE EDITOR DELIVER MESSAGE OF NEW MOOD TO THE KREMLIN

Dusko Doder

Under glasnost, the letters that have been pouring into all Soviet newspapers have, if anything, increased. Furthermore, Soviet law requires that all letters be answered within ten days. The Soviet government feels that people need an outlet to vent their frustrations, and letters to the editor serve as that safety valve.

Perhaps the clearest indication of a new mood in Moscow is a voluminous flow of letters to Soviet newspapers.

During the past few months such letters have become unusually outspoken and full of surprises. They talk about "dishonesty" of unnamed leaders, or advance such heretical ideas as the need for abolishing centralized planning.

The country's largest weekly newspaper, *Literaturnaya Gazeta*, recently summarized its weekly mailbag by saying that "as we can see, the authors of many letters are advocating a system of economic relations which would be significantly different from the existing one. The letters also talk about another thing, namely that a new type of economic thinking is in the process of formation."

Letters published in the Soviet press probably carry more weight than those that appear in American newspapers. This is partly because of differences between a free society and a closed society. A local official seeing a complaint against him published in *Pravda* is likely to think twice before dismissing the grievance again. *Pravda*, after all, is the official paper of the ruling party.

Another reason, however, is historical. For centuries any Russian with a grievance sought to take his case to the czar. In the early days of the empire, a special basket used to be lowered at regular intervals from a window in the old Kremlin palace to collect petitioners' letters.

The tradition continues to be practiced in a new form. For residents of Moscow, it can be done by dropping petitions in a special box at the Communist Party Central Committee headquarters. For most of the population, however, the favored route is to write a letter to *Pravda, Izvestia* or other newspapers.

In recent years, the party has regarded letters as an important safety valve and a way of allowing public opinion a legitimate and quasi-independent outlet. Moreover, the letters play a vital role in assessing the mood of the country and keeping the leadership informed about social and economic grievances and ways to solve them.

The volume of letters is enormous. *Pravda* and *Izvestia*, the two principal newspapers, receive between 9,000 and 11,000 letters from readers each week. The mailbag of other Soviet newspapers ranges between 10,000 and 13,000 such missives per month for each.

By law, every letter has to be answered within 10 days. Because of their official status, the newspapers have the right to carry out investigations and subpoena and inspect any official documents they want to check, including police and Communist Party records.

As an indication of how seriously the letters process is viewed, the largest editorial section in any Soviet newspaper is the letters department. *Izvestia*, for instance, has 65 staffers who read letters. Each letter is supposed to be read.

The letters are classified by topics and forwarded

Dusko Doder, "Candid Letters to the Editor Deliver Message of New Mood to the Kremlin." *The Washington Post*, August 14, 1983. Reprinted by permission.

The author is a *Washington Post* Foreign Service Reporter.

to relevant ministries. A small number deemed "typical" by the staff are published. The answer most frequently received by petitioners is a card acknowledging receipt of the letter.

As a result, the letters page serve a dual function. On the one hand, they provide the Kremlin with information about public opinion while, on the other, they allow it to shape that opinion by carefully and deliberately selecting how much information is to be doled out to the public—the process that allows the authorities to define the issues and cast them in a way of their choosing.

Some newspapers have established a reputation for championing their readers' causes by sending reporters to investigate typical grievances ranging from unfair punishments inflicted by obtuse local leaders to poor services, instances of corruption and other personal problems.

Some newspapers have also featured an "agony column" aimed at young people whose letters reflect confusion about new social and sexual attitudes. Typical is a sad story recently of unwanted pregnancies in a high school in a small Siberian town. The newspaper *Komsomolsakya Pravda* investigated the case and denounced the school's sanctimonious condemnation and ignorance of sexual activities.

A novel feature in the letters page, however, is a new focus on large and previously taboo subjects.

Pravda, for instance, printed a letter last week written by G. Varina, a factory worker in Chita, in Siberia. She talked about "dishonesty" among leaders, poor working conditions and official "lies" about production goals.

"Everything is allegedly going fine," she wrote. "But that is a pure lie. We have to live with the truth no matter how bitter it may be. The lies are a corrosive which undermine the human spirit and destroy the people." . . . A writer from Moscow, V. Agayev, proposed a new incomes policy based on economic performance and "rewarding those people who seek out customers and better meet their needs."

A young woman from Kalmna, in the Moscow region, described in her letter how students are being drafted to join the Komsomol, the Young Communist League. She said, "We simply received a call from the local office of Komsomol to immediately send 15 persons to join the organization." This presumably was to allow the local office to meet its quotas.

A group of university students denounced the educational system, saying they are learning very little and that they are studying in "a terrible atmosphere that fosters passivity and silence" and prevents them from becoming "self-reliant and independent" persons.

Yet another student said in her letter than although she was a member of the Komsomol she believed in God. "I do not see anything bad in this," the student, 16, said. "But if I say that I believe in God, they will expel me from the Komsomol. Why?"

Soviet journalists say that the newspapers have received similar letters in the past but they were not printed. Traditionally no measures are taken to intimidate those expressing dissenting views, presumably because the mailbag is one of the few reliable means the party has to gauge reactions to its policies.

The fact that such letters are printed reflects an attempt by the new Kremlin leadership to mobilize public opinion behind its plan to revitalize the Soviet economy and society. Such public support may be necessary, at least in part, to overcome bureaucratic resistance to changes.

In retrospect, it may be significant that one of the first published Politburo statements since Yuri Andropov became Soviet leader last November was devoted almost entirely to letters. The document, published Dec. 11, said that the letters should be regarded as "political activity of the working people and their direct participation" in the improvement of economic management system.

"The letters are the instruction of the working people to the party and Soviet organs," it added.

MEDIA DEVELOPMENTS IN THE SOVIET UNION

Nicholas Daniloff

Soviet media have not been good at reflecting Soviet reality nor have they given a favorable picture of the United States to Soviet citizens. *Glasnost* has opened things up a bit in the U.S.S.R., but that does not extend to revealing what decisions are being taken in the Politburo.

. . . . There are two aspects of the Soviet media that have traditionally concerned U.S. observers. The first is, How good a reflector of Soviet reality is the Soviet press? And second, How well does the Soviet press portray the United States to the Soviet people?

In the past—say 10 or 20 years ago, when I first went to Moscow—we Moscow correspondents relied to a great extent on what the Soviet press published and, specifically, what TASS published. And so, it is legitimate to question whether the Soviet press is, in fact, providing Western journalists with an accurate picture of what is going on. The Soviet press in the past—although not as true today— was less than a mirror of the surrounding world. I think part of this is because Lenin viewed the press as one of the tools of government. The role of the press was to be a handmaiden in constructing socialism and, eventually, communism. Believing that people would be demoralized, the Soviet press did not attempt to report that accidents had happened, that there had been an earthquake, that a ship had sunk and many people had died. Rather, the press tried to give a very bright a rosy picture of the world.

The problem with that approach is that ordinary citizens could see very clearly that what the Soviet press was portraying often was not really accurate. And over the course of many years, an enormous credibility gap arose. One of the things Gorbachev is addressing these days is that credibility gap.

During the time I worked in Moscow, three general secretaries—Andropov, Brezhnev, Chernenko—died. Yuri Andropov, who was one of the most promising of those general secretaries, received a delegation of U.S. senators in August of 1983 and then suddenly disappeared. We all began wondering, particularly after experiencing Leonid Brezhnev's demise, whether Andropov had become ill. At that point, nothing much happened. August went by; September went by; October went by; and, finally, at the end of October, Leonid Zamyatin announced that Andropov had a cold and could not receive a group of visiting doctors. Well, that was probably the most serious cold that world history has ever known, because within a few months Andropov was dead. Zamyatin's personal reputation as a spokesman of Soviet reality went way, way down. He also left a rather negative legacy for his successors.

The kind of disrepute into which Soviet journalism has fallen and the skepticism about what is being portrayed in the Soviet media has found its way into a number of jokes currently told among Soviet citizens. Radio Armenia is one of those jocular, mythical radio stations in the Soviet Union that accepts questions from its listeners and gives witty answers.

| ONE QUESTION: | Which is more useful, newspapers or TV? |
| ANSWER: | Newspapers, of course, because at least you can wrap your garbage in them. |

Nicholas Daniloff, ''Media Developments in the Soviet Union.'' Andersen Lecture, sponsored by the World Press Freedom Committee in association with the Center for Strategic and International Studies. Reprinted by permission.

The author was *U.S. News & World Report* correspondent in Moscow for many years.

ANOTHER QUESTION: Can you wrap a bus in a newspaper?

ANSWER: Yes, if the newspaper has just published a lengthy speech of the general secretary.

QUESTION CONCERNING FOREIGN AFFAIRS: How do we find out what's going on in the world?

ANSWER: We believe the opposite of what TASS is denying.

The most famous joke plays on the words "Izvestia" and "Pravda." Pravda means "truth" and izvestia means "news," and both are the names of prominent newspapers. The joke is, "There's no news in Pravda, and no truth in Izvestia."

This gives you an idea of how the Soviets viewed their press and held it askance. In other words, the Soviet press was not, and has not been, a very good reflector of current reality—until Mikhail Gorbachev came to power.

On the other topic—how well the United States is portrayed in the Soviet press—I would say that in bad times the United States has gotten very bad press in the Soviet Union. The United States is portrayed as an unjust society with a few very rich people and a lot of very poor people. The poor people have no chance; they have no future; everything is bleak; and, furthermore, the United States is bent on military superiority and essentially wants to crush the Soviet Union.

In good times—that is, in times of détente or in the period that we seem to be entering now—you might think that the image of the United States would improve, but here a paradox occurs. When relations between the United States and the Soviet Union get better, people loosen up in the Soviet Union, and their natural curiosity about the West makes them very receptive to what is happening abroad, in fact, too receptive, from the Soviet leadership's point of view. So again, the Soviet press, even in good times, tends to paint a rather negative picture of the United States. The United States is portrayed as a country trying to take advantage of the new openness in the Soviet Union, to undermine the Soviet Union by infiltrating subversive mi-

crobes. It is a country that is locked in a long struggle for power with the Soviet Union.

These, then, are my two starting points—the Soviet media has not been a good reflector of Soviet reality and the Soviet press does not favorably portray the United States to its citizens. I will now meander a little bit through by memories of my experience in Moscow and come back to these two points at the end.

When I went to Moscow in 1981 as a correspondent for U.S. News & World Report, I found considerable disillusionment. If any of you have been reading Mikhail Gorbachev's new book, you will see that he describes this stagnation, this falling behind, this demoralization that was afflicting the Soviet Union in the later years of Leonid Brezhnev. Again, a joke illustrates the current sentiment at the time that I was leaving the Soviet Union. Although the joke was a little premature, it is now very topical. The joke is about Gorbachev's forthcoming meeting with President Reagan in the Oval Office.

Mr. Reagan, anxious to impress Mr. Gorbachev, decided he would call up the devil because, as you know, the United States is in league with the devil. He wanted to convince Mr. Gorbachev of the great technological superiority of the United States in being able to telephone Lucifer.

He asked one of his aides to call the number. The aide gets the devil on the line, hands the telephone to Mr. Reagan, who talks to the devil for 15 minutes and hangs up.

Gorbachev is suitably impressed. An aide comes in and says, "Mr. Reagan, you spoke for 15 minutes; that will cost the American taxpayer $1,500."

Well, Gorbachev thought this was a fascinating experience. He went back to Moscow, and said to his aides, "Get me the devil on the telephone. If the United States can do it, the Soviet Union can do it."

And so the aide got the devil on the line and handed the telephone to Mr. Gorbachev, who spoke for about 15 minutes. He hung up, and Gorbachev looked at the aide and said, "Well now, how much did that cost?" The aide replied, "Well, that cost two kopeks."

And Gorbachev said, "What? Two kopeks? You mean about five cents? The Americans paid $1,500, and we're only paying five cents?''

And the aide said, ''Yeah, you have to understand, that when you call the devil from Moscow, it's a local call. When you call from Washington, it's long distance.''

That joke reflects the sort of negative attitude that existed in Moscow. Another example is the play that was put on in 1982. It was called ''*Tak Pobedim*'' (''Thus Shall We Win'') and centers on Lenin's last days. Originally it was thought to be a good play for the Twenty-sixth Party Congress. The playwright, Mikhail Shatrov, thought it would be fascinating to write because Lenin's last days reflected a man who was losing his power—a similarity to Leonid Brezhnev. Lenin clearly saw, by the way, that Stalin was an evil influence on the Communist Party of the Soviet Union. He had been rude to Lenin's wife, Krupskaya, and Lenin had written, in what has been known as his testament, words to the effect that after my death, Stalin should not be allowed to become the general secretary. He is too rude; he doesn't know how to handle the comrades properly; he doesn't take account of all the different points of view.

It was very difficult to get this play on the stage. Plays, as well as books, go through a type of censorship before they are shown to the public. In this particular case, a report on the play was sent to the Marxism-Leninism Institute, and the report came back that this play should not be shown under any circumstances. The objections were that Lenin was shown as a dying man, mortal, and about to disappear—all negative aspects. In the play, Lenin says of one of his colleagues, ''And Martov is also dying.'' Behind the scenes there was great objection to this phrase, because it emphasized Lenin's mortality.

Finally, Mikhail Suslov, then the number-two man in the Politburo and the ideological czar, got wind of the play and canceled it. Only after Suslov's death did a movement arise to get the play back on stage. And, here again, a new struggle began. Could you put on this play at a time when a leader like Leonid Brezhnev was actually dying? Brezhnev's aides came to see the play; then other important party figures saw it; and finally they agreed that the play could go on. Apparently the play was permitted for two reasons: First, it showed Lenin as a more human person, as a real individual, not as God—as he is often looked upon in ordinary Soviet propaganda. Lenin was presented as an individual who had to face different points of view from his colleagues and who had to make decisions by persuading. Second, like Brezhnev, Lenin was leaving the political scene. In those days of 1982, many rumors were circulating that Brezhnev could not really govern anymore. So for the whole Politburo to show up at the play, along with Brezhnev, was a provocative, oblique way of telling the world that Brezhnev had not left the political scene, that he was there and governing.

This story gives you a sense of some of the intellectual ferment going on below the surface. The intellectuals wanted to put on something about Lenin more truthful than had been permitted in the past, and they had to struggle very hard to accomplish it.

Shifting from that particular example of ferment to several years later, I had an interview with Roy Medvedev, a very interesting and unusual Soviet historian, who styles himself as a dissident Marxist historian. He is somebody who has not wanted to leave the Soviet Union; he feels rooted there. (His twin brother, incidentally, did leave and lives in England today.) In the interview, Medvedev told me something very interesting and very applicable to the situation Gorbachev faces today. Medvedev said, ''The Communist Party does not have to share power, but it must allow an opposition. It could be an opposition within the party, or there could be opposing factions. There should be an open political debate.'' He went on to say, ''In almost 70 years, we have not developed personnel capable of working in such an environment—neither at the highest political levels nor at the lowest. The party has turned into a bureaucratic organism. It cannot and does not want to live in an environment of free speech and democracy.''

These are interesting statements because, for one thing, this is not what the Communist Party wanted the world to hear in 1985. Yet, as you examine Gorbachev's actions, he seems to be considering Medvedev's point of view in his policies of *glasnost*: an opening up, allowing many different views to come to the surface.

Let me just say a word about Gorbachev and his perspective on *glasnost*. Mikhail Gorbachev, of course, is the new generation, following three decrepit leaders who died in office: Brezhnev, Andropov, and Chernenko. Gorbachev represents new dynamism. Among recent Soviet leaders, he is one of the best educated and has traveled a fair amount abroad. Although we did not know it until very recently, Gorbachev made a private trip to France in 1966, in which he traveled all over the country in a car by himself. Later, he traveled to Great Britain and to Canada. He is a man who has seen and appreciated how productive the Western world is. It seems to me that he understands that free circulation of ideas is absolutely crucial to the development of any industrialized society, and he has initiated a policy of greater openness, greater truthfulness, in public discourse in the Soviet Union for some very specific reasons.

First, it is important for the creative process to have this free discussion. Second, Gorbachev wants very much to bring Soviet intellectuals to his side. He wants the intelligentsia to back him. He wants them to be a counterweight to a 20-million-strong bureaucracy, which is extraordinarily picayune and protective of its own privileges. Third, Gorbachev wants to get Soviet intellectuals to identify problems in the Soviet economy; and, finally, he wants to get them to suggest constructive solutions.

These, it seems to me, are the aims of Gorbachev's *glasnost*. The aim of *glasnost* is not, however, to bring about the kind of democratic reform that would make the Soviet Union similar to the United States or another Western country. It is an effort to get the intellectual resources of the Soviet Union working to improve Soviet socialism and, in the end, Soviet communism.

Glasnost has arrived in a rather uneven way, as you might expect, because there are people who do not support *glasnost* nearly as much as Gorbachev does. The following few examples show the evolution of this policy.

Shortly after Mikhail Gorbachev became the general secretary, in March 1985, he made a trip to Leningrad where he spoke at the former Smolny Institute, which was Lenin's headquarters during the revolution. Choosing that forum for his first appearance was not accidental. By making that choice Gorbachev was saying that he was the true inheritor of Lenin's mantle, and he buttressed this notion extraordinarily by speaking openly about the shortcomings of Soviet industry. His words were quite dramatic and shocking at the time and inspired a lot of enthusiasm among people whom I call the ''colonels''—people in mid-career, with a future to look forward to, who were depressed at the demoralization and stagnation of the Soviet Union in recent years.

At the same time, Gorbachev's speech was a rather depressing statement for the people whom I call the ''generals''—those who had found a niche in Soviet society, had won their privileges, and didn't want to see those privileges undermined by some young whippersnapper who had become general secretary.

After his remarks in Leningrad, Gorbachev began traveling to other parts of the Soviet Union where he spoke more openly; he walked the streets of the Soviet Union and the Soviet people confronted him, airing their complaints in a very direct fashion. Then, in the summer of 1985, an event occurred that demonstrated the fragility of *glasnost*.

The event was the defection to the United States of Vitalii Yurchenko and his return to the Soviet Union. It was a mysterious affair. The United States maintained that Yurchenko had voluntarily come to the United States. The Soviet Union portrayed it as quite another matter. The Soviet version of the Yurchenko affair was that he had been kidnapped while on an assignment in Rome, that Yurchenko had been brought against his will to the United States, and then, finally, through his own ingenuity he managed to get out of clutches of the Central Intelligence Agency (CIA) from a restaurant in Georgetown and make his way to the Soviet embassy. I was at Yurchenko's press conference in Moscow when he came back and told his tale in great detail. I would like to quote to you some of what he said, describing his abduction. He recalled he had been in Rome on an assignment; he was sitting on a park bench; he was drinking some boiled water out of a Coca-Cola bottle when, all of a sudden:

> I was reaching to put the top back on, when I felt something like liquid splashed on me, a feeling as if I had been plunged in water. Everything went dark, and I felt like I was falling . . . then someone grabbed me.

When I came back to the United States, I did some research on the book that I am writing and in the course of this research I came across an affidavit submitted by a Department of Justice official to the Walker-Whitworth trial. In that affidavit, John Martin, chief of the internal security section of the Department of Justice, says, and I quote from the affidavit, "Vitalii Yurchenko defected by voluntarily walking into the U.S. embassy in Rome, Italy, in July 1985."

There are two totally different versions of Yurchenko's defection. I think you know which version I believe. Sworn documents submitted to a U.S. court are more likely to hold the truth than statements by Yurchenko at a press conference supervised by the Soviet Foreign Ministry. Let me add that the man who presided over that press conference was Vladimir Borisovich Lomeyko, who was then head of the Soviet press department of the Foreign Ministry—a man who I respect. Lomeyko subsequently left his post, and I think that he did so because he found that being chief of the press department of the Soviet Foreign Ministry required him, on occasion, to sanction boldfaced lies.

A very important moment in bringing the policy of *glasnost* into existence was the Chernobyl nuclear accident. Someday, when we have the minutes of the Politburo debate on that subject, I believe you will find that Gorbachev argued strenuously for full disclosure. The fact could not be hidden because radiation had gone across international borders. You will also find a group of people who argued strenuously against disclosure, probably making the argument that it would undercut the Soviet Union by harming its image.

Although today we have a more open press policy in the Soviet Union than we have ever had before—except possibly in the 1920s—clearly there are forces in Moscow that would like to limit that openness. Those limitations are evident in the political process, for example, which still remains extraordinarily hidden. The Politburo meets, it is true, every Thursday and issues a communiqué, but that communiqué is merely an agenda of items discussed. It never explains who took what position or how a decision was resolved.

The ouster of Boris N. Yel'tsin is another very interesting and, at the same time, rather depressing development. Yel'tsin was found to be unaccept-

able. By whom he was found to be unacceptable is not totally clear. Why he was found to be unacceptable has not really been revealed. His speech to the Central Committee—which was found to be unacceptable—has not been published. Yet, Yel'tsin was made to stand up and say that he was arrogant, to grovel abjectly before those people who were about to dismiss him, apparently so he could then get another job—a responsible, but not politically prominent, job.

I am reminded in the Yel'tsin affair of a joke that I heard in Moscow as I was sitting in the Lefortovo "Hotel." In the joke, an interrogator was putting questions to Ivan Ivanovich for holding views that were not really acceptable to the topmost leadership of the Soviet Union.

INTERROGATOR:	"Ivan Ivanovich, what do you think of Soviet-American affairs?"
IVAN IVANOVICH:	"Well, I think what *Pravda* writes about it. What *Pravda* says is what I believe."
INTERROGATOR:	"Ivan Ivanovich, what do you think about relations with China?"
IVAN IVANOVICH:	"Well, what *Izvestia* says about relations with China totally reflects what I believe."
INTERROGATOR:	"And what do you think about President Reagan?"
IVAN IVANOVICH:	"Well, what *TASS* put out on its wire yesterday is exactly what I think about President Reagan."
INTERROGATOR:	"Ivan Ivanovich, don't you have any ideas of your own?"
IVAN IVANOVICH:	"I do, but I don't agree with them."

Forcing a person who is critical of you or who has different views than yours into a position where he has to abjectly grovel is the sort of thing that happened with Yel'tsin. It is not an inspiring example of political freedom. Furthermore, top Soviet leaders seem to voice criticisms of their own toward the policy of *glasnost*.

Mr. V. M. Chebrikov, the head of the KGB, sees an increased threat to Soviet security from *glasnost*. He says, "Needless to say, in the Soviet Union there is no, and cannot be any, class base that the adversaries of socialism could regard as a springboard for conducting subversive activity. At the same time, and this must be said bluntly, we do have some bearers of ideas and views that are alien and even openly hostile to socialism. Some of them are embarking on a path of committing antistate and antisocial activity."

Alexander N. Yakovlev, another member of the Politburo and adviser to Gorbachev, says, "Certainly, the more we open to the West, the stronger walls we will erect against things like pornography and movies in which violence is rampant."

In a speech July 14, 1987, Gorbachev seemed to take a view that is more liberal than those just quoted. He says, in his remarkable address in Moscow, "We are now, as it were, going through a school of democracy afresh. We are learning. Our political culture is still inadequate. Our standard of debate is inadequate. We are an emotional people, but we shall doubtless get over it; we shall grow up . . . I have no reason for any great political reproaches. If extremes have made their appearance anywhere—and incidentally, they have, and we have seen them—this nevertheless happened in the context of the struggle for socialism and the struggle to improve it."

The point I am getting at is there is a new policy of media management called *glasnost*. It is a policy of being more truthful and more open about events inside the Soviet Union. At the same time, there are forces within the Soviet Union that are concerned that *glasnost* might go too far. In closing, I would like to comment on the two points that I began with: How good a reflector is the Soviet press today of the current reality in the Soviet Union? and What kind of an image does the United States today have in the Soviet Union?

On the first point, there has been a sea change in the way the Soviet press describes what happens in the Soviet Union. There are articles today about the seamy side of Soviet life, the sorts of things that were never written about before—drug-taking, prostitution, and police abuse of power. There are also articles about Afghan veterans who are not acknowledged when they come back to the Soviet Union, although many of them have been maimed and others have given their lives in what, from Moscow's point of view, is a legitimate activity in support of the Soviet Union.

Those who have been in the Soviet Union recently tell me that the picture of the United States still has not markedly improved. There are still enormously descriptive pictures of the injustices of American society—homeless people generally merit one photograph on the front page, or inside, of a Soviet newspaper every day. It has a very dramatic effect.

In regard to the Soviet portrayal of the United States, some developments should be recognized and perhaps cheered. For example, the Soviet television program "International Panorama" recently ran a rather informative description of the U.S. presidential candidates without a lot of ideological interpretation.

Under Gorbachev's *glasnost* there have been many more American appearances in the Soviet media, even by those individuals, such as Richard Pipes of Harvard University, who are quite critical of the Soviet Union.

Finally, there have been the "space bridges" in which groups of Americans have conversed with groups of Soviet citizens through television hookups. These space bridges leave something to be desired. Sometimes one feels that the Soviet participants perhaps are not being as truthful as they might be, and the U.S. side is sometimes a bit naive and badly informed. Nevertheless, this kind of dialogue is quite unusual and is something we should be pleased to see happening.

COMMUNIST VERSION OF CANDID CAMERA LETS AUDIENCE VOTE WHETHER TO ACCEPT ANSWERS

Jackson Diehl

In other Communist countries in Europe, too, glasnost has had its effect. Hungarian television has been in the vanguard among Communist satellite media in its daring. In this period of openness, television is giving the public an opportunity to express itself.

BUDAPEST—Cornered on national television, a Hungarian trade union chief recently admitted that work stoppages had occurred in factories despite official intolerance of strikes. Under similar pressure, the managing director of the national savings bank abandoned attempts to justify low interest rates on consumer accounts.

But the favorite revelation for Janos Ban, moderator of the popular program "66," came when a government labor official was bluntly advised that socialism's tenet of full employment ought to be abandoned.

"His answer began with something like, 'Do you know what you are saying?' " Ban fondly remembers.

What caused these outbursts on Hungary's communist-controlled television was not the provocative questioning of professionals, but the spontaneous pressure of average Hungarians. Under Ban's guidance, 66 citizens are regularly invited on the air to grill top officials about domestic issues—and to vote on whether their answers are acceptable.

The result is one of the more remarkable examples of how Hungarian television has been changed by the slow political liberalization of this most reformist of Soviet Bloc countries. Under the watchful eye of communist party authorities, society's most powerful news medium is airing popular concerns

and divergent views to an extent unthinkable in most Eastern European countries.

"It's simple: I don't believe there are questions that can't be answered on television," Ban said of his four-year-old program, which was inspired by American audience-participation shows. "On my program, the top officials are forced to discuss with the public. And if changes are needed, then they are forced to outline solutions."

Once considered daring, Ban's show is now only one of several Hungarian programs designed to call government to account. A recent entry, "Windows," invites consumer complaints about products and government services and then investigates them.

Another program, "Background to the News," also features aggressive questioning of government officials. When the national postmaster refused to appear, a host journalist responded by excoriating the mail service in front of an empty chair.

Television officials say the new programs, although ultimately faithful to the socialist system, are providing a rare channel for Hungarians to pressure and influence government.

"These programs are a kind of forum where people can voice their own opinions," said Denes Damjan, vice president of programming for the two government-run channels. "At the same time, they are a kind of test-tube for the government, a way of

Jackson Diehl, "Communist Version of Candid Camera Lets Audience Vote Whether to Accept Answers." *The Washington Post*, March 20, 1986. Reprinted by permission.

The author is a *Washington Post* Foreign Service correspondent.

finding out what people's problems are and what measures ought to be taken.''

This approach fits into a more general effort by Hungary's leadership to expand the bounds of participation and expression without giving up ultimate control of public life. ''The authorities no longer care about dictating expression in culture, but about defining its limits,'' said Miklos Haraszti, a dissident writer. ''And there's a widespread belief that those limits have to be slowly expanded, even as you exclude the development of real alternatives.''

The twin goals of this policy have most recently emerged in the government preparation of a law regulating journalism, expected to be approved this month. Journalists have praised the law's provision that requires all government officials to answer requests for information, opening the way for more coverage of sensitive subjects in newspapers and on television.

At the same time, officials point out that the law will provide a firm legal basis for cracking down on Hungary's *samizdat* industry, which now includes a half-dozen clandestine political journals and an equal number of book publishers. In what dissidents have interpreted as a signal of a harder line, police have sought to halt work by two *samizdat* activists, Jeno Nagy and Gyorgy Gado, by repeatedly conducting all-day ''searches'' of their homes in the last month.

While few observers here expect that the government will eliminate independent cultural activity in the near future, authorities have succeeded in keeping most of Hungary's artists and intellectuals active within the official limits—an accomplishment that Eastern European governments no longer can take for granted.

In contrast, underground publishing and other independent arts are far more widespread in Poland, while Warsaw's emaciated officially sponsored culture, despite frequent claims of liberalism, has in many areas been quietly surpassed in tolerance by Hungary.

Television offers one of the clearest measures of that evolution because it is the medium most jealously protected by Soviet Bloc governments. Even in the 1970s, when Hungary was well embarked on its widely watched program of relaxing central control of the economy, television was still dominated by a dull fare of ''educational'' programming and communique-controlled news.

In the past several years, many of the old programs have been canceled and replaced by popular entertainment, while programming on domestic affairs has been radically upgraded. In the most recent step, the nightly television news has undergone its first reorganization in two decades. Young producers have replaced bulletin-reading with a more westernized format of fast-paced, film-oriented coverage.

Television critics who complained of boring didacticism in the past now have more familiar gripes about what they see as television's materialism and superficiality.

''Television now wants to please and entertain the public at all costs,'' said Gabriella Locsei, a critic for the official newspaper *Magyar Nemzet*. ''It's simply adjusting to the general changes that have gone on in society.''

Ban's program seems to combine the trend toward pleasing audiences with the expansion of expression on public affairs. After choosing topics for his programs, he makes appearances on news shows to invite letters from viewers on the subjects. He and his staff then review the letters—which number up to 20,000—and invite 66 of the letter writers to appear on the show.

Guest officials are first questioned by Ban, who may ask them to explain prickly issues of policy. Later, questions are put by members of the audience.

In both cases, the audience uses pushbuttons to vote on whether the answer is satisfactory. If a majority is displeased, the invited dignitary is obliged to offer further argument or change his position.

MAJOR DEVELOPMENTS IN CHINESE TELECOMMUNICATIONS: AN OVERVIEW

WANG RENZHONG

China has always been an enigma to the West. This article presents an overview of its long communication history, "from beacon fire to satellite communication."

The focus of this article is on the development of telecommunications in China, particularly recent activities dealing with telephone, television, and communication satellites.

In general, the evolution of telecommunications in China may be divided into three eras: before 1949; 1949–1979; 1980–present.

Telecommunications as modern means of communication appeared in China as early as the latter part of the 19th century. In 1877 and 1878 the last dynasty in China's history, the Quing government, began to run official telecommunication and postal undertakings. When radio broadcasting went on the air in a few countries of the world in the early 1920s, it also attracted Chinese attention. In 1928, the first official radio station was established by the Guomindang government. Certainly this was not the first radio station in China. The first radio station operated by a foreigner emerged in China even earlier. Following developments were rather slow because of the endless civil wars and the military occupation by the Japanese. From the 1920s to 1949 little had been achieved in the telecommunication area.

Since the founding of the People's Republic of China in 1949, the telecommunication industry has been expanding gradually in both scope and variety. However, developments during the three decades since 1949 are still not as rapid as they could have been. Although a national postal and telecommunication service network was built, it did not work efficiently. The Communist Party of China and the government attached importance to the de-velopment of radio broadcasting as the most important means of propaganda, but radio sets were far beyond the financial ability of most Chinese. Television had been developed, but was regarded as a luxury before the end of the 1970s. A satellite was launched successfully, but was used for communication until 1984. These examples illustrate the slow development of telecommunications.

In addition, there are two major factors which are also responsible for the delay of China's telecommunications industry. One was the withdrawal of a great number of Russian science and technology experts when the friendship between China and the U.S.S.R. was broken at the beginning of the 1960s. Another is evident in Mao's policies from 1957 to 1976, when military matters and production were emphasized at the expense of most economic development, including telecommunications.

The year 1978 was a major turning point for China, when the principle of "seeking truth from facts" was proposed and established, and the development of productive forces was considered "as the center of all work." The following quote illustrates this change of the Chinese ideology. "Whatever is good for the development of the productive forces and the improvement of the people's life should be recognized, experimented with and explored." In fact, the idea is just the reflection of Deng Xiaoping's idea which was presented in this way: "I do not care what color the cat is, as long as it catches mice."

According to the new recognition, the new lead-

Wang Renzhong, "Major Developments in Chinese Telecommunications: An Overview." *International Communication Bulletin*, Volume 23, Numbers 3–4, Fall 1988, pp. 4–9. Reprinted by permission.

The author is an instructor in journalism at Heilongjiang University in Harbin, China, and a visiting scholar at the University of Calgary, Canada.

ership of China's Central government has made a series of new, open policies aimed at promoting the rapid development of the national economy. Among the overall aspects of the nation's economy, the vital importance of sufficient and efficient telecommunication network has been recognized and emphasized. As result, the telecommunication industry as a whole has been growing in the past few years.

TELECOMMUNICATIONS IN CHINA

Telephone

The history of public communications in China is considerably long. About 2,500 years ago, courier horses and carts appeared in China.

In the early years of the Han dynasty, the government used beacon fires to send messages. Later, the canals provided an alternative network. Telephone communication did not make its appearance in China until after it had appeared in many other countries. In 1877 and 1878 the Quing government began official telecommunications and postal undertakings. In 1882 the government established the Chinese Telegraph Administration. However, the development was slow and little had been achieved in the 70-odd years prior to 1949. When the People's Republic of China was founded, there was only one post office for every 370 square kilometers.

In the cities, there were only 310,000 telephone exchanges under the management of the post and telecommunication department, of which only 200,000 were automatic. In 13 provinces, there were no automatic telephones.

At the same time, there were just over 2,800 single- and three-channel long-distance carrier cables and 3,000 telegram lines, most of which were in big cities such as Shanghai, Nanking, and Peking. Post and telecommunications facilities simply did not exist in the countryside.

Since the founding of the People's Republic of China, the situation in telecommunications has been gradually transformed. After 30 years of construction, a national postal and telecommunication service network, centered in Beijing and linking all the cities and rural areas, has been built. By 1979, China had increased the number of telephones to 3.7

million. In urban areas, the number of telephones increased from 310,000 in 1949 to more than 1.7 million in 1979. Although great achievements were made, the telecommunication service in China was still at a rather low level as compared with other major nations. The majority of telephone exchanges was step-by-step. The transmission network consisted mainly of open wires (usually iron) with 1, 3, or 12 carrier systems. Most of the networks were old and primitive.

With the further reform developments in the past eight years, the Chinese government has fully realized the vital importance of efficient communications. New policies have been made in favor of faster development of a modern telecommunication infrastructure. Various efforts have been made by both the central government and local governments. More state funds have been set aside for upgrading telecommunication facilities. More foreign funds have been invested in telecommunication than ever before. As a result, the process of modernizing telecommunication systems has been quickened.

The total number of telephones has been increased from 3.7 million in 1979 to more than 7 million in 1986. In urban areas, the number of telephones has been increased from 1.7 million in 1979 to 3.7 million in 1986. In addition, optic fiber links are utilized in cities' telecommunication systems. Long-distance telephone calls can be made automatically, or semiautomatically, through cable or microwave line in 241 cities.

An international telecommunication network has been established, which consists of satellite ground stations, microwave lines and relay stations, with Beijing and Shanghai as the major outlets. So far, China has already established direct telecommunication relations with 44 countries and regions. There are more than 50 thousand international direct dialing telephones with which 19 countries and regions can be called directly. In return, the telephone users outside China can directly make telephone calls to more than 60 regions in China. Moreover, except for Israel, South Korea and South Africa, China also has already established satellite telecommunication contacts with all parts of the world via three satellite ground stations in Beijing and Shanghai, and the international telecommunication satellite over the Indian and Pacific Oceans.

Nevertheless, compared with major developed

countries, it is obvious that China, at its present stage of development, is still rather backward in terms of the entire telecommunication network despite its significant progress made since 1979. The United States has approximately 155 million telephones, which means that 97% of the households have telephones, or there are approximately 70 telephones per hundred people. In industrialized nations, such as Japan and U.K., the numbers decrease, but are still sizable. In countries where average per capita annual income reaches US$800, the rate of telephone penetration is around 10%. And the average density of telephone in the world is about 12 telephones per hundred people. China with its population of more than 1 billion, has only 0.8 telephones per hundred persons.

Zhu Gaofeng, China's Vice Minister for Post and Telecommunication, has noted, ''Post and telecommunication is one of the foundations for society,'' He acknowledges that ''the gap between China and developed countries is quite big'' in these areas. The current reform in China is aimed at reducing the gap between China and developed countries in order to improve the economic level of the nation. To ensure the realization of the strategic objective, the post and telecommunication industry must be developed at a somewhat quicker pace than the national economy as a whole. Based on such analysis, China has an ambitious plan to develop its telecommunications:

By the year of 2000, the entire number of telephones will reach 33.6 million, or 2.8 telephones per 100 people. The emphasis of telephone's development will be placed in urban areas. Thus, telephone penetration in urban areas will be 10%. In Beijing, Shanghai, Tianjin, Guangzhou and provincial capital cities, the rate of owning a telephone will probably be over 25%. In other words, it may be possible that every applicant (as a household) can get a telephone in all the big and medium cities in China. The national telecommunication network will be automatic. All long-distance telephone calls in cities above and at county level will be made automatically.

Will the plan be realistic and achieved by the end of this century? The answer is ''yes''. Gaofeng expressed his confidence in a journalist interview from *Guang Ming Daily* on September 14, 1987. To achieve this goal, the central Government of China has taken some effective measures such as increas-

ing the proportion of investment for the development of the post and telecommunication; giving permission to both the Ministry of Post and Telecommunications and local bureaus to retain 90 percent of their profits and foreign exchange income to update their equipment; trying to attract and search for more foreign investment in telecommunication industry in China; encouraging collective and individual investment in the construction of local post and telecommunication network; urging the import of advanced telecommunication equipment and technology; making an increase of joint-venture in relation to telecommunication and promoting the development of the nation's own telecommunication technology and industry.

Television

In contrast with other industrialized countries, the initiation of television in China is certainly late. As television was very popular in the USA in the late 1950s and 1960s, and became common in Japan in the 1970s, it was still a rare-seen thing in China. China did not start to experiment with television until 1956. Two years later, on May 1, 1958, TV broadcasting started in Beijing, the capital of China. Regular telecasts went on the air on September 2 of that year. The following December another station opened in Shanghai. A station established at Harbin in late 1958, however, did not go on the air until 1960, to be followed by other stations in Shenyang, Changchun, and Guangzhou.

Although the abrupt withdrawal of Russian technical experts from China in 1960 greatly hampered the development of television, a rough framework of television network in China was constructed. By mid-1961, there were 29 stations and relay centers and 16 stations were still in the experimental stage. However, television was still unpopular in the first two decades of its development because television sets were too expensive for most Chinese. The case is illustrated by a story about China's former President Lu Shaoqi. One day in 1958, Lu's family received a TV set. The children were excited with the unusual device and put the set in their room. When their father Lu came in, they told him the good news. But Lu educated the children to live as ordinary people, and persuaded them to forgo the privilege, and put the TV set in the public room to share the new device with the security guards.

Television penetration had been very slow before the Cultural Revolution. In 1960, there were only 12,700 TV sets which were used only in public places such as railroad stations, parks, hotels, schools, etc. Estimated number of television receivers per 100 persons in 1964 was 0.003. The situation became much worse during most of the Cultural Revolution (1966–1969). The development of television even stopped entirely at that period of Chinese history. The few moves toward international agreements (such as an exchange agreement with Visnews in 1965) were sabotaged by the Cultural Revolution when all contacts with foreigners, especially in cultural matters, were banned. The situation became somewhat better after 1969 when foreign contacts were reestablished and the development of television continued.

In 1973, China started to experiment with color television. The first station to switch to color was the China Central Television Station (CCTV), which came on May 1, 1987, from Beijing Television. CCTV has been appointed to be responsible for both a national service and regional service. At the end of 1978, China became a member of the Asian-Pacific Broadcasting Union (ABU), and since then has been taking a leading role in ABU affairs.

One of the major reasons for the slow development and low penetration of television in China in the early stage of its development is television's identification with the military industry, and its use for military purposes. The current government elite, however, have placed great emphasis on the use of television as a major communications medium with the citizens. As a result, public television services and the manufacture of domestic TV receivers have expanded greatly. At the same time, large scale plans for further expansion via both terrestrial and satellite service are already formulated and being implemented.

The government invested 128 million yuan in the radio and television industry in 1979, twice the allocation made the previous year. In the same year, there were 38 TV centers with 238 transmitting and relay stations with transmitters of more than 1 kilowatt.

At the beginning of 1980, one in every 280 Chinese had a TV set, compared to one in 16,400 ten years earlier. At the end of 1980, TV service

reached some five million TV sets, and most stations were capable of transmitting color, although black-and-white programs were still being used. The increasing number of TV sets and telecasts over a larger area made television an important part of city life. In 1980, in Beijing, one-third of the families had TV sets. In Shanghai there was an average one set for every 4.2 households.

Taken as a whole, it was still a luxury to have TV in the countryside where 80 percent of Chinese people lived at the beginning of the 1980s, and many doubted that China could achieve high television popularity among its large population.

The situation has been changing rapidly in the past seven years. "The China of 1980 and 1987 are quite different countries, and I have seen changes every year," said Joseph E. Stepanek, a founders of the United Nations Industrial Development Organization who has worked as an American government advisor on economic planning. In his latest visit to China in 1987, Stepanek observed many dramatic changes in living standards, one of which is the popularity of TV sets in Chinese homes.

"In 1980, we brought a Chinese friend a color television set which we bought in Hong Kong. I think it was the first color television set in Wuhan (the capital city of Hubei province). Now everyone has one," Stepanek said.

A 1988 national TV audience survey has revealed that the Chinese own 112 million TV sets. This means that nearly 50 percent of the Chinese households own TV sets, compared to only two percent in 1978. In urban areas, the percentage is much higher—almost 85 percent of urban households have TV sets while there are about 20 TV sets per 100 in the countryside.

With the improvement of the Chinese people's living standard, the need for TV sets has been increasing rapidly in both rural and urban areas. To meet the increasing demand from the huge market, China has made solid efforts. Traditional radio equipment factories have begun to focus on civil products; joint ventures have been encouraged; advanced technical equipment has been imported. The productive network for TV sets has been formed. As a consequence, the Chinese ability of producing TV sets and other television equipment has been improved greatly. Annual output of TV sets in China now reaches 16 million. In 1987, the entire number of TV sets made in China, reached 19,370,000. 6,710,000 of these are color sets. Now China has become the country with biggest output of black and white TV sets in the world, and third in color-set production.

Television programming has also changed significantly, both in appearance and context, over the last few years. While educational programming is the major category in terms of time allocation, more entertainment, some imported from abroad, is now in evidence. The transformation of television programming has naturally resulted in the increase of television viewers. Thus, China today has 600 million television viewers, which makes China the country with the greatest absolute number of television viewers in the world.

Now, the strategic target for Chinese-made color TV sets has been confirmed and also is proceeding. The examination of quality of Chinese-made color TV sets conducted by the Ministry of Electronic Industry show that over 80 percent of components used in Chinese-made color TV sets are made by Chinese.

Radio

In 1928, the Guomindang government established its first radio station—the Central Broadcasting Station at the capital, Nanjing. The radio started as a 500-kilowatt station and was increased four years later to 750 kilowatts. From the beginning, the station was used for newscasts.

As government-owned and -operated stations were founded at other points in China, privately owned stations also sprang up. Between 1932 and 1936, 16 new noncommercial stations were established, three of which were under the Central Broadcasting Administration (it was organized in 1932 by the Guomindang government to make a national broadcasting policy), eight operated by provincial governments, four by special municipal governments, and two controlled by the Ministry of Communications. Within the same period, 63 privately owned commercial stations were established in metropolitan areas.

The Japanese occupation of Chinese territory and anti-Japanese war dislocated and stopped much broadcasting activity, but by September 1947 there were 41 stations under Central Broadcasting Admin-

istration's supervision, 48 privately-owned commercial stations, and four allied armed forces stations were in operation. However, broadcasting was still an infant medium in 1949 because there were less than one million radio receiving sets in the entire country, averaging about 0.3 sets for every 100 persons.

The first radio station of the Chinese Communist Party started transmitting on September 5, 1945. It was the Yanan Xinha Broadcasting Station with only two-hours of programming daily. The small station beamed on its 300-watt transmitter propaganda messages for the consumption of the Guomindang leaders and the people in the cities controlled by Guomindang government. Later, its programs were improved slightly, and time on the air was increased also.

In March 1949, the station was moved to Beijing where the Chinese Communist Party set up the organization that on October 1, was renamed the Central People's Broadcasting Station.

Although the Chinese Communist Party was operating a network of 16 radio stations when the People's Republic of China was founded in 1949, the importance of radio to the Party and the government ensured that it expanded rapidly, both at the national level and in the distribution of services to communes, bridges, and teams. By 1950, there were 83 radio stations established and owned by the government, in addition to the former National Stations and some 33 privately owned stations in China. As in the case of the press, the privately owned and operated stations were controlled and eventually were to be absorbed by the State.

Because of the low economic level of China, for most Chinese people, radio sets were too expensive to purchase. The number of radio sets increased slowly in China during the 1950s and 1960s. In order to increase access to radio more evenly over the entire country and to make it available in areas that formerly lacked it, the Chinese government stressed production of loudspeakers which were cheaper than radio sets. A number of factories were designated to produce loudspeakers. Thus, a national wired-speaker system was gradually formed. By the end of 1958, wired stations were in operation in some 1,800 counties and cities and 5,800 people's communes.

In 1951, there were only about 2,000 wired-speaker exchanges in the urban areas; by the end of the second Five-Year-Plan, in 1962, the number was increased to 5,400 exchanges with about 7 million loudspeakers. With the development of wired-speaker system, the production of radio sets was also developed. In 1964 UNESCO estimated that in 1962, China had 4.5 million radio sets, namely one radio receiver for every 100 persons. Since China opened its doors in 1978, the production of radio sets, like the whole electric industry of China, has been developing rapidly. According to a *Xinha Bulletin* (18 February 1980), at the beginning of 1980 there were about 88 million radio sets capable of receiving over-the-air broadcasts, along with 120 million loudspeakers in the wired network.

There are no recent figures about the penetration of radio sets disclosed in the past few years, because radio broadcasts are losing their dominant position in mass communication; instead, TV is now playing an increasingly important role in mass communications in China, and receives more attention from the government.

Communication Satellites

China has a short history of space technology. The government first drew up plans in the mid-1950s for space exploitation, together with plans to establish rocket research and experimental space centers. By the 1960s, China had succeed in developing rockets for space exploitation. In 1965, China first drew up a technical plan for a manmade satellite, and in 1970 launched its first satellite. China became a member of the Universal Postal Union in 1971 and of the International Telecommunication Union in May 1972. Since then, there has been constant progress in this field.

China had not had satellites aimed at communications until 1984. Then how did China handle long-distance communications over its vast distances? By depending largely on land-based microwave transmissions.

However, microwave, like light waves, can only travel in a straight line and for a certain distance. To make microwave telecommunications work in very large areas, numerous relay stations are required. Although more than 15,000 kilometers of microwave trunk lines and 270 relay stations had built by 1984, they still did not totally satisfy the demands of China's domestic telecommunications. In some border and remote areas, problems were extremely serious. It was recognized that the fundamental answer to the problem was highly advanced technology—a synchronous communications satellite—that would maintain a relatively fixed position in space over China.

The success in launching an experimental communications satellite in 1984 and particularly an applied communication and broadcasting satellite in 1986, marked a new breakthrough in China's telecommunication and space technology. As a result, China's domestic satellite communication network officially went into operation on July 8, 1986, signaling a new stage in the country's communication industry, one of the bottlenecks hindering the country's long-run economic development.

The overall network is composed of five ground stations—Beijing, Guangzhou, Lhasa, Urumqi and Huhhot, which are linked by an international satellite over the Indian Ocean (See map, Figure 1). The network makes daily transmissions of CCTV programs and special education programs throughout the country with the help of thousands of satellite receiving stations and ground stations. The network also provides both public and special user of industry or economy with more efficient telephone, telegraph and facsimile communication services.

China has developed, manufactured, and operated satellite systems with minimal help from other countries. Yet, China is one of three countries (with the United States and the Soviet Union) who have mastered the satellite re-entry technology. This ability has made China an international marketer of satellite services as well as having increased the pace of its modernization of domestic telecommunication. On August 5, 1987, two micro-gravity experimental devices belonging to SaMatra Limited of France, carried into space by a Chinese Long March rocket, marked the first time China has provided satellite piggyback service for a foreign company. Furthermore, from the second half of 1986 to August 1987, more than 10 companies from the Federal Republic of Germany, France, Belgium, Sweden, Britain, Italy, the United States and Canada have approached China about providing piggyback service for their scientific experiments. Some have already signed memorandums of agreement with the Chinese space agency, and still others

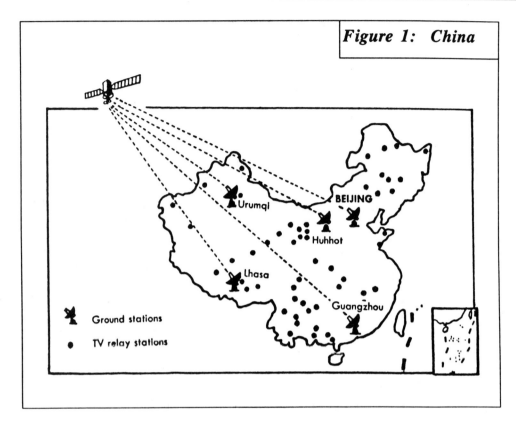

Figure 1   China

are considering signing long-term agreements with China.

CONCLUSIONS

From beacon fire to satellite communication, China has made a great leap in the communication area, which is pushing the ancient nation into entering the modern world and in the long run becoming an information society.

The increasing number and improved quality of the telephone network has provided an efficient communication service, which is one of the crucial stimulus to the rapid growth of the national economy in China.

With the popularity of television for Chinese families, outside pictures are being brought in. As a result this new medium is making the people more open-minded, more active in thinking, and more creative. They are beginning to think not only historically or vertically, but also perpendicularly.

The communication satellite has closely tied the once isolated country to the outside world. Once a forbidden land for the West, China is now welcoming Westerns. The traditional mysterious nation is learning from other nations and becoming known by others.

The advanced information system is also promoting an encourageable two-way dialogue among the government, the party, and the public. Thus, a more democratic atmosphere is being formed.

The development of the telecommunication industry has also changed the structure of the traditional mass media in which radio broadcasts and loudspeakers occupied the dominant position. Now television is playing a more important role in mass communication while various print publications are also flourishing.

On the whole, the impact of telecommunication's growth is penetrating almost every aspect in a vast changing society. In return, telecommunications will also benefit from the society and be growing more rapidly.

REFERENCES

Books: James W. Markham, *Voices of the Red Giants: Communications in Russia and China*, Ames, Iowa: Iowa State University Press, 1967; John Howkins, *Mass Communication in China*, New York: Longman, 1982; *China*, Information Gatekeepers, Inc., 1979; Yu, Timothy, "Communication Research Priorities in China," in Sarath Amunugama, Abdul Rahman b. Mohd. Said, *Communications Research in Asia.* Singapore: Asian Mass Communication Research and Information Centre, 1982.

Serials: "Changing Functions of Mass Media in the People's Republic of China" by D. C. Robinson, in *Journal of Communication* (Autumn 1981); "A New Line in China" in *Far Eastern Economic Review* (April 17–23, 1981); *Beijing Review* (April 5, 1982, p 14–15; October 31, 1983, p 18–21; April 30, 1984, p 23; May 7, 1984, p 22–25; September 30, 1985, p 9; May 12, 1986, p 28; June 16, 1986, p 30–31; July 21, 1986, p 9; October 12, 1987, p 6–7; March 2, 1987, p 23, 29; March 23, 1987, p 21–22; August 24, 1987, p 24; September, 1987, p 75–76; January, 1988, p 4–10.); *Xinha Monthly Report* (September, 1987, p 75–76; August, 1987, p 118–119; September, 1987, p 120); *People's Daily—Overseas Version* (October 9, 1987; October 30, 1987; December 23,24, 1987; January 8, 1988; January 23, 1988; January 26, 1988; January 29, 1988; February 4, 1988).

RECENT DEVELOPMENTS IN CHINESE JOURNALISM

Qian Xinbo

This article examines recent developments in Chinese journalism from the point of view of a Chinese journalism educator. Everything is developing rapidly, according to him, but there is still much to be done in terms of upgrading equipment and finding ways to finance mass media in a country the size of China. Since it is a Communist country, its mass media cannot depend on advertising for its financial support.

Two years have passed since the first Sino-Australian Press seminar was held in Beijing in November 1981. During this period, all sectors in China have been undergoing reforms. Playing its role as a shaper of public opinion, the Chinese mass media have contributed to the reforms in other sectors while carrying on their own reforms. They have made rapid progress in the process.

Browsing through Chinese newspapers, one gets the impression that marked changes have taken place in both form and content compared with two years ago. The reform in journalism started with

Qian Xinbo, "Recent Developments in Chinese Journalism." *Australian Journalism Review*, Volume 6, Number 1, January 1984, pp. 36–39. Reprinted by permission.

The author is Deputy Director of the Institute of Journalism of the Chinese Academy of Social Sciences.

how news was written. News must be factual, brief, fresh, timely and abundant. Papers carry shorter items, and their news coverage is more timely and wider in scope. A page used to carry only a few items. Now there are often more than 15. The pages look busier, with more pictures.

They look livelier and have a greater variety of stories. Each newspaper seeks to have its distinctive flavor and caters to the needs and interests of its own readers. This marks a departure from the uniformity that used to characterise Chinese newspapers.

Statistics on the national economy were seldom published in the past. Now, they appear regularly in our newspapers. Spokesmen have been designated by the State Council and its ministries and commissions who brief Chinese and foreign journalists from time to time. Overcoming the one-sidedness in our coverage of international events in the past, we have been trying to be more balanced, objective, fair and timely. The increased advertising in our newspapers and radio-TV programs has helped to promote the exchange of economic information.

Endeavors have also been made to improve financial management and upgrade equipment. But in this connection, much work needs to be done to catch up with the advanced countries.

The pace of development in Chinese journalism has been quite rapid during the last two years. There were 476 newspapers with an overall circulation per issue in excess of 60 million at year's end in 1981. By the second quarter of 1983 however the number of newspapers has increased to 818, and overall circulation per issue increased by 50 percent to more than 90 million copies. Several papers were inaugurated in Beijing this year. These include the *Economic Daily* (formerly the *Finance and Trade Journal*, published three times a week), the *Huasheng Journal* (Voice of China), the *Zhengxie Journal* (organ of the Chinese People's Political Consultative Conference), and the *Education Journal*. Some put out a bigger paper or increased their issues, like the *Unity Journal* (organ of the Revolutionary Committee of the Kuomintang), the *Athlete*, the *Legal System Journal* and the *Health Journal*. The English-language *China Daily* added a North American edition.

With the implementation of the responsibility system in the countryside, the peasants are anxious to practise scientific farming in a bid to increase production. Science and technology journals have become quite popular. There are 43 such publications. Early in 1982, Hebei Province published a scientific and technology tabloid known as the *Happy Farmer*. Initial circulation was from 30 to 40 thousand, but jumped to more than 200,000 by the year's end. To meet the needs of China's family planning program, many localities have published journals on this general topic. They are all very popular. The *Family Planning Journal* of Henan Province has had a circulation in excess of 200,000 from the very beginning.

The circulation of evening papers is growing rapidly. They cover more local news and stress informative and interesting stories, so they are very popular. Guangzhou's *Yangcheng Evening News* has a circulation of 1.5 million. Shangai's *Xinmin Evening News* and the *Beijing Evening News* have circulations of 1.4 and one million respectively.

The paper with the biggest circulation in China is the *Chinese Children's Journal* (more than 10 million copies). Another children's paper, published by a group of youngsters, appeared in Shanghai last July 15. Entitled *Young Masters of China*, the editorial board has an average age of only 12, and its contributors range in age from 5 to 14. It is indeed a unique paper.

Looking into the future, journalism in China will see greater growth as the rural economy develops. There is a division of labor and coordination between Chinese newspapers at the national, provincial and county levels, between general and specialised, morning and evening newspapers. They cooperate and compete with each other, forming an integral whole that works together to give full coverage of China's modernisation program and helping to push it forward.

The formal establishment of a radio and TV ministry under the State Council in 1982 is an indication of the growing role played by those two branches of the mass media. As of the end of 1982, there were 118 broadcasting stations, 47 TV stations and 180 million radio receiver sets in China. Owing to its vast geographical expanse and large rural population, it was found necessary to set up 2,600 cable broadcasting stations with more than 90 million loudspeakers, thereby establishing a broad network of mass communications. The Central People's Broadcasting Station has increased its programs from five to seven. Its international service, Radio Beijing, has begun a special English transmission for the local international community.

There are more than 27 million TV sets, mostly in urban areas, TV programming is still inadequate with no broadcasts during the day, except for holidays. Work began on building a national color TV centre last May. When completed in 1986, this modern building will be the tallest in Beijing, and TV channels will be increased from two to five. Broadcast hours will be extended to daytime. The university courses offered on TV, begun in 1979 and operated jointly with the Ministry of Education, have graduated 160,000 people. More than 340,000 are enrolled in these courses at present.

There are two news agencies in China: the Xinhua News Agency and the China News Agency. Xinhua sends copy to national news organisations running into 50 to 60 thousand Chinese characters a day. It sends 50,000 characters to provincial and municipal news organisations. It has correspondents in 87 countries and sends copy abroad in six languages. Its director-general Mu Qing has set the goal of turning Xinhua into a world news agency with a distinctive Chinese characteristic. Xinhua is working towards this goal by improving its news reporting and editing and its technical facilities.

The China News Agency sends copy mainly to newspapers run by overseas Chinese or compatriots in Hong Kong and Macao. It feeds them with news about developments in China. It services some 200 Chinese-language newspapers in 13 countries and in Hong Kong and Macao, supplying them with news items, features and photos.

The teaching of journalism has not kept pace with the development of journalism and cannot meet the growing needs for trained personnel. In the past 32 years, only some 5,200 people have graduated from schools or departments of journalism. There are some 1,500 undergraduates and 100 or so post-graduates studying journalism. Projections show that 90,000 graduates in journalism will be needed from now until the end of the century, meaning an average enrollment of 5,000 a year. At the national conference on the teaching of journalism last May, a program was adopted providing for an expansion

from 16 to 30 universities with a department of journalism, an enlargement of enrollment and the founding in the near future of a journalism institute. It also called for the training of journalists by a variety of other means. From this, it can be surmised that it won't be long before the teaching of journalism in China will see a substantial development.

A new phenomenon is the establishment of research centres devoted to the study of journalism. More than 50 such centres have been set up in Beijing and other localities in recent years. Various academic societies of journalism have also been founded and symposia held on the topic of reforming journalism. Meetings to exchange experience and books and other publications about journalism have become more common. Two large-scale computerised samples have been conducted since 1982 to study our readers, listening audience and viewing public. One was a survey in the Beijing area last summer, and the other was the one in Zhejiang Province last October. Data gathered through these surveys provide a clearer picture for reforming and developing the media in China.

China's national policy of opening to the outside world applies equally to the field of journalism. There have been numerous contacts between Chinese journalists and their counter-parts abroad during the last two years. In the 18 months from January 1982 to June 1983, the All-China Journalists' Association played host to 137 journalists from 31 foreign countries and sent 111 people on visits to 21 countries. Contacts between major national and some local journalistic organisations with foreign colleagues are also quite numerous, and the trend seems to be for ever closer ties.

Our professional publications have been introducing developments in the Western mass media. The Journalism Research Institute of the Chinese Academy of Social Sciences held a seminar on Western communication theories in November 1982. It discussed the history of communication, its substance and relationship with journalism. Our attitude is, through a fuller understanding and analysis of Western communication theories, to absorb what is useful and rational to the Chinese situation and not to copy things lock, stock and barrel. We Chinese journalists have learned from our own experience that we can copy neither the Soviet nor the Western model, but must try and find a path to socialist journalism suited to Chinese conditions.

Journalism in China is different from that practised in the West and is often misunderstood by our Western colleagues. They accuse us of being "government-controlled" and having "no freedom of the press." Let me touch briefly on the nature of Chinese journalism and on some of its principles in the hope that this might further our mutual understanding.

China is a socialist country under the leadership of the Communist Party. We do not disclaim the fact that Chinese journalism is an integral part of China's socialist cause. Chinese newspapers are not pitted against the Government because they share common interests and strive for a common goal. We see journalism as a bridge between the Government and the people, helping the two to communicate with one another. Government policies and laws and decrees are conveyed to the people through the mass media. The wishes and views of the people are transmitted to the Government through the media. The function of the mass media in China is to inform the people and help channel public opinion. It is not motivated by profit-seeking, but by serving the people and serving socialism. These are the characteristics of Chinese journalism.

Chinese journalism has certain traditions of which it is proud. It has also developed some unique features over the years. These can be characterised as:

1. News must be truthful. We have always held that credibility can be built up only through honest reporting, through sticking to the facts. That was what we did for a long time. It is a deplorable fact that this principle was violated to the discredit of Chinese journalism during the Great Leap Forward in 1958 and the decade of the "cultural revolution." We have put in a lot of effort in recent years to re-establish the tradition that news must be truthful and to restore the credibility of the Chinese media among the people. Nowadays, if an item of news is found to be untrue, whoever is responsible will be criticised. We will continue to fight for the principle that news must be truthful.*

2. To channel and spur popular enthusiasm toward the cause of China's socialist modernisation and of defending world peace. That news has an impact on its audience is an undeniable fact. It is the aim of Chinese journalism to build morale and inspire people to work together for the early realisation of China's modernisation. Of course we believe that news should be informative and interesting too, but news must help to foster a healthy inquisitiveness, uplift values and broaden horizons. We are opposed to catering to the baser interests of some people, and we refrain from pornography and gory descriptions of violence. We are against crass commercialism in journalism.

3. To keep in close touch with the people and with reality, journalism must serve and be run by the people. The people provide our newspapers and radio stations with many news leads, articles, criticism and suggestions. *Renmin Ribao* (*People's Daily*) receives about 2,000 letters a day from its readers. Between three to four hundred letters are received each day by both the *Workers' Daily* and the *China Youth Paper*. The Central People's Broadcasting Station received 238,000 letters in 1982. The letters to the editor column of newspapers and the letter box program of the radio stations are very popular because they give expression to the views and wishes of the people.

Many letters cite good deeds as well as criticise evil-doings. There is room only for a small fraction of these letters to be published in the papers or broadcast over the air. Most of the other letters are forwarded to departments concerned for them to deal with. But journalistic organisations are obliged to check that action is taken in every case. This involves a lot of work, but has a big social impact. Criticisms of red tape and misconduct on the part of some people appear almost daily in our newspapers and radio programs. The *Economic Daily*, for example, carried a series of reports from March 23 to April 15 this year on irregularities in the allocation of housing by some people in charge of the first light industry bureau of Baoding city in Hebei Province. In those 22 days, it printed some 30 news items, commentaries, features, pictures and cartoons.

---

*Editor's note: As is so often the case with basic laws, constitutions, canons, and resolutions of all types, people as well as governments do not always live up to their aspirations. China may or may not have been truthful in what it told the world about what transpired in Tiananmen Square in June, 1989. Suffice it to say that most of the rest of the world did not believe the official story.

Likewise, from last February to July, the Central People's Broadcasting Station focused on the incident of the uncivilised unloading of a consignment of goods by the Shuangchengpu Station under the Harbin Railway administration in Northeast China.

Both these cases of investigative reporting produced good results. Using the media for criticism and self-criticism has turned the media into an important channel for exercising socialist democracy.

THE CHINESE COMMUNIST PRESS AS I SEE IT

Lu Keng

From the point of view of this Chinese journalist now working in Hong Kong, Chinese mass media have grave shortcomings. The author analyzes the Chinese press using Western criteria and finds many shortcomings. News in China is scarce, slow, wasteful, and lacking in news value, according to this emigre reporter.

. . . The People's Republic of China is a country under the leadership of the Chinese Communist Party. Since the polity of this country is proletarian dictatorship, its press is also inscribed with dictatorship.

Mao Tse-tung said: "The force at the core leading our cause forward is the Chinese Communist Party. The theoretical basis guiding our thinking is Marxism-Leninism." Thus, the ideology guiding the press under the Chinese Communist Party was copied from the Soviet Union. Or, more appropriately, given by the Soviet Union. In his "On the People's Democratic Dictatorship," Mao said: "The salvos of the October Revolution brought us Marxism-Leninism." The very basis of this ideology is the grasp of class struggle as the key link. Everything is for class struggle. Everything must obey the principle of class struggle. In the west, journalism reflects more or less the social responsibility theory, in which the function of the press is to satisfy the people's cultural needs, to promote understanding and social progress, and to improve the well-being of the people. From the Communist point of view, however, the major function of the press is to carry out class struggle between the proletariat and the bourgeois. In his "On the Nature of Our Newspapers," Lenin iterated that class struggle will be carried out in the newspapers against the protectors of the bourgeois. He said that the proletarian press should look like a "revolutionary press," and "the mouthpiece of class dictatorship." "This class is now using actions to demonstrate that the resistance of the bourgeois and the protectors of the bourgeois will be smashed by its iron fists," Lenin said.

Mao Tse-tung fully subscribed to Lenin's concept of proletarian dictatorship. Not only did he inherit Lenin's conceptualization of the press as a tool for class struggle, he developed it further. In his "Talks at the Yenan Forum on Literature and Art," Mao said that "in the world today all culture, all literature and art belong to definite classes and gear-

Lu Keng, "The Chinese Communist Press As I See It." *The Asian Messenger*, Volume 4, Numbers 2–3, Autumn 1979/Spring 1980, pp. 44–53. Reprinted by permission.

The author is a journalist who came to Hong Kong from China in 1978 and was chief commentator of *The Centre Daily*, a Hong Kong-based independent newspaper.

ed to definite political lines.'' ''To defeat the enemy, we must rely on the army with guns. But this army alone is not enough; we must also have a cultural army, which is indispensable for unity our own ranks and defeating the enemy.'' During the Cultural Revolution, Mao's hand-picked heir-apparent, Marshal Lin Piao, further elaborated this concept. He said, ''carrying out a revolution is inseparable from two barrels, one is the barrel of a gun and the other, the barrel of a pen. To establish a political power, we must depend on these two barrels. To consolidate a political power, we must also depend on these two barrels.'' Thus, from this viewpoint, the press is a component part of the proletarian dictatorship machine. Like the army, police, jails and courts, the press is a tool and weapon for proletarian dictatorship. It would be a great honor if a journalist should become a small ''screw'' in this machine of dictatorship. In the eyes of the proletariat, the so-called ''crownless king,'' and ''voice of the people'' are nothing but lies used by the bourgeois to cheat the people. In Mao Tse-tung's words, ''this windy nonsense'' must be stopped.

FUNCTIONS OF THE CHINESE COMMUNIST PRESS

In scholarship, we usually begin by learning from others. This is also true with running a newspaper. From the very beginning, the Chinese Communist press has been learning from the Russians. It is neither the traditional intellectual endeavor, nor the western free enterprise, but an organ of proletarian dictatorship. Its propaganda functions, as prescribed by the Party, are to carry out the Party's intentions and to look upon the materialization of Communism as its highest goal. During the present stage, it must struggle for the materialization of socialism and the consolidation of proletarian dictatorship.

Generally speaking, the Chinese Communist press has four functions:

1. *To propagate policies:* In his ''Talk to the Editorial Staff of *Shansi Suiyuan Daily*'' Mao Tse-tung said, ''Questions concerning policy should as a rule be given publicity in the Party papers or periodicals.'' ''The role and power of the newspapers con-

sists in their ability to bring the Party program, the Party line, the Party's general and specific policies, its tasks and methods of work before the masses in the quickest and most extensive ways.''

2. *To educate the mass:* In the same talk, Mao unequivocally pointed out: ''You comrades are newspapermen. Your job is to educate the masses.'' In the inaugural statement of *China's Worker*, (Chung Kuo Kung Jen Pao), a daily launched in Yenan in 1940, Mao made it clear that ''*China's Worker* should become a school for the education and training of workers.''

3. *To organize the mass:* Mao Tse-tung always emphasized that ''the people need us (Communists) to organize.'' In addition, Mao also regarded the press as a tool for organizing the mass. He said, ''to strengthen the Party's ties with the masses through the newspapers—this is an important question of principle in our Party's work which is not to be taken lightly.''

4. *To mobilize the mass:* In the talk to the editorial staff of the *Shansi Suiyuan Daily*, Mao also said that ''we must arouse the people to fight for their own emancipation.'' Later in Yenan and Peking, Mao said several times that the goals for struggle and the slogans for fighting should be advocated through the newspaper to unite the people and mobilize the people.

What then is the purpose of propaganda, education, organization and mobilization? The purpose is to ''attack the enemy and eliminate the enemy.'' Or, in a word, to carry class struggle to the end.

There was one vivid example. In 1957 around the time of the anti-rightist struggle when Mao Tse-tung was masterminding his ''open plot,'' under Mao's direct instruction the Chinese Communist newspapers were engaged in a series of ''insidious plots.'' On June 8, 1957, Mao drafted for the Communist Party Central Committee an ''inner-Party directive,'' entitled ''Muster Our Forces to Repulse the Rightists' Wild Attacks.'' In this ''directive'' Mao said:

Get each of these parties to organize forums with the Left, middle and Right elements all taking part, let both positive and negative opinions be voiced, and *send reporters to cov-*

er these discussions. We *should tactfully encourage* the Left and middle elements to speak out at the meetings and refute the Rightists. This is very effective. The Party paper in each locality should have dozens of articles ready and publish them from day to day when the high tide of the attacks begin to ebb there . . . But before the tide is on the ebb, Party papers *should restrict the number of articles expressing positive views* . . . Better let the reactionary professors, lecturers, assistants and students *spew out their venom and speak without any inhibitions*. (emphasis added by the speaker)

This resulted in the trapping of an uncountable number of intellectuals known all over the world.

Wasn't this unbashful use of the newspaper as a tool for class struggle too exciting? Well, according to Mao Tse-tung's thought, it was not a question of excitement. He would do it whether it was exciting or not because they were all reactionaries. "Only by boosting our own morale and dampening the enemy's can we isolate the reactionaries so as to defeat them or replace them."

THE CHINESE COMMUNIST PRESS SYSTEM

Basically, the Chinese Communist press includes two levels: the central press and the local press. The local press can be further divided into the provincial, district, and county press. In fact, there are very few district newspapers. And the county newspapers are even more few and far between.

Major central level newspapers are the *People's Daily, Kuang Ming Daily, Worker's Daily, Liberation Army Daily* and the *China Youth Daily*, plus the small *China Pioneers Daily*. Each of these newspapers is under a different command system. The *People's Daily*, the mouthpiece of the Party Central Committee, is under the jurisdiction of the central Politburo. Its editorials, which toward the later half of the Cultural Revolution were jointly published in the *People's Daily*, the *Liberation Army Daily* and the *Red Flag* journal, speak for the Party Central and

must be studied by all of the people. It had then become an unwritten law for all the other newspapers to reprint its editorials. Sometimes even periodical journals were reprinting its editorials. At that time the Party Central iterated that even such specialized journals as *Health News* (Chien Kang Pao), or *Oral Cavity Journal* (Kuo Chiang Ko Cha Chi) also had to carry out propaganda in line with major political events.

Kwang Ming Daily, formerly the mouthpiece of the Democratic League, was taken over by the Chinese Communists in the 1957 anti-rightist struggle. Run by the Party Central's Department of Propaganda, this daily focuses on the propaganda of cultural, educational and scientific content.

The *Liberation Army Daily* is run by the General Political Department of the Ministry of Defense. The paper is distributed to military units and state institutions. No individual subscription is permitted.

The *Worker's Daily* is the mouthpiece of the National Workers Union. The *China Youth Daily* is the mouthpiece of the Central Committee of the Chinese Communist Youth League. The *China Pioneers Daily*, also run by the Chinese Communist Youth League, is published for the young pioneers (generally known as the "red scarfs"). All these newspapers are under the unified leadership of the Party Central Committee.

As for the local level press, each of the 29 provinces and municipalities has a daily of its own under the direct leadership of the respective Chinese Communist Party Committees. Before the Cultural Revolution, some of the Party's regional bureaus also published their own newspapers. For instance, the South China Bureau published the *Southern Daily* (Nan Fong Jih Pao) in Canton and the Central-south Bureau published the *Yangtze Daily* (Chang Chiang Jih Pao) in Wuhan. The *Southern Daily* and *Canton Daily* (Kwang Chou Jih Pao) were later merged into one to become the mouthpiece of the Kwangtung Provincial Party Committee.

Each provincial newspaper is named after the province and is published in the provincial capital. Thus, *Hopei Daily* is published in Shihchiachuang, *Chekiang Daily* in Hangchow, *Szechuan Daily* in Chengtu, *Shensi Daily* in Sian, *Liaoning Daily* in Shengyang, *Honan Daily* in Chengchow, etc. However, there are exceptions. The mouthpiece of the

Kiangsu Provincial Party Committee published in Nanking, for instance, is not called ''Kiangsu Daily'' but *Hsinhua* (New China) *Daily*. The mouthpiece of the Shangtung Provincial Party Committee published in Chinan is not called ''Shangtung Daily'' but *Ta Chung* (Popular) *Daily*. These newspapers have kept their historical names. To the Chinese Communists, the *Hsinhua Daily* has a glorious history in the struggle against the Nationalist Party. At the time of the Huannan (Southern Anhui) Incident, Chou En-lai himself peddled the *Hsinhua Daily* on Chungking streets. *Ta Chung Daily*, established in 1947 in Shangtung's liberated areas, was the brainchild of Gen. Chen Yi.

Before the Cultural Revolution, there were six evening newspapers in the country. Among the better-known were *Peking Evening News* (Pei Jing Wan Pao), Shanghai's *Hsinmin* (New People) *Evening News*, Canton's *Yangcheng* (Canton) *Evening News*. Chengtu, Lanchow and Harbin each had an evening daily.

Besides the *Worker's Daily*, other specialized newspapers include the quarto-sized *China Farmer's Daily* (Chuang Kuo Nung Min Pao), the *Physical Education Daily* (Ti Yu Pao, issued daily except Sunday), and the *Health News* (issued every three days).

Local Newspapers

Generally, each province or municipality has a newspaper. In places where economy and culture are more developed, there are more than one. In Shanghai, for instance, in addition to the *Liberation Daily* (Chieh Fang Jih Pao) and the *Wen Hui Pao*, there are other smaller quarto-sized papers like the *Youth News* (Ching Nien Pao). A few provinces also publish a local farmer's paper. In Yunnan, for instance, there is a quarto-sized *Yunnan Farmer's Daily* (Yunnan Nung Min Pao), published in Kunming. In areas populated by the minority nationalities, newspapers are also published. In Hungtai and Chinpo Autunomous Chow, there is the *Unity News* (Tuan Chieh Pao), which propagates unity

among nationalities and socialist constructions in areas populated by minority nationalities.

From the central to the local level, there are a little bit more than forty newspapers in the country, averaging about one for every 20 to 25 million people. Compared to Hong Kong, where there are more than 120 newspapers, the number is far too small. Except the *People's Daily* which publishes one and a half sheet, the rest only contain one sheet a day. In addition to the limitations imposed by policies, there is a severe shortage of newsprint. The Cultural Revolution, in particular, saw the almost crazy printing and issuing of *Selected Works of Mao Tse-tung* and the so-called ''Red Treasure Book'' (*Quotations from Chairman Mao Tse-tung*)* as well as the almost crazy posting of *tatzepao* (big character posters). These activities had drained the country's domestically produced paper. Even with paper imported from abroad in great quantities, the demand still far exceeded the supply. As a result, even school textbooks could not be printed.

During the first few years after the liberation, the Chinese Communist newspapers allowed circulation abroad included the *People's Daily* and the *Kwang Ming Daily* in Peking, plus the *Liberation Daily* and *Wen Hui Pao* in Shanghai. In addition to these four newspapers, now the *China Youth Daily, Peking Daily* and *Nan Fang Daily* are also permitted for export.

Before and during the Cultural Revolution, no local newspapers were allowed for sale overseas. They were classified as ''third degree secret'' (san chi chi mi). Some of the less capable Nationalist agents, being unable to obtain any Communist intelligence, paid a high price for these local newspapers in Hong Kong, Macao, or the Yunnan-Burma border area. During the Cultural Revolution, in the Yunnan-Burma border area, a copy of *Yunnan Daily* could sell for 100 Jen Min Pi or 300 Hong Kong dollars. Copies with special features were even selling for as high as 1,500 Hong Kong dollars each. Through this channel the agents could easily report to the Nationalist's Mainland China Work Committee that mission had been accomplished. For the

---

*About one billion copies of the *Quotations from Mao Tse-tung* of various sizes were printed, approximating one copy for every member of the population. This was really a great disaster for the people.

speculative but needy residents, however, as long as they were not caught, one bundle of used newspapers might bring them a bag full of Seiko watches. Thus, the attraction was still very great.

The *People's Daily* is the newspaper with the largest circulation. In addition to free and exchange copies, it has a circulation of 6,200,000 copies. However, there is a quarto-sized paper whose circulation exceeds the *People's Daily*'s by some three million copies. This paper is called *Reference News* (Tsan Kao Hsiao Hsi). It was a semi-public paper suggested by Chou En-lai and authorized by Mao Tse-tung. Chou had wanted to "open the eyes of the people" a little bit more. He said, "we have neglected our left and right neighbors too much." A closed-door policy was too dangerous. Though Mao Tse-tung had given his approval, at one meeting he sarcastically referred to the endeavor as "a case of a Communist Party publishing a newspaper for imperialism." At first, the circulation of this paper was strictly restricted, but was later gradually expanded to more than 10 million copies by 1977 and 1978, becoming the paper with the largest circulation in China.

In addition to *Reference News*, there is the *Reference Materials* (Tsan Kao Tse Liao), generally known as "ta tsan kao" or "big reference." A bound sextodecimo, with a morning edition and an afternoon edition, it is especially edited for the eyes of high ranking Communist cadres (the 13th rank and above). What then is the difference between the "big reference" and the "small reference"? The "small reference" reprints stories by the various international wire services and important articles in foreign newspapers. The "big reference," with a much higher confidentiality, carries a lot more stories or articles about Taiwan and Hong Kong. Reports sharply critical of the Communists are also often printed.

"Internal Reference"

Since the Chinese Communist press puts the Party in the first place and demands a strict secrecy, there are some conditions which they would like to have the high ranking personnages informed, but not the common people. Thus, both Hsinhua (New China) News Agency and the *People's Daily* issued their own "internal reference" (nei bu tsan kao), abbreviated as "nei tsan." For instance, Hsinhua's internal publication is called *Trends of Journalistic Work* (Hsin Wen Kung Tso Tung Hsiang), which stipulates Hsinhua duties as follows: 1. to report to the Party Central, 2. to guide the work of lower levels. This publication also frequently carries the opinions of the various provincial and municipal Party committees, usually about some touchy problems. The internal publication of the *People's Daily* is called *Brief Reports on the People's Daily's Work Conditions* (Jen Min Jih Pao Kung Tso Chin Kuang Chien Pao). Problems not suitable for publication or those whose publication yet to be decided for some time are included in it. As for minor problems, they are published in the *Life in the Editorial Department* (pien chi bu sheng ho). These problems include letters from readers as well as the exchange of experience.

If someone should ask: Is there any privately owned newspaper in the mainland? The answer is: no.

In the first few years after the liberation, *Ta Kung Pao* and *Hsin Min Pao* (New People's Daily) were still permitted to publish. The Democratic League also used *Wen Hui Pao* and *Kwang Ming Daily* as its mouthpieces. Before long, however, the Chinese Communists launched a total "adjustment." *Hsin Min Pao* was assigned to publish as an evening paper in Shanghai. *Ta Kung Pao*, on the other hand, was assigned to cover news about light and handicraft industries. Later, it was renamed *Ching Pu Pao* (Progress News). But, there was not much "progress." The paper soon ceased publication. Luckily, Fei Yi-ming had some foresight, for he had also started a Hong Kong edition. Otherwise, this once Missouri Journalism award winner paper would have become a historical name. Both *Wen Hui Pao* and *Hsin Min Pao* were taken over by the Chinese Communists after the anti-rightist struggle.

One episode deserves mentioning. When Mao Tse-tung went to Shanghai for the first time after the liberation, out of whim, he asked about *Sheng Pao*. Mao was told that it had been closed. Mao shouted, "What a pity!" To flatter him, someone said: shall we resume the paper? Mao replied, "Forget it! Resumption of the paper will be restoration of the old!" Thus, one of China's oldest papers can only be viewed in the library of officials who have obtained permissions.

Therefore, when we talk about the press system in mainland China, there is only one system. That is, the Chinese Communist press system. This was at least the case in the seventies. We can only hope that it will become different in the eighties. Recently, it was said that *Ta Kung Pao* and *Hsin Min Pao* had requested for permission to resume their papers. Their reports had been forwarded to the Party Central Committee's Politburo, though no further word has been heard yet.

ORGANIZATION AND PERSONNEL OF THE CHINESE COMMUNIST PRESS

The *People's Daily* is not run by the Director, but rather by an editorial committee headed by the Editor-in-Chief. Membership of this committee has varied from time to time, ranging from five to more than ten. Receiving instructions from the Politburo, this editorial committee decides the paper's policies, and personnel and supervises the daily operation.

Inner-organization of the paper is confidential. There are two channels through which we become to know about it, though still very little. First, we know through cumulated material scattered here and there. Second, we know through the exposes during the Cultural Revolution when many Chinese Communist inside stories were being dragged out.

The Office of the Editor-in-Chief in the *People's Daily* gives out orders and serves as the command headquarters. The editorial division is the executive unit. It includes the following departments:

Theory Propaganda Department: This department is responsible for the materialization of "politics taking command." For instance, the study of "using practice to test truth as the sole criterion" is now its major thrust.

Reporters Department: It commands the paper's reporters stations. The *People's Daily* dispatches correspondents and establishes stations in all provinces and municipalities as well as major agricultural and industrial bases like Tachai and Taching.

Other departments are Politics and Law, Rural

Villages, Industry and Transportation, Finance and Economy, Cultural and Educational, Literature and Art, International, and Mass Work. The Literature and Art Department edits the "literary supplement page" (*fu kan*) while the International Department handles international news and the Mass Work Department, letters from the readers.

In addition, there are a Domestic Morgue and an International Morgue.

The paper has a gigantic administrative structure. Under the Editor-in-Chief and the Deputy Editor-in-Chief, the secretary general supervises all the routine work. In the Office of the Editor-in-Chief, the director handles all the administrative routines within the editorial division. As for the editors, some are responsible for rewriting and polishing, others for editorial layouts or post-publication checks.

In a recent talk with Mr. Watanabe, Director of Japan's *Asahi Shimbun*, Hu Chi-wei, Editor-in-Chief of the *People's Daily*, said in the Mass Work Department alone some eighty persons were responsible for the handling of letters from the readers. Still the staff was too small for the job. It is not unusual at all for the whole newspaper to have more than two or three thousand people.

Unlike their counterparts in Taiwan or Hong Kong, all editors and reporters in the *People's Daily*, the Hsinhua News Agency, and other newspapers, agencies, radio or television stations are state employees, enjoying privileges as Party or State cadres and they are paid according to their ranks in the Party or the government.

Originally, there were thirty ranks in the Chinese Communist cadres; now there are twenty-five. The first rank cadres are paid 600 Jen Min Pi while the 30th rank, 22 Jen Min Pi. The first rank is further divided into two levels. Only Mao Tse-tung was classified as a first rank first level cadre. The rest five vice chairmen, Liu Shao-chi, Chou En-lai, Chu Teh, Chen Yun and Lin Piao, and Party Secretary General Teng Hsiao-ping were classified as first rank second level cadres so as to distinguish slightly the latter from the chairman, since Mao never wanted anyone equal to him. Below the second rank, there are no divisions into levels. Teng To, one time Editor-in-Chief of the *People's Daily*, was said to be an eighth rank cadre, paid 300 Jen Min Pi a month. In the mainland, quite a few of the provincial governors are only ninth rank cadres. This illustrates the importance of the unique role the *People's Daily* occupies.

The recruitment of personnel is based on political backgrounds, usually requiring a three-generation political clearance.

Where do these journalist cadres come from then? There are three sources: The first group of journalistic cadres were trained during the Yenan years by the various newspapers in liberated areas or by the Hsinhua News Agency. These newspapers included *Liberation Daily* (Chieh Fang Pao), *Shansi Suiyuan Daily* (Chin Sui Jih Pao), *Chin-Cha-Chi Daily* (Chin Cha Chi Jih Pao), and the *Ta Chung Daily* in Shangtung. Quite a few of these journalists were the students of Hu Chiao-mu while many others were trained by persons like Teng To, who was well versed in Chinese classics. The second group consists of underground Chinese Communist journalistic workers in Nationalist-controlled areas. Quite a few of them were able to penetrate into Nationalist newspapers or newspapers run by Nationalist reporters. These Communist journalists later were charged with very important duties. For instance, a young journalist who worked for me was a Chinese Communist underground agent assigned to the Nanking *Central Daily News*. A graduate of the Department of Journalism of the National Cheng-chi University, Lee Lien-chun changed his name to Li Lien when the Chinese Communist troops entered Nanking on April 23, 1949. On behalf of the Communists, Li took over the Nanking *Central Daily News*. The third group are those recruited after the liberation among college graduates with relatively good family backgrounds (workers, peasants and soldiers). After the liberation, college departments responsible for the training of journalistic workers were the Department of Journalism of Futan University in Shanghai and the Department of Journalism of Peking University, which had incorporated the department at Yenchin University. Later, journalism departments were established at the Chinese People's University and the Peking Broadcasting Institute. Students at these institutions all have to go through a very selective screening procedure. The Chinese Communist policies stipulate that "Backgrounds are important, but not by themselves only. The important thing is political performance." But, in fact, all the people entering the journalistic teams are picked first of all for their

backgrounds. Political performance comes second, and talents, last. This was at least the case before the Cultural Revolution.

CONTROL OVER THE PRESS BY THE CHINESE COMMUNISTS

In short, the control is absolutely strict.

The tight control over the Chinese Communist press is inseparable from Mato Tse-tung's conceptualization of the functions of the press. Mao said,

> To overthrow a political power, it is always necessary first of all to create public opinion, to do work in the ideological sphere. This is true for the revolutionary class as well as for the counter-revolutionary class.

Thus, to the Chinese Communists, or at least to Mao Tse-tung, the press has become a very sensitive issue.

Facts also have proved the importance of "grabbing the barrel of a pen." When the Gang of Four were rampaging in the mainland, under their control was really nothing but the media. With the propaganda tools in their hands, however, they were able to turn the whole mainland upside down.

Having fully understood the importance of the media, Mao Tse-tung maintained that all propaganda tools be under the absolute leadership of the Party. The first principle the media must observe is "tang hsin," or Party allegiance. From a given viewpoint, Mao's call for "the whole Party to run the press" has been accomplished. In this respect, it must be admitted that the Communists have done better than the Nationalists. At least, the Communists were far more serious and paid far more attention to the media than the Nationalists. . . .

Not only does the Party Central attach much importance to the media, but also do the provincial and municipal Party committee secretaries. In the autumn of 1956, at a dancing party in Tsui-hu (Grassy Lake) Guest House in Kunming of Yunnan, I met a party secretary in charge of propaganda by the name of Ma Chi-kung. During intermissions, I saw Ma reviewing an editorial to be published the following day in the *Yunnan Daily*.

The Chinese Communist press emphasizes leadership by the Party secretary. Besides taking directive from him, all newspaper workers, in their relationship with leadership units, are required to assume a responsible attitude in seeking instructions, in discussion with him, in reporting the situations to him and in voicing opinions. In the Communist eyes, the press not only can be helped by the leadership institutions but also can help the leadership institutions. In fact, the press itself is a gigantic investigation, research, and control institution. The press not only seeks instructions from the Party secretary but also research results it has obtained to use the investigation and report and make suggestions to him.

Before the Cultural Revolution, not a single news story or article in the Chinese Communist press ever violated the intentions of the Party secretary. Hu Feng's criticism that there was a "Uniformity of Public Opinion" was not without any basis. During the Cultural Revolution, because of the intensification of faction struggles, especially after the Gang of Four's slogan of "grasping revolution by kicking away the Party secretary," were there cases of violations. But still, the press was under the absolute control of the factions.

OPERATION OF THE CHINESE COMMUNIST PRESS

Operation of the press follows the practice of "walking on two legs." In the *People's Daily*, for example, on the one hand it depends on Hsinhua for news, while on the other hand it also reprints all the good materials in local newspapers. Besides, the paper also utilizes its correspondence network, e.g., the various reporters stations. As for international news, all comes from Hsinhua.

As for local newspapers, they are cast in the same "mold" as the *People's Daily*'s. There is very little local uniqueness. When the Gang of Four was at its height, there was a widely circulated saying in the mainland: "The big papers (referring to the *People's Daily* and other local papers) copy the small papers (referring to *Journal of Peking University* and *Journal of Tsing Hua University*); small papers copy Liang Hsiao (referring to the writers group organized by Chiang Ching at Peking University and Tsin Hua University. Members included such well-known professors as Chou I-liang and Fung Yu-lang.)."

During this period, Liang Hsiao's articles were guiding the whole political life in the mainland. As for news, the soul of a newspaper, it was compressed to a very miserable position.

In 1958, Mao Tse-tung proposed a socialist general line: "muster all energies, swim up the stream and construct socialism in a massive, quick, good and economic way (to, kwai, hau, sheng)." The opposites of "massive, quick, good and economic" are "scarce, slow, bad and wasteful (shao, man, cha, fei)." These four words can best describe the news in Chinese Communist newspapers and radio broadcasting. This was especially the case during the Cultural Revolution.

Scarce

According to statistics obtained by the Department of Journalism of the People's University, before the Cultural Revolution, news only accounted for about 60% of all the newspaper space. During the Cultural Revolution, it dropped to about 40%, and sometimes to as low as 30%. Nevertheless, what could be regarded as news was in fact very meager. Most of the space was "hegemonized" by lengthy and dull articles.

Slow

That the Chinese Communist news is slow has been a widely known fact. The Lin Piao incident was not announced until a full month later. The arrest of the Gang of Four on October 6, 1976, was first broadcast on October 9, 1976, in London. However, the people in the mainland were still kept in the dark. It was not until October 15, did we people in Kunming see tatze-pao saying "hail the crash of the 'Gang of Four'."Still, people were half suspicious and half believing. It was not until October 18 was Hua Kuo-feng's talk on this incident circulated. By then the people had already lost their interest in knowing the exact date the newspaper first carried the story.

Bad

Quality of the news is so bad that it can hardly be regarded as news. When Chou En-lai died, the mainland was in a mourning atmosphere. To divert the people's attention, the Gang of Four ordered their "running dog" at Tsing Hua University, Chih Chun, to orchestrate a news story headlined "Great Debates Bring Great Changes." At the very beginning, the story said that people were very concerned with the debates at Tsing Hua University, suggesting that they did not care about Chou's death. Then, several thousand words were used to describe the debates at Tsing Hua. This was no news at all. It was nothing but playing political games and sheer nonsense. From a journalistic point of view, it was not news at all. Headlines like "Grasp Spring Ploughing," "Resist Drought and Protect Saplings," "Great Harvest Expected," or "Annual Quota Surpassed" would appear annually in the newspapers in turns and in the same format. Even by proletarian journalistic standards, such news could not be regarded as "good." It can only be regarded as "bad."

Wasteful

It is not uncommon for the Communist press agencies to spend mountains of efforts on a single meaningless item. For instance, in covering a certain provincial conference, the reporter must submit his completed report to the conference secretariat. It will first be reviewed by a secretary in charge of news release, and then passed on to the conference secretary general, who will then submit the article to the Provincial Party Secretariat's office. If the secretary general of the Party Secretariat's office is also very careful, he will ask a provincial Party secretary to review it. When the article returns to the newspaper, it goes to a department head first, who then passes it on to the editor-in-chief. The editor-in-chief then assigns an editor to handle the "news". If it should be published at all, the item would have gone through several checkpoints and been "chopped up" several times. In this tedious reviewing process, the persons in charge, to show that they are responsible, will have changed a few words or deleted a couple of sentences.

This is the handling of ordinary news. When it comes to important news, before publication both Hsinhua and the *People's Daily* will have to submit it to the Party Central for review and approval. As for local newspapers, articles will have to be submitted to the standing committee of the provincial Party Committees for discussion. Thus, news has already become "old" or even history.

THE CHINESE COMMUNIST REPORTERS

Since all Chinese Communist reporters are classified as Party or state cadres, they lack the independence of professionals. During the Nationalist years in Chungking and Nanking, reporters were often seen walking proudly in and out of the residences of powerful personnages. This scene can no longer be found in the present-day mainland. Nevertheless, the Communists have adopted a different system, in which news not suitable for publication is released as "internal reference news". Much of this "internal reference news" covers the dark side of Party and state cadres and can often reach the "heaven". i.e., the highest leadership. It was said to be Mao Tse-tung's must for daily reading. Even when he was too ill to do any reading, he had it read by his niece, Wang Hai-yung. In addition to Mao, members of the Politburo also read it. Since the articles by Hsinhua or *People's Daily* reporters may be read by the "heaven", they occupy a very special status in the people's eyes. In fact, when people want to "kao yu chuang" (that is, "make a plea with the emperor", meaning pleading with the highest authorities), they will try all means to get their complaints to a Hsinhua or *People's Daily* reporter.

SOVIET SCHOLARS LOOK AT U.S. MEDIA

JAMES R. BENNETT

Soviet writers are all highly critical of American journalism, just as most American writers are critical of Soviet journalism. In a review essay of several Communist books, this author points out that the Communist authors all base their information on American sources, just as most American critics of Soviet mass media use Communist sources to make their point. One important difference, of course, is that there are many more Americans who find fault with their own press than there are Russians who make negative comments about theirs.

Americans are often assured of the free flow of ideas in our democratic society, of the diversity of views that command access. By comparison with Chile or Czechoslovakia, for example, the U.S. press does indeed fare well. But the best test of a free press is not always comparative. A free press can be measured by our own ideals: by James Madison's faith in a self-governed people armed with the power of knowledge, by the Hutchins Report's insistence upon the availability of a truthful and comprehensive account of the day's events in a meaningful context, or by Justice Black's interpretation of the First Amendment to mean full access of antagonistic points of view. By these internal tests the United States may be less "free" because of the lack of general availability of a broad range of critique in American discourse on political topics.

Consider, for example, the books under review here, books printed in English in ideologically competitive countries and critical of our reputation for a free press. They are not listed in the *Book Review Index* or the *New York Times Book Review Index*.[1] A few reviews turned up in the *Social Sciences Citation Index*, but these mainly were in highly specialized journals published abroad. (I learned about the books through the unsolicited catalog of Imported Publications in Chicago.)

Because they have been so little reviewed in U.S. periodicals, these books have been virtually invisible in spite of their great importance as a window into ways Soviet scholars perceive the United States. Admittedly, the books were written originally in Russian and therefore apparently primarily for a professional Russian audience to acquaint them with the history and methods of aspects of U.S. global power. But their translation into English and their distribution outside Eastern Europe and the Soviet Union offer an opportunity to see how outside critics portray the United States and an image that may contribute to the formation of both policy and public opinion.

In *The Monopoly Press*, Petrusenko sets forth, by both summary and case studies and with support from U.S. scholarship, why the standards of the Hutchins Report have never been achieved and why the expression "free and fearless press" must be taken with many grains of salt. Chapter 2 recalls the often low opinion of the press held by the Founding Fathers. The growth of government influence over the press is traced in chapters 3 and 4. Chapter 5 focuses on the close ties between news reporting, business, and advertising. Local news monopoly and newspaper chains are covered in chapters 6 and 7. Chapter 8 summarizes the extent of control of the monopoly business/government system over television—"commercial television's constant drive to cement the American way of life." Chapter 9 returns to government management of

James R. Bennett, "Soviet Scholars Look at U.S. Media." From the *Journal of Communication*, Volume 36, Winter 1986, pp. 126–132. © 1986, *The Journal of Communication*. Reprinted by permission.

The author is professor of English at the University of Arkansas.

news by close relations with news personnel, lying, and other manipulations of news "objectivity." Chapter 10 pursues the various sources of the "crisis of credibility" in U.S. media, and the final chapter discusses the past role of muckraking journalism in this crisis.

Petrusenko inflates the implications of his evidence according to his own ideological and personal needs and constraints. The press "fully cooperates with the propaganda machinery of the executive branch, helping it to carry out administration policies and manipulate public opinion" (p. 39). There are "people not entirely displeased with the portrayal of violence on U.S. television: reactionary and military circles, to be precise. They would like to have young Americans determined and ruthless enough to carry out their ambitious plans" (p. 90). The author bristles at times with such overgeneralizations and simplistic conspiracy theories, both actually contradicted by his own evidence of complexity. But I found no examples of falsification of quotations or illustrations, most of which came from reputable U.S. sources. And his basic theses are hardly earthshaking. Many Americans share the author's skepticism about the genuineness of a free press in the United States and accept his description of a mass media system designed to shape public opinion by the promotion of corporate values through denigration of the Soviet Union (see, e.g., 1).

Petrusenko's thesis in *A Dangerous Game* is carefully accurate: the mass information media "attract the intelligence service of the main imperialist powers like a magnet." "Covertly and overtly," he continues, "it [intelligence] seeks to use to its advantage newspapers, magazines, book publishing houses, the radio and television. To this end it establishes contacts with journalists, making them willing or blind promoters of subversive plots" (introduction). (His "magnetic" hyperbole is not intended "to shed suspicion on *all* journalists working" in capitalist-owned news media.) No informed person in the United States denies CIA designs on the media and contacts with journalists, for many books and articles in addition to those cited by the author corroborate his argument.[2]

Since CIA archives are secret, Petrusenko depended "completely on published materials from news media in the United States, Great Britain and

other countries." U.S. sources predominate: *The Invisible Government* and *The Espionage Establishment* by David Wise and Thomas Ross, *The CIA and the Cult of Intelligence* by Victor Marchetti and John Marks, *Inside the Company* by Philip Agee, *Give Us This Day* by Howard Hunt, and various U.S. newspapers and magazines. Are these sources reliable? And does Petrusenko quote them accurately?

A check of reviews cited in *Book Review Digest* for each of the first four books listed above— thirteen reviews in all—revealed five positive, six neutral (i.e., pro and con, two of them more favorable than negative), and two negative (by T. W. Braden and W. F. Buckley). And Petrusenko quoted and summarized his sources accurately. Chapter 1, dealing with U.S. media efforts to undermine Cuba, draws mainly upon Wise and Ross's *The Invisible Government* (chapters 2–4 and 24), Hunt's *Give Us This Day*, and Agee's *Inside the Company*, with further information taken from *Anatomy of Anti-Communism* (American Friends Service Committee, 1969), Marchetti and Marks, and a few other sources. I checked all of the quotations from Hunt, Marchetti and Marks, Wise and Ross, and *Anatomy of Anti-Communism*, and found no errors of substance. Nor did I find any changes in the spirit of Petrusenko's sources as the result of his selective quoting and s mmarizing. The book thus provides a good instruction to its subject.

Like the other authors, Biryukov in *Television in the West and Its Doctrines* needs some instruction in how to conduct an argument addressed to a hostile audience, if indeed it was his intention eventually to reach Western readers. Embedded within a respectable survey of Western scholarship (including Green's *The Universal Eye*, Barnouw's *The Image Empire*, Emery's *National and International Systems of Broadcasting*, etc.) appear too many evidentially unsupported claims for the superiority of the socialist over the capitalist way of life. From the beginning Biryukov refers to "bourgeois ideology," "monopoly bourgeois and their ideological apparatus," "class interest," and "ruling class" without defining the terms or bothering to cite evidence. Too little or no evidence is adduced to support the claims that the "crisis of bourgeois cinema" is attributable to "its inability to genuinely win the hearts and souls of the rising generation in the face of the more impressive successes scored by world socialism" (p. 25) and that the "monopoly bourgeois" try to "regulate mass media" (p. 28). For the first four chapters Biryukov rushes his case that monopoly ideology and interests, the "ruling class," control television in the Western countries to the detriment of their own and the world's people. The quantity of blustering, indignant, unsubstantiated pronouncements in the first third of the book, though it may hearten a loyal Soviet, certainly discourages even a determined book reviewer.

His evidence is accretive, however. In chapter 5 he finally confronts directly the issue of ruling class control of television, explaining what he means by ideology and control, giving more evidence (though some is not germane, e.g., pp. 88–89 illustrating nationalism, not ideology; or not persuasive, e.g., p. 103, on why Fred Friendly was fired). The book improves until the chapter's rather unprepared-for final sentence: "Bourgeois television is in essence anti-popular and anti-human inasmuch as it is called upon to defend an unjust, exploiting system" (perhaps he meant "insofar," or the translator erred).

The next chapter, dealing with principles and methods for the research and analysis of television, again advances his thesis. But why isn't it the opening chapter? It sifts the failure of Western media sociologists to recognize ideology and class as fundamental forces in media and blames their adherence to Lasswell's research paradigm. Herbert Schiller's *The Mind Managers* provides Biryukov with his major U.S. scholarly support. How much more persuasive his earlier chapters would have been had this chapter come first.

Finally, he turned in chapters 7–9 to the "doctrines" of his title: "impartiality," "mass culture," and "free flow of information." In chapter 7 he suggests how feeble the Fairness Doctrine has been in practice, though his allegation that it "is little more than a cover-up for the bourgeois partiality, class bias of television broadcasting in capitalist countries" (p. 152) is a book-length issue in itself. That television is largely chewing gum for the eye to induce people to consume and keep up with the Joneses, with consequent diminution of high culture and significant knowledge, is hardly an original idea, but he gives considerable substantiation of it, though again he overstates the implications of his evidence (p. 166). Chapter 9 on Western and especially U.S. media imperialism sticks fairly closely to

reporting previous studies without outrageous extrapolations.

Television in the West could have been a better book, not only by more appropriate arrangement of the chapters but also by more tactful restraint from absolute generalizations. And had Biryukov searched more thoroughly he would have found additional evidence in support of many of his arguments. He does draw heavily from Green and Barnouw, and he cites briefly Skornia's *Television and the News*, Brown's *Television: The Business Behind the Box*, a newspaper article by Herbert Gans, an interview of Nicholas Johnson, and other sources, all of which agree with him in significant ways. But he does not refer to other available books by Johnson, Herbert Schiller, Robert Cirino, or G. William Domhoff, Richard Bunce's *Television in the Corporate Interest*, Fred Cook's *The Warfare State*, J. William Fulbright's *The Pentagon Propaganda Machine*, Herbert Gans's *Deciding What's News*, Todd Gitlin's *The Whole World Is Watching*, Stuart Hood's *On Television*, Dale Minor's *The Information War*, Vance Packard's *The Hidden Persuaders*, Gaye Tuchman's *The TV Establishment* and *Making News*, or the many other books and articles published prior to his book which support his case. His (and Petrusenko's) thesis that the mass media in capitalist societies are instruments of a ruling class and ideology is much better established in U.S. publications than he knew. Yet, despite Biryukov's summary of the evidence on the subtleties of domination from the very country he is critiquing, the book could have been more original if he had tried to show how, as he claims, Western television is *designed* by the "ruling class."

Panfilov's constant reference to the "imperialist" United States in *Broadcasting Pirates* is similar to the "communist" or "Marxist-Leninist" labels of some U.S. journalists. Once the spot ads for the author's ideology are ignored, what remains is a generally reliable history of U.S., British, and West German radio propaganda. However, zeal trips up Panfilov now and then. He exaggerates CIA subornation of U.S. journalists when he says, "It is not a matter of indicating American reporters and commentators who are CIA agents, but finding at least a few journalists who do not work for the CIA" (p. 174). (Petrusenko's *A Dangerous Game* provides a more precise allegation.) And his denigration of President Woodrow Wilson's Fourteen Points to the level of selfish imperialism reveals a streak of hard intolerance, ironical in a person advocating détente.

But if reality—not merely national aggrandizement and power—is to be a foundation of U.S. and Western policies, then Panfilov's book on the growth of "saboteur" radio propaganda during peace time is all the more important as a reminder of other facets of that reality. Panfilov recounts Senator William Fulbright's futile efforts at one committee hearing to induce a member of the government to tell the public the extent to which the CIA controlled our propaganda radios (Radio Free Europe, Radio Liberty/Liberation, etc.). He cautions how much the glorification of a free flow of news as an achieved fact of national greatness sometimes masks obstruction of access and flow by government officials. And he tells how others perceive U.S. propaganda—as subversion, as sabotage, even as war, and increasingly threatening on an ever-enlarging global scale. Whereas David Sarnoff thought a change in the name of "Voice of America" to "Voice of America—For Freedom and Peace" would be a reminder of what the United States stands for, Panfilov with good reasons sees it as threatening his way of life.

These books together carry the reminder that news personnel live inside the bellies of their ideological whales. U.S. news organizations affirm the American way of life and omit or oppose hostile ideologies. They further the process of cultural consolidation only less directly than do the government and the corporations. That is why the socialist authors of these outside books so deride U.S. "free press" bragadoccio. Inside the whale, yes, you can discern diversity and options. But, from a critical perspective, the choices the press offers the American people are "free" only within the condition that capitalism be overwhelmingly affirmed and socialism systematically condemned. Thus, these books from Eastern Europe deserve attention because a democracy, if it is to thrive with the vigor envisioned by Madison and Hutchinson and Black, needs outside criticism.

Some of these books are poorly edited. They lack indexes and bibliographies. The pages of one of the paperbacks came apart. All, though in greatly varying degrees, leap to exaggerated conclusions. All

miss the full subtleties and nuances of the system they decry. Diatribe and dogma too often substitute for proof. Several of the authors mechanically repeat the words "imperialism" and "ruling class" as though speaking to already converted fellow socialists, a rather inept rhetorical strategy to persuade American readers, at least.

But the books, by and large, are factually accurate, employ reliable Western sources, and, although they offer little new to scholars, together their consolidation of published information challenges the complacent American myth of a "free press."

NOTES

1. Other, comparable books missing from these listings are *The War of Ideas* by Georgi Arbatov (Moscow: Progress, 1973), *Professional Codes in Journalism* edited by Lars Bruun (Prague: International Organization of Journalists, 1979), *The CIA in the Dock* edited by V. Chernyavsky (Moscow: Progress, 1983), *The CIA in Latin America* by Konstantin Tarasov and Vyacheslav Zubenko (Moscow: Progress, 1984), and *A World Without Arms?* by Igor Usachev (Moscow: Progress, 1984).

2. These include *The CIA File* by Robert Borosage and John Marks (1976), *The CIA and the Media* (U.S. congressional hearings, 1977–1978), *Final Report of the Select Committee to Study Governmental Operations with Respect to Intelligence Activities* (1976), *The Lawless State* by Morton Halperin et al. (1978), *The CIA in Guatemala* by Richard Immerman (1982), *The Man Who Kept the Secrets—Richard Helms and the CIA* by Thomas Powers (1979), *The CIA's Secret Operations* by Harry Rositzke (1977), and articles in *More* and other magazines. My bibliography on the intelligence agencies and information control in the United States appeared in the *National Reporter*, Winter 1986, pp. 41–47.

REFERENCE

1. Dorman, William. "The Image of the Soviet Union in the American News Media: Coverage of Brezhnev, Andropov and MX." *War, Peace & the News Media* [New York University], 1983, pp. 44–76.

BOOKS REVIEWED IN THIS ESSAY

The Monopoly Press, or *How American Journalism Found Itself in the Vicious Circle of the "Crisis of Credibility"* by Vitaly Petrusenko. Vladimir Leonov (trans.). Prague: International Organization of Journalists, 1976. 143 pages.

A Dangerous Game: CIA and the Mass Media by Vitaly Petrusenko. Nicolai Kozelsky and Vladimir Leonov (trans.). Prague: Interpress, n.d. (ca. 1978). 189 pages.

Television in the West and Its Doctrines by N. S. Biryukov. Yuri Sviridov (trans.). Moscow: Progress, 1981 [1977]. 207 pages.

Broadcasting Pirates, or *Abuse of the Microphone: An Outline of External Political Radio Propaganda by the USA, Britain and the FRG* by A. Panfilov. Nicholas Bobrov (trans.). Moscow: Progress, 1981. 200 pages.

6 THIRD WORLD SYSTEMS

In April 1955, four countries that considered themselves to be nonaligned with either the Western powers or with the Communist nations, called a conference of similarly situated nations in Bandung, Indonesia. The five conveners of the conference were India, Indonesia, Egypt, Ceylon and Yugoslavia—known as the Colombo powers. These were countries that had achieved their independence mainly during the late 1940s, but included some states which had never been colonies, such as China and Turkey. Beside the conveners, 24 other countries attended, plus a number of observers. The purpose of the conference was to declare the solidarity of "Third World" countries. The focus was mainly economic. At the United Nations Conference on Trade and Development (UNCTAD) in 1964, the "Group of 77" came into existence, comprising nonaligned countries interested in speaking with "one voice" in the United Nations. This group had grown to include about 125 countries by the late 1980s.

These so-called Third World countries realized, however, that economic development must go hand-in-hand with development in communication. Starting in 1972, therefore, they began to agitate, both through UNESCO and at conferences of the nonaligned countries, for a new world information and communication order that would provide a "free and balanced information flow" in the world. To achieve this, it was felt, Third World countries needed access to communication hardware, especially satellites.

The first tangible outcome of these conferences was the inauguration in 1976 of the Non-Aligned News Agencies Pool (NANA), administered by the Yugoslav news agency, Tanjug. It has never been very successful. Then in 1980, at its 21st General Conference in Belgrade, Yugoslavia, UNESCO unanimously adopted a recommendation by Sean MacBride for a New World Information Order. That same year, the International Program for the Development of Communication was established within UNESCO to help developing nations with the development of their information programs.

THIRD WORLD JOURNALISM

L. JOHN MARTIN

Mass media in the West are no longer as unbalanced as they used to be until the 1960s. Yet many criticisms of Western media are based on outdated facts and figures. News judgment, according to this report, is changing in all countries, but there are certain rules of newsworthiness, such as proximity and timeliness, that have not changed. People's interests, apart from being influenced by what they are used to reading in their press, are fairly similar worldwide.

. . . At the time of independence in the early 1960s, the media in the now independent countries [of the Third World] were still serving mostly colonially organized systems. The international wire services hadn't yet adapted to the new needs of these countries—in fact it was still unclear what these new needs were. And the Western press was still treating the newly independent countries as though they were European dependencies.

When these now nonaligned countries at various conferences and at UNESCO complained about this treatment, they had plenty of evidence of unbalanced coverage by the Western press. They did not even need to point to the dozens of studies by Western researchers showing the lack of balance. When the balance is as skewed as it was at the time, you didn't need statistics to prove your point. It was obvious to anyone reading the press.

I can't blame the Third World countries for calling for a New World Information Order under the circumstances. As newly independent countries, they found that news continued to be defined in Western terms, and the mass media in the newly independent countries borrowed heavily for their entertainment materials from the West. This may not have bothered the general public as much as it bothered their leaders, since people learn to expect certain things in their media and miss it if it is not there. But Third World leaders looked to the mass media as a rallying point. They wanted to use the media for nation building, and they felt that Western definitions of news and the cultural values on which Western entertainment is based failed to support their concept of national development. Nor can I blame the international wire services or the press. They provided the news that they thought would sell, since news agencies and most newspapers in the West—and, for that matter, in many Third World countries—are a business.

But as is true of any company that wants to stay in business, when the wire services heard the complaints of the Third World countries, they quickly reexamined their content and proceeded to change it. . . . Thus, if the complaints of the Third World were true in the sixties, when most of the studies on which the MacBride Commission based its report were done, by the mid-seventies they no longer were true.

Let us look at some of the complaints and some of the findings of a study done for UNESCO by IAMCR in 1979, and one done at the University of Wisconsin last year. A major complaint of Third World countries is that the news flow to and from the Third World is dominated by Western wire services. In fact, news from Burundi in a neighboring Zambian paper generally comes to it via London. This is true, and it is very unlikely that in the foreseeable future, Zambia or Sweden or Japan or Brazil will have correspondents all over the world who can gather their news for them. What they do

L. John Martin, "Third World Journalism." Abstracted from a talk by Dr. Martin at a seminar for Third World journalists, July 6, 1984. Reprinted by permission.

The author is a professor in the College of Journalism, University of Maryland.

have, however, is their own national news agencies which buy international wire service news and distribute it nationally. What the IAMCR study found is that most of the news distributed by these global wire services is neutral and remarkably little of the news that gets into the Third World press shows any bias at all. Between 20% and one-half of all foreign news is credited to a national wire service in all countries of the world. Between 10 and 40 percent and one-half of all foreign news is credited to a national wire service in all countries of the world. Between 10 and 40 percent is credited to the media's own correspondents. About a fourth of all foreign news comes from one of the four Western global wire services. Newspapers can and do select their foreign news from a wide variety of sources. The problem is not that they are limited in the news available to them, but what to leave out. As for bias, the media can and do edit the news to inject their own biases.

Another complaint is that the Western media set the news agenda. They define what is news, excluding the kinds of news that the Third World considers important. The IAMCR researchers found it difficult to find definitions of news other than Western definitions. All over the world, news is an unusual, unexpected event. Proximity and timeliness appear to be universal news values. Thus, news of Asian countries is more likely to appear in the Asian press, of Africa in the African press, of Europe in the European press—than in the press of other areas. Timeliness is also valued in all countries, although some countries tend to be more concerned about minutes and seconds than others. They did find, however, that few countries outside of the Soviet sphere of influence carried news of the Communist World. And, furthermore, Third World countries show remarkably little interest in Third World countries outside of their own immediate geographic region.

A third complaint is that the little information about the Third World that does appear in Western media tends to emphasize negative news. This simply is no longer true. There is no evidence, says the IAMCR report, "that more attention was paid to this [negative] category of news in the Third World than in any other part of the globe." However, most foreign news is political news rather than news of private citizens, and in recent times, political disruptions have been more predominant in the Third World than in the West. But when similar events occur in the West—as for instance racial violence in the United States, religious disruptions in Ireland, terrorism in Germany and Italy—they receive at least as much coverage as do comparable events in the Third World.

Fourthly, development news is lacking. Researchers have found it difficult to pin down what is meant by development news. Some have suggested that it means the struggle against poverty and illiteracy. This kind of news certainly is not as plentiful as foreign news in the press of any country. It is quite frequently covered as domestic news in the press of each country, however. One reason is limited time and space; another is that our definition of news requires some kind of news peg, and development news seldom has a news peg. A third is that editors sense that their readers would not spend much time on a story of this kind that did not have an immediate impact on themselves. Thus, they would read a story about a new vaccine being developed to eradicate some common illness, regardless of what country it occurred in, but they would be less likely to read a story about higher examination scores in the fourth grade in some country outside their regions. . . .

THE LATIN AMERICAN CONCEPT OF NEWS

Fernando Reyes Matta

The Latin American press sees news through foreign eyes, having to buy most of its international news from Western wire services. The result is that Latin American media "cannot provide the insight needed to portray the processes of development as they are taking place within Latin America or in the Third World."

A look at the development of the Latin American press since the middle of the last century shows that the concept of news was originally understood as a current of opinion, with newspapers presenting ideological debates and political positions on the growth of new nations. With the changing economic structures brought on by colonial independence and shifting international dependencies, the Latin American concept of news gradually changed. After 1870, Latin American news agencies were legally tied with the French news agency Havas. The French influence lasted until 1920, when the first agreement between United Press (now United Press International—UPI) and the daily *La Prensa* of Buenos Aires was signed. New factors—an eager market, the need for information with impact, and an interest in the immediacy of information—then gradually affected the concept of news. The affect was strengthened by the growing dominance of North American news agencies (12), which in turn led to a strong emphasis on "professionalism" along the lines of the North American model. The result was a concept of news which moved from the task of interpreting events and presenting opinion to the daily process of selecting events deemed "newsworthy" and commercially interesting.

After World War II, the United Nations debate on human rights and advocacy of the "free flow of information" principle resulted in the expansion of the United Press and Associated Press (AP) role in Latin America. Technological advances which rat-

ified news "objectivity," in which the facts were the news, upheld the North American "professionalism" and strengthened the imported news values.

The current status of the Latin American press manifests the continuing dominance of North American news values, as institutionalized in the transnational news agencies. The transnational news agencies produce and process nearly 60 percent of the information published in Latin America (11, p. 189). UPI and AP alone provide 39 percent and 21 percent of the information received by the principal Latin American dailies. Another large percentage is covered by the large European agencies, leaving only an insignificant amount of the total information flow to be covered by Third World news agencies (11, p. 189). A good example of how the transnational agencies are used as sources for news is given below in Table 1, which gives a breakdown by news agencies of the origin of the stories for the major Latin American dailies on one day.

The Latin American dependency on transnational news agencies results in part from a scarcity of capital and resources with which the Latin Americans could form a news agency of their own to satisfactorily compete with the transnational news agencies. As Diaz Rangel (4) points out, in the case of Venezuela, "no daily maintains permanent correspondents abroad, not even in neighboring countries." This problem may be observed in several other Latin American countries.

Yet economic difficulties do not entirely explain

Fernando Reyes Matta, "The Latin American Concept of News." From the *Journal of Communication*, Volume 29, Number 2, Spring 1979, pp. 164–171. © 1979, *The Journal of Communication*. Reprinted by permission.

The author is director of the Division of Communication Studies of the Instituto Latinoamericano de Estudios Transnacionales (ILET) in Mexico.

Table I SOURCES OF NEWS COPY FOR LATIN AMERICAN DAILIES
ON ONE SAMPLE DAY IN 1965 (IN COLUMN CENTIMETERS)

	UPI	AP	Reuter	AFP	Ansa	Other
El Universal	507	—	—	209	—	69
El Nacional	—	545	—	150	—	14
El Tiempo	83	92	—	85	—	—
El Espectador	322	—	—	—	—	35
Excelsior	—	455	—	109	—	18
Novedades	102	295	—	138	—	23
Diario de Noticias	94	—	—	—	15	15
O Globo	124	125	—	94	—	—
El Comercio (Quito)	540	—	—	140	—	30
La Nación	—	186	—	61	—	40
La Prensa	544	—	—	—	—	—
El Comercio (Lima)	227	—	57	63	3	—
El Mercurio	244	220	58	110	—	152
La Mañana	—	217	—	114	69	30
Total centimeters	2783	2135	115	1273	87	426
% of total coverage	40.8	31.3	1.6	18.6	1.2	6.2

Source: (4)

the lack of a Latin American news-information structure, for certain countries like Argentina, Brazil, and Mexico, and to a lesser extent, Chile, Venezuela, and Colombia have become sophisticated enough in information services and have the resources to have set up one for themselves. However, this has not occurred because the concept of the "journalism industry" and the concept of news held by the Latin American press is primarily North American. Therefore, the modification of the prevailing dependence on transnational (primarily U.S.) news agencies does not constitute one of their objectives. The constant flow of news which fits easily into the North American concept of news has produced an inertia in those responsible for journalistic decisions, especially in the selection of what is news.

The prevailing structure of the Latin American news media, then, can be explained in terms of economics and professionalism. The vast majority of the news organizations are monopolies, controlled by the entrepreneurial, dominant classes of

society. In this respect, states Elsy Bonilla de Ramos (3), "the characteristics of the foreign information monopolies are only reproduced in the country to the extent that national information monopolies exist which give them space and free access to the internal information networks."

In addition, the professional structure is deeply rooted in the practice of many years, which has implied a dependence of the media on the values of what are called the "central" countries, or those countries which dominate the world scene economically, politically, and militarily. There has been a tacit acceptance by journalists that events in these countries are more relevant than those in the "periphery," or those countries who are considered to be on the sidelines of world influence.

We found that not one Latin American country sent correspondents to cover this event and only some of the newspapers had printed background information which had been supplied in a UPI cable. The day independence was formalized, November 26, 1975, not one newspaper carried the story on the front page. The Brazilian daily, *O Estado*, gave it three columns on an inside page, with less importance than a New York jewelry robbery. The rest of the Latin American papers studied treated the story similarly, as shown by the following examples:

La Prensa (Argentina): 2 columns of UPI information on an inside page.

El Diario (Bolivia): 6 centimeters of AP information, at the bottom of the front page. The event was given the same importance as a small fire in Tijuana, Mexico.

Excelsior (Mexico): Published an AP radio photograph on the front page. The inside pages provided a good synthesis, albeit of information from Reuters, AFP (Agence France Presse) and AP. This was the only paper to point out the Third World content of Premier Henk Arron's speech.

La Prensa (Nicaragua): No coverage.

Critica (Panama): No coverage.

La Prensa (Peru): UPI and AFP information on inside pages.

These papers not only did not give the event prominence, but also simply transcribed the agency dispatches word for word (see Table 2). Thus the Latin American coverage of this event reflected the negative slant of the news agency reports which predicted racial conflicts, tacitly implying that the people of Surinam were incapable of governing alone

and reinforcing the journalistic tendency to underline the negative aspects of the event. The possible racial conflicts, no doubt, were more competitive in the news markets than the strategic importance of the country as the third largest world producer of bauxite.

This devaluation of regional news applies not only to Latin America but also to all Third World countries. The imbalance of Third World news coverage in the Latin American papers we studied is dramatic, as shown by Table 3 which lists the total material by region on November 24–27, 1975. The importance of Western Europe is magnified at this particular time because of the coronation of Juan Carlos of Spain, the subsequent demonstrations in Madrid against Pinochet, and the political crisis in Portugal. Even so, stories concerning the United States alone still account for 20.2 percent of the stories. If expressed in terms of world population, the panorama would be even more striking. Asia is undoubtedly the region of the world with the largest volume of inhabitants, but did not account for more than 3.6 percent of the information, confirming for the reader in Caracas or Buenos Aires that it is indeed a distant and impregnable continent.

The subordination of Third World news can also be illustrated by one of the stories from the United Nations on November 23 about excess mercantilism and profit-seeking occurring in the pharmaceutical industry. The AFP cable, in mentioning the uselessness of the majority of the products on the market, pointed out that a Brazilian study revealed that of

Table 2	COVERAGE OF SURANIM INDEPENDENCE ON NOVEMBER 26, 1977			
	Agency Used	*Column Cms.*	*Number of Columns*	*Page Numbers*
La Prensa (Argentina)	UPI	56	3	2
El Imparcial (Guatemala)	UPI	38	2	1
La Prensa (Nicaragua)	Reuter Latin	27	5	3
La Nacion (Costa Rica)	UPI	27	1	25
La Prensa (Peru)	UPI	24	4	15
El Dia (Uruguay)	UPI	20	1	2
Critica (Panama)	UPI	15	3	2

Source: (6)

Table 3   TOTAL AMOUNT OF NEWS COVERAGE BY WORLD REGION FOR 16 LATIN AMERICAN NEWSPAPERS, NOVEMBER 24–27, 1975

	Column Centimeters	Percentage
Western Europe	9,264	40.5
United States	4,636	20.2
Latin America	4,479	19.6
Middle East	1,579	6.9
Africa-Arab States	—	—
North Africa-South Africa	806	3.5
Asia	836	3.6
U.N.-CEPAL	531	2.3
Socialist Europe	701	3.0

Source: (6)

14,000 drugs sold, only 116 were considered fundamental and only 52 basic (11, p. 195). The story was transmitted to Latin American papers not only by AFP, but also by AP and Prensa Latina. However, except in Mexico where it was given slight coverage, the story was systematically ignored by all the Latin American papers studied. Thus the rejection of the information came from the newspapers themselves. They chose instead a story about Caroline Kennedy's photographs.

This example shows how both the agencies and the newspapers perpetuate the traditional information structure in the Latin American press. The local reporters send the New York offices what they think is wanted, and then the news sent to Latin America is that which the newspapers usually "consume" (5). Thus the local papers consistently reinforce the expectations of their readers, expectations created by the news structure. As a Latin American observer has pointed out, "the information calms [one] down, since the daily with which [one] identifies, permanently ratifies the correctness of [one's] view which is reinforced through being reproduced in the structure of the newspaper. . . . A survey has shown how during its first months, *La Opinion* generated a dependency similar to that which a patient establishes with his analyst: Mondays, when there is no edition (like its model *Le Monde*) produce anxiety in its reades who lose the rationality of the outside world" (13, p. 232).

The current information model was forged within the "liberal" view that individuals naturally and freely choose and demand what they need, forgetting that in reality the environment conditions needs. The circle closes in this way: (a) "News" is selected by the reporters of the national media from all available events or facts, according to the dominant criteria and values of their journalistic practice. (b) The transnational news agencies collect information from the national media and from their local representatives and then make a selection according to what is traditionally accepted by the central/regional office. (c) The central office in New York, Paris, or wherever, provided with the material preselected by their own representatives, send their clients the material, supposedly demanded by them, which coincides systematically with what the media are accustomed to receive and fits perfectly with the dominant values of the journalism of the continent. (d) The local media receive the cable information from the news agencies, *which they originally selected themselves*, and the circle is closed (5, p. 176). Finally (e) the public confirms the reigning journalistic practice by consuming the information to which it is accustomed.

Thus the seriousness of the current problem goes far beyond economic solutions. The answer is not the simple and mechanical nationalization of the media, since inherent in the concept of news value currently in force is a commercial and industrial concept of news. As Mattelart has said, "we will not fully solve the question of cultural dependence simply by suppressing foreign, especially North American, programs. A Chilean program can reproduce the same ideological structure and thus, albeit camouflaged, suffer from the same vices as foreign material" (8, p. 175). It is therefore necessary, both empirically and theoretically, to look critically at the foundations of the entire concept and structure of news.

News not only used by Latin America but also about Latin America comes primarily from UPI and AP. A synthesis of the situation is expressed by two ex-presidents of Venezuela. Rafael Caldera, during a 1970 press conference at the National Press Club of Washington, D.C., pointed out that

[p]erhaps the phrase "no news is good news" has become "good news is no news." Only the most deplorable incidents, be they caused by nature or by man, receive prominent attention in the media (of the United States); little or nothing is mentioned about literary or scientific achievements; little or nothing is said about the efforts of man to dominate nature and to put it at the service of his needs; little is said about social achievements and the defense against the dangers which threaten our peace and development. It is much easier to present the Latin American as a disorderly and difficult neighbor, incapable of achieving those objectives achieved by others in the economic and technological fields (2).

Years later, Carlos Andrés Pérez considered the struggle for a new information order and especially for an improved concept of news as a main priority of his presidency. In his message to UNESCO during the 1976 San Jose conference he declared:

The international press only selects information that detracts from the image of our countries: the major press and the broadcast media from the developed world ignore our struggles, efforts, and fair demands for a just international system (9).

Hester's (5) large study of international news supports this assessment of agency news priorities. In a table ranking those topics AP correspondents perceived their editors were interested in, stories involving the United States ranked first and all "crisis" stories closely followed. Revolutions or coups ranked second, natural disasters third, crime or criminal violence fourth, and domestic politics and foreign relations tied for fifth place. While U.S.-related news, catastrophe, and violence were overvalued, news referring to development, cultural events, religion, science, or education ranked at the very bottom of the scale.

The version of Latin American news in which North American interests generally predominate has been documented by other researchers. For example, according to Markham (7), ". . . revolution is needed for Latin America to appear in the news." Whitaker (15) arrives at the conclusion that the information which appears "concentrates on what the tourist should see, eat, drink or buy, or tells of the discomforts (not to say direct dangers) of living and travelling in Latin America."

Despite the profound nature of the political and social changes occurring in Santo Domingo in 1965 and Chile in 1970, which could have reoriented reporting towards a more sophisticated appraisal of Latin American life, that has not happened. As expressed by one observer: "One thing remains constant in the North American press: an apparent implacable hostility to social change in any part of the region, be it accompanied by violence or not . . . . magazines and newspapers in the United States have resorted principally to sensationalism and ridicule when informing or commenting on the social revolutions which occurred in Mexico after 1910, in Bolivia in 1952, in Cuba in 1959, in Peru in 1968 and in Chile between 1970 and 1973" (6).

Thus, it is clear that the transnational news agencies not only determine what the Latin Americans read, but what other nations read about them. The ways in which that image has been distorted have been classified by Somavia (14). Distortion in this case does not necessarily imply a false presentation of the facts, but rather an arbitrary selection of facts according to an inaccurate news model. It can mean that an exaggerated sense of importance is given to anecdotes or events considered "folkloric," or a presentation of events isolated from the whole. It can also mean distortion by "implication," when events are reported so that their implicit consequences are favorable to the interests of the transnational agency or country doing the reporting. Distortion can also occur by a report "preconditioning the facts" for the purpose of conditioning the future behavior of people, firms, social groups, or governments, or by the silence surrounding situations which have ceased to interest the transnational agencies or countries. News practice in Latin America provides multiple examples of each one of these categories (see 1, 3, 10).

Several efforts to develop alternatives to the current dependency on the transnational news agencies have been tried in Latin America. The news agencies EFE, Prensa Latina, and Inter Press Service have tried from a number of angles to provide a different view of Latin America and its current development, as in their coverage of the events in Chile from 1970 to 1973, the nationalization of Venezuelan oil, the Panama Canal question, and the political evolution of Jamaica. In addition, Latin American newspapers are making an effort to break away from the tendency toward inertia by using other sources of information, in addition to news agencies, to give events the broadest, most informative coverage. The best of the papers are trying to limit the verbatim printing of news agency dispatches.

Better and more accurate news coverage also requires an awareness on the part of the professionals that relying on the "old" news values cannot provide the insight needed to portray the processes of development as they are taking place within Latin America or in the Third World. The kind of reporting that has been done should not be devalued but rather revised, and alternative news models and news treatment sought. News professionals must experiment widely with news forms which might supply attractiveness and dynamism to social issues which traditionally have not been considered as newsworthy. Finally, the public must be re-educated to the alternative news values, so that they can exercise critical vision of news coverage and participate more fully in the news process.

These fundamental questions about news values and news coverage and the need for alternative news processes and structures are part of the larger issue of information policies which, through UNESCO and other international forums, is now concerning the countries of the entire globe.

REFERENCES

1. Beltrán, Luis Ramiro and Elizabeth Fox de Cardona. "La influencia de los Estados Unidos en la Communicación Masiva en América Latina: El Mito del libre flujo de la información." Honolulu: East-West Communication Institute, 1976.

2. Caldera, Rafael. "Versión resumida de la conferencia de prensa con los periodistas en el Club Nacional de Prensa en Washington, D.C." *Alianza para el Progreso: Carta Seminal*, June 15, 1970.

3. de Ramos, Elsy Bonilla. "Las agencias internacionales de noticias y sus sistemas informativos: el estudio de un caso." *Comunicación y Cambio Social*. Quito: Ildis Cicspal, 1975.

4. Díaz Rangel, Eleazar. *Pueblos Subinformados*. Caracas: Monte Avila, 1976.

5. Hester, Al. "The Associated Press and News from Latin America: A Gatekeeper and News Flow Study." London: University Microfilm International, 1977.

6. Knudson, Jerry W. "The Inter-American Press Association as Champion of Press Freedom: Reality or Rhetoric? The Experience, 1962–73." Unpublished paper, Temple University, Dept. of Journalism, 1973.

7. Markham, James W. "Foreign News in the United States and South American Press." *Public Opinion Quarterly* 25, Summer 1961, pp. 249–262.

8. Mattelart, Armand. "Lucha de clases, cultural socialista y medios de comunicación masivos." *Cuaderno de la Realidad Nacional* 8 (Santiago).

9. Pérez, Carlos Andrés. "Discurso inaugural in la 30a Asamblea General de la SIP." Caracas, Venezuela, Octubre 1974.

10. Reyes Matta, Fernando. "América Latina, Kissinger y la UPI: Errores y Omisiones desde México." *Comunicación y Cultura* 4 (Buenos Aires), September 175, pp. 55–72.

11. Reyes Matta, Fernando. "El encandilamiento informativo de America Latina." *La Información y el Nuevo Orden Internacional*. Mexico City: ILET, 1977.

12. Reyes Matta, Fernando. "La evolucion histórica de las agencias transnacionales de noticias hacia la dominación." *La Información y el Nuevo Orden Internacional*. Mexico City: ILET, 1977.

13. Schumcler, Hector. "Dependencia y Política en la Prensa Argentina, el Caso de La Opinión." *Communicación y Cambio Social*. Quito: Ildis Ciespal, 1975.
14. Somavía, Juan. "Las Agencias Transnacionales de Noticias." La Noticia Internacional. Mexico City: ILET, 1977.

15. Whitaker, John R. "The Image of Latin America in U.S. Magazines." Report of the Magazine Publishers Association, 1969.

THE FREE AND NOT-SO-FREE PRESS OF LATIN AMERICA AND THE CARIBBEAN

Bruce Garrison and Julio E. Munoz

A country by country report on press freedom in Latin America indicates that not only are there problems of censorship in many countries in the region, but there are many physical risks to covering news in the area. Some improvements have been reported in recent years, but Latin America still has a long way to go.

Journalist and writer Carlos Loret de Mola died in a car accident, official reports stated about his death in Mexico in late 1985. His family believes he died because he was preparing a book, "My Colonel," about former Mexican President Luis Echeverria, Colonal Jose Garcia Valseca and new UPI owner Mario Vasquez Rana.

Newspaper columnist Manual Buendia was shot to death outside his office. Loret de Mola and Buendia died fighting a problem they had worked to solve: corruption.[1] On the same day Buendia was shot, on the border of Nicaragua and Costa Rica, two reporters were killed in the bombing of a press conference of Nicaraguan rebel leader Eden Pastora. This time the dead journalists were Linda Frazier, a reporter for San Jose's *Tico Times*, and Jorge Quiros, a reporter for Costa Rican television.[2]

In still another case, Salvadoran journalist Rafael Hasbun, 56, was murdered as he walked toward his San Salvador office where he wrote his column for *Diario de Hoy*. Despite his popularity as a conservative, three men gunned him down. It was one more assassination in a war zone. There have been many. Hasbun, a lawyer and journalist, reached thousands through his column. But the gunmen silenced his opposition voice.[3]

Working in Latin America remains an extremely dangerous assignment for U.S. journalists as well. A *Newsweek* photographer was shot to death in an ambush in fighting between leftists rebels and government troops just northeast of San Salvador. A *Time* magazine photographer was luckier; he was not hit.[4]

Many other journalists died in Latin America trying to do their jobs. According to the Committee to Protect Journalists, five working journalists died in Peru and Guatemala in 1985. A total of 13 journalists died on assignment in Latin America in the

Bruce Garrison and Julio E. Munoz, "The Free and Not-So-Free Press of Latin America and the Caribbean." *Newspaper Research Journal*, Volume 7, Number 4, Summer 1986, pp. 63–69. Reprinted by permission.

Bruce Garrison is associate professor of journalism and director of graduate studies in the School of Communication at the University of Miami in Coral Gables, Florida. Julio E. Munoz is director of the Technical Center of the Inter American Press Association in Miami.

first six months of 1984. At least 21 journalists were killed in 1983 in Latin America, 12 more than the number who died in incidents of political violence in 1982.

After looking at annual reports by worldwide organizations monitoring freedom of the press, Fram concluded, "journalism is still dangerous, and freedom of the press continues to be limited in vast areas of the world. . . ."[5]

It is apparent when the news media in some Latin America and Caribbean region countries have felt pressure to support the prevailing ideology of the nation's government, and when they have resisted both political and social revolutions, violence and restrictions on freedom of the press and information increase.

In developing countries where press freedom is at a transitional stage, political instability is a prevailing characteristic of the social system. The power structure in such nations is compelled to exert strict control over the flow of ideas, especially over the mass media system. Different types of control represent the various functional alternatives available to national governments to regulate and constrain the free operation of mass media outlets.

This macroscopic approach to communication research has been inherent to the work of Tichenor, who in recent years has developed a structural model in which information control is seen as a mechanism of system maintenance.[6] Habte notes these conformity pressures are both subtle and direct.[7]

In the world press freedom review, International Press Institute Director Peter Galliner said, "some of the worst places to be a reporter today are Central and Latin America. Overseas and domestic correspondents have faced danger daily from a variety of sources."[8]

Argentine editor Federico Massot said political violence was one of the main problems facing the press in Argentina during the military regime that ended in December 1983: "There has been a lot of it (violence) in the past 35 years and I don't see how it will disappear overnight. The first attacked are the journalists and papers."

Another problem Massot identified is self-imposed censorship. While there has never been outright censorship in Argentina, except during the Peron era, the danger during the past 35 years, Massot said, was in self-imposed restrictions on information flow because journalists have been intimidated by violence against them and their newspapers and the weakness of the economy.[9]

Costa Rican publisher and editor Manual Jimenez agrees with Massot. "With the exception of Costa Rica, Honduras, and to a certain degree, Panama, Central America is an area where journalism has become a dangerous profession. In Nicaragua, Guatemala, El Salvador, many of our colleagues have been killed, kidnapped, or forced into exile.

"In general, we can no longer think of journalism as a profession that would bring about a special status . . . or provide a certain immunity. War and political turmoil do not honor credentials. . . ."[10]

Freedom House officials said print media freedom, as known in democratic states, exists in only about one-third of the world's countries. While there are serious problems elsewhere, incidents of violence against Latin America and Caribbean journalists demand concern for this region remain serious.

Of the 21 journalists killed by acts of violence in 1983, eight were killed in a single incident in Uchuraccay, Peru. While a government committee concluded the journalists were mistaken by villagers as a band of hostile terrorists, questions remain unanswered.

Beyond this, the Inter American Press Association (IAPA) indicated at least four other journalists were kidnapped, ten threatened with death, 80 arrested, 19 expelled from 17 countries, and two dozen beaten or had their offices bombed in 1983.[11]

Obviously, concern for press freedom and freedom of access to public information in Latin America is not new. Alisky notes this topic has concerned scholars for several decades. He wrote: "Press freedom became one of the basic criteria for measuring degrees of democracy and dictatorship in the various Latin American nations in the continuing surveys. . . ."[12]

Alisky says press freedom is a concept which has interested scholars. A more difficult and illusive factor is freedom of information: 1) the freedom of reporters and editors to gather facts from official and unofficial sources for news stories and 2) the news media's ability to protect sources of information which must remain confidential.

This commentary's authors make their evaluations of freedom of the press and information using the free system of the Western World as a baseline.[13]

Former Inter American Press Association President Herman Ornes, publisher of *El Caribe* of Santo Domingo, Dominican Republic, said entering the 1980s many Latin American governments were using a language that was at best superficial. It did not really give any substantial freedom of the press and information in Latin America and the Caribbean.[14]

The literature reviewed includes final reports from the Inter American Press Association's 41st general assembly in Colombia in October 1985 and the mid-year meetings in Brazil in March 1986 and in Panama in March 1985,[15] as well as earlier meetings' reports from 1982 to 1984. Literature from the International Press Institute, the Index on Censorship, and the Committee to Protect Journalists was also consulted.[16]

The following country-by-country summaries illustrate the situation in much of Latin America and the Caribbean:

Argentina. There are increased import duties on newsprint and other production materials and proposed laws making the right of reply mandatory. Various draft bills on the right of reply are before the National Congress, one of which has already been passed by the Chamber of Senators. Newspapers in Argentina are not permitted to bid for radio and television channels. Official advertising placement is discriminatory, punishing opposition newspapers.

Bolivia. Three journalists were jailed, accused of doubling as political and union leaders. Newspapers still suffer from financial problems connected to the nation's economic difficulties.

Brazil. A law regulating the press continues in effect, but there are moves to repeal it or weaken it. A journalist who reported on a death squad was murdered in Brasilia; a former public security official has been indicted for the murder. Working journalists are now required to have a college or university degree. The right of reply is established by the Brazilian constitution.

Chile. There is no press freedom under the current government. A state of emergency succeeded a state of seige, bringing some relief to journalists in Chile, but legislative limits on freedom of expression are expected to be tightened further.

Establishment of new publications remains restricted and threats against reporters and editors continue. The government has ordered lawsuits filed against several journalists. Finally, the ailing economy of Chile has put many media organizations into heavy debt to official financial institutions.

Costa Rica. In one of the major developments in Latin America in 1985, the Inter-American Court of Human Rights upheld the position of the Inter American Press Association by condemning the practice of obligatory licensing of journalists in Costa Rica. This important decision was contained in a unanimous advisory opinion issued by the court, which is a body of the Organization of American States, in mid November 1985.

Mandatory licensing was found to be incompatible with an article of the American Convention on Human Rights. Furthermore, foreign correspondents must be accredited from the journalism collegium to which local journalists must belong if they wish to cover news in Costa Rica. Initially, the collegium denied accreditation to a journalist there on a one-year IAPA fellowship, later it granted a 30-day permit.

Cuba. There is still no freedom of the press. All news media are the property of the state and represent the government's point of view. There are no independent journalists working in Cuba. Two newsmen are jailed there, one for 18 and the other for 25 years.

Dominican Republic. Newspapers in the Dominican Republic are challenging the obligatory licensing of journalists in court on constitutional grounds. Like some other Latin American and Caribbean nations, placement of advertising is arbitrary and at times politically inspired.

Ecuador. Newspapers may publish without restriction in this democratic nation. There are government attempts to manipulate the news by withholding advertising from those it regards as opponents, including *Hoy*. The Ecuadorian information minister says the new government seeks a free press, but

IAPA members have found evidence of government attempts to suppress some news.

Contractual, political and press freedom issues have been raised in the grant of licence to operate a television channel by the previous administration and the current government's cancellation of it.

El Salvador. The elected government is committed to a free functioning press, but an extreme climate of violence dampens the practice of an unfettered news media. Official advertising placed in *Diario de Hoy* has been cut back because of political reasons, editors there believe.

Guatemala. Self-censorship prevails at newspapers here, even though there has been a change of government. The new constitution guarantees freedom of information and expression.

Guyana. There is no press freedom at present. Intimidation and harassment of the *Catholic Standard* and its editor, Fr. Andrew Morrison, continue. The government also controls the supply of newsprint here. Because of this, IAPA feels his ability to publish the newspaper remains "precarious."

Haiti. In the government of Jean-Claude Duvalier, there was no press freedom. In early 1986, the Duvalier regime fell and was replaced first by a six-person transitional ruling council and later by Gen. Henri Namphy.

The new government's intentions toward free press and information in Haiti is not yet known. Under Duvalier, it was common for arbitrary detention of journalists. Persons exercising free speech had been jailed.

Mexico. The government is indifferent to physical aggression against newsmen and their newspapers, including two newspapers which had published reports compromising government authority.

A Mexican government monopoly manufactures and distributes newsprint, which may be a threat to freedom of the press. The government also decreed the automatic appropriation of satellite communication equipment.

Netherlands Antilles (Aruba). Journalists here are being threatened and harassed by officials. The government reportedly discriminates against *The Buers, La Prensa* and *The News* in decisions about placement of official advertising.

Nicaragua. The leading independent opposition newspaper, *La Prensa*, continues to receive harassment from the government. The government still forces prior censorship upon the editors of *La Prensa*.

While the government here repeatedly pledges to allow freedom of expression and respect plurality, this has not been the case in the past year. Copies of the first issue of the Catholic weekly *Iglesia* were seized in only one example.

The military of the Sandinista government took over *Iglesia's* printing plant and closed the church's radio station, Radio Catolica. Furthermore, the government still does not permit closed radio stations and news programs to return to the air.

Panama. The government still controls a confiscated publishing company and two radio stations. Compensation payment is still pending for damaged *La Prensa*, which was occupied by government forces in 1982. A law empowering the government to shut down publications and summarily jail their editors remains on the books.

The independent press is subject to a systematic campaign of intimidation. It is so serious that a columnist went into hiding after learning about threats against him.

Paraguay. There is no press freedom. *ABC Color*, the leading newspaper, remains shut down after two years. Furthermore, the government refused to allow a weekly to be published by the Chaco Catholic diocese.

Radio Nanduti broadcasts were suspended for 10 days and a reporter who taped a speech by an opposition political leader was charged with complicity in inciting riots. Foreign correspondents' news copy is censored and foreign publications referring to the Paraguayan situation are seized. An Argentine reporter covering the Mengele story was expelled.

Uruguay. Virtually all laws restricting freedom of the press and information have been repealed. Import duties have been scrapped as well.

While these positive developments highlight activity in Uruguay, the press law, providing for a far-reaching right of reply, remains in force. The law also empowers the administration to seize foreign publications deemed dangerous to morality, national security or the public order. Finally, there have been reports of discriminatory placement of official advertising here.

While some governments continue to harness the press, the status of freedom of the press and infomation in Latin American and the Caribbean is improving. The fall 1985 report of the Committee on Freedom of the Press and Information said the decrease of dictatorships and return to democratic government in some countries has been offset by severly depressed economies which "threaten the vitality and at times the very existence of a free press."

The spring 1986 committee report from Bahia, Brazil, said . . . "with the end of the Duvalier family dictatorship in Haiti, Latin America finds itself with just four major dictatorial governments. Cuba and Nicaragua are at one end of the political spectrum while Chile and Paraguay are at the other extreme."[17]

However, the change in Haiti shows how quickly things have changed in at least one country in Latin America and the Caribean. An IAPA General Assembly recently concluded: "a depressing and sometimes alarming story of a free press under attack from all directions emerged from reports . . . (of the Freedom of the Press and Information Committee)."[18]

The trend restricting freedom of the press and information seems to be unchanged in some places—there still is substantial harassment, imprisonment, expulsion, violence, censorship and conspiracy to restrict the flow of news. Increasing costs are becoming a more serious problem in Latin American and Caribbean countries as well.

As in Uruguay, there are certain bright spots. Elected governments in several countries have replaced military dictatorships and there is more press freedom in nations such as Peru, Ecuador and Bolivia as a result. Brazil is moving in that direction. And with democracy restored in Granada, a free press functions on that island today.

Another recent positive event has been the ruling of the Inter-American Court of Human Rights that licensing of journalists in Costa Rica violates Article 13 of the Inter-American Convention on Human Rights.[19]

On the downside, there is a dangerous trend toward more and more discriminatory use of official advertising in some countries. Governments seem to use official advertising to reward friendly newspapers and punish opposition ones. And if the governments' assignment of advertising is not a problem, the economy has forced some governments to eliminate or cut back advertising. This has affected the private sector as well, as companies have been forced to reduce advertising budgets.

Regardless of the cause, these revenue shortfalls have led to economic difficulties for many publications and others have had to go out of business. The effect is obvious: Fewer voices make access to information more difficult for the citizen. Advertising is one problem. Taxes and international exchange also remains a problem for these publications.

Furthermore, there already exists in many countries, such as in Argentina, legislation which forces newspapers to open their pages for right to reply for those who feel injured by published stories.

Concern for Latin American news media seems to be growing parallel to the importance of the region in world affairs in this decade. In June 1983, the Council on Hemispheric Affairs and the Newspaper Guild issued what they hope will be the first of a series of annual reports on press freedom throughout Latin America. The objective is to focus more attention to the professional status of Latin American journalists.[20]

South American governments have shown growing interest in a free press by hosting American journalists and scholars to discuss media responsibility and performance in democratic governments.

Even for American journalists working in Latin America, the dangers and limitations are apparent. Risk may be part of the job, yet for newspapers sending reporters and photographers to cover breaking stories, caution is necessary.

Clearly, policies of the governments restrict flow of information back to the United States. Licensing is but one example of such widespread restriction. Dangers to the health and safety is of foremost concern, however, and measures such as the International Committee of the Red Cross (ICRC) is taking will be necessary for those on dangerous assignments. In 1985, the ICRC agreed to provide help through a 24-hour hot-line to Geneva for assistance in urgent situations. It also will help create a clearing house on dangerous areas.[21]

The hope in 1986 that the American continents—including the Caribbean—could show a better freedom of the press situation is endorsed by a few but important changes:

1. Return of Democracy in Brazil;
2. End of total censorship in Uruguay;
3. End of Duvalier regime in Haiti; and,
4. Maintenance of democracy in the three traditional democratic countries: Venezuela, Colombia and Costa Rica.

Unfortunately there is still a long way to go before the continent becomes fully free in terms of expression and government harassment of independent news media. But there are some good signs in the middle of the fray, and we are encouraged. We see each step forward as a victory in the war for this free speech cause.

NOTES

1. See "Report of the Freedom of the Press Committee," Inter American Press Association, Board of Directors meeting, Bahia, Brazil, March 6, 1986. See also "Noted Columnist, Weekly Editor Slain in Mexico," *IAPA News*, No. 295 August 1984, p. 9. For more information, see Report No. 2 in Bruce Garrison and Julio Munoz, "An Update on Freedom of the Press and Information in Latin America and the Caribbean," paper presented to the Mass Communication Division, International Communication Association, Honolulu, Hawaii, May 1985. See also Report No. 1, Bruce Garrison and Julio Munoz, "Freedom of the Press and Information in Latin America and the Caribbean," presented to the second annual Intercultural Communication Conference, University of Miami, Coral Gables, Fla., February 1985.
2. "The Pain of Reporting the Death of Colleagues," *IAPA News*, No. 295, (August 1984), p. 8.
3. Sam Dillon, "Salvadoran Gunmen Kill Right-Wing Journalist," *The Miami Herald*, (April 2, 1984).
4. Associated Press, "U.S. Journalist Slain in El Sal-
vador Gunfire," *The Miami Herald*, (March 17, 1984), p. 14a.
5. Telephone interview with Eric Goldstein, Committee to Protect Journalists, New York, (April 2, 1986). See also Marcia Fram, "Nineteen Journalists Slain in 1983 Attacks," *presstime*, (February 1984), 6:2, p. 7.
6. P.J. Tichenor, G.A. Donohue, and C.N. Olien, "Mass Media Functions, Knowledge, and Social Control," *Journalism Quarterly*, 50:652–59 (Winter 1973).
7. Amde-Michael Habte, "The Mass Media Role in the Third World," in L. John Martin and Auju Grover Chaudhary, eds., *Comparative Mass Media Systems*, (New York: Longman, 1983), p. 107.
8. Peter Galliner, "World Press Freedom Review," *IPI Report*, 32:12 (December 1983), p. 1. Taking such situations quite seriously, the Inter American Press Association has produced a brochure for journalists working in dangerous areas. The brochure, "Surviving Dangerous Assignments," is available by request from the IAPA headquarters, 2911 NW 39th St., Miami, FL 33142.
9. Federico Massot, "The News Media in Argentina." Address before students and faculty, School of Communication at the University of Miami, Coral Gables, Fla., (Feb. 2, 1984).
10. Manuel Jimenez B., "Press Without the First Amendment," Region 3 conference of the Society of Professional Journalists, Sigma Delta Chi, Miami Beach, Fla. (April 7, 1984).
11. Fram, *op. cit.*
12. Marvin Alisky, *Latin American Media: Guidance and Censorship*, (Ames, Iowa: Iowa State University Press, 1981), pp. 19–20.
13. See Sunwoo Nam, "Press Freedom in the Third World," in L. John Martin and Anju Grover Chaudhary, eds., *Comparative Mass Media Systems*, (New York: Longman, 1983), p. 310.
14. "Ornes Warns of Dangers," *IAPA Updater*, (March 1, 1979), p. 2.
15. The authors use reports on violence against journalists, freedom of press and freedom of information from the Inter American Press Association mid-year Board of Directors meeting in Bahai, Brazil, March 1986; the 41st General Assemby at Cartagena, Colombia, October 1985; and the mid-year meeting in Panama City, Panama, March 1985.
16. Reports cited are International Press Institute's *IPI Report*, the *Index on Censorship* and the Committee to Protect Journalists' *CPJ Update*.

17. Raul Kraiselburd, remarks of the chairman, "Report on the Committee of Freedom of the Press and Information." Unpublished report prepared for members of the Inter American Press Association, 40th General Assembly, Los Angeles, October 1984.

18. "Conclusions." Unpublished report prepared by the Inter American Press Association, 40th General Assembly, Los Angeles, (Nov. 1, 1984).

19. "Conclusions." Unpublished report prepared by the Inter American Press Association, mid-year meeting, Bahia, Brazil, (March 6, 1986).

20. Charles A. Perlik Jr., "Introduction," in Council on Hemispheric Affairs and the Newspaper Guild, "A Survey of Press Freedom in Latin America" (Washington, D.C.: Council on Hemispheric Affairs, June 1983), p. 1.

21. "Red Cross takes lead in safety issue, hotline for newsmen at risk proposed," *IAPA News*, (June 1985), No. 299, p. 1, 6.

TELEVISION NEWS IN SAUDI ARABIA

JERRY C. HUDSON AND STEVE SWINDEL

Saudi Arabia, as an example of a country in another Third World region, also depends heavily for its foreign news on international—mainly Western, but no Communist—sources. Because the Saudi press "borrows" so heavily from foreign sources, it is limited in what it can relay to its readers about the outside world. At the same time, it screens very carefully the content of foreign news stories to avoid topics that are contrary to Islamic social and political beliefs.

The Western world seems to know very little about the characteristics of broadcast programming and news in Saudi Arabia. There are two major reasons for this lack of information. First, the government of Saudi Arabia has been reluctant to allow foreign companies or researchers to come into the Kingdom for the purpose of conducting research. Second, researchers who are permitted to engage in research activities must adhere to rigid research guidelines that could easily bias the data. For instance, women may not participate in any organized research.[1]

About 15 percent of the Saudi Arabian domestic audience is literate while more than 90 percent of the Saudi homes have radio and/or television sets; therefore, broadcasting has the greatest potential for disseminating news and information to a large number of people.[2] However, the Saudi government maintains strict control of all broadcast activities, including news, through the Ministry of Information. News programs are screened and reviewed for objectionable content. The government believes that it must regulate the Saudi cultural and social trends by reinforcing Islamic and political beliefs in the media. Two illustrations exemplify the government's control. Gatekeepers must give preferences to news items and information about the Saudi Royal Fami-

Jerry C. Hudson and Steve Swindel, "Television News in Saudi Arabia." *Journalism Quarterly*, Volume 65, Number 4, Winter 1988, pp. 1003–1006. Reprinted by permission.

Jerry C. Hudson is an associate professor of Mass Communications at Texas Tech University. Steve Swindel is an assistant professor of Mass Communications at Texas Tech University. Hudson spent thirteen months in Riyadh, Saudi Arabia, with the U.S. Department of Labor.

ly, and scenes that show men and women embracing and/or kissing must be edited.[3] Yet, with these stringent guidelines, gatekeeping decisions in Saudi Arabia may be no different from decisions made in other countries. Kurt Lewin and others[4] suggest that the gatekeeper, or news selector, is greatly influenced by social and psychological factors that affect the boundaries of choice and mirror the perceptions of the society in which he lives.

Borrowed news stories or items are reports used by the domestic media, in which the news items are taken from other reports disseminated previously by foreign news media or services.[5] News borrowing is a common practice for media in many developing countries.[6] Systematic news borrowing may become more important and more common for developing countries because of restrictions placed upon the number and mobility of available international news sources.[7] In some countries, an increase in news borrowing may also increase the difficulty in news selection or gatekeeping.

The Saudi Ministry of Information may select from many external sources for international news. Gatekeepers may choose from stories provided by Agence France Presse, the Associated Press, Middle East News Agency (Egypt), Reuters, and many specialized news services. However, there are no news services from Communist countries.[8]

The purpose of this study is to examine the subject and country of origin of news stories broadcast on television in Saudi Arabia.

METHOD

The research method employed in this study was content analysis. The units of analysis consisted of news story subject and news story origination. These analyses were conducted within the framework of ten English language television newscasts that were videotaped at 10 P.M. on Channel 2 in Riyadh, Saudi Arabia, May 18, 1985, through May 22, 1985, and March 31, 1986, through April 4, 1986. The news content for the Arabic and English language newscasts was identical in order of the news stories and in story content. In an attempt to guard against clustering of stories that could have dominated the news during a weekly broadcast, one

week was randomly selected during the first three-month period of the study, and the second week was randomly selected from the final three-month period of the study.

The sample of television news stories was analyzed through the use of a coding instrument that examined story subject and story origination. The instrument was similar to those used in previous television news research.[9] The news story subject was classified into 10 categories: Saudi Royal Family (His Royal Highness Crown Prince Fahd ibn 'Abd al-'Aziz and His Royal Highness Prince 'Abd Allah ibn 'Abd al-'Aziz), other Saudis, government leaders from other countries, economic (unemployment, inflation, monetary values, etc.), violence (defined by Gerbner et al.[10]), health, religion/Islamism, sports, military (any activity by a nation's armed forces that did not include acts of violence), and others.

Stories were also categorized according to their geographic origin. The origination categories were: Saudi Arabia, the United States, Europe, the Soviet Union, the Middle East (excluding Saudi Arabia), and others.

Undergraduates enrolled in a broadcast journalism class were employed as coders. All of the news stories ($N = 188$) were coded by each of the 10 coders. The reliability of the coding instrument was assessed using Krippendorff's coefficient of agreement.[11] Both measures were highly reliable. The measure for country of origin yielded a coefficient of .999. The coefficient for the subject category was .997. In the event of disagreement, stories were assigned to categories according to the majority judgment of the coders. There were no more than two disagreements for any news story.

RESULTS

A total of 188 news stories were broadcast in the 10 newscasts ($N = 82$—May 85 and $N = 106$—March/April 86). Table 1 shows the percentages of stories that originated from six geographical areas. About 35 percent of the stories originated from Saudi Arabia followed by stories grouped from ''other countries'' (20%). More stories originated from Saudi Arabia during the March/April 86 week

Table I   PERCENTAGES AND ORIGINS OF NEWS STORIES

Origin	May 85 (N = 82)	March/April 86 (N = 106)	Row Totals (N = 188)
Saudi Arabia	29.3%	42.5%	36.7%
United States	19.5	10.4	14.4
Europe	17.1	11.3	13.8
Soviet Union	2.4	4.7	3.7
Middle East	12.2	10.4	11.2
Other countries	19.5	20.8	20.2
Column totals	43.6%	56.4%	100.0%

than during the May 85 week. The United States (14.4%), Europe (13.8%), and the Middle East (11.2%) were about equal in frequency of story origination. However, there were fewer stories from the United States and Europe during the second week than during the first week. Stories originating from the Soviet Union comprised only 3.7 percent of the 188 stories broadcast on Channel 2. The origin differences between the two weeks were not statistically significant (χ^2 = 6.798, df = 5, $p < .236$).

An analysis of the subject categories (see Table 2) indicates that 19.1 percent of the stories focused on the Saudi Royal Family. The frequency of news stories related to other Saudis, economics, and violence increased during the second week. Stories related to government leaders of other countries, religion/Islamism, and the military decreased in frequency during the second week of the study. The frequency of the remaining subject categories was about the same. The news subject category differences between the two weeks were not statistically significant (χ^2 = 15.592, df = 9, $p < .076$).

The final analysis identified the news subject category with the country in which the news story originated. A statistically significant difference existed between the subject categories and the origination categories (χ^2 = 182.48, df = 45, $p < .0001$). Table 3 shows that Saudi Arabia was the only origin for stories related to the Saudi Royal Family, other Saudis, and religion/Islamism. However, no stories about violence or sports originated in the Kingdom

of Saudi Arabia. The Soviet Union was the source for only three types of stories: government leaders of other countries, economics, and the military. Of the stories concerning economics and the military, 14.3 percent had origins from the Soviet Union. More than 50 percent of the stories that originated from the Middle East related to violence and the military. Yet, more than 60 percent of all the stories related to violence (N = 27) originated from the United States and Europe.

CONCLUSIONS

This study identifies two major characteristics of Saudi television news. First, the Saudi Ministry of Information depended heavily on the "news borrowing" concept for its newscasts. Only 37.7 percent of the news stories originated in Saudi Arabia. The news sources in the United States, Europe, and the Middle East contributed almost 40 percent of the total news stories.

Second, the Saudi gatekeepers seemed to conform to their political and Islamic beliefs. Stories related to the Royal Family were broadcast more frequently than those on any other subject. Additionally, Islamism was the only religious subject broadcast, and there was no Saudi violence portrayed in the newscasts. This tends to support Lewin's concept of gatekeeping that news selection is greatly influenced by social and psychological factors.

Table 2   PERCENTAGES AND SUBJECTS OF NEWS STORIES

Origin	May 85 (N = 82)	March/April 86 (N = 106)	Row Totals (N = 188)
Royal Family	20.7%	17.9%	19.1%
Other Saudis	2.4	12.3	8.0
Government leaders of other countries	15.9	7.5	11.2
Economics	8.5	13.2	11.2
Violence	11.0	17.0	14.4
Health	2.4	.9	1.6
Religion/Islamism	3.7	.0	1.6
Sports	11.0	10.4	10.6
Military	11.0	8.5	9.6
Other	13.4	12.3	12.8
Column totals	43.6%	56.4%	100.0%

Table 3   PERCENTAGES OF NEWS STORY SUBJECT AND COUNTRY OF STORY ORIGIN

News Subject	Saudi Arabia (N = 69)	United States (N = 27)	Europe (N = 26)	Soviet Union (N = 7)	Middle East (N = 21)	Others (N = 38)	Row Totals (N = 188)
Royal Family	19.1%	0.0%	0.0%	0.0%	0.0%	0.0%	19.1%
Other Saudis	8.0	0.0	0.0	0.0	0.0	0.0	8.0
Government leaders of other countries	5.8	18.5	15.4	28.6	9.5	10.5	11.2
Economics	10.1	7.4	15.4	14.3	14.3	10.5	11.2
Violence	0.0	33.3	30.8	0.0	23.8	13.2	14.4
Health	33.3	33.3	0.0	0.0	0.0	33.3	1.6
Religion/Islamism	4.3	0.0	0.0	0.0	0.0	0.0	1.6
Sports	0.0	3.7	23.1	0.0	14.3	26.3	10.6
Military	1.4	3.7	7.7	14.3	28.6	18.4	9.6
Other	2.9	29.6	7.7	42.9	9.5	18.4	12.8
Column totals	36.7%	14.4%	13.8%	3.7%	11.2%	20.2%	100.0%

NOTES

1. Douglas A. Boyd. *Broadcasting in the Arab World* (Philadelphia: Temple University Press, 1982), p. 143.
2. Richard F. Nyrop, Beryl Lieff Benderly and Laraine Newhouse Carter. *Saudi Arabia: A Country Study* (Washington: U.S. Government Printing Office, 1982), p. 196.
3. Boyd, *op. cit.*
4. Kurt Lewin, "Psychological Ecology (1943)" in *Field Theory in Social Sciences* (New York: Harpers, 1951) and Richard M. Brown, "The Gatekeeper Reassessed: A Return to Lewin," *Journalism Quarterly*, Vol. 56, Autumn 1979, p. 679.
5. Daniel Riffe, "Second-hand News Risky?" *Grassroots Editor*, Summer 1980, p. 3–4, 17.
6. Glorisa J. Canino and Aletha C. Huston, "A Content Analysis of Prime-Time T.V. and Radio News in Puerto Rico," *Journalism Quarterly* Vol. 63, Spring 1986, pp. 150–154; Drew McDaniel, "Development News in Two Asian Nations," *Journalism Quarterly*, Vol. 63, Spring 1986, pp. 167–170; Stuart J. Bullion and Randall Bytwerk, "U.S. News Media Citations in Neues Deutschland," *Journalism Quarterly*, Vol 63, Spring 1986, pp. 170–174; C. Anthony Giffard, "Developed and Developing Nation News in U.S. Wire Service Files to Asia," *Journalism Quarterly*, Vol. 61, Spring 1984, pp. 14–19 and Daniel Riffe, "International News Borrowing: A Trend Analysis," *Journalism Quarterly*, Vol. 61, Spring 1984, pp. 142–148.
7. Mort Rosenblum, "Information Please," *Columbia Journalism Review*, January–February 1981, pp. 59–63.
8. Nyrop, Lieff and Carter, *op. cit.*
9. Doris Graber, "Is Crime News Coverage Excessive?" *Journal of Communication*, Vol. 29, Summer 79, pp. 81–92; Robert Rutherford Smith, "Mythic Elements in Television News," *Journal of Communication*, Vol. 29, Winter 79, pp. 75–82; Richard Budd, "U.S. News in the Press Down Under," *Public Opinion Quarterly*, Vol. 28, Spring 1961, pp. 39–56 and Clifford R. Bush, "A System of Categories for General News Content," *Journalism Quarterly*, Vol. 37, 1960, pp. 206–210.
10. George Gerbner, Larry Gross, Michael Morgan and Nancy Signorelli, "The 'mainstreaming' of America: Violence Profile," *Journal of Communication*, Vol. 30, Summer 1980, pp. 10–20.
11. Klaus Krippendorff, *Content Analysis: An Introduction to Its Methodology.* Beverly Hills: Sage Publications, 1980.

WHY CHERNOBYL WAS A NONSTORY AND OTHER TALES OF INDONESIAN JOURNALISM

MARSDEN EPWORTH

Journalism is a popular profession in Indonesia, despite many constraints that are placed on reporters. Government sensitivity to what the press says is common in the Third World, and the experiences of an American journalist in Indonesia provide a good example of what it is like to be working in a Third World country.

Marsden Epworth, "Why Chernobyl Was a Nonstory and Other Tales of Indonesian Journalism." *Columbia Journalism Review*, September/October 1988, pp. 41–43. Reprinted by permission.

The author worked as a journalist in Indonesia for two years. She now lives in Lakeville, Connecticut.

Jakarta is jammed with people, all kinds: bureaucrats, strutting and plump; generals, like the bureaucrats except for their monumental Rolexes; and matrons—the Asian ones in bright silks, a servant trailing with mineral water and magazines, the American ones with cropped hair, red nails, tight lips, plunging through the want and the mess on their way to the Jakarta Hilton for aerobic exercise and a glass of white wine.

On Jalan Sangaji, a street lined with government offices, the peddlers sell ornamental fish. Somebody sells drugs, hash mostly and marijuana. And the *Indonesian Observer*, an English-language newspaper, sells information there, of a sort.

Shortly after coming to Jakarta in 1985, I applied to all three English-language dailies for work. The *Observer*, though homely and idiosyncratic, was my favorite. Its editorials twitting unnamed politicians and generals were the liveliest reading in town. The other two papers, the *Indonesia Times* and *The Jakarta Post*, churned out the government line with unwavering seriousness.

I met the publisher, B.M. Diah, in his office, a European sitting room with a Victorian couch covered in amber velvet. He wore a black cap—a *peci*, the mark of a Moslem and a patriot—and we talked about the *Observer*.

He founded the paper after the 1955 Asia-Africa Conference in Bandung, at which the country's first president, Sukarno, created the nonaligned movement. The idea, says Diah's wife, Herawati, whose title is general chairman of the *Observer*, was to give Indonesia an international presence, and to give the Third World a voice.

Since then, Diah, once a journalist, then a diplomat, and later a government official, has become director of the Jakarta Hyatt. He is a respected man, a member of the civilian elite that shares power in Indonesia with the military. Now the publisher wanted to transform this crowded inky daily into something handsome and, well, "Western." I suggested a few changes, and he hired me. My job was to edit copy, set style, clean up the layout, write a little, teach a little, and make sure that the same story did not appear twice. I asked who wrote the editorials. Diah did not say.

We went upstairs to the newsroom, a seedy place

where stray cats wandered. The windows were open and a half dozen fans pumped the smoke and the dust and the heat from the street around the newsroom, slowly, so as not to disturb papers on long tables set in a square. Teletypes clattered—Associated Press and Agence France-Presse in English, and Antara, usually described as "the quasi-government news service," in Indonesian. At the center of the squared tables the front-page editor, Gurbaks Singh, turbaned, bearded, and remote, a Sikh born in Sumatra, presided, a glass of tea and a typewriter at his elbow. He had the best typewriter in the newsroom. When it broke down, Singh would get the next best. He was in his fifties, the oldest man there and the most influential.

It was Singh who breathed a dated Britishness into the *Observer*, and a sense of classism and sometimes racism as well. It was a Singh who made the paper crowded and hard to read. It was Singh who insisted that photos of President Suharto, Sukarno's successor, greeting his ministers or visiting a cement plant, embellish every front page. And it was Singh who had to be convinced that change would be a good thing.

Diah introduced me and left. I never saw him in the newsroom again.

The *Observer*, with a stated circulation of 36,000—a number no one working there believed—was read by government officials, the military, embassy people, expatriates working in the archipelago, and, of course, the Department of Information. The paper had little advertising, one telephone, and five reporters. The covered foreign news, domestic news, city news, business news, and sports. Two of the reporters were employed part-time by the government, one in the Foreign Office, the other in the Department of Information. All of them were men. (Officials, it was thought, would not speak to women.) The roof leaked. The typesetters knew no English. One of the teletypes was always down. And the reporters took money from people they wrote about.

Singh explained how that worked. In the 1950s, after independence, government officials and businessmen paid reporters, usually free-lancers, a dollar or two at the end of a press conference. For carfare. Over time, however, reporters were expected to do more than write news. They were expected, along with every other segment of Indonesian society—the military, the professions, business, and the arts—to take a hand in nation building.

Naturally, a lot of Indonesian journalists have not always seen things this way. Mochtar Lubis, a contemporary of Diah's, wrote about government corruption and about student dissent during the sixties and seventies. His paper, *Indonesia Raya*, was closed repeatedly, first by Sukarno and then, permanently, by Suharto. He spent years in jail.

Other journalists who put a free press above nation building have lost the government licenses that permit them to work on a newspaper. Decades later they still may not work for any publication. So journalists who want to stay in the profession are careful not to antagonize the government or any of its supporters. The oldtimers know this. The newcomers learn fast.

In mid-1986, while I was at the *Observer*, the police dragged a young reporter for *Merdeka* ("Freedom"), another paper published by the Diahs, out of a news conference. His offense was repeating a question that military chief L. B. Murdani was disinclined to answer. And I was interviewed twice by an officer in the Department of Information after writing a story about East Timor, the island nation that Indonesia annexed in 1976. The government, which confuses order with progress and criticism with heresy, has an unrestrained right to get the kind of press it wants. In return, the government gives papers a license to publish and a break on the price of newsprint.

But for all the constraints and occasional dangers of Indonesian journalism, the profession attracts people. As anywhere else, a reporter's job in Indonesia is interesting. It is also fairly secure. And in a country where information is guarded and much of it is secret, reporters are special. They are insiders. They are in possession of something valuable. They know things other people do not. This gives them position. They inspire awe. Like spies.

They also have little or no college education and no special training. If they can read and write, if they can get a security clearance, and if they can tell what news bolsters the regime and what news does not, they've got a job. And in a country with very few jobs, no welfare system, a fondness for intrigue, and a lively distrust of imported abstractions, report-

ers do not complain about a government-managed press.

What Indonesian officials call "a free and responsible press" is not only acceptable, it is celebrated by many reporters and editors. A free press like the Western press, they say, which would write about attacks on Chinese Indonesians, student demonstrations, and wasteful, government-arranged import monopolies, would create dissension and chaos in Indonesia. This country has seen factions and conflict and bloodletting, they say. It has seen riots and coups and plots and the murder of children. Now the country has order. And the press has a responsibility to help the government preserve that order.

When Antara reported a plane crash in Sumatra that killed a high-ranking military man, the information department ordered us to drop the wire story. No one argued about it. We just waited for the press release from the military that arrived, a day later, minus the eyewitness reports of a fireball breaking up the plane. In the official story the plane simply crashed into a Sumatran mountain. That prevented talk of a secret war between militant Moslems and the government, Singh explained. We never report anything that could be construed as dissent, he said. Not from Moslems, not from students, not from anyone. Never. Enemies of the state, communists, might use such a story to weaken what President Suharto calls his New Order.

Of course, this does not prevent English-language papers and magazines printed in Bangkok, Singapore, or Hong Kong from writing about dissent. But foreign publications are screened at the airport. The *International Herald Tribune*, *The Asian Wall Street Journal*, *Far Eastern Economic Review*, *Time* magazine—all are censored.

Sometimes stories are snipped or whole pages are missing. Sometimes the print is slathered with pitch and covered with plain paper. (Whenever foreign papers or magazines are delayed, readers know the censors are at work.) As for wire services, the Department of Information monitors them, and although the department is said to have the technology to block stories from entering newsroom teletypes, Indonesian journalists do not think this technology is used. Indonesian journalists censor themselves.

When François Mitterrand came to Indonesia in

1986, he went to Bandung, a university town in West Java, to address students who had studied in France. Officials said later they had been apprehensive about this junket, but the French president had insisted. Suharto accompanied his guest to the Bandung Institute of Technology. We expected a routine story. When the Agence France-Presse story clattered into the newsroom describing 2,000 students chanting ''*Liberté, Liberté,*'' and waving placards denouncing the government, the reporters were thrilled.

I wondered how we could get a photo of the two presidents awash in student protesters. I did not wonder long. Singh dumped the story even before the man from the Department of Information called. Students are not allowed to demonstrate in Indonesia. And, if they do, newspapers are not allowed to report what happened. Not a single major Indonesian newspaper carried the story.

The government is as sensitive about the foreign press as it is about its own. In April 1986 a story in *The Sydney Morning Herald* sparked a crisis in Australian-Indonesian relations. The piece by David Jenkins, who had worked in Indonesia for five years, likened Suharto to ousted Philippine President Ferdinand Marcos. Jenkins's story described a business empire fashioned out of banking, steel, shipping, manufacturing, agriculture, real estate, and movie making, a $2 billion empire nurtured by the Suharto family—the president's children, his brothers, and his wife.

The reaction from Jakarta was harsh and prolonged. The Indonesian government banned the paper, banned Australian journalists, refused entry to a planeload of Australian tourists bound for the Indonesian island of Bali, canceled seabed boundary talks between the two countries, withdrew from an Australian training program for Indonesian army officers, and called off technology minister B. J. Habibie's scheduled trip to Canberra.

Soon afterward, the government also barred two journalists working for Australian news organizations from covering President Reagan's meeting with Suharto in Bali.

Then the government ousted Barbara Crossette of *The New York Times*, in Indonesia to cover the Bali meeting, because a story about Asian governments in the *Times's* Sunday magazine by A. M. Rosenthal vexed Suharto. She returned in 1987 for a brief visit and was barred again when she tried to come back for the parliamentary elections. Again she had displeased the president, a government official said: she had quoted a man named Slamet Bratanata in one of her stories.

Bratanata is a member of the Petition of 50, a group that periodically asks the House of Representatives for ''a little more democracy, a little less corruption,'' as he puts it. Many of the group members are former government and military men who are sometimes characterized as disappointed outsiders. They cannot work in their professions and they cannot travel. Their phones are probably tapped and their mail is certainly read. Still, they are not in jail, as some of the government's critics are. And they are not in hiding.

They live like Bratanata, a sixty-year-old computer teacher, who resides in an old residential section of Jakarta. Bratanata, like Mochtar Lubis the journalist and like Diah the newspaper publisher, backed Suharto's rise to the presidency, and in 1965 Suharto, during his ascent to power, made Bratanata minister of mines. His job was overseeing Indonesia's richest resource, oil.

What was not part of his job was criticizing the military's reckless plundering of this resource. Oil money poured without accounting into the pockets of army chiefs who controlled the state-owned oil company, Pertamina, and Bratanata insisted on reforms. Foreign aid depended on it, Bratanata said. Finally, Suharto fired him. And twenty years later he is still being punished, he says. Bratanata cannot get a job. He cannot get a bank loan. He cannot get a passport. He cannot leave the country. He is officially barred from writing, and his name cannot appear in print.

But he can talk. And he can listen. Everyone trusts Bratanata. He is a dissident, but not a malcontent. He is educated, but not foreign. He has held high office, but he is no thief. He is a faithful Moslem, but not a radical Moslem. He believes in democracy, but not Western democracy.

And when *The New York Times* and *Newsweek* and *The Asian Wall Street Journal* and other Western publications want information, their reporters go to Bratanata. So do government officials, military men, businessmen, bureaucrats, diplomats, and the Moslems. Bratanata deals in information. Censored information. Information no paper will print. For Bratanata, an unfree press is more than a fact of life. It's a living.

The *Observer*, like every other paper, was writing a lot of stories about the breach in Australian-Indonesian relations. But, like every other paper, we were not saying what caused it. We did not know what caused it. All we knew was that an Australian news story had offended the president. I went to Bratanata to find out why.

He had the story of course, along with an Indonesian translation.

I brought a copy of the *Herald's* article to the office and the reporters read it with great interest, but no one seemed disturbed by it. They had heard this before—perhaps not in such detail, but the president's business triumphs were not entirely unknown. The president has certain rights, Singh told me, rights that foreigners do not understand.

A prince plunders. And if a prince plunders a lot, his subjects can plunder a little. So can reporters. The two dollars news people once got for carfare have turned into twenty dollars for applause.

Once I asked a reporter if he ever turned down the "gift" at a news conference. Never, he said. No one does that. At *The Jakarta Post*, editor Sabam Siagian collects this money from reporters and puts it into an emergency fund for the staff. But he never tells them to turn it down. Breaking custom is hard anywhere.

A few weeks after joining the *Observer* I started going to press conferences. My first was for Rabo Bank, a Dutch firm expanding its investments, particularly its agricultural investments, in Indonesia. True, commodity prices were low, explained the bank officers, but cocoa and rubber and palm oil prices would not be depressed forever. And when the market improved, Rabo would be in a position to profit.

The news conference was held in one of Jakarta's new commercial towers, glassy, hard, and cool, homages to Western-style development. A dozen reporters drank tea and ate cake and asked questions, good questions, I thought. As my 6 P.M. deadline neared I packed up, leaving the others at the table, and headed for the elevator. The floor was

marble, the walls were concrete, and the sound of every footfall bounced off the hard surfaces. I heard steps behind me. I moved faster. So did the steps. Heading for the elevator, I broke into a trot. So did the steps.

A bank officer was calling after me. He was running. I was running. "Wait. Your gift. Your gift," he called.

What I wanted to do, of course, was to turn suavely and deliver a brief but gracious word on the independence of the press. Instead, I escaped into the elevator. Mortified.

This money does not buy an obedient press. It buys a laudatory press, a fawning press, a press that manipulates information just as the government does, not for order, not for the president, not for nation building, but for personal gain. The press in Indonesia has gone into business for itself.

One day, Diah called upstairs and ordered Singh to attend a press conference for Indomilk, an Australian-Indonesian milk-processing plant in Jakarta. Before Citibank and Unilever and Fairchild and 3M and Exxon and Johnson & Johnson, and all the other corporations attracted to Indonesia by its cheap labor and its political stability, sent Westerners to this tropical archipelago, milk was rare. By the mid-eighties, though, thousands and thousands of expatriates stationed all over Indonesia wanted milk. And they got it: dried milk, canned milk, irradiated milk, and, best of all, fresh milk. Indomilk was the major fresh-milk processor in the country. So when most of the International School population in Jakarta succumbed suddenly to a bacterial infection, Indomilk was named the culprit. The government closed the plant for two weeks and, when it reopened, the company called a press conference.

All the major dailies sent reporters. All the major dailies wrote stories. But Singh's alone ignored the medical reports and the laboratory analyses and the closing of the plant. Instead, his piece elaborated on the company's fastidious procedures, its spanking clean equipment, and its rigorous supervision of its staff. The story, which went to press on my day off, stunned me. Singh, however, was mute on the subject until a few weeks later, when he told me the paper was docking his pay for two months in connection with the Indomilk story.

It was, as Herawati Diah later observed, " a

promotional piece.'' Indomilk paid Singh for this promotion, she told me, and that was wrong. Indomilk should have paid the paper. As she explained in a memo, ''No one is allowed to write promotional articles on products without [obtaining] ads.'' Indomilk did not take an ad. So Singh's pay was docked the amount that the promotion, in management's view, merited.

In the end, Indomilk took an ad, but not as big an ad as Diah had anticipated. Singh got his ''gift'' and went back on salary. The *Observer* took in a little extra revenue. And nobody worried about the readers, which is the way things generally worked.

Reporters were usually willing to manage the news for cash, or maybe for lunch at a five-star hotel. But sometimes they did it just to exercise power.

When news of an explosion at a Russian nuclear power plant came clattering over the teletype, I asked Singh to call his friend the press secretary at the Soviet embassy for comment. The press secretary told Singh the story was false, fashioned to embarrass the Soviet Union. There had been no explosion at Chernobyl.

I cut his remarks into the wire copy, which was slated for page one, and went home. But next morning the *Observer* had no Chernobyl story, not on the front page, not on any page. The Soviet embassy denied the story, Singh explained. So he killed it. The *Observer* was probably the only paper in the world that had the story and did not use it because the front-page editor wanted to do a favor for a friend. He liked attending embassy receptions.

Maybe the publisher did, too.

Like other foreign reporters, I befriended Indonesia's public dissenters. Bratanata I saw often. Sometimes in the afternoon, before evening prayers, I visited him in his dark sitting room with the stone floors. We ate cake his wife had made and drank tea. He would bring to events information he had picked up from all the people he talked to all the time. He enjoyed this. He held court. Sometimes he grumbled about foreign reporters not paying him for his time and his information. When I asked if he worried about the risks, he shrugged, saying that a man can only live with what is right.

One day as I left his house for the paper he handed me an envelope, a familiar envelope, sealed and unmarked, exactly like an envelope I opened every day at the *Observer*. In the car I opened it. It was an editorial for the *Observer*. This dissident whose mail was opened, whose phone was tapped, whose driver probably reported regularly to KOPKAMTIB (the military branch in charge of security and order), as drivers were reputed to do, this maverick who implicated the Suharto circle in the murder of a young woman, who told reporters how Suharto joined the military (it was either the army or prison), this nonperson whose name could not be mentioned, even in a foreign newspaper, was not only writing, he was writing all the editorials for a newspaper, a government-supported newspaper. He was shaping policy at a major daily and meeting foreign diplomats and complaining to the legislature with the knowledge and approval of the government.

Bratanata is part of an opposition that serves the government. When the West wants dissidents it goes to Bratanata and his friends. It does not go to the artists or the intellectuals or the Catholic priests or the radical Moslems or the students. It does not go to the people in jail.

It goes to people like Bratanata who have a stake in the way things are run in Indonesia. It goes to people who benefit from a managed press, whose status and livelihood depend on it.

A GHANAIAN COVERS EAST AFRICA

Isaac Fritz Andoh

Here is a brief report by an African on the problems of covering another African country. Because of government suspicions, being a foreign correspondent in Africa is a frustrating experience not only for Westerners, but for Africans themselves.

One of the most exciting, but difficult, assignments is to be based in Africa as a foreign correspondent. Even to me as an African it has been no less so.

In Khartoum, Sudan, I covered the ministerial meeting and summit of the Organization of African Unity; in Lusaka, Zambia, the Commonwealth Heads of Governments meeting; in Arusha, Tanzania the Group of 77 meeting and in Kampala, Uganda during the regime of ousted Ugandan leader, Idi Amin, the O.A.U. Ministers of Information conference.

The common thread that runs through all these assignments is the difficulty in getting to the main source of news, either as a result of officialdom or improper preparation by those expected to cater for the press.

A case in point is the Nairobi Summit and ministerial meeting of the Organization of African Unity, where African journalists complained about poor arrangements by the O.A.U. information office. A Nairobi paper wrote. "Throughout the Council of Ministers meeting, from the opening of the heads of state summit to the closing moments, newsmen had to put in extra hours of waiting close to information offices, hoping to get releases on the closed-session talks, which dominated the entire two-week summit." For white journalists, access to news sources is even more difficult, especially in the coverage of day-to-day events that need immediate clarification.

Unlike a number of developed countries where one can get "official spokesmen" to clarify in cases of doubt, in most African countries this kind of arrangement does not exist. The nearest to "spokesmen" are public relations officers attached to government departments, which in some cases are even worse than civil servants.

Seeking clarification of copy requiring immediate attention is sometimes an ordeal for a correspondent. The process drags so much that a correspondent either loses his temper or simply has to make do with the available information at his disposal. One is inclined to believe that public relations officers attached to government departments are tailored to operate within certain laid-down regulations.

It should be borne in mind that in a continent where leaders are most sensitive to criticism and "biased" reporting, misinformation can lead to expulsion. With a little caution one could avoid being declared a persona non-grata. To be expelled from a country as a result of deliberate distortion amounts to inefficiency.

To be effective, especially as a news agency correspondent in Africa, it is necessary to subscribe to the news agency of the country in which one is operating. The other alternative is to maintain a network of local correspondents or stringers. But this attracts the ever-watchful eyes of the intelligence agencies, with the possibility that the stringer will be branded a "capitalist agent" or "a communist agent." Because of this, highly qualified and efficient African journalists invariably refuse to earn extra money stringing.

Reprinted from *Topic* (published by the World Press Institute at MacAlester College), March 1986. Reprinted by permission of the author.

The author lived in Nairobi, reporting on East African affairs for the Ghana News Agency. He was a Fellow at the World Press Institute when this article was written.

NEWS FROM THREE WORLDS IN PRESTIGE U.S. NEWSPAPERS

W. James Potter

In this study of eight American dailies covering ten randomly selected days in 1913, 1933, 1963, and 1983, the author finds that the Third World has been getting more coverage in recent years than it did 70 years earlier. However, more than half of the Third World coverage was found to be sensationalistic. This he did not find in front page headlines about the Western world.

The press in the United States has been criticized for providing so little international news,[1] especially in comparison with the proportion of international news appearing in the newspapers of other countries.[2] The empirical studies which have been conducted to determine if this criticism is valid, conclude that somewhere between 5% and 78% of news coverage is concerned with international news.

This wide range can be attributed to the methods used to define and measure international news. For example, in an analysis of the Associated Press wire copy in the early 1950s, it was reported that only about 5 percent to 10 percent dealt with foreign news.[3] The New York *Times* in 1970 was found to have about 16 percent of the total news space given to foreign news content.[4] In 1982, a study of front pages of five daily newspapers found a wide range of space devoted to international/national news with a high of 78 percent of all content in the *Charlotte Observer* to a low of 31 percent of all content in the *Milwaukee Sentinel*.[5] It is difficult to identify a reliable figure of how much international news is being presented to readers on a daily basis.

Within this amorphous international news hole, there has been an ongoing debate concerning the treatment of news from Third World countries. A wide variety of content analyses has been conducted, and the literature displays conflicting percentages which range from a low of 15 percent to a high of 59 percent of international news featuring Third World countries.

Critics of Western newspapers complain that too little space is given to the coverage of happenings in the Third World.[6] Among the severest critics is Masmoudi who describes Third World news coverage as a "flagrant imbalance" toward Western developed countries. He claims that 80 percent of the international news flow is about events in the "developed world," and that events in the less developed countries, which account for about three fourths of all people on earth, are virtually ignored.[7]

Semmel analyzed the total editorial print content of four prestige newspapers (the *New York Times*, *Chicago Tribune*, *Miami Herald* and the *Los Angeles Times*) in the fall of 1974.[8] He found that the proportion of international stories which referred to the 67 nations of the Third World was 15 percent while the proportion of stories which referred to the "developed" nations ranged from 47 percent to 65 percent of all foreign news items. He concluded, "the foreign news attention pattern of each daily is similar: each pays far greater attention to countries which are economically affluent, politically powerful and culturally similar to the United States."[9]

Also newspapers published in some other parts of the world are just as Western news oriented. For example, Matta analyzed the content of 16 Latin American newspapers and found that 60.5 percent

W. James Potter, "News from Three Worlds in Prestige U.S. Newspapers." *Journalism Quarterly*, Volume 64, Spring 1987, pp. 73–79. Reprinted by permission.

The author is assistant professor in the College of Communication at Florida State University.

of the coverage was for Western Europe and the United States, while 19.6 percent was for Latin America, 16.3 percent for the rest of the Third World and 3.0 percent for Socialist Europe.[10]

However, there is another set of content analyses which indicate that the Third World receives a great deal of coverage in the U.S. press. For example, Weaver and Wilhoit analyzed the AP and UPI wire services for foreign news content in 1979 and report that of the 339 stories they identified as foreign news content, 139 (41%) referred to the more developed countries (Europe, USSR, North America, Japan, Australia and South Africa) while 197 stories (59%) referred to less developed countries.[11] They also found that stories on the less developed countries were significantly longer than the stories on the more developed countries.

Haque, who analyzed the front page content of three elite newspapers (*New York Times*, *Washington*, *Post* and the *Christian Science Monitor*) for ten days in early 1979, also found that 82 percent of all foreign news stories were of the Third World.[12] In a comparison of international news coverage of the *New York Times* and the *Chicago Tribune* from 1970 to 1979, Riffe and Shaw report that between 35.9 percent and 41.5 percent of all international news stories dealt with the Third World, and 10.8 percent to 13.2 percent dealt with the Second World (Soviet and socialist countries.)[13]

Perhaps the range in the reported figures reflects changes in the amount of news presented over time. The literature has been criticized for lacking a longitudinal approach.[14] Over a long time span, the amount of Third World news would possibly be seen in a state of change which might better explain the discrepant findings in the literature. This strategy seems promising especially since Riffe and Shaw found a difference over a relatively short 10-year period from 1970 to 1979. They reported that the *New York Times* showed a balance between First and Third World news coverage throughout that period while the *Chicago Tribune* went from a domination of First World news to a balance near the end of that period. Thus the first two research questions in this study are: How is international news coverage distributed among the areas of the world, and does the proportion change over time?

There is yet a third question of interest relevant to this topic which has not yet been addressed in the empirical literature, i.e., has the *type* of content changed over time?

Several studies have reported that Third World news coverage is dominated by topics concerning destructive actions such as natural disasters, accidents and crime; but no study has examined this qualitative aspect of coverage over time.

Weaver and Wilhoit analyzed wire service copy in 1979 and report that a significantly higher percentage of stories from the less developed countries is concerned with ''elections, political violence, internal conflict or crisis and armed conflict,'' and that a significantly higher percentage of stories from developed countries is concerned with ''prices, labor relations, and culture.''[15] The authors also observe that most of the wire service stories they analyzed ''concentrated on political and military activity and crime. Economic matters, international aid efforts (except for military aid), social services, culture, scientific and medical achievements, and ecological issues such as energy and pollution were all but neglected.''[16]

METHOD

Eight newspapers were selected from among the nation's prestige press. This was an expansion beyond the four prestige newspapers analyzed by Semmel.[17] The additional newspapers were taken from a list of prestige newspapers provided by Stempel and Windhauser[18] so that a larger sample of geographically balanced newspapers could be used. They were *the New York Times, Washington Post, Chicago Tribune, St. Louis Post-Dispatch, Atlanta Constitution, Miami Herald, Los Angeles Times,* and *Christian Science Monitor*. These eight newspapers were chosen because each has a very large circulation, each is regarded as a very high quality newspaper and the group reflects a geographical balance throughout the country. Because of these characteristics, it was felt that these newspapers could serve as a fairly accurate reflection of the agenda being set by the press in this country.

All stories with a headline and at least two inches of copy on the front page were coded for the following characteristics: newspaper, year, level of news and type of news story. The level of news included international/national, local/state, or neither. If the story was international/national it was further coded as being West, East or Third World. In order for a story to be coded West it had to have a primary focus on a developed, industrialized, non-Communist country such as the United States, Canada, Western Europe, Israel, Greece, Japan, Australia, and South Africa. Eastern countries were U.S.S.R., the Soviet bloc and China. Third World countries included all of South and Central America, Africa (except South Africa), Asia (except those mentioned above), and Oceania.

An important feature of the methodology is that stories could be coded as belonging to more than one of the three subcategories. For example, negotiations between the U.S. and the Soviet Union was coded as belonging to both the subcategories of West and East.

The qualitative balance was measured in this study by adapting a content categorization which was developed by Burgoon, Burgoon and Wilkinson.[19] The categories are government, sensational, business, science/technology, and popular. The government category refers to stories about the normal workings of a government, the executives, legislators and judges.

The sensational news category includes four subcategories (natural disasters, accidents, crime, and military/war). The first three were based on the Burgoon, Burgoon and Wilkinson scheme. The military/war subcategory was added as a result of a pilot test. This is a very broad category which includes high profile type events usually involving life and death situations such as earthquakes, famine, terrorist attacks, leaks of poison gas and the like.

The business category includes stories about particular industries or businesses and consumer issues. The category of science/technology includes four subcategories: energy, conservation/environment, health or other.

The popular category in essence is a measure of the soft or feature-type news that cannot be included in any of the already discussed categories. Popular stories were coded as being included in one of three subcategories: people features, entertainment/culture and sports.

Multiple assignment of stories to categories was permitted. For example, a story about the United States President meeting with French business executives who were going to develop a new communication satellite would be coded as having important features in three story categories: International/national (West), Business (industry) and Science/technology (other). A composite week of the front pages of each newspaper from 1920 and 1980 were constructed for a pilot test of categories.

For the actual study, 10 randomly selected weekdays were chosen from each of the following years: 1913, 1933, 1963, and 1983. These four years were chosen because they did not include major wars or national election activity in the United States. For each week, the front pages of the five weekday editions were coded thus yielding a sample of 320 front pages.

Coders were graduate and undergraduate students at Florida State University. Ten percent of the entire sample was coded twice to test intercoder reliability. Scott's pi coefficients ranged from .79 to .97.

RESULTS

Of the 3,469 front page stories identified, 1,515 stories (43.7%) were international in focus. The range of international news focus among the eight newspapers was quite large. The *Miami Herald* gave only 21.3 percent of its front page newshole to international news while the *Los Angeles Times* gave 72.9 percent.

Within the total set of 1,515 international news stories, 1,100 (73.6%) featured the West exclusively, 113 (7.5%) featured the Third World only, and 42 (2.8%) featured the East only. The remaining 260 stories were coded as having a dual focus: 156 were West-Third; 73, West-East; and 31, East-Third. Because of the dual or multi focus of many stories, the coding units displayed in Table 1 will sum to a figure greater than the total number of stories. While the proportion of stories which feature the Third World exclusively is low (7.5%), when all stories about the Third World are added together, the proportion of international stories referring to the Third World increases to 20.6 percent.

The *Miami Herald* displayed the highest percentage of Third World coverage with 54.9 percent of its

Table I   COMPARISON OF WEST, EAST, AND THIRD WORLD COVERAGE IN EIGHT PRESTIGE U.S. DAILY NEWSPAPERS, IN PERCENT

Newspaper	Third World		West		East		Number of Stories	N
	Single	Dual	Single	Dual	Single	Dual		
Miami *Herald*	22.1[a]	32.8	39.3	34.4	1.6	6.6	21.3[b]	122
New York *Times*	12.8	35.4	47.4	33.1	5.7	10.3	31.2	175
Christian Sci. *Monitor*	10.6	15.3	60.0	24.1	2.4	14.7	37.6	170
Washington *Post*	10.8	8.2	71.4	11.3	5.6	4.8	52.4	231
St. Louis *Post-Dispatch*	1.5	10.9	75.2	16.3	3.0	13.4	47.9	202
Atlanta *Constitution*	3.3	7.1	83.6	7.1	2.2	3.6	51.5	183
Los Angeles *Times*	5.0	1.8	87.8	4.7	2.2	3.6	72.9	278
Chicago *Tribune*	2.6	3.2	81.2	10.4	5.2	8.4	51.7	154
Total coding units	119	192	1072	242	57	124	1806	1806
	7.9%	12.7%	70.8%	16.0%	3.8%	8.2%		

Chi Square = 328.81 with 35 degrees of freedom, p < .001

[a]Percentages in the cells indicate the proportion of a newspaper's total stories which were coded as belonging in that column. Their sum across the row will total to a figure higher than 100% because of the multiple coding of stories.

[b]Percentages in this column refer to the proportion of international news stories relative to a newspaper's total number of front page stories.

122 stories in this category. The *New York Times* had the largest number of stories in this category, but since it also had the largest number of coding units, it was ranked second behind the *Miami Herald* in percentage, with 48.2 percent of its coding units referring to the Third World. The *Chicago Tribune* (5.4%), *Los Angeles Times* (6.8%), *Atlanta Constitution* (10.4%), and *St. Louis Post-Dispatch* (12.4%) were substantially under the median in quantity of Third World coverage.

There is a strong negative relationship between the proportion of news space devoted to international news and the proportion of international news space devoted to Third World countries. The newspapers with the smallest proportion of international news are much more likely to use that small space for Third World coverage. Newspapers with much larger international news space present a much smaller proportion of Third World news in that space.

For example, the *Miami Herald, New York Times*, and *Christian Science Monitor* displayed a total of 1,572 news stories; only 467 (29.7%) of these stories were categorized as international news. Within this group of 467 international news stories, 195 (41.8%) have a Third World focus. In contrast, the *Los Angeles Times, Chicago Tribune*, and *Atlanta Constitution* displayed a total of 1,034 news stories; 615 (59.5%) of these stories were categorized as international news.

Within this group of 615 international news stories, only 47 (7.6%) have a Third World focus. Therefore, newspapers with a relatively large international news hole are much less likely to use that space to present Third World stories, as measured both in absolute number of stories and in proportions of news stories.

The trend in the number of international stories on the front pages of the sample exhibits a curvilinear pattern with the highest numbers of stories in 1933 and 1963 and much lower numbers in 1913 and 1983 (see Table 2). The curvilinear shape of this relationship appears to be influenced by two separate trends. First, the *absolute* number of stories on

Table 2   COMPARISON OF CHANGES IN WORLD NEWS COVERAGE, IN PERCENT

Year	Third World		West		East		Number of Stories
	Single	*Dual*	*Single*	*Dual*	*Single*	*Dual*	
1983	16.6%[a]	24.3	50.6	25.9	6.2	7.7	259
1963	6.3	18.2	64.7	21.2	3.9	12.4	411
1933	5.7	4.3	80.9	9.0	3.7	6.6	512
1913	6.3	9.6	78.4	12.6	1.8	5.7	333
Total coding units	119	192	1072	242	57	124	1806

Chi Square = 143.54 with 20 degrees of freedom, p < .000
[a]Percentages in the cells indicate the proportion of a newspaper's total stories which were coded as belonging in that column. Their sum across the row will total to a figure higher than 100% because of the multiple coding of stories.

the front pages of these newspapers has been declining. In 1913, there were a total of 1,069 front page stories; in 1933 there were 1,163, then there was a drop to 744 in 1963 and 493 in 1983.

Over the same period, there has been an increase in the *proportion* of international stories on the front page. In 1913 only 33.9 percent of the front page stories were international news; in 1933 it increased, to 45.7 percent; in 1963, 57.4 percent; and 1983, 55.4 percent.

Within the set of front page international stories, there has been an increase in the proportion focusing on the Third World. In 1913, only 15.9 percent of international stories were Third World related, and in 1933 only 10 percent were. But by 1963, 24.5 percent of stories were Third World related and by 1983, 40.9 percent were. The proportion of Western stories indicates a slight decline during that period; 1913, 91.0 percent; 1933, 89.9 percent; 1963, 85.9 percent; and 1983, 76.4 percent. It is interesting to note that the number of stories about Eastern countries has remained low. In 1913, only 7.5 percent of stories were about the East. In 1933, it was 10.3 percent; 1963, 16.3 percent; and 1983, 13.9 percent.

The qualitative balance among story types which is shown in Table 3 indicates support for the hypothesis that Third World coverage is skewed to the sensational. More than half of all Third World coverage (57.4%) was categorized as belonging to one

of the sensational subcategories, with crime being the most frequently coded subcategory. In contrast, only about one-third of the coverage of the West was categorized as sensational. The most coded category of Western news was government, which received 36.0 percent of all coding units to the Third World category's 23.4 percent. Another point of contrast is the business category. About 14.2 percent of Western news was in this category while only 5.8 percent of the Third World news was. The news about the East followed a pattern much closer to the Third World balance than the West: sensational, 51.9 percent; government, 30.7 percent and business, 5.5 percent.

DISCUSSION

In this study, the proportion of international news was about 44 percent, which is very close to the 47 percent median reported by Todd[20] in his analysis of front page news.

While the literature provides a range of 15 percent to 59 percent of international news being Third World coverage, in this study the proportion was found to be very close to the lower limit of this range at 20.5 percent; but this figure reflects an average over four time periods. Until 1933, the percentage of stories referring to a Third World country was between 10 percent and 16 percent, but by 1963 it

Table 3   ANALYSIS OF THIRD WORLD, WEST AND EAST STORIES BY TYPE OF STORY

Story Type	Third World Single	Third World Dual	West Single	West Dual	East Single	East Dual	Coding Units
Government							
Executive	30	35	283	44	10	21	373
Legislative	3	10	145	15	1	5	164
Judicial	1	1	61	10	5	9	77
Exec.-Jud.	3	2	46	5	1	3	55
	85[a](23.4%)[b]		609 (36.0%)		55 (50.7%)		
Sensational							
Nat. Disaster	4	1	14	1	0	0	19
Crime	43	126	204	138	22	52	427
Military/War	15	13	122	26	3	13	166
Accidents	2	5	56	6	1	3	66
	209 (57.4%)		567 (33.5%)		94 (51.9%)		
Popular							
People Feat.	7	10	109	9	1	5	129
Ent/Culture	8	2	40	5	2	3	55
Sports	0	0	3	0	1	0	4
	27 (7.4%)		166 (9.8%)		12 (6.6%)		
Science/Technology							
Health	8	2	21	2	1	0	32
Cons/Environ.	0	2	17	1	0	1	19
Energy	0	0	5	0	0	0	5
Other	4	6	58	5	3	5	73
	22 (6.0%)		109 (6.4%)		10 (5.5%)		
Business							
Industries	5	10	195	14	1	6	216
Consumers	4	2	25	7	0	3	34
	21 (5.8%)		241 (14.2%)		10 (5.5%)		

[a]Total number of coding units in the block of sub-categories above.
[b]Percentage of coding units in the block above compared to total number of stories in the category.

had grown to almost 25 percent and by 1983 it was over 40 percent of all front page stories. This trend would indicate that in the 1970s the proportion of Third World coverage would be as high as 36 percent to 40 percent as Riffe and Shaw[21] report, even though the average over the 70-year span is as low as 20.5 percent.

The growth in Third World news coverage on the front page of prestige newspapers is exhibited both in stories exclusively about a Third World country, and in the number of stories about a Third World country in conjunction with a country from one of the other two categories. While Third World news coverage has increased proportionately, Western coverage has declined from about 90 percent of stories in 1913 to 76 percent in 1983.

An unexpected finding in this study was the very low proportion of news coverage of Eastern countries. Only about one story in eight referred to an Eastern country, and Eastern coverage has been relatively static at a low level. So while Third World coverage may be slighted as critics contend, Eastern countries are being ignored even more. Should the news value of Eastern coverage be less than the news value of Third World countries? It will be interesting to monitor the proportions into the future to determine if Third World coverage will continue to grow and if the proportion of coverage of Eastern countries will continue at a relatively low level.

One must be careful when comparing the number of Third World stories across time periods, because the number of stories on the front page has declined dramatically since 1933. During that time the number of international stories and the number of Third World stories has also declined. However, the *percentage* of stories which are international in focus and which feature the Third World countries has increased, especially since 1963.

While the quantitative analysis of news stories reveals an imbalance in news coverage, the qualitative analysis which focuses on the differences in the type of news story, indicates a different kind of imbalance. The pattern of Western news coverage shows an important focus on both government and sensational topics and a fair emphasis on business. However, Third World and Eastern news coverage (which share a similar pattern) is much more likely to be sensational. With Third World news coverage, sensational stories are more than twice as prevalent than are government stories. In fact, with Third World news coverage, the number of stories about crime were as prevalent as stories about government, business and science/technology combined.

In summary, the proportion of international news coverage is fairly large, especially considering the journalistic criterion of proximity. The prestige American press devotes about 44 percent of the newshole to international news with the remaining 56 percent split among regional, state and local coverage.

The proportion of Third World coverage is growing (especially in the past few decades) at the expense of Western news coverage. Coverage of the East remains at a low level. The differences in type of coverage may be even more significant than the differences in quantity. News coverage about the Third World and the East (when it appears) is much more likely to be sensational in nature, while the coverage of Western events is more likely to display a balance between government stories and sensational stories.

NOTES

1. Herbert I. Schiller, "Decolonization of Information: Efforts Toward a New Information Order," *Latin American Perspective* 5:35–48 (1978).
2. James Hart, "The Flow of News Between the United States and Canada," *Journalism Quarterly*, 40:70–74 (1963); James Hart, "Foreign News in U.S. and English Daily Newspapers: A Comparison," *Journalism Quarterly*, 43:443–449 (1966); Ibrahim Abu Lughod, "International News in the Arabic Press: A Comparative Content Analysis," *Public Opinion Quarterly*, 26:600–611 (1962); James W. Markham, "Foreign News in the United States and South American Press," *Public Opinion Quarterly*, 25:249–262 (1961).
3. Scott M. Cutlip, "Content and Flow of AP News—From Trunk to TTS to Reader," *Journalism Quarterly*, 31:434–446 (1954).
4. George Gerbner and George Marvanyi, "The Many World's of the World's Press," *Journal of Communication*, Winter, 1977, pp. 52–66.
5. Rusty Todd, "The New York *Times* Advisories and National/International News Selection," *Journalism Quarterly*, 60:705–708 (1983).
6. Schiller, loc. cit.
7. Mustapha Masmoudi, "The New World Information Order," in Jim Richstad and Michael H. Anderson, eds., *Crisis in International News* (New York: Columbia University Press, 1981).
8. Andrew K. Semmel, "Foreign News in Four U.S. Elite Dailies: Some Comparisons," *Journalism Quarterly*, 53:732–736 (1976).
9. *Ibid.*, p. 736.
10. Fernando Reyes Matta, "The Latin American Concept of News," *Journal of Communication*, Spring 1979, pp. 164–171.
11. David H. Weaver and G.C. Wilhoit, "Foreign News Coverage on Two U.S. Wire Services," *Journal of Communication*, Spring 1981, pp. 55–63.
12. S. M. Mazharul Haque "Is U.S. Coverage of News in Third World Imbalanced?" *Journalism Quarterly*, 60:521–524 (1983).
13. Daniel Riffe and Eugene F. Shaw, "Conflict and

Consonance: Coverage of Third World in Two U.S. Papers," *Journalism Quarterly*, 59:617–626 (1982).

14. Al Hester, "Theoretical Considerations in Predicting Volume and Direction of International Information Flow," *Gazette*, 19:238–247 (1983); K.K. Hur, "A Critical Analysis of International News Flow Research," *Critical Studies in Mass Communication*, 1:365–378 (1984).

15. Weaver and Wilhoit, loc. cit.

16. Ibid., p. 63 see also Peter Golding and Phillip Elliot, "Mass Communication and Social Change: The Imagery of Development and Development of Imagery," in E. de Kadt and G. Williams, eds., *Sociology and Development* (London: Tavistock, 1974); John A. Lent, "Foreign News in the American Media," *Journal of Communication*, Winter 1977, pp. 46–51; Riffe and Shaw, loc. cit.

17. Semmel, loc. cit.

18. Guido H. Stempel III, and J.W. Windhauser, "The Prestige Press Revisited: Coverage of the 1980 Presidential Campaign," *Journalism Quarterly*, 61:49–55 (1984).

19. Judee K. Burgoon, Michael Burgoon, and Miriam Wilkinson, "Dimensions of Content Readership in 10 Newspaper Markets," *Journalism Quarterly*, 60:74–80 (1984).

20. Todd, loc. cit.

21. Riffe and Shaw, loc. cit.

PART

3 INTERNATIONAL PROBLEMS

With roughly 70 percent of the 159 members of the United Nations considering themselves in the Third World, it is easy to see why the problems of the Third World loom so large among the concerns of mass communication scholars. A very large proportion of published research in the field of international communication in recent years has had to do with the Third World in one way or another.

One set of topics, which we have labeled "Global Impact," focuses on the powerful cultural, economic, political, and psychological influences that the media of dominant nations—especially the United States—exert over developing nations in various stages of advancement. Jeremy Tunstall, in *The Media Are American* (1977, p. 273), concludes that "the more media each country has the more each bit of the media must compete, the more each country must either import or imitate competitive American practices." And the result is that "the world, by adopting American media formats, has in practice become hooked on American-style media whether these are home-made or imported" (p. 18).

Other countries have begun to develop excellent entertainment fare of their own domestically, but much of it is patterned after the American model. The question that intrigues international communication researchers is the extent to which this may lead to a global melting pot, and, normatively, whether this is at all desirable. What are the pros and cons of ethnic distinctiveness in the global village?

Activists in the Third World have a ready answer. They press aggressively for recognition of the uniqueness of the often artificial entity that comprises their individual nation states. Through the United Nations Educational, Scientific and Cultural Organization, in which they are overwhelmingly represented (at least numerically), they have pushed for a new world information and communication order that brings both political and cultural recognition to each and every member state. What they want is access to modern communication technology. They complain of being slighted by Western media both by being completely ignored most of the time and by being noticed only when disaster strikes or when they are involved in some negative news. They resent multinational companies that are interested in them only to the extent that they can be exploited either as a market for foreign products (including news and entertainment), or as a source of materials (including news and entertainment) that can be profitably sold to wealthier countries.

It has been suggested that the New World Information Order (NIWO)—a product of UNESCO—is no longer of current interest to the communication scholar. This is patently incorrect, as witness the many articles on the subject that are still appearing in professional journals. But even if American researchers have moved on to greener pastures, NWIO is still a passionate topic of debate in the Third World.

Equally important to that area is the problem of using the mass media to promote national development. A developing country cannot afford the luxury of phatic communication—a term that anthropologist Bronislaw Malinowski invented to denote communication without substance, like asking "How are you today?" The mass media must be harnessed to help in national development. To the extent that they are not fostering national development, a large proportion of the content of the mass media should report on the development of the nation, termed developmental communication by some.

Much of the literature of development and developmental communication stems from the Third World itself. Most of it is normative rather than empirical although some excellent work has been done.

7 IMPACT OF GLOBAL COMMUNICATIONS

The Bible says that after the flood that destroyed the people living on earth at the time of Noah, each of his sons (Shem, Ham and Japheth) had descendants who formed "the nations . . . in the earth." The Bible goes on to say that "the whole earth was of one language, and of one speech." But they decided they would build a tower reaching into heaven, which God was opposed to. So "the Lord said, Behold, the people is one, and they have all one language; . . . and now nothing will be restrained from them." And God said, "let us go down, and there confound their language, that they may not understand one another's speech." (Genesis chap. 11) This is the story of the tower of Babel.

International communications appears to be reversing the scattering of people. It is creating what has been referred to as the "global village." What is turning the world into a huge melting pot is the homogenizing effect of exposure to similar experiences. These experiences stem from exponential increases in travel and tourism (probably around 400 million people travel abroad each year at this time of writing); the dependence of world media on a limited number (five, to be exact) of international wire services, so that a growing number of people are exposed to the same news, in the same format; the cloning of the world's entertainment by television, videocassettes, and the motion picture industry; and, probably most importantly, the standardization of our everyday lives by the international mass marketing of industrial goods and services.

And although we kick and scream at being dumped into this melting pot, we also inveigh against any effort to deprive us of the artifacts that modernize our neighbor's lives. As people, we hate to give up our ethnic, national, tribal, or community identities that set us apart from our neighbor, but we covet every convenience that our neighbor has—the modern technology that will ultimately turn us into clones of one another.

FROM "MODERNIZATION" TO CULTURAL DEPENDENCE: MASS COMMUNICATION STUDIES AND THE THIRD WORLD

John Sinclair

This article by an Australian scholar traces the development of communication research on the global impact of mass media over the past 40 years. It looks especially at the impact of modern technology on communication models.

The image of the television aerial reaching up from the roof of a stark hovel somewhere in the 'Third World' is already becoming a contemporary cliche. But while it stands as a clear symbol of the far-flung penetration of the world achieved by mass media in recent decades, the real meaning and consequences of that penetration are far from understood. This article outlines how social scientists' approaches to understanding the process or their 'paradigms' have made important shifts in response to world events, and provides a guide to the literature through which these shifts may be traced.

MODERNIZATION

In the 1950s and 1960s, it all seemed quite simple—mass media were seen as the means of diffusing technological 'progress' from the West and for breaking down the 'backward' and 'traditional' structures and attitudes which were holding up 'development' or 'modernization'. This was the view institutionalized in academic research and teaching and adopted in actual policies of communication and economic development by Western countries, Third World countries and UNESCO alike. Daniel Lerner's studies in the Middle East focussed on psychological changes in the modernized individual (Lerner, 1958), Everett Rogers concerned himself with psychological responses to the diffusion of

technological innovations (Rogers, 1969), and Wilbur Schramm urged the adoption of Western media systems in Third World countries in a book (Schramm, 1964) widely influential in those countries and distributed under US and UNESCO sponsorship (Tunstall, 1977, ch 12).

In this way academic work contributed to the actual spread and growth of media systems in Third World countries and also established the Western model of theory and research in the field. However the failure of the media to bring about the instant modernization which this paradigm promised, compounded with the more general failure of 'economic development' policies over the so-called 'Development Decade' of the 1960s, led to critical re-evaluations in every quarter of the media's relation to economic development. By 1976, even Everett Rogers had to acknowledge that the 'dominant paradigm' of development/modernization has 'passed' (Rogers, 1976). In fact it still survives in a greatly modified form, as in a fairly recent study by Katz and Wedell which is still concerned with 'the problems of harnessing broadcasting to national development' (Katz and Wedell, 1978, p vi).

DEPENDENCY

It is significant that whilst the major figures of the modernization approach had come from the eco-

John Sinclair, "From 'Modernization' to Cultural Dependence: Mass Communication Studies and the Third World." *Media Information Australia*, Number 23, February 1982, pp. 12–18. Reprinted by permission.

The author is Senior Lecturer in Sociology at Footscray Institute of Technology, currently on leave in the Sociology Department at La Trobe University.

nomically, politically and culturally dominant USA, the first attempts to challenge their perspective and its real consequences in media development were from the Third World, and particularly the region upon which 'modernization' policies had had most effect, namely Latin America. This challenge can be seen as part of a broader movement amongst Latin American academics during the 1960s which sought to account for the increased social inequality, national indebtedness, technological dependency and economic domination by rapidly expanding transnational corporations, to which economic 'development' policies had led. It was in this context that 'dependency theory' arose, a theory focussed upon the historical emergence of an unequal world system which served as the framework for understanding these problems (O'Brien, 1975). In a similar way Latin American communication researchers began to analyze the nature and perceived effects in their region of the rapid spread of mass media, particularly commercial television, as a foreign cultural influence grounded in economic and political domination. A corresponding awareness grew of the need to free themselves of the model of analysis provided by US social science (Corradi, 1971).

The earliest studies within this new approach were conducted in Venezuela in the 1960s and Chile during the Allende years (1970–1973). By the early 1970s however, the modernization paradigm also came to be challenged in the UK and USA as a result of different developments, and many fine Latin American works never became available to English speakers. A notable exception is the pioneering *How to Read Donald Duck*, an analysis of the imperialist ideology found in the Walt Disney comics widely distributed in Latin America (Dorfman and Mattelart, 1975).

The Venezuelan studies included critical content analyses of violence and fatalistic ideology in television programs, especially in the *telenovela*, the popular Latin American genre based originally on US soap operas. A study by Santoro concerning children's perceptions of US 'good guys' in television programs skilfully combined content analysis with audience research of an imaginative kind, while Díaz Rangel made an early study of Western distortion of Third World news. These studies and other are reviewed briefly in English by Luis Ramiro Beltrán, himself an early researcher and bibliogra-

pher in the region (Beltrán, 1978a and 1978b).

In Chile, the election of Allende in 1970 created an intense climate for practical research into the role of mass media and culture generally in the struggle for effective social change. Although the ideas of European structuralism and semiology (the science of signs) were influential, particularly in the work of Veron, and in spite of the contributions made by dependency theory, the study of mass media became a question of political practice based on the concept of the media as an 'Ideological State Apparatus' in the international context of the 'ideological offensive' of 'cultural imperialism'. The most important figure in the communication field to emerge at that stage was Armand Mattelart whose work from the period has recently become available in English (Mattelart, 1980a and 1980b). Mattelart's most recent work, still involved with cultural imperialism, will be considered below.

Political events elsewhere also were changing the nature of communication studies. By the end of the 1960s in the USA, the experience of Vietnam had greatly sharpened both popular and academic awareness of US government policies and corporate activities overseas, and the ideological role played by the mass media in the polarized domestic political situation also came under critical analysis. This scrutiny was soon extended to US government and business involvement specifically in communications overseas, first of all in Herbert Schiller's *Mass Communications and American Empire* (Schiller, 1969). Research groups soon were giving their attention to the documenting of US corporate expansion into the domination of Third World media systems, advertising and markets (Frappier, 1968 and 1969), revealing a structure of US 'cultural imperialism' in the Third World against which the blinkered optimism of the modernization paradigm was thrown into relief and subjected to criticism accordingly.

Alan Wells' *Picture-tube Imperialism?* is an interesting transitional work from this period. While critical of the development/modernization theorists, Wells' critique is conducted in terms of the scholarly conventions of North American social science, thus contrasting with the more polemical but no less empirical style of Schiller. Wells incorporates some of the ideas of the dependency theorists concerning the effects of 'consumerism' upon social inequality and dependent economic organization in Latin

America, and systematically presents data collected by government, industry and progressive sources on the extent to which Latin American broadcasting systems and economies had been brought under US corporate and government control in the previous decade (Wells, 1972).

Such documenting of the activities in the US and abroad of US broadcasting networks, communication transnationals such as ITT and RCA, transnational advertising agencies such as J Walter Thompson and McCann Erikson, consumer goods manufacturing transnationals and US government agencies proceeded into the 1970s. The 'Network Project' produced a series of pamphlets, Schiller's work continued (Schiller, 1973 and 1976) and Barnet and Muller's *Global Reach* gave due attention to the transnationals' 'Control of marketing and the dissemination of ideas' (Barnet and Muller, 1974).

On the theoretical side, dependency theory was becoming known in the US, albeit in an Americanized form (Cardoso, 1977). As in Europe however, most communication theorists were slow to recognize the implications which this basically economic theory held for the study of communication and culture. An important exception is a paper by Evelina Dagnino which interprets dependency theory in the light of European theories of ideology and culture current at the time, notably those of the 'Frankfurt School' and of Althusser. She nevertheless arrives at a dialectic view of 'cultural dependence' which recognizes the active role of both the ruling elites in creating dependence and of the dominated classes in resisting it. This view stands in contrast to the more mechanistic versions of 'cultural imperialism' which assume that Third World countries passively submit to foreign manipulation and control (Dagnino, 1973).

Around the same time in the UK where dependency theorists were also becoming known, particularly A G Frank, communication scholars there too began to challenge the development/modernization paradigm. Philip Elliot and Peter Golding of the Centre for Mass Communication Research at the University of Leicester published a cogent critique backed up with a study of Western dominance of the international flow of news, particularly between Britain and African countries (Elliot and Golding, 1974). Golding subsequently published a more ex-

tended version of the critique of the paradigm, rejecting it on the grounds of its inadequacy to Third World reality and the ahistorical and ethnocentric assumptions of the North American functionalist sociology from which it had grown (Golding, 1974).

'TRANSFER' AND MEDIA IMPERIALISM

At the Institute of Development Studies at Sussex University where international scholars had been working with dependency theory and monitoring the activities of transnational corporations for some time, Rita Cruise O'Brien was developing her studies of 'institutional transfer'. These involved the nature and extent of transnational corporations' control over technology and its 'transfer' to Third World countries, including the transfer of institutional forms and professional practice in broadcasting, and the 'taste transfer' of demand for advertised products and orientation to Western life-styles shown in imported programs. In outlining these transfers, she notes the differences between Third World regions in the patterns of transfer which they have experienced, in particular distinguishing the Latin American commercial model of broadcasting transferred from the US with the BBC and ORTF models adopted in the British and French spheres of influence in Africa (Cruise O'Brien, 1975 and 1979).

For Oliver Boyd-Barrett, the various kinds of transfer could be organized under the general concept of 'media imperialism'. Relating them to the classic theories of imperialism, the four 'modes' of media imperialism were specified by Boyd-Barrett as: the technology of the media system; the set of industrial arrangements, including patterns of ownership and control and the relation of the media to advertising; the professional values and practices of media personnel; and media contents themselves, both information and entertainment (Boyd-Barrett, 1977a). A useful discussion by Golding of the transfer of the ideology of professionalism, especially as it concerns African countries, is published in the same source (Golding, 1977). Boyd-Barrett has also written a unit in the Open University *Study of Culture* series which thoroughly explores for teaching purposes the issues of mass communication in various Third World regions from the point of view of media imperialism (Boyd-Barrett, 1977b).

The question of 'mass imperialism' is also taken up by Jeremy Tunstall in his *The Media are American*, by now a well-known but still indispensable reference for teaching and research as well as a useful starting point for the general reader. Tunstall is critical of 'media imperialism', especially the 'television imperialism thesis' of Schiller and Wells, for although his own work documents the influence which US and British development have had in every region of the world, Tunstall sees the 'tide' as having passed and predicts a proliferation of Third World production centres and new 'hybrid' forms of media content (Tunstall, 1977).

An important European contribution in the early 1970s came from Tapio Varis in Scandinavia, where much academic interest has developed in mass media in the Third World. Based on questionnaire responses by programmers in more than fifty countries, this study documents the structure of programming categories, the percentage and source of imported material, and the directions of the 'international flow' of programming on television, evidencing as one would expect the dominance of the US and Europe (Nordenstreng and Varis, 1974).

This study was supported by UNESCO, and represents an early move in UNESCO's shift away from supporting the 'free flow' doctrine and the development/modernization policies noted earlier and towards the campaign for a 'New International Information Order'. This really began in 1973 when a meeting of the Heads of State of the Non-Aligned Countries declared "the need to reaffirm national cultural identity" in the face of cultural imperialism. The issue of news rather than entertainment was their main concern, the right to a 'balanced' flow of information being seen as instrumental to achieving the 'New International Economic Order' already being pursued by Third World nations, increasingly powerful in the UN. A series of international meetings in this campaign have since been organized by UNESCO. A brief history of the meetings and a resume of the questions involved will be found in a special issue of *Latin American Perspectives* on cultural imperialism (Schiller, 1978). UNESCO is concerned with many aspects of communication and

'new technology', and has in recent years published an annual annotated and indexed bibliography, *List of Documents and Publications in the Field of Mass Communication*. It has sponsored the International Commission for the Study of Communication Problems under Sean MacBride which recently published a major report (UNESCO, 1980), it maintains a working relationship with the International Association for Mass Communication Research, the only truly international organization of professional researchers, and supports a number of documentation centres in various regions of the world.

We have seen how the issue of news has become a major international concern, and how it figures amongst the earliest research in the field of international communication. In addition to the Venezuelan and British studies already noted there is an early US study on news 'flows' (Hester, 1971) and a more recent study of the regional situation in Latin America (Reyes Matta, 1976). An article by Somavia in the last-cited source puts the Third World's case against Western news domination, while a specific study of an international news agency's distortion of events is available from the important independent research centre in Mexico where much of this work has been carried out or reported, the Instituto Latinoamericano de Estudios Transnacionales (ILET) (Reyes Matta, 1974). A brief outline of the development and degree of control held by the world news agencies is provided by Tunstall (Tunstall, 1977, ch1), and a full treatment by Boyd-Barrett has just become available in English (Boyd-Barrett, 1981). The case in defence of the news agencies is made by Righter (Righter, 1978).

TRANSNATIONALS

The monitoring of the activities of transnational corporations which began in the late 1960s has been maintained. A brief outline and bibliography is provided by Varis (Varis, 1976) whilst a comprehensive if fragmentary collection of extracts from pertinent documents and articles on many aspects of transnational communications is *The Corporate Village*, a useful source of teaching (Hamelink, 1977). On specific media, there is Guback's work on the international film industry (Guback, 1974), and Bunce's book on communication transnationals in television (Bunce, 1976). Sauvant has studied the effects of transnationals upon the 'business culture' of nations where they operate, particularly on business education and advertising (Sauvant, 1976). In turn, the monitoring of 'progressive' work of all kinds on many aspects of international communication is maintained by the International Mass Media Research Centre which has now published seven volumes of bibliography (IMMRC, 1972–1980).

The impact of transnational consumer goods manufacturing and transnational advertising upon Third World media systems and economies has attracted increasing attention, as in Fejes' useful outline of the Latin American situation (Fejes, 1980), and a study of the economic effects of 'taste transfer' in Kenya (Langdon, 1975). A general account of the growth and effects of transnationals and their advertising upon Third World dependency will be found in an article published as part of continuing work in ILET in Mexico (Roncagliolo and Janus, 1979).

But by far the most comprehensive, and but for the price, accessible account of transnationals in international communication in Mattelart's *Multinational Corporations and the Control of Culture*. Originally published in French in 1976, this work provides detailed documentation of such trends as the growth of communications transnationals in the electronics and aerospace industries; the 'transnationalization' of book publishing and the supply of educational materials; corporate control of children's and educational television; transnational concentration and diversification in the press and the film/telefilm industry; the nature and extent of overseas expansion by US advertising agencies; and the political role which these agencies increasingly perform (Mattelart, 1970b).

Whereas this work concentrates on empirical detail, Mattelart goes further towards establishing a theoretical framework in another recent publication. Proposing a 'class analysis' of communication, he provides a critical history of communication research in the Third World, and calls for research into the models of 'modernity' which media cultivate, and into the resistance rather than the submission of peoples subject to cultural domination. However,

whilst convincing in his identification of the directions which research should take and stimulating in particular observations and theoretical initiatives, Mattelart does not provide a consistent enough theoretical framework. The book of readings which this essay prefaces contains a number of classic Marxist readings; studies in the historical development of selected media; readings on current industrial developments; articles on new manifestations of cultural imperialism, including some Latin American works not previously translated, and further essays by Mattelart, covering his Chilean experience, the 'geopolitics of paper', and the ideology of the military state in Latin America (Mattelart, 1979a). While the monograph (1979b) is useful for reference, the book of readings is more worthwhile for those interested in theory and teaching.

Mattelart remains committed to the concept of 'cultural imperialism', specifying as examples the most direct and manipulative forms of foreign influence in Third World countries, and seeing it behind 'clandestine fronts' in Europe. Whilst asserting that cultural imperialism 'must be understood as a correlation of forces, a combination of national and international forces', he rejects dependency theory as being unable to account for the specific class character of foreign influence in each country, or to explain the 'State apparatus' character of mass media. At the same time, he insists that his view is not a conspiracy theory (Mattelart, 1980b).

RECENT CRITICS

But for all Mattelart's contribution to the development of a critical awareness of international communications, the concepts of cultural imperialism and its derivative, media imperialism, are under challenge. Again, there is no dispute about the facts of Western dominance of Third World communication but about how they are to be interpreted.

Those who see this dominance as a neutral or even positive influence in the world have shown one of the major weaknesses in the cultural/media imperialism concept, namely the way in which its vagueness and rhetoric render it vulnerable to misinterpretation. A recent study by Lee concerns itself with the international 'flow' of television programs and systems, taking Canada and Taiwan as case studies, but in its theoretical argument rejects both the cultural imperialism view, which Lee takes to be the current paradigm, and the view put by the surviving theorists of the former modernization paradigm. Treating these two views in a simple dichotomy of "neo-Marxist" and "non-Marxist", Lee easily refutes the cultural imperialism view by insisting on the separation of culture as an autonomous order from what he calls 'the political and economic functions of the media'. This deprives the concept of its entire rationale, which is that cultural phenomena are complexly mediated consequences of economic and political structures: Lee's refutation dismisses this as 'reductionism' and easily shows that what remains is untenable (Lee, 1980). An earlier critique by Read runs a similar argument: because foreign media penetration is motivated by economic rather than cultural factors, he says, and because Third World markets are poor, they are not exploited but at worst, neglected (Read, 1976, 78–79, 163–167).

But if the concept of cultural imperialism has these 'non-Marxist' critics, so are there 'neo-Marxist' theorists concerned to rethink the problem of the cultural dimension of foreign domination on a more rigorous basis. This basis is again being found in dependency theory which has been refined over the last decade in a way which now places less emphasis upon the internal consequences of external domination as in Frank's well-known formulation, and is more concerned with the internal dynamics of class structure in the historical development of specific societies, particularly those which are experiencing the contradictions of 'dependent development' (Cardoso, 1977).

MULTIPLE LEVELS

An article which largely defines this new formulation of cultural dependence comes from Raquel Salinas and Leena Paldan in a recent book of readings edited by Nordenstreng and Schiller, a book which in general provides a useful guide to current concerns in the critical understanding of international communication (Salinas and Paldan, 1979). Salinas has elsewhere presented an analysis of culture in dependent societies in relation to the problem of 'national culture' (Salinas, 1978), whilst Paldan has recently written critically of the cultural imperialism approach in Mattelart's work (Paldan, 1980).

Their joint article rejects both cultural imperialism and media imperialism preferring the concept of 'multiple levels of determinancy', that is, the analysis of the mediation of domination by the class system and the state, which dependency theory offers. Their class analysis of dependent societies sees a fundamental division between the 'internationalized sectors' (the local ruling class and its middle-class allies) and the 'marginalized' masses. The cultural incorporation of these groups is seen as both contradictory and incomplete: in particular, they point to a potential clash of interests between media owners and the state, and to the likelihood of resistance by the masses to alien cultural content in media.

This is a dynamic and rigorous line of analysis which promises to do more justice to the complex reality of mass communication in Third World societies than the simple images either of an externally controlled 'cultural imperialism' homogenizing all before it, or of the 'modernization' theorists' view of the media as inducing enthusiasm for the wholesale adoption of Western technology, values and structures.

REFERENCES

Barnet, Richard J and Muller, Ronald E (1974), *Global Reach*, Simon and Schuster, New York.

Beltran, Luis Ramiro, (1978a), 'TV etchings in the minds of Latin Americans: conservatism, materialism and conformism', *Gazette* (Netherlands) XXIV, 1:16–85.

Beltran, Luis Ramiro (1978b), 'Communication and cultural domination: USA–Latin American case'. *Media Asia* 5, 4 183–192.

Boyd-Barrett, Oliver (1977a), 'Media imperialism: towards an international framework for the analysis of media systems', in Curran, J, Gurevitch, M and Woolacott, J (eds) *Mass Communication and Society*. Edward Arnold/Open University Press, London, 116–135.

Boyd-Barrett, Oliver (1977b), 'Mass communications in cross cultural contexts: the case of the Third World' Unit 5 in *The Study of Culture 2*. The Open University, Milton Keynes.

Boyd-Barrett, Oliver (1981), *The International News Agencies*, Constable, London (Original publication in French, 1978?)

Bunce, Richard (1976), *Television in the Corporate Interest*, Praeger, New York.

Cardoso, Fernando Henrique (1977), 'The consumption of dependency theory in the United States'. *Latin American Research Review* XII, 3 7–24.

Corradi, Juan Eugenio (1971), 'Cultural dependence and the sociology of knowledge: the Latin American case'. *International Journal of Contemporary Sociology* 8, 1 35–55.

Cruise O'Brien, Rita (1975), 'Domination and dependence in mass communications: implications for the use of broadcasting in developing countries'. *Institute of Development Studies Bulletin*, 6, 4 85–99.

Cruise O'Brien, Rita (1979), 'Mass communications: social mechanism of incorporation and dependence' in Villamil, J J, (ed), *Transnational Capitalism and National Development*, Harvester, Brighton, Sussex, 129–143.

Dagnino, Evelina (1973), 'Cultural and ideological dependence: building a theoretical framework' in Bonilla, Frank and Girling, Robert, (eds) *Structures of Dependency*. Stanford University, Stanford, 129–143.

Dorfman, Ariel and Mattelart, Armand (1975), *How to Read Donald Duck: Imperialist Ideology in the Disney Comic*. International General, New York. (First published in Spanish in Chile, 1971).

Elliot, Philip and Golding, Peter (1974), 'Mass communication and social change: the imagery of development and the development of imagery' in de Kadt, Emanuel and Williams, J, (eds) *Sociology and Development*. Tavistock, London, 229–254.

Fejes, Fred (1980), 'The growth of multinational advertising agencies in Latin America', *Journal of Communication*, Autumn, 36–49.

Frappier, John (1968), 'US Media Empire/Latin America' *NACLA Newsletter* II, 9, 1–11.

Frappier, John (1969), 'Advertising: Latin America' *NACLA Newsletter* III, 4, 1–11.

Golding, Peter (1974) 'Media role in national development: critique of a theoretical orthodoxy' *Journal of Communication*, Summer, 39–53.

Golding, Peter (1977), 'Media professionalism in the third world: the transfer of an ideology' in Curran, Gurevitch and Wollacot, (eds) *op cit* 291–308.

Guback, Thomas H (1974), 'Film as international business' *Journal of Communication*, 24, 1, 90–101.

Hamelink, Gees (1977), *The Corporate Village*, IDOC International, Rome.

Hester, Al (1971), 'An analysis of news flow from developed and developing nations', *Gazette* (Netherlands) 17, 29–43.

IMMRC, (1972–1980), *Marxism and the Mass Media: Towards a Basic Bibliography* (7 vols) International General, New York and Paris.

Katz, Elihu, and Wedell, George (1978), *Broadcasting in the Third World: Promise and Performance*. Macmillan, London.

Langdon, Steven (1975), 'Multinational corporations, taste transfer and under-development: a case study from Kenya', *Review of African Political Economy*, 2, 12–35.

Lee, Chin Chuan (1980), *Media Imperialism Reconsidered*, Sage, Beverley Hills.

Lerner, Daniel (1958), *The Passing of Traditional Society*, The Free Press, New York.

Mattelart, Armand (1979a), 'For a class analysis of communication' in Mattelart, A and Siegelaub, S (eds), *Communication and Class Struggle*, vol 1 *Capitalism, Imperialism*, International General, New York, 23–70.

Mattelart, Armand (1979b), *Multinational Corporations and the Control of Culture: the Ideological Apparatuses of Imperialism*. Harvester Press, Sussex.

Mattelart, Armand (1980a), *Mass Media, Ideology and the Revolutionary Movement*, Harvester Press, Sussex. (First published in French in Paris, 1974.)

Mattelart, Armand (1980b), 'Cultural imperialism, mass media and class struggle: an interview with Armand Mattelart', *The Insurgent Sociologist* IX, 4, 69–79.

Nordenstreng, Kaarle and Varis, Tapio (1974), *Television Traffic—A One-way Street?* UNESCO, Paris.

O'Brien, Philip J (1975), 'A critique of Latin American theories of dependency' in Oxaal, I, Barnett, T, and Booth, D, (eds) *Beyond the Sociology of Development*. Routledge and Kegan Paul, London, 7–27.

Paldan, Leena (1980), 'Multinational corporations and the control of culture, by A Mattelart' (review) *Media, Culture and Society* 2, 2, 193–198.

Read, William H (1976), *America's Mass Media Merchants*, Johns Hopkins University Press, Baltimore and London.

Reyes Matta, Fernando (1974), 'Latin America, Kissinger and the UPI: errors and omissions despatched from Mexico', mimeograph, Instituto Latinoamericano de Estudios Transnacionales, Mexico (ILET, Apartado 85-025, Mexico 20 D F, Mexico.)

Reyes Matta, Fernando (1976), 'The information bedazzlement of Latin America: a study of world news in the region', *Development Dialogue* (Sweden), 2, 29–42.

Righter, Rosemary (1978), *Whose News?* Deutsch, London.

Roncagliolo, Rafael and Janus, Noreen (1979), 'Advertising, dependency and mass media', *Development Dialogue* (Sweden), 1, 81–97.

Rogers, Everett M (1969), *Modernization Among Peasants: The Impact of Communications*, Holt, Rinehart and Winston, New York.

Rogers, Everett M (1976), 'Communication and development: the passing of the dominant paradigm', *Communication Research* 3, 213–240.

Salinas, Raquel (1978), National culture in peripheral societies: promise or reality. Paper presented to the XI Congress of the International Association for Mass Communication Research, Warsaw.

Salinas, Raquel and Paldan, Leena (1979), 'Culture in the process of dependent development: theoretical perspectives'. In Nordenstreng, Kaarle and Schiller, Herbert I (eds), *National Sovereignty and International Communication*, Ablex, Norwood, New Jersey, 82–98.

Sauvant, Karl P (1976), 'The potential of multinational enterprises as vehicles for the transmission of business culture' in Sauvant, Karl P and Lavipour, F G (eds),

Controlling Multinational Enterprises: Problems, Strategies, Counter-strategies. Wilton House, London, 39–78.

Schiller, Herbert I (1969), *Mass Communications and American Empire*, Kelley, New York.

Schiller, Herbert I (1973), *The Mind Managers*, Beacon Press, Boston.

Schiller, Herbert I (1976), *Communication and Cultural domination*. New York, International Arts and Sciences Press.

Schiller, Herbert I (1978), 'Decolonization of information: efforts toward a New International Order'. *Latin American Perspectives*, 16, 35–48.

Tunstall, Jeremy (1977), *The Media are American: Anglo-American Media in the World*, Constable, London.

UNESCO (1980), *Many Voices, One World*. International Commission for the Study of Human Communication Problems, UNESCO, Paris. ('The MacBride report'.)

Varis, Tapio (1976), 'Aspects of the impact of transnational corporations on communication', *International Social Science Journal* 28, 4, 808–830.

Wells, Alan (1972), *Picture-Tube Imperialism?* Orbis, Maryknoll, New York.

CULTURE CLASH: IMPACT OF U.S. TELEVISION IN KOREA

JONG GEUN KANG AND MICHAEL MORGAN

Viewing American television programs on the American Forces Korean Network has a differential effect on Korean males and females. The authors feel that watching American television may create divisions within a nation among those who want to retain and those who want changes in cultural traditions and values.

Jong Geun Kang and Michael Morgan, "Cultural Clash: Impact of U.S. Television in Korea." *Journalism Quarterly*, Volume 65, Number 2, Summer 1988, pp. 431–438. Reprinted by permission.

Jong Geun Kang is an assistant professor in the Department of Speech communication at Augustana College, Sioux Falls, and Michael Morgan is associate professor in the Department of Communication at the University of Massachusetts/Amherst.

The impact of American television programs on viewers in other countries has been a topic of intense debate among researchers, theorists and policy-makers. But until fairly recently the actual impact of U.S. programs on foreign viewers' cultural values, beliefs and ideologies has been mostly either taken for granted or ignored.[1] A small but growing number of studies, however, have begun to provide empirical evidence about the influence of U.S. television in other countries. In this paper, we attempt to contribute to this debate by exploring relationships between exposure to U.S. programs and conceptions of social reality among college students in Korea.

Conceptually, this study is based on the hypothesis that heavy exposure to television entertainment "cultivates" images and attitudes which reflect television's most stable and repetitive portrayals.[2] As developed by Gerbner and his colleagues, cultivation assumes reciprocal relationships between television exposure and audience conceptions, rather than simple one-way casual processes.[3] It also assumes not that television is the most powerful influence, but potentially the most common.[4] Cultivation analysis has examined television's contributions to viewers' conceptions of a wide variety of topics and issues, but it has rarely been applied outside the U.S.

The Korean context provides an ideal setting for examining cultivation. There are sharp differences between the images portrayed on American programs and traditional Korean values, for example, in terms of "proper" roles of men and women, of family values, and of respect for parents and elders. While many institutions and "Westernizing" social forces may be generating an erosion of traditional Korean values, this study was conducted to see if U.S. television programs make a contribution in this direction. Our goal is thus to shed light both on the cultivation hypothesis and on the debate over U.S. cultural imperialism.

BACKGROUND

Despite an increase in the amount of international program exchange in the past decade,[5] the U.S. remains by far the world's leading exporter of television programs, selling between 100,000 and 200,000 hours of programming to other countries each year. Recent estimates of the revenue from U.S. program sales abroad exceed half a billion dollars, or about 20% of total sales.[6] According to the trade press, international growth in new technologies such as cable and satellites has created a "significant increase in the demand for American TV product," and sales are "thriving."[7]

Schiller,[8] Tunstall,[9] and others have charged that American entertainment augments U.S. economic power and reduces the cultural uniqueness of the importing societies. Chenchabi[10] proposed that such "cultural invasion" increases the frustration of a large majority of the population in Africa, Asia, and elsewhere. In particularly strong terms, Masmoudi[11] condemned American television programs as

> instruments of cultural domination and acculturation, transmitting to the developing countries messages which are harmful to their cultures, contrary to their values, and detrimental to their development aims and efforts.

Others, however, argue that cultural diffusion and the dynamic integration of foreign elements may have their benefits which cultural isolation is an illusion which results in squandered resources.[12] Moreover, Katz, et al.[13] criticize the more dramatic versions of the media imperialism thesis and suggest that such strong claims are overstated.

As noted above, this debate has been characterized largely by anecdotes and measures of "program flow," and by the almost total lack of data about actual effects. The little previous empirical research on the effects of U.S. television programs in other countries that does exist provides contradictory findings.

In an early study in Taiwan, Tsai[14] found that television-viewing children had a more favorable attitude toward elements of American culture and a less favorable attitude toward their own culture than did their non-viewing counterparts. More recently, Weimann[15] surveyed high school and college students in Israel, and found that heavy viewing was strongly associated with a "rosier," idealized perception of "living in America."

Pingree and Hawkins[16] found that for Australian children, amount of exposure to U.S. television programs was correlated with television-biased conceptions of reality about Australia, though not about the U.S. Finally, in the Phillippines, Tan, et al.[17] reported that frequent viewing of American television programs among high school students went with an emphasis on a non-traditional value (pleasure), and with a de-emphasis of some traditional values (salvation, forgiving and wisdom).

On the other hand, research in Iceland[18] concluded that U.S. television has a minimal effect in generating favorable attitudes about the U.S., or in creating attitudes of fear, anger or sadness which Icelanders commonly associate with U.S. culture. And, Sparkes' U.S.-Canadian study[19] found very little (if any) attitudinal differences associated with exposure to foreign news programs. Other conflicting examples from other countries are reported in Melischek, et al.[20]

Some of the discrepancies in these studies may reflect the fact that different dependent variables are employed; some studies examine the influence of American television on images of the U.S., others look at images of the native culture, and still others deal with "traditional" values and beliefs. Furthermore, any effects of U.S. television programs may vary from different types of viewers (for example, in terms of age and education) in different countries. Also, the impact of American television programs should not be expected to be uniform across diverse cultures. All this clearly introduces numerous complicating factors which make it unlikely that any consistent, generalizable effects of American television on importing countries will be found.

KOREAN TELEVISION AND AFKN

Koreans own close to eight million television sets, a penetration rate of 97.5%.[21] The Republic of Korea has 78 television stations. Of these, 51 are connected to the government-run KBS network, and 21 are affiliates of the Munhwa Broadcasting Company, which is partially owned by the Korean government. The remaining six stations are part of the American Forces Korean Network (AFKN), which is run by the U.S. military.

We focus on AFKN in this research because it broadcasts nothing but U.S. programs and because

Korean officials play virtually no role in its programming. AFKN, therefore, provides a relatively "pure" and unrestricted source of non-Korean images and messages.[22] Although AFKN treats American servicemen and their families as its primary audience, its signal reaches the entire nation through a sophisticated cable and microwave system.[23]

Our examination of a typical *AFKN TV Guide* shows that AFKN broadcasts 132 hours weekly, of which 80 hours consists of entertainment programs, such as "The Tonight Show," "Hee Haw," "Three's Company," "M*A*S*H," "The Love Boat," "Dallas," and others. Many young Koreans watch these American programs on AFKN, and journalists and scholars in Korea have increasingly expressed concerns about the possible reduction of Korea's cultural uniqueness from AFKN viewing.[24]

Any possible impact of AFKN must of course be seen in the context of the larger political and cultural climate of Korea. Korea has changed dramatically since the "economic miracle" in the early 1970's, in which it became one of the United States' largest trading partners.[25] Trade with the U.S. has brought on a massive influx of Western culture, exacerbating the American military presence and often heightening conflicts with Korean culture. While the messages of American television programs present clear conflicts with many traditional Korean values, watching AFKN programs is likely to be at most only one small aspect of any larger process of Westernization.

If we accept the assumption that the images and values expressed in AFKN television programs are in conflict with traditional Korean perspectives, then *a priori*, AFKN viewing could show any of several patterns of relationships with Korean viewers' conceptions. First, heavy AFKN viewers could be more likely to endorse Western (and less likely to endorse Korean) views, which would strengthen both the cultivation and cultural imperialism arguments. (Since our data are cross-sectional, this finding would also be consistent with the notion that those who are more Western-oriented choose to watch more AFKN).

Second, there could be no associations at all between AFKN viewing and attitudes, which would weaken both arguments. And a third possibility is that heavy AFKN viewers could be *less* likely to endorse Western (and *more* likely to endorse Korean) views, which would suggest some kind of "boomerang" effect not previously explicated in the literature. (There could also be systematic subgroup variations within any of these possibilities.)

Given the inconsistencies in previous studies, we chose to explore the data to see if they conform to any of these patterns, rather than to test hypotheses in a formal sense.

METHOD

A self-administered questionnaire (in English) was given in April 1984 to 226 Korean college students attending a well-known language institute in Seoul, Korea. College students were chosen because of their accessibility and because they are likely to watch AFKN television programs regularly; most such language institutes use AFKN broadcasts for instructional purposes.

The survey was conducted in classes over a two-week period. Trained instructors were present to answer any questions raised by respondents, although they did not reveal the specific purposes of the study.

The sample is 46% male and 54% female. Most respondents are in their 20s. (A fifth are younger than 20 and a tenth are over 30; the mean age is 24.6 years.) In terms of religion, 40% indicated they were "Christians," 18% Buddhists, 21% Catholics, and 21% "other."

The independent variable in this study is amount of AFKN viewing, and is measured by the question, "On an average day, how many hours do you spend watching AFKN-TV?" By American standards, exposure to AFKN is relatively low; less then 20% reported spending two or more hours viewing AFKN "on an average day." For some analyses, the sample was partitioned at the median, into light (less than an hour daily; 48%) and heavy (an hour or more daily; 52%) AFKN viewers; continuous data were used in partial correlations. Viewing of Korean programs (or of American programs on Korean stations) was not measured.

Dependent variables were derived from a series of statements, such as "It is natural that we should obey our own parents all of the time." Response

categories were five-point Likert scales (from "strongly agree" to "strongly disagree," with "no opinion" as the midpoint). The statements were designed to reflect possible tensions between Western and traditional Korean values in two key cultural areas: marriage and family, and sex-role attitudes. Several other discrete items which did not fit into any neat category were also examined.

Among numerous demographic and control variables, only sex appears to be related to amount of AFKN viewing, with females watching significantly more; 41% of males compared to 62% of females were classified as heavy AFKN viewers (gamma = .40, p<.001). Thus, all analyses were conducted for males and females separately.

RESULTS

The dependent statements attempt to measure whether respondents support what are essentially more "liberal" American perspectives or more "conservative" Korean views. The following analysis examines associations between amount of AFKN viewing and respondents' positions on these statements. If AFKN viewing cultivates conceptions based on images in American programs, then those who watch more AFKN should be less likely to support traditional Korean positions.

To begin with, five items measured students' orientations toward marriage and the family. The items concern filial piety, preference for the Korean or American family system, and attitudes toward traditional "match-making" marriages, unrestricted dating and the importance of discussing dating with parents. The associations between these variables and amount of AFKN viewing are shown in Table 1.

The table shows the percent of light and heavy AFKN viewers who endorse each statement, separately for males and females. Partial correlations controlling for age and religion (a dummy variable representing whether or not the respondent is a Buddhist) are also presented for males and females.[26]

It should be noted that males and females give clearly different responses to these items. Somewhat surprisingly, females are more "progressive" and "liberal" while males are more "traditional" and "conservative." Yet while Korean females overall

Table 1   AMOUNT OF AFKN VIEWING AND ATTITUDES TOWARD MARRIAGE AND FAMILY

	Percent Who Agree with Each Statement by Amount of AFKN Viewing[a]				Partial Correlations[b]	
	Males		Females		Males	Females
	Light	Heavy	Light	Heavy		
It is natural that we should obey our parents all of the time	69	48	53	41	−.18*	−.17*
The Korean family system is better than the American family system	68	81	64	64	.19*	.04
I want a match-making marriage (disagree)	47	55	51	71	.00	.18*
Unrestricted dating is unethical	54	48	70	60	−.08	−.09
People should talk to their parents about dating	54	48	66	55	−.14	−.19*

[a]Light = less than 1 hour of AFKN viewing per day; Heavy = 1 hour or more per day; based on median split
[b]Based on continuous data, and controlling for age and whether respondent is Buddhist
*$p < .05$
**$p < .001$

are sharply and significantly less likely than males to endorse strict adherence to traditional norms about *obeying* parents (46% vs. 72%) and more likely to object to the idea of an arranged marriage (63% vs. 50%), they remain more likely than males to uphold certain "moral" perspectives, such as the belief that unrestricted dating is unethical (64% vs. 51%), or the perceived importance of *discussing* dating with parents (59% vs. 40%).

These baseline differences produce different patterns of association with AFKN viewing for males and females. Compared to males, AFKN viewing is more strongly related to females' perspectives, and in a direction away from the traditional values. Among females, heavy AFKN viewers are less likely to endorse the traditional view on four of the five items, and significantly so (after controls) on three.

Both males and females who watch more AFKN are significantly less likely to uphold the traditional value of filial piety, compared to lighter viewers. At the same time, heavy male AFKN viewers are significantly more likely to agree that the "Korean family system is better" (an item which shows no association at all among females). Inasmuch as ob-

eying parents is arguably a central tenet of the Korean family system, the results for these two items represent an intriguing contradiction: heavy male viewers feel less inclined always to obey their parents yet still prefer the Korean family system.

Thus, while AFKN may cultivate some acceptance of non-traditional values for males, it may also sharpen their opposition to what they perceive to be inadequacies in the American system and their allegiance to the Korean system. While females are clearly more predisposed to breaking with the traditions, greater AFKN viewing seems to intensify those predispositions, but not to the point of explicitly disavowing the Korean family system.

Less pronounced patterns are found in Table 2, which shows the relationship between amount of AFKN viewing and attitudes about sex-roles. Items include "Husbands should do some household chores like cooking, cleaning the house and washing dishes," and "Married women should be able to work outside the home if they want." While these propositions are by no means universally accepted in the United States, they are strongly in opposition to traditional Korean role prescriptions.

Table 2   AMOUNT OF AFKN VIEWING AND SEX-ROLE ATTITUDES

	Percent Who Agree with Each Statement by Amount of AFKN Viewing[a]				Partial Correlations[b]	
	Males		Females			
	Light	Heavy	Light	Heavy	Males	Females
Husbands should do some household chores, like cooking, cleaning the house and dishes	65	74	91	90	.08	.10
Married women should be able to work outside the home if they want	78	79	98	97	.03	.14
Women should share dating expenses	76	86	87	92	.15*	.07
I sympathize with the Women's Movement in Korea	45	52	80	78	.14	.02

[a]Light = less than 1 hour of AFKN viewing per day; Heavy = 1 hour or more per day; based on median split
[b]Based on continuous data, and controlling for age and whether respondent is Buddhist
*p < .05
**p < .001

Overall, those who watch more AFKN-TV are more likely to take more "liberal" positions on these sex-role attitudes, and three of the four items show significant overall associations (data not shown). The within-group analysis, however, shows only weak associations, indicating that sex makes most of these relationships spurious. In other words, females are more "liberal" and watch more AFKN; controlling for sex essentially eliminates the associations.

Baseline differences between males and females are again dramatic. Females are more likely to assert that husbands should do household chores, that married women should be able to work outside the home, and to strongly support the women's movement in Korea.

Males are slightly more likely than females to believe that women should share dating expenses. This belief is positively related to AFKN viewing for males, but this is the only significant association in the table. As a group, females show no associations between these variables and their level of AFKN viewing; their extremely high levels of agreement with these items may have produced a ceiling effect. The relationships for males, while consistently positive (i.e., heavy AFKN viewers are less traditional), are quite weak. In general, the data provide scant evidence that U.S. programs influence Korean students' attitudes about sex-roles.

Relationships between amount of AFKN viewing and several other dependent variables, concerning Western and traditional values and behaviors, are shown in Table 3. The patterns are highly congruent with those observed above for attitudes toward marriage and the family (in Table 1). Compared to males, females are predisposed to think and behave in certain "non-traditional" ways—e.g., to like rock 'n' roll music, to wear jeans, and to be more willing to discount Confucianism—and the more AFKN they watch, the more they agree with Western values.

On the other hand, males who watch more AFKN are more concerned that "Western culture might reduce Korea's cultural uniqueness," even while they are more likely than light viewers to wear jeans—another apparent contradiction. As is the case with their support for the Korean family system (above), exposure to AFKN among males may serve to heighten perceptions of the risks and undesirable consequences of cultural dissipation, rather than me-

Table 3   AMOUNT OF AFKN VIEWING AND OTHER ATTITUDES

	Percent Who Agree with Each Statement by Amount of AFKN Viewing[a]				Partial Correlations[b]	
	Males		Females		Males	Females
	Light	Heavy	Light	Heavy		
I like rock 'n' roll music	52	55	56	74	.03	.21*
I mostly or often wear jeans	8	17	20	40	.15	.33**
Confucianism is an old-fashioned philosophy that should not be important any more	8	7	14	19	.08	.18*
Western culture might reduce Korea's cultural uniqueness	72	88	67	70	.20*	.07

[a]Light = less than 1 hour of AFKN viewing per day; Heavy = 1 hour or more per day; based on median split
[b]Based on continuous data, and controlling for age and whether respondent is Buddhist
*p < .05
**p < .001

chanically generating acceptance of Western culture.

DISCUSSION

What, then, might we conclude about the impact of U.S. television programs on Korean viewers? Above all, there are striking differences for males and females, not only in terms of how much they watch but also in the implications of their viewing.

As a group, the females in the sample are far more likely than the males to endorse non-traditional Korean viewpoints regarding roles, norms, and values. In most cases, females who watch more AFKN are even *more* "liberal," although AFKN viewing makes no difference in the case of sex-role attitudes.

For males, greater AFKN viewing goes with (and may heighten) an intensely protective attitude toward Korean culture. Males who watch more are more likely to favor the Korean over the American family system, and more likely to believe that Western culture might "reduce Korea's cultural uniqueness." It is possible that their relative "conservatism" filters their interpretation of AFKN content in

a way that leads them to perceive U.S. culture as more threatening and dangerous and to increase their attachments to the traditions. At the same time, males who watch more AFKN are more likely to endorse several *non-traditional* Korean norms, such as questioning one's parents or sharing dating expenses. Thus, greater AFKN viewing for males goes with an apparent conflict between having more hostile views toward Westernization yet embracing some of its manifestations.

Of course, no inferences about the direction of causality can be made. It is likely that those students who are more Western-oriented will watch more AFKN in order to learn more about Western ways. This may explain why females, who are more progressive than males (and highly restricted in Korean society), watch more. Indeed, our entire sample—college students who are learning English—can be considered to be unusually Western-oriented, and that in itself may explain the findings, at least for females. It is equally likely, however, that these relationships are reciprocal: certain predispositions may lead females to greater AFKN viewing, but their viewing may in turn consolidate and amplify their support of non-traditional norms and values.

Still, the argument that AFKN viewing is merely symptomatic of Western sympathies does not in any way explain the results for males. Indeed, the results for males suggests an outcome rarely considered by critics of U.S. cultural domination—namely, that exposure to Western images and values can have a "backlash" effect by engendering opposition to the imported culture and raising nationalistic cultural consciousness.

Of course, politicized college students may be more likely than a more general population to manifest this reaction. But if this interpretation is correct, it suggests that AFKN may have helped in some small way to *intensify* the recent violent strife among Korean students, which developed an increasing level of anti-Americanism.[27]

All this suggests that, as in the United States, the contributions of U.S. programs abroad are not likely to be uniform across the population. In fact, support for *all* of the patterns hypothesized above can be found in the data: while some items show no association with AFKN viewing at all, heavy AFKN viewers hold less traditional views on some topics and more traditional views on others, and all of this varies considerably for male and female subgroups. The sharply divergent patterns provide some support for cultivation among females but vividly suggest that "hypodermic" models of cultural imperialism are inadequate.

In sum, within the clear limitations of our sample and our measures, our findings do suggest that American programs may indeed be contributing to the Westernization of traditional cultures, but not always in the manner "intended." Increased nationalism and anti-Americanism—which are quite contrary to the usual assumptions about cultural imperialism—may have profound social, political, and economic consequences; at the same time, a decline in the absolute authority of parents, the sharing of dating expenses, and the wearing of jeans are not necessarily trivial cultural transformations. The point is that the impacts of U.S. programs abroad may be more diverse than we have so far acknowledged. As American television continues to "tighten its grip on the world,"[28] it may unwittingly be contributing to conflicts between those who wish to retain and those who wish to reject diverse cultural traditions and values.

NOTES

1. See Jonathon F. Gunter, *The United States and the Debate on the "World Information Order"* (Washington: Academy for Educational Development, 1979).
2. George Gerbner, Larry Gross, Michael Morgan, and Nancy Signorielli, "The 'Mainstreaming' of America: Violence Profile No. 11," *Journal of Communication*, Summer 1980, pp. 10–29; "Charting the Mainstream: Television's Contributions to Political Orientations," *Journal of Communication*, Spring 1982, pp. 100–127.
3. George Gerbner, Larry Gross, Michael Morgan, and Nancy Signorielli, "Living with Television: The Dynamics of the Cultivation Process," in Jennings Bryant and Dolf Zillman, eds., *Perspectives on Media Effects* (Hillsdale, N.J.: Laurence Erlbaum, 1986).
4. Michael Morgan, "Television and the Erosion of Regional Diversity," *Journal of Broadcasting and Electronic Media*, 30:123–129 (1986).
5. Tapio Varis, "The International Flow of Television Programs," *Journal of Communication*, Winter 1984, pp. 143–152.
6. Peter Caranicas, "American TV Tightens Its Grip on the World," *Channels*, January/February 1984, pp. 27–30; Diane Mermigas, "U.S. TV Industry Seeking Global Production Ties," *Electronic Media*, February 16, 1985, pp. 1, 26.
7. Colby Coates, "World Sales Good Despite Strong Dollar," *Electronic Media*, March 7, 1985, p 12.
8. Herbert Schiller, *Mass Communication and American Empire* (New York: Augustus M. Kelly, 1969); *Communication and Cultural Domination* (White Plains, N.Y.: International Arts and Sciences Press, 1976).
9. Jeremy Tunstall, *The Media are American* (London: Constable, 1977).
10. Rachid Chenchabi, "Media, Culture and Self-reliant Development," *Development*, Winter 1981, pp. 65–73.
11. Mustapha Masmoudi, "The New World Information Order," *Journal of Communication*, Spring 1979, pp. 172–185.
12. Ithiel de Sola Pool, "The Changing Flow of Television," *Journal of Communication*, Spring 1977, pp. 139–149.
13. Elihu Katz, E.G. Wedell, M.J. Pilsworth, and Dov

Shinar, *Broadcasting in The Third World* (Cambridge, Mass.: Harvard University Press, 1976).

14. Michael K. Tsai, "Some Effects of American Television Programs on Children in Formosa," *Journal of Broadcasting*, 14:229–238 (1970).

15. Gabriel Weimann, "Images of Life in America: The Impact of American TV in Israel," *International Journal of Intercultural Relations*, 8:185–197 (1984).

16. Suzanne Pingree and Robert Hawkins, "U.S. Programs on Australian Television: The Cultivation Effect," *Journal of Communication*, Winter 1981, pp. 97–105.

17. Alexis S. Tan, Gerdean K. Tan, and Alma Tan, "American Television in the Philippines: A Test of Cultural Impact," *Journalism Quarterly*, 64:65–72, 144 (1987).

18. D.E. Payne and C.A. Peake, "Cultural Diffusion: The Role of U.S. TV in Iceland, *Journal of Communication*, Summer 1977, pp. 254–261.

19. Vernone Sparkes, "TV Across the Canadian Border: Does It Matter?" *Journal of Communication*, Fall 1977, pp. 40–47.

20. Gabrielle Melischek, Karl Erik Rosengren and James Stappers, eds., *Cultural Indicators: An International Symposium* (Vienna: Austrian Academy of Science, 1984).

21. "Korea," *Electronic Media*, Jan. 10, 1985, p. 49.

22. AFKN is an affiliate of the American Forces Radio and Television Service, and the second largest of five networks managed by the Army Broadcasting Service. AFKN started operating in 1950, the first year of the Korean War, and began television broadcasting in 1957. According to General Robert W. Sennewald, Commander-in-Chief, U.S. Forces Korea, "No one organization in Korea contributes more to the quality of life than AFKN." See American Forces Radio and Television Service, "AFKN Fact Sheet," mimeo (Seoul, Korea, 1983).

23. *Ibid.*; also Jae Won Lee, "Korea," in Marjorie B. Bank and James Johnson, eds., *World Press Encyclopedia: Vol. 1* (New York: Facts on File, 1982).

24. Concerns over the possible effects of AFKN programs have intensified since the Korean government in 1983 approved the connection of AFKN with SATNET, the U.S. Department of Defense Satellite Network. AFKN is now linked to the U.S. via satellite around the clock. SATNET programming comes from the American Forces Radio and Television Service Production Center in Los Angeles; approximately 40% of the AFKN program week is now received in this manner. See "Satellite Network to Expand AFKN Schedule," *The Korea Herald*, Oct. 1, 1983, p. 5.

25. Tom Ashbrook, "Beyond Japan: Asian Economies on the March," *the Boston Globe*, Nov. 6, 1983, pp. 1, 94.

26. For the percentage data, the independent and dependent variables are recoded; they are used in unrecoded, continuous form for the simple and partial correlations.

27. Nicholas D. Kristof, "Anti-Americanism Grows in South Korea," New York *Times*, July 12, 1987, Section 4, p. 3.

28. Caranicas, *op. cit.*

TV ON ICE

Martin Lucas

The author concludes that "the experience of the Inuit (Eskimos in Canada) contradicts the more pessimistic theories about television's cultural effects . . . [raising] hope for other communities—the possibility that the very technologies that seemed poised to complete the destruction of their way of life can be made the tools to reaffirm its validity."

In 1972 the Canadian government launched the world's first commercial domestic television satellite "Anik A." One immediate effect of the first transmissions in 1973 was to make television broadcasts available for the first time to the people who live in the vast area of Canada north of the tree line, whom we call Eskimos and who call themselves Inuit, "the People."

It would not have been surprising if uncontrolled exposure to this powerful colonizing force had finally finished off what indigenous culture remained among the Inuit. Instead the Inuit's readiness not only to watch TV but to make their own seems to be leading to a resurgence of confidence in traditional languages and lifestyles which might have seemed impossible a few years ago.

The Inuit relationship with Europeans began in the late 19th century as they traded first with New England whalers and then with the Hudson Bay Company. Right up to the 1930s the Inuit seemed able to maintain a traditional migrant hunting way of life, but they became precariously dependent on the medicines and guns which they obtained through trading skins and furs. After the second world war, as fur prices collapsed, and faced with rising levels of poverty and disease, the Canadian government elected to concentrate the remaining Inuit in 40 settlements, scattered in a band stretching for over 3,000 miles from the Labrador coast to Alaska and as far north as the 75th parallel. In these tiny communities, provided with heated accommodation and education and health services, the decline of the population reversed and currently the 25,000 Inuit have a birth rate of 32.1 per 1,000—twice the Canadian average and one of the fastest growing in the world.

Despite the dramatic changes in their circumstances, many of the deeper structures of Inuit life seemed untouched. Unlike other native groups in southern Canada and the United States the Inuit were in the majority in their homelands and were largely shielded from intensive contact with southern culture by the sheer distances of trackless tundra and ice which separated them from it and from each other. Even in the late 60s, especially in the eastern arctic, almost all Inuit still spoke Inuktitut as their first or only language. They continued to pass onto their children the rich repertoire of survival skills which enabled them to live comfortably in a climate which commonly touches $-50°$ centigrade during the winter, they continued to live in the densely sociable and supportive extended family groups which were the centers of every day law, custom and belief, and they continued to build their lives around the central principle of unselfish and cheerful cooperation.

But then in 1973, as the Telesat receiving dishes were installed in all but the smallest communities, television arrived. The Inuit took to this new southern import even more enthusiastically than they had in earlier times accepted the rifle, religion and alcohol. To a people brought up in a silent almost

Martin Lucas, "TV on Ice." *New Society*, January 9, 1987, pp. 15–17. Reprinted by permission.

The author is a free-lance writer.

monochromatic world where the senses are tuned to make fine discriminations between colors of ice and levels of windsound, full color TV was a sensual supercharge. Observers noted that in many Inuit households the TV stayed on continuously from the day it arrived. The Inuit quickly adapted their communal lives to their viewing habits, and it often became the job of smaller children, taught English at school, to provide a running translation for the elders.

The Inuit became obsessed in turn with ice hockey, soaps and *Sesame Street*, as it became more imperative to them to absorb the new experience. When VCRs arrived they took to them with the same enthusiasm, and a recent survey of one community shows that 75 percent of households own VCRs. New video titles arrive by plane in the far north at just about the same time and in the same quantity as they hit corner shops in Britain. In the easygoing atmosphere of the Inuit home toddlers will stay up all night with their parents to watch *Alien, Terminator* and other gory favorites.

But as the Inuit have absorbed TV into their everyday lives they have had to absorb other changes. As fur prices have collapsed again following Greenpeace's successful lobbies to the EEC, fewer and fewer Inuit can depend for their income on hunting, once the focal activity of all Inuit life. Each generation of Inuit, as its involvement with government services or mining companies increases, spends more time in the settlements and less on the land than the one before it. Despite 50 percent unemployment levels the Inuit have become increasingly affluent and they are no longer dependent on each other for every service from survival to entertainment. Children spend less time with their parents, use Inuktitut less often, and no longer have that unquestioning respect for elders and their ways on which the transmission of language and culture depends. Many young Inuit are either timid about venturing onto the vast dangerous country which their elders so enjoyed, or foolishly cocksure about their ability to survive in it. They are not impressed by the subtle discords of throat singing or the endless repetitive drum dancing of the elders. In recent years the first Inuit pop groups have begun to appear, and in one or two communities, like creatures from a distant planet, Inuit punks. Increasing numbers of alienated young people have begun to join

the shifting population of Frobisher Bay, the Inuit's main point of contact with white culture, and problems of heroin and cocaine addiction have now been added to the perennial Inuit problem of alcoholism.

Changes like this deeply distress older Inuit, and many feel that TV must be a major factor in their decline. One Inuit leader declared publicly "television has meant that the last refuge of the Inuit, the home, has been invaded by an outside culture," and one of the more conservative communities, Igloolik, refused to accept television broadcasts at all for several years. The Inuit felt bitterly that they were not consulted about the way that television was introduced, nor about its content. But during the seventies the Inuit began to gain political weight. In the stable setting of the new hamlets, the briskly democratic traditions of the family groups extended to create active and vocal lobby groups. In 1975 the Inuit Tapirisat of Canada, one of the most fiercely determined Inuit groups, was set up, and one of its immediate objectives was to get at least part of the television broadcast to the Inuit under their own control.

In 1978 the Canadian government agreed to fund the experimental use of its new Anik B satellite by Inuit in the north west Territories and Quebec. In one project, called "Inukshuk," newly trained Inuit technicians and producers put out 16 half-hour programmes a week for eight months. Many of them involved a complicated tele-conferencing network that allowed Inuit groups, separated by thousands of miles, to meet and talk to each other for the first time. It was a highly successful project, and a real indication to the majority of Inuit that they could take an active role in the broadcasts they received. When government money ran out and the project came to a close, the increasingly self-confident Inuit leaders made new efforts to obtain a regular regional television service.

IBC REFLECTS TRADITIONAL BELIEFS

Since 1983 the IBC, the Inuit Broadcasting Corporation, has been a practical reality—a non-aligned, non-profit making corporation with seven directors elected from Inuit organizations across the arctic. Although most Canadians have never heard of it, it is the most substantial of 13 similar native bodies funded by the Northern Native Broadcasting Access Programme (NNBAP). It employs about 50 staff using 20 lightweight cameras to make five and a half hours of programming a week. The network produces a 30-minute current affairs show twice a week, frequent phone-ins, and even the occasional drama, from its center at Frobisher Bay in the east arctic. Documentaries and cultural programs are produced in four other centers spread across the central arctic. These programs are flown into Frobisher Bay on video cassette and then "up-linked" to a CBC satellite where they are inserted into the schedules coming up from the south and redistributed. All the programs are in Inuktitut and all of them directly reflect traditional Inuit ideas and beliefs.

The IBC operates with a tiny budget, about $1.6 million a year and the programs are produced by a fairly inexperienced and hastily trained Inuit staff who often have to act as cameraman, interviewer, editor and producer in one, and this sometimes shows. To European eyes, some of the current affairs programs seem hastily conceived and edited and of low technical quality, but others, like the lovingly detailed documentaries on making equipment or hunting, could stand comparison with broadcast programs produced anywhere in the world.

Both the IBC and the federal government have commissioned surveys of the impact of IBC programs. The IBC claims that these demonstrate that their programs are welcomed by the Inuit and that they are learning new skills and improving their use of Inuktitut. A more detailed examination of the surveys suggests an almost direct relationship between age, previous use of Inuktitut and a preference for IBC programs. This may reflect older Inuits' continuing obsessions with hunting, the land and the old songs and traditions. All-time favorite programs in 1984, for example, had titles like *Old Places For Walrus, Skin, Rope and Whip, Whale Hunt* and *Marriage The Old Way.*

It has, however, been shown that young people do enjoy the coverage of the community events and music which are typical of life in the settlements, and about three quarters of all the nine to 15 year olds watch at least one hour a week of IBC. Aware of the crucial nature of this section of their audience, the IBC are now pressing ahead with the formation of a children's unit which will present a regular Inuit *Blue Peter* style program aimed at the three to nine year olds. If the resources and staff were available they would try to produce more programs explicitly directed at young people.

But the IBC faces many problems. It is expected to compete with the other highly expensive and professional channels on a budget per hour equivalent to less than a third of that available to the CBC, itself the object of serious government cuts. It has to produce programs of professional quality using inexpensive equipment, which often has to be protected in home-made fur cases in order to cope with almost unbelievably hostile and erratic conditions, which even now kill a number of people each year. One IBC crew were recently isolated by a freak storm for over two weeks, surviving only on a caribou that they were able to shoot. Staffing is a perennial problem and IBC has to draw its staff from a tiny pool of capable young people who may abruptly interrupt their expensive training in Frobisher Bay in order to return permanently to a settlement where they feel at home.

IBC producers have become far more sophisticated, adopting many of the priorities and practices of more conventional broadcasters, but some still resist the kind of objective analysis that we take for granted in British television and they've been criticized for it. It may well be that the Inuit way of looking at the world shapes both the kind of television programs that are made and the way in which they are received. IBC have discovered that their viewers tend to be more concerned about people and their feelings than they are with facts and statistics. Viewers will happily watch long-drawn out interviews which wander freely around the main topic, and if the interviewee is older than the interviewer, his questions will always be deferential and he will never interrupt, whatever the issue.

In cultural and documentary programs, the IBC uses far less rapid editing than conventional European or American producers and this is not just the result of an easygoing approach to production values. The Inuit like to watch real events happen in real time. A famous and favorite IBC program about making rope follows exactly the tortuous process by which the stomach skin of a seal is slowly cut into one long ribbon, stretched and dried. The whole process takes about half an hour, and so does the program.

Some observers are sceptical, believing that the formats of IBC programmes reflect the competence of their makers more than their psychology, but whatever the kind of programs that the Inuit make, the very fact that they exist at all has the major effect of altering their understanding of themselves. In their efforts to preserve the culture they see slipping away, the Inuit have to an extent become anthropologists of themselves, and that new understanding has had to be formalized into language classes, and dance and song schools, as well as radio and TV programs.

It can be argued that there is an inherent flaw in these efforts to use the media artificially to preserve and propagate a culture, and that the IBC is simply turning the traditional life of the Inuit into a television program, ultimately no more relevant to the real life of its Inuit viewers than *Coronation Street* is to viewers in the north of England. Such a pessimistic view, however, ignores that wider context in which IBC operates.

The IBC came into existence as part of a much larger movement in which native minorities in Canada, as in other countries, are struggling to achieve self-determination and self-confidence. The most significant aspect of the IBC's programs is that they are conceived and produced by the Inuit themselves. The culture of television may seem very far removed from traditional Inuit culture, but it is still essentially an oral one and it brings a new authority to the old oral culture.

When IBC producers first approached elders in order to record songs and stories from their childhood, they took a lot of persuading because many believed that these activities had been officially banned by the missionaries. But now, as old crafts and skills have appeared on the IBC screens, so they have proliferated in the settlements. Watching the fabric of their everyday lives, organized into adequate if not glossy TV packages introduced by titles set in Inuktitut syllabics, has helped to weaken for the Inuit the idea that only the whites, with the unrelenting authority of the literate and educated south, can make the final decisions on the value of the Inuit lifestyle.

The IBC, along with CBC's Northern Radio Service which now has an extensive Inuktitut component, has undoubtedly helped to draw together the scattered Canadian Inuit communities into one political and cultural force, and it's generating a new received Inuktitut from the six original dialects. But IBC programs aren't the only ones that are changing the Inuit's attitudes to the rest of the world. The surveys of Inuit viewing patterns show that one of the most popular and frequently viewed programs is *The Journal*, CBC's big budget equivalent of our *Newsnight*. As the Inuit find out more about the rest of the world, they're becoming increasingly aware that they are not alone in facing the problems raised by the impact of rapidly changing technologies generated by other more powerful cultures.

It is easy to assume that a remote and tribal people, whose favorite TV supper is still raw seal meat, must somehow be specially vulnerable to the rash of game shows and cops and robbers serials. But the vicissitudes of *Miami Vice* are as remote to viewers in the home countries as they are to those in the high artic—and no less compelling. The Inuit respond like television viewers everywhere. Their older people worry about sex and violence, the parents want more education and serious programs, and the children apparently approve of everything.

But the Inuit sometimes respond to the programs they view with a directness that reminds the rest of us of the values which they retain and which we sometimes have difficulty recalling. When the Inuit were shown the Ethiopian famine on the TV screens, they reacted as they always have when someone else is in need, by trying to give everything. Whole communities had to be restrained from pledging all their income. They gave a great deal of money and sent an IBC unit to Ethiopia to record how that money was spent and meet local people. Through television the people of two underdeveloped countries were able to make direct and useful contact without the controling mediation of modern urban culture.

The experience of the Inuit contradicts the more pessimistic theories about television's cultural effects. And it raises hope for other communities—the possibility that the very technologies that seemed poised to complete the destruction of their way of life can be made the tools to reaffirm its validity.

IN CANADA'S ARCTIC, JOINING THE GLOBAL VILLAGE

HERBERT H. DENTON

Bringing radio and television to Canada's Eskimos poses problems of communication. Much of what goes on in the world is incomprehensible to people who have never traveled more than 500 miles from the place of their birth. Here news must be recounted in allegories.

YELLOWKNIFE, Northwest Territories, Canada— Radio commentator Allan Adam struggles to interpret for his fellow Chipewyan Indians in their native language the meaning of some of the frequently confusing images they see on television.

The ancient tribes of the Canadian Arctic have come eagerly into the "global village" of the video age, courtesy of new satellite technology that allows them to switch from the news in Edmonton and Vancouver to "Dallas" or Dan Rather with a click of the remote gun.

In large ways not yet fully comprehended, this has wrought profound change among these people, many of whom still return for months on end to the cold, harsh solitude of the northern wilderness to fish, trap, chase moose and caribou and lead a primitive, nomadic existence much the same as that of their ancestors.

In his daily Chipewyan-language program on Canadian Broadcasting Corp. (CBC) radio here, the 29-year-old Adam is attempting to bridge a linguistic and cultural chasm. Among other endeavors, he tries to explain the conflict in the Persian Gulf to scattered societies where one in three persons does not understand English and most have not traveled 500 miles from their place of birth.

There is no word in the native language for Persian Gulf, nor are there names for Iran, Iraq or the Middle East. So Adam must improvise. He locates the Middle East generally by describing it in Chipewyan as "the place where Jesus walked." Discuss-

ing Washington's role in the gulf presents thorny enough problems for his listeners, but he first must locate Washington. The term he uses comes from the description that the Chipewyans gave to the white explorers who came here more than a century ago. Washington is called "the land of the people with the big knives."

Some events defy translation. Bob Rhodes, area manager for CBC radio here, recalls how one of the other native-language broadcasters decided that the way to handle the Air Florida crash in Washington in 1982 was to assure his listeners that the disaster was no cause for alarm.

"You may see big plane crash on television," the radio announcer told them. "Not here. Far, far away to the south. In white man's country."

Slightly fewer than 80,000 persons inhabit the Canadian North, a landscape half the size of the United States. Canadian governments, which have spent millions to bring radio and television to the northern regions, brought radio there in the late 1950s because they wanted to counteract English-language Radio Moscow, which boomed in from the other side of the North Pole, and to reestablish Canadian sovereignty over territory dominated by Americans during World War II. Canadian television came 20 years later.

The major American networks and public broadcasting are arriving now, because of a Canadian government policy known by the shorthand phrase "three plus one." It is a strict commitment to extend

Herbert H. Denton, "In Canada's Arctic, Joining the Global Village." *The Washington Post*. Reprinted by permission.

The author is a *Washington Post* Foreign Service correspondent.

to all Canadians, regardless of their distance from the U.S. border, access to the three American networks plus one public television channel.

Some communities, such as the tiny settlements on the coast of the Beaufort Sea above the Arctic Circle, resisted this cultural invasion for a few years, but in time they also succumbed to the irresistible new kaleidoscope of images that altered their perceptions from the first day.

"That morning they didn't have anything," Rhodes said, remembering the capitulation of the final holdouts in the late 1970s. "By suppertime, they had 16 hours of TV and 24 hours of radio."

Rhodes, his protégé Allan Adam and several others interviewed here falter when asked about the impact of these and other changes.

While television and radio have been the most profound changes, the old cultures also have been affected by factors as diverse as the work of Catholic missionaries, the replacement of the dogsled with the snowmobile and the use of small aircraft to reach distant areas. More recently, the video games in Radio Shack emporiums, the Reeboks and stone-washed denims at the omnipresent Hudson Bay Co.—now more involved with its new role as the mall-style department store of the North than with the traditional and diminishing fur trade—testify to modern inroads.

Nostalgia for the traditional way of life is strongest among the '60s generation of politicians now in power. College-educated, native-born Rita Cli, the chief administrator for the Northwest Territories government in the Mackenzie River town of Fort Simpson, occasionally will escape the ringing phones and other pressures of her job to spend a weekend in "the bush" with her father and brothers.

"You know, you go out there and you have a heck of a good time," she says. "You come back and you feel like you have enough energy to go on for a year. Whatever anger you have when you go out there is left there when you come back."

The chasm confronting the native peoples of the Canadian North is perhaps best illustrated by the most popular programs on radio and television. "Dallas" and "All My Children" are big television draws, according to the informal surveys of CBC executives here. "Bush Radio," which airs from 6 to 8 a.m. and delivers personal messages over transistor radio to peddlers, dog drivers, hunters, canoe-

ists and trappers, is the favorite radio show. Trappers on the tundra, for example, learn about major family events such as the birth of children on "Bush Radio." Vital information such as the times and touchdown locations of airplanes bringing supplies is also aired.

One of the mysteries is just what the native peoples make of what they see on television. "In some of the smallest communities, you can see a satellite dish," noted George Tuccarro, a Cree Indian who is a CBC radio staff producer. "In some Inuit communities [where] they don't speak English, they turn the volume down and watch the image on the screens. I don't know what that does to people's heads."

Many believe the television set serves mostly as a kind of electronic fireplace of pretty, flickering images that—whether sitcom or news footage—are perceived as fiction or myth. A perhaps apocryphal story is told of an elderly Inuit man who erupted in laughter when it was explained that the pictures of the men in spacesuits jumping up and down on a cratered surface were of American astronauts making the first moon landing in 1969. Recovering, the elderly tribesman is said to have dismissed the event as nothing new. The Inuit's shamans had been going up to the moon for ages, he said.

Other responses indicate that people do distinguish the real from the fanciful and that they react with empathy to some of what they see through the prism of their own traditions and values. Rhodes said Inuit reporters have told him that their people crave more interpretation of the events they see on their small screens. He said they told him that the Inuit were very disturbed when they saw women and children suffering or being hurt. That was the meaning for them of the pictures of starvation they saw from the famine in Ethiopia. It is what is important to them in the footage of the chaos and violence in Beirut.

Contact with the outside world has been a jolting experience for the Indians and Eskimos of the North. Even a man as successful in forging a bridge between native culture and the white man's world as the senior CBC native-language broadcaster, Joe Tobie, expresses feelings of ambivalence.

In a long conversation one recent afternoon, Tobie, 55, who is descended from both the Chipewyan and Slavey tribes, mused about his show. As much as he tries to interpret the bigger world, he said he is convinced that community news and the country-and-western songs he intersperses in his commentary are the most popular features on his show. "I used to play Hank Snow," he says, "but the people would say, 'that old music again.'" So, he plays the favorites, Loretta Lynn's "Coal Miner's Daughter" and Lacy J. Dalton's "Sixteenth Avenue."

Tobie considers with a certain aloofness any questions about where he thinks all this will lead. While his younger fellow Chipewyan, Allan Adam, talks enthusiastically about the possibilities for modernizing the Chipewyan language and the other five native languages of the Arctic and sub-Arctic regions of Canada through the six hours of programming each day on CBC radio, Tobie says he looks forward to the time when he can retire, with a pension. Then, he said, at least once a month he can "stay out of the big city" of Yellowknife (population 11,000), go back to the bush where there is "none of this 8 o'clock, on time," routine, and just "mind my own business."

Western influences have produced mixed results for the native peoples of the Canadian North. Better health care has raised life expectancies while education, first by Catholic missionaries and now by the territorial government, has boosted literacy rates. But along with them have come generational conflict between illiterate parents and educated children and an erosion of self-esteem among males as traditional roles are being redefined. Women are speaking out more and voicing their complaints. Boredom, brawling and wife abuse are major problems here, exceeded only by the pervasive scourge of alcoholism.

"The thing is, everything's tumbling so fast you never get ahead of it," Dr. Ross Wheeler, chairman of the Alcohol and Drug Coordinating Council of the Northwest Territories, says not just of the influence of television but also of all the other unsettling changes. "It moves so quickly that in a lot of ways all we've been doing is playing catch-up—catching the people who have fallen off the edge of the cliff."

But there are the success stories. In the 1950s and 1960s, Catholic missionaries here assiduously culled the best and brightest and sent them off to Grandin College in the village of Fort Smith, about 300 miles south. Radicalized by the ultimately abortive plans to lay the Alaskan oil pipeline across their lands, they have emerged as a persuasive and able force.

They were responsible for the planning of the visit of Pope John Paul II in September. On behalf of the natives here, they are negotiating with Canada for self-government. The aspirations, says Fort Simpson Chief Jerry Antoine, are neither to be assimilated or to be rigidly separate from the rest of Canada.

"We as native people can contribute to the mosaic of Canada if the federal government recognizes that," Antoine said. A political rapprochement "will greatly increase the Boy Scout image of Canada," he added.

But the still murky aspirations influenced by television are another factor that the young political leaders will have to deal with. "There's a very strong possibility that we will get swallowed up," says Steve Kakfwi, former president of the Dene Nation, an association of the Indian tribes of the western part of the Northwest Territories.

"That's the danger of the dance," Kakfwi continues. "We may end up at the end of this process as nice, brown white people—just part of the melting pot—or we may end up as a strong Dene Nation which has no problem being part of the larger society but is strong enough to stand on its own."

NEW ZEALAND TV NETWORK SNAPPING UP U.S. TV SHOWS

RICHARD MAHLER

New Zealand has recently added its first privately owned television service—
Network 3. Although there is a quota system that limits the proportion of non-
domestic programs that may be shown, the network plans to buy 45 percent of
its programs from the U.S. and 25 percent from England.

New Zealand TV executives, preparing to face competition for the first time, are buying U.S. TV series and movie packages at a rapid pace.

Spurring the buying spree is the anticipated end of the government TV monopoly in New Zealand early next year.

On March 31, Network 3 is slated to sign on as the first privately owned TV service available to the 1.2 million households (3.4 million viewers) in this South Pacific island nation.

New Zealand has had a government TV monopoly since the medium was introduced there more than 25 years ago.

"They cannot understand competition," Tom Parkinson, Network 3 North chief executive officer, says of the rival state-run TV 1 and TV 2 networks. "But they'll soon learn."

Auckland-based Mr. Parkinson and Network Programing President Kel Geddes were joined here by Trevor Spitz, chief executive of Network 3 South in Christchurch, for the annual May screenings of new prime-time shows.

"We picked up 'Law and Order,' 'Roseanne,' 'Murphy's Law' and 'The Wonder Years,' " Mr. Geddes told *Electronic Media*, "as well as film packages from Paramount, Warner Bros., Fox, Columbia and other studios."

Shows such as "Amen," "Airwolf," "Hunter" and "227" have also been purchased by the new network.

The executives have obtained licensing rights to "60 Minutes" from CBS and will weave New Zealand stories among U.S. and Australian segments. An agreement with England's Channel 4 will provide a steady flow of dramas and documentaries.

Network 3, backed by a large group of prominent New Zealand investors, will offer about 45 percent U.S.-made programing when it signs on, with about 30 percent produced domestically and 25 percent from England and neighboring Australia. The eventual goal is 47 percent domestic fare.

Russell Watkins, president of Russell Watkins International, is the U.S. representative for Network 3, based in Los Angeles. "We're looking for prime-time series, made-for-TV movies and theatrical films," says Mr. Watkins.

Network 3 has also made "a major output deal" with NBC News whereby the two networks will trade news and sports, he adds.

A similar arrangement exists with Australia 7 Network, which will also lease studio and satellite facilities to Network 3 in Sydney and Los Angeles.

Unlike TV 1 and TV 2, the state-owned networks operated by the New Zealand Broadcasting Council, Network 3 will be completely advertiser supported in a structure similar to the United Kingdom's ITV system. Each of four regions has separate ownership and management, although Mr. Geddes serves as overall network program director.

"We want to have a strong mix of U.S. program-

Richard Mahler, "New Zealand TV Network Snapping Up U.S. TV Shows." *Electronic Media*, June 20, 1988. Reprinted by permission.

The author is the Los Angeles bureau chief of *Electronic Media*.

ing and shows from other sources," Mr. Watkins explains.

A quota system will limit the amount of non-domestic fare allowed on Network 3.

The Network 3 consortium is jointly funding a news organization based in a new 75,000-square-foot Auckland studio. Studios in three other regional capitals will turn out children's series, dramas, public affairs programs and farm shows.

Although Network 3 officials won't talk prices, other sources estimate they are spending at least $2,000 per hour for prime-time shows and more than $3,000 for made-for-TV movies. New Zealand license fees have been kept low due to a lack of marketplace competition and are expected to rise quickly.

"The James Bond and Walt Disney movies haven't even been sold (to existing networks) here," noted Mr. Spitz.

The new broadcast TV service will eventually shift from the government-controlled microwave system to fiber optics, allowing Network 3 to introduce cable TV service to the country for the first time.

"We are building a state-of-the-art broadcast sys-tem with digital stereo and all the other bells and whistles," Mr. Geddes says.

Excess capacity on the fiber-optic system will be sold to business users.

Initial terrestrial penetration will be about 80 percent of New Zealand homes, expanding to 98 percent within 10 years. During its first year, Network 3 will broadcast from noon to midnight, adding morning shows in 1992 and 24-hour service in 1994.

The backers expect Network 3 to obtain 10 percent of New Zealand's total media dollars within its first year of operation, or about $163 million. National ad sales are being handled through a centralized office in Auckland headed by Maurice Urlich.

Annual revenues for TV 1 and TV 2, which obtain money from license fees as well as advertising, were not available at press time.

The government networks employ about 2,000 people, compared to 600 employees at Network 3.

Mr. Geddes emphasizes the need to attract the more than 50 percent of New Zealanders who now own videocassette recorders.

"The number of homes using television has dropped to the 40 percent level, and we intend to change that trend," he said.

8 NEW WORLD INFORMATION ORDER

As children, we often were told that "sticks and stones may break my bones but names can never hurt me." But of course we never believed it, since "names" can and do hurt. Third World countries are especially sensitive about whether and how they are portrayed in Western media. They want to be depicted as equals in the world community. If they have problems, they want the problems aired in a balanced fashion, the listing of their positive traits and accomplishments along with their shortcomings.

The West, on the other hand, says that's all well and good, but it's not news. No one wants to read about the cats that did *not* get marooned up a tree. Furthermore, the West does not want anyone to dictate what news to cover, how it should be used, or who may cover it. The West wants both free access to news and the freedom to define what is news. The Third World and the Communist countries say, "What kind of freedom is it, if only the wealthy may decide what is newsworthy or have the means to gather and disseminate the news?"

The New World Information Order was designed to bring order into the "chaos and anarchy" of news gathering and dissemination. Most Western journalists and publishers, however, say they would prefer chaos and anarchy to managed news, since in the free marketplace of ideas, truth will emerge, but if news is managed, it can lead only to propaganda.

THE NEW WORLD INFORMATION ORDER

Mustapha Masmoudi

The case for a change in the international communication and information order is articulately presented by this Tunisian diplomat. He says economic progress is impossible without development in communication technology and in the control of one's own communication system. Developing countries must be self-reliant and self-regulating, according to the author.

Information plays a paramount role in international relations, both as a means of communication between peoples and as an instrument of understanding and knowledge between nations. This role played by information is all the more important and crucial to present-day international relations in that the international community now possesses, thanks to new inventions and major technological breakthroughs, highly sophisticated and very rapid means of communication which make it possible to transmit information almost instantaneously between the different regions of the globe. . . . [However], information in the modern world is characterized by basic imbalances, reflecting the general imbalance that affects the international community. They occur in a wide range of fields, particularly in the political, legal, and technico-financial spheres.

In the political sphere, that is, in respect of the conception of information, these imbalances take many forms:

1. *A flagrant quantitative imbalance between North and South.* This imbalance is created by the disparity between the volume of news and information emanating from the developed world and intended for the developing countries and the volume of the flow in the opposite direction. Almost 80 percent of the world news flow emanates from the major transnational agencies; however, these devote only 20 to 30 percent of news coverage to the developing countries, despite the fact that the latter account for almost three-quarters of mankind. This results in a veritable *de facto* monopoly on the part of the developed countries.

2. *An inequality in information resources.* The five major transnational agencies monopolize between them the essential share of material and hu-

Mustapha Masmoudi, "The New World Information Order." *Journal of Communication*, Volume 29, Number 2, Spring 1979, pp. 172–198. Reprinted by permission.

The author was Tunisia's Secretary of State for Information and is First President of the Intergovernmental Coordinating Council for Information of the Non-Aligned Countries. He is at present Tunisia's Ambassador, Permanent Delegate to UNESCO, and Member of the International Commission for the Study of Communication Problems.

man potential, while almost a third of the developing countries do not yet possess a single national agency. Inequality also exists in the distribution of the radio frequency spectrum between developed and developing countries. The former control nearly 90 percent of the source of the spectrum, while the developing countries have no means of protecting themselves against foreign broadcasts. It is frequently difficult for them to compete, particularly since some of these broadcasts are transmitted from stations located within developing countries. In respect of television, not only do 45 percent of the developing countries have no television of their own, but this disparity is aggravated still further by the broadcasting in these countries of a large number of programs produced in the developed countries.

3. *A de facto hegemony and a will to dominate.* Such hegemony and domination are evident in the marked indifference of the media in the developed countries, particularly in the West, to the problems, concerns, and aspirations of the developing countries. They are founded on financial, industrial, cultural, and technological power and result in most of the developing countries being relegated to the status of mere consumers of information sold as a commodity like any other. They are exercised above all through the control of the information flow, wrested and wielded by the transnational agencies operating without let or hindrance in most developing countries and based in turn on the control of technology, illustrated by the communication systems satellites, which are wholly dominated by the major international consortia.

4. *A lack of information on developing countries.* Current events in the developing countries are reported to the world via the transnational media; at the same time, these countries are kept "informed" of what is happening abroad through the same channels. By transmitting to the developing countries only news processed by them, that is, news which they have filtered, cut, and distorted, the transnational media impose their own way of seeing the world upon the developing countries. . . . Moreover, [they often] present these communities—when indeed they do show interest in them—in the most unfavorable light, stressing crises, strikes, street demonstrations, putsches, etc., or even holding them up to ridicule. If and when the press in the

industrialized countries does present the Third World's problems, achievements, and aspirations in an objective light, it does so in the form of special supplements or issues, for which high rates of payment are charged.

5. *Survival of the colonial era.* The present-day information system enshrines a form of political, economic, and cultural colonialism which is reflected in the often tendentious interpretation of news concerning the developing countries. This consists in highlighting events whose significance, in certain cases, is limited or even non-existent; in collecting isolated facts and presenting them as a "whole"; in setting out facts in such a way that the conclusion to be drawn from them is necessarily favorable to the interests of the transnational system; in amplifying small-scale events so as to arouse justified fears; in keeping silent on situations unfavorable to the interests of the countries of origin of these media. In this way, world events are covered only insofar as it suits the interests of certain societies. . . .

Likewise, information is distorted by reference to moral, cultural, or political values peculiar to certain states, in defiance of the values and concerns of other nations. The criteria governing selection are consciously or unconsciously based on the political and economic interests of the transnational system and of the countries in which this system is established. The use of labels and persuasive epithets and definitions, chosen with the intention of denigrating, should also be stressed.

6. *An alienating influence in the economic, social, and cultural spheres.* In addition to dominating and manipulating the international news flow, the developed countries practice other forms of hegemony over the communications institutions of the Third World. First of all, they have possession of the media through direct investment. Then, there is another form of control, one which today is far more decisive, namely, the near-monopoly on advertising throughout the world exercised by the major advertising agencies, which operate like the media transnationals and which earn their income by serving the interests of the transnational industrial and commercial corporations, which themselves dominate the business world. A further form of domination is represented by the influence used to oppose social

evolution; this is practiced quite openly by the institutions engaging in propaganda. Moreover, advertising, magazines and television programs are today so many instruments of cultural domination and acculturation, transmitting to the developing countries messages which are harmful to their cultures, contrary to their values, and detrimental to their development aims and efforts.

7. *Messages ill-suited to the areas in which they are disseminated.* Even important news may be deliberately neglected by the major media in favor of other information of interest only to public opinion in the country to which the media in question belong. Such news is transmitted to the client countries and is indeed practically imposed on them, despite the fact that readers and listeners in these countries have no interest therein. The major mass media and those who work for them take no account of the real relevance of their messages. Their news coverage is designed to meet the national needs of their countries of origin. They also disregard the impact of their news beyond their own frontiers. They even ignore the important minorities and foreign communities living on their national territory, whose needs in matters of information are different from their own. . . .

All such political and conceptual shortcomings are worsened—when they are not actually justified—by inadequate international legal structures. The present international legal framework is defective and even non-existent in certain fields. Moreover, the application of present-day legislation is arbitrary. It favors a small number of countries at the expense of the majority, thanks to a conception of liberty peculiar to those who own or control the communication media and who are frequently the very same people who own or control the means of production. In this context, questions need to be raised on many issues:

1. *Individual rights and community rights.* The philosophy which has prevailed to date has given prominence to the rights of a small number of persons or bodies specializing in this field. As a result, the rights and concerns of groups have been more or less disregarded. Yet, if it is true that the right to information is intrinsic to the human condition, it is nonetheless a natural right of every human community, in the sense that each people feels an overpow-

ering urge to communicate with "the other," not only in order to come to terms with and to preserve its own personality but also in order to know and understand other peoples better; and so, through the communication channels established in this way, to create conditions likely to foster a climate of mutual understanding and respect, and cooperative relations that will be beneficial to all.

2. *Freedom of information or freedom to inform.* Freedom of information is presented as the corollary of freedom of opinion and freedom of expression, but was in fact conceived as the "freedom of the informing agent." As a result, it has become an instrument of domination in the hands of those who control the media. In legal terms, it has resulted in the enshrining of the rights of the communicator, while disregarding his duties and responsibilities owards those to whom he is communicating.

3. *Right of access to information sources.* This right is understood in a one-sided manner, and essentially benefits those who have the resources to obtain and impart information. This *de facto* situation has allowed certain major transnational corporations to turn this right into a prerogative, and enabled the wealthy powers to establish their domination over the information channels.

4. *The ineffectiveness of the right of correction.* In contrast to the domestic law of certain countries, the right of correction is regulated very ineffectively by international law. With the exception of the convention of 1952, no valid means exist of enabling states to have false or inaccurate information concerning them corrected. Moreover, the 1952 convention is itself not very effective (cf. Articles 3 and 4). Regulations in this area are in fact restrictive and unfavorable to developing countries.

5. *The absence of an international deontology and the defective character of the regulations governing the profession.* In this context, the imbalance is also fostered by the absence of an international deontology. Attempts made to date by UNESCO and the United Nations to institute an international code of ethics suited to the needs of the individual and the community have proved ineffectual.

6. *Imbalance in the field of copyright.* Matters of copyright have long been regulated by the Berne Convention of 1886, which is protectionist in its scope of application, in the duration of the validity

of copyright, and in the fewness of the waivers that may be applied to these provisions. The Universal Convention of 1952, revised in 1971 and administered by UNESCO, provides for a less rigorous degree of protection. As regards the Florence convention, because of the protectionist effects which it may generate while at the same time fostering the circulation of intellectual works from the industrialized countries to developing countries, it has benefitted the latter not at all. Altogether, the international publishing and distribution system operating today has led, on pretext of protecting copyright, to the predominance of certain commercial interests in the developed countries and has indirectly contributed to the cultural and political domination of these countries over the international community as a whole.

7. *Imbalance in the distribution of the source of the spectrum.* The objective must be to denounce the provisions of Article 9 of the Radio Regulations, which enshrine vested interests in respect of the distribution of the spectrum, and so deprive in particular recently independent countries of satisfactory means of making their voices heard.

8. *Disorder and lack of coordination in telecommunications and in the use of satellites, compounded with flagrant inequalities between states in this field.* In the absence of any effective regulation, the present inequalities in this field are likely to increase, while the rights of the more powerful will become consolidated in a manner beyond remedy. It hardly needs stressing that such great progress has been made in this field that, without adequate regulation, a veritable invasion of radio broadcasts and television programs must be expected, amounting to a violation of national territories and private homes and a veritable form of mental rape. . . .

The developed countries' technological lead and the tariff system for international communications which they have instituted have enabled them to benefit from monopoly situations and prerogatives. [This has occurred] both in fixing the rates for transport of publications and telecommunications and in the use of communications and information technology. The advent of satellites is likely to intensify this imbalance if decisive international action is not taken and if technological aid is not furnished to the developing countries. This imbalance is particularly apparent in the following fields:

1. *Telecommunications.* The present structures and patterns of telecommunications networks between developing countries are based solely on criteria of profitability and volume of traffic, and so constitute a serious handicap to the development of information and communication. This handicap affects both the infrastructure and the tariff system.

With regard to the infrastructure, in addition to the absence of direct links between developing countries, a concentration of communication networks is to be observed in the developing countries. The planning of the infrastructure devised by the former colonial powers precludes, for certain developing countries, all possibility of transmitting information beyond their frontiers (earth stations allowing only reception of television programs produced in the industrialized countries, with no possibility of broadcasting towards these countries).

With regard to tariffs the situation is even more striking and in certain respects quite irrational. Designed so as to disadvantage small outputs, the present tariff system perpetuates the stranglehold of the rich countries on the information flow. It is strange, to say the least, that, over the same distance, communications should cost more between two points within developing countries than between two others situated in developed countries.

Similarly, nothing can justify the fact that the same communication should cost less when transmitted from a developed to a developing country than in the opposite direction. The survival of anachronistic practices is in itself sufficient to explain certain operating norms: why, for example, a telegraphic press circuit sometimes costs as much as or even more than a telephone circuit. How can we accept the privileges enjoyed by the major news agencies, which secure, thanks to the density of their traffic, fulltime use of circuits at a cost that in certain cases does not exceed that of a daily average use of one hour? The situation is aggravated still further in certain countries by the leasing of the telecommunications network to foreign companies whose *raison d'être* is profiteering, and the channeling of international traffic to their country of origin.

2. *Satellites.* Although the 1977 Geneva conference endeavored to establish main heads of a pro-

cedure designed to prevent abuses in the rational use of satellites, the developing countries are still threatened by the anarchic use of extra-atmospheric space, which is liable to worsen the imbalance affecting the present telecommunications system.

3. *Distribution of radio frequencies.* The problem of allocating the frequency spectrum, which is a universal but limited natural resource, arises today with particular urgency. The developing countries are in fact more determined than ever to challenge vigorously the rights that the developed countries have arrogated to themselves in the use of the frequency spectrum. They are also determined to secure an equitable sharing out of this spectrum.

It is common knowledge that almost 90 percent of the source of the spectrum is controlled by a few developed countries, and that the developing countries, although covering far more extensive areas, possess fewer channels than the developed countries. The power density per square kilometer is four times less in the developing countries than in the developed.

4. *Transport of publications.* The imbalance observed in the telecommunications field also occurs in the flow of newspapers and publications:

tariffs and distribution rates for newspapers are governed, as are those for all other mail, by the Universal Postal Convention, and all member countries of the Universal Postal Union are obliged to respect them;

with regard to newspapers, and bearing in mind their role as a means of information, culture, and education, the Universal Postal Convention allows member countries the option of granting a maximum 50 percent reduction in the tariff applicable to printed materials in respect both of newspapers and periodicals, books and pamphlets;

in addition to the optional nature of this reduction, air mail is subject to a bottom rate which does not favor the transport of small-circulation publications, i.e., precisely those produced in the developing countries. . . .

How, then, can this new world information order be established and in what does it consist? . . . It should be emphasized that this new order

entails a thorough-going readjustment. It is no ready-made recipe, which could enable an unjust situation to be transformed overnight into one less unjust. Because it is the product of a long history, the present situation cannot be put right quickly. The aim must be rather to initiate a process at the national, regional, and international levels. Effective, concrete measures are called for, rather than academic discussion. . . .

The new world information order founded on democratic principles seeks to establish relations of equality in the communications field between developed and developing nations and aims at greater justice and greater balance. Far from calling in question the freedom of information, it proposes to ensure that this principle is applied fairly and equitably for all nations and not only in the case of the more developed among them. . . .

From the political viewpoint, the hopes, concerns, and struggles of communities, groups, and nations must be treated on equal terms and with complete honesty and objectivity, while avoiding provocations, supporting the causes of liberty and justice, defending human rights in their full, universal dimension, and making every effort to eliminate the sequels of colonialism, racialism, apartheid, and all other discriminatory practices and serving the cause of peace in the world. Such measures should be taken at three levels, and concern each of the different media.

In respect to developing countries, the aims must be:

to define national communications policies, as being necessary to each country's economic and social development and of a nature to motivate its citizens on behalf of such development;

to make provision, in the formulation of such national communications policies, for measures favoring optimum exchanges of new programs at the regional or sub-regional level, and fostering active and determined participation on the part of all developing countries in the operation of international communications and information centers and networks;

to multiply exchange agreements between information bodies, training and research institutes, and national, regional, and international organizations directly or indirectly involved in the communications sector. In this context, the exchange of journalists and technicians should be intensified with a view to fostering between mutual understanding;

to consolidate and develop the established structures, particularly among the non-aligned countries, while at the same time, helping, in cooperation with the developed countries and the international organizations concerned, to establish communications media, to train qualified personnel, and to acquire suitable materials and equipment in a spirit of collective self-reliance;

to institute and strengthen assistance to the least developed countries;

to pay particular attention to the information supplied by the national news collection centers or news pools of the developing countries, on the problems which concern their respective regions or countries;

to alert the media of the developed countries to the imbalances, deficiencies, and imperfections of the present communications system, by arranging for meetings (conferences, seminars, or symposia) between those responsible for the different media in the developed and developing countries;

to launch a wide-ranging campaign in the field of communications in the universities of both developing and developed countries, aimed at training or retraining professionals and inculcating the values of the new international economic order and the new world information order;

to democratize information resources and structures. At the horizontal level, this implies setting up national news agencies and machinery for cooperation and mutual assistance between developing countries, such as the Press Agency Pool of the Non-Aligned Countries or the regional unions (African, Arab, Asian, Latin American), and on the vertical plane, curtailing the monopolies of the major press agencies by promoting the conclusion of international agreements aimed at equal and fair utilization of all communications media, including satellites;

to establish a system fostering a free and equitable flow between developed and developing countries, from the point of view of content, volume, and intensity;

to implement a national policy to promote literary and artistic creation by instituting a tax system that is as favorable as possible;

to encourage the setting up or development of national societies of authors aimed at ensuring optimimum management for the countries concerned of the resources deriving from the exploitation of intellectual works in all their diversity.

In respect to the developed countries the aims must be:

to call public attention to the action taken by the developing countries, emphasizing the ever-increasing interdependence of the different nations of the world. It is indeed unthinkable that public opinion in the developed countries should continue to be unaware of the widening gap between these and the deprived countries, or to adopt an attitude of indifference to the matter; . . .

to help "decolonize" information by taking a more objective approach to the aspirations and concerns of the developing nations, while at the same time eschewing all incitement to hatred or racial, religious, political, or any other kinds of discrimination, and all initiatives liable to misrepresent, distort, or show in an unfavorable light the measures taken by the developing countries;

to help establish a balance in the information flow by devoting more space in newspapers and in radio and television programs to news concerning developing countries as well as to news concerning immigrants working for the development and well-being of host countries;

to promote better mutual understanding by encouraging the media in the industrialized countries to devote greater attention to the content of their transmissions in order to better satisfy the needs of listeners, viewers, and subscribers both in and outside their national territory as also to make the cultures and civilizations of other peoples, especially those to whom the transmissions are addressed, more widely known;

to ensure that journalists and writers show the utmost prudence and themselves verify the reliability and authenticity of all material, data, or arguments used by them which might tend to intensify the arms race;

to ensure that journalists respect the laws of the country and the cultural values of the different peoples, and acknowledge that the right of peoples to make known their own concerns and to learn about those of other peoples is as important as respect for individuals;

to put an end to the pernicious activities of foreign stations established outside national frontiers;

to give particular attention to information supplied by national news-gathering centers or news pools in the developing countries on events concerning their respective regions or countries, and to encourage the mass media to subscribe to these pools and to the main news gathering centers, with a view to balancing and diversifying the news concerning these countries and in general increasing the space allotted thereto;

to ensure that, prior to each mission, special correspondents acquire as comprehensive a knowledge as possible of the countries to which they are sent, so as to be able to assess problems and concerns correctly and not see merely the sensational or anecdotal aspects of events, refrain from hasty judgments, free themselves of any distorting ideological lens through which they might be tempted to judge events and people, guard against all bias or prejudice, and endeavor to ensure that their conclusions correspond to reality.

In respect to the international organizations, efforts should be aimed at:

enlarging and diversifying the scope of the aid given by UNESCO and the other international organizations to developing countries and supplying means for linking up multilateral and bilateral assistance to these countries so as to step up such assistance and render it more effective;

helping to promote the development of the media in developing countries both at the national and regional levels, in a spirit of collective self-sufficiency;

enabling the developing countries to take advantage of the forums open to them in the international organizations in order to make known their demands and to bring about the establishment of a new world information order;

supporting the efforts of developing countries to formulate and adopt national communications policies, to promote research, particularly on the implications of transfers of technology, and to set up documentation centers on communications;

instituting a tax in the developed countries which are exporters of literary and artistic works of all kinds, the proceeds from which would help to finance the international copyright fund which is to administered by UNESCO;

enlarging and diversifying the range of the aid granted to developing countries, and helping them to use the communication sciences to promote social evolution by undertaking studies based on assumptions and methods which reflect the realities and correspond to the needs of the developing countries;

granting maximum technical and financial assistance to institutions carrying out research on communications, in accordance with the needs emerging in each country and each region;

implementing with all due dispatch and in collaboration with the mass communications training centers which exist in all developing countries, a program to draw up and coordinate the curricula of mass communications institutes and departments and special vocational training courses in this field. The essential purpose of this program would be to adapt studies to the specific, practical needs of each country and each region in respect of communications. To this end, a board or consultative panel should be set up on which directors of institutes, departments, or university courses in mass communications would serve;

promoting, through the grant of fellowships and similar measures, an advanced university training course in the communication sciences. Such training should be given in accordance with the needs, objectives and potentialities of developing countries: . . .

helping to formulate research programs and to establish training centers so as to enable developing countries to produce radio and television programs designed to serve the aims of the New International Economic Order;

granting the mass communications sector a status that corresponds to its undoubted importance and to its evident influence on all other sectors of activity, so as to develop an easy and harmonious relationships not only with the cultural sector but also with the education sector and with others that are today less closely linked thereto;

devising a clear-cut policy on the use of satellites transmission systems, respecting in all cases the sovereign rights of individual states;

encouraging the testing, evaluation, and dissemination of new, low-priced, and easy-to-use communications technology so as to enable the message of development to reach the masses at present cut off from all such information;

helping to establish historical documentation and archives centers in the developing countries.

From the legal viewpoint, there can be no justice in international communications unless and until rights in this field are redefined and applied on an extensive scale. Information must be understood as a social good and a cultural product, and not as a material commodity or merchandise. Seen in this perspective, all countries should enjoy the same opportunities of access to sources of information as well as to participate in the communication process. Sociocultural considerations should prevail over individual, materialistic, and mercantile considerations. . . .

Information is not the prerogative of a few individuals or entities that command the technical and financial means enabling them to control communications; rather, it must be conceived as a social function intrinsic to the various communities, cultures, and different conceptions of civilization. . . .

The need to establish an international deontology governing information and communications is becoming ever more strongly felt. The self-regulation of professional media organizations must, to be sure, be given recognition in such a deontology. However, it cannot replace a more wide-ranging formula, since no social group should have the pre-

rogative of not being held accountable to the community to which it belongs. . . .

The protection of journalists is a key element in the world communications and information system. Such protection should extend to the relations between the journalists and employers and should enable them to safeguard freedom of thought and analysis against all potential pressures. It must cover the journalist in the performance of professional duties. . . .

This right of correction should be reinforced by calling to account the individual or legal entity guilty of violating the principles of professional deontology or of propagating false or biased information before an international tripartite body grouping together representatives of states, representatives of the profession, and neutral figures known for their moral integrity and competence in matters of information.

As has been pointed out by the international organizations responsible for the assignment of frequencies, the national resources of both the electromagnetic spectrum and the geostationary orbits are limited. This limitation makes it essential to revise the present allocation of the resources of the spectrum and to regulate the use of extra-atmospheric space for telecommunications purposes. This task is all the more urgent in that direct broadcasting by satellite is, according to present forecasts, likely to come into operation in the next decade.

For this purpose, it is essential to provide for:

the safeguarding of the rights of countries still under domination to equitable access to the frequency spectrum;

the revision of Article 9 of the Radio Regulations and the reappraisal of the rule of "first-come, first-served" where the frequency spectrum is concerned;

a "moratorium" on the free-for-all use of extra-atmospheric space pending the conclusion of an international agreement which satisfactorily guarantees the supply and use of modern telecommunications technical resources in general; the Final Acts of the World Satellite-Broadcasting Administrative Radio Conference, held in Geneva in 1977, should serve as a basis for the drafting of this agreement. . . .

The developing countries must coordinate their action within the overall framework of the United Nations system so that matters lying within the competence of the ITU may be given a significance which transcends the purely technical context.

From the technical and financial viewpoints, . . . the steps to be taken include the following:

rethinking the present pattern of the international telecommunications network;

fostering the establishment of centers or nodes of communication in developing countries and setting up direct links whenever possible between developing countries;

working for the lowering of communication tariffs between developing countries;

ensuring that satellites are seen primarily as a means of alleviating certain telecommunications functions hitherto discharged by point-to-point, short-wave transmission;

using satellites for transmitting radio and television programs of developing countries which have hitherto been unable to ensure their adequate diffusion solely by conventional means;

assigning a predominant role to the developing countries at the next World Administrative Radio Conference (WARC) scheduled for October 1979;

ensuring equitable redistribution of the spectrum, without taking any *faits accomplis* into consideration, on the basis of a balanced allocation between all regions of the globe;

taking joint action in order to obtain new favorable terms for newspapers at the next congress of the Universal Postal Union;

doing away with the minimum tariff and inducing air transport companies and postal administrations to take joint action in order to reduce the air freight surtax on publications;

formulating an international code of conduct governing the transfer of technology which corresponds to the specific needs and conditions of developing countries.

The technical advances achieved during the recent decades in all sectors of economic activity have not been equitably distributed between members of the economic community. The income of the developing countries, in which 75 percent of the world's population is concentrated, at present represents only 30 percent of the world income. Average per capita income in the industrialized countries today stands at $2400 per annum, whereas that of the developing countries, in which three-quarters of the world's population live, is a mere $180. More serious still, the 24 poorest countries have an annual per capita income not exceeding $100. This disparity is bound to increase: it is estimated that in ten years these figures will be $3400 and $280 respectively.

The developing countries' share in world trade, already limited to 32 percent in 1950, has continued to diminish, dropping to a mere 17 percent. . . . The deterioration in [trade] . . . has been attended by a considerable increase in the Third World's debt, which rose to $233,000 million in 1977. These phenomena were perceived by the developing countries as a continuation of political hegemony and an expression of the will to pursue neo-colonialist exploitation. Conscious of the grave implications of this ever-widening gulf between Third World countries and industrialized countries, the United Nations proclaimed on May 1, 1974, their common determination to undertake the urgent ask of establishing a new international economic order founded on equity and capable of redressing the flagrant inequalities of the present system.

However, the failure of these appeals for equity to produce a response or to gain a hearing has soon proved their essential inefficacy. The media have even conditioned public opinion in the developed countries to such an extent as to render it allergic to all claims and demands emanating from the Third World.

Accordingly, the establishment of a new world information order must be considered as the essential corollary of the new international economic order. In order to give concrete reality to this new approach and to enable the media to fulfil their task of educating and informing, measures must be taken both by the industrialized and the developing countries, as well as by the international organizations concerned. . . .

The process initiated is a complex one, and transformations will take time. What is essential is to familiarize public opinion with change and to promote a responsive awareness of it. For the develop-ing countries, self-reliance must be the watchword; this they can achieve by developing cooperation at the horizontal level so as to enable them to establish a balanced flow with the developed countries.

AFRICAN NEWSPAPER EDITORS AND THE NEW WORLD INFORMATION ORDER

CONNIE ROSER AND LEE BROWN

African editors hold contradictory views about the New World Information Order. They support both a balanced and a free flow of information; they are dissatisfied with Western wire service news but are ambivalent about the value of regional and local news agencies; they want both freedom of expression and regulation of expression through right of reply laws; they want newspapers to be responsible for promoting national development but also to be free to report news that threatens development.

For more than a decade now, advocates and oppo-nents of the New World Information Order have clashed over the imbalance in the flow of news and entertainment between the North and South.[1] In the continuing exchanges between the Western media and UNESCO, the Third World journalist is caught between Western journalistic ethics and the growing nationalism of the Third World countries.

Supporters of the new order are principally aca-demics and politicians from Third World or Eastern European nations who participate in UNESCO-sponsored research and conferences; opponents are mostly journalists from the United States and West-ern Europe. The journalists of the developing na-tions, a third group with a stake in the debate's outcome, have had little voice thus far.[2]

This paper is an analysis of the attitudes of some members of this third group toward some of the issues involved in the new order debate. Divided between their sense of national pride and the jour-nalism values into which they were socialized, Third World journalists may be forced to reconcile con-flicting values; equality or freedom in the flow of news between North and South; developmental jour-nalism and/or the Western role of government watchdog.

The Third World representatives at UNESCO conferences where information flow is discussed have typically been government officials, the media experts the organization invites to participate in its research are academics, and opposition to the new order has typically come from Western media orga-nizations.[3] Thus, policies with far-reaching implica-tions for journalists are being debated with little input from a population that is directly affected by any restrictions placed on the flow of news.

The entire population of African news editors was surveyed during the summer of 1981 to (1) learn

Connie Roser and Lee Brown, "African Newspaper Editors and the New World Information Order." *Journalism Quarterly*, Volume 63, Number 1, Spring 1986, pp. 114–121. Reprinted by permission.

Connie Roser is a doctoral candidate at the Institute for Communication Research, Stanford University. Lee Brown teaches in the Department of Journalism, San Diego State University.

their opinions on some of the proposals for the New World Information Order, and (2) discover which of various influences on editors (e.g., training, work socialization and ownership of their newspapers) are associated with attitudes toward the new order. (Table 1)

Just what the new order is, however, remains problematic. As a Latin American proponent has said, "The New World Information Order is not a perfectly definable concept."[4] Because the idea is evolving, many different approaches have been suggested to solving the problems it addresses. These range from structural change in news flow at the international level to interpersonal exchange.

For the purposes of this paper, the New World Information Order was defined as a proposed state in which the flow of news between the Southern and Northern Hemispheres would be equalized; in which the dominance of the world's five largest news agencies would be broken down by the development of regional and national news agencies in the Third World; in which much more attention would be given by the media to development news rather than violence and conflict; and in which government control of the media for developmental purposes would sometimes be acceptable.[5]

STUDY DESIGN

Ten topics of debate formed the basis for the questionnaire:

1. inequality in the flow of news between the North and South;
2. development of national and/or regional news agencies to compete with or replace the Western wire services;
3. government control of the media for development purposes;
4. basic changes in the news values of the media to emphasize positive development news rather than conflict and natural disasters;
5. establishment of an international agency to regulate news flow and content;
6. redistribution of the electromagnetic spectrum;
7. licensing of journalists;

8. ownership of the media by governments or foreigners;
9. establishment of an international right of correction;
10. negative effects of foreign advertising.

Attitudes toward these propositions were then compared to several socialization variables to assess whether:

1. Journalism training in Western schools imparted Western concepts of the press' roles and functions to these Third World editors;
2. More experience working at a newspaper is associated with a stronger acceptance of Western news values, and hence, with less favorable attitudes toward the New World Information Order;
3. Values of the African editors reflect the ownership and sources of support of their newspapers (i.e., do editors of government-owned and supported newspapers favor more government control over news?);
4. The editors' concepts of the press' roles and functions are consonant with the political systems under which they live.

We expected that formal training in Western schools and more years of work experience would be associated with opposition to the New World Information Order, as a result of socialization into Western values. We also expected that the work context would be related to values such that support for the new order would be associated with government support or ownership of the newspaper, and that support would be associated with a restrictive political system. Finally, we hypothesized that editors of newspapers with foreign owners would show more opposition to the new order.

The names of editors and newspapers and their addresses were obtained from the 1980 Editor & Publisher *Yearbook*,[6] which contains a complete listing of the daily newspapers of Africa. Editors of 171 newspapers in 45 countries were sent a two-page questionnaire with return postage in the form of international reply coupons.[7]

The questionnaires were printed in one of three languages: English, French or Portuguese, in accor-

Table I   ATTITUDES OF RESPONDENTS TOWARD PROPOSALS
FOR A NEW WORLD INFORMATION ORDER

Attitude Item	Mean	Standard Deviation
1a) The flow of news between the Northern and Southern Hemispheres should be equal and balanced.	6.05	1.81
1b) The free flow of news should not be restricted in any way.	6.64	1.57
2a) The wire services report Third World news adequately.	2.59	1.70
2b) Coverage of the Third World by the wire services has improved over the last five years.	4.45	1.90
2c) The Western media do not carry enough accurate information about Africa.	6.07	1.40
2d) A Pan-African news agency is needed to provide Africans with more objective news about Africa.	5.21	2.25
2e) National news agencies in most African countries would produce propaganda instead of news.	5.33	2.25
2f) A Pan-African news agency would not be able to function freely from government interference.	5.59	2.05
2g) A national news agency could operate independently of the government in most African countries, even if it was supported by the government.	3.74	2.49
3a) African governments should ensure that the media assist in national development.	5.07	2.37
3b) Instances in which government censorship is justified:		
1) never	3.50	1.97
2) wartime	4.81	2.23
3) national crisis	4.26	2.26
4) national development is threatened	2.93	2.07
5) national values/cultural identity is threatened	2.98	1.99
6) national image is threatened	3.07	1.97
7) always	2.33	1.57
4a) Governments own the news of events that happen within their own nations.	2.19	1.64
4b) No one owns the news.	6.62	1.15
4c) It is a journalist's responsibility to print all the news, good or bad, regardless of what he thinks about the news.	5.57	2.30
4d) African journalists should support government programs and policies to aid national development.	5.00	2.35
4e) The same news values apply in developing countries as in the developed countries.	4.86	2.39
4f) Too much emphasis by the media on national conflicts and problems can be a threat to national development.	4.33	2.47
5a) An international agency should be established to ensure that the flow of news between the developed and developing nations is balanced and the content is fair.	4.71	2.47

Table I   (*Continued*)

Attitude Item		Mean	Standard Deviation
6a)	Journalists should be licensed to maintain high standards within the profession.	3.33	2.58
6b)	Journalists do not need the protection of a license.	5.17	2.37
7a)	African countries are entitled to a fair share of the electromagnetic spectrum, even if they are not able to use the space allotted to them yet.	5.36	2.05
8a)	At the present level of economic development of my country, it is impossible for the news media to support themselves without government assistance.	3.69	2.75
8b)	Foreign ownership of African media is not detrimental to the functioning of the media or to the fulfillment of their purpose	4.10	2.40
8c)	A privately owned press only reflects the views of the wealthy—not the views of the common people.	2.38	2.05
9a)	When false or biased news about a country is printed in the newspapers of another country, the country that has been wronged should have the right to print a correction in the newspapers that carried the false information.	6.43	1.31
9b)	Newspapers should be able to print what they like about other countries.	4.21	2.54
10a)	Foreign advertising hastens development.	4.55	2.00
10b)	Foreign advertising introduces destructive foreign values.	3.55	1.86

The number preceding each item indicates the topic of the debate to which it relates.
Entries are means on a seven-point scale in which 1 is "strongly disagree" and 7 is "strongly agree."

dance with the language of the editor's newspaper or former colonizer of the editor's country.[8] The use of colonial rather than African languages was necessary in the light of more than 800 languages spoken on the continent; detribalized Africans also use the colonial languages for this reason, and the bulk of mass media content is presented in English, French or Portuguese.[9]

Mailings of the questionnaire were made in April and June of 1981; from the first mailing 23 responses were received and from the second, 19.[10]

The dependent variable for the tests of the hypotheses was an index of support for the New World Information Order. This index was formed by weighting the items related to each debate topic, giving each topic equal weight; the topic scores were then summed. Thus, the two items relating to the

free flow of information together carried as much weight in the index score as the eight censorship items.

A total of 42 responses were received from 20 different countries. The preponderance of responses came from the Republic of South Africa, and from other former British colonies. Respondents were spread thinly over most of the African continent with several noticeable gaps. Only two Arab nations were represented: Morocco and Tunisia. None of the former Portuguese colonies, and none of the socialist nations responded.[11]

The influence of the South Africans on the results is formidable. Their 31 newspapers accounted for 18% of the total mailing to 171 newspapers. Their 16 responses, however, made up 38% of the total responses. Because South Africa remains a white-ruled country, because it is substantially more industrialized than the rest of Africa, and because South Africans showed a significantly different pattern of responses than the other Africans, South Africa has been considered separately on the attitude measures.

RESULTS

The editors were strongly in favor of a balanced flow of news, and, at the same time, a free flow of the news (see Table 2). That the respondents did not see an inherent contradiction in agreeing with both of these statements is, perhaps, one of the most interesting results of this survey.

They favored the establishment of a Pan-African news agency, but regarded local and regional agencies with some ambivalence—as sources of more objective news about Africa on one hand (62%) and as sources of government propaganda on the other (67%).[12] Nonetheless, dissatisfaction with the Western wire services' reporting on Africa was widespread (69%).

Opposition to foreign advertising and foreign ownership of the media was more limited than might have been expected. Forty-one percent opposed foreign ownership of African newspapers and less than a fifth opposed foreign advertising. Perhaps the editors recognized that their newspapers require these sources of support.

While only one editor agreed that censorship is justified all the time, opposition to censorship in general was not strong, with almost two-thirds agreeing that governments should ensure that the media assist in national development.

A pervasive concern of the editors was the desire for equality with their Western counterparts in information reception and transmission capabilities. This could be seen, not only in the support for a balanced news flow and a Pan-African news agency, but also in the editors' support for redistribution of the agency controlling news flow (55%). The latter finding was particularly surprising because it represents an infringement on the right to transmit information freely, a right the editors believed should not be restricted (93%).

A second surprising result was the strong support found for an international right of correction (88%).

Yet close to half agreed that newspapers should be able to print what they like about other countries. The apparent discrepancy is perhaps attributable to the belief of many Africans that their countries are misrepresented in the Western press as lands of perpetual "coups and earthquakes."

Licensing of journalists was opposed by three-fifths of the editors. On one of the licensing items (#7a), however, the Black Africans and Arabs scored slightly above the middle of the scale, showing mild support and indicating that opposition may not be strong among these groups.

In each case, the South Africans showed less support for the proposal (See Table 2).

The index scores served as the dependent variable in a series of tests to identify predictors of the editors' attitudes. Scores on the dependent variable ranged from 1.85 to 5.35 on a seven-point scale on which seven normally distributed with a mean of 3.62 and a standard deviation of 0.69; reliability of the index was 0.77, as estimated by Cronbach's alpha. Without the South Africans, the mean rises to 4.02.

Among the independent variables, the most powerful predicator of editors' attitudes was the ownership and source of support of their newspapers, although several other variables also showed some relationship to the attitude index. In more detail, the findings were:

Training and Work Experience

An analysis of variance comparing attitudes of untrained editors and editors trained in the First, Second or Third Worlds and South Africa showed no significant relation ($F = 1.66$; $df = 4,31$; n.s.); nor did length of training show a relation to attitudes (standardized beta = .10; $R^2 = .01$). Work experience, however, was significantly associated with attitudes. Regressing the index scores on the editors' years of work experience yielded a standardized beta of $-.29$ ($R^2 = .10$). Thus, editors with more journalism training or who studied journalism in a Western nation do not show significantly stronger opposition to the new information order than other editors. Those who have had more work experience, however, are less likely to support the new order.

Table 2

ITEMS ON WHICH THE SOUTH AFRICANS DIFFERED FROM OTHER RESPONDENTS

Attitude Items		South Africa	Others	t
2d)	A Pan-African news agency is needed to provide Africans with more objective news about Africa.	4.06	5.92	3.03[b]
3a)	African governments should ensure that the media assist in national development.	3.25	6.19	4.29[c]
3b)	Instances in which government censorship is justified: 6) national image is threatened.	2.25	3.58	2.22[a]
4a)	Governments own the news events that happen within their own nations.	1.44	2.65	2.47[a]
4d)	African journalists should support government programs and policies to aid national development.	3.31	6.04	4.40[c]
4f)	Too much emphasis by the media on national conflicts and problems can be a threat to national development.	3.31	4.96	2.20[a]
5a)	An international agency should be established to ensure that the flow of news between the developed and developing nations is balanced and the content is fair.	3.06	5.73	3.96[c]
6a)	Journalists should be licensed to maintain high standards within the profession.	2.13	4.08	2.53[a]
6b)	Journalists do not need the protection of a license.	6.19	4.54	2.30[a]
7a)	African countries are entitled to a fair share of the electromagnetic spectrum and satellite space, even if they are not able to use the space allotted to them yet.	4.31	6.00	2.81[a]
8a)	At the present level of economic development of my country, it is impossible for the news media to support themselves without government assistance.	2.13	4.65	3.20[b]
9a)	When false or biased news about a country is printed in the newspaper of another country, the country that has been wronged should have the right to print a correction in the newspapers that carried the false information.	5.81	6.81	2.74[a]
Number of Observations		(16)	(26)	

The number preceding each item indicates the topic of debate to which it relates.
Entries are means on a seven-point scale in which 1 is "strongly disagree" and 7 is "strongly agree."
t statistic is for a two-tailed test.
[a]$p < .05$ [b]$p < .01$ [c]$p < .001$

Political Systems

We hypothesized that editors from countries with a more democratic political system would express less support for the new order than editors from countries with an authoritarian political system. Countries were divided into four groups: multi-party systems, one-party systems, military governments and dictatorships, and South Africa. South Africa was categorized separately because it fits none of the categories, combining as it does a multi-party system and little political representation for blacks. The means for the four groups were as follows: military governments and dictatorships, $\bar{X} = 4.95$ (n = 4); one party governments, $\bar{X} = 4.06$ (n = 9); multi-party governments, $\bar{X} = 4.39$ (n = 12); South Africa, $\bar{X} = 3.20$ (n = 16) (F = 8.33; df = 3,37; p<.001).

Editors from countries with military governments or dictatorships show significantly more support than editors from countries with one- or multi-party governments (p<.01). Thus, living in a country with less political freedom appears to correlate with acceptance of controls on the media. This finding, of course, is based on a very small number of observations; it is, however, a sufficiently intriguing finding to merit further research.

Ownership and Support

Our hypotheses stated that editors working for newspapers that were owned and/or supported by the government would show more support for the new information order, and that editors of newspapers with foreign owners would show less support. The first hypothesis was strongly supported, while the second was not for lack of data. Only two questionnaires were returned from editors of foreign-owned newspapers, making any analysis impossible.

Because the data were not normally distributed, we used a nonparametric test for these hypotheses. Wilcoxon rank-sums and a Kruskal-Wallis test (a chi-square approximation) for the rank sums yielded a probability of .01. Means for the three groups were: privately owned newspapers, $\bar{X} = 3.44$ (n = 29); papers that are 80% owned by the government $\bar{X} = 3.85$ (n = 3); papers that are wholly owned by the government, $\bar{X} = 4.57$ (n = 7). Thus, government ownership appears to be associated with its editor's support for the new information order.

Similar results were obtained in the comparison of editors whose newspapers received no support from the government with editors whose newspapers did receive government support. Probability for the chi-square approximation was .01. Editors receiving no support averaged 3.41 (n = 28), while editors who received government funding averaged 4.62 (n = 11). Although our number of observations is small, the difference in means is large enough to suggest that a real difference exists. And the difference is not merely an artifact of the lower scores of South Africans (whose newspapers receive no government support and are privately owned), for the relationships remain when the South Africans are removed from the analysis.

There are several possible explanations for the relationships between support, ownership and attitudes. It may be that some of the editors of government-owned and supported newspapers in our sample are political appointees or have closer ties to the government than to the journalism community. For such editors, government involvement in media flow and content may seem less objectionable than it does to other journalists. Perhaps these editors have a strong sense of nationalism that carries more weight than their journalistic values. Or perhaps—and this is the most interesting possibility—working in an atmosphere of government dependence leads to more acceptance of governmental restrictions and controls on news transmissions.

CONCLUSION

Government ownership and subsidization of an editor's newspaper are associated with support for the New World Information Order, as are military control and dictatorships. Opposition is related to years of experience working in the media, while journalism training shows no relation to attitudes.

Based on these data, then, we find no support for Golding's contention that Western training imparts to Third World journalists an ideological framework that inhibits their countries' development and promotes neo-colonialism.[13] We found no evidence that Western training led to the adoption of Western values regarding news flow and censorship. Instead, economic and political factors within the editor's own newspaper and country were the strongest predictors of professional attitudes.

Given that the sample was biased toward pro-Western nations, the extent of support for radical change in current news practices is remarkable. More than half the respondents favor establishment of an international agency to regulate flow and content of news; almost all favor an international right of correction; and the majority believe governments should ensure that the media assist in national development.

Finally, an unexpected outcome has been the discovery of apparent inconsistencies within the responses of the editors. They feel that news flow should be free and equal at the same time; that newspapers should be able to print what they want about other countries, but be regulated by an international right of correction; that it is their responsibility to aid in national development, and, at the same time, to print all the news—even though some news can threaten development. These contradictions speak of an idealism about their role and responsibility, and reflect, perhaps, the conflicting influences to which the editors are subject.

Because of the low response rate, the apparent contradictions and the heavy impact of the South African respondents, the findings must be viewed with caution. At the same time, with politicians and Northern hemisphere journalists occupying both front and back bench seats in the debates about information flow, even this less-than-definitive survey of African editors may be considered a contribution to mutuality of purpose, to understanding and to an expansion of dialogue.

NOTES

1. Elie Abel, ''International Communication: A New Order?'' in Everett Rogers and Francis Balle, eds., *The Media Revolution in America and in Western Europe* (Norwood, N.J.: Ablex, 1985).
2. Rosemary Righter, *Whose News? Politics, the Press and the Third World* (New York: New York Times Book Co., 1978).
3. *Ibid.*
4. Philip Power and Elie Abel, ''Third World vs. the Media,'' *The New York Times*, 21 Sept. 1980, p. 123, 128.
5. This definition draws on several sources, including: Mastapha Masmoudi, ''The New World Information Order.'' In George Gerbner & Marsha Seifert, eds., *World Communications: A Handbook* (New York: Longman, 1984); Jeremy Tunstall, *The Media Are American: Anglo-American Media in the World* (New York: Columbia University Press, 1977); International Commission for the Study of Communication Problems, *Many Voices, One World: Communication and Society, Today and Tomorrow* (New York: Unipub, 1980).
6. *Editor & Publisher International Yearbook for 1980* (New York: Editor and Publisher, 1980).
7. Countries lacking a daily newspaper were omitted from the survey. They were the Central African Republic, Djibouti, the Gambia and Rwanda. A fifth country, Chad, had no mail service at the time due to its civil war, and was therefore also omitted.
8. If the editor's country had been colonized by both the French and English, two questionnaires were sent, one in each language.
9. William Hachten, *Muffled Drums: The News Media in Africa* (Iowa: Iowa State University Press, 1970).
10. The long time-gap between mailings was necessary due to the slowness of international mail.
11. It might be argued that editors of large, major newspapers should be considered separately from editors of smaller newspapers; the correlation of circulation and attitude, however, was non-significant (r = .15, n.s.). We feel justified, therefore, in grouping all editors together.
12. Percentages were calculated by collapsing the 7-point scale into 3 categories: agree, disagree and no opinion.
13. Peter Golding, ''Media Professionalism in the Third World: The Transfer of an Ideology.'' In James Curran, Michael Gurevitch & Janet Woollacott, eds., *Mass Communication and Society* (Beverly Hills: Sage, 1979).

THE U.S. POSITION ON THE NEW WORLD INFORMATION AND COMMUNICATION ORDER

COLLEEN ROACH

While the United States has been strongly opposed to stated and implied government controls that the New World Information Order proposes, the author points out that the U.S. government itself imposes a variety of controls on both domestic and foreign communication. While the U.S. government promoted the free flow of information principle at UNESCO meetings, it has been limiting the flow of information among its own citizens.

As the decade of the 1980s draws to a close, one might rightfully ask: why should anyone still be interested in the debate on a New World Information and Communication Order? After all, the United States has withdrawn its membership from UNESCO. And many Third World countries, distracted by the economic crisis of recent years, have abandoned their earlier militancy. Nonetheless, this issue still merits analysis for two reasons.

First, the U.S. withdrawal, if properly understood, should provide us with some guidelines on future U.S. policy toward the United Nations system. Second, the fact that the controversy over the NWICO towered over the issues this movement hoped to raise gives the false impression that with the U.S. withdrawal from UNESCO the issues have disappeared. This is obviously incorrect. In short, although the NWICO is simply "off the agenda" of the U.S. press,[1] the international call for a New Order is still very much alive, and the disparities between developed and developing countries that gave rise to the demands for equality in global communications have not been resolved.

The objective of this article is, in a broad sense, to assist in keeping the NWICO on the international communications agenda. Specifically it analyzes both the "context" and "contradictions" of the major arguments used by the United States to attack the NWICO.

By "context" I refer to the conjunction of main politico-ideological argument used by the United States to attack the NWICO—its supposed intent of promoting government-controlled media—with the global privatization/deregulation movement. Within the "closed system" of U.S. arguments on the NWICO, of course, whether made by the State Department, the U.S. press, or the interest groups, one finds a fairly consistent and uniform position: an unequivocal countering of the NWICO umbrella principle with the principle of "free flow of information" and the linking of all tenants of UNESCO's position to that principle's presumed opposite, "government control of the media."

However, the contradictions of this position become manifest when one steps "outside" to examine seemingly unrelated events or policy statements. An obvious contradiction would arise, for example, if the U.S. government promotes the "free flow of information" principle in international forums while limiting the flow of information to U.S. citizens; or if the U.S. government or media are found to have endorsed concepts and slogans that, in the NWICO debate, have been taken up by UNESCO. The most ironic contradiction would arise were it to be dem-

Colleen Roach, "The U.S. Position on the New World Information and Communication Order." From the *Journal of Communication*, Volume 37, Number 4, Autumn 1987, pp. 36–51. © 1987, *The Journal of Communication*. Reprinted by permission.

The author is assistant professor of communications at Fordham University.

onstrated that certain NWICO concepts and slogans actually originated in the United States. Given the polemics that the NWICO movement has generated and the great variety of actors involved—the press, government officials, politicians, researchers, etc.—in examining these contradictions I rely on a wide range of sources.

As will be demonstrated, the U.S. position on the NWICO was largely determined by economic considerations. Certainly, the best-known writers on the NWICO, such as Hamelink, Nordenstreng, and Somavia, have examined, to varying degrees, the economic interests of the transnationals and the U.S. private sector at stake in the NWICO debate. However, the specific question of how these interests have been linked to the articulation of the "government control" argument has not been analyzed in any detail.[2] Although I do not advocate an analysis based upon "economic determinism," I assume that the "government control" argument is largely a politico-ideological construct serving primarily, though not exclusively, to defend the economic imperatives of private sector expansion on a global basis.

To state that virtually every NWICO-related issue or subject ("social responsibility of the press," "protection of journalists," "right to communicate," etc.) was reduced to the slogan of "government control of the media" is no exaggeration. The reason for this strategy is not merely the U.S. predilection for over-simplification of complex issues, or even the historical commitment to the First Amendment, although these factors are certainly not to be neglected. The emphasis on the "government control" argument reflects, above all, the need to ensure that the NWICO would not reinforce government-run or public sector communications media at the expense of the private sector.

For it is the protection of the private sector that is most critical. The imperative for U.S. transnational telecommunications business interests is concretely reflected in the "deregulatory fever" and the move toward the privatization of the public sector. This coupling of the deregulatory and privatization movements necessarily undermines a strong public sector of the economy whether on a national or international basis. One can better appreciate why the "government control" argument came to be the platform of

the U.S. position on the NWICO by understanding the linking of these forces.

Within the international context, the U.S. backing for privatization and deregulation at the global level was, of course, most evident in negotiations at UNESCO. The evolution of the U.S. position on the NWICO from 1976 to 1984 has been marked by the increasing importance accorded to private sector concerns. The creation of the World Press Freedom Committee (WPFC) in 1976 brought together in one large umbrella group most of the representatives of the private sector who had some stake in the NWICO debate. The adversarial role played by the *New York Times* and the *Washington Post* should also be kept in mind.[3] And one of the main reasons that the United States has been lukewarm toward its own creation, the International Program for the Development of Communications (IPDC), is precisely the lack of guarantees that top priority will be given to projects designed to promote the U.S. private sector in developing countries.

As the NWICO story unfolded, the decisive role played by the U.S. private sector in negotiations with UNESCO took on a certain symbolic significance. The speech of the representative of the U.S. delegation to the Communications Commission of the 1982 UNESCO General Conference, James Philips, opened "in the name of his government and the private sector" (31). The choice to head the U.S. delegation to the last UNESCO General Conference in which the United States participated (in 1983) was Edmund P. Hennelly, Director of the Mobil Oil Corporation.

However, it would be a major error to conclude that UNESCO was singled out for this type of strategy. The United States promoted privatization and the enhancement of 'free market forces," particularly in the developing world, to the entire United Nations system. This strategy was clearly in operation at the second U.N. International Conference on Population, held in Mexico and August 1984, where the United States linked resolution of population problems to the promotion of a "market economy" and the "necessity of encouraging private investment"(14). According to one report, the U.S. delegates suggested that, "if the free enterprise system is allowed to work, there will be sufficient economic growth to forestall crisis''(4). Robert McNamara, former president of the World Bank, commented that ''Americans will be laughed out of the conference if they stress that theme. It's absurd''(4).

The United States has continued to take this position. At the special U.N. General Assembly on the Economic Crisis in Africa, held in New York in June 1986, the United States made no specific commitment in aid or debt relief, but with the assistance of the other ''donor nations'' it was nonetheless able to have the following sentence inserted in the final document of the General Assembly: ''The role of the private sector is also to be encouraged through well-defined and consistent policies''(44). And although African delegates were understandably disappointed at the meager results of the conference, Secretary of State George Shultz praised what he called the Africans' ''new willingness to employ market-oriented measures in dealing with their economic difficulties'' that ''will amount to a total restructuring of African economies''(2).

The deregulation/privatization movement in telecommunications is, of course, of international scope, most notably in Japan and in the United Kingdom. The state broadcast monopoly has also been broken down in France, Italy, and Spain. In France, the return of the Right to power (or rather ''power sharing'') has not only consolidated the movement to eliminate the state broadcast monopoly but has taken on a much larger significance. There is now a Minister of Economics, Finances and Privatization, and the plan to sell 65 state-owned banks and industrial companies to private investors provoked the first serious clash with President François Mitterand (26).

Given that the public sector is being undermined in the industrialized world and that the developing countries are viewed as a source of expanded markets, it seems no accident that the ''government control'' of communications media was used as the main argument to attack the NWICO in the mid to late 1970s. Its ascendancy also coincided with the championship of that other cherished American freedom: the freedom to expand global markets.

The ''government control of the media'' argument assumes that U.S. media are completely free from state intervention. But of course this is not exactly the case. In broadcasting, with its notable definition of ''public'' airwaves, the Federal Communications Commission (FCC) had, until very recently, two central means of control: the Equal Time Rule and the Fairness Doctrine. Although commercial broadcasters, allied with the FCC, succeeded in having the Fairness Doctrine repealed, its possible resuscitation by sympathetic members of Congress, along with the continued survival of the Equal Time Rule, serves to remind us of the government role in media regulation.[4] The print media in the United States appear ''unregulated,'' but, as Picard notes, ''the U.S. government has, with the support and encouragement of the newspaper industry, regularly entered the economic arena to correct and replace the marketplace so highly regarded by libertarians'' (32). Such government supports are not acknowledged by critics of state intervention because, according to Picard, they support ''the infrastructures of the corporatist commercially-based industry and help[s] make the newspaper industry one of the most profitable industries in the United States'' (32, pp. 9–10).

The American public too supports ''positive'' government regulation of the media. A survey on freedom of expression carried out by the Public Agenda Foundation in 1980 documents this observation. For example, respondents favored laws requiring that opponents of a controversial policy be given as much coverage as proponents, in both newspapers (73 percent to 17 percent) and on television (74 to 18 percent; 34, p. 29). According to the study,

> although people reject laws they perceive as censorship, they favor a different type of law—what might be called ''traffic cop'' regulations—designed to guarantee a *balanced, diversified flow of information*. People view fairness in the media as more than a laudable goal. They are willing to back their commitment to fairness with the force of law. Laws requiring fairness, from the public's point of view, increase freedom of expression (34, p. 29, emphasis added).

The American public's belief in a ''balanced,

diversified flow of information" is of particular relevance to the NWICO debate. One of the early victories of the Third World forces was UNESCO's adoption of the formula in 1974 referring to the need for "a free and *balanced* flow of information" (later modified to a "wider and better balanced flow of information") in their description of the NWICO. Although in UNESCO negotiations the U.S. delegation acquiesced to this term, the idea of "balance" was never really accepted by U.S. hard-liners, who tied "balance" to "government control" by posing the rhetorical question: "Who will do the balancing?" As answered by a *New York Times* editorial referring to the 1978 UNESCO Mass Media Declaration, "For all its talk of 'free' and 'objective' information, what it really champions is something called 'balance'—as defined by the declarers, who are governments" (41).

In spite of such objections, it is more than likely that the term "a free and balanced flow of information" originated in the United States. In congressional hearings in June 1977, before the International Operations Subcommittee of the Senate Committee of Foreign Relations, William Harley, a communications specialist and former Vice-Chairman of the U.S. National Commission for UNESCO, stated: "In 1968—largely at the initiative of the United States—the concept of a 'balanced and free flow of information' was adopted as part of Unesco's amended Declaration on Human Rights" (45). Diplomatic terminology used in resolutions and declarations is often old wine in new bottles. It is quite probable that Third World diplomats were familiar with the 1968 terminology (or perhaps even present at the negotiations that gave birth to this phrase) and later adopted it for their own use within a different context. In any case, this would not be the last time that Americans would strenuously object to a term or concept that they themselves had originated.

Another contradiction in the U.S. position on "government-controlled media" is evident in examining U.S. government-sponsored international broadcasting outlets. For example, the WORLD-NET program, with a $1.6 million service for transmitting U.S. Information Agency programs by satellite to Europe, began broadcasting in April 1985.

Although the U.S.I.A. has called it an enormous global "diplomatic opportunity" (46), other reactions have been less sanguine. Even during its experimental phase, a West German broadcaster stated that the initial offerings were "very close to propaganda" (19).

Another controversial U.S.I.A. activity was the launching of Radio Marti, voted into existence by Congress as a branch of the Voice of America in 1983 and designed to be the equivalent of a "Radio Free Cuba." Negotiations to forestall the inevitable radio war between the United States and Cuba over this new propaganda strategy are at a standstill (15, 36). Radio Marti has also been subject to criticism within the United States because of its openly propagandistic nature and the administration's efforts to operate it independent of congressional oversight (16, 50).

Other examples of intervention by the U.S. government relate to military censorship and the increasing blanket of "national security" being thrown over what are deemed to be overly controversial issues. The military censorship imposed during the invasion of Grenada in late 1983 is perhaps the most striking example of how "national security" and "security concerns" are increasingly being invoked to curb journalistic access to information. Subsequent to the news blackout during the Grenada invasion, an outcry was raised by numerous media organizations within the United States, notably the American Society of Newspaper Editors, the American Newspaper Publishers Association, Sigma Delta Chi, Associated Press Managing Editors, and the Reporters Committee for Freedom of the Press (3). The contradiction between this blackout and the U.S. position on the NWICO was apparent to several well-placed observers. For example, Seymour Topping, managing editor of the *New York Times*, observed that "the extraordinary restriction imposed on the press in the coverage of the Grenada invasion prejudices the position the United States has taken in international forums on freedom of the press" (33). Another minor flap ensued after the *Challenger* disaster in January 1986 when the National Aeronautics and Space Administration (NASA) impounded the film of some of the country's largest news organizations (including AP and UPI). This action came after protests had already been voiced over NASA's tight control of information (27).

Even television networks have not been immune from government assaults. In February 1986, ABC received a strongly worded written rebuke from the White House Director of Communications after the network had allowed a Soviet reporter to rebut without challenge the president's nationally televised speech on his plans for increased military spending. ABC backed down and publicly admitted its wrong-doing (1). And relations between the CIA and access to intelligence information are continually brought to the fore, from various "spy trials" to Irangate.

How do these shadings of the argument in the United States illuminate the "government control" argument applied to the developing countries? Most defenders of the "balanced" flow account for the obvious presence of government in their media systems according to one of three arguments. First, since the colonial powers, particularly in Asia and Africa, left behind very centralized communications systems controlled by the colonial governments, the newly independent states merely perpetuated inherited structures. Second, since the private sector is most developing countries is very weak, the state is the only source of capital for building communications systems. Third, since many developing countries have yet to consolidate their national unity, the government must make use of the media for this purpose. Thus, these spokespersons stress the necessity of some national government participation for historical reasons in order to encourage any type of media organization.

Ironically, the communications paradigms of the 1950s and 1960s promoted in the Third World by the Americans, notably Wilbur Schramm, favored development projects planned and executed by national governments, with a largely one-way information flow from government development agencies to the people. However, in the logic of today's critics, there is but one short step between government participation and control. As Charles Wick suggested in a Paris speech during the UNESCO 1983 General Conference,

This complaint about "imbalance" in the flow of information was coupled with another,

more radical view. To some—and I hasten to add, fortunately not all—Third World countries there is a conviction that the media should be used as tools of development. This, of course, leads them to the unacceptable conclusion that media should be controlled by the State (51, p. 4).

Obviously, times had changed. What the United States advocated following World War II as part of the process of modernizing the Third World was no longer applicable in the 1980s.

Of course, the Third World's desire to use media for development does not justify those regimes that do indeed use UNESCO rhetoric to reinforce strict, at times even total, control of the media. This is the main "contradiction" in the position of the NWICO advocates. UNESCO, however, has made no attempt to skirt the issue. The Director-General of UNESCO has stated on numerous occasions that the countries of the developing world must improve their own national situations before demanding action at the international level.

However, if consistency is demanded from one side it should also be required from the other. U.S. criticism, within the NWICO context, of countries that control the press and persecute journalists has not prevented the United States from supporting regimes whose survival depends on restrictions on freedom of the press.

The corollary of the "government control of the media" slogan is the "free flow of information" doctrine. Although there was some slight room for negotiations on the free flow doctrine under President Carter, it has been uncompromisingly defended in the Reagan administration. In September 1981, President Reagan sent a letter to the Speaker of the House of Representatives stating that "the United States has long regarded the principle of the free flow of information as a cornerstone of any democratic political order." And in Secretary of State Shultz's letter of December 1983 to UNESCO, announcing the U.S. decision to withdraw, the only mention made of the communications question was a reference to the necessity of respecting the free flow of information.

However, what is less well known is that within

the United States, civil liberties groups, sympathetic lawmakers, and journalists had been attacking the administration because of its domestic violation of the free flow of information principles (see 11). In 1981, for example, U.S. customs agents began seizing written materials arriving from Cuba and announced that citizens who wanted their mail must report to the government who they were and why they wanted it. The law invoked to justify such actions was the "Trading with the Enemy Act," the logic being that the U.S. government is within its rights in "restricting the dollar flow to hostile nations."

In February 1983, the U.S. government attempted to restrict the distribution of three Canadian films (a documentary against nuclear war and two films on the dangers of acid rain). The Justice Department declared that the three films were "political propaganda" and that therefore their projection in theaters had to be preceded by a communique indicating the disapproval of the U.S. government. A related government directive stipulated that it must receive a list of all organizations requesting copies of the films. Mobilization against this action by ecology groups, civil liberties associations, members of Congress, and even the Canadian government led to the annulment of the Justice Department action in 1983 by a federal judge in California (6, 22, 47). However, in April 1987, in a decision widely criticized by civil liberties groups, the U.S. Supreme Court upheld the right of the administration to label the three Canadian films "political propaganda" (9).

In a related area, that of the free flow of scientific information, the U.S. policy has also provoked criticism from the academic community. In February 1984, the National Academy of Sciences published a report condemning the current regulations applying to technology exports. The members of the National Academy stated that the new rules went beyond what had been judged necessary in a 1982 study on the subject carried out by a group of eminent scientists and military advisors. The earlier report, while recommending greater vigilance, had strongly urged that the free flow of scientific information be preserved. The 1984 report stated that this advice had not been followed and that the govern-

ment is now keeping a very close watch on scientific exchanges, even going so far as to send agents to scientific congresses (35). Even the *New York Times* made an impassioned plea for "open channels of scientific communication":

> The Pentagon has been conducting a virtual guerilla war against the academic tradition of open scientific communication. The presidents of Cal Tech, MIT, and Stanford recently warned that they would refuse Pentagon-funded research if military reviewers insisted on the right to stop publication (40).

The most important group in the United States to mobilize against the restrictions on the free flow of information is the American Civil Liberties Union (ACLU). The Spring 1986 issue of the ACLU's newsletter is aptly entitled "Opening America's Borders to a Free Flow of Information." The ACLU has launched a special "Free Trade in Ideas Campaign" that emphasizes "access to information" as its key point. The backers of the campaign stress that, since 1981, American rights have been seriously restricted in four areas: the right to travel, the right to import ideas from abroad, the right to export ideas to other countries, and the right to invite foreign speakers to the United States regardless of their political beliefs and associations. The ACLU campaign's goal is the passage of legislation in both the Senate and House that would remove restrictions in the above areas (30).

One of the most obvious contradictions in the U.S. defense of the free flow of information doctrine involves the flow of television programs, the issue that in the opinion of many observers launched the debate on a NWICO. A study by Kaarle Nordenstreng and Tapio Varis, published by UNESCO in 1974, concluded that over a five-year period the United States dominated the international TV export market, selling more than twice as many programs as all other countries combined (28). This evidence of U.S. cultural domination (mentioned even in U.S. congressional documents) virtually obscured the fact that the United States itself imported almost nothing: the 16 U.S. commercial stations examined imported a total of only 1 percent of their programming and the 18 public stations only 2 percent. An update of this project in 1983 showed virtually no change—an overall figure of 2 percent for total imports of both commercial and public broadcast stations (48, 49). Thus, in the limited TV landscape of the United States the virtues of a "free flow of information" are unidirectional. The irony of this situation has not been lost on a number of well-placed scholars, among them the Executive Director of International and Allied Arenas in the Harvard Program on Information Resources Policy, who observed that "this is mainly a commercial question, but in some ways it makes the United States, the world's richest nation in communication and information resources, one of the world's most culturally deprived nations" (18, pp. 67–68).

Another corollary of the free flow doctrine directly related to media is the "freedom of the press." In the NWICO debate, this concept was presented as the universal ideal of democracy and the antithesis of "government control of the media." It was also closely related to the defense of the First Amendment. Notwithstanding specific assaults on freedom of the press in the 1980s, the most serious impediment to a genuine realization of this democratic principle is the monopolistic structure of the press itself. It is almost a commonplace to state that freedom of the press in the United States applies only to those who are wealthy enough to have a press. The wide range of newspapers available in many Western European countries has not been sustained in the United States because of the increasing concentration of the industry (5, pp. 8–9).

One of the few Americans to have questioned the sacrosanct principle of U.S. freedom of the press in connection with the NWICO discussions was U.S. Representative George Crockett from the State of Michigan. In casting the only dissenting vote during 1981 congressional hearings to consider a vote of censure against UNESCO, he stated that the United States has

a press that operates in an increasingly monopolistic market and seems to be more and more responsive solely to the interests of its corporate boardrooms. It therefore seems somewhat hypocritical for anyone to introduce

a simple resolution that proposes to condemn the entire Unesco operation because some of its members' notion of a free press may differ somewhat from ours, especially when our hands are not clean. Let's first remove the mote from our eyes. Then we can better help other nations do the same (10, p. 203).

As expressed within the context of the NWICO, UNESCO's position has been that press freedom goes hand in hand with press responsibility. Nonetheless, the United States once again strongly objected that any mention of responsibility was a cover-up for government control of the media.

There are many examples of how this position was articulated by U.S. spokespeople. As Rosemary Righter reports, in 1978 a State Department diplomat at negotiations on what was then still a Draft Declaration on the Media said, "we are just basically opposed to *any* connection between the media and responsibility, however expressed" (37, emphasis in original).[5] During the 1980 UNESCO General Conference, the *Washington Post* carried an editorial entitled "International Big Brother" that also presented U.S. objections to this concept: "Their [UNESCO's] new "order" would amount to order, imposed and policed by them. Unesco is said to be ready to anoint itself as arbiter of world communications, to establish standards for 'responsible' reporting" (21).

However, as writers such as Schiller and Nordenstreng have pointed out, the origins of the "social responsibility" theory are to be found in the United States itself. The institutional expression of the "social responsibility" theory was that of the Hutchins Commission on Freedom of the Press created in the United States in the mid-1940s. This commission of prominent academics concluded that the importance of the press in modern society warrants an equivalent obligation of social responsibility and that some type of government regulation might be necessary to ensure that the press accept its responsibility (8). Although the main conclusions of the Hutchins Report were never accepted by the U.S. media, the work of the commission, and particularly its advocacy of the media's "social responsibility," has had a considerable and long-lasting effect on Western journalism. A seasoned observer of the international communications debate, Dinker Rao Mankekar, even went so far as to state that the movement for a New Order called for a "rehabilitation" of the Hutchins Commission (23).

Moreover, "social responsibility" is far from being a dead theme in U.S. journalism. A number of well-known figures in the journalistic and political communities have made reference to it in recent years. In the 1970s, for example, U.S. Vice President Spiro Agnew admonished the press for not exercising more social responsibility. Almost ten years later, William Randolph Hearst, editor-in-chief of the Hearst Newspapers, insisted that "freedom is not enough. A sense of responsibility must go with it. The Founding Fathers had that in mind when they added the Bill of Rights to the Constitution in 1791" (13). The concept of a responsible press is cited in the official code of ethics of Sigma Delta Chi (the best-known professional association of journalists in the United States). And, paradoxically, the establishment of "responsible media" is cited as one of the objectives of the World Press Freedom Committee, the U.S. group formed in 1976 expressly to combat the NWICO. The official stationery of the WPFC states that the organization is dedicated to "responsible and objective media."

A final illustration of U.S. adherence to norms of "responsibility": When a private media commission was formed in the United States in 1983, it was named the National Committee on a Free and Responsible Media (*Editor & Publisher*, July 9, 1983).

The pattern of origin and opposition continues with the slogan "the right to communicate." U.S. objections to "the right to communicate" surfaced during the 1980s, when UNESCO also began to support a new generation of "people's rights." Since "the right to communicate" was presented as one of these new rights, it became enmeshed in the larger controversy over "collective rights" versus "individual rights." The U.S. polemics were clearly spelled out in the AP coverage (October 25, 1983) of the 1983 UNESCO General Conference. After referring to "the right to communicate" as "one of the 'collective or people's rights,' " the AP correspondent reported, "Many nonindustrialized nations maintain that peoples' rights should have equality

with individual human rights. Western nations maintain such a concept could be used by authoritarian governments to abridge individual rights." Similar objections are presented in a 1983 editorial which maintains that UNESCO's commitment to "the right to communicate . . . means an end to private ownership of the means of communication. It means that these media become organs of official propaganda. . . . Unesco must back off. Control is not the answer" (17).

Such criticism ignores the fact that most of the conceptual work for "the right to communicate" was elaborated in the 1970s in the West. The London-based International Institute of Communication did pioneering work in this area, the father of "the right to communicate" was the late Frenchman, Jean D'Arcy, and the East-West Communication Institute at the University of Hawaii took a leading research role. According to Harms and Richstad, who were most active in the early stage of research, "the right to communicate" was based upon notions such as interactive, two-way communication, with an emphasis on social participation (20)—references that were later to become almost synonymous with the demands for a NWICO.

Leonard Sussman, who was an early and adamant critic of UNESCO and the NWICO, also admits the Western origin of "the right to communicate":

> The concept of this still theoretical "right" originated in the West, as did most human rights guarantees now written into universal covenants. . . . Though most of the theoretical work on the formulation of this "right" in international law has been done in Europe and the U.S., the developing countries fully support the general approach (42).

A final issue connected to the "government control" argument is the protection of journalists. In February 1981, at a UNESCO-sponsored meeting, the major U.S. interest groups, aided by key U.S. newspapers, succeeded in equating "protection of journalists," "licensing of journalists," and "government control of the media." Since then, any mention of protection of journalists has been stigmatized as being a cover-up for government control of the media.

The notion of "licensing" has never been defined. If "licensing" simply means a journalist's accreditation, granted by the government, then such a procedure exists everywhere in the world. In the United States, federal agencies normally issue special documents accrediting members of the journalistic community. Moreover, for the last several years a debate has been going on within the United States on the use of entry visas as a means of establishing a *de facto* licensing system for foreign journalists. Frank Campbell, then Minister of Information of Guyana, raised this question in a February 15, 1981 interview with the *New York Times*:

A journalist from Guyana wanting to go to the U.S. has to comply with normal visa requirements. Very often he is refused. But if we refuse a visa to a U.S. journalist, then it's a press freedom matter. Let's have universality.

This issue was even raised by one of the organizations that has led the campaign against UNESCO and the NWICO: the Inter-American Press Association (IAPA), whose Executive Committee has considered examining "whether or not the U.S. Immigration and Naturalization Service is using visa issuance as a means of accrediting or licensing foreign journalists working in that country" (*IAPA News*, February 1984, p. 2).

Robert Rutka, a Canadian journalist who had been an accredited Washington correspondent for four years, working for the Cuban news agency Prensa Latina, was informed in 1984 that under U.S. jurisdiction people are barred from dealing with Cuba—dubbed an "enemy nation"—unless they have a license. He was also informed that "under present conditions" he would not be granted a license (7). The contradiction between this action and the Reagan administration's position on the alleged promotion of licensing at UNESCO did not go unremarked. The conservative Montreal *Gazette* published an editorial in February 1984 arguing that by ordering Rutka to leave Washington, the United States was undermining its own argument about press freedom by refusing to grant a license to a

journalist (7). The sentiment was echoed by the conservative U.S. magazine *Editor & Publisher*:

One of the reasons why the U.S. government said it is resigning from Unesco is because of some of the things proposed for the New World Information Order. Licensing of reporters is one of them. Now we're doing the same thing (12).

The liberal New York magazine *The Nation* has also become involved in the licensing controversy. In a 1984 editorial responding to a *New York Times* editorial criticizing the licensing of journalists in Latin America, *The Nation* wrote:

The odd thing about the story is the unstated assumption that no such licensing system exists in the United States, similarly impairing freedom. It exists, of course, the only difference being that in the United States the orthodox media are trusted by the government to maintain and police the system informally, thus sparing the government much time and expense (29).

Although the United States had criticized UNESCO's concern for the protection of journalists, in 1981 a U.S. Committee to Protect Journalists was established in New York City. In addition to Walter Cronkite, who serves as honorary chairman, a number of other U.S. media personalities are on the board of directors, such as Ben Bagdikian, Anthony Lewis, and Dan Rather.

Do the numerous contradictions in the U.S. "government control" argument necessarily indicate that economic considerations have formed the basis of the U.S. position on the NWICO? Most researchers, no matter what their political orientation, would readily concede that contradictions do, in fact, indicate "something." The polemics arise over the nature of this "something" and whether or not it matters.

In my view, this "something" does not simply point to the vagaries of policy making or the difficulty of reconciling national with international objectives. The economic importance of international communications, since the 1970s, for the United States and most Western economies is indisputable. Coupled with the momentum of the privatization/ deregulation movement, this observation provides a plausible "something" to explain why the "government control" argument, despite its contradictions, has been and continues to be the main politico-ideological element in the official U.S. position on the NWICO.

The remaining question is: does it matter? If one is completely cynical about the role of researchers in effecting meaningful social change, then obviously it does not. But insofar as the NWICO movement has been sustained by sincerely motivated members of the critical research community, it represents one of our finest hours. Few issues supported by any other area of the social sciences have generated as much interest and discussion over real, concrete matters such as exploitation, power, dominance, dependence, and the construction of a more humane social order.

If policy-makers are ever to be held accountable for discrepancies such as those cited in this article, then an informed public opinion must play a key role in this process. Thus far, public opinion in the West has received only the "official version" of the NWICO story. It is essential that the community of international communications researchers not allow this version to go uncontested.

NOTES

1. There are a few notable exceptions. For example, Mario Vazquez Raña, the new head of UPI, told *Newsweek*: "UNESCO has enough problems and should leave journalists alone. We are going to punch out at UNESCO" (June 16, 1986). President Reagan, in his speech to the U.N. General Assembly, also made mention of the NWICO: "We cannot permit attempts to control the media and promote censorship under the ruse of a so-called New World Information Order" (*New York Times*, September 22, 1987).
2. An analysis based on this linkage is certainly in step with the work of Mattelart and Schiller, whose conceptual work has been of decisive importance for the NWICO debate. Indeed, most recently both have been

concerned with the importance of the privatization/ deregulation movement of international communications (see 24, 25, 38, 39).

3. These two giants of the U.S. press, and not, as is commonly believed, the U.S. State Department, were the most extreme "hard-liners" among the actors involved in elaborating the U.S. position. For example, after the 1978 UNESCO General Conference, when over six years of prolonged negotiations finally produced a consensus on the Mass Media Declaration, both the *New York Times* and the *Washington Post* published extremely critical editorials, openly disavowing the position taken by the U.S. diplomats (see *New York Times*, November 27, 1978, and *Washington Post*, November 27, 1978).
4. It should be acknowledged that certain observers of the NWICO debate referred to this contradiction. For example, the late Leonard Theberge, former director of the Media Institute, in referring to the "government control" argument, wrote: "broadcasters have always been regulated by the FCC and are required to adhere to the Fairness Doctrine" (43, p. 87).
5. Righter, who has been one of the most vitriolic critics of UNESCO and the NWICO, nonetheless describes the U.S. position on responsibility of the media as "crude and cliché-ridden confrontationalism" (37).

REFERENCES

1. "ABC News Says It Erred in Airing Russian's Views." *New York Times*, February 28, 1986.
2. "Africans Unhappy at Replies at UN Aid Session." *New York Times*, May 29, 1986.
3. "Around the Hemisphere." *IAPA News*, February 1984, p. 10.
4. "Bad Population Politics." *International Herald Tribune*, August 9, 1984.
5. Bagdikian, Ben H. *The Media Monopoly*. Boston: Beacon Press, 1983.
6. "Canada Asks U.S. to Reconsider Ruling on Three 'Propaganda Films.'" *International Herald Tribune*, February 28, 1983.
7. "Canada: Prensa Latina Reporter Surprised, Angry by U.S. Ouster." IPS New Service, February 21, 1986.
8. Commission on Freedom of the Press. *A Free and Responsible Press*. Chicago: University of Chicago Press, 1947.

9. "Court Backs Propaganda Label for Three Canadian Films." *New York Times*, April 29, 1987.

10. Crockett, Hon. George W. "Prepared Statement of Hon. George W. Crockett in Opposition to House Resolution 142." In *Review of U.S. Participation in UNESCO*, Hearings and Markup before the Subcommittees on International Operations and on Human Rights and International Organizations of the Committee of Foreign Affairs, House of Representatives, 97th Cong., March 10, July 9 and 16, 1981. Washington, D.C.: U.S. Government Printing Office, 1982.

11. Demac, Donna. *Keeping America Uninformed: Government Secrecy in the 1980s*. New York: Pilgrim Press, 1984.

12. "E&P Takes Issue with U.S. 'Licensing' Case." *IAPA News*, August 1984, p. 5.

13. "Editor's Report." *San Francisco Examiner*, May 9, 1982.

14. "Les Etats-Unis s'engagent à ne pas verser de fonds qui seraient utilisés pour l'avortement." *Le Monde*, August 8, 1984.

15. "For Cuba's Radio Marti Fans, It's Soap Opera, not Soapbox." *New York Times*, August 27, 1985.

16. Frederick, Howard. *Cuban-American Radio Wars: Ideology in International Telecommunications*. Norwood, N.J.: Ablex, 1986.

17. "Freedom to Communicate." *Daily American* (West Frankfurt, Ill.), June 29, 1983.

18. Ganley, Oswald and Gladys Ganley. *To Inform or to Control: The New Communications Network*. New York: McGraw-Hill, 1982.

19. "Global U.S. Press Conference." *IPTC News* No. 56, March 1984, p. 35.

20. Harms, L. S. and J. Richstad (Eds.). *Evolving Perspectives on the Right to Communicate*. Honolulu: East-West Communications Institute, 1977.

21. "International Big Brother." *Washington Post* (published in the *International Herald Tribune*), October 21, 1980.

22. "Judge Lifts Label on Canada Films." *International Herald Tribune*, May 25, 1983.

23. Mankekar, Dinker Rao. "The Evolution of Social Accountability in Communication." *Media Development* 27(4), 1980, pp. 10–11, 14.

24. Mattelart, Armand. *Transnationals and the Third World: The Struggle for Culture*. South Hadley, Mass.: Bergin & Garvey, 1983.

25. Mattelart, Armand. *Communication and Information Technologies: Freedom of Choice for Latin America?* Norwood, N.J.: Ablex, 1985.

26. "Nationalization vs. Denationalization." *New York Times*, July 27, 1986.

27. "News Groups Protesting NASA's Seizing of Film." *New York Times*, January 31, 1986.

28. Nordenstreng, Kaarle and Tapio Varis. *Television Traffic—A One-Way Street?* Reports and Papers on Mass Communication No. 70. Paris: UNESCO, 1974.

29. "Old World Information Order." *The Nation*, July 7–14, 1984, pp. 6–7.

30. "Opening America's Borders to a Free Flow of Information." *Civil Liberties* (Newsletter of the American Civil Liberties Union) No. 357, Spring 1986.

31. Philips, James. Remarks before the Communications Commission, 4th Extraordinary Session of the UNESCO General Conference, November 26, 1982.

32. Picard, Robert G. "State Intervention in U.S. Press Economics." *Gazette* 30(1), 1982, p. 4.

33. "Press Sees Grenada News Curbs Hurting U.S. Stand on Controls." *International Herald Tribune*, November 9, 1983.

34. Public Agenda Foundation. *The Speaker and the Listener: A Public Perspective on Freedom of Expression*. New York: Public Agenda Foundation, 1980.

35. Quatrepoint, J. M. "Un rapport de scientifiques américains critique la politique de limitation des exports technologiques." *Le Monde*, February 29, 1984.

36. "Radio Free Cuba." *Detroit News*, April 22, 1985.

37. Righter, Rosemary. *Whose News? Politics, the Press and the Third World*. London: André Deutsch, 1979.

38. Schiller, Herbert. *Who Knows: Information in the Age of the Fortune 500*. Norwood, N.J.: Ablex, 1981.

39. Schiller, Herbert. *Information and the Crisis Economy*. Norwood, N.J.: Ablex, 1984.

40. "Security and Secrecy." *New York Times* (published in the *International Herald Tribune*), April 30, 1984.

41. "A Simple No to UNESCO." *New York Times* (published in the *International Herald Tribune*), September 11, 1978.

42. Sussman, Leonard. *Warning of a Bloodless Dialect: Glossary for International Communications*. Washington, D.C.: Media Institute, 1983.

43. Theberge, Leonard. "Comments: Journalism in the Service of the State." *Political Communication and Persuasion* 2(1), 1982.

44. "UN in Agreement on Steps to Bring Recovery." *New York Times*, June 2, 1986.

45. United States Congress. *Congressional Record*. Proceedings and Debates of the 95th Cong., 1st Sess. Washington, D.C., June 13, 1977.

46. "U.S. Agency Transmits TV Programs to Europe." *New York Times*, April 23, 1985.

47. "U.S. Restricts Three Films as Propaganda." *International Herald Tribune*, February 26–27, 1983.

48. Varis, Tapio. "International Flow of Television Programs." *Journal of Communication* 34(1), Winter 1984, pp. 143–152.

49. Varis, Tapio. *International Flow of Television Programmes*. Reports and Papers on Mass Communication No. 100. Paris: UNESCO, 1985.

50. "A Victory on Marti." *New York Times*, September 27, 1983.

51. Wick, Charles Z. "UNESCO: A Time for Change." Remarks prepared for delivery at the French Institute for International Relations, Paris, October 27, 1983.

FOR BETTER JOURNALISM, NOT MORE PROPAGANDA

Leonard R. Sussman

In this article, the author spells out some of the arguments offered by the United States and other Western representatives at UNESCO conferences for opposing various provisions of the New World Information Order document.

A better system for transmitting news and information world-wide is needed. Journalism can always be improved. Yet many proposals for a New "Information Order" sound to independent journalists like a "new world propaganda order."

It must be possible to improve the volume and quality of news moving among developing countries—and between them and the industrialized nations—without implicit threats to the professional integrity or personal safety of the independent journalist.

In 1981, for example, 21 journalists were murdered and 14 others assaulted by guerrillas or governments. Another 58 were imprisoned. Seven countries expelled journalists, and 45 journalists fled just one country. Countless newspersons were harassed, many more censored, and most—not some, but most—worked under the direct influence or control of governments.

The independent, the free journalist, is in the minority. Yet governments of every political hue depend on the free journalist to provide an objective account of the day's news around the world. Even the most oppressive countries buy the daily reports of the independent world-news services.

No report, to be sure, can be entirely free of some

Leonard R. Sussman, "For Better Journalism, Not More Propaganda." *Freedom House*, List Number 26, July 1982. Reprinted by permission.

The author is executive director of *Freedom House* in New York and was Commissioner of the U.S. National Commission for UNESCO.

subjective influence. By striving for neutral news-writing, however, one can come close to it. By seeking the opposite one can only produce propaganda. Independent journalists therefore fear governments setting objectives for reporters. Even noble sounding objectives—opposing war and apartheid—open the door to governments henceforth dictating to journalists all manner of political "responsibilities."

The "use" of journalism for governmental propaganda has become implicit in the highly emotionalized news-media debates at United Nations Educational, Scientific and Cultural Organization (UNESCO) and elsewhere. The Soviet Union in 1970 began to exploit for its own ideological and political objectives the Third World's criticisms of the four major Western news media. The Soviet Union's agency is seldom mentioned by the Third World because TASS is merely an extension of the USSR's geopolitics, and not a journalistic undertaking. To be journalistic, as are the four Western news services and other smaller agencies, TASS would have to employ neutral criteria in seeking and reporting news. TASS makes no claim to neutrality or objectivity. It serves the interests of the Soviet Union at all times.

That is not to suggest that East-West conflicts necessarily dominate the news media controversies. Many Third World countries, whether or not they have journalists independent of their governments, want better communication facilities tying them to the rest of the world. They also ask that their developments be reported more extensively—and more *sympathetically*—by international news services. Providing better national and international communications facilities, however, is quite different from assuring that the *content* of newsreporting hereafter will satisfy a hundred diverse developing countries.

Yet too often the UNESCO debates sound to independent journalists as though the two demands are tied together: share communications technology and report Third World news as a UNESCO resolution may decide. No self-respecting independent journalist can accept the latter commitment.

Many proposals discussed at UNESCO would describe the journalist's responsibilities. Indeed, the MacBride Commission (International Commission

for the Study of Communication) in 1980 found of equal value two opposing political systems. One requires the journalist to be exclusively the servant of the state. The opposite system—that of independent journalism—expects professional integrity and a seeking for truth to be the highest authority. By equating these diametrically opposed political and journalistic systems the MacBride report further fueled the fears of independent newspersons.

The commission placed on an agenda for "further study" the licensing and inter-governmental monitoring of newsreporting as part of the "protection of journalists." A consultation in February 1981 at UNESCO's Paris headquarters provided a formal paper espousing licensing, codes, monitoring and penalties for journalists as part of a proposed "protection" commission. The issue failed when free-press advocates at the last moment refused to join the consensus.

The defining of "a New World Information and Communications Order," however, remains on the agenda of UNESCO's 1983 general conference. Seeking to define a "new order" can deteriorate into a bitterly propagandized debate. UNESCO's 1976 general conference faced irreparable division over the news media issue.

The "new order" debates inevitably raise erroneous arguments along with some valid criticism of the present news flow around the world. It is these false claims that arouse suspicions, indeed fears, among journalists who are independent of their own governments. Free-press representatives, even in the freest countries, constantly assert their independence of all governments, including their own. They regard the press as a servant of the people, not the government. Whether the free press performs well or not, it is distinguished by its ability to alert citizens to all aspects of life, including the functioning, for better or ill, of their government.

The free-press system relies not only on legal protection for its independence, but as well on financial independence. A newspaper supported by commercial advertising need not rely on governmental financing which often leads to official influence or control of the press. The best American newspapers have long avoided commercial influences over the news and editorial columns, even while warding off governmental intrusions into journalistic prerogatives. Such independence-giving financial support has been repeatedly derided in UNESCO documents as "commercialism," and the organization is committed to further studies of this factor.

The challenges to the present news flow continue. Now, however, the charges are being systematically questioned by trained specialists. Early findings are revealing. Professor Robert L. Stevenson of the University of North Carolina's Center for Research in Journalism and Mass Communications checked whether—as charged—the major world-news services neglect the developing countries and favor news of their own countries. Stevenson found that in all 16 countries examined, news of the immediate region dominates the foreign-news columns. Africans get more African news than any other; Asians get more Asian news. In most places, North American news was less used than European news. The majority of all news flowing into Latin America from the four world-news services is news about the Third World: from 52 to 69 percent in the four agency files was from developing countries. Hardly neglect!

It is frequently charged that world services choose mainly negative aspects of developing-country news—a caricature of reality. Stevenson found that developing countries relying on the world services carry mainly reports of international and domestic politics, with between 14 and 18 percent devoted to economic matters and a major segment set aside for sports. Indeed, Latin Americans published a higher proportion of "disasters" and "negative" news about North America than their own countries.

That is not to say that coverage of the developing countries cannot be improved. Even ardent defenders of independent journalism—this writer among them—believe there should be:

1. *Constant efforts to improve the quality, and increase the variety of reporting about the developing countries.*This will require greater access by journalists to unofficial as well as official news sources in the developing countries, and an end to the harassment, imprisonment, expulsion, and even murder of journalists in the line of duty.

2. *The redefining of "news" to enlarge the social- and economic-development coverage that dominates Third World concerns.*These tend to be long term issues that do not readily fit current criteria for "hard" news or "today's" stories. Yet improved strains of rice or close-planting of maize can crucially affect food production—no small matter in any society—and certainly newsworthy at every stage of development, not only when its absence spells hunger.

To renew their commitment to a free and fair flow of information, 63 independent news-media leaders from 21 countries met at Talloires, France, in May 1981. Their Declaration of Talloires supported the "universal human right to be fully informed, which right requires the free circulation of news and opinion." They added, "Denying freedom of the press denies all freedom of the individual."

They acknowledged that governments in developed and developing countries "frequently constrain or otherwise discourage the reporting of information they consider detrimental or embarrassing, and that governments usually invoke the national interest to justify these constraints." But, they said, "the people's interest, and therefore the interests of the nation, are better served by free and open reporting."

If a society cannot afford diverse independent-news media, said the declaration, "existing information channels"—even if government operated—"should reflect different points of view."

The declaration strongly opposed all forms of censorship, international codes of journalistic ethics (though it did not object to national codes created by journalists themselves), and licensing of journalists.

The most influential group of news-media leaders ever assembled pledged "cooperation in all genuine efforts to expand the free flow of information worldwide." The time has come, said the declaration, for "UNESCO and other intergovernmental bodies to abandon attempts to regulate and formulate rules for the press."

The Congress of the United State formally applauded the Talloires Declaration. Congress went further. It approved by overwhelming votes two amendments to the U.S. State Department appropriations bill that would cut off American financial support of UNESCO if it "implements any policy or procedure the effect of which is to license journalists or their publications, to censor or otherwise restrict the flow of information within or among countries, or to impose mandatory codes of journalistic practice or ethics.''

President Reagan wrote Congress that he supported the amendment and commended the Talloires Declaration ''to the attention of all nations.'' President Reagan added, ''We do not feel we can continue to support a UNESCO that turns its back on the high purposes this organization was originally intended to serve.''

The congressional and presidential actions served a clear warning that Americans were deeply troubled by the UNESCO news-media controversies.

Such warnings can be useful. U.S. funding of UNESCO would not be ended unless the organization formally ''implemented'' censoring or press-control measures. That is not likely to happen. But great damage to independent journalism continues to be caused by repeated ''studies,'' conferences and statements by that disparage government-free journalism and directly or indirectly support the ''use'' of the mass media for government-specified objectives. Programs ''studying'' such steps continue apace at UNESCO.

In early 1982, at Acapulco, Mexico, at a UNESCO sponsored meeting, a 35-nation Inter-Governmental Council was forced to trim its expectations to fit a budget of less that $1 million for 1982. The United States, concerned about the emphasis placed on government owned news outlets, did not contribute directly to the International Program of Development of Communications. Instead, the United States offered increased cooperation by both the federal government and the American private sector. The chief U.S. Delegate, William G. Harley, said that the ''mature and responsible'' tone

of debate at the meeting had ''inspired confidence'' for the future.

Fifty-four ideas were proposed to the 35-nation council. Twenty-four regions and three intraregional projects were approved. Discussion of 27 national projects was postponed until the council's next meeting at Paris in December 1982. Of those projects approved, only 14 received direct financing, in most cases far less than requested.

Many projects considered at Acapulco would, indeed, provide basic technological assistance. But others would strengthen governmental controls over existing world-news channels. For example, an Asia-Pacific News Network (ANN) that requested $350,000 received only $80,000. ANN would link several government-run news agencies in the region and tie them to TASS in Moscow. ANN would also ''recommend'' that newspapers in Asia and the Pacific hereafter be forbidden from taking the independent news services—such as the Associated Press and Reuter—but rely soley on the government's screening of the news from these world-news services.

This prior censorship linked to the expansion of technical facilities may prove damaging and retrogressive. Such steps are not likely to generate open-hearted financial support from the developed countries.

Even that, however, should not relieve developed countries of responsibility to seek constantly to improve the flow of Third World news. On the contrary, free-press advocates in both the developed and developing worlds should, if necessary, combine inside or outside UNESCO to share more widely the fruits of modern communications.

All people need to know more about one another—but not at the cost of propagandistic distortions under the guise of technology-sharing.

9   DEVELOPMENT COMMUNICATIONS

One example of the importance of managing news, say Third World countries, is in connection with national development. Once a nation becomes wealthy, literate, conscious of its national identity, with a responsible population, it can be fully democratic. The nation can then afford to have the kind of aimless press that the West has, where everyone pulls in whatever direction the spirit moves him or her. In the meantime, and until national development has been achieved, development journalism must be practiced.

While this may sound very reasonable, it founders in the execution. For one thing, there is little agreement by anyone as to what is and what is not development communication. There also is some controversy over the difference between development and developmental communication. And, finally, while there is some evidence that when the opportunity arises, media in Third World countries are more likely than Western media to cover development news that concern them, it also appears that Third World readers like to read non-development and negative news just as do Western readers.

In the meanwhile, the West is trying to help Third World countries in improving and strengthening their communication systems so that they at least have what they call "the infrastructure" that it takes for development communication.

DEVELOPMENT AND DEVELOPMENT NEWS

Leonard R. Sussman

Because of the importance of these terms in the vocabularies of developing countries, we begin with some definitions—admittedly from the viewpoint of the United States.

Leonard R. Sussman, "Development and Development News," *Glossary For International Communications*, Washington, D.C.: The Media Institute, 1983. Reprinted by permission.

The author is executive Director of *Freedom House*, New York, and commissioner of the U.S. National Commission for UNESCO.

DEVELOPMENT

Third World

This is the most important single word in the political vocabulary of developing countries. All governmental activities are tied to development in some manner. As a consequence, all communications channels, including (or especially) the news media, are expected to participate in the development process. That premise leads in varying degrees—depending on the political structure of the country—to more or less freedom for the journalist to serve as an independent observer and reporter.

UNESCO

The economic, social and political development of the Third World is regarded as the most vital concern of UNESCO. For ten years, the complex, often bitter debates over international news media issues have been closely linked to the demands of Third World countries to "use" mass media—international, and domestic—to advance their development. In that process, many press-freedom traditions of Western journalism were challenged; sometimes to alter the system of international communication so that the content of messages could be controlled; sometimes to gain communications technology that would, in turn, assist domestic development.

First World

Broadly defined, the term suggests the process of improving existing, or creating new, structures or concepts. The United States has long recognized the need to assist the process of agricultural and industrial development abroad. The Agency for International Development (AID) is one arm of government devoted to such assistance. AID and the U.S. Information Agency (USIA) are now committed to providing aid for communications development abroad. The United States also was a prime mover in the creation of the International Program for the Development of Communication (in UNESCO).

Second World (Marxist)

The Soviet Union ties development assistance to the degree of ideological or geopolitical support received from Third World countries.

DEVELOPMENT NEWS

Third World

The term development news originated in Asia in the sixties as an effort—with private U.S. foundation help—to introduce new farming and industrial technologies into developing societies. Journalists were trained in covering scientific and economic changes and relating them to the development needs of their countries. The effort failed ultimately when governments either feared the spread of new information or the discussions of the problems and failures sometimes associated with economic development. Soon, governments took over the process and used it mainly as a channel to disseminate governmental views. The Nonaligned Press Agencies Pool carries some development information. Inter Press Service regularly covers development news from United Nations agencies as well as Third World governments.

UNESCO

Without emphasizing the term, UNESCO meetings have exhorted the communications systems to carry more information related to economic development. UNESCO seldom distinguishes between the flows of news and information. That places on Western journalism the burden of conveying information not generally regarded as subjects for broad journalistic coverage. News channels can become easily overburdened with "today's" coverage, leaving little space for longer term "process" stories (which may be defined as "information" and not "news" unless written with sophistication). Process stories, however, can herald important changes ahead, and forecast next year's "hard" news.

First World

This term has little meaning in Western journalism though it is regularly employed in Europe and the United States. Development news concentrates on the issues, problems, alternatives, and opportunities in using modern methods, training and technology to advance agricultural, industrial or economic development. Western journalism covers such matters close to home, but (except for several major newspapers) seldom report in depth on such subjects in developing countries. Serious investigative reporting of the Third World examines the long-term process of development, whether or not related to issues currently deemed newsworthy.

Second World (Marxist)

Second World publications and broadcasts devote a major share of space and time to the mobilization of the citizens for labor and other activities. This is designed to muster factory or farm workers to follow new procedures, make better use of equipment or generally be more productive.

A META-RESEARCH CASE STUDY OF DEVELOPMENT JOURNALISM

Jo Ellen Fair

Meta-Research is a research technique that looks over a field of study to see what generalizations may be made about the findings of various researchers. Here it is applied to development journalism. Most research in the field has assessed only the quantity of development journalism and concluded that there is too little development journalism for it to have an impact on national development.

As the international communication field continues to proliferate both in number of topics and volume of research articles, evaluating research observations and trends through traditional narrative literature reviews for the field as a whole or even for one particular area of study has become increasingly difficult. The purpose of this paper is to begin to explore how observations and trends cumulating through a body of research literature can be integrated and assessed systematically.

Using meta-research techniques in which conceptual explication, methodology, findings and conclusion are examined and grouped, this study will analyze the research done on development journalism as a means of demonstrating how research in a particular area of international communication might be synthesized. The value of using meta-research to synthesize a research domain such as development journalism lies not so much in the technique's quantitative nature. Rather, the strength of the technique is that it facilitates the development of a replicable set of criteria to analyze studies and

Jo Ellen Fair, "A Meta-Research Case Study of Development Journalism." *Journalism Quarterly*, Volume 65, Spring 1988, pp. 165–170. Reprinted by permission.

The author was a doctoral candidate in mass communication in the School of Journalism at Indiana University when this article was written.

the emergence of general, it not more theoretical, conclusions about the body of research.[1]

META-RESEARCH TECHNIQUES

Simply put, meta-research involves the analysis of previous analyses in which several primary studies are integrated with the goal of obtaining general or theoretical conclusions about a body of research.[2]

Meta-research comprises two different techniques. The first technique called meta-analysis is the systematic integration and statistical re-analysis of original data from a set of studies.[3] A second meta-research technique is called propositional inventory. Though less powerful than its counterpart, this technique involves a synthesis of a set of studies and their conclusions based on what is reported in the studies.[4] In a sense, propositional inventory involves a content analysis of a number of studies.

The goal of both meta-research techniques is to gather information either quantitatively (through statistical re-analysis) or qualitatively (through information reported about conceptualization, operationalization, methods findings and conclusions) so as to allow the identification of trends occurring within a set of studies.

As with any research method, meta-research techniques used to collect data across a set of studies have not been free of criticism. Critics of meta-research argue that techniques require subjective judgments similar to those made in traditional literary reviews. Though subjective judgments are made in meta-research with regard to the information that is coded, these judgments must be made explicitly. Moreover, researchers must pay close attention to concept explication, operationalization and measurement of the independent and dependent variables used in the studies.[5] The difference, then, between subjective judgments made in traditional literature reviews and meta-research is one of using "private" rules selectively and "public" rules across studies.

Much of the criticism of meta-research techniques has focused on the biases introduced by selecting for analysis only published studies, by the inclusion of both methodologically weak and strong studies and by the inclusion of studies with different

concept explications, operationalizations and measurement techniques.[6]

The bias introduced by including only published studies may be ameliorated by including convention papers, dissertations, theses and the unpublished works of colleagues.[7] As for the synthesis of a variety of studies, the inclusion of methodologically "poor" studies and the inclusion of methodologically "different" studies introduces no bias into the meta-research in that heterogeneity in conceptualization, methods and measurement merely increases the need for analysis.[8] As Glass, McGraw and Smith point out, "The claim that only studies that are the same in all respects can be compared is self-contradictory; there is no need to compare. . . . The only studies that need to be synthesized or integrated are different studies."[9]

Despite the criticisms aimed at meta-research, to the extent that it is rigorously carried out, meta-research can be an important enterprise in that: (1) It can synthesize a vast body of research, which allows a wider audience to make use of (social) scientific information; (2) It can provide information about a research domain that cannot be discovered through primary or secondary studies; (3) It can produce information about the reliability of a research finding (i.e., it can produce evidence confirming or contradicting a finding); (4) It can help direct future research by the formation of general or theoretical conclusions; (5) It can facilitate the application of research to practical, administrative or policy problems; and (6) It can advance theory formation in a particular discipline of study.[10]

METHOD

The use of development journalism research represents a "case study" of how meta-research techniques might be applied in the international communication field. The unit of analysis used in this meta-research was the study. Though the term "study" is somewhat ambiguous because it can represent differences in planning, size and complexity,[11] the study is used here so that in addition to results, several other aspects of development journalism studies could be coded.

The development journalism studies selected for analysis were those that carried out an analysis of content presented in print, wire or broadcast media. The studies that were included in the meta-research were those that labeled media content as development journalism or discussed media content as being involved in, a part of or helping with national development. Studies that discussed only the concept of development journalism or the role of the media in developing countries were excluded. The number of development journalism studies analyzed was 20.[12] These studies were published between 1967 and 1986.

To obtain as many studies as possible, multiple sources were used to discover the various development journalism studies. There sources were: *Communication Abstracts, Journalism Abstracts*, programs from AEJMC and ICA conventions, computerized bibliographic searches, as well as citations in research articles and books.

Each article included in the study was coded for descriptive information, conceptualization, review of literature, method, findings and discussion. Descriptive information included where the article was published and the year of publication.

The variables used to examine the framework of the studies included the type of theoretical framework, the purpose of the study, the conceptual and operational definitions of development journalism and national development, and the role of journalism/mass media in national development.

Each study also was examined in terms of whether it contained a literature review, as well as the number of citations and whether non-communication citations were included. The method variables included the medium analyzed, the unit of analysis and other sample features. In the findings section, variables included whether studies assessed the quantity or quality of development journalism and the influences on the production of this content. Lastly, conclusions about development journalism and generalizations about the role of development journalism in national development were coded.

Since the meta-research undertaken here is a content analysis of a set of studies, a check was made of coding reliability. Using one other coder, who analyzed four studies (20%), the reliability coefficient was .90.[13] Also, to improve coder objectivity, articles included in the meta-research were coded in random order so that coders would not be influenced by systematic trends occurring across studies.[14]

FINDINGS

Descriptive Information

Of the 20 studies analyzed, 12 appeared as journal articles or convention papers. *Journalism Quarterly* and *Gazette* each carried three articles, while *Media Asia* carried one. Four papers dealing with development journalism were presented at ICA, and one paper was presented at AEJMC. The remaining eight articles of the 20 appeared as book chapters or as monographs.[15] The earliest study labeling media content as development journalism appeared in 1967 in Lerner and Schramm's *Communication and Change;* the latest study was published in 1986 in *Journalism Quarterly.*

Only four of the research projects had been funded either fully or in part by a university (N = 2, 10%), private foundation (N = 1, 5%) or government/intergovernmental organization (N = 1, 5%). In the remaining 16 studies (80%), no references were made to funding sources. It was assumed that individual scholars were responsible for the expenses of their research. Interestingly, Weaver and Gray[16] found a similar pattern of funding in the journalism/mass communications field as a whole from 1954 to 1978. They found roughly a quarter (26.2%) of all journalism/mass communication studies to be funded as compared with the 20% of development journalism studies reported above.

Framework of the Studies

Fifteen of the 20 studies (75%) were coded as being descriptive in that they described development journalism without linking the media or media content to a theoretical framework. Of the other five studies, one was primarily historical; two attempted to determine the extent in which development journalism content could stimulate national development; and two put development journalism content into context by linking the content to either the government's national development policies or to information needs and expectations of a rural audience.

Given that most articles were descriptive in nature, it is not surprising that in the majority of cases, the purpose of the studies was to determine the amount and/or type of development journalism (N = 12, 60%) presented in the media or to illustrate how development journalism content might help national development (N = 3, 5%).

Generally, the role of the mass media in the national development process was discussed as one in which the media served to spur development or act as agents of change (N = 9, 45%). In 10 cases, however, no role of the media was specified. This finding is interesting when it is considered that the study of development journalism implicitly assumes some kind of role for the media and their content in national development.

Because of its perceived relationship to national development, development journalism has been studied as a separate category of news. For this reason the conceptual and operational definitions as set out in the studies were examined. In terms of conceptualizing development journalism, no consensus was found among the 20 studies. In three cases, the concept develooplopment journalism was explicated as any news that relates to the primary, secondary or tertiary needs of a country's population. Similarly in another three cases, development journalism was defined as news that satisfies the needs of a country's population and contributes to self-reliance. In two studies, development journalism was defined very generally as news that related to development or to social, economic or political problems. Defining development journalism as positive or good news occurred in only two cases, while one case defined development journalism news for neo-literates.

Though the 20 studies revealed several different conceptual definitions of development journalism, in nine cases (45%), no conceptual definition was put forth. Despite the absence of conceptual definitions, 18 studies presented operational definitions of development journalism. In 15 of these 18 cases, development journalism was operationalized by topics or categories of news that were considered to be development journalism.[17]

The conceptual and operational definitions of national development also were examined since the term ''development'' in development journalism assumes communication used for national development purposes. It was found, however, that in 13

cases (65%) national development was neither conceptualized or operationalized. No doubt the absence of conceptual and/or operational definitions of development journalism (N = 11) and national development (N = 13) reflects the difficulty of defining such terms, but it also may reflect a lack of clarity or rigor in organizing the framework of the study.

Literature Review

It was decided to examine the literature review sections of the 20 studies for two reasons: to discover whether the development journalism studies were building upon research done previously, and to find out whether an agreement existed among scholars concerning the types of studies cited. An even split occurred between the number of studies citing and not citing previous development journalism studies or related communication works.

The number of citations ranged from three to 13. Fifty-five authors were cited in 10 literature reviews. The most frequently cited works were Mustapha's study of Malaysian development news (four citations), Osae-Asare's study of the Ghana press' coverage of development (four citations), Vilanilam's study of development content in India (three citations), and Lerner's *Passing of Traditional Society* (three citations). Lerner's book, published in 1958, also was the earliest citation.

Additionally, four of the 10 studies with literature reviews cited studies in disciplines other than communication. In these four literature reviews, political science studies were cited three times; sociology was cited twice, and anthropology and economics were cited one each.

METHOD

Nineteen of the 20 studies used content analyses to examine the development journalism content of the media. Probably because of their availability to researchers, newspapers were the most frequently examined medium. In 12 studies, newspapers were the only medium studied, in five other studies, newspapers were examined in addition to another medium or media. After newspapers, wire services were examined in four studies, and television examined in three studies. Newsmagazines and radio each were analyzed in two studies.

The sample features—the unit of analysis, period of analysis and type of sample—also were examined. The units of analysis most commonly used were the story (N = 12) and the percentage of news hole (space or time) devoted to development journalism (N = 12). The length of the sample period ranged from less than a week (N = 5) to a year (N = 4). Other frequently used sample periods were two weeks (N = 5) and one (N = 4). In five cases, however, the sample period was not mentioned. Purposive samples—samples chosen because of data availability or convenience—were used in 11 cases, while 6 cases used random samples.

RESULTS

Perhaps because the studies relied methodologically on a quantitative method (content analysis), all but two of the 20 studies (90%) assessed only the quantity of development journalism. The most frequently cited influences affecting the production (or lack thereof) of development journalism were: news values (i.e., development journalism was less newsworthy than other topics; N = 11); organizational factors (e.g., media ownership and control; N = 8); journalistic factors (e.g., lack of trained personnel, N = 7); and resources (e.g., lack of funding or materials; N = 4).

Conclusions and Generalizations

Following the examination of the studies findings, the conclusion and generalizations made about development journalism content were analyzed. When necessary, multiple conclusions and generalizations were coded. In the 20 studies, researchers concluded seven times that too little development journalism was published for it to have an impact or influence on national development. Moreover, five times researchers concluded that one medium carried more development journalism content than another medium. Other conclusions mentioned were that a "watchful" or "responsible" press could help in the development process (four mentions) and that development journalism was not as newsworthy as other news stories (three times).

Lastly, generalizations about the media and/or media content and national development were coded. Eleven of the 20 studies advanced at least once this kind of generalization. Because of the different purposes, conceptual and operational definitions, methods, results and conclusions, there was a variety of generalizations. The only generalization made more than once or twice (four of 12 mentions) was that development journalism must be present in the media to support or help in the national development process.

CONCLUSIONS

The task of meta-research is to synthesize a set of studies so that general or theoretical conclusions can be offered about a research domain. This meta-research has revealed a number of very different conceptualizations, operationalizations, measurements, findings and conclusions occurring within 20 development journalism studies. Variety in these studies indicates little consensus as to what development is, how to study it, and what it means in a national development context.

Variety within a set of studies is not necessarily "wrong" or "bad," as differences in studies can represent competing schools of thought, paradigms or theories. In the case of development journalism, it seems that the variety within these studies represents a fragmentation of thinking about development and development journalism. It is frequently assumed in these studies that development journalism is important to national development. Yet, the role of the media and their content in national development in the majority of cases was not discussed explicitly.

In several instances, the rigor of these studies must be questioned not only in terms of the absence of conceptual and operational definitions of development journalism, but also in terms of the absence of definitions for development. It seems that if development journalism is a special type of communication in relation to national development, then national development must be defined to study the nature of that relationship.

Moreover, if the goal of research is to advance knowledge about a particular topic or area of study, the research must be replicable. It is difficult to ask the same research questions or posit similar hypotheses when no guidelines are present for the concept being examined or tested, or for the reliability of measurements.

The descriptive nature of nearly all of the studies may have served to fragment the ways in which the studies were organized and carried out. Without a primary theoretical framework to guide research, studies tended to examine descriptively many different facets of development journalism. Generally, studies done on development journalism do not cite each other and do not seem to build one another. The result of this research fragmentation may point to a lack of maturity in the study of development journalism, whereby studies do not fit coherently into a larger body of research.

In future meta-researches of development journalism particularly, or international communication generally, the combining of quantitative measures used in meta-research and qualitative reviews of individual studies may help researchers to assess better the strengths and weaknesses of individual and grouped studies. Through meta-research techniques, specific areas of interest may be linked to more general area: development journalism to international communication or international communication to mass communication. From this linking of research interests, the identification of similar concerns about methods, findings, conclusions and generalizations across specific, smaller areas of study and general areas of study may be enhanced.

NOTES

1. Gene Glass, Barry McGraw and Mary Lee Smith, *Meta-Analysis in Social Research* (Beverly Hills: Sage, 1981), pp. 2–24; Everett Rogers, "Methodology for Meta-Research," in Howard Greenbaum, Susan Hellweg and Joseph Walter, eds., *Organizational Communication, Volume 10* (Beverly Hills: Sage, 1985), pp. 15–16.
2. Rogers, *op. cit.*, p. 14.
3. J.R. Light and P.V. Smith "Accumulating Evidence: Procedures for Resolving Contradictions Among Different Research Studies," *Harvard Educational Review*, 41:429-471 (1971), p. 443; Glass, McGraw and Smith, *op. cit.*, p. 21.
4. Rogers, *op. cit.*, pp. 17–18.
5. Brain Mullen and Robert Rosenthal, *BASIC, Meta-Analysis: Procedures and Programs* (Hillsdale, N.J.: Lawerence Erlbaum Associates, 1985) p. 15.
6. Glass, McGraw and Smith, *op. cit.*, pp. 226–229; Fredric Wolf. *Meta-Analysis: Quantitative Methods for Research Synthesis* (Beverly Hills: Sage, 1986), p. 14.
7. Glass, McGraw and Smith, *op. cit.*, pp. 226–229.
8. *Ibid.*, pp. 217–226.
9. *Ibid.*, pp. 22–23.
10. Mullen and Rosenthal, *op. cit.*, pp. 1; Rogers, *op. cit.*, pp. 14–16; Wolf, *op. cit.*, pp. 10–11.
11. Gene Glass,"Integrating Findings: The Meta-Analysis of Research," in L.S. Schulman, ed., *Review of the Research* (Itasia, I.: Peacock, 1977), pp. 354–355; Harris Cooper, *The Integrative Research Review* (Beverly Hills: Sage, 1984), p. 75.
12. Generally, when dealing with content analysis or surveys, 20 cases would be too small a sample or even a census for researchers to work with quantitatively. However, with meta-research techniques, as long as a body of research can be identified and collected, meta-research can be used. In fact, meta-analyses have been performed on as few as two or three studies. See Gene Glass, "Primary, Secondary and Meta-Analysis of Research," *Educational Reporter* 10:3-8 (1976), p. 3; Mullen and Rosenthal, *op. cit.*, pp. 5–7.
13. Holsti's formula for coder reliability was used to measure the amount of agreement between coders analyzing the development journalism articles. See Ole Holsti, *Content Analysis for the Social Sciences and Humanities* (Reading, Mass.: Addison-Wesley Publishing, 1969), p. 137.
14. Rogers, *op. cit.*, p. 25.
15. The following articles were used in the meta-research: L.R. Nair, "Private Press in National Development: The Indian Example" in Daniel Lerner and Wilbur Schrammn, eds., *Communication and Change in Developing Societies* (Honolulu: East-West Center Press, 1967), pp. 168–189; Robert Simmons, Kurt Kent and Vishwa Mishra, "Media and Development News in the Slums of Ecuador and India," *Journalism Quarterly*, 45:698-705, Winter 1968); Ralph Barney, "Mass Media Roles in Development: A Descriptive Study From Four Developing Areas," *Gazette*, 19:222-238, (1973); Shawki Barghouti, "The Role of Communication in Jordan's Rural Development," *Journalism Quarterly*, 51:418-424 (Summer 1974); John Vilanilam, "Developmental News in Two Leading Indian News-

papers." *Media Asia,* 2(1):37-40 (1975); John Lent and Shanti Rao, "A Content Analysis of National Coverage of Asian News and Information," *Gazette,* 25:17-22 (1979); Hamina Dona Mustafa, "A Comparative Analysis of the Use of Development News in Three Malaysian Dailies During 1974," in John Lent and John Vilanilam, eds. *The Use of Development News,* (Singapore: AMIC, 1979), pp. 56–70; Emmanuel Osae-Asare, "The Ghana Press and National Development: A Comparative Content Analysis of Development News in the National Daily Newspapers and the Wire Services, April-September 1976," in Lent and Vilanilam eds., *op. cit.,* pp. 72–90; Oranuj Yunjanondh, "A Content Analysis of Newscasts of Three Radio Stations in Thailand, July-August 1977," in Lent and Vilanilam , eds., *op. cit.,* pp. 92–110; J.S. Yadeva and A. Mohnot, *Press Portrayal of Development News of International Significance in India* (New Delhi: Indian Institute of Mass Communication, 1980); Wilbur Schramm and Erwin Atwood, "The Coverage of Development News," in Wilbur Schramm and Erwin Atwood, eds., *The Circulation of News in the Third World: A Study of Asia* (Hong Kong: Chinese University Press, 1981), pp. 87–99; Georgina Encanto, "Development Journalism in the Philippines," in Erwin Atwood and Wilbur Schramm, eds., *International Perspectives on News* (Carbondale and Edwardsville, IL: 1982), pp. 33–48; Christine Ogan and Clint Swift, "Is the News About Development All Good? A Content Analysis of Selected Foreign Newspapers." Paper presented to the annual meeting of the Association for Education in Journalism and Mass Communication, Athens, Ohio, August 1982; Ishadi Sutopo, *Development News in Indonesian Dailies,* Occasional paper number 15. (Singapore: AMIC, 1983); Christine Ogan, Joe Ellen Fair and Hemant Shah, " 'A Little Good News' ": The Treatment of Development News in Selected Third World Newspapers," *Gazette,* 33:173-191 (1984); Christine Ogan and Ramona Rush, "Development News in CANA and Interlink: The Role of Women and Other Topics." Paper presented to the annual meeting of the International Communication Association, Honolulu, Hawaii, May 1985; Christine Ogan, "The International Population Conference as Development News," paper presented to the annual meeting of the International Communication Association, Honolulu, Hawaii, May 1985; Aurobindo Mazumdar, "Development Communication Through the Press: A Case Study of Newspapers in Assam." Paper presented to the annual meeting of the International Communication Association, Honolulu, Hawaii, May 1985; Ralph Barney "Media Development in a Transitional Situation: A Time-Lag Example." Paper presented to the annual meeting of the International Communication Association, Honolulu, Hawaii, May 1985; and Drew McDaniel, "Development News in Two Asian Dailies," *Journalism Quarterly,* 63:167-170 (1986). Vilanilam also has another article on development journalism in India. (John Vilanilam, "Ownership versus Development News Content: An Analysis of Independent and Conglomerate Newspapers in India," in Lent and Vilanilam, eds., *op. cit.,* pp. 31–54). However, this last article was not included in the meta-research because it is nearly identical to Vilanilam's 1975 article.

16. David Weaver and Richard Gray, *Journalism and Mass Communication Research in the United States: Past, Present and Future* (Bloomington, IN: Center for New Communications, 1985), p. 24.

17. The studies coded a variety of development-related news topics. The most frequently coded topics were economics, with eight mentions, rural/agricultural information, with six mentions; social change, with four mentions, and education and physical projects, with three mentions.

MEDIA SUBSERVIENCE AND DEVELOPMENTAL JOURNALISM

SHELTON A. GUNERATNE

Here a Third World journalist defines developmental journalism and says that it is compatible with the social responsibility theory of a free and responsible press. It is incompatible, says the author, either with the libertarian theory of a completely free press or with the authoritarian or Communist theory of a press controlled by the government.

DEVELOPMENTAL JOURNALISM

. . . This brings us to consider the meaning of developmental journalism, Shalklow (1975) says that its meaning is not the retailing of the government rallying cries, but rather "the formation of a new class of newspaper and broadcasting and magazine reporters who were fully trained and informed in the general economic field, as specialists."

Sarkar (1973: 41) calls it a new frame of reference and the new education for the craft of journalism. Chowdhury (1976: 2) defines it as the coverage of "news beats that are new in concept and designed to be relevant to social and economic changes" without a direct confrontation with the government news managers. Coats (1973: 7–8) believes it to be the reflection in the press of "traumas, upheavals, problems and progress encountered and achieved from the grass roots to the high seats of government" and the meaningful stage-by-stage coverage of the progress on "new bridges, schools, hospitals, houses, villages, industrial estates, offices, hotels and roads" and other such projects.

Golding (1977: 303) has discussed the origin of developmental journalism in terms of four ways in which it was produced:

First, by stressing the generally educative function of news either about specific pieces of informa tion or by arousal of general awareness of events and their implications.

Second, by producing stories which displayed particular social needs or problems it was hoped that government would be provoked into action.

Third, by giving prominence to local self-help projects news could encourage emulation of such activities in other communities. Finally, the news could tackle specific problems, such as elite corruption, often with prudent obliqueness.

However, one defines developmental journalism its aim goes much further than the information and entertainment function assigned to the mass media under the libertarian ideology. It could be looked upon as an integral part of today's new journalism which involves analytical interpretation, subtle investigation, constructive criticism and sincere association with the grass-roots (rather than with elite). The authoritarian concept of the press imposes some negative limits on the possible contribution of developmental journalism to social betterment by forbidding criticism of political machinery and the officials in power and by adopting the top-down approach to problem solving.

The first three ways of developmental journalism, discussed by Golding, are in keeping with the social responsibility theory of the press as well as the new paradigm of communication and development. The fourth way is incompatible with the au

Shelton A. Guneratne, "Media Subservience and Developmental Journalism." *Unilag Communication Review*, Volume 2, Number 1, January/June 1980, pp. 97–102. Reprinted by permission.

The author is a Sri Lankan who is on the journalism faculty at Moorhead State University, Moorhead, MN.

thoritarian concept but quite consistent with the social responsibility concept.

Developmental journalism of the second variety was adopted by India's *Hindustan Times* to bring about vast changes in the village of Chhatera in Haryana, some 25 miles north-west of Delhi. The newspaper played the role of "catalyst, planting new ideas in the minds of villagers and articulating their aspirations" and enlisted the support of about 20 other agencies, public and private institutions to bring about these changes. A regular fort-nightly column was started in 1969 to report on the village's progress. The editor, Verghese (1976: 11), says "The team of reporters and photographers . . . who have covered Chhatera at various times became better journalists . . . it was for almost all of them an altogether new experience that has enriched their careers".

The *Hindustan Times* project was undertaken with adherence to the principles of social responsibility. It is a clear demonstration of how the mass media could contribute to development without being subservient to the government.

SUBSERVIENCE DEBUNKED

The media subservience theory is nothing but the authoritarian theory of the press put in a new form in terms of the Third World's need for rapid development, national unity and other attractive concepts. It is old wine in a new bottle. It has provided solace to Third World leaders who like power but dislike criticism and investigative reporting. It has given some academics the opportunity to theorise. It has also given some journalists the grand opportunity to repent their abuse of journalism based on the libertarian concept.

The questions may well be asked whether the subservience of the mass media to those in power has produced the ideal kind of developmental journalism as expected by the subservience protagonists.

Quebral (1974) . . . was elated at the transformation of the mass media following the declaration of martial law in the Philippines. But the media are forbidden to criticise the President and his family, the military and the polices of the government, and they are expected to reflect the goals of the New Society. Self-regulation is observed by an association of the publishers of the leading dailies and magazines, the Philippine Council for Print Media, which recently denounced the country's press as "one of the world's most corrupt" and compared the newspaper offices to versatile dens of thieves (Rebamontan, 1977: 23), Mercado (1973) says, "Many political leaders . . . believe that the press has a duty to assist official policy. The establishment in most of our countries want a press they can use. A 'used' press is, obviously, bound to be a timid and passive press whose staff members will accept docilely pompous government statements and grandiose economic programmes without embarrassing questions".

The taming of the press in Sri Lanka under the Sirimavo Bandaranaike Government led to the fall of professional standards and to media-clogging by politicians, bureaucrats and party functionaries (Wickremesinghe, 1977: 18). This happened within a professed democratic political framework.

The Malaysian mass media are strictly guided by the national ideology, *Rukunegara,* and newspapers devote considerable space to stories on national development. In so doing, the mass media practice "strict self-restraint, steer away from investigative reporting, fill the pages with government speeches and campaigns (and) ignore the opposition." (Lent, 1977:20). The media are also restricted by the 1971 amendment to the Sedition Ordinance which prohibits the discussion of four so-called sensitive issues: (i) the Bahasa Malaysia language policy; (ii) the special rights granted to the Malay ethnic community; (iii) the special roles of Sultans and other royalty in the society; and (iv) the citizenship policy for the non-Malays (Lent, 1975: 7). These issues affect the lives of the Chinese and the Indians who comprise half of Malaysia's population. By denying the right of expression on vital issues, the Malaysian Government has adopted the authoritarian press concept within a professed democratic political framework.

The Indonesian mass media are also guided by the national ideology, *Pancasila.* But Anwar, an Indonesian journalist, has lamented the media's subservient role which has necessitated the practice of "existential journalism" a method of criticism using Aesopian language. Journalist Oetama says, "Only if the press plays an independent role within the national framework can it exercise some kind of control over misuse of power, whether by the government or by the people''; and he adds that the Indonesian press criticism of the government is mostly ''indirect, covered with symbolism and found between the lines.'' By imposing too many restrictions, the Indonesian Government also has adopted the authoritarian press concept with a professed democratic framework.

The implication of the above examples is that developmental journalism may not necessarily reach its fullest potential within a media subservience set-up while it has a better chance of reaching that potential within a social responsibility setup which recognises the moral right of freedom of expression encompassed in democratic political theory.

Within the non-Communist Third World, only a few countries would admit themselves to be in the authoritarian fold in the sense of Franco's Spain and Salazar's Portugal. But clear examples exist such as Amin's Uganda, Pinochet's Chile, Duvalier's Haiti and Bokassa's Central African Empire. What exists in these countries is government-say-journalism operating under the media subservience theory. A streak of authoritarianism runs through the power-holders in many countries in Latin America, Africa, Asia, and the Middle East even though many constitutions boast of freedom of expression guarantees and democratic trappings. They have fostered a subservient media systems for their own ends. . . .

SUMMARY AND CONCLUSION

This essay has attempted to establish that media subservience to government is not a prerequisite for fostering development journalism. . . .

the libertarian, concept of the press, which defines the function of the mass media as providing information and entertainment, does not fit the concept of developmental journalism;

the authoritarian and communist theories of the press are compatible with developmental journalism but with non-democratic limitations; and

the social responsibility theory provides the most fertile ground for reaping the full potential of developmental journalism in keeping with the democratic political philosophy as well as the new thinking on bottom-up development and self reliance. . . .

REFERENCES

Chowdhury, Anitabha, ''Fiesta of Asian press freedom seen at an end. . . .'' *IPI Report*, 25 (July), 1–2. 1976.

Coats, Howards, ''Development Journalism or plotting the march of progress,'' *Leader—Malaysian Journalism Review*, 2 (No. 3), 7–11. 1973.

Golding, Peter, ''Media Professionalism in the Third World: the transfer of an ideology,'' Pp. 291–308 in James Curran, Michael Gurevitch and Janet Woollacott (eds.), *Mass Communication and Society*, London: Edwin Arnold, 1977.

Lent, John A., ''A Third world news deal? The guiding light,'' *Index on Censorship*. 6 (September–October), 17–26. 1977.

Lent, John A., ''The guided press,'' Media, 2 (November), 6–7. 1975.

Mercado, Johnny, ''Development reporting: some observations,'' *Leader Malaysian Journalism Review*, 2 (No. 1), 41–45. 1973.

Quebral, Nora C., ''The Making of a Development Communicator,'' *Media Asia*, 1 (No. 2), 12–13. 1974.

Rebamontan, Lucino, ''The mud is flying at Filipino journalists,'' *Media*, No. 1 (November), 23. 1977.

Sarkar, Chanchal, ''Development and the new journalism,'' *Leader—Malaysian Journalism Review*, 2 (No. 1), 35–41. 1973.

Verghese, B. George, ''Project Chhatera—an experiment in development journalism,'' *Media Asia*, 3 (No. 1), 5–11. 1976.

Wickremesinghe, Esmond, ''A Call For Sri Lankan Free Press,'' *Media*, 4 (June), 18. 1977.

A THIRD WORLD PERSPECTIVE ON THE NEWS

Narinder K. Aggarwala

One of the best discussions of the meanings of development and developmental journalism by a Third World journalist was written in 1977 as a conference paper. We reprint it here because it states clearly why the Third World feels it needs a new information and communication order. The author gives examples of what kinds of development news he would like to see in the world's press.

Ever since the UNESCO sponsored San José Inter-Governmental Conference on Communication Policies in Latin America and the Caribbean in July 1976, the public debate on the question of press freedom and the information/communication needs of the developing countries has assumed a surrealistic quality. In what appears to be a no-holds-barred brawl, the adversaries—championing either the "free" or the "balanced" flow of information—seem to be railing at, rather than talking to, each other, and often on different planes. They have made the issues involved appear incompatible and irreconcilable.

But do the appearances reflect the truth? Is the fundamental principle of freedom of the press really in conflict with the developing countries' desire or demand for a better share, or say, in the world news flow, both quantitatively and qualitatively? Is their demand that the new disseminated internationally by the transnational wire services should reflect the realities, true concerns, and views of the developing countries irreconcilable with the right of the media to collect and disseminate news without government intervention? Does the developing countries' pressing need for using communication media for furthering social and economic development automatically dictate government control of national news media? Or does the developing countries' objective of setting up national news agencies represent a sinister threat to free flows of news?

I do not think so. I qualify this assertion by emphasizing that I am addressing myself to only one of the two issues involved in the current debate on the subject of press freedom—information flows across international borders. The view from the other perspective—of information flows within a country—may be quite different. By narrowing my focus, I do not in any way want to give the impression that I attach less importance to the vital issue of press freedom at policies of his/her newspaper or agency and the news preferences and quirks of his/her editor. The adaptation to the correct angle, slant, and treatment follows as a natural corollary.

Unquestionably, the world news disseminated by the international wire services has, in the milieu of the great North-South divide, a Northern orientation. This is what the developing-country leaders generally refer to when they decry the"one-way" flow of news. They do not mean that the developed countries are not getting any news from the developing countries, or vice versa. This is also what Louis Penalver, then Venezuela's education minister, meant in late 1976 when he asked: "Why should we rely exclusively on foreign news sources, which represent powerful economic interests, to hear about our own neighbors?" Developing countries' demand for measures to correct the existing "imbalance" in world news flows is a call for change from one (Northern) perspective to multi-(Northern/Southern) perspectives on world news. Third World

Narinder K. Aggarwala, "A Third World Perspective on the News." *Freedom At Issue*, May–June 1978. Reprinted by permission.

The author is an Indian journalist working with the UN Development Program as regional information officer for Asia and the Pacific.

countries want to establish a counter-flow of world news with Third World perspective—which need not and should not be an official one—to supplement the present primarily Northern perspective of world news.

The lack of a Third World perspective is obvious in the manner in which Western journalists, rightly or wrongly, discuss the problems, such as employment, food, population, etc., confronting the developing countries. Their reports, more often than not, either ignore or belittle the efforts of developing countries to alleviate the problems, often against seemingly insurmountable odds. It is not suggested or implied that the media should become subdued or less critical in its exposure of the enormity, as well as the urgency, of problems bedeviling the Third World. But the developing countries do deserve passing recognition of their development efforts, something strangely missing from the Western media reports.

At present, all social, economic, and political developments in the Third World are reported in terms of right of leftward shifts in government policies. Land reforms, measures to weaken the stranglehold of a few indigenous business groups over national economies or to encourage the development of national industries to the immediate or potential disadvantage of transnational corporations, and legislation to ensure better monitoring and supervision of national banking and trade institutions are all presented as portents of a country's slide into the communist or socialist ambit. (No matter that such measures are necessary for a nation's economic survival or the well-being of its people. No matter also that many of these measures have been in force in most of the Western countries for decades, without any one of these countries becoming communist or socialist.)

The same format, however, is not used when reporting similar developments in the Western world. For example, after the recent local government elections in France, in which the leftist coalition made a near sweep, no international wire service carried a story proclaiming the imminent danger of a socialist/communist takeover of France. True, it would have given a false picture of the political situation in France. But such generalized, interpretive reporting, which does not reflect the

reality as it exists but which does make the news more "sexy," is the norm in the case of dispatches filed from the Third World. This is all the more true of "authoritative reports and commentaries" of roving Western correspondents who claim to become experts on a developing country's complex situation after only a few days' visit.

The intention here is not to challenge the journalistic credentials of the Western media representatives or to downgrade the quality of their work. Nor is it desired to teach them how to write or report news (we are a very sensitive lot about such things!). The purpose is to emphasize that interpreting Third World developments, Western correspondents seem to (1) lack a proper perspective and/or (2) give preference over accuracy to making news more interesting or saleable to its Western users. It is this which is behind a recent remark of Philippine Foreign Secretary Carlos P. Romulo that "the governments of most of these (developing) countries have come to feel that, for whatever reason, events there are not being reported fairly, that their policies and actions are being misinterpreted or misrepresented in the Western mass media."

"SPOT" VS. "SOFT" NEWS

When the Third World leaders criticize the Western press for biased and distorted reporting, they are not, generally speaking, questioning the factual accuracy of Western news agencies or the honesty of their correspondents. Distortion, as Juan Somavía, Director of the Latin American Institute for Transnational Studies in Mexico City, points out, "does not necessarily mean a false presentation of events but rather an arbitrary selection and a slanted evaluation of reality." The alleged objectivity of news presentation, according to him, is belied by an arbitrary use of language, overemphasis on events of no real importance, and the general practice of "making news" by presenting isolated facts as a nonexistent whole.

Pressed by the limitation of space (in the case of printed media) and of time (in the case of radio and television), Western correspondents tend to select only the news that they think is of interest to their readers/subscribers in the industrialized countries, either because it is "sensational" or the national level. To the contrary. I believe that a free press is one of the essential, fundamental human rights. A free press generally guarantees that all other fundamental rights will be respected in a country, at least on the surface. Any attempt to whittle down press freedom in a country is a foreteller of the curtailment and ultimate elimination of all fundamental human rights. Contrary to what may have been said in some quarter or the other, there is nothing exclusively Western in the concepts of fundamental rights and freedoms. They are universal.

The battle for press freedom is, as is true in the case of all other human rights, a continuing one. The freedom of the press should not be allowed to be diminished in any form or disguise, and not the least in any international declaration which, with the passage of time, may assume the importance or force of international norm or law. We need to persuade all countries—and not only those of the Third World— that government control of the media, howsoever attractive in the short run, will be nationally catastrophic in the long run, and that a free press is vital to the future of a country and its people. In the case of the Third World, the task of persuading governments to support the cause of a free press could be made substantially easier if ways could be found to redress the so-called "imbalance" in the world news flows—the reason most commonly cited by many of the Third World countries currently supporting or leaning toward the doctrine of government control of the media for the national good. Western media leaders are bound to jeer, and claim that Third World countries are using this as an excuse, as a camouflage, to control media and to silence domestic criticism. This may be so, but the fact remains that there is considerable validity in the developing countries' complaint about "one-way" flow of information and ideas.

The Third World's complaint against the international news media is two-fold. First, only a quarter of the news that goes on the wires of the four major Western news agencies emanates from, or deals with, developing countries, although they make up nearly two-thirds of humanity. Second, most of the Third World news is negative and deals with such subjects as shortages, famines, natural disasters, and political and military intrigues. The news dissemi-

nated by the four transnational news agencies is meant primarily for the users in the developed countries and has a very strong Northern orientation. What the developing countries want is world news by Third World journalists for developing country media use. There is a genuine need for creating a channel through which developing nations can get news about each other, and the industrialized world, from their own perspective.

In this brief paper, I have attempted to suggest a model for such a mechanism—an independent Third World News Agency (TWNA), a loose conglomerate of several autonomous regional news agencies. News to be useful and effective will have to be factual, honest, and above all, credible. Without credibility, which in the case of news media translates into freedom from official and vested interest intervention, any news distribution mechanism will prove ineffective and fail.

The model provided is merely a bare-bone one. Many details will have to worked out and investigated. But all this can be done, once the idea of TWNA is found feasible and practicable. I think it is. I have also attempted to work out a structural model of the proposed TWNA. With the suggested structure, the TWNA will be able to provide a machinery for the collection and dissemination of world news with multiple Third World perspectives.

I agree with the general tenor of developing countries' criticism of the Western media (particularly as it relates to the coverage of the Third World), but I disagree with the solutions that have been suggested or agreed to by the developing countries so far—including the Non-Aligned News Agency Pool—to redress the situation. I think the proposed TWNA constitutes the best approach to providing better coverage of the developing countries and, if implemented, will go a long way in meeting the information needs of the Third World.

NEEDED: THIRD WORLD PERSPECTIVE

Developing countries primarily depend on four Western news agencies—AP, UPI, Reuters, and Agence Frances Presse (AFP)—for news about each other. News about Botswana, more often than not, reaches the people of Zambia through one of the four Western wire services. Worse still, until recently, the Caribbean countries used to receive much of their news about themselves via London through Reuters. The news that the developing countries' media receives from the international wire services is the news written and selected for the Western media. The style, the content, the treatment, and the perspective of practically all the news flowing in and out of the Third World reflects the personality, preferences, and the needs of the Western media.

Except for a few stringers and second-level reporters and sub-editors, all the news representatives and bureau chiefs of the four Western news agencies are the nationals of either the United States, Britain, or France. As the selection and the perspective of news is generally user-oriented (in the case of four transnational wire services, the Western media), even the employment of a substantial number of developing country reporters by the international wire services will not make any meaningful difference in the kind of news disseminated by these agencies. A case in point is the UPI which recently claimed that its Latin American news is written primarily by Latin nationals. Developing-country nationals working for international wire services become conditioned to writing news with primarily a Western audience in mind. It is one of the least stated but most fundamental survival axioms of the journalistic professions that a reporter learns, as quickly as possible, the editorial deals with something "strange" or "exotic." Wars, disasters, famine, riots, and political and military intrigues do make better copy than economic development. The primary concern of Western correspondents reporting from the Third World is with "spot" news and not with "soft" or "development" news. This practice is followed as well by the correspondents of the four major Western news agencies on which the Third World media depend for international news. In this process, they tend to forget or give short shrift to the information needs of the Third World.

For example, Tanzania's efforts to organize basic rural health services by using paramedics (the Tanzanian version of "barefoot doctors") may not be "sexy" enough for the Western media, but it does present a model to many developing countries. Similarly, the development of inland fisheries in Nepal,

the introduction of animal traction for farming in West Africa, and the establishment of the first forest ranger training institute in Honduras may not warrant Western media attention, but they are of great interest to developing countries, showing as they do certain movements on the development front in the problem-ridden Third World. Such news is also important to the developing countries as an agent of change, since an individual's first motivation toward change often comes from "hearing it on the radio," "seeing it on film" or "reading it in the paper." Development news, dealing with technical know-how available in or being acquired by developing countries, will assume even greater significance for the Third World as the developing countries' efforts to promote technical cooperation among themselves gain momentum in the coming years.

Developing countries feel chagrined about the lack of appreciation of Third World information needs in the news disseminated by the Western news agencies. "If Swaziland," stresses Adnan Z'merli, Tunisia's representative to UNESCO, "implements a successful new system for irrigating orange groves, we'd like to hear about it. We also want to know what is happening in Kenya—not just what goes on in Paris, Washington, and Moscow." Mr. Z'merli's statement, voicing as it does a sentiment commonly expressed by Third World countries, underscores the insufficiency of the North-oriented international news agencies in serving the Third World information media.

DEVELOPMENT NEWS

Admittedly, it is difficult to make development news interesting, but it can be, and is being, done. So long as an action or development has any bearing on people (all economic and social development activities do), it can make interesting copy. But it needs special skills and training. It requires journalists—both at junior and senior levels—who can understand highly complex economic, technical, scientific, and sociological information and translate and interpret it to their generally lay audiences. "High professional skills, higher than ever before, will be needed to make other (development) news interesting and not dull, and credible to the public.'' acknowledges Chakravarti Raghavan, former chief editor of the Press Trust of India, India's largest news agency prior to its government-dictated merger with other Indian news agencies to form "Samachar" in 1976. There is also urgent need to evolve criteria for assigning appropriate weightage to development factors in grading day-to-day news.

Some Western correspondents and commentators have erroneously equated the increasing Third World demand for development-oriented news with government-controlled news and information handouts. This may be the hidden motive of some developing countries, but development news should not be damned as synonymous with government-dictated news. Development news is not identical with "good" or "positive" news, lack of which is constantly bewailed by the politicians and government officials of not only the developing but also developed countries. Development news if not an official PR handout, issued by Third World countries concerned with image-building. In its treatment, development news is not, and should not be, any different from regular news or investigative reporting. It can deal with development issues at macro- or micro-levels and can take different forms at national and international levels. In covering the development newsbeat, a journalist can, and should, critically examine, evaluate, and report (1) the relevance of a development project of national and, most importantly, local needs; (2) the difference between a planned scheme and its actual implementation; and (3) the differences between its impact on people as claimed by government officials and as it actually is. Thus conceived, a development news story will be markedly different from a government handout.

It is not easy to provide an all-inclusive definition of development news which covers the entire spectrum of socio-economic and cultural development— even non-development—and problems as well as prospects. One can only cite examples. In 1969, when George Verghese, then the editor of the *Hindustan Times,* assigned a team of reporters to write periodically about the people, the problems, and the development prospects of a small Indian village, he introduced a new form of development journalism at the national level in India. "Our Village, Chhatera,'' as the project was called, was a bold attempt to give rural orientation to the predominantly urban-based and elite-oriented newspapers in the country. It is the form of journalism that can prove of immense help in bridging the rural-urban communication gap in the Third World.

Development journalism can also be the story about Wayen—a small village not far from Upper Volta's capital, Ouagadougou. Wayen, which literally means "the village of the sick,'' symbolizes the problems of poverty, sickness, and development— almost in their totality—in the Third World. Wayen's inhabitants are afflicted with endemic diseases—blindness, malaria, leprosy, to name a few. They have no clinic, no school, no roads, no sanitation. Development seems to have passed them by. Yet, the people of Wayen are a proud and a hopeful lot. They want help, but not pity or charity. With a little effort, Wayen's story can be told interestingly at national, regional, and international levels, because this tiny, dusty African village is what all the development—trade, aid, global campaigns against tropical diseases, and the New International Economic Order—is about.

Or, development journalism can be the kind of article that appeared in the *New York Times* recently, in which the author, Pat Orvis, described how a small water pump had changed the life in a Pakistani village which is typical of thousand upon thousands of remote, disease and poverty-ridden villages in the Third World. I can give scores of examples of national and international development journalism. It is not much different from what usually appears in Western newspapers in community or general news sections. But, unfortunately, an international counterpart of community news is missing from the Western media files. In the West, particularly the United States, media managers are constantly searching for, and experimenting with, ways to make the news relate to the people. In the Third World, development journalism is essential to make the media—and the decision-makers—relate to, and relevant to, the people.

Development journalism is a relatively new genre of reporting in the Third World. Not all Third World newspapers and editors have taken to it kindly or eagerly. They have failed to changed their highly political orientation, acquired during the anticolonial struggle, and have failed either to recognize and/or communicate their changed information needs to the transnational news agencies serving them. This is behind the claim of the international news agencies—particularly Reuters—that they do carry development-oriented features for "regional" distribution, but that there is not much demand for such fare even in the developing-country media. But the market for this kind of journalism is expanding at a relatively rapid pace in the Third World, as is evident in the increasing use of the material distributed by such development-oriented news feature syndicates as the Manila-based DEPTH news (operated by the Press Foundation of Asia), the London-based Gemini News Service, and the Rome-based Inter-Press Service.

DEVELOPMENT*AL* JOURNALISM

There is a general tendency in the Western media to confuse development journalism with "development*al* journalism," A term coined by Leonard R. Sussman, executive director of Freedom House, to describe the use of mass media by Third World countries for economic development and national integration. One very often finds Western media leaders condemning development journalism when in fact what they have in mind is developmental journalism as defined by Sussman. It is of utmost importance that we distinguish between development journalism and developmental journalism, or what in United Nations circles is generally referred to as Development Support Communication (DSC) programs. The UN term, although a bit more cumbersome than "developmental journalism," is more convenient and descriptive of the use of various media—not just mass, but any media—for promoting economic and social development. Development news reporting is only a very minor element of DSC, which in recent years has won many new converts among Third World planners and leaders, primarily due to the efforts of various UN agencies, including the UNDP (United Nations Development Program), UNESCO, and UNICEF. Dr. Paul Fisher, Director of the Freedom of Information Cen-

ter, Columbia, Missouri, is probably referring to the DSC phenomenon when he says: "There is a tendency among leaders of developing countries to favor the view of technicians and specialists who see communication as a tool to achieve certain goals.They are talking about using journalism, using communication to predetermined ends."

Although Dr. Fisher's evaluation is accurate his inferential criticism and apprehensions are misplaced. There is nothing Machiavellian or alarming in the developing countries' desire to use communication for furthering economic and social development. Communication media have been so used in the Western countries for many decades, particularly in agricultural extension work. The problems arises when the distinction between development communication, primarily a government activity planned and carried out as part of a country's national development program, and the new media whose effectiveness as a DSC component is inversely related to the degree of government intervention, is blurred. To most Third World leaders, information and communication unfortunately have become synonymous and interchangeable, hence both subject to government influence and direction.

This is what Sussman refers to as the development litany of the Third World. This litany, according to him, goes like this: "Economic development is essential to assure the well-being of a society and the sovereignty of the state. Effective communications to all sectors of the citizenry is a concomitant of economic development. Only the government is responsible for, and can assure, the proper use of communication for this purpose. Therefore, governments must control the *mass media* in the name of economic development" (emphasis added).

Partly, the desire of Third World governments to control the news media may be due to a lack of, or inadequate, perception of the distinct but vitally supplementary roles that the news media and the other media can play in development. What is needed is a concerted drive by media leaders, both from the developing and the developed countries, to convince the Third World leaders that, while the governments (particularly in the developing countries) have the right to use communication media for economic development, the news media can provide effective support to national economic development programs only if allowed to discharge their peripheral DSC role free of government intervention. Such a drive will serve the cause of free press much better than repeated and loud denunciations of Third World leaders for subjugating the news media.

MEDIA CONTROLS

Contrary to what some critics of the Third World's demand for a New Information Order would like us to believe, the flow of news in the world today is not totally unfettered, or *absolutely* free. Media operations in almost all countries are subject to certain regulations which prohibit the publication of official secrets and news endangering national security. In most industrialized countries, news management, which has been elevated to a fine art, is an everyday phenomenon. Governments can, and do, expel or deny a visa to any foreign correspondent, at any time, and for almost no reason. Examples of such actions are plentiful, one of the most recent being the expulsion of an American journalist by Britain. Short-notice expulsion is, and will continue to be, an accepted hazard of foreign news-reporting. Even now, in many developing countries, foreign news agencies are barred from supplying news directly to a newspaper or a radio station and have to go through a national news agency. Thus many developing countries already possess the means, if they so desire, to excise or rewrite any news article that they deem unfavorable or slanted. This option is exercised more often than not in "killing" (as against rewriting to correct any discernible slants) some of the stories supplied by the Western wire services.

This is not to minimize the danger, in my personal view, of the growing trend in the Third World toward direct government control of the news media. The danger is accentuated by the need for government subsidy for the national news agency, particularly in the first few years of its operation, in a developing country. But a government-subsidized agency does not necessarily have to be government controlled. The possibility, as well as the level, of official intervention in the operations of a news agency depends very much upon the political philosophy and survival needs of those in power. There is also the fear that a national news agency, in the

absence of competition, may willy-nilly become purveyor of official news. To some extent, this is a justifiable apprehension, but it need not always come true. After all, most developed countries, including Britain and France, have only one national news agency covering the domestic scene, but nobody accuses them of being official mouthpieces.

Some of the more extreme proposals for media control, such as those calling for "the imprisonment of foreign correspondents who insult or misrepresent host countries" or the "licensing" of journalists, are merely a reflection of the tremendous frustration which Third World leaders feel about domestic as well as foreign media. It is not too difficult to understand. After all, it was not very long ago that some of the top government leaders in a major Western country, besieged by an unrelentingly critical media, were questioning the credentials of nationally known news commentators to analyze and criticize government actions in the name of the general public. They even initiated measures which were openly denounced as "intimidatory" by the media.

Few developing countries will agree with the statement attributed to an African diplomat in Nairobi that "we do not want Western journalists in our countries. They should take their news from us." Among those who advocate the institution of a code of social conduct and professional responsibility for news correspondents and call for the establishment of a New Information Order, many are quick to disown any idea of government control over the media. Many others defend the need for such government control "only at the present stage of their national development," and "to check the externally funded forces of political and social disequilibrium."

"We are not," says Somavia, who is an ardent critic of the Western media, "advocating government control over the agencies' news flows." The same view is voiced by Raghavan, who contends that national news agencies should be "free of governmental or bureaucratic control, direct or indirect . . . (and should be run) professionally in such a manner that they evoke respect for their professional competence, integrity, and credibility. They should not be vehicles of propaganda."

The Development Dialogue, a Swedish journal

advocating Third World causes, had this to say in its 1976 Autumn issue in supporting the call for a New Information Order:

> While it cannot be said that there is no role for governments in information, a role that is as varied as the circumstances, it should be remembered that societies are permanent, and governments—though they may be devoted to the public good—are transient. Societies and the individuals who constitute them are richer in their diversity, needs, and aspirations than the states and their bureaucratic machineries—which should only be their servants. A New Information Order and *another* (development) information are not designed to replace the domination of the transnationals by that of national bureaucracies, however well intentioned, they are not a move towards "a more restricted press," but toward a freer one, which would really meet the need to inform and to be informed—one of the fundamental human needs.

DEVELOPMENT NEWS ON ALL INDIA RADIO: ASSESSMENT OF QUANTITY AND QUALITY

HEMANT SHAH

Very little development news is broadcast by All India Radio, this research has found, and what there is of it is not of high quality.

Researchers have examined the use of development news by print and electronic news media in a wide variety of settings. The studies are generally informative and provide much descriptive information about the performance of the news media in terms of producing development news. However, taken as a whole, the studies of development news suffer from several conceptual and methodological problems.

One of the problems with development news studies is the failure to recognize that all news could be development news. The problem stems from differing operational definitions of development news. Some studies have used fairly crude definitions, such as all "good" news[1] or all news about economic and social problems,[2] to identify development news items, while others use lists of development news topics based on a survey of audience needs,[3] the opinions of experts,[4] an existing theoretical framework,[5] or pretests conducted by the researchers.[6]

While some of these methods of identifying development news can be quite useful, they all result in ignoring subjects that may be relevant to development.

Most development news studies have assessed only the quantity of development news appearing in a selected medium. Using content analysis, the studies have found there is generally little quantitative emphasis given to development news. The exceptions were the native-language newspapers of Malaysia[7] and Indonesia[8]—some of which devoted as much as 50% of their space to development news.

Hemant Shah, "Development News on All India Radio: Assessment of Quantity and Quality." *Journalism Quarterly*, Volume 65, Summer 1988, pp. 425–430. Reprinted by permission.

The author is an assistant professor in the Department of Journalism and Mass Communication at Iowa State University.

The quality of development news has rarely been assessed. Studies by Ogan and Swift,[9] and Ogan, Fair and Shah,[10] assessed development news quality by comparing newspaper items with some of Aggarwala's suggestions for effective development reporting and found not only poor quality but worsening quality over time. A study by Ogan and Rush[11] examining the quality of development news produced by two of the so-called "alternative news services" found the quality of development news in these news services to be better than in Third World newspapers. However, none of these studies examined quality by using the reporting criteria in conjunction with the placement of development news items.

By ignoring the quality of development news, researchers assume that (1) the mere presence of development news will contribute to development; (2) each item can contribute equally to development; and (3) the greater the quantity of development news, the greater the contribution to development.

Most development news studies have focused largely on print news. Only a few studies have examined development news produced by broadcast media. For example, Barghouti[12] examined Jordan's radio and television networks, Yunjanondth[13] studied the radio network of Thailand, and McDaniel[14] studied the television networks in Malaysia and Pakistan. The lack of attention to radio news is somewhat surprising because of its importance as an effective channel of mass communication in developing countries where literacy rates are low.

Taking into account the weaknesses of previous development news research, this study was designed to study *broadcast* news on AIR and examine the *quality* (in terms of development news reporting criteria and the placement of development news items) as well as the quantity of all news items, acknowledging the possibility that all news potentially can be development news.

Development news should examine critically, evaluate and interpret the relevance of development plans, projects, policies, problems and issues. It should indicate the disparities between plans and actual accomplishments, and include comparisons with how development is progressing in other countries and regions. It also should provide contextual and background information about the development process, discuss the impact of plans, projects, policies, problems and issues on people, and speculate about the future of development.

Development news should also refer to the needs of people, which may vary from country to country or from region to region, but generally include primary needs, such as food, housing and employment; secondary needs such as transportation, energy sources and electricity; and tertiary needs such as cultural diversity, recognition and dignity.[15] News items that do not at least partially fulfill these criteria cannot be considered development news.

The study addressed the following four research questions:

1. What proportion of AIR news items are development news?
2. In terms of length of story, what is the quantity of development news items?
3. In terms of satisfying development news reporting criteria and placement of news items, what is the quality of development news items?
4. What topics are covered as development news?

METHOD

To investigate the research questions, a content analysis of the scripts of AIR newscasts was undertaken. The study analyzed all news items broadcast in nightly central bulletins on one randomly chosen day from each month in calendar year 1985. In addition, nightly central bulletins from three consecutive days in December 1985 also were analyzed. The randomly chosen dates were: January 23, February 10, March 26, April 15, May 9, June 28, July 9, August 14, September 8, October 19, November 1 and December 9. The consecutive days were December 4, 5 and 6.

The coding protocol required coders to make decisions about the size or quantity and the quality of each item as well as the topics covered by each item. The questions and categories in the protocol were developed after consulting three sources. Much of the protocol resembles the instrument used in studies of development news conducted by Ogan and colleagues.[16] Categories and questions were also borrowed from the UNESCO/IAMCR "Foreign Images" project.[17]

Adjustments were made to accommodate coding of the Indian news media. Some of the categories pertaining to the topics covered in the news items were created after a review of India's Sixth Five Year Plan, in order to reflect the Indian government's emphasis on specific development sectors.

A total of 243 news items were analyzed. Coder reliability between two independent coders was established at .86.[18]

One dimension of the quality of news items was measured by comparing each item with the following 10 criteria for development news suggested by Aggarwala and others.[19]

1. Does the item emphasize development processes rather than events?
2. Does the item contain content critical of development projects, plans, policies, problems or issues?
3. Does the item discuss the relevance of development projects, plans, policies, problems or issues to national, regional or local needs?
4. Does the item provide contextual or background information about development projects, plans, policies, problems or issues?
5. Does the item speculate about the future in relation to development needs?
6. Does the item discuss the impact of projects, plans, policies, problems or issues on the people?
7. Does the item discuss development processes in other regions or countries?
8. Does the item compare the subject with original development goals?
9. Does the item compare the subject with government claims for success?
10. Does the item make any references to development needs of the people?

An affirmative answer to a question resulted in one point for the development news item under consideration. Ten affirmative answers, therefore, resulted in a score of 10 for a given item on this qualitative dimension. A score of 10 was unlikely, however, because some items were not relevant for some stories. Only news items scoring at least one point were considered to be development news.

Another aspect of development news quality is its placement. Items prominently placed in the newscasts may publicize development efforts and goals better than items not given prominence. Thus, a second qualitative dimension was a measure of the prominence assigned to each development news item by AIR news editors. If the development news item was in the first one-third of the broadcast, the item was coded as having high prominence; an item in the second one-third of the broadcast was coded as having medium prominence; and an item in the last one-third of the broadcast was coded as having low prominence.

Development news items having high prominence were treated as having better quality of placement than items of medium or low prominence. The AIR newscasts were 15 minutes in duration with breaks at 5 and 10 minutes into the broadcast, thereby breaking up the newscast into three distinct sections. Therefore, it was easy to determine whether each news item was in the first, second or last one-third of the newscast.

The quantity of development news items on AIR was determined by calculating the proportion of the total newscast taken by each news item. The total number of words in each news item was divided by the total number of words in the entire news broadcast.

RESULTS

Of the 243 AIR news items analyzed, 36 (or 14.8%) satisfied at least one of the development news reporting criteria and were coded as development news. Clearly, AIR newscasts contain relatively little content that can be called development news. The remainder of the analysis will focus primarily on the items that were coded as development news.

The average proportion of the newscast given to development news items was 7.25% while non-development news items occupied an average of 5.58%. The average length of the development news items was 147 words. The average length of the non-development news items was 115.5 words. In terms of quantity, then, when AIR does broadcast development news items, they appear to receive more air time, on average, than do non-development news items.

Placement of news items within the newscast was one measure of the quality of the news items. A similar proportion of development and non-development news items were given high prominence by the news editors at AIR: Only 16.7% of development news items and 17.9% of non-development news items were broadcast in the first one-third of newscasts. However, a greater proportion of development news items were given medium prominence than were non-development news items. About 53% of the development news items, as opposed to about 35% of the non-development news items, were given medium prominence. Nearly 7 of every 10 development news items were broadcast before the second break in the newscast, whereas only slightly more than half of the non-development news items were broadcast before the second break. (See Table 1).

A second measure of the quality of each development news item used in this study was a comparison of each item with the 10 criteria for reporting development news. The range of scores for this measure was 1 through 10—a "1" indicating that the item satisfied only one reporting criterion and a "10" indicating that the item met all the criteria. Table 2 shows the distribution of development news items along the range of criteria scores.

Development news items scored fairly low in terms of satisfying the development news reporting criteria. Three-fourths of the development news items satisfied only three reporting criteria or fewer, indicating that most development news items on AIR were low in quality.

In the 36 items coded as development news, 34 different topics were mentioned a total of 90 times (because multiple coding was allowed). In Table 3, the 34 topics mentioned in development news items are collapsed into 12 general categories. To get an idea of the importance these topics received as development news, the number of times these topics were mentioned in development news items is compared to how often they appeared in all news items.

Some important categories of national development issues were covered in AIR newscasts. Agriculture and rural development, education, employment and labor, and health and medicine were mentioned 40 times overall. And well over half the news items in which these four categories appeared were coded as development news items. The other eight topic categories appeared proportionately less frequently in development news items, although overall, these eight topic categories were mentioned a total of 287 times.

Among these eight topic categories were trade, tariffs and other economic matters, energy, industry and science, transportation and communication and human rights. Issues vital to development in India but never appearing in items coded as development news included irrigation and flood control, India's minimum needs program, water supply, hill area development, relations between industry and labor, economic aid and nuclear issues.

An important finding revealed in Table 3 is that political, diplomatic and military topics are sometimes covered as development news. Previous studies, because they have ignored the possibility that all news has the potential to be development news, have ignored political, diplomatic and military news items in their analyses of various news media.

Table I	PLACEMENT OF ITEMS: PERCENTAGE OF DEVELOPMENT AND NON-DEVELOPMENT ITEMS GIVEN HIGH, MEDIUM AND LOW PRIORITY	
	Development News Items *(n = 36)*	*Non-development News Items* *(n = 207)*
High	16.7	17.9
Medium	52.8	34.8
Low	30.6	47.3
	N = 36	N = 207

Table 2   CRITERIA SCORES OF DEVELOPMENT NEWS ITEMS

Scores	Percentage of Items	Cumulative Percentage
1	33.3	33.3
2	16.7	50.0
3	25.7	75.0
4	16.7	91.7
5	5.6	97.2
6	2.8	100.0
7–10	0	
Totals	N = 36	

DISCUSSION

Based only on quantitative measures of the average length and space occupied by development news items, it would be easy to conclude that when development news is covered by AIR, it is covered fairly well. If the first of the qualitative measures—placement of development news items within the broadcast—also is considered, one could still conclude that AIR covers development news fairly well because a fairly large proportion of development news items was broadcast before the second break. But to draw this conclusion would be to make the mistake of earlier studies by ignoring a second aspect of the quality of development news.

Table 3   TOPICS MENTIONED IN ITEMS CODED AS DEVELOPMENT NEWS

	Total Mentions	Number of Times Mentioned in Development News	Percent of Times Mentioned in Development News
Agriculture, rural development	14	11	78.6
Education	7	5	71.4
Employment, labor	13	9	69.2
Health, medicine	6	4	66.7
Trade, tariffs, cost of living, 5 year plans, prices, aid, economic performance	50	19	38.0
Social welfare, nutrition, food, family planning, environment, caste issues	29	10	34.4
Energy, industry, science	32	8	25.0
Culture, religion	26	5	19.2
Nat'l integration	12	2	16.7
Transportation, communication	18	3	16.7
Politics, diplomacy, internal conflict, int'l treaties, military matters	97	13	13.4
Human rights	23	3	13.0
Totals	327	90	27.5

When the quality of development news items was judged according to the criteria for development news reporting, it was apparent that development news items on AIR did not reflect the thorough, investigative-style reporting advocated by the development news reporting criteria suggested by Aggarwala and others.

Further, only 12 topic categories appeared in development news items, and among them, only four appeared in development news items most of the time they were mentioned. Overall, the topics in the 12 categories were mentioned 327 times and appeared in development news items only 27.5% of the time (see Table 3).

The low quality of development news on AIR suggests a need for improved reporting of development news. Needed is coverage of some topics that are ignored completely by AIR but are potentially important to national development and more frequent coverage as development news of some topics that AIR does report regularly. In general, more thorough and more frequent reporting of a wider range of development issues is likely to improve the quality of AIR development news.

Because this study examined all news items on AIR, it was discovered that political, diplomatic and military issues were sometimes covered in items coded as development news. And because this study emphasized quality of coverage as an important facet of development news, it was discovered that topics traditionally associated with national development, although they may have received coverage, are not always treated as development news.

Earlier studies had coded as development news any item that dealt with development topics, regardless of the quality of coverage. The findings of this study suggest that future studies of development news should not limit their scope to a limited list of development news topics and should consider the quality of development news, not only the quantity.

NOTES

1. Wilbur Schramm and Erwin Atwood, *The Circulation of News in the Third World: A Study of Asia* (Hong Kong: Chinese University Press, 1981).
2. L.R. Nair, "Private Press in National Development: The Indian Example," in Daniel Lerner and Wilbur Schramm, eds., *Communication and Change in Developing Societies* (Honolulu: East-West Center Press, 1967).
3. A. Mazumdar, "Development Communication Through Press: A Case Study of Newspapers in Assam." Paper presented to the annual meeting of the International Communication Association, Honolulu, May 1985.
4. John Vilanilam, "Ownership Versus Development News Content: An Analysis of Independent and Conglomerate Newspapers of India," in John Lent and John Vilanilam, eds., *The Use of Development News* (Singapore: AMIC, 1979, pp. 31–54. Also see in Lent and Vilanilam, studies by Emmanuel Osae-Asare, "The Ghana Press and National Development: A Comparative Content Analysis of Development News in the National Daily Newspapers and the Wire Services, April–September 1976," pp. 72–90; Hamima Mustapha, "A Comparative Analysis of the Use of Development News in Three Malaysian Dailies During 1974," pp. 56–70; and O. Yunjanondth, "A Content Analysis of Newscasts of Three Radio Stations in Thailand, July–August 1977," pp. 92–110; and Mazharul Haque, "Is Development News More Salient Than Human Interest Stories in Indian Elite Press?" *Gazette*, 38:83–99 (1986). All these studies use Vilanilam's list of development topics.
5. Two such studies of development news are by Ralph Barney, "Mass media Roles in Development: A Descriptive Study From Four Developing Areas," *Gazette* 19:222–238 (1973), and Ralph Barney, "Media Development in a Transitional Situation: A Time-Lag Example," *Gazette*, 38:171–185 (1986). Barney uses the "Inspector-general" framework proposed in Lucian Pye, *Communication and Political Development* (Princeton, N.J.: Princeton University Press, 1963).
6. Robert E. Simmons, Kurt Kent and V.M. Mishra, "Media and Development News in the Slums of Ecuador and India," *Journalism Quarterly,* 45:698–705 (1968).
7. Mustapha, in Lent and Vilanilam, *op. cit.*
8. Ishadi Sutopo, *Development News in Indonesian Dailies* (Singapore: AMIC, 1981).
9. Christine Ogan and Clint Swift, " Is the News About Development All Good? A Content Analysis of Selected Foreign Newspapers," paper presented to the annual meeting of the Association for Education in Journalism and Mass Communication, Athens, Ohio, August 1982.

10. Christine L. Ogan, Jo Ellen Fair and Hemant Shah, " 'A little good news': The treatment of development news in selected Third World newspapers," *Gazette*, 33:173–191 (1984).

11. Christine Ogan and Ramona Rush, "Development News in CANA and Interlink: The Role of Women and Other Topics," in Walter G. Soderland and Stuart H. Surlin, eds., *Media in Latin America and the Caribbean: Domestic and International Perspectives* (Windsor, Ontario: University of Windsor, 1985) pp. 95–118.

12. Shawki Barghouti, "The Role of Communication in Jordan's Rural Development," *Journalism Quarterly,* 51:418–424 (1974).

13. Yunjanondth, *op. cit.*

14. Drew McDaniel, "Development News in Two Asian Nations," *Journalism Quarterly,* 63:167–170 (1986).

15. Narinder K. Aggarwala, "What is Development News?" *Journalism of Communications,* Spring 1979, pp. 181–182 (1979); Aggarwala "A New Journalism," *Intermedia,* 8:26–27 (1980); P.R.R. Sinha, "Review of Asian Media Performance and Activity in the '70s." *Media Asia,* 8:49–54 (1981); Sinha "Towards a Definition of Development Communication," in Peter Haberman and Guy De Fontgalland,

eds., *Development Communication: Rhetoric and Reality* (Singapore: AMIC, 1978), pp. 18–28; Everett Rogers, "Passing of the Dominant Paradigm," in Everett Rogers, ed., *Communications and Development: Critical Perspectives* (Beverly Hills: Sage, 1976), pp. 121–148; Erskine Childers, "Taking Humans Into Account," *Media Asia* 3:87–90 (1976).

16. See for example, the studies by Ogan and Swift, *op. cit.;* Ogan Fair and Shah, *op. cit.;* and Ogan and Rush *op. cit.*

17. Annabel Sreberny-Mohammadi, Kaarle Nordenstreng, Robert Stevenson and Frank Ugboajah, "Foreign News in the Media: International Reporting in 29 Countries," Reports and Papers on Mass Communication, No. 92 (Paris: UNESCO, 1985).

18. The reliability coefficient for two independent coders was calculated as the percentage of agreement on coding decisions for a sample of AIR news items.

19. Aggarwala, "A New Journalism"; Aggarwala "What is Development News?"; Sinha, "Review of Asian Media Performance and Activity in the '70s"; Sinha "Toward a Definition of Development Communication"; Rogers, "Passing of the Dominant Paradigm"; Childers, "Taking Humans Into Account."

COMMUNICATION FOR DEVELOPMENT: AND WHY IS PRINT MEDIA GROWTH SO SLOW?

DANIEL LERNER

The author, one of the first scholars in the field of communication and development, calls for improvements in the mass media. Without these, he says, the media cannot contribute to national development.

Daniel Lerner, "Communication for Development: And Why Is Print Media Growth So Slow?" *Leader, Malaysian Journalism Review*, Number 2, July 1972, pp. 21–24.

The late author was Ford Professor of Sociology at Massachusetts Institute of Technology at the time this article was written.

A general view of communication assigns it the key role of shaping and maintaining a "dynamic equilibrium."

This assignment is difficult, for communication lends itself as readily to *accelerating* tempo—in developing countries more readily—as to maintaining balance. What is needed is a basic reformulation of the role communication can play *for* development administration.

Some years ago, in describing the impact of communication upon empathy (psychic mobility), I examined the view that "the modern style of life can nowadays be acquired *as a whole* by individuals living in modernizing societies. This interpretation is quite plausible, but it does not clarify what happens to empathic individuals who are ready and able to modernize more rapidly and completely than their social environment permits. Our data on 73 countries in all continents indicate that many millions of persons everywhere are in this position."

This referred to the transformation of rising expectations into rising frustrations then already becoming visible in the less-developed countries.

More recently, reviewing his observations in Asia, Dr. Hahm Pyong Choon has focused our attention directly upon the effect of inflationary communications upon populist ideology and economic policy in the less developed countries.

He writes that "in a country where capacity to absorb information about the good life of the outside world, and hence to feel miserable and dissatisfied with their present living conditions, far outstrips material means to meet their expectations, amassing of individual fortunes will not be allowed even under the sanction of the profit motive."

A compatriot and colleague of Dr. Hahm has converted this diagnosis into a prescription for the press.

The supreme task of less developed country communication, according to Dr. Ki Uk Han, is "to persuade and convince the people to help discipline themselves to compromise their slow material progress with the spiraling of mental expectancy, with the means available to them at a given state of national development."

These, then, are the objectives of development communication:

- to meet the demand for social justice,
- to shape expectations in ways that maximize satisfactions and minimize frustrations, and
- to sustain a dynamic equilibrium between the socioeconomic and the psychocultural components in a rapidly changing situtation

These objectives are often compromised by the ideological extremism of its allies as well as its adversaries.

The allies oversell; the adversaries over-kill. A PR man for government information services in an SEA country illustrates oversell; "Communication should be a key word in the vocabulary of development in newly emergent nations. With it most things could be made possible *(sic!)*, but without it most things *(sic!)* would be practically impossible." Overkill is illustrated daily by the denunciamentoes of the New Left.

In terms of coercion *versus* consensus as the organizing principle of civil order and administration, we accept the judgment of Professor Shils that the "Quasi-Marxists have contributed very little (to our understanding of consensus) because of their inclination to regard power, and above all coercive power, as the sole means of producing coordinated action."

In this respect we add as an hypothesis to be explored on another occasion the probability that Quasi-Marxist regimes often are even more damaging to development communication than military regimes.

The use of development communication to sustain dynamic equilibrium is difficult even in less developed country regimes that pronounce their allegiance to the democratic ideal based on social justice, economic growth, political participation, and personal freedom.

Consider this statement by a "Number One Voice" whom it is no longer fashionable to quote, Chiang Kai Shek: at the entry to the Journalism Building of Chengchi University in Taipei is inscribed in marble these words: "The launching, development and maturing of our National Revolution in the past fifty years had everything to do with the application of mass communication."

"The progress or lagging behind depended on the insights extended and the efforts made by the mass media. When the endeavour of the media was congruent with the national development policies, the revolutionary process was accelerated; otherwise it was slowed down."

But such sound thoughts are not enough. The money must go where the mouth is.

In many countries of Asia the media are starved; in others they are stifled. Development communication is starved when the system overloads it with freight it is not equipped to carry.

Thus, Professor Hirunyaboosh, Chief of Information in Thailand, writes that "a cause that made the second plan incomplete and may well down the third plan is the inadequacy of public information services."

If development communication is starved by inadequate allocation from government, it is stifled by excessive demands from government.

The general South-East Asia situation is described by Tarzie Vittachi, managing editor of the Asian News Service, as follows; "The liberty of the Asian press is being increasingly subverted. The Asian press now stands—some might say totters—in the twilight zone between the authoritarian and libertarian concepts of its role in society."

The bright spots of press freedom in Asia, according to Vittachi, are Japan, India and the Philippines. None of these is South-East Asia by strict construction, except the Philippines—which its friendliest critic has described as "a watchdog which can only bark but not bite," because, among

other reasons, it competes, outside Manila, with 200 radio stations and 13 stations.

Now let us look at the interaction of literacy, print, and the audiovisual media.

In general, literacy has been increasing throughout South-East Asia though at a slower rate than population in some countries. While there have been some serious failures to accelerate education, there have been some conspicuous successes.

These provide heartening evidence that rationally planned and programmed accceleration can work.

As literacy grows in Asia, however, a strange lack of comparable growth in the printed media becomes apparent. In virtually all South-East Asian countries, as Amitabha Chowhury points out, there is a "widening gap between actual and potential circulation."

In Indonesia—where film production has zoomed from 10 in 1969 to 19 in 1970 and 67 in 1971—daily circulation stands at 1.2 million, about 1% of the nation's population of over 120 million. A similar situation exists in the Philippines, where there are over 200 radio and 113 television stations, but daily circulation barely maintains itself at a half-million (for 28 million literates). Table 1 illustrates the present position in SEA:

In any case, SEA is far from the *minimum* standard of 10 copies per 100 persons set by UNESCO. The South-East Asia rate hovers around, and often falls below, one copy per 100 persons.

Some correction needs to be made in terms of readership, which is said to be substantially higher than circulation in all SEA countries. Because the

Table I   LITERACY AND NEWSPAPERS (IN MILLIONS)

						In School	Literates	Daily Circulation
India	(1964)	...	...	...	...	45.5	114.0	5.
Philippines	(1963)	...	...	...	...	6.0	28.0	0.5
Thailand	(1963)	...	...	...	...	4.5	14.0	0.3
Indonesia	(1972)	...	...	...	...	10.0	50.0	1.2
Malaysia	(1972)	...	...	...	...	2.0	7.0	0.8

(N.B. These figures are the best estimates I could obtain in rapid transit. There is a high probability of substantial error. Take seriously only the orders of magnitude represented.)

cost of a newspaper is relatively high, each copy sold passes through many hands.

But the situation is still dismal, and the worsening ratio of circulation to literacy offers little promise in the years ahead.

It is clear that even readership, not to mention circulation, has not kept pace with increasing literacy. The daily press grows only fractionally, the weekly press remains inert, and the monthly press actually declines over the three year period—while radio and television show substantial growth. A clear and cogent analysis of this situation has been made by Jack Glattbach, director of the SEA Press Centre in Kuala Lumpur.

The result, in many SEA countries, is an impoverished and deteriorating press. Newsmen are ill-paid and survive only by moon-lighting.

Filipino "travails" are epitomized by Sabah Singh, who writes: "My income as an insurance agent is ten times more than what I get as a correspondent."

In Laos, the editor-publisher of the only daily paper has ceased to distribute outside of Vientiane because the circulation is so low that revenue does not balance costs—and, he ruefully adds, "at that, they often don't pay me at all."

While there are some success stories, and I will tell them on another occasion, the prospects for development communication in SEA are generally dim in the absence of new policy initiatives.

I shall spare you my prescriptions for the future and close by citing the view of some perceptive Asian communicators. Mr. Sumadi, of the Indonesian Department of Information, put the matter incisively to an East-West Center seminar on "The Role of Government Information in Development" earlier this year: "there can be no effective development information without information development."

At the same seminar Aslam Siddiqi, director of the Information Services Academy in West Pakistan, took the high ground that is needed if communication *for* development is to improve significantly in the visible future: "The training of government information officers should start by clearing cobwebs in their minds . . . The thinking processes have to change and new cognitive values and structures have to be acquired. This is a difficult task. And all the time, the national environments of those GIO's will generate cognitive dissonance and will be working against them."

Accordingly, Siddiqi proposes that training give priority to the clarification and amplification of perspectives among Asian communicators.

He would require all trainees to acquire a sense of their own role as rearrangers of the environment through a sequence of four basic courses: (1) the Role of I.O.'s in Government and in the Community of Communicators; (2) Communication and Society; (3) Totality in Communication; (4) Effectiveness in Human Communication. Only then would he allow them to proceed to the techniques and mechanics of their trade.

Only by rapid and widespread implementation of proposals such as these can communication *for* development become operative.

COVERAGE OF DEVELOPMENT NEWS IN DEVELOPED AND DEVELOPING COUNTRIES

Christine Ogan

Some Westerners have charged, says this author, that Third World media are no different from those in the West when it comes to covering development news: both prefer to cover political news. In this study, however, of the coverage by Third World and Western media of an international conference on population, Third World media discussed population issues significantly more often than the political issues, while developed countries focused more on the political issues than did the media in developing countries.

Some authors have attempted to conceptualize development news.[1] Others have tried to measure it.[2] Everyone who has researched the concept has tried to wrestle with the question, "What is development news?" Even researchers who have written what they feel to be definitive answers to that question have not been in agreement. And the inability to agree on a definition has made the measurement of development news difficult.

Part of the more basic problem in the research is that few scholars can agree on the definition of development. So studies of development news can include all the news in a mass media product, with the argument that if an event occurred in a developing country, news about it relates to that country's development. Other studies have excluded what the authors considered to be information that is either anti-development, such as war or political squabbling, or unrelated to development, such as sports and entertainment news.

About the only thing on which researchers have agreed is that there is little development news included in the press of developing countries and that what does exist is not often critical of the shortcomings of development efforts.

This study attempts to alleviate some of the problems inherent in development news research by tak-

ing a different measurement approach. Instead of trying to isolate and describe the portions of a news media product devoted to development news, as has most frequently been done, this study focuses on an event related to the development process and analyzes the coverage of that event in a number of newspapers and news magazines in the United States, Western Europe, Africa and Latin America.

The event was the United Nations International Conference on Population in Mexico City from August 4 to 14, 1984. The conference came 10 years after the first United Nations sponsored population meeting in Bucharest, Romania. Unlike many other problems of developing countries, rapid population growth is not characteristic of the developed countries of the world. An estimated 90% of the world's population increase in the next 15 years will occur in the developing countries.[3] So analysis of the proceedings and outcome of this meeting should have much more significance to developing countries that are trying to understand and deal with the problem.

It was not expected, however, that this significance would necessarily be recognized by the press in developing countries, as will be later explained. It was hoped that by examining an issue that most people would agree was important to the process of development, one might focus on the specific nature

Christine Ogan, "Coverage of Development News in Developed and Developing Countries." *Journalism Quarterly*, Volume 64, Spring 1987, pp. 80–87. Reprinted by permission.

The author is associate professor of journalism at Indiana University.

of coverage without having to redefine development or development news.

HYPOTHESES

The study had two general purposes. The coverage of the population conference by the press of developed and developing countries was compared. Based on the results of previous research, it was expected that there would be no difference in the way reporters from developed and developing countries covered the conference. It was also expected that the conference would be covered more as a political event than a development event. Research findings that led us to this null hypothesis are described below.

The second purpose was to determine if the press exercised the discretionary latitude in coverage attributed to it in the results of previous research. By examining the degree to which reporters covered the actual speeches listed on the conference agenda, it could be partially determined whether reporters were sticking to the agenda outlined by the conference organizers, or establishing their own agenda by consulting other available sources. The results of previous research, also described below, led us to expect that the actual speeches would be covered infrequently

The following hypotheses were tested:

1. Newspaper coverage of the International Conference on Population (ICP) by developed and developing countries will be similar in approach, use of sources and topics addressed.
2. Coverage in the newspapers of both developed and developing countries will be concentrated on political, rather than population issues.

Although the population issue has been described as one that should concern developing more than developed countries, a major study of the world's press, conducted in 1979, found very few differences in the way countries cover the news, regardless of their stage of economic development. In that study, a team of researchers conducted a content analysis of the international news in the press of 29 different countries, to determine the pattern, source

and nature of that coverage. One of the basic findings was that "politics dominated international news everywhere."[4] Of the international news hole in the 29 countries, an average of 46% of the space/air time was taken up by political news.

The researchers also concluded that countries devote most attention to news occurring within their national boundaries; that news in all countries is defined as oriented toward "exceptional events," such as coups and earthquakes; and the "soft" news gets little attention in the press of any nation.[5]

Since the population conference occurred outside the borders of all nations whose newspapers or news magazines were included in the study (with the exception of Mexico), and since the population conference could not be classified as an "exceptional event," it was expected to be covered similarly by all news media in the study. In addition, since the population conference had a political agenda as well as a development orientation, it was expected that politics would be emphasized over the population issue.

Several content analyses of development news have found that such news is covered more as spot news (about events) than features (about processes), that it is usually given low priority and written in little detail. Development news is more often about economics than related to social services and is not often critical.[6] These findings also lead to a hypothesis of no difference. The population issue is considered a process, while the conference itself is an event. Coverage was expected to be limited to such things as voting results and highlights of major speeches, with little depth coverage of the population problem itself.

3. Official conference speakers and their speeches will get little coverage compared to other sources and topics.

This hypothesis is based on some previous and ongoing research in political agenda setting. In the conclusions to a study of media agenda setting in the 1980 presidential election, researchers Weaver, Graber, McCombs and Eyal report, "It also appears that reporters and editors exercise considerable discretion in choosing certain issues to emphasize over time. This means that not all of the issues stressed by the leading candidates or the major political parties will be heavily covered by newspapers and televison."[7] Candidates stress what Colin Seymour calls the "diffuse" issues, or broad policy proposals, while the media cover "clear cut" issues, or ones "that neatly divide the candidates, provoke conflict and can be stated in simple terms."[8]

Although the population conference was not very much like an election, some people said the United States was more interested in political success of its policy, and its impact on American voters, than in the conference. *Washington Post* reporter William A. Orme Jr., noted that 700 journalists had been accredited for the conference, "raising the suggestion that the U.S. team might be aiming at a home audience."[9] And there were other political issues, unrelated to population control, brought to the conference by several Arab countries and by the Soviet Union.

There is no simple answer to the problem of overpopulation—and even disagreement over whether high population growth rate is an obstacle to economic development. So it would be easier for reporters to focus on the "clear cut" political issues brought to the conference than to try to tackle the complexities of the impact of world population growth—the "diffuse" issues more often raised in speeches.

Four main political issues were expected to be brought up at the conference in addition to the controversial U.S. policy statement.[10] The Soviets proposed a "peace" recommendation that linked the solution to population problems with disarmament. Another recommendation, backed by Arab states and made specifically with reference to settlements on the West Bank, would forbid the occupier of a territory from transferring parts of its own population into the territory it occupies. Several recommendations specified the rights of host countries and immigrants to those countries regarding both legal and illegal migration. Other recommendations dealt with different ideological perspectives on socio-economic development. These perspectives reflected the differences between East and West approaches.

Finally, the most talked about policy issue, was the U.S. policy to discontinue funding of agencies supporting abortion as a means of population control. This was not a specific recommendation, although Recommendation 13 urged governments to help women "avoid abortions and whenever possible to provide for the humane treatment and counseling of women who have had recourse to illegal abortions."[11]

METHOD

This study was undertaken as a class project for a graduate seminar in Communication and National Development. Class members assisted in the development of the coding procedure, and each student content analyzed newspaper or news magazine coverage of the International Conference on Population. Newspapers and magazines were selected on the basis of availability in the university library and the foreign language proficiency of the students.

Publications in both developed and developing countries were examined from about mid-July to late August 1984. The following publications were included in the study: From the developed countries: *The Irish Times*, Dublin, Ireland; *The Times*, London, England; *Le Monde* and *Le Figaro*, Paris, France; *The Globe and Mail*, Toronto, Canada; *The London Free Press*, Canada; the *New York Times*, the *Chicago Tribune*, the *Los Angeles Times*, and the *Christian Science Monitor*, all U.S. papers. In addition, the following magazines from developed countries: *L'Express*, *Le Nouvel Observateur* and *Actuel Developpement*, all from France; *MacLeans* from Canada; and *Newsweek* and *Time* from the United States. Publications from the developing countries included: *Uno Mas Uno*, Mexico City; *El Tiempo*, Bogota, Columbia; *La Prensa*, Buenos Aires, Argentina; *Granma*, Havana; *The Daily Nation*, Nairobi, Kenya; and *The Rand Daily Mail*, Johannesburg, South Africa.

Taken together, the foreign papers represent commercial interests (with the exception of *Granma*, as do the U.S. publications. This fact lends support to the argument that no difference will be found in coverage from the developed and developing countries' publications. The content analysis included all stories about the population conference or on a population issue appearing during the specified time period. A few issues of one paper, *El*

Tiempo, were missing from the library's collection.

Coders answered 34 questions related to news sources, priority, size, tone and content of each item. After training sessions, coders achieved an inter-coder reliability coefficient of .96.[12] Reliability was based on coded items in English language publications from several countries, since all coders were not fluent in French or Spanish.

World Bank guidelines were used to classify the United States, the United Kingdom, France and Canada as developed nations, or industrial market economies (in the World Bank's terms) and Argentina, Colombia, Cuba, Kenya, Mexico and South Africa as developing nations. Of that group, the World Bank categorizes Kenya as a low-income country; Colombia and Cuba as lower-middle-income economies; and Mexico, Argentina and South Africa as Upper-middle-income economies.[13]

FINDINGS

A total of 221 stories and editorials were coded from the 23 publications, 83 from newspapers in developing countries and 138 from publications in developed countries. The coverage was competing with at least one major international event during the period—the summer Olympics, held in Los Angeles. This perhaps accounts for the small number of stories (6) in the *Los Angeles Times*. Later in August, the Republican National Convention was held in Dallas, an event for which the U.S. media were gearing up; and in early September, the Pope paid a visit to Canada. Although all these events might have had an influence on the ICP coverage, it can be argued that news events always compete for attention.

Contrary to Hypothesis I, there were differences between the coverage of the conference by news media of developed and developing countries. Newspapers and news magazines in developed countries were more likely to cover the political issues raised at the conference—both the one related directly to the subject of the conference (the Reagan administration's policy of withdrawal of funding for organizations that provide assistance for abortions) and the less related political issues of resettlement,

immigration, and the ideological differences between East and West.

Coders coded one main topic and two subsidiary topics if found in the articles. The specific topics were collapsed into political issues, population issues and straight news coverage (for example, the result of a vote or the coverage of a speech only). Differences between developed and developing countries were found for the primary and secondary topics coded. (See Table 1).

Pearson's correlation coefficient was used to indicate whether each of the four political issues was mentioned more or less often by the news media in developed or developing countries.[14] Of the four unrelated political issues predicted to be brought up at the conference, only the disarmament issue was not raised more often by the media of the developed countries than the media of the developing countries. Pearson's r ranged from .13 for the immigration issue to .20 for the East-West development philosophy differences, to .30 for the resettlement issue.

Developed country media also criticized the new U.S. funding policy more often than did developing country newspapers (r = .21). And developing country newspapers were slightly more critical of the failure to find solutions for the population problem at local or international levels than were the developed country publications (57.1% vs. 44.9%; r = .11). But the tone of stories and editorials in both types of media was about equally critical overall. About 41.0% of developing country newspaper articles and 34.1% of developed country articles were negative. Only 6.0% of developing country stories and 8.7% of developed country stories were positive in tone. The rest were judged to be either neutral or balanced.

Developing country media have been found to rely heavily on government sources in the reporting of development news.[15] In their coverage of the ICP, developing country newspapers relied solely on government sources more often than did developed countries. (Cramer's V = .37) One primary and up to two subsidiary sources were coded. In all cases, the sources were more likely to be government sources than non-government or international government organization representatives. (See Table 2) Male sources were more often consulted than female by both types of media. A mean of 1.23 men in the

Table 1 ISSUES COVERED AT THE INTERNATIONAL CONFERENCE ON POPULATION BY DEVELOPED AND DEVELOPING COUNTRIES, IN PERCENT

Primary Topic of Article	Developed Country	Developing Country
Political Issue	49.6	31.3
Population issue	38.5	56.6
Straight News	11.9	12.0
	N = 135	N = 83
Cramer's V = .20		

Secondary Topic of Article	Developed Country	Developing Country
Political Issue	52.2	26.6
Population Issue	37.2	59.4
Straight News Event	10.5	14.1
	N = 86[a]	N = 64
Cramer's V = .26		

Other Political Issues Discussed	Developed Country	Developing Country
International resettlement	23.9	1.2
r = .30		
International immigration	14.5	6.2
r = .13		
East-West Development Ideological Differences	28.3	11.1
r = .20	N = 138	N = 83

[a]N is smaller because many stories did not include a secondary topic.

developing media as against 1.97 in the developed media were consulted compared to .11 women.

Several questions related to the depth of the stories. Stories from developed country newspapers were longer (mean length of 16.8 paragraphs) than those from developing country newspapers (mean of 9.8 paragraphs). Magazines were eliminated from this comparison since no news magazines were included in the developing country sample and news magazine stories tend to be longer. But developed country media were not more likely to include population statistics than developing country newspapers, while stories about population issues not raised at the conference were slightly more often raised by developed country media. (See Table 2) Little information about population plans or progress made in controlling growth was included by either type of medium.

Specific mention of women's issues in the population question—such as birth control, consequences of abortion, responsibility for family planning, etc.—was more often made in developed countries (50.7% vs. 22.9%; r = .27)

Finally, there were differences related to the priority given the item. The developed country media tended to place "medium" priority on conference stories (below the fold on the front page or inside the paper up high), while developing country newspapers gave the conference coverage either "high" priority (front page above the fold) or low priority (inside the paper toward the end with a small headline) (See Table 2).

Developing countries apparently thought conference coverage was important, however, because 72.3% of the stories included in their newspapers were written by a native reporter or covered by their

Table 2   SOME CHARACTERISTICS OF COVERAGE BY DEVELOPED
AND DEVELOPING COUNTRY PUBLICATIONS

	Developed	Developing	Measure of Association
Type of Article			
News	46.7	74.7	No Statistical
Opinion	13.9	15.7	Difference
Analysis	39.4	9.6	
Tone of Article			
Positive	8.7	6.0	No Statistical
Negative	34.1	41.0	Difference
Neutral/Balanced	57.2	53.0	
Priority of Article			
High	16.7	30.1	Cramer's
Medium	56.5	19.3	V = .36
Low	26.8	50.6	
Provider of Article			
Foreign	15.2	15.0	No Statistical
Native	76.1	72.3	Difference
None listed	8.7	12.0	
Sources Consulted			
No Source cited	34.7	23.3	Cramer's
Only Gov't and	20.2	56.2	V = .37
Both Gov't and Non-Gov't Source	45.2	20.5	
(The rest were unattributed sources)			
Critical of Failure to Solve Local or World			
Problem	44.9	57.1	r = .11
Critical of New U.S. Funding Policy	31.9	13.3	r = .21
Used Statistics	42.8	33.3	no difference
Raised Women's Issue	50.7	22.9	r = .27
Included Solutions	44.9	49.4	r = .17
	N = 138	N = 83	

own wire services. Developed country media also sent their own correspondents to cover the conference. About 76.1% of their stories were written by their own correspondents or came from a Western wire service.

Hypothesis 2 was supported. With the exception of two or three principal conference speakers, most stories did not make reference to one of the speakers on the official conference program. In the stories or editorials from the two types of media, a total of 359 sources were consulted in the developed country publications and 111 sources in the developing country publications. In the developed country pub-

lications, 97 sources were cited who were on the official conference speaker agenda, or 27.0% of the total number of the sources consulted.[16] In the developing country newspapers, 26 sources on the agenda were cited, or 23.4% of the total. Although about 13 women were listed as speakers on the program, none was cited in any of the articles.[17]

If reference to the speech made by the source was included in the story, that information was coded also. Many of the conference agenda speakers cited in stories were interviewed or otherwise consulted rather than quoted from their official speeches. This further reduced the percentage of citations of official conference speeches to 19.2% of the total number of sources consulted in developed country media. All references to speakers by developing country newspapers were from actual speeches.

As in previous studies, reporters appeared to have considerable latitude in covering this conference. Of the stories or editorials written about the conference, 38.4% of those from developed country publications, and 25.3% of those from developing countries included references to conference speakers.

When reference to conference speakers was broken down by topic—political issue, population issue or straight news event—about ⅔ of all stories including the speaker as a source were about political issues or straight news events in the developed country media. In developing country newspapers, about half the stories were about political issues or straight news events, and the other half were about population issues. As found in previous studies, the "clear-cut" issues were more frequently covered—speeches and political issues—than the "diffuse" issue of solving the world's population problem.

That finding is also supported when we observe the person who was cited most often—James L. Buckley, head of the U.S. delegation who delivered the U.S. position. For both types of media Buckley received the most citations.

Although great reporter latitude may account for the nature of the conference coverage, it may also be true that reporters had difficulty gaining entrance to the conference hall to hear the speeches and went elsewhere for their news. Student reporters in Mexico City said that there was no room for them to attend any of the official sessions. It is not known which reporters from which media were admitted to the conference sessions, however.

CONCLUSIONS

This is the first study that has shown differences in coverage of development issues between media of developed and developing countries. The charges from the West and the findings of previous international news flow studies have indicated that Third World media are no different from media in the West in their preoccupation with political news.

This study of coverage of one event by 22 newspapers and magazines in five developed and six developing countries shows the Western media concentrating more on the political issues and less on the population issue at the International Conference on Population.

It is probably not wise to generalize much from this study. Results should be taken for what they represent—some differences in approaching coverage of a single event by selected news media in a small number of countries.

Although more stories related to population issues in the developing country newspapers and fewer stories concentrated on extraneous political issues, little depth or analysis was found in the coverage, either at the international or the local level. Each member of the class who coded stories from developing countries expressed his/her disappointment at the superficiality with which the population issue was covered. To some extent, that impression is substantiated in the length of the stories—a mean of 9.8 paragraphs (with a mode of 7).

On the other hand, it can be said that the media in the developing countries did a better job of covering the conference for what is was intended to be than as a political event.

In both types of media, reporters wrote minimally about the official speeches given at the conference, and cited the speakers in low proportion to the total number of sources cited. Though this can be said to support the findings of studies that grant reporters great freedom to set the agenda for a particular event, other explanations are also possible. Certainly the agenda for the American delegation to the conference was to carry the message that a free enterprise economy is the answer to economic development and that the world population problem will take care of itself when a strong economy is achieved. Members of the Population Institute and many of the United Nations delegates had the reduction of world population as their agenda for the conference. And selected delegates from Arab nations, the Soviet Union and some other countries were more concerned with the disarmament, resettlement and immigration issues.

So there were several source agendas for the meeting, and it was found that reporters picked up on all of those in their coverage. But only limited coverage was given to the conference agenda and purpose. Future studies are needed to determine whether this finding is an artifact of this particular event, or typical of the latitude reporters have in most of their work.

Though limited in focus, this study shows that developing countries are concerned about the population problem, and reporters did their part in covering the population issue at this conference.

NOTES

1. See Narinder K. Aggarwala, "Media, News and People: A Third World View," *Media Asia,* 5:78–81 (1978); "Humanizing International Views," *Media Asia,* 5:136–39 (1978); "News with Third World Perspectives: A Practical Suggestion," in Philip C. Horton, ed., *The Third World and Press Freedom,* (New York: Praeger, 1978), pp. 197–209. Also see Frank Campbell, "The Practical Reality of 'Development Journalism,' " *InterMedia,* 12:24–29 (March 1984); Shelton Gunaratne, "Media Subservience and Developmental Journalism," *Communications and Development Review,* 2:3–7 (Summer 1978); John A. Lent, "A Third World News Deal? Part One: The Guiding Light," *Index on Censorship,* 6:17–26 (September/October 1977); Christine L. Ogan, "Development Journalism/Communication: The Status of the Concept," *Gazette,* 29:3–13 (1982); and Nora C. Quebral, "Development Communication: Where Does it Stand today," *Media Asia,* 2:197–202 (1975).

2. See Hamima Dona Mustafa, "A Comparative Analysis of the Use of Development News in Three Malaysian Dailies During 1974," in John A. Lent and John V. Vilanilam, eds. *The Use of Development News,* (Singapore: AMIC, 1979), pp. 56–70; Christine L. Ogan and Clint Swift, "Is the News About Development All Good?" presented to the Association for Education in Journalism and Mass Communications at the annual convention in Athens, Ohio, August 1982; Christine L. Ogan, "Development News in CANA and Interlink" in Walter G. Soderland and Stuart H. Surlin, editors, *Media in Latin America and the Caribbean: Domestic and International Perspectives,* Windsor, Ontario: University of Windsor, 1985, pp. 95–119; Christine L. Organ, Jo Ellen Fair

and Hemant Shah, " 'A Little Good News': The Treatment of Development News in Selected Third World Newspapers," *Gazette,* 33:173–91 (1984); Emmanuel Osae-Asare, "The Ghana Press and National Development: A Comparative Content Analysis of Development News in the National Daily Newspapers and the Wire Service, April–September 1976," in Lent and Vilanilam, *op. cit.,* pp. 72–90. Ishadi Ks. Sutopo, "Development News in Indonesian Dailies," Occasional Paper 15. (Singapore: AMIC, 1983), and John V. Vilanilam, "Ownership versus Development News Content: An Analysis of Independent and Conglomerate Newspapers of India," in Lent and Vilanilam, *op. cit.,* pp. 31–54.

3. Text of Declaration by International Population Conference in Mexico, the *New York Times,* August 16, 1985.

4. Annabelle Sreberny-Mohammadi, "The World of the News' Study," *Journal of Communication,* Winter 1984, pp. 121–142.

5. *Ibid.*

6. See Ogan, *op. cit.;* Ogan and Swift, *op. cit.,* and Ogan *et al., op. cit.*

7. Doris Graber, Maxwell McCombs and Chaim Eyal, David Weaver, *Media Agenda-Setting in a Presidential Election,* (New York: Praeger Publishers, 1981). p. 199. See also Thomas Patterson, *The Mass Media Election: How Americans Choose their President,* (New York: Praeger Publications, 1980). pp. 31–42.

8. See Weaver *et al., op. cit.*

9. William A. Orme Jr. "U.S. Foresees Defeat on Population Policy," *The Washington Post,* Aug. 11, 1984, p. A15.

10. "Issues to Watch at ICP," *Popline,* July 1984, p.4.

11. *Ibid.*

12. Holsti's composite reliability coefficient was used for this study. See Ole Holsti, *Content Analysis for the Social Sciences and Humanities,* (Reading, Mass.: Addison-Wesley, 1969), p. 137.

13. The World Bank, *World Development Report 1984,* (New York: Oxford University Press, 1984).

14. For nominal level data, Pearson's correlation between is considered a suitable measure of association when a 2 x 2 table is computed. See H.T. Reynolds, *Analysis of Nominal Data,* (Beverly Hills: Sage Publications, 1977), p. 28.

15. See Ogan and Swift, *op. cit.,* and Ogan, Fair and Shah, *op. cit.*

16. Multiple citations of the same person are reflected in the large number.

17. Since the composition of the official delgations was not fixed right up until time of the conference, and since it could not be determined how long it would take to get through conference recommendations, all official speakers were not listed on a program. To the extent that it could be determined, a list of official speakers was made and provided to the coders. Since an official roster from the Strategic Planning Seminar for the conference was available, those speakers, many of whom also spoke at the ICP, were included on the coders' lists.

DEVELOPMENT COMMUNICATIONS

AGENCY FOR INTERNATIONAL DEVELOPMENT (A.I.D.)

The final paper in this chapter is from an A.I.D. report on what the U.S. government has been trying to do to help developing countries improve and update their communication technology. It also discusses how communication is helping developing countries support their education, health, agriculture and other developmental programs.

I. INTRODUCTION

For most the world over most of its history the main means of communication have been the human voice, the written word and various systems of signs and symbols. Over the past few decades additional communications systems which once seemed only remote possibilities have begun to be familiar in developing country towns and villages.

Radio and newspaper coverage has increased. One or both now reach most developing country towns and villages. Telephones and television are available in most of the larger cities. Satellite TV receiving stations are proliferating and telephonic communication systems (terrestrial, microwave and satellite) have begun to link institutions and individuals thousands of miles apart. Increasing use is made of video and audio recording equipment in training and extension systems. Microcomputers, photocopiers and other information technologies are beginning to be available in public and private sector offices.

Over the next decade there is every reason to expect declining costs, increasing availability and diversified application of these and related communications technologies. Communications capabilities will grow dramatically in some countries and much more slowly and unevenly in others.

The emerging technologies, and combinations of these with more familiar technologies, present both major opportunities and new problems throughout the developing world. They are powerful tools for development which can be used to enrich the development environment with diverse types and sources of information. However, they are only tools. Their potential impact on the processes of development depends on the problems to which they are applied and the relevance of the information being communicated. Extending information which is not fully relevant to people's needs or through channels which people do not trust to be factually correct and

Reprinted from A.I.D. document, *Policy Determination*, PD-10, February 17, 1984. This is followed by a summary of A.I.D.'s activities in the art of communications, from *A.I.D. and Development Communications*, S&T/Office of Education, August 1983.

unbiased is likely to be a very expensive and relatively futile exercise at best and can seriously distort and impede the development process.

A.I.D. has made extensive use of radio as a cost-effective means of extending information for diverse populations (e.g. rural mothers, farmers and primary school students) and diverse subjects (e.g. mathematics, agriculture, family planning and oral rehydration therapy for diarrheal diseases). A.I.D.-supported experimentation with both satellite and terrestrial telecommunications systems is helping to speed the exchange of developmentally important information and data over great distances and among multiple participants, linking research institutions and universities, facilitating technical and business teleconferencing. In short, the potential for using communications technologies to help resolve a wide range of development problems has been demonstrated.

This policy determination provides guidance on the objectives and conditions under which A.I.D. will support the fuller application of these technologies in U.S. development assistance programs. This guidance applies to all Development Assistance-funded programs, and unless otherwise authorized, to programs supported with Economic Support Funds. A.I.D. will seek to assist developing nations in using these technologies as tools in their own development programs and in making informed consumption and investment choices among the available technologies. A.I.D. will also make use of these technologies to reduce costs, extend services and information and increase the effectiveness of projects it supports in all sectors.

II. OBJECTIVES OF A.I.D. COMMUNICATIONS ASSISTANCE

Communications technologies are powerful tools for development, with substantial potential for (1) reducing rural isolation, (2) in-creasing the productivity and effectiveness of economic and social development programs, (3) strengthening key private and public sector institutions, and (4) advancing the basic human right of people to have the information needed to make informed personal choices.

The priority for A.I.D. will be "development communications," defined as the application of existing communications technologies and media to problems of development. A.I.D. will also give attention to "communications development," defined as the development of new or additional communications infrastructure and capacity, but will not give priority to investments in infrastructure. . . .

III. A.I.D.'s DEVELOPMENT COMMUNICATIONS EMPHASES

The largest part of A.I.D. assistance to communication is expected to be as integral components of projects in each of the development sectors in which A.I.D. works. While a substantial increase in support for communications activities is anticipated, A.I.D. does not expect to support communications as a distinct program sector. . . .

IV. GUIDELINES FOR INFRASTRUCTURE SUPPORT

A.I.D.'s development communications activities will limit direct investment in infrastructure development and will concentrate instead on technical assistant designed to ensure that infrastructure projects are effectively implemented and utilized (e.g., training for key technicians and managers, technical assistance to organizations making use of existing infrastructure). . . .

INDEX

Figures are indicated by italic page numbers and tables by italic t after the page number.

MAKE it WORK!

DINOSAURS

Andrew Haslam

written by
Dr. Mike Benton

Consultant: Dr. Arthur Cruickshank
Honorary Research Assistant at Leicestershire Museum

Scholastic Canada Ltd.,
123 Newkirk Road, Richmond Hill, Ontario, Canada L4C 3G5

MAKE it WORK!
Other titles

Body
Building
Earth
Electricity
Flight
Insects
Machines
Photography
Plants
Ships
Sound
Space
Time

First published in Canada in 1997 by
Scholastic Canada Ltd.
123 Newkirk Road
Richmond Hill
Ontario L4C 3G5

Copyright © Two-Can Publishing Ltd, 1996
Series concept and original design
© Andrew Haslam and Wendy Baker

Canadian Cataloguing in Publication Data

Haslam, Andrew
    Dinosaurs

(Make it work!)
ISBN 0-590-24974-6 (bound) ISBN 0-590-24975-4 (pbk.)

1. Dinosaurs – Juvenile literature. I. Title. II. Series.

QE862.D5H373 1997   j567.9'1   C96-931956-8

Printed in Hong Kong

1 2 3 4 5 6 7 8 9 10 99 98 97 96

Text: Dr. Michael Benton
Editor: Jennet Stott
Senior Designer: Lisa Nutt
Managing Designer: Helen McDonagh
Project Editor: Kate Graham
Managing Editor: Christine Morley
Managing Art Director: Carole Orbell
Photography: John Englefield
Production: Joya Bart-Plange

Contents

Words marked in **bold** in the
text are explained in the glossary.

A person who studies **dinosaurs** is called a **paleontologist**. Paleontologists work like detectives, uncovering clues to the past by digging for **skeletons** and **fossils**. By studying dinosaurs, we can begin to understand what the world was like millions of years ago.

MAKE it WORK!

In this book we show you how to make lots of dinosaur models. These help you to understand how their bodies worked, how strong their bones were, and how fast they moved. The models are painted in various colours. Although no one knows what colours dinosaurs really were, we have used camouflage shades, such as green and yellow, for the plant-eaters, and bright shades for the meat-eaters.

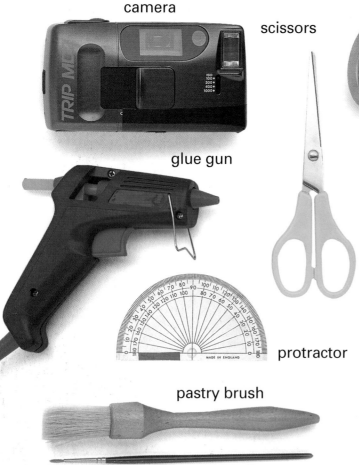

camera

scissors

glue gun

protractor

pastry brush

paintbrush

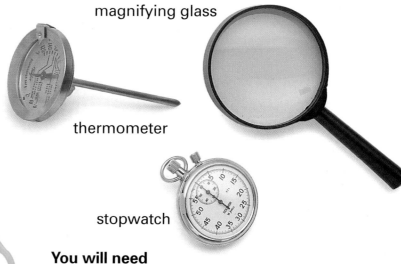

magnifying glass

thermometer

stopwatch

You will need

You can make most of the models out of simple materials, such as cardboard, wood, plastic bottles and wire. You will also need a craft knife and scissors to cut some of the materials. Throughout the book, we mention enlarging shapes on a photocopier. You may have to ask an adult to help you with this.

Paleontologists use many different scientific techniques in their work. When they find a dinosaur skeleton, they remove the rock that surrounds it. To do this, they use special tools to pick away at the rock, or chemicals, such as acid, to dissolve it.

notepad and pencil

pencil sharpener

ruler

Safety!

If you are using sharp tools, remember that they can be very dangerous! Be careful when you use them and ask an adult to help you. Make sure that anything you are cutting or drilling is held firmly, so that it cannot slip.

hacksaw

Making dinosaurs to scale

The models in this book are made to a scale of about 1:30. This means that the dinosaurs would be 30 times longer and taller in real life.

hand drill

belt punch

clamp

pliers

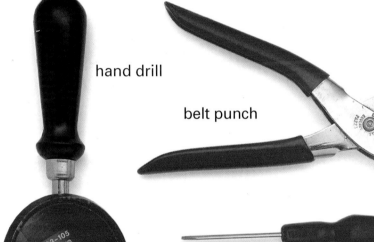

screwdriver

bradawl

tenon saw

hammer

Keeping records

Paleontologists work very slowly and carefully. They keep detailed records of every stage of their work with photographs, drawings and notes. It doesn't matter if you don't have a camera. Using a notebook to draw and write about your finds is an excellent way of keeping a record.

Naming dinosaurs

When paleontologists discover a new dinosaur, they give it a name. This name is often made up of Latin and Greek words that describe the dinosaur. So, *Tyrannosaurus rex* means "tyrant reptile king." The first name—*Tyrannosaurus*—is the name of the **genus** (group with the same characteristics). The second name—*rex*—is the name of the **species**.

6 Geological Time

The Earth is about 4.6 billion years old. Life appeared about 3.5 billion years ago in the form of tiny single **cells**, something like viruses. Fossils of these cells can be seen only under a microscope. Dinosaurs first roamed the Earth 225 million years ago and humans emerged less than 5 million years ago!

MAKE it WORK!
Make yourself a **geological** time scale. You can make a clock or a time chart. The 12 hours of the clock face represent the age of the Earth from 4.6 billion years ago to the present. It shows that dinosaurs appeared in the last hour and humans in the last few seconds.

You will need
glue	a compass
scissors	a protractor
stencils	coloured pencils
a paper fastener	coloured cardboard
paints and paintbrushes	
a clock motor with battery, hands, nut and plastic cap	

To make a clock
1 Using a compass, draw a circle 20 cm in diameter on green cardboard, then cut it out. Now make a hole in the middle of the circle.

2 Use a protractor to divide the circle into 12 equal divisions. Mark each one with a short line in white pencil. Stencil on the numbers 1 to 12 for the hours with yellow paint. At each hour, stencil the number of years in white paint using the clock below as a guide. Each hour represents one-twelfth of 4.6 billion years.

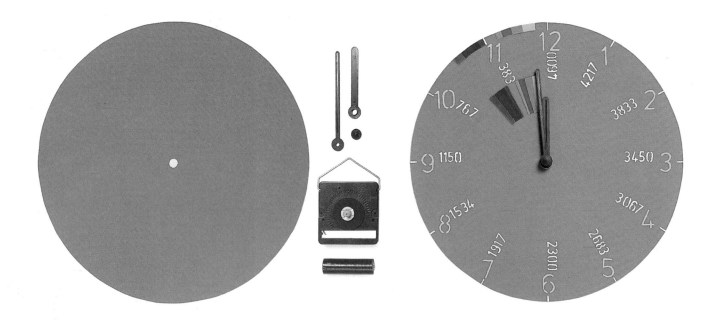

3 Draw a line to mark the beginning of the past 570 million years. From this line up to the number 12 (present day), you will need to paint coloured strips representing the different geological periods shown opposite. Each colour represents a different period. The colours should follow the order shown in the time chart, opposite.

4 Remove the nut and the hands from the central spindle of the clock motor. Put the spindle through the hole in the clock face from the back of the cardboard. Replace the nut on the spindle, then put the hands on. Fit the plastic cap over the hands. If you don't have a clock motor, use a paper fastener to attach the hands.

To make a time strip

1 Take a 230 cm length of green cardboard. Starting with 0 at the top, divide it into periods of 100 million years using thin strips of red tape, as shown right. Each 100-million-year period should be 5 cm deep.

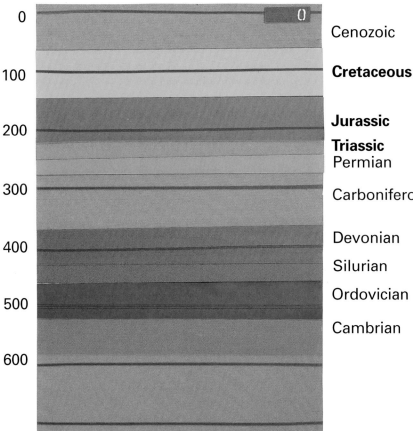

Millions of years	Geological periods
0	Cenozoic
100	**Cretaceous**
200	**Jurassic**
	Triassic
	Permian
300	Carboniferous
400	Devonian
	Silurian
500	Ordovician
	Cambrian
600	

2 Using the colours in the picture above as your guide, cut out thin strips of cardboard of varying widths—these mark the geological periods of the past 570 million years. Glue the strips of cardboard to the top end of the green strip, following the order of colours above. Now label each billion-year period with red cardboard.

Dinosaurs lived during the Triassic, Jurassic and Cretaceous periods. Triassic dinosaurs included Coelophysis *and* Plateosaurus. Stegosaurus *and* Brachiosaurus *lived during the Jurassic period.* Triceratops *and* Deinonychus *lived during the Cretaceous period.*

We know that dinosaurs existed because their fossil bones and footprints have been found. Fossils, the preserved remains of ancient plants and animals, are often found in rock. When a dinosaur died, the soft parts of its body rotted away, leaving only the bones and teeth. Some skeletons were preserved in layers of sand and mud. **Minerals** carried in water soaked into the bones and, over millions of years, turned them to stone.

1 Roll out a large piece of Plasticine until it makes an even slab about 1 cm thick. Make sure the surface of the Plasticine is smooth and even, as any cracks or marks may spoil the look of your finished cast.

2 Trace the skeleton of the dinosaur shown opposite, then enlarge it on a photocopier. Lay the enlarged photocopy on top of the Plasticine sheet and prick through the paper with a pushpin to mark the outline of the dinosaur on the Plasticine. Lift the photocopy off and use the modelling knife to join the dots and shape the outline of the dinosaur. Then carve the bones neatly out of the Plasticine.

3 Make a frame for the mould by cutting off the base of a cardboard box. The rectangular frame should be at least 5 cm deep.

4 Press the frame into the mould. Make sure no gaps are left between the Plasticine and the sides of the frame.

5 Mix up some plaster of Paris (it should be pourable, but not watery). Pour it into the frame, so that it completely covers the Plasticine and forms a layer 1-2 cm deep. Let the plaster harden.

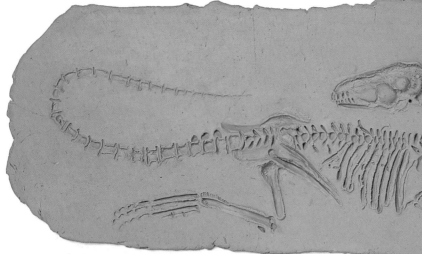

MAKE it WORK!

Make your own model of a fossil dinosaur skeleton, and then make a cast—a shape created by pressing material into a mold. This is the fossil of a theropod, a two-legged meat-eater from the Late Triassic.

You will need

a pushpin
a pencil
Plasticine
tracing paper
a modelling knife　　a rolling pin
a cardboard box　　plaster of Paris

6 Carefully peel off the Plasticine to reveal the cast (you can use the mould again to make another cast). Flip the plaster over and you should have a perfect dinosaur cast.

Dinosaur fossils look very different from the flesh-and-blood creatures that walked the Earth millions of years ago. In the fossil model above, for example, the neck is bent back because all the **ligaments** have dried up.

When an animal dies, its body usually breaks down quickly. In the first four weeks, fluids, such as blood, disappear. Within a year, all soft tissues, such as flesh, will have decomposed. In one to two years, the collagen, or bone protein, is lost. Only if the body is quickly covered in sediment, such as sand or mud, does it stand a chance of being preserved.

ammonite
fossil

leaf fossil

Ammonites were a type of shellfish. Their fossils are found in rocks formed millions of years ago during Jurassic and Cretaceous times. Their coiled shells are among the fossils most often found.

Fossilized plants, such as the leaf above, are usually found in limestone and sandstone rocks, or in coal deposits. Coal deposits are the remains of forests that rotted down millions of years ago, and were covered by many layers of sand or mud.

10 The Dinosaur World

When dinosaurs were alive, the world was much warmer than it is today. There were three main ages of dinosaurs—the Triassic, Jurassic and Cretaceous. Different dinosaurs lived during each of these times, and a variety of plants and other animals existed alongside them.

MAKE it WORK!

Make your own dinosaur landscapes and put plastic dinosaur models in them. Find out which dinosaurs lived when (the chart on pages 6 and 7 will help you) and put them in the landscape for that period. Add plastic palm trees to the landscapes, or make your own trees.

You will need

paints	tape
scissors	glue
thin green cardboard	dried moss
plaster of Paris	newspapers
wooden skewers	strips of cloth
plastic dinosaur models	
three wooden boards 30 cm x 45 cm	

1 Build a landscape on each board by crumpling newspaper into different shapes as shown below. Give the Triassic landscape large mountains and add a volcano to the Cretaceous landscape. Tape to hold the newspaper firmly in place.

2 Mix some water and plaster of Paris to make a very wet paste. Soak strips of cloth in this paste.

3 Spread the cloth strips over each landscape frame you have made. Smooth the surface carefully with your hands and let dry.

▲ Triassic—hot, dry, vast deserts

▲ Jurassic—warm, with lush vegetation

4 Make the Triassic landscape look like a desert by using orange, red and yellow paint. Paint the Jurassic landscape with green, brown and yellow paint to look like plants and soil. Add rivers and lakes with blue paint to both. Paint the bare, volcanic landscape of the Cretaceous with shades of brown, yellow and purple paint.

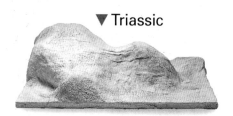

▼ Triassic

▼ Jurassic

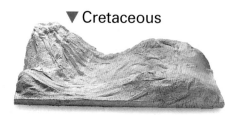

▼ Cretaceous

5 To make your own trees, cut out a rectangle of lightweight green cardboard 6 cm x 3 cm. Make 20 equally-spaced cuts along one long side of the cardboard. Glue the uncut edge around the top of a skewer and spread the leaves.

6 Make 20 palm trees and push them into the landscapes. If you are using model palm trees, glue these to the landscapes at this point.

7 Make some bushes with the dried moss and glue them to each of the landscapes, especially along the river banks. The Triassic deserts should be scattered with thin bushes, while the Jurassic landscape should have plenty of large bushes. The landscapes are now ready for your dinosaurs.

8 Arrange the dinosaur models so that the plant-eaters are feeding from the tops of the palm trees or from the low bushes. Some of the meat-eaters could be lurking behind the trees, ready to pounce on their prey.

The dinosaur world was very different from our own. When dinosaurs first appeared, the great land masses were all joined together. They later drifted apart to their present positions. Climates were hotter since there were no polar ice caps. Triassic dinosaurs lived in hot, dry conditions, but the climate became wetter in the Jurassic and Cretaceous.

▶ Cretaceous—warm, with volcanoes in some areas

Dinosaurs were **reptiles** that lived only on land. They could not fly, nor could they live in water. They belonged to the **Archosauria**, or "ruling reptiles" group. This group includes ancient flying reptiles, or **pterosaurs**, as well as present-day crocodiles and birds. All dinosaurs lived during the **Mesozoic** era, 250 million to 65 million years ago.

mya = million years ago

Dinosauria 235 mya

Ornithischia 230 mya

Genasauria 225 mya

Cerapoda 225 mya

Marginocephalia 130 mya

Ornithopoda 225 mya

Thyreophora 190 mya

Fabrosauridae

Ceratopsia

Pachycephalosauria

Hadrosauridae

Iguanodontidae

Hypsilophodontidae

Heterodontosauridae

Ankylosauria

Stegosauria

Lesothosaurus

MAKE it WORK!
This model of the dinosaur evolutionary tree shows how dinosaurs evolved over 160 million years on Earth and which types are most closely related. After making your tree, add plastic dinosaurs in their correct positions.

You will need
a pencil
a compass
coloured cardboard
scissors and glue
32 cm-square wooden board

1 Make the tree as shown above, using coloured cardboard. Put it together on the board and glue in place. Add the names of the dinosaur groups on cards and arrange your plastic models on the correct "branch" of the tree.

The branches of the evolutionary tree
At the top of the tree is Dinosauria—the whole class of dinosaurs. Below it are the two main groups of dinosaurs—the Ornithischia and the Saurischia. **Ornithischian** dinosaurs have birdlike hips. **Saurischian** dinosaurs have lizardlike hips.

Putting dinosaurs into groups

Ornithischian dinosaurs are all plant-eaters and some of them, such as *Triceratops*, have horns, spines and other kinds of armor. Saurischians include the meat-eating **theropods** and the long-necked, plant-eating **sauropods**.

Once you know whether a dinosaur is a Saurischian or Ornithischian, you need to find out what kind of skeleton it has to move further down the tree. For example, dinosaurs are placed in different groups according to the shape and structure of their skulls or backbones. Some of this information can be very difficult to find, especially without a complete skeleton to study.

look up bold names in the glossary on pages 46 to 47

Saurischia 230 mya

Sauropodomorpha 230 mya

Theropoda 225 mya

Tetanurae 205 mya

Coelurosauria 180 mya

Maniraptora 170 mya

225 mya

Prosauropoda

Sauropoda

Ceratosauria

Carnosauria

Ornithomimidae

Dromaeosauridae

Birds

Some dinosaurs and their groups

Triceratops
● Ceratopsia

Iguanodon
● Iguanodontidae

Scelidosaurus
● Thyreophora

Stegosaurus
● Stegosauria

Apatosaurus
● Sauropoda

Brachiosaurus
● Sauropoda

Diplodocus
● Sauropoda

Tyrannosaurus
● Carnosauria

14 Digging up Dinosaurs

Dozens of dinosaur skeletons are dug up every year. Paleontologists search for them along ancient rivers, lakes and desert dunes. An **excavation** may be sparked off by the discovery of a few small bone pieces that have been washed out of the ground by rain or floods. Months of digging may follow to find out if there is a whole skeleton buried, or just a few fragments.

To make the drawing

1 Carefully place the cast you have already made on a photocopier and make a copy of it. Using thin tape, make a grid of squares over the photocopy as shown in the picture below (paleontologists use grids to make their drawings more accurate).

2 Trace the dinosaur from the photocopy using the grid squares as a guide. Once you have completed the tracing, add a white and red line to show the scale—each block represents about a metre. Glue the drawing onto a piece of white cardboard, as shown.

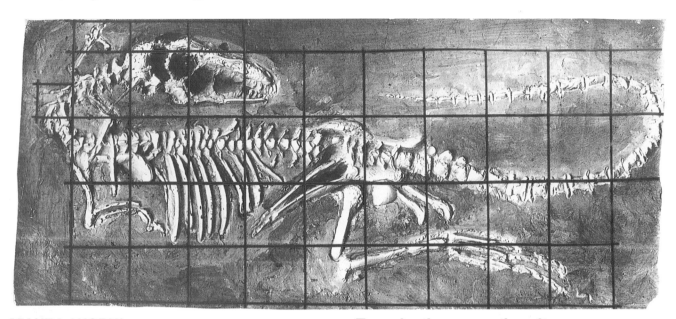

MAKE it WORK!

When a skeleton is discovered, paleontologists work on-site, first photographing the skeleton and then drawing it. Here we show you how to draw a grid of a meat-eating dinosaur cast and make a model excavation site. First you will need to make the fossil cast on pages 8 and 9.

You will need

fine sand	a dowel rod
red thread	scissors
a craft knife	tracing paper
modelling clay	pushpins and tape
a drinking straw	a small hammer
green and white cardboard	a modelling knife
paints and paintbrushes	a ruler and a pencil

To make the excavation site

1 Use modelling clay to build soil and rocks around the dinosaur cast to make it look like an excavation site. Sprinkle fine sand all over the surface, except on the skeleton, and press it into the clay.

2 To make the grid, lay a ruler across the area immediately surrounding, and over, the skeleton. Using a small hammer, gently knock pushpins in at regular intervals. Take care not to crack the surrounding plaster. Tie lengths of red thread between the pushpins to make a model grid, just like a paleontologist's grid. Place a drinking straw at the back of the grid to act as a surveyor's pole.

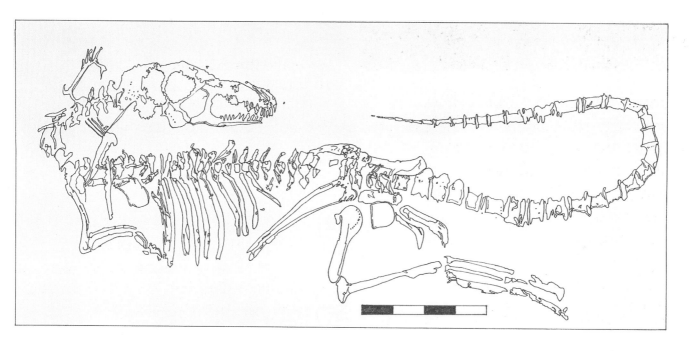

3 Add model trees to the site, or make them using various lengths of dowel rod for trunks. Use green cardboard for the leaves (see page 11 for instructions on how to make them). Push the trees into the clay on the board and build up clay around the base to fix them in place.

4 Paint the edges of the plaster base to look like sand and soil. Place model people at the site—these are the paleontologists.

Digging up a dinosaur skeleton is a huge task. It might take a team of five to ten paleontologists several weeks to carefully dig up all the pieces. A complete skeleton can weigh 20 tonnes or more.

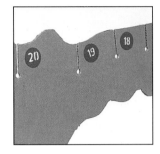
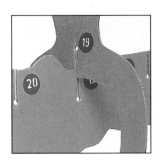

Dinosaur skeletons contain hundreds of bones, just as ours do. In fact, you can match the shape and position of most dinosaur bones with bones in human skeletons. Like us, dinosaurs had skulls, backbones, and arm and leg bones.

MAKE it WORK!
Make a large, simple skeleton of a four-legged dinosaur. This is a model of *Apatosaurus*, one of the biggest dinosaurs. It was a plant-eater that may have weighed as much as 30 tonnes.

You will need
a craft knife
tracing paper
masking tape
corrugated cardboard
coloured gummed labels

1 Trace the outlines of all the bones shown at right. Enlarge the backbone until it is about 115 cm long. Then enlarge the other pieces by the same percentage.

2 Lay the tracings over the cardboard. To prevent the tracings from sliding as you cut, tape them to the cardboard with masking tape. Ask an adult to help you cut out the shapes with a craft knife, then remove the paper tracings. Cut deep slits in the shapes, as shown at right.

3 Number the coloured gummed labels and stick them to the bone shapes in the positions shown.

4 The neck and backbone are made out of one piece of cardboard. Push the rib sections with red labels numbered 12 to 20 into the matching red slots along the backbone, as shown above. Make sure the rib sections are in the right order: the ribs should be longest in the middle of the backbone, and become shorter as they reach the front of the neck.

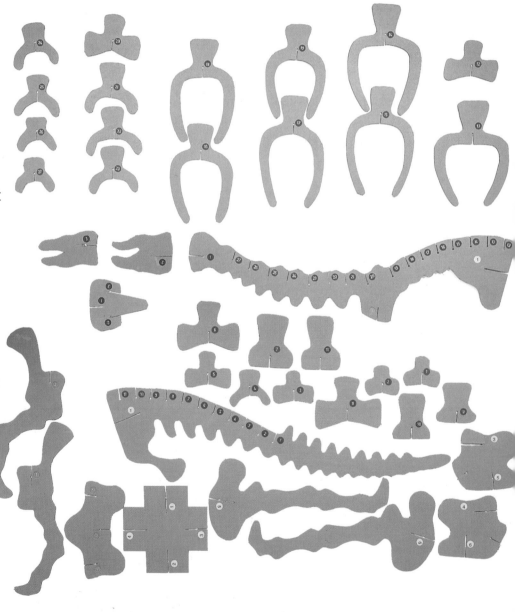

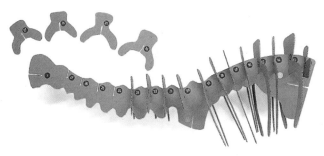 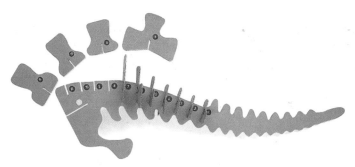

5 Slot the remaining rib sections with red labels numbered 21 to 27 into the front of the neck and backbone, as shown above.

8 Fit the rib sections with red labels numbered 1 to 11 onto the tail region as shown above. Now put all the pieces together as shown below and slot the two halves of the skeleton together.

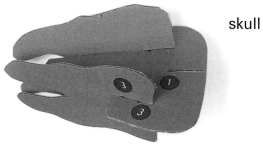

skull

6 Make the skull by slotting together the three skull pieces with blue labels numbered 1 to 3. Make sure the pieces are pushed into the slots with the matching numbers.

7 Now make up the front legs with green-labelled pieces numbered 1 to 3 and back legs with yellow-labelled pieces numbered 1 to 6. Make sure the legs face in the right direction. Adjust the final fitting of the legs when the model is complete to make it stand steady.

Dinosaurs like Apatosaurus had up to 450 bones. There were dozens of bones in the backbone and just as many in the tail. Two ribs were attached to each bone in the backbone, and there were up to 50 or 60 bones in the skull.

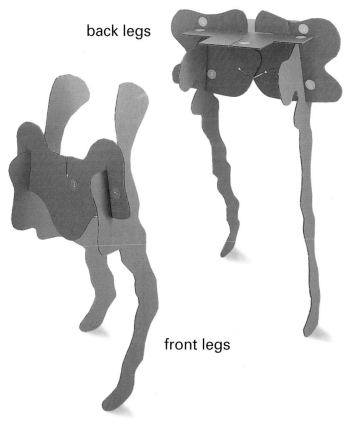

back legs

front legs

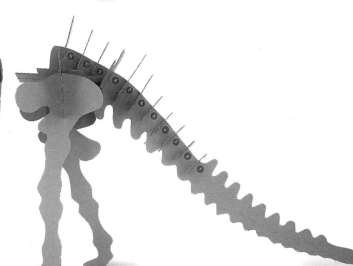

How the skeleton works

Dinosaur skeletons had to support a lot of weight, so they had to be very strong. The leg bones of a large dinosaur, for example, had to be thick enough to bear the dinosaur's enormous weight without breaking. Although the bones were thick, the skeleton was designed so that the animal could move freely.

You have made a model of the skeleton of the *Apatosaurus*, one of the largest dinosaurs that ever lived. It weighed 10 times as much as an elephant! Now you can look at each part of the *Apatosaurus* skeleton to see how such an enormous animal worked.

The backbone and legs

The backbone and the legs are the engineering marvels of the giant sauropods. In *Apatosaurus*, the distance between the shoulder and the hips is quite short. Notice how the backbone arches up to give it the strength to hold the weight of all the internal organs inside the ribcage. The backbone is particularly strong in the hip region.

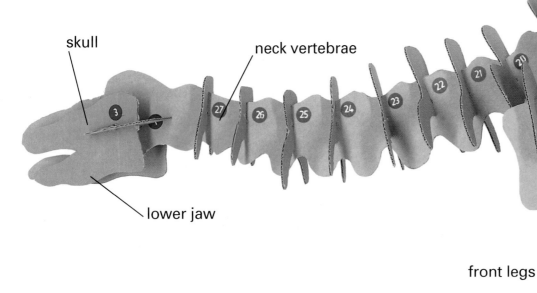

skull

neck vertebrae

shoulder blade

lower jaw

front legs

The head and neck

The head of *Apatosaurus* had to be small, otherwise the long neck would never have been able to support it (animals with large heads have short necks). Still, with such a small mouth, it is difficult to see how *Apatosaurus* could eat enough to feed its huge body.

Paleontologists believe that *Apatosaurus* moved its neck slowly from side to side in search of food. It could probably raise its neck a little to grab leaves from the trees. The long neck worked like a crane. It was probably moved by powerful muscles and ligaments along the top of the neck, rather like the steel cables that move the arm of a crane.

The spines on the backbone are very high around the hips—sometimes as much as half a metre in height. This would have provided support for the strong muscles and ligaments that helped the backbone carry the weight of the stomach and other internal organs.

The tail as a weapon

The tail acted as a counterbalance to *Apatosaurus'* long neck, and also helped to hold up the heavy middle section of its body. *Apatosaurus* also may have used its tail to defend itself from meat-eaters. It could do this by swinging it from side to side like a whip.

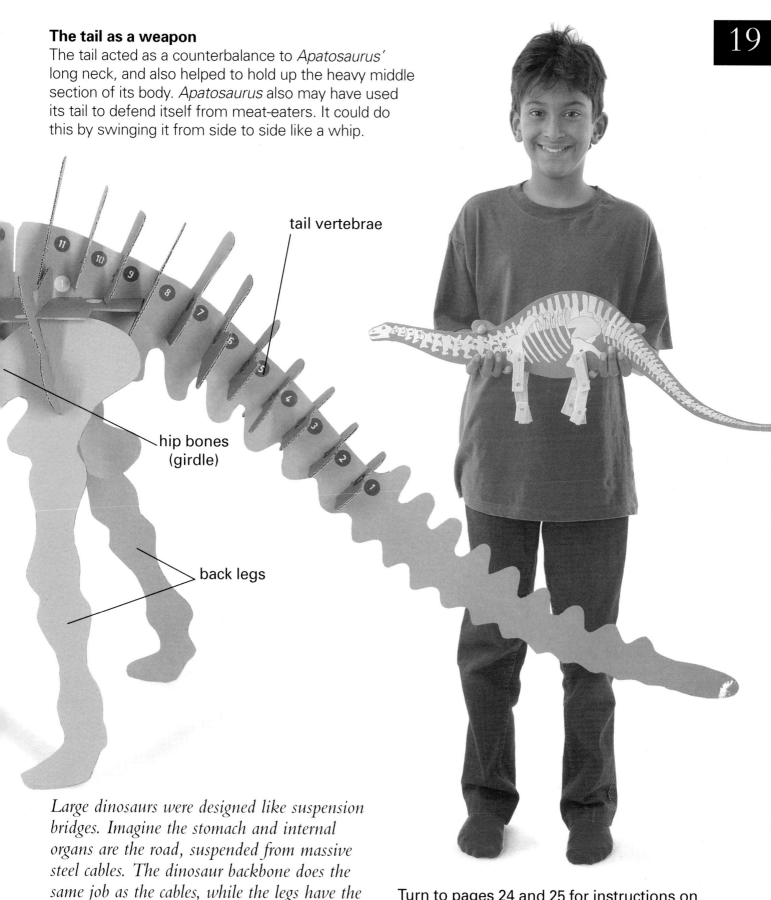

tail vertebrae

hip bones
(girdle)

back legs

Large dinosaurs were designed like suspension bridges. Imagine the stomach and internal organs are the road, suspended from massive steel cables. The dinosaur backbone does the same job as the cables, while the legs have the same function as bridge supports.

Turn to pages 24 and 25 for instructions on how to make the sauropod model above.

20 Dinosaur Skulls

You can tell a great deal about a dinosaur by looking at its skull. Look at the teeth first: meat-eaters had long, sharp teeth; plant-eaters had shorter, blunt teeth. The jaws are also important: deep jaws mean huge muscles and a powerful bite, typical of the giant meat-eaters.

1 Trace the bone shapes below. Enlarge the lower jaw pieces on a photocopier to around 50 cm long. Enlarge the other pieces by the same percentage. Copy the shapes onto cardboard and cut them out. Take care when cutting out the tabs. Curve the two lower jaw pieces carefully as shown above. Glue the ends together. Slot the lower jaw spacer in the middle and glue in place.

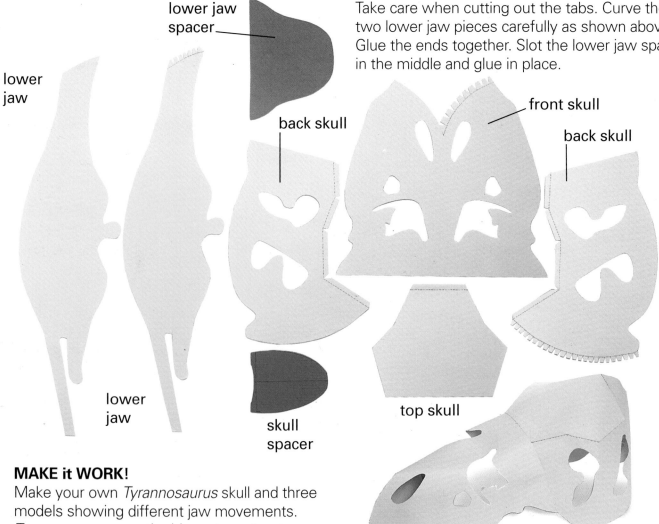

lower jaw spacer

lower jaw

back skull

front skull

back skull

lower jaw

skull spacer

top skull

MAKE it WORK!

Make your own *Tyrannosaurus* skull and three models showing different jaw movements. *Tyrannosaurus* was the biggest meat-eater on land and could have eaten any plant-eater.

You will need

glue	a pencil
a craft knife	scissors
tracing paper	
cream, brown and white cardboard	

2 Bend the front skull shape in half so that the tabs fit under the opposite side. Glue them in place. Now glue the tab on the top skull to the middle of the front skull. Next, glue the two back skulls to the front and top skull, and to each other. Fit the skull spacer behind nostrils.

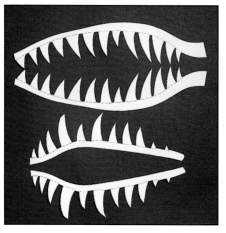

lower

upper

3 Place the skull you have just made on top of the lower jaw. Trace the four rows of teeth above and use a photocopier to enlarge them so that they fit the jaws. Trace them onto white cardboard and cut them out. Glue the longer row of teeth to the upper jaw, and the shorter one to the lower jaw.

Dinosaur jaws

The early reptiles had simple jaws that opened and shut to cut food into pieces. However, both meat-eating and plant-eating dinosaurs had jaws that were shaped and hinged differently from early reptiles. This different design made them much more powerful and efficient.

jaws of a primitive reptile

jaws of a plant-eating dinosaur

jaws of a meat-eating dinosaur

You will need

glue	soft wood
a saw	a craft knife
a hand drill	pink and white cardboard
5 mm dowel rod: 3 dowel rods 2.5 cm long	

To make a primitive reptile's jaws

Cut two pieces of wood 17 cm long. Drill two 5 mm holes in each piece, 4.5 cm from the ends. Push a piece of dowel rod through the holes to make the hinge as shown. Glue a piece of white cardboard onto the jaws as shown above. This shows where the reptile's bite is strongest.

To make a plant-eater's jaws

Cut wood as above and glue together. Join the jaws with a 5 mm dowel rod. Glue on the pink cardboard as shown. As you can see, these jaws are lower than the hinge point. This gives the plant-eater a more powerful bite along the whole jaw, not just at a single point, as on the primitive reptile's jaw.

To make a meat-eater's jaw

Using wood 31 cm long, make jaws as before. The pink cardboard shows how the jaw is slightly curved. The bite is strongest here, where the largest teeth are. They pierce the flesh of prey.

Dinosaurs had straight legs that were held underneath the body. This meant they stood fully upright on two or four legs. With straight legs, they could move faster and walk farther than sprawling animals. Also, they were able to grow much larger, because their legs could support a lot of weight.

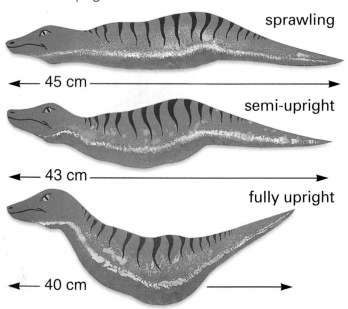

sprawling reptile, such as a modern lizard

For the bodies you will need

scissors	pencil
paints and paintbrushes	thick cardboard

1 Draw the three body shapes and cut them out of thick cardboard. Paint the faces and bodies to match the colours shown below.

semi-upright reptile, such as a modern crocodile, or dinosaur **ancestor**

MAKE it WORK!

To compare different ways of walking, make models of a **sprawler** (a reptile with arms and legs that stick out sideways), a semi-upright reptile (with legs tucked partly under the body), and an upright dinosaur.

sprawling
← 45 cm →

semi-upright
← 43 cm →

fully upright
← 40 cm →

For the sprawling reptile's legs, you will need

a hand drill	glue

2 cm-wide softwood: 12 pieces 6 cm long, 12 pieces 3 cm long
5 mm dowel rod: 12 pieces 15 mm long

1 Drill two 5 mm holes in the longer pieces of wood, 0.5 cm from each end. Drill one hole in the shorter pieces, 0.5 cm from one end. Place a 3 cm piece of wood between two 6 cm pieces. Line up the holes and push a dowel rod through. Put one 6 cm piece between the open end of the joined pair and secure with a dowel rod. Sandwich the 6 cm piece between two 3 cm pieces and secure with a dowel rod.

2 Glue the legs to the body. Each leg should sit flat against the body as shown at far left.

For the semi-upright reptile's legs you will need

a hand drill   glue
2 cm-wide softwood: 12 pieces 6 cm long,
   12 pieces 3 cm long
5 mm dowel rod: 12 pieces 15 mm long

1 Put the legs together as you did for the sprawling reptile. Glue the legs at an angle, so that the body is raised off the ground.

2 For each leg, sandwich one end of a 7 cm piece between two 4 cm pieces, and the other end between two 8.5 cm pieces. Secure with two 15 mm-long pieces of dowel rod.

3 Make two holes in the body for the arms and legs. Push a 33 mm length of dowel rod through the open end of the arms, the hole in the body, and the other arm. Repeat this to attach the legs.

Dinosaurs grew very large because of their upright legs. Today's sprawling reptiles cannot hold their bellies off the ground, so they never grow bigger than a lizard.

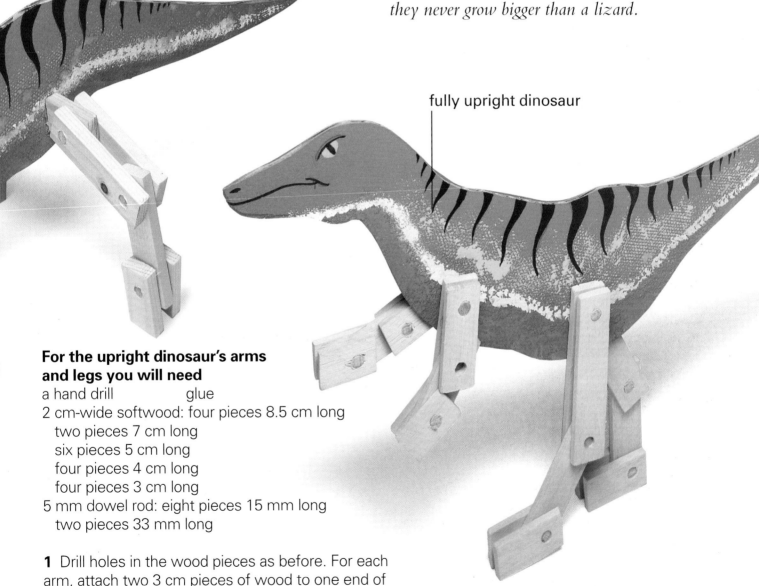

fully upright dinosaur

For the upright dinosaur's arms and legs you will need

a hand drill   glue
2 cm-wide softwood: four pieces 8.5 cm long
   two pieces 7 cm long
   six pieces 5 cm long
   four pieces 4 cm long
   four pieces 3 cm long
5 mm dowel rod: eight pieces 15 mm long
   two pieces 33 mm long

1 Drill holes in the wood pieces as before. For each arm, attach two 3 cm pieces of wood to one end of a 5 cm piece, and two 5 cm pieces to the other end. Fix with two 15 mm-long pieces of dowel rod.

24 Four Legs or Two?

The first dinosaurs stood up on their hind legs. These early dinosaurs were the size of humans and they caught and ate small animals with their hands. Later dinosaurs were much larger and could no longer support all their weight on their hind legs. They had to go down on all fours.

MAKE it WORK!
Make a four-legged (**quadrupedal**) sauropod dinosaur and a two-legged (**bipedal**) ornithopod to see how each dinosaur walked.

You will need

scissors   corrugated cardboard
a hand drill   paints and a paintbrush

For the sauropod you will need
5 mm dowel rod: eight pieces 15 mm long
   two pieces 33 mm long
2 cm-wide softwood:
   twelve pieces 6 cm long
   eight pieces 3 cm long

For the ornithopod you will need
2 cm-wide softwood:
   four pieces 12 cm long
   two pieces 9 cm long
   eight pieces 6 cm long
   two pieces 4.5 cm long
   two pieces 4 cm long
   four pieces 3 cm long
5 mm dowel rod:
   two pieces 33 mm long
   ten pieces 15 mm long

1 Copying the finished models, draw the ornithopod and sauropod body shapes onto corrugated cardboard. Then cut the shapes out. Trace the skeleton outlines onto the cardboard and paint the bones white or pale yellow.

2 Drill 5 mm holes in all the pieces of wood as shown below at left. To make each sauropod leg, take one 6 cm piece of wood and sandwich it between two 3 cm pieces. Line up the holes and secure with a 15 mm-long dowel rod. Now sandwich the free end of the 6 cm piece between two 6 cm pieces. Line up the holes and secure with a 15 mm-long dowel rod.

3 Take the open end of each of the sauropod's back legs and secure to the cardboard body with a 33 mm-long dowel rod. Repeat for the front legs.

4 For each of the ornithopod's arms, take one 4.5 cm piece of wood and sandwich it between two 3 cm pieces. Line up the holes and secure with a 15 mm-long dowel rod. Now sandwich the free end of the 4.5 cm piece between two 6 cm pieces. Line up the holes and secure with a 15 mm-long dowel rod.

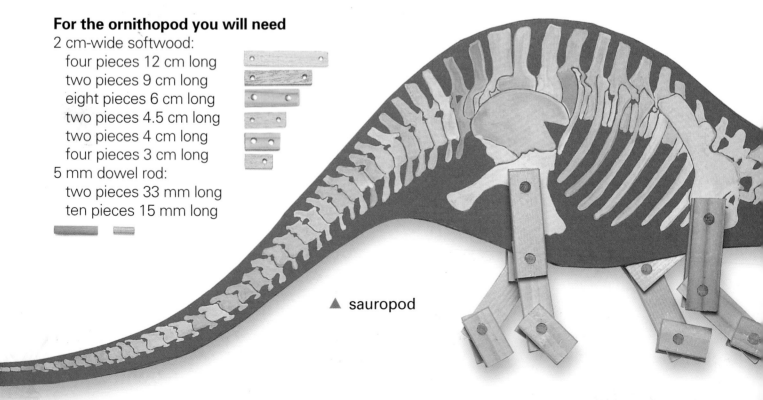

▲ sauropod

5 For each of the ornithopod's legs, take a 4 cm piece and sandwich it between two 6 cm pieces. Line up the holes and secure with a 15 mm-long dowel rod.

▲ These pictures show the sequence of an ornithopod's stride.

▼ ornithopod

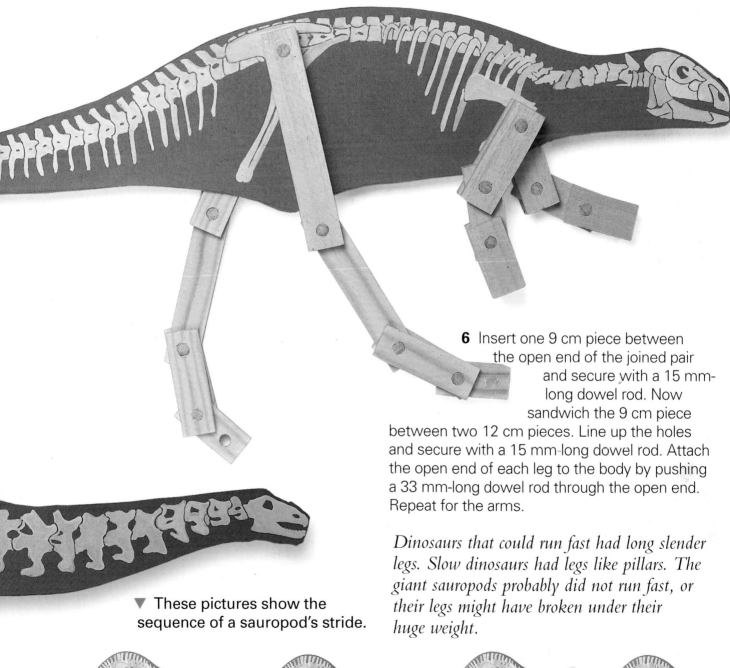

6 Insert one 9 cm piece between the open end of the joined pair and secure with a 15 mm-long dowel rod. Now sandwich the 9 cm piece between two 12 cm pieces. Line up the holes and secure with a 15 mm-long dowel rod. Attach the open end of each leg to the body by pushing a 33 mm-long dowel rod through the open end. Repeat for the arms.

Dinosaurs that could run fast had long slender legs. Slow dinosaurs had legs like pillars. The giant sauropods probably did not run fast, or their legs might have broken under their huge weight.

▼ These pictures show the sequence of a sauropod's stride.

Some meat-eating dinosaurs used amazing weapons to attack their prey. The **raptors**, a group of human-sized dinosaurs, had a fearsome claw on each back foot. These claws were held up when the animal was attacking, and could be flicked down quickly to tear at flesh.

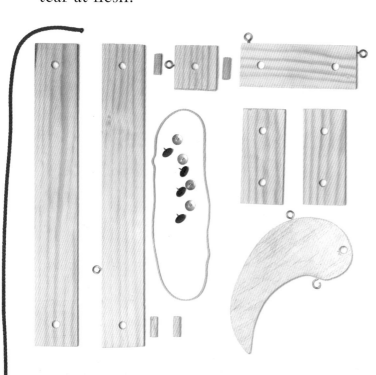

1 Ask an adult to help you cut four pieces of dowel rod, 2 cm long. Then drill holes in the pieces of wood, as shown below left. These holes should be 5 mm in diameter, so that the pieces of dowel rod fit into them exactly.

2 Screw the eyelets into the sides of the softwood strips: three on the medium strip, as shown at left, one on a long strip, one on the square piece, and one on the claw's top edge, as shown below. Screw a hook on the underside of the claw, opposite the eyelet.

3 Place a dowel rod into the hole at each end of the long strip with the eyelet. Put a pushpin into each dowel rod on the outside only.

4 Fit the medium strip over the dowel rod at one end of the long strip. Then fit the square at the other end of the long strip, as shown above. Position the short strips at the other end of the medium strip, one on each side. Line up the holes and slot in a piece of dowel rod. Put a pushpin through each end of the dowel rod.

5 Sandwich the claw between the other end of the short strips. Line up the holes and slot in a piece of dowel rod. Secure with a pushpin pushed through both ends.

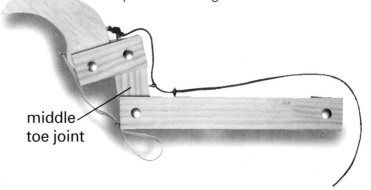

middle toe joint

MAKE it WORK!

This flick-claw model is based on *Deinonychus*, a raptor from the early Cretaceous of North America. The model claw is designed to move quickly, just like the real thing.

You will need

a craft knife
5 mm dowel rod
one brass hook
six brass eyelets
string
a hand drill
eight pushpins
a long rubber band

strips of 5 mm softwood:
   two long, 25 cm x 3.5 cm
   one medium, 10 cm x 3.5 cm
   two short, 8 cm x 3.5 cm
   one 3.5 cm square
   balsa-wood claw, 13.5 cm long x 5 mm deep

6 Position the remaining long strip onto the model, as shown below left. Fit onto the dowel rods and secure with pushpins.

7 Thread a long piece of string through the eyelets along the top of the claw, as shown below left. Knot the string at the claw end.

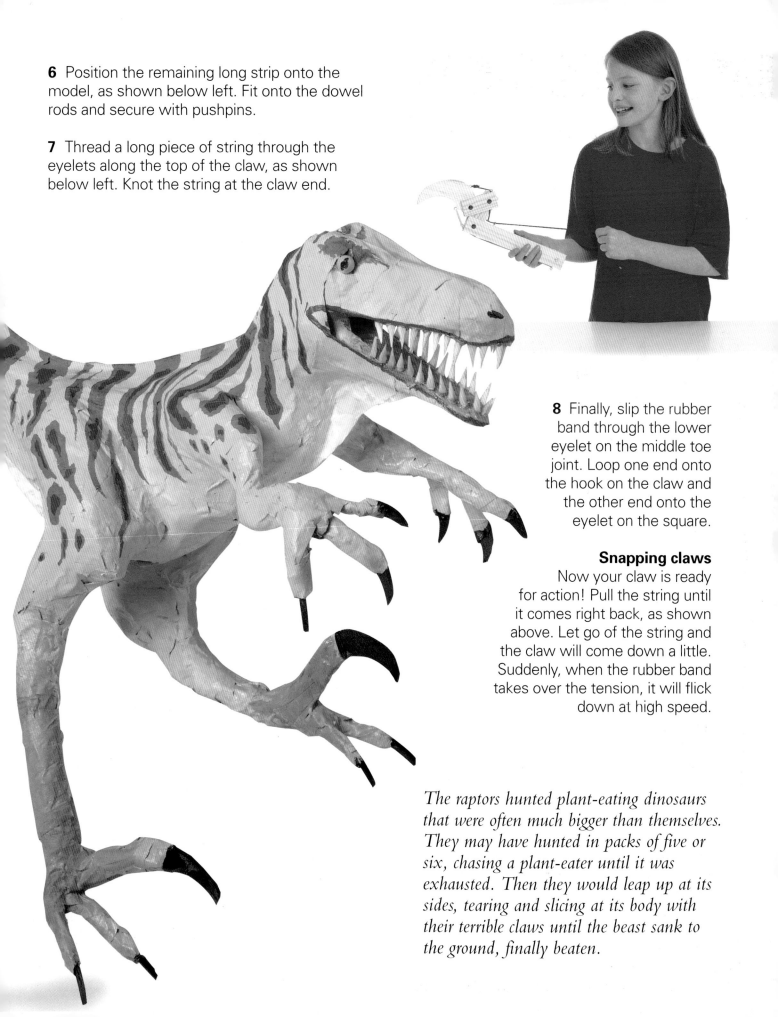

8 Finally, slip the rubber band through the lower eyelet on the middle toe joint. Loop one end onto the hook on the claw and the other end onto the eyelet on the square.

Snapping claws
Now your claw is ready for action! Pull the string until it comes right back, as shown above. Let go of the string and the claw will come down a little. Suddenly, when the rubber band takes over the tension, it will flick down at high speed.

The raptors hunted plant-eating dinosaurs that were often much bigger than themselves. They may have hunted in packs of five or six, chasing a plant-eater until it was exhausted. Then they would leap up at its sides, tearing and slicing at its body with their terrible claws until the beast sank to the ground, finally beaten.

The plant-eating dinosaurs had to find a way of defending themselves from the meat-eating dinosaurs. The large plant-eaters could not escape by running quickly, so many of them developed body armour—bony plates that grew in the skin—to protect themselves.

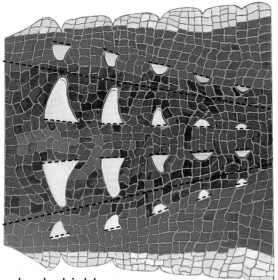

back shield

MAKE it WORK!

Make your own suit of ankylosaur dinosaur armor. The ankylosaurs were large plant-eaters, some of them as big as army tanks. They had bony plates all over their bodies—on the back, around the sides, over the tail, and all over the head. Some ankylosaurs also had a bony club at the end of their tail, which they may have used to fight off meat-eaters.

You will need

string
a pencil
a craft knife
masking tape
paints and paintbrushes
large sheets of cardboard

glue
scissors
paper clips
a long ruler
newspaper

1 To make the back shield, lie down on a sheet of cardboard and ask a friend to draw around your body. Now copy the shape below left onto the cardboard (use your body outline as a guide to make sure the shield will be large enough to fit on your back). Cut out the shield.

2 Now ask an adult to help you trim the edges with a craft knife. Make sure you cut carefully, so that all the edges are smooth.

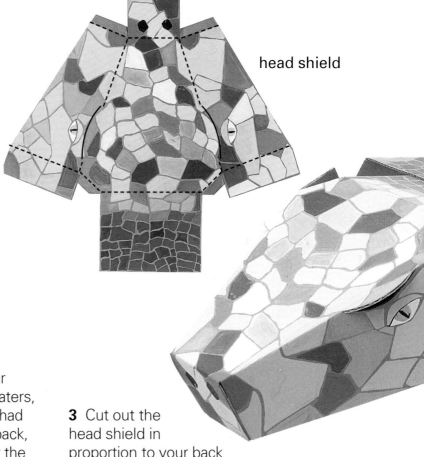

head shield

3 Cut out the head shield in proportion to your back shield, as shown above. For the tail, cut a long, thin, triangle shape, as shown above right. Draw some triangular shapes on the body and the tail as shown in the pictures, for the ankylosaur's spines.

4 Draw the bony plate shapes on the back shield and paint them green. Then paint a border of yellow and white scales to show the ankylosaur's underside. Finally, paint the spine shapes pale yellow.

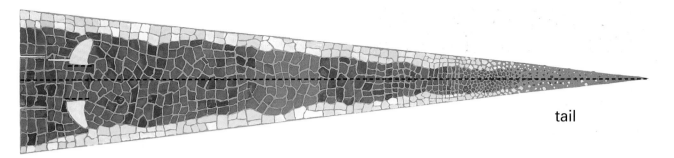

tail

5 Draw bony plate segments on the head shield and paint them in shades of brown. Paint on yellow eyes and black nostrils. Paint the section at the back of the head in green shades. Now paint the tail in shades of green, with the edges (the underside) in yellow. Finally, paint the spine shapes pale yellow.

6 Ask an adult to help you cut around the spine shapes on the back shield and tail. Fold them back along the dotted line, so they stick up.

7 Ask an adult to help you cut a semicircle above the eyes, as marked opposite. Fold the head shield into shape, using a long ruler to help fold along the dotted lines, as shown opposite. Glue the flaps together at the snout. Use paper clips to hold the pieces until the glue is dry. Fold the back shield and tail in the same way.

8 Crumple up some sheets of newspaper into two balls. Wind masking tape around them, then paint them green or blue.

9 Tape the newspaper balls to the tail as above. Make two slits at the top of the tail and slot the tail onto the back shield. Tape it in place underneath.

10 Glue and tape the head shield to the back shield. Make four holes in each side of the back shield. Thread the string through the holes and tie the shield around your body.

When attacked, ankylosaurs often curled up and tucked their arms and legs under their tough back shields. At other times, they used their tail clubs to strike meat-eaters.

The ornithopods, or two-legged plant-eaters, were among the fastest dinosaurs. These long-legged creatures often raced along in herds, reaching speeds of up to 50 km/h when they were being chased by meat-eaters. Their long tails helped them keep their balance as they ran.

2 Wrap newspaper around the wire body, neck and tail and tape in place. Leave the feet, hands, head, and end of the tail uncovered. At this point, you can keep on bending the wire covered with masking tape until your *Hypsilophodon* looks similar to the one above.

MAKE it WORK!

Make a model of *Hypsilophodon*—a small ornithopod that lived in the early Cretaceous in southern England. Its relatives lived throughout the world—in Europe, North America, Africa and Australia.

You will need

wire
pliers
Plasticine
strips of thin cloth,
  such as cotton
paints and paintbrushes

scissors
a rolling pin
newspaper
masking tape
plaster of Paris

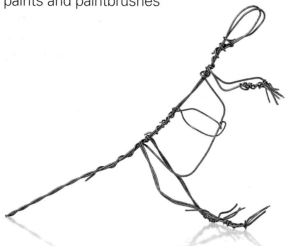

3 Mix some plaster of Paris with water. Make sure the mixture is thick, but not stiff.

1 Using pliers, twist two long lengths of wire together to make the backbone, leaving a loop for the head. Add loops of wire for the ribcage. Twist short lengths of wire onto the backbone for the arms and legs, carefully shaping the ends into five fingers and four toes.

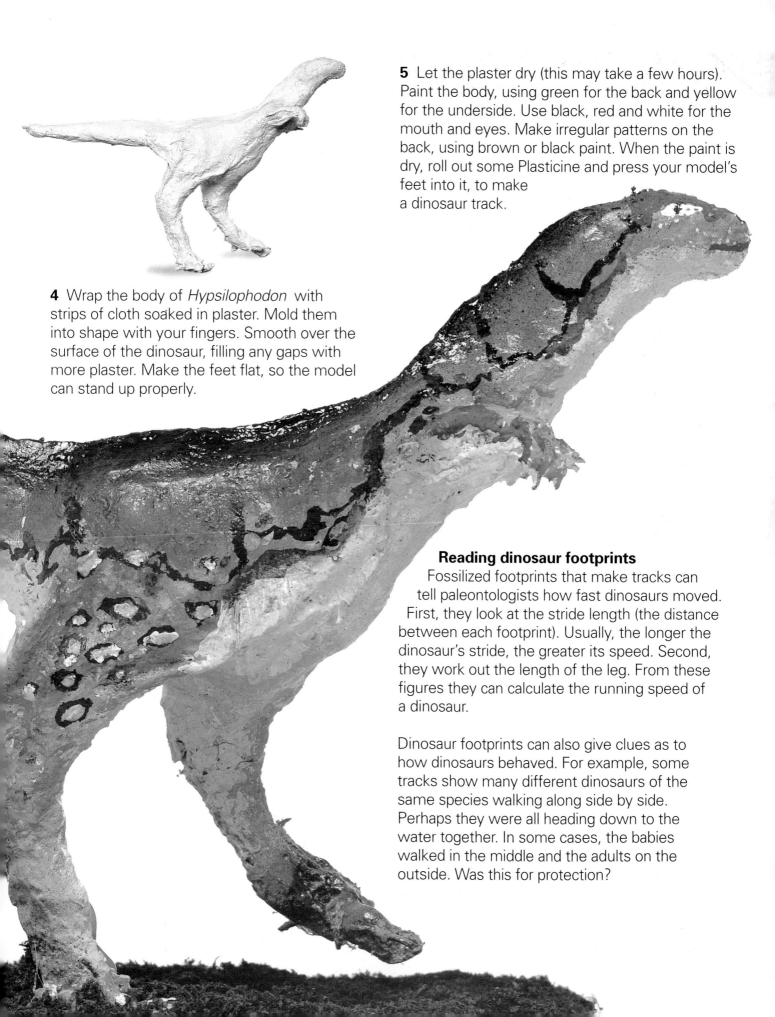

5 Let the plaster dry (this may take a few hours). Paint the body, using green for the back and yellow for the underside. Use black, red and white for the mouth and eyes. Make irregular patterns on the back, using brown or black paint. When the paint is dry, roll out some Plasticine and press your model's feet into it, to make a dinosaur track.

4 Wrap the body of *Hypsilophodon* with strips of cloth soaked in plaster. Mold them into shape with your fingers. Smooth over the surface of the dinosaur, filling any gaps with more plaster. Make the feet flat, so the model can stand up properly.

Reading dinosaur footprints

Fossilized footprints that make tracks can tell paleontologists how fast dinosaurs moved. First, they look at the stride length (the distance between each footprint). Usually, the longer the dinosaur's stride, the greater its speed. Second, they work out the length of the leg. From these figures they can calculate the running speed of a dinosaur.

Dinosaur footprints can also give clues as to how dinosaurs behaved. For example, some tracks show many different dinosaurs of the same species walking along side by side. Perhaps they were all heading down to the water together. In some cases, the babies walked in the middle and the adults on the outside. Was this for protection?

Brachiosaurus was the largest dinosaur. The evidence came from a complete skeleton. It was 25 metres long and probably weighed 50 or 60 tonnes. Larger dinosaurs, such as *Supersaurus*, may have weighed twice as much, but no one has found a complete skeleton of this creature.

MAKE it WORK!

Make your own giant sauropod *Brachiosaurus* (in the same way as you made *Hypsilophodon* on pages 30 to 31). Now do an experiment that will tell you the approximate weight of *Brachiosaurus*.

You will need
wire
pliers
newspaper
masking tape
strips of cloth
plaster of Paris
7 cm-wide softwood:
   one piece 38 cm long
   two pieces 20 cm long
   two pieces 16 cm long
paints and a paintbrush
pieces of wood for spacers

1 For the body, glue two small wood spacers on each side of the 38 cm piece of wood. Add the legs by gluing the four remaining pieces of wood to the spacers, angling one so that it looks like the leg is moving. Make sure the longer legs are at the front.

2 Using pliers, twist two lengths of wire together to make the backbone. Tape in place on the wooden body. Make the head by looping a short piece of wire and twisting the ends onto the backbone. Add more pieces of wire to make the outline of the neck and tail. Tape the wire in place as shown above.

3 Wrap newspaper around the frame and secure with tape. Now mix some plaster of Paris with water. Make sure the mixture is thick, but not stiff. Wrap the body with strips of cloth soaked in plaster and mold them into shape with your fingers. Add more plaster to fill any gaps and make a smooth surface. Make the feet flat, so that the dinosaur will stand up. Let it dry.

4 Paint the body of the *Brachiosaurus* grey or dark blue, with a yellow underside. Use black for the mouth and red for the eyes.

Working out the weight

To find out how much *Brachiosaurus* weighed, you will need a plastic model that is accurately modelled on a full-size reconstruction. You also need to know the scale of your plastic model.

1 Put some weighing scales in a large tray. Fill the weighing dish with water right up to the brim. Be careful not to spill any in the tray.

2 Put the dinosaur into the weighing dish and allow the water to flow over the edge into the large tray underneath.

3 Empty the weighing dish. Now pour the the water that spilled into the large tray back into the dish. Write down the weight of this water in grams. Now multiply the weight of the water by the scaling factor of the dinosaur (x 100, for example), which is usually printed on its stomach. This will give you the approximate weight of the dinosaur in grams. Now convert this into kilograms, or tonnes.

Sauropods, such as Brachiosaurus, *were ten times bigger than an elephant. Some experts think they were* **cold-blooded**. *Cold-blooded animals need less food and use less energy than* **warm-blooded** *animals do. This is because their body temperature is controlled by how hot or cold it is outside. Warm-blooded animals, such as humans, convert food into energy to heat their bodies from the inside. Some experts say that if* Brachiosaurus *had been warm-blooded, it could not have eaten enough to survive.*

Paleontologists have debated whether the dinosaurs were warm-blooded or not. Did dinosaurs have constant body temperatures like birds and **mammals**, or did their body temperatures simply match the air temperature? The bony plates of *Stegosaurus* give us some clues.

MAKE it WORK!

Make a model of the dinosaur *Stegosaurus* and think about how it might have used the bone plates on its back. These plates were set into the skin, rather than into the skeleton.

You will need

wire	plaster of Paris
pliers	cardboard and scissors
newspaper	masking tape and glue
strips of cloth	paints and paintbrushes

1 Twist two pieces of wire together with pliers to make the backbone. For the legs, twist smaller pieces of wire together and attach these to the backbone. Use extra pieces of wire to make the rest of the body shape.

2 Stuff the body and tail with newspaper, then wind masking tape around the body, neck and tail. Fill the shape out so it looks well rounded.

3 Make up some plaster of Paris, following the instructions on the package. Soak strips of cloth in the mixture. Stretch the cloth strips over the wire frame, building up several layers. Now build up a small head shape with an open mouth, by carefully shaping the damp plaster.

4 Smooth the surface of the model with your fingers to make the correct body shape. Add plaster to fill any gaps, then let it dry.

5 Draw back plates in three different sizes on cardboard and cut them out. Glue the plates along the spine as shown above. Draw four long spikes on cardboard and cut them out. Glue them onto the end of the tail.

6 When your *Stegosaurus* is completely dry, paint it. Use contrasting colours, such as yellow and red, or green and brown. Paint one color all over the body, and let it dry. Then add irregular shapes in another colour. You can sprinkle soil or wood shavings around the base of the model if you like.

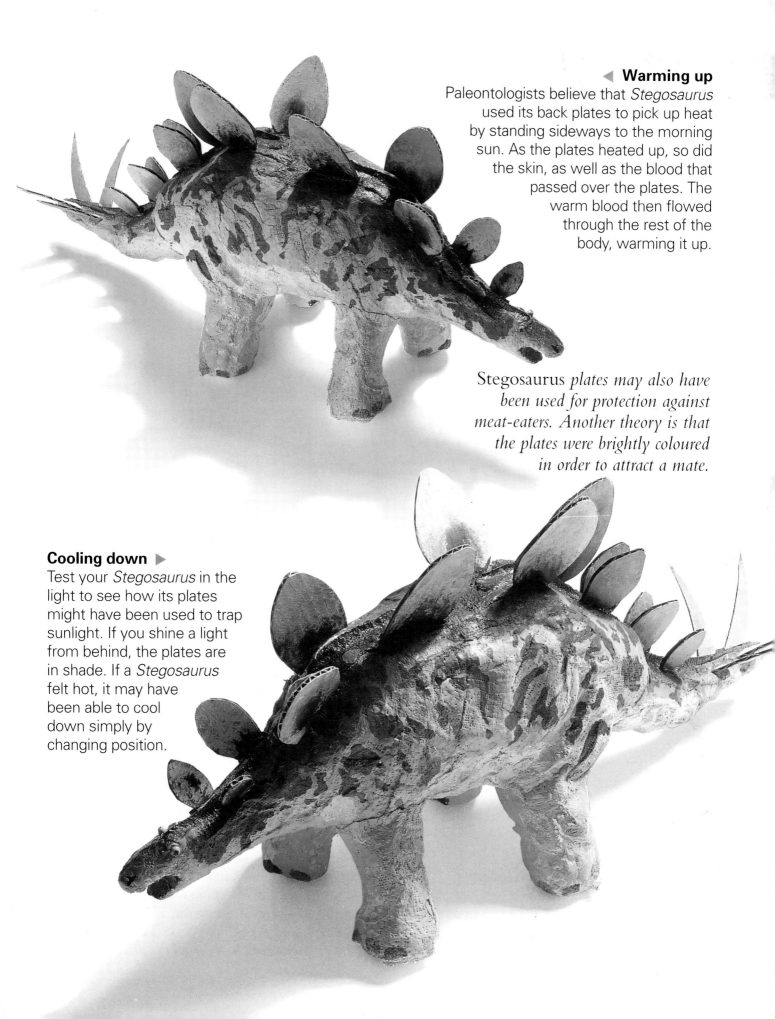

◀ Warming up

Paleontologists believe that *Stegosaurus* used its back plates to pick up heat by standing sideways to the morning sun. As the plates heated up, so did the skin, as well as the blood that passed over the plates. The warm blood then flowed through the rest of the body, warming it up.

Stegosaurus plates may also have been used for protection against meat-eaters. Another theory is that the plates were brightly coloured in order to attract a mate.

Cooling down ▶

Test your *Stegosaurus* in the light to see how its plates might have been used to trap sunlight. If you shine a light from behind, the plates are in shade. If a *Stegosaurus* felt hot, it may have been able to cool down simply by changing position.

36 Dinosaur Nests

Like birds and reptiles, dinosaurs laid eggs. They made a nest on the ground and laid 20 or 30 eggs that looked like long, narrow hens' eggs with a hard, chalky shell. Dinosaurs often laid their eggs in mud or sand nests and covered them up to keep them warm and safe from predators.

MAKE it WORK!

Make a model of a *Triceratops* and its nest. *Triceratops* was a ceratopsian or "horn-faced" dinosaur. Ceratopsians were plant-eaters with horns on their noses and foreheads, which they used to protect themselves from meat-eaters. Their neck frills were thought to act as shields.

You will need

pliers	wire
dried moss	hen's eggs
plaster of Paris	newspaper
scissors and cardboard	masking tape
paints and paintbrushes	strips of cloth

1 Twist two pieces of wire together to make the backbone, the head and the belly, as shown below. Twist two short pieces of wire together for each pair of legs and attach to the body. Now add extra wire to shape the body.

3 Twist two short lengths of wire onto the top of the head to make two long horns. Now add a loop of wire around the back of the head to make the frill. Cover these with pieces of newspaper and masking tape.

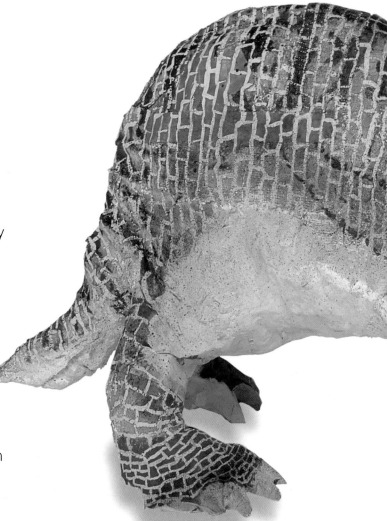

2 Stuff the body with crumpled-up newspaper and wind masking tape round the body, neck and tail, as shown above right. Make the body round, and make the head with an open mouth.

4 Make up some plaster of Paris and soak strips of cloth in the mixture. Make sure the plaster is runny, but not stiff. Stretch the cloth over the wire frame and build up several layers. Add more plaster to fill in any gaps.

5 Continue adding plaster around the horns, so that they are rounded. Smooth the surface of the model with your fingers to make the correct body shape, as shown below left. Using stiff plaster, add a short horn to the nose and a hooked beak to the mouth.

8 Use green and yellow paint to give your *Triceratops* model a thick, scaly skin. Paint the horns, edges of the frill, toes and underside in yellow and white. Use brown and black for the eyes, and red and white for the tongue and teeth.

9 Make a *Triceratops'* nest from dried moss. Put several hens' eggs in the nest and place the nest next to your finished model.

In life, *Triceratops* measured up to nine metres long. Their eggs were a maximum 30 cm long, a little larger than an ostrich egg. In our model below, the eggs are much larger than they should be in proportion to the model.

6 Using stiff plaster that has nearly dried out, shape five toes on each foot. Do this carefully, so that the *Triceratops* will stand properly. Roll up two tiny balls of newspaper for the eyes and press into the plaster. Let the plaster dry.

7 To finish the frill, cut out several triangle shapes from cardboard. Glue these around the neck shield as shown above. Let the glue dry.

Some dinosaur babies could run about and find food almost as soon as they hatched. Others had to wait in the nest for their parents to feed them. Paleontologists discovered this when they studied nesting sites in the state of Montana and in Mongolia. They found bones of parents and one-year-olds near the nests, along with the remains of leaves and berries.

38 Dinosaur Brains

Dinosaurs had small, reptile-sized brains (a bird or a mammal the size of a dinosaur would have a brain 10 times as big). The dinosaur brain was good enough to tell them where to find food and how to escape danger, but they were unable to learn as well as birds and mammals. Only the small meat-eaters, such as the raptors (see pages 26 to 27) had as much brain power as birds.

1 Twist two long pieces of wire together to make the backbone, tail and a head with an open mouth. Then twist two smaller pieces of wire together for the arms and legs. Attach these by twisting them around the backbone. Now add more pieces of wire to fill in the body, as shown below left.

2 Stuff the body, neck and head with crumpled-up newspaper. Wind masking tape around the body, head, and neck, as well as the upper part of the legs and the tail.

MAKE it WORK!

Make a model of *Tyrannosaurus*, the biggest meat-eating dinosaur. Although *Tyrannosaurus* had a huge body, its brain was much smaller than yours. Like all dinosaurs, its brain was protected by a tough, bony case.

3 Make up some plaster of Paris and soak strips of cloth in the mixture. Stretch these over the wire frame and build up several layers of strips over the whole body as shown below. Make sure the model can stand upright.

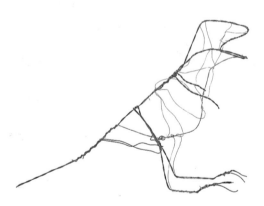

You will need

wire	pliers
scissors	newspaper
craft knife	toothpicks
masking tape	two large plastic beads
strips of cloth	paints and paintbrushes
plaster of Paris	

4 To make the teeth, cut several toothpicks into short points. Push these firmly into the damp plaster around the edges of the mouth. Let the plaster dry.

5 Paint the *Tyrannosaurus* in shades of orange, red, brown and black, or colours of your choice. Use bright red for the mouth. You can paint on the eyes, or glue on two large plastic beads. Sprinkle soil or wood shavings around the base.

This matchbox inside a shoebox shows the size of *Tyrannosaurus'* brain in relation to its skull.

Reptiles have a tiny brain contained inside a small bony box at the back of the skull. A dinosaur's brain did not have a "thinking" part. It simply sent nerve messages to the eyes, ears, mouth and muscles to make the body work.

Dinosaurs lived only on land. However, there were giant reptiles in the seas during the time of the dinosaurs. The most unusual were the **plesiosaurs**, which had broad bodies and long necks and tails. The plesiosaurs swam by using their broad limbs as huge paddles.

MAKE it WORK!

Plesiosaurs were reptiles, which means that they had to breathe air. They could probably have remained underwater for up to 10 minutes in search of fish to eat, but then they had to surface for air. We show you how to make your own plesiosaur—this one sinks and swims!

2 Pierce a hole in the lid of the bottle, thread in the plastic tube, and fix the tube to the neck with tape. The other end of the tube should reach right to the head, as shown above.

3 Bend some wire into paddle shapes for the plesiosaur's limbs, as above. Tape them in place under the bottle. Wrap newspaper around the neck, body and tail, twisting it tightly to get a neat shape. Tape the newspaper firmly in place.

You will need

wire
pliers
a plastic tube
masking tape
strips of cloth
a plastic bottle with lid

paints
varnish
scissors
newspaper
plaster of Paris

1 Fold a long piece of wire in half, and twist it together with pliers, leaving a loop for the head. The twisted wire will be the backbone. Now fix the plastic bottle below the backbone, about halfway along with masking tape. Make sure the bottle top points to the mouth.

4 Cover the whole body with cloth strips soaked in plaster of Paris. Mould carefully around the head, body and tail, so that your model looks like the one above. Leave an opening in the mouth for the end of the tube and take care not to let any plaster block it up.

5 Let the plaster dry. Paint the plesiosaur, using green or blue for the back, and yellow for the belly. You can add rough stripes or spots to the back. This colour pattern acts as camouflage in the water. Once the paint is dry, apply four coats of varnish. Allow plenty of drying time between each coat.

Plesiosaurs moved their paddles down and backward to push themselves forward in the water. Then they turned the paddle so that the narrow side faced forward, and brought it up to the front again. The tip of the paddle followed a figure-eight pattern, like the wing of a bird in flight. Penguins use a similar paddle action when they swim.

Taking a dive
Make your plesiosaur sink by filling it with water. Simply place it underwater or carefully pour water into a funnel fitted into the plastic tube. Your model will float when there is no water in the bottle—use the plastic tube for pouring water out. When real plesiosaurs wanted to dive, they probably blew all the air out of their lungs to make themselves heavier. When they were breathing normally at the surface, they floated.

Pterosaurs were neither dinosaurs nor birds. They belonged to the archosaur group and were perhaps related to the dinosaurs. They ruled the skies when the dinosaurs ruled the Earth—from the late Triassic to the end of the Cretaceous, the time of the great **extinction** (see pages 44 to 45). Some, such as *Pteranodon*, were huge, with a wingspan of seven metres.

1 Trace all the body and wing parts below. Ask an adult to enlarge the wings on a photocopier, until they measure around 50 cm long. Enlarge the other pieces by the same percentage.

2 Tape the photocopy onto the cardboard. Ask an adult to help you cut out the shapes with a craft knife. Make sure the grooves in the cardboard run along the length of the wings.

3 Cut slits into the cardboard shapes, as shown below. They must be wide enough for the shapes to fit together firmly.

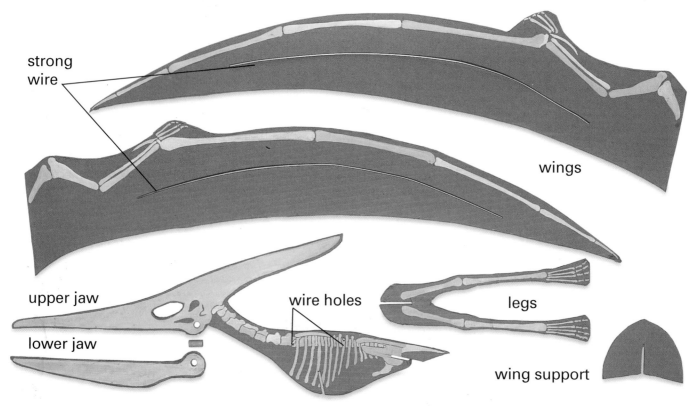

strong wire

wings

upper jaw

lower jaw

wire holes

legs

wing support

MAKE it WORK!

You can make a gliding model of *Pteranodon* (in life, it flapped its wings, like a giant bird).

You will need

Plasticine	a pencil
two strong wires	a craft knife
a 5 mm dowel rod	glue and tape
corrugated cardboard	tracing paper
paints and a paintbrush	a bradawl

4 Paint the *Pteranodon* skeleton onto the cardboard, using the picture above as a guide. Trace the shapes in pencil first and then paint bone shapes either cream or yellow. Ask an adult to help you cut out an eye socket and a 5 mm hole in the upper and lower jaws. Use the bradawl to make two small wire holes in the backbone, as shown.

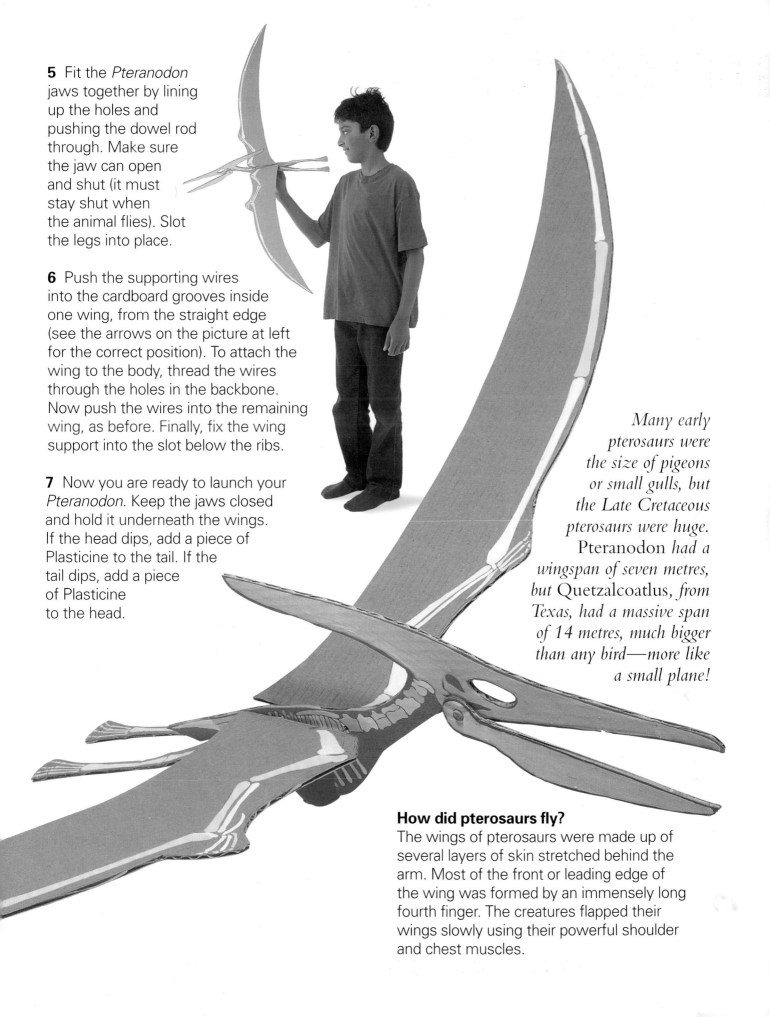

5 Fit the *Pteranodon* jaws together by lining up the holes and pushing the dowel rod through. Make sure the jaw can open and shut (it must stay shut when the animal flies). Slot the legs into place.

6 Push the supporting wires into the cardboard grooves inside one wing, from the straight edge (see the arrows on the picture at left for the correct position). To attach the wing to the body, thread the wires through the holes in the backbone. Now push the wires into the remaining wing, as before. Finally, fix the wing support into the slot below the ribs.

7 Now you are ready to launch your *Pteranodon*. Keep the jaws closed and hold it underneath the wings. If the head dips, add a piece of Plasticine to the tail. If the tail dips, add a piece of Plasticine to the head.

Many early pterosaurs were the size of pigeons or small gulls, but the Late Cretaceous pterosaurs were huge. Pteranodon had a wingspan of seven metres, but Quetzalcoatlus, from Texas, had a massive span of 14 metres, much bigger than any bird—more like a small plane!

How did pterosaurs fly?
The wings of pterosaurs were made up of several layers of skin stretched behind the arm. Most of the front or leading edge of the wing was formed by an immensely long fourth finger. The creatures flapped their wings slowly using their powerful shoulder and chest muscles.

Sixty-five million years ago, the dinosaurs died out. There have been many theories about this great extinction. Some scientists believe the climate changed from warm to cold. Others think the Earth was hit by a giant **meteorite** that sent up clouds of dust and blacked out the sun.

MAKE it WORK!

You can make a game to re-create the extinction of the dinosaurs. Throughout the game, players lose dinosaurs, trees and bushes until all that's left is a barren, volcanic landscape.

You will need

glue	thin tape
a pencil	scissors
coloured cardboard	Plasticine
a pencil sharpener	paper clips
48 cm-square board	a long ruler
paints and a paintbrush	tracing paper
thick and thin dowel rods	white stickers

1 Cut out 2 cm strips of thin red, white, blue and green cardboard. Glue these to the borders of the baseboard. Now make a grid of 4 cm squares. This will make 11 squares along each side. Using a ruler and a pencil, join up the marks so that you end up with 121 squares, each measuring 4 cm square.

2 Copy the volcano shape shown above. Cut out the shape from cardboard and bend the edges along the fold lines as above. Make one large volcano (to occupy nine squares), two medium (four squares) and three small (one square).

3 Glue the volcano shapes together (secure with paper clips until the glue dries). Paint the volcanoes white with red and orange lava.

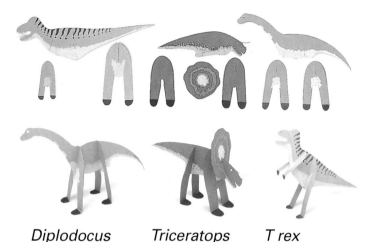

Diplodocus   *Triceratops*   *T rex*

4 To make the dinosaurs, trace the shapes as above. Enlarge the tracings about 300 percent, so that each dinosaur fits inside one square. Copy the shapes onto cardboard and cut them out. Make slits in the legs and bodies, then slot them together. Paint the models and bend their feet so that they can stand. Each player should have three plant-eaters (one *Triceratops* and two *Diplodocus*) and one meat-eater, *Tyrannosaurus rex*.

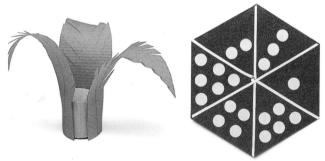

5 Make five palm trees and six bushes. Cut palm fronds from cardboard and glue to lengths of thin dowel rod. Fix the palms to the baseboard with Plasticine. Make bushes by sticking leaf shapes to pieces of thick dowel rod as shown above. Cut a pond shape out of blue cardboard.

6 Make the spinner as shown above. Sharpen one end of a thin dowel rod with a pencil sharpener and push it through the middle of the spinner. The spinner will spin on the sharp end.

Playing the game:

1 Up to four people can play the game. Each player takes one side of the board. Place the pond in position on the board, then make a pile of bushes, palms and volcanoes. Players take turns removing one of these from the pile and placing them on the board.

3 The player spins the spinner and moves a dinosaur along that number of squares, in any direction. If the dinosaur lands on a square with a tree or bush, it can remove it. A meat-eater can remove a plant-eater or another meat-eater by landing on its square. If a plant-eater lands on a meat-eater's square, it will be eaten.

2 When the landscape is complete, players take turns placing their dinosaurs on the board. Place your meat-eater last and try to put it next to a plant-eater, so it can eat it! The last person to place a dinosaur on the board starts.

4 The game ends when there are no dinosaurs or plants left on the board. The volcanoes stay on the board all the time (a dinosaur must move around the volcanoes and the pond). The player who ends up with the greatest number of plants and dinosaurs is the winner.

Ammonite A swimming shellfish with a curved shell. It was common in the Jurassic.

Ancestor An early type of animal from which another, later type of animal is descended.

Ankylosauria A dinosaur subgroup containing armored plant-eating dinosaurs, such as *Euoplocephalus*.

Archosauria A group of animals containing archosaurs, the "ruling reptiles." The archosaur group includes dinosaurs, crocodiles, pterosaurs and birds.

Bipedal Walking on two legs, like humans and many dinosaurs.

Cell A unit of living matter so small that it can be seen only under a microscope.

Ceratopsia A dinosaur subgroup containing ceratopsians, or "horn-faced" creatures, such as *Triceratops*.

Cold-blooded An animal, such as a reptile, that has no internal way to control its body temperature. Instead, it heats itself by basking in the sun.

Cretaceous
The period from 145 million to 65 million years ago. The last dinosaurs lived during this time.

Dinosaur An extinct reptile and member of the Dinosauria, a group of generally large, land-living reptiles that had straight limbs.

Excavate To dig up the soil carefully in order to find buried objects, such as skeletons. It may take paleontologists several months to excavate a complete dinosaur skeleton.

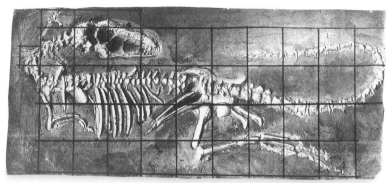

Extinction The death of a species. A mass extinction takes place when many species, like the dinosaurs, die off at the same time.

Fossil The remains of a once living thing, usually preserved in rock.

Genus A group of closely related species.

Geological Relating to the study of rocks and other substances that make up the Earth's crust. Dinosaur fossils preserved in rock can be dated by finding out the age of the rock.

Jurassic The second period in the age of the dinosaurs, from 205 million to 145 million years ago. Ammonites and plesiosaurs were common in seas during this time. It was the time of the largest dinosaurs.

Ligament A tough tissue that connects bones and muscles in the body.

Mammal An animal that has hair and is warm-blooded. Mammals feed their young on milk. Humans, dogs, cats, horses, bats and whales are all mammals.

Mesozoic The era of geological time from 250 million to 65 million years ago, which includes the Triassic, Jurassic and Cretaceous periods. It is also known as the Age of the Dinosaurs.

Meteorite The remains of a rock from space that has burned up on entering the Earth's atmosphere.

Mineral Any substance found in the earth that is not a vegetable substance. Common minerals are calcite and quartz.

Ornithischian A "bird-hipped" dinosaur that is a member of the suborder Ornithischia. Ornithischians include the plant-eating ornithopods, ceratopsians, stegosaurs and ankylosaurs.

Ornithopoda A group of two-legged, plant-eating dinosaurs with many rows of grinding teeth, such as *Hypsilophodon*.

Paleontologist A person who studies fossils.

Plesiosaur A sea reptile of Jurassic and Cretaceous times. It was an air-breathing animal that ate fish and laid its eggs on land.

Prosauropoda A group of medium-sized, plant-eating dinosaurs with long necks, such as *Plateosaurus*.

Pterosaur A flying reptile with leathery wings stretched along elongated fingers. Pterosaurs lived during the Triassic, Jurassic and Cretaceous periods.

Quadrupedal Walking on all fours.

Raptor A small hunting dinosaur with a curved claw, such as *Deinonychus*.

Reptile An animal with scaly skin and four legs that usually lives on land. Turtles, lizards, crocodiles and snakes are all modern reptiles.

Saurischian A "lizard-hipped" dinosaur that belongs to the suborder Saurischia.

Sauropod A giant, long-necked, plant-eating dinosaur, such as *Brachiosaurus*.

Sauropodomorpha A group of long-necked, plant-eating dinosaurs, most of which walked on all fours.

Skeleton The bony framework that supports animals' bodies and protects delicate organs, such as the heart.

Species A group of plants or animals whose members share the same characteristics and can breed together successfully.

Sprawler An animal that walks with its limbs stuck out to the side, such as a lizard.

Stegosauria A group of "plated," plant-eating dinosaurs, such as *Stegosaurus*.

Theropod A dinosaur that belonged to the Saurischia group. They were all bipedal meat-eaters.

Triassic The period from 250 million to 205 million years ago. Evidence of the first dinosaurs dates from this period.

Warm-blooded A type of animal that can keep its body temperature constant by using heat generated inside itself.

48 Index